T0318348

This book is a selection of Jacques Drèze's work over the last ten years on the topics of lasting unemployment, stagflation and unused capacity. At the theoretical level, the author has contributed to the formulation and analysis of general equilibrium models which allow for price rigidities and excess supply and lend themselves to econometric implementation, thus helping to pull together separate branches of economics. The book also contains papers focussing on policy analysis at a Belgian and European level. This collection thus represents an attempt to integrate micro- and macroeconomics, and to use theory for empirical and policy purposes.

Underemployment equilibria

Underemployment Equilibria
Essays in Theory, Econometrics and Policy

JACQUES H. DRÈZE

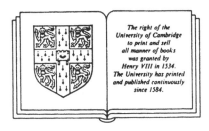

The right of the
University of Cambridge
to print and sell
all manner of books
was granted by
Henry VIII in 1534.
The University has printed
and published continuously
since 1584.

CAMBRIDGE UNIVERSITY PRESS

Cambridge
New York   Port Chester
Melbourne   Sydney

CAMBRIDGE UNIVERSITY PRESS
Cambridge, New York, Melbourne, Madrid, Cape Town, Singapore,
São Paulo, Delhi, Dubai, Tokyo, Mexico City

Cambridge University Press
The Edinburgh Building, Cambridge CB2 8RU, UK

Published in the United States of America by
Cambridge University Press, New York

www.cambridge.org
Information on this title: www.cambridge.org/9780521435246

First published 1991

A catalogue record for this publication is available from the British Library

Library of Congress Cataloguing in Publication Data

Drèze, Jacques H.
    Underemployment equilibria: essays in theory, econometrics, and
    policy/Jacques H. Dreze.
        p.   cm.
    Includes index.
    ISBN 0 521 39318 3
    1. Underemployment – Mathematical models. 2. Equilibria (Economics) –
Mathematical models. 3. Prices – Mathematical models. I. Title.
HD5707.5.D74   1991
331.13 – dc20   90-1848   CIP

ISBN 978-0-521-39318-8 Hardback
ISBN 978-0-521-43524-6 Paperback

To my students

Contents

Preface

Economics is an endless challenge. It is intellectually demanding, and practically important. The intellectual challenge can only be met through basic research – the patient construction of knowledge, which has advanced dramatically over the past decades, yet remains grossly inadequate today. The practical challenge calls for making the best possible use of whatever knowledge we have, in order to assess or suggest policies. That practical challenge also leads economists, occasionally, to redefine research priorities, in an attempt at understanding better the policy issues of the day. But even then, the long-run goal of constructing economic knowledge creeps under the surface, ready to take precedence again.

Except for Chapter 2, which was written in 1972 and published in 1975, all the essays collected in this volume have appeared over the decade 1979–89. They are representative of my attempt, starting in 1978, at understanding better the nature of, and likely remedies to, the macroeconomic problems of Europe – in particular persistent unemployment.

The quest for a better understanding was definitely practical, as it became increasingly clear that the recession born in 1974–75 would not be short lived; but it was also intellectual, as the reading of Malinvaud's *Theory of Unemployment Reconsidered* (1977) had revealed to me how a new synthesis of microeconomic and macroeconomic thinking could be sought.

With welcome support form the *Fonds National de la Recherche Scientifique*, I took sabbatical leave during academic year 1978–79 and set to work – knowing well that 'learning-by-doing' was the only realistic way. I was fortunate on several counts: first, in renewing my fruitful association with Franco Modigliani, as evidenced by Chapter 14; next in entertaining constructive contacts with a generation of creative French theorists, like Jean-Pascal Bénassy, Jean-Michel Grandmont, Guy Laroque and Yves Younès; then, in being surrounded by imaginative graduate students, like Henri Sneessens, Jean Dermine or Jean-Paul Lambert; and more recently, in participating in such collective activities as the European Unemployment Program or the Macroeconomic Policy Group (about which more below).

Altogether, it was an exciting decade, in spite of the intellectual frustrations awaiting a microtheorist trying to learn macroeconomics, and of the practical frustrations linked to the elusiveness of the policy issues. Of course, my initial goal of understanding the nature of the day's macroeconomic problems could only be fulfilled to a limited extent; and the long-run goal of expressing the little I have learned in a form contributing to the construction of economic knowledge remains to be fulfilled. The desire to communicate with others towards further advancement of these two goals prompted the decision to publish this collection of essays, which makes available in one place the scatter of minor findings which have fed my broader reflexions.

The title of this volume is borrowed from that of my Presidential Address to the European Economic Association in 1986. The address itself is reproduced as Chapter 1[1] and provides an overview of the book's contents. I do accordingly urge readers to use that chapter for orientation purposes. The remaining parts of the book are largely self-contained.

A special comment should be made about Chapter 2, and its fate. As said above, that paper was written in 1972, and according to footnote 1, 'was motivated by research in progress on the rational aspects of wage rigidities and unemployment compensation, viewed as a form of income insurance for which market opportunities offer no substitute' (p. 34). I was at the time concerned with risk-sharing and second-best efficiency in an incomplete markets set-up.[2] I realised that price flexibility, geared to continuous clearing of spot markets, could be less efficient than suitable forms of price stability, commonly labelled 'price rigidities'. In order to investigate that issue formally, I needed to specify how trade would take place at non-clearing prices. Chapter 2 contains such a specification, and thus serves as foundation for many other chapters.

---

[1] With a couple of editorial notes (Ed. note) updating the references.
[2] See Drèze (1974 b); the theoretical work on incomplete markets has recently become more formal – see Duffie et al. (1988) – but the same issues remain in the foreground.

In writing that paper, with realistic applications in mind, I endeavoured to establish, for simple types of price rigidity (inequality constraints on nominal or real prices), the consistency of suitable forms of quantity determination (rationing of supply under downward price rigidity, of demand under upward rigidity). It came as a surprise to me that more macroeconomically oriented colleagues concentrated their attention on the special case of fixed prices – so that their work was labelled 'fixed-price equilibrium macroeconomics', and was eventually discounted on grounds of insufficient rationale for the fixed-price assumption. I still feel that income insurance, in a dynamic incomplete markets set-up, is a convincing rationale for downward wage rigidities. I realise now, in the light of Chapters 12 and 13, that the issues are more complex than I had thought at first. In particular, they involve time, uncertainty and successive (overlapping) generations of workers in an essential way.

Hopefully, readers of Parts V, VI and VII will convince themselves that I regard prices and wages as economic variables, the determination of which needs to be explained – though not invariably in terms of spot-markets clearing. Other parts, especially III and IV, contain papers based on a fixed-price model, because they deal with technically difficult issues, that could not be handled at once in a more general setting. Thus, as noted on p. 95, 'when individual money prices are only subject to inequality constraints ..., the set of feasible allocations is not convex' and this introduces a major additional complication. Thus, the characterisation of Shapley-value allocations in large markets is obtained in Chapter 6 for fixed-price economies at considerable technical difficulty; extending that analysis to economies with limited price flexibility – hence with a non-convex feasible set – raises another layer of technical complications. For the purpose of understanding the phenomenon of stagflation, fixed-price models are easily disqualified. But for the long-run objective of constructing economic knowledge, the analysis of general equilibrium models with fixed prices *was* a necessary intermediate step; the stability analysis of Chapter 10, which could not dispense from a specification of quantities traded at non-clearing prices, bears witness to the usefulness of that intermediate step, also for students of inflation ...

Although most of the theoretical chapters (2–13) rely on a microeconomic approach, the motivation and the applications are of a macroeconomic nature.

The last fifteen years have been a period of intense activity in macroeconomics. In the words of Blanchard and Fischer (1989, pp. 26–7), 'the field is now too large and fragmented' for a unified presentation; 'the Keynesian framework ... is in theoretical crisis, searching for micro-foundations; no new theory has emerged to dominate the field, and the time is one of explorations in several directions ...'. I quite agree; and I cannot claim more, for the work presented or referred to here, than a place among these directed explorations.

Yet, even when research explores alternative directions, the mind attempts to bring the separate contributions together, to envision how they might fit into a unified broader picture. There remains a long way, from the first glimpses of consistency among separately developed theories, to their formal integration. But the intuition of the unified theory is already valuable.

General equilibrium theory has for a number of years provided a unified framework for microeconomics. The more recent developments of a 'non-Walrasian' general equilibrium theory,[3] as exemplified in Parts II–V of this volume, holds the promise of providing a framework sufficiently broad and versatile to encompass a good deal of macroeconomics as well. I claim in Chapter 1 that general equilibrium theory, suitably developed in that broader perspective, 'covers macroeconomics automatically, sparing us the need to need to develop two separate fields' (p. 7). Hence the reference to 'general equilibrium macroeconomics'. One clearcut illustration (multiplier analysis) is offered in Chapter 8. Other chapters, like 4 or 10, deal with microfoundations rather than with 'macroeconomic implications of microeconomics'; but the potential overall consistency is clearly discernible.

The major limitation of the models in Parts II–V is that they do not come explicitly to grips with uncertainly and incomplete markets – hence with information, expectations and dynamics. Yet the need to do so is omnipresent, and sometimes recognised explicitly (for instance in Chapters 10, 16 or 18). The difficulties, and promise, are illustrated in Part VI, devoted to the central theme of wage flexibility.

The next step is to search for the macroeconomic implications of non-Walrasian *temporary* general equilibrium theory, a framework designed to deal explicitly with uncertainty, expectations and so on in an incomplete markets setting.[4] That step is suggested by the work collected here. It is

---

[3] The term 'non-Walrasian' is non-appealing to me, in particular because it seems to exclude the Walrasian special case; in chapter 1, I refer to 'general equilibrium with rationing', but I have learned from readers that these words prompt an unduly narrow interpretation.

[4] See Grandmont (1977, 1988) for a survey and selected readings.

also suggested, I think, by many alternative explorations (dealing, for instance, with rational expectations, bubbles, real business cycles ...). Thus Blanchard and Fischer (1989, p. 29) note that 'modern approaches can be defined as the study of dynamic general equilibrium under uncertainty, with incomplete (and possibly imperfect) markets'. Again, I agree. Because macroeconomics has not reached a standstill, the task of retrieving major results as implications of a suitably extended general equilibrium theory is an endless challenge, and will never be complete. In my opinion, the most appealing avenue for basic research at this time remains, in spite of the formal difficulty, temporary-general-equilibrium macroeconomics. I hope that others may share that view, so that good company be enjoyed down that avenue.

The subtitle of Chapter 1 (*From* theory *to* econometrics and policy) claims more than the subtitle of the Book (Essays *in* theory, econometrics and policy). One must choose style for a Presidential Address, and I thought that the occasion (the launching of the European Economic Association) called for punch. Yet, between the theory of Parts II–VI, the econometrics of Part VII and the policy assessments or recommendations of Part VIII, the links remain somewhat informal. It is, of course, an ultimate ambition of economists to develop theoretical models that are susceptible of precise empirical implementation leading to specific and quantified policy recommendations. Most of the time, that ambition seems just as remote as the ambition to fit most current research orientations into a single unified framework ... In the present case, the ambition seems no more remote than with other approaches to macroeconomics.

The logical filiation goes from non-Walrasian general equilibrium theory to the macroeconomic models with quantity rationing of Barro–Grossman (1971, 1976) and Malinvaud (1977), then to the econometric work outlined in Section 4 of Chapter 1 and culminating in Chapters 15 and 16. These two chapters stand a long way from naive fixed-price models. They present a sparse econometric specification that was found flexible enough to fit consistently the data for ten countries both over a period of fast balanced growth (until 1974) and over a period of slow growth with unemployment. But the precision of the estimations is not uniformly impressive, and the specifications could be improved in several directions. I hope that the work will continue.

That cooperative venture by researchers in ten countries, known as the European Unemployment Program, seems to have made quite efficient use of sparse means. It is a sign of hope that a 'Stimulation Program for Economic Science' (SPES) has recently been set up by the EEC to promote international research cooperation.

The two papers selected for the 'Policy' Part VIII were written for the Macroeconomic Policy Group, a revolving group of five economists advising the Directorate for Economic and Monetary Affairs at the Commission of the European Communities, with the logistic intermediation of the Center for European Policy Studies (CEPS) in Brussels. The theoretical sections of Chapter 17 are closely related to Chapters 12 and 13 in Part VI. (Actually, Chapter 13 was developed from a blueprint initially published as an appendix to Chapter 17 – not reproduced here.) Chapter 18 is a group report; it is interesting that so much agreement could be reached among economists with so diverse backgrounds and theoretical frameworks. That paper addresses itself to contemporaneous issues, and should accordingly become outdated fast. It seemed nevertheless worthy of inclusion, both because it contributes to the picture of economic thinking in Europe over the past decade, and because it stresses some points of lasting interest – like the link between openness and fiscal policy effectiveness (Section 5).

Both the econometrics and the policy studies feed back into the theoretical research, because they suggest specifications that can be retained, or raise problems that can be studied, in further theoretical work. For instance, as noted in Chapter 10, the empirical record suggests concentrating attention on excess supply equilibria. It also suggests that European economies are characterised by multiplicity of stable, or nearly stable, equilibria – a characteristic that students of general equilibrium theory can easily accept ...

The work brought together in this volume has a distinctly European flavour. During the past fifteen years, the research interests and methodology of macroeconomists in Western Europe, and in North America, drew further apart than had been the case in earlier years. Although that trend seemed unfortunate at the time, it may have been a manifestation of the emergence of independent macroeconomic research in Europe – a phenomenon less visible in earlier years. I guess that the gap was also deepened by the importance attached to policy issues on both sides. As the long-run objectives of basic research regain prevalence, we may expect that the more significant advances on both sides will be recognised by all concerned, and that the gap will be filled progressively. In particular, recognition of a unifying framework should improve communication.

At the time of resigning from my teaching position at Université Catholique de Louvain, I take pleasure in dedicating this volume to my students. I wish thereby to thank them for all that I have learned from them, for the continued inspiration and motivation which they have provided. I also wish to encourage them, and their contemporaries, to meet the endless challenge of economics. I hope that we may still meet for a while along the avenues of research.

Similarly, I wish to thank my co-authors for their intellectual contributions as well as for the fun of working together. And I hope that we may continue to cooperate in research.

All the work underlying this volume was carried out at the Center for Operations Research and Econometrics (CORE), Université Catholique de Louvain, in close cooperation with the Department of Economics there. I am grateful to my colleagues and to the staff of CORE for the generous provision of intellectual stimulation, logistic assistance and warm friendship. My special gratitude goes to Ginette Vincent, who not only processed all the papers when initially written, but also prepared this manuscript for the printer, and merged all the references into a single combined list[5] while I was sailing around ...

Archipelago de Cabo Verde, November 1989

---

[5] In the combined list of references, discussion papers that are quoted at a later date in print are not listed separately, and all references are to the published version. But no systematic effort is made to trace discussion papers through publication generally.

Acknowledgements

The author would like to thank the publishers of the following articles for their kind permission to reprint them in this book.

Chapter 1: 'Underemployment equilibria: from theory to econometrics and policy', *European Economic Review*, 31, 1987 (North-Holland).

Chapter 2: 'Existence of an exchange equilibrium under price rigidities', *International Economic Review*, 16, 1975 (University of Pennsylvania).

Chapter 3: 'On supply-constrained equilibria', *Journal of Economic Theory*, 33, 1984 (Academic Press).

Chapter 4: 'Competitive equilibria with quantity-taking producers and increasing returns to scale', *Journal of Mathematical Economics*, 17, 1988 (North-Holland).

Chapter 5: 'Optimality properties of rationing schemes', *Journal of Economic Theory*, 23, 1980 (Academic Press).

Chapter 6: 'Values of markets with satiation or fixed prices', *Econometrica*, 54, 1986 (Tieto Ltd).

Chapter 7: 'Public goods with exclusion', *Journal of Public Economics*, 13, 1980 (North-Holland).

Chapter 8: 'Second-best analysis with markets in disequilibrium: public sector pricing in a Keynesian regime', in *The Performance of Public Enterprises: Concepts and Measurement* (edited by M. Marchand, P. Pestieau and H. Tulkens), North-Holland, 1984.

Chapter 9: 'Demand estimation, risk aversion and sticky prices', *Economic Letters*, 4, 1979 (North-Holland).

Chapter 11: 'The role of securities and labour contracts in the optimal allocation of risk-bearing', in *Risk, Information and Insurance: Essays in Memory of Karl Borch* (edited by H. Loubergé), Kluwer, 1989.

Chapter 12: 'Wages, employment and the equity-efficiency trade-off', *Recherches Economiques de Louvain*, 55, 1989 (Université Catholique de Louvain).

Chapter 13: 'Labour management, contracts and capital markets: some macroeconomic aspects, and conclusions', in *Labour Management, Contracts and Capital Markets*, Basil Blackwell, 1989.

Chapter 14: 'The trade-off between real wages and employment in an open economy (Belgium)', *European Economic Review*, 15, 1981 (North-Holland).

Chapter 15: 'A discussion of Belgian unemployment, combining traditional concepts and disequilibrium econometrics', *Economica*, 53, 1986 (London School of Economics and Political Science).

Chapter 16: 'Europe's unemployment problem: introduction and synthesis', in *Europe's Unemployment Problem* (edited by J.H. Drèze, C.R. Bean, J.P. Lambert, F. Mehta and H.R. Sneessens), M.I.T. Press, 1991.

Chapter 18: 'The two-handed growth strategy for Europe: autonomy through flexible cooperation', *Recherches Economiques de Louvain*, 54, 1988 (Université Catholique de Louvain).

Overview

1 Underemployment equilibria
From theory to econometrics and policy*

1. Introduction

Over the years, I have had a number of interesting dreams. But I had not dreamt that I would stand in front of such a large and distinguished audience to address the first Congress of the European Economic Association.

Unbeknown to them, students often figure in my dreams. (On one occasion, I dreamt that I had fallen asleep while lecturing – and woke up in a nightmare, to realise that I was indeed standing in front of my undergraduate statistics class...) Recurrently, I dream about students at the University of Nirvanah, taking up different subjects – like microtheory, macrotheory, welfare economics, business cycles and economic policy – all taught within the same methodological framework and fitting nicely together, like the pieces of a jig-saw puzzle, to form a coherent picture. I wish to share with you today some glimpses of that dream, and my hope that it may come true.

My topic is 'underemployment equilibria', meaning situations where substantial unemployment, as defined in statistical practice, persists with no clear tendency to disappear. 'Equilibrium' is thus defined by absence of movement, not by conformity to some concept.

Today, most European countries are in a situation of underemployment equilibrium; this is a *fact*, a distressing fact (see table 1.1). Unemployment rates among the young are alarmingly high (see table 1.1). The social cost of letting one out of three or four young adults out of work for a prolonged period is hard to assess. To economists of my

* *European Economic Review*, 31 (1987), 9–34. Presidential Address to the First Congress of the European Economic Association,Vienna, August 1986.

Table 1.1   *Unemployment rates*

	Total %		Young (< 25 years of age) %		Long term (> 1 year) % of total	
	1978	1985	1979	1983	1979	1983
Belgium	8.1	14.8	14.0	30.0	38.1	49.9
Denmark	7.1	9.9	14.7	27.9	6.8	5.6
West Germany	3.8	8.3	4.5	13.3	22.2	29.9
France	5.2	12.6	17.5	21.7	19.4	24.4
Italy	7.1	12.9	26.2	35.7	35.0	40.2
Netherlands	5.4	14.8	11.5	31.0	28.9	49.4
United Kingdom	5.3	11.7	10.5	25.9	30.4	41.5
EC 10	5.5	11.5	13.5	24.5	28.4	38.8

Source: European Economy 22, November 1984, p. 16 (Table 8).

generation, it is a disappointing fact. We had indeed been trained to believe that severe unemployment, of the kind experienced in the thirties, would not occur again: Keynesian economics had supplied the explanation and identified remedies, built-in stabilisers (in particular, social security transfers and unemployment benefits) had rendered our economies immune to demand deficiencies, the experience of the thirties had revealed what policy blunders should be avoided. As we all know, these hopes were vain. Underemployment equilibrium is with us again, we do not know for how long.

Explanations which are held useful today differ from those available fifteen years ago. At that time, the only relevant theoretical framework was that of Keynesian macroeconomics, pointing to the demand side as both the culprit and potential saviour. Today, many agree that underemployment equilibria in our open economies exhibit a mixture of Keynesian and classical features, which bring both demand and supply considerations to bear on explanation and remedy alike. The broader theoretical outlook has resulted from important contributions, inspired by the seminal work of Clower (1965, 1967) and Barro and Grossman (1971, 1976) in the U.S., but developed by European economists in the past fifteen years. The distinctly European flavour of these contributions, for which many speakers at this Congress deserve credit, makes them a natural theme for my Address. Given the scope of these contributions, I shall concentrate on those with which I have been associated in one way or another, in particular through the work of my students. This easy option is not meant to belittle the numerous contributions not cited.

2. Theory of unemployment reconsidered: An orientation ToUR

2.1.

To orient ourselves, I will first remind you of the basic message conveyed by the best known among these contributions, namely Malinvaud's *Theory of Unemployment Reconsidered*. That message is easily captured at the level of a single firm, producing a single output y by means of given facilities and a quantity of labour l. The technology and size of the facilities define a production function relating output to labour input: $y = y(l)$. If the output price p and the wage cost w are given, and if we disregard inventories, there will under standard assumptions exist profit-maximising levels of output and employment, that I shall refer to as notional levels and denote by y^* and l^* respectively; they satisfy $y^* = y(l^*)$ and, assuming differentiability, $y'(l^*) = w/\tilde{p}$, where $\tilde{p} = p$ for a competitive firm, $\tilde{p} = p(1 + \eta_{p \cdot q})$ for a monopolistic firm.

Actual levels of output and employment will correspond to these in a static equilibrium where prices, quantities and production facilities are mutually adjusted. But when we study the impact of short-run fluctuations, like shifts in input prices or aggregate demand, we must consider two additional conditions, namely (i) that output y can be sold, at the going price – which may not be the case if supply and demand have shifted away from the positions to which price and capacity were adjusted; and (ii) that the supply of labour l^S to the firm is at least as high as l^*. Otherwise, the firm will be *constrained* on either the goods market or the labour market, and its actual output will fall down to either the level corresponding to demand, y^D, or the level corresponding to full use of available labour, $y(l^S)$, whichever is smaller. That is

$$y = \min(y^*, y^D, y(l^S)). \tag{1}$$

Writing $l(y)$ for the inverse production function, we obtain similarly

$$l = l(y) = \min(l^*, l(y^D), l^S). \tag{2}$$

These two relations embody the common sense observation that goods will only be produced if that is profitable and if the goods can be sold. Similarly, workers will only be employed if there exist suitable places of work, if there is a demand for what they produce, and if they offer their labour.

That straightforward reasoning can be reproduced at the aggregate, macroeconomic level, with the help of fig. 1.1. The aggregate production function of the economy is drawn there as $Y = Y(L)$, displaying the

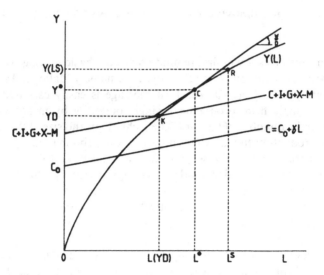

Figure 1.1

neoclassical features of smoothly diminishing returns. Aggregate labour supply is *LS*. Aggregate demand is now partly endogenous and defined as the sum of consumption *C*, which I have for simplicity drawn as increasing linearly with employment; and other components treated provisionally as exogenous, namely investment *I*, government expenditures *G* and the trade balance $X - M$. Aggregate demand is $YD = C + I + G + X - M$.

To complete the picture, there remains to locate the point (Y^*, L^*) corresponding to the notional output supply and labour demand. It is defined implicitly by the condition $Y'(L^*) = w/\tilde{p}$ (marginal revenue product of labour equals real wage) and is found at the point *C*.

We now have three interesting points on the production function, namely the point *K*, where $Y = YD$; the point *C*, where $Y = Y^*$; and the point *R*, where $Y = Y(LS)$. If the economy could be treated as a single firm producing a single commodity by means of a single type of labour, then one could conclude from the reasoning at the firm level that

$$Y = \min(Y^*, YD, Y(LS)). \tag{3}$$

The main modification is that now $YD = YD(Y)$.

Fig. 1.1 is drawn with $YD(Y) < Y^* < Y(LS)$, leading to the Keynesian solution $Y = YD$. But that is only one among several possible orderings, and the three points K (for Keynesian), C (for classical) and R (for repressed inflation) define solutions associated with alternative data. (Thus, increasing G would eventually lead to $YD > Y(LS)$, and lowering $w/\tilde{p}$ would similarly lead to $Y^* > Y(LS)$, in my figure.)

2.2.

In comparison with the Keynesian multiplier, fig. 1.1 contains two important innovations.

First, it brings in the supply side explicitly and from the start – a step postponed to ch. 21 in Keynes (1936). Macroeconomics thus becomes intrinsically two-sided, and a proper framework is at hand to study the balance of supply-side policies and effective demand policies, or to meet such concerns of policy-makers as the limitations placed on fiscal expansion by latent inflationary pressures and capacity constraints. *The substantive theme of this address is that supply and demand both matter, today.*

A second innovation relates to the multiplicity of solutions, at the aggregate level (K, C, R) or at the firm level. The different solutions carry different policy implications. Also, in an economy with many firms, making up diverse industries or service sectors, there is no reason to expect that all firms will be simultaneously in similar situations. Casual observation suggests that European steel producers satisfy demand with excess capacities, whilst producers of equipment goods quote long delivery lags.

Thus aggregation over firms means aggregation over non-homogeneous units, some of which realise their notional trade offers, whilst others cannot – just as in the case of households. This consideration has important implications for econometric work – to be mentioned later. It may also be related to the methodological comment by Malinvaud (p. 4 of ToUR) that progress in macroeconomics had been held back by 'the lack of a general equilibrium framework concerning an economy with rationing'. Indeed, general equilibrium is the limiting framework where each firm and each household appears as a separate entity. Recognising microeconomic heterogeneity is thus a definite step towards what I shall call 'General Equilibrium Macroeconomics' – or GEM for short. *The methodological theme of this address is that general equilibrium with rationing covers macroeconomics automatically, sparing us the need to develop two separate fields.*

Of course, macroeconomics had been a general equilibrium venture all along, and Keynes belongs right next to Walras as a founder of that approach. But Walrasian and Keynesian economics had for many years developed along parallel, disjoint paths – an unfortunate development, reflecting the segmentation of our profession, and making life difficult for our students. Keynes was obviously right in attempting to develop a theoretical framework in which the undisputed fact of persistent unemployment could be fitted. It was up to microeconomists to extend their own models accordingly. It is surprising that it took them so long to do so. It is also surprising that, once that step was taken, in particular by Yves Younès (1975) and Jean-Pascal Bénassy (1975), the integration with Keynesian macroeconomics came so easily, as illustrated by ToUR or more systematically by Bénassy's treatment in *The Economics of Market Disequilibrium* (1982). I hope to convince you that both general equilibrium and macroeconomics benefit from the integration.

2.3.

Before turning to that task, I must first consider in what sense the alternative solutions to the firm's problem define 'equilibria', i.e. situations which do not call for any adjustments in *quantities*, *prices* or *production capacities*.

To begin with the goods market, if $y^* = y^D$, the firm realises its desired production plan, and the market for its output clears, so there is no natural inducement to a change and equilibrium prevails. If $y^* < y^D$, unsatisfied demand invites buyers to bid up the price, or the firm to raise price so as to boost profits. Such a situation is not an equilibrium. It should only be observed temporarily, pending an increase in price and/or an expansion of production capacities. And indeed we do not observe prolonged rationing of demand. Yet, elimination of excess demand need not result in higher employment, if it is achieved through a price increase and additional imports. Such cases of stagflation are particularly likely if the excess demand initially resulted from a supply shock rather than from a demand shock.

The third possibility, $y^* > y^D$, is more interesting. Could it happen that a firm's notional supply exceeds its sales, without this creating a tendency for the price to fall, or for the production capacities to be reduced? The answer is: yes – if the firm is operating under increasing returns to scale! For in that case the firm would prefer to sell more at the same price, but it would not supply the same output at a lower price, nor could it reduce costs by producing the same output from smaller facilities. And such conditions may have a competitive flavour, with price equal to average cost (plus markup), as in 'contestable markets' – see, e.g. Baumol, Panzar and Willig (1982); or they may have a monopolistic flavour, with marginal revenue equal to (non-increasing) marginal cost.

To my eyes, increasing returns are the rule rather than the exception – a conclusion already drawn 25 years ago from a study of the qualitative attributes of Belgium's exports and imports (Drèze (1960)). Increasing returns arise whenever the technology entails economies of mass production (through assembly lines, high-speed machine tools, etc....); whenever commodities (like clothing and durables, but also bread or processed foods) are produced or procured in batches subject to set up costs; they result from the overhead costs of opening up and maintaining facilities, from the economies of bulk transportation, from the law of large numbers in storing spare parts, etc..... These are all circumstances where equilibrium – either competitive or monopolistic – is consistent with excess supply.

By contrast, under diminishing returns, excess supply would induce the firm to reduce price, or capacity, or both. If it reduced capacity, the Keynesian unemployment would eventually become classical.

Turning to the labour market, I would again suggest that excess demand – $y(l^S) < y^*$ – is not a candidate for lasting equilibrium, as firms will then outbid each other to attract additional labour, will train less skilled workers internally or will substitute capital for labour. But excess supply of labour, i.e. unemployment, is a widespread phenomenon. It does not lead to significant adjustments in labour supply. I shall return later to reasons why it does not lead to wage cuts.

2.4.

The foregoing should help dispel two misconceptions. First, excess supply, but not excess demand, is consistent with equilibrium. In particular, 'classical unemployment', i.e. a situation where employment is determined by the notional labour demand of firms rather than by the effective demand for output, need not carry any connotation of demand rationing, if prices are flexible upwards and imported substitutes are available. It is a characterisation of the unemployment which arises when weaving mills or shipyards close down, under the competition of lower cost producers in Newly Industrialised Countries. It is a reminder of the simple fact that employment requires places of work, hence an appropriate capital stock created and maintained by appropriate investment. In the *Price Theory* textbook of my entertaining teacher George Stigler (1942), there was a student problem reading as follows: 'With a Cobb–Douglas production function, one could grow the world's output of corn from a flower pot. Comment.' I may have commented at the time that the world's labour supply would not suffice. I appreciate better today the simple wisdom of the question. Employment definitely requires work places – which flower pots do not provide.

Second, equilibrium of the firm concerns not only quantities but also prices and capital investments. Thus, GEM is not restricted to fix-price models. On the contrary, the more flexible framework should open new avenues for the study of price dynamics – as illustrated below (Section 3.2).

I thus hope to share with you my conviction that GEM provides a theoretical framework sufficiently broad and general to be used effectively by most of us, with contributions from many sides fitting together naturally. I shall consider first the contributions of general equilibrium theory.

3.   General equilibrium with rationing

The general equilibrium model of Walras, Arrow and Debreu has contributed much elegance and clarity to economics. But its program remains unfinished, and some extensions – in particular to increasing returns, price dynamics and uncertainty – involve rationing in a natural way. (The term 'rationing' is here understood broadly, and covers in particular situations of 'voluntary' or 'efficient' excess supply of goods, as well as situations of unemployment.)

3.1.

Starting with increasing returns, it stands to reason that firms operating with declining average costs will typically wish to sell more at the same price, precluding existence of competitive equilibria where firms maximise profits at given prices. But competitive equilibria can also be characterised by an alternative set of properties, namely (i) that firms minimise their production costs, (ii) that they supply their output voluntarily (meaning that profits could not be increased by reducing sales), and (iii) that lower output prices would not sustain the same supply. Under diminishing returns, the second condition says that output prices should cover marginal costs, and the third says that output prices should not exceed marginal costs – hence the equality of output prices and marginal costs, characteristic of competitive equilibria. Under increasing returns, or more generally under U-shaped average costs, the second condition says the output prices should cover both average and marginal costs. That is still a reasonable condition. And the third condition says that output prices should not exceed the *maximum* of average and marginal cost, in the absence of monopolistic exploitation.

The alternative characterisation can be applied under increasing as well as constant or diminishing returns. Pierre Dehez and I (1988a) show that equilibria so defined exist, at the general equilibrium level, under minimal assumptions. For the firms with convex production possibilities, they correspond to competitive profit maximisation at given prices. For the firms with increasing returns, they correspond to profit maximisation at given prices *subject to a sales constraint* (thus allowing for excess supply); and the sales constraint is only binding when downward price rigidity sets in, because lower prices would not cover overhead costs. Rationing thus comes in naturally when we extend general equilibrium theory to the realistic case of increasing returns. (I may mention in passing that rationing comes in equally naturally when we introduce public goods with exclusion – see Drèze (1980b).)

3.2.

It also stands to reason that interesting price dynamics should allow trades to occur during the process of price adjustment. To assume that prices adjust continuously and instantaneously to clear all markets is not only unrealistic; it is very restrictive. Allowing for price rigidities yields a more flexible framework to study price dynamics. But when trades occur at non-market-clearing prices, some form of temporary rationing is unavoidable. Concepts of general equilibrium with rationing are thus indispensable to study price adjustments.

The idea that quantities adjust faster than prices, along such a process, has been stressed by Keynes and some of his commentators, in particular Leijonhufvud (1968). That idea finds its natural expression in the requirement that all advantageous trades compatible with given prices take place, before prices adjust. That requirement in turn finds expression in the condition that only one side of a given market, the short side, should be subject to quantity rationing. The theory of general equilibrium with rationing has established the feasibility of that condition: Given an arbitrary set of prices, all markets can be made to clear through voluntary trading by imposing quantity constraints on the short side only, and no constraints on the numeraire (money). That result is robust relative to the precise definition of rationing equilibria; see Bénassy (1975, 1982), Drèze (1975), Younès (1975), Malinvaud and Younès (1977a, b).

That existence result does not specify how the appropriate levels of one-sided rationing constraints emerge. And it does not bring in the spontaneous price increases which, we observe, eliminate excess demands. For a framework (introduced by Morishima (1976) in his 'Bastard Keynesian Theory') where production is described by a capacitated activity analysis model and where prices of final goods are derived from input prices through a markup formula, I have studied (Drèze (1983)) a simple tâtonnement process defined on the prices of inputs (including rents on installed capacities) and the quantities of these inputs which the owners can sell or use. The nominal prices of inputs are downward rigid and adjusted upward in case of excess demands. No price adjustments take place so long as desirable adjustments in the rationing constraints exist – thereby expressing the Keynes–Leijonhufvud idea. (The order in which the allowed adjustments take place is otherwise unrestricted.) Under natural assumptions, such a process converges to an equilibrium with constraints on the supply of inputs only (with unemployment and excess capacities). If arbitrarily small discrepancies between effective supplies and demands are tolerated, a strong finite convergence result is obtained. (I need not assume any substitutability, but well that no input is inferior, in the sense of being used less when aggregate demand expands. A nontâtonnement version is under study.)* That work corroborates the otherwise unfilled promise that adjustment processes in prices and quantity constraints would be more naturally stable than price tâtonnements. (It was inspired by a pioneering contribution of van der Laan (1980), later extended by Kurz (1982), Dehez and Drèze (1984) and van der Laan (1984) again.)

3.3.

Uncertainty and incomplete markets suggest another link between rationing equilibria and price dynamics.

There are, in my opinion, two main sources of persistent downward rigidities of prices and wages.

A first source is the non-competitive behaviour of firms and labour unions attempting to maximise revenues against demands perceived as inelastic. It is always difficult to estimate demand elasticities – and it is

---

* (Ed. Note) See Chapter 10 below.

not clear whether, and how, elasticity estimates should be revised when demand shifts. Under constant marginal costs or reservation wages, monopolistic prices and wages fail to respond to downward shifts.

This is illustrated in fig. 1.2, borrowed from Sneessens (1987). The figure is drawn for a canonical example. The technology entails a fixed cost and constant variable (marginal) costs C, up to a rigid capacity y^*. A constant elasticity demand function is subject to multiplicative shocks, which leave the monopoly price unchanged at $\tilde{p} = C.(1 + \eta_{p \cdot q})^{-1}$ so long as demand at that price does not exceed capacity. For demand realisations like D or D' inducing output levels inferior to capacity, there is *excess supply* with *downward price rigidity*.[1]

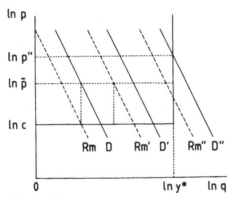

Figure 1.2

In a world of uncertainty and incomplete insurance markets, a second source of rigidities lies in the advantages of maintaining a degree of price stability across uncertain contingencies, as a risk-sharing and information generating device. There are many situations where continuous market-clearing through prices would make economic life as hectic as a rodeo.

The clearest illustration of this point comes from wages; the application to commodity prices is less transparent – see, however, the classic treatise by Okun (1981). In capitalist economies, one may expect wage-earners to be more risk-averse than asset-holders, because the latter can diversify risks through the stock market, whereas the former cannot. There is thus scope for mutually advantageous risk-sharing. But there is no organised

---

[1] The figure is drawn in logs to obtain linear relationships; from the demand function $q = Ap^{-\alpha}$, we obtain $\ln p = (1/\alpha)\ln A - (1/\alpha)\ln q$, $\ln Rm = \ln (\mathrm{d}pq/\mathrm{d}q) = (1/\alpha)\ln A + \ln (\alpha - 1)/\alpha - 1/\alpha \ln q = \ln p + \ln (\alpha - 1)/\alpha$.

insurance against deficient labour incomes, other than downwards wage rigidity and unemployment benefits. In such a world, efficiency considerations call for linking wages to national income and wealth; they do *not* call for letting wages fluctuate to clear labour markets continuously.* The argument to that effect, initially discovered in implicit contracts theory,[2] extends to the markets for new hirings as well, when labour demand is relatively inelastic; see Drèze (1986b, section 4 and appendix).† In this context, inelastic demand does not mean scope for monopolistic exploitation, but rather limited output losses under non-market clearing prices.

Typically, the two sources of rigidity are intertwined, and it is difficult to separate the inefficient use of *ex post* monopoly power from the efficient provision of *ex ante* income insurance. Expectations and time consistency raise additional difficulties. The wage elasticity of labour demand is low in the short run, substantial in the long run.[3] Wage rigidities that make sense in the face of a short-lived recession may become severely harmful in the face of a prolonged depression. The proper response may be both difficult to diagnose, and inconsistent with the expectations rationally held prior to a genuine surprise.

These considerations, to which I shall return in drawing policy conclusions, help us understand the existence and asymmetry of wage rigidities, as well as the difficulty of reaching agreement on wage policies.

3.4.

By way of conclusion to this section and of transition to the next one, let me move to a domain where general equilibrium theory has been put to practical uses, namely second-best analysis. In the methodology of the second-best, as pioneered by Ramsey (1927) and Boiteux (1956) and developed for instance by Diamond and Mirrlees (1971) or Guesnerie (1980), one uses the abstract general equilibrium model to trace out the implications of specific policies, like indirect taxes or public utility rates, under conditions where the realisation of a Pareto optimum as a competitive equilibrium is not feasible (for instance because overhead

---

* (Ed. Note) See Chapter 11.
[2] See in particular Azariadis (1975), Baily (1974), the informal exposition by Drèze (1979a) or the survey by Rosen (1985).
† (Ed. Note) See also Chapters 12 and 13.
[3] See e.g. Drèze and Modigliani (1981).

government expenditures must be covered by indirect taxes; or because the public utility operates with increasing returns, under a budget constraint ruling out marginal cost pricing). Traditionally, the competitive equilibrium framework has been used, whereas Keynesian macroeconomics was the dominant approach to fiscal policy. Why use two mutually inconsistent frameworks to study respectively the desired level of tax revenue and the desired structure of tax rates? There is no logical justification for such schizophrenia.... .

I have found the study of public sector pricing in a Keynesian regime particularly instructive. The program was to retrace the steps of Boiteux who, assuming all private agents to be in competitive equilibrium, discovered the well-known 'inverse elasticity rule' for public utility pricing. Assume instead, as a simple alternative, that the private agents are in Keynesian equilibrium, with unemployment, excess supply of commodities and sticky prices. The public utility pricing rule is then derived from a cost–benefit calculation, where the relevant costs and benefits come from the effects of price changes on the rate of inflation, the rate of unemployment and profits; these total effects are computed through a matrix multiplier operating on direct effects. In other words, the general equilibrium methodology leads naturally to evaluate costs and benefits by means of the 'comparative statics' approach of macroeconomics, taking all multiplier effects into account (Drèze (1984b), section 3.3). Furthermore, the trade-off between inflation, unemployment and profits is derived from primitive welfare weights assigned to individuals. There is no need to specify a global trade-off directly. These features reveal the intimate consistency between general equilibrium with rationing and standard macroeconomics. They suggest that the macroeconomic implications of microeconomics may be a more fruitful research topic than the microeconomic foundations of macroeconomics.... .

I will consider next how that program can be realised at the empirical, econometric level.

4. General equilibrium macroeconomics and econometrics

4.1.

The step from the detailed general equilibrium model, with many goods and many agents, to an operational macroeconomic model, has been taken boldly by some European econometricians. The path which they were to follow had been prepared by two significant sets of contributions, one empirical and one theoretical.

On the empirical side, the simple aggregate model of ToUR had been estimated as such for several European countries, with an employment relation derived from the min-condition:

$$L_t = \min\left[L_t^*, L(YD_t), LS_t\right], \tag{4}$$

up to disturbance terms and lagged adjustments.

The seminal contributions seem to have come from Benelux, with the work of Kooiman and Kloek (1985) for the Netherlands and of Sneessens (1981) for Belgium; see also Artus et al. (1984) and the Quandt Bibliography (1986).

These pioneering efforts demonstrated the workability of the approach. But they met with the objection that a model whereby the whole economy switches, between one year and the next, from a regime of Keynesian employment to a regime of classical unemployment or repressed inflation is too crude. It would be more realistic, and more germane to GEM, to view the national economy as a patchwork of individual markets for goods and for types of labour, some of which may be characterised by excess demand while others experience excess supply. Over time, the *proportion* of markets in the different regimes changes; for instance, a fall in aggregate demand is accompanied by an increase in the proportion of markets for individual goods or labour services where excess supply prevails.

A *description* of the state of the national economy should thus be given in terms of *regime proportions* for individual markets rather than in terms of a single regime prevailing at the aggregate level.

That pertinent observation was given content in theoretical papers by Muellbauer (1978) and Malinvaud (1980, 1982a), which inspired empirical econometric work, starting again with the Netherlands – Kooiman (1984) – and Belgium – Lambert (1988).

4.2.

The approach taken by these authors consists in postulating a *statistical distribution* of supplies and demands on micromarkets for goods and types of labour. The means of the distribution are related to the standard definitions of aggregate supply and demand for the national economy. The deviations from the mean reflect the idiosyncrasies of individual markets.

The authors mentioned above, and several others – Gourieroux *et al.* (1984), Martin (1986) – make a specific assumption about the form of the statistical distribution. The lognormal distribution, or a close substitute, is theoretically appealing and analytically tractable, especially when a convenient structure is imposed on covariances. It has led to the following approximate expression:

$$Y_t = [(Y_t^*)^{-\rho} + (YD_t)^{-\rho} + (Y(LS_t))^{-\rho}]^{-1/\rho}, \tag{5}$$

which 'explains' actual aggregate output Y_t in terms of the three standard quantities: notional supply Y_t^* (usually called potential output), final demand YD_t (usually called Keynesian demand) and full employment output $Y(LS_t)$. The parameter ρ, derived from the covariance matrix of deviations from the means, is a measure of the 'mismatch' between supply and demand across micromarkets – that is, of the extent to which firms supply iron rods while consumers buy Japanese video sets to watch the Mundial. For finite ρ,

$$Y_t < \min(Y_t^*, YD_t, Y(LS_t)). \tag{6}$$

When ρ tends to infinity, the mismatch disappears and the min is attained in the limit.

The proportions of micromarkets in the different regimes – say, π_K, π_C and π_R with $\pi_K + \pi_C + \pi_R = 1$ – are related as follows to the arguments of the output equation in the lognormal case:

$$\pi_{Kt} = \left(\frac{YD_t}{Y_t}\right)^{-\rho} = \eta_{Y_t \cdot YD_t}, \quad \pi_{Ct} = \left(\frac{Y_t^*}{Y_t}\right)^{-\rho} = \eta_{Y_t \cdot Y_t^*},$$

$$\pi_{Rt} = \left(\frac{Y(LS_t)}{Y_t}\right)^{-\rho} = \eta_{Y_t \cdot Y(LS_t)}. \tag{7}$$

In models of the manufacturing sector, like those of Kooiman and Lambert, these proportions are measured directly from business survey data, at a substantial gain in estimation efficiency.

It follows in particular from (5) and (7) that

$$\dot{Y}_t = \pi_{Ct}\dot{Y}_t^* + \pi_{Kt}\dot{Y}D_t + \pi_{Rt}\dot{Y}(LS_t), \tag{8}$$

a simple relationship between the rate of growth of actual output and the rates of growth of its determinants, weighted by the regime proportions describing the state of the economy.

All these expressions have natural counterparts for employment with

$$L_t = [(L_t^*)^{-\rho} + (L(YD_t))^{-\rho} + (LS_t)^{-\rho}]^{-1/\rho}. \tag{9}$$

An illustrative implication would be

$$\eta_{L_t.w_t} = \pi_{C_t}.\eta_{L_t^*.w_t} + \pi_{K_t}.\eta_{L(YD_t).w_t} + \pi_{R_t}.\eta_{LS_t.w_t}. \tag{10}$$

Let us look at an empirical application. fig. 1.3, reproduced from Sneessens and Drèze (1986a), presents empirical estimates of the four variables in (9) for the Belgian economy over the period 1955–82. We observe balanced growth during the sixties and early seventies, when potential employment L^*, Keynesian labour demand $L(YD)$ and labour supply LS followed the same trend. The Keynesian series displays less regularity, reflecting the greater short-run volatility of demand in comparison to capital and labour supply. Over that period, actual employment follows a parallel path, yet at a slightly lower level, with a growing structural mismatch between the supplies and demands for specific goods and labour services. A sharp break occurs in 1975, from which date onward the three basic series diverge. Labour supply continues to grow on the same trend. Potential employment (notional labour demand) stagnates from 1975 to 1980 and thereafter begins to fall, a tendency which extends to the present. Keynesian labour demand falls abruptly in 1975 and again in 1981. At the end of the period, actual employment is close to the level induced by final demand, with a large number of unemployed, of which less than half could be put back to work under a reflation of aggregate demand. This is due to the insufficient capital formation over the past decade, compounded by accelerated scrapping, due in particular to bankruptcies. The picture reveals the complex nature of our current predicament, where insufficient demand appears as the immediate constraint on employment, but where insufficient productive capacities lurk in the background as another potential constraint standing in the way of a return to full employment.

4.3.

At the risk of losing readers in a technical maze, I have summarised in the appendix the structure of a 'streamlined' GEM econometric model.[4]

---

[4] Taking the liberty to quote myself from the pages of the respectable *Economic Journal*: 'Models basically play the same role in economics as in fashion: they provide an articulated frame on which to show off your material to advantage...; a useful role, but fraught with the dangers that the designer may get carried away by his personal inclination for the model, while the customers may forget that the model is more streamlined than reality' (Drèze (1985a, p. 3)).

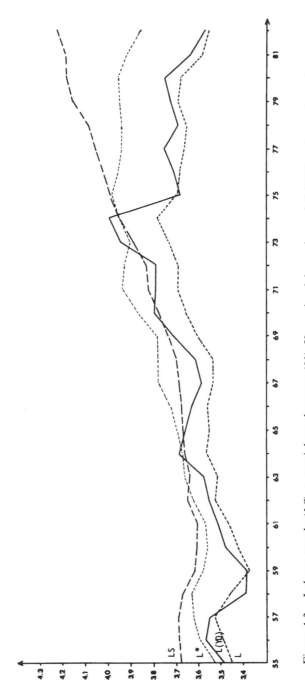

Figure 1.3. Labour supply (*LS*), potential employment (*L**), Keynesian labour demand (*L(YD)*) and actual employment (*L*) (millions of man years).

Source: Sneessens and Drèze (1986a)

It corresponds to the model of the Belgian economy estimated by Sneessens and Drèze (1986a, b), where however investment and exports are treated as exogenous. Lag structures are left out to simplify exposition.

The output equation appears as (A.7), next to the standard accounting identity (A.6). The specific difficulty associated with that equation is that YD_t, Y_t^* and $Y(LS_t)$ are *not observed*. They must be replaced by estimates in terms of observables, as suggested by (A.8).

On the supply side, potential output Y_t^* is estimated from an aggregate production function, into which the capital stock and relative factor prices are plugged. Our modelling of the production function in (A.1) and (A.2) is quite simple – the Leontief–Cobb–Douglas technology already found in Sneessens (1981). More ambitious approaches are possible, as illustrated by Kooiman and Kloek (1985) for instance. I would hope that the new challenges of GEModelling may inspire new developments on the production front(ier).

On the demand side, the logic of the model is that $Y_t < YD_t$. In the case of the small open economy of Belgium, we felt safe in assuming that consumer demand was always satisfied, with excesses relative to domestic supply spilling over into additional imports beyond the 'normal' or 'structural' import demand MD. To simplify exposition I have assumed in the appendix a unitary elasticity of these imports to final demand, and solved for YD in eq. (A.5). Consumption and import demands receive traditional specifications in (A.3) and (A.4).

The price and wage equations are quite simple. The price equation (A.10) combines a component of demand-pull inflation, introduced by the ratio YD_t/Y_t, and a component of cost-push inflation, introduced by the first differences of average costs. The wage equation (A.11) is more problematic, as one could expect. It lacks the theoretical underpinning of a theoretical bargaining model and relates instead wages to labour productivity. This is at best a 'reduced form' representation, where the twin causation from technological progress to wage demands and from wage concessions to labour saving technologies is left unstructured. We naturally introduce unemployment as an explanatory variable.

Although investment and exports are treated as exogenous variables in Sneessens and Drèze (1986a), one should, and easily could, introduce additional structural equations, like (A.12) and (A.13), to endogenise them (and the capital stock). This would lead to a system of 7 structural equations for the endogenous observed variables C_t, I_t, X_t, Y_t, L_t, P_t and W_t – namely equations (A.3) and (A.8)–(A.13).

4.4.

An attempt at estimating such a model in several European countries is under way, coordinated by Richard Layard and myself, and sponsored by the Commission of the European Economic Community.* We are in acute need of imaginative empirical work along such lines. Europe suffers from its segmentation in national economies. Models of individual countries are not directly comparable, and of limited interest to foreigners. This holds back the accumulation of empirical knowledge, in comparison with the U.S. where the large army of applied economists and econometricians works with the same data set. Let me mention in passing the instructive experiment under way at the Commission of the European Communities, where André Dramais (1986) has estimated a macroeconometric model directly on aggregate data for the community as a whole.[5] The same specification will be estimated on country data, and the simulations of the aggregate model will be compared with the simulations of the linked country models. Clearly, if we could work with aggregate European data, empirical research would leap forward. More realistically, we should aim at making a data base covering at least the four major European countries widely available for systematic replications of empirical studies. And we should watch closely the experience of the Macromodelling Bureau at the University of Warwick, which documents and makes accessible to outside users a set of British models. A similar initiative at the European level would make sense, and might be worth promoting by the European Economic Association.

Returning to the model of the appendix, let me mention briefly a few problems. The approach of aggregating over microunits by means of a statistical distribution is not entirely new. It has been used by Houthakker (1955) and his followers to construct aggregate production functions. Imaginative related work by Hildenbrand (1981, 1983) on both production and consumption should also be mentioned. In the present context, that approach smooths out the min condition, thereby reducing considerably the computational efforts. There are several important open issues. One of them relates to the robustness of the aggregate specifications *vis-à-vis* the choice of distributional form (lognormal, logistic, Weilbull, . . .). Another relates to the restrictive assumptions on covariances, leading in the model presented here to a single mismatch parameter ρ. One would like at least to distinguish the mismatch on labour markets from the mismatch on

---

[5] Interestingly, the employment function in that model uses the min specification (4).

*(Ed. Note) See Chapter 16.

goods markets. (My suspicion is that the latter is much more important than the former.) Another still relates to the statistical flexibility of the approach for dynamic specifications – a point (over)emphasised by Hendry (1982) – for full information estimation or for Bayesian analysis. And the 'small economy' assumption will need to be relaxed when we move from Belgium or the Netherlands to more significant areas.

Two more fundamental issues should be mentioned. They concern respectively aggregation and integration. There is no doubt that aggregation of microrelationships by means of statistical distributions entails a substantial loss of potential information. We know a lot about the tensions or latitudes on individual markets, and would prefer to use that information. A simple meaningful step would call for separating the manufacturing sector from the services and the public sector. (One advantage of that step comes from the availability of business survey data for manufacturing firms.)

The integration issue is altogether different – although related as well to efficient use of information. The model of the appendix uses explicitly the aggregation over micromarkets to derive the aggregate output and employment expressions. But several other equations are specified in a more or less *ad hoc* – though plausible – way. Such is the case in particular for the price and wage equations, and for the investment equation (to be added). And the concept of 'micromarket' itself remains ambiguous. The logic of General Equilibrium Macroeconomics would call for aggregating relationships describing the behaviour of individual agents – an 'integrated' behaviour which, in the case of firms, bears simultaneously on output, employment, prices and investment. That idea is partly, but imperfectly, reflected in the presence of the variable YD_t/Y_t in the price equation, or the variables YD_t/Y_t and Y_t^*/Y_t in the proposed investment equation. A more satisfactory approach would call for deriving the demand-pull term of the price equation directly from the aggregation of 'excess demand' terms of the micromarkets – thereby probably bringing in the parameter ρ; and similarly for the investment equation. There should result a more efficient integration of the information contained in the output, employment, price and investment data. That approach remains to be worked out. A preliminary exploration is found in Sneessens (1987).

4.5.

On the positive side, the model outlined in the appendix has a number of interesting implications for macroeconomic theory.

This may be illustrated with reference to the short-run multiplier of autonomous expenditure. From (5), with $YD = CD(Y) + I + G + X - MD(Y)$, we obtain easily

$$\frac{dY}{dG} = \frac{1}{\left(\dfrac{YD}{Y}\right)^{\rho+1} + \dfrac{\partial MD}{\partial Y} - \dfrac{\partial CD}{\partial Y}} < \frac{1}{1 + \dfrac{\partial MD}{\partial Y} - \dfrac{\partial CD}{\partial Y}}$$

$$\simeq \frac{1}{\dfrac{1}{\pi_K} + \dfrac{\partial MD}{\partial Y} - \dfrac{\partial CD}{\partial Y}}. \tag{11}$$

This formula calls for two comments. First, the multiplier is reduced – in comparison with the standard Keynesian formula – because the response of actual output to demand is dampened by the extent of classical unemployment and repressed inflation in the economy.

Second, even if the marginal propensities to import and to consume were estimated as constants, the multiplier would not be constant; it would vary over time with the proportion of Keynesian unemployment in the economy – being an increasing function of that proportion.

Another interesting application concerns the inflation–unemployment trade-off, for which bringing in the supply-side also makes a difference. Much use is made, in some macroeconomic literature, of the concept of 'non-accelerating-inflation rate of unemployment', or NAIRU. But NAIRU also stands for 'Not Always Instructive Rate of Unemployment'. If the aggregate economy were predominantly in a classical regime, the NAIRU as usually defined would be a 'Now Altogether Irrelevant Rate of Unemployment', because the main source of price inflation would originate in the pressure of excess demand.

The kind of Phillips curve associated with our model is more general. The relationship between unemployment and wage or price inflation is twofold. On the one hand, there is the causation from the rate of unemployment to wages: the higher unemployment, the slower the rate of increase of wages – hence of prices, through cost-push inflation. On the other hand, there is the demand-pull inflation, associated with high levels of demand, hence with low levels of unemployment. Here the causation is from excess demand to high inflation and low unemployment. Empirically, the two relationships are entangled. The natural identifying variable is the degree of capacity utilisation, Y^*/Y or DUC, and the reduced form equation, which endogenises shifts in the Phillips curve, is

$$d \ln P = -\alpha \ln [1 - DUC^\rho - (1 - UR)^\rho] - \beta UR. \tag{12}$$

All these points may have been known to enlightened macrotheorists for some time. But GEM provides a rigorous framework within which the needed qualifications and extensions to Keynesian economics fit naturally – and emerge from microeconomic reasoning.

5.   Policy conclusions and agenda

5.1.

I may not have convinced you that macroeconomics should best be taught within a 'General Equilibrium Theory' course, as I do in Louvain-la-Neuve. And the unity of the theoretical framework may stand out more clearly in my own mind, where it has been at work for ten years, than I could express in one hour today. But hopefully you may share my conviction that macroeconomic thinking and teaching requires due attention to the supply side, and to the constraints placed on output and employment by productive capacities and the number of work places.

If the estimates obtained for Belgium and reproduced in fig. 1.3 are at all typical, or if the estimates obtained by Dramais (1986) for the Common Market as a whole are correct, we must conclude: on the one hand, that an insufficient level of effective demand is the main factor holding back employment in Europe today; but on the other hand, that only part of our shocking level of unemployment could be eliminated by a demand revival, due to capital shortages and structural mismatches.

We thus need two-handed policies,[6]* where the demand side and the supply side both receive due attention. There is little point in arguing about which side is the more important – in the same way that there is little point in debating whether the ham or the cheese is more essential to the preparation of a ham and cheese sandwich. For the purpose of defining an appropriate mix of demand-side and supply-side policies, econometric work of the kind outlined here seems definitely helpful. An immediate usefulness emerges at the diagnostic level, to evaluate the strength of inflationary demand tensions and the threats of classical unemployment, The relevant quantities are not observable, so that we need imaginative use of all available information (including business surveys, I would say). I see here a major role for GEM econometrics, in addition to the usual role of providing the quantitative orders of magnitude without which policy recommendations remain platonic.

[6] 'A two-handed approach', in the words of Blanchard et al. (1985).
* (Ed. Note) See Chapter 18.

In these conclusions, the supply side is not done full justice, because no reference is made to the relevance of supply factors in the determination of effective demand. Given the magnitude of imports and exports in relation to GDP for Europe as a whole, competitiveness vis-à-vis the rest of the world plays an important role in the determination of final demand for domestic output. It also plays an important role as a determinant of investment. My conclusions point to an investment boom as being particularly welcome – if only we knew how to engineer it. Demand expectations put on investment the same lid that effective demand puts on output – pointing again to the need of a two-handed approach. Work on investment, to fit it properly in the theoretical framework of General Equilibrium Macroeconomics, and to fit appropriate econometric relationships, continues to deserve a high priority on the research agenda. Our policy needs point in the same direction as more theoretical considerations. As for stimulating desirable capital widening investment without at the same time stimulating undesirable capital deepening, I am afraid that the dilemma is genuine. In sectors open to international competition, the more capital intensive technologies seem to offer the better long-run prospects to European producers. And recent technological advances offer prospects for capital–labour substitution in services that seem difficult to counteract. Overall stimulation of demand and investment are thus likely to offer the better chances for employment recovery.

5.2.

An important area of uncertainty concerns incomes policies – a prudish name for wage moderation. In this respect as well, we need to keep an eye on both the demand side and the supply side. There is no doubt that aggregate consumption remains a prime determinant of effective demand, for Europe as a whole. And I have not seen any evidence yet pointing to a spending propensity higher for profits than for wages. At the same time, spending on investment is more desirable today than spending on imported consumables. And I am convinced that the short-run elasticity of employment with respect to real wages is small, whereas the long-run elasticity is substantially negative, so that the issue of time horizon mentioned in Section 3.3 is essential.

The GEM framework and the econometric work reviewed here suggest two propositions. If it is indeed the case that only half of our unemployment could be eliminated by demand reflation, with capital widening investments indispensable for attacking the other half, then: (i) a fairly long time is bound to be needed before Europe attains again a reasonable degree of full employment – so that a middle to long-term time horizon is definitely relevant; (ii) although indispensable in the long run, wage restraint could not be fully effective in the short run, due to the insufficient number of working places resulting from the low investment levels of the past decade.

Many of us feel that real wages rose abnormally in the mid seventies, when Europe was struck by the conjunction of worsening terms of trade, increased competition from the NIC's and a slower growth of world imports. We struggle today with the consequences of that mistake, in which all participants to the wage bargaining process share responsibility. It is not a pleasant struggle. If my two propositions are correct, we must combine structural measures that prevent the repetition of such a mistake with short-term remedial measures that alleviate the burden of unemployment, especially unemployment of the young – and, I shall argue in a moment, of the less skilled. The relevant structural measures are those which will keep our real wages on a suitable path, whether the recovery unfolds or whether the recession continues.

A genuine hazard of the present situation still lies with the temptation of beggar-thy-neighbour policies of intra-European competition through exchange rates *and wage levels*. We need instead concerted reflation with stable real wages that can be maintained in the longer run in the face of a long-awaited recovery. In some countries, a more realistic pattern of indexation, combining in suitable proportions nominal GDP with consumer prices, belongs in such a policy. The temporary disappearance of inflation offers an exceptional opportunity for negotiating such a structural change, which strikes me as more promising and less fraught with deflationary hazards than nominal wage cuts of uncertain longer-run consequences. Expectations of stable wage developments are also more relevant to hiring decision than short-lived concessions. Additional structural measures aimed at greater efficiency of our productive sphere and of our market mechanisms, measures promoting investment and reducing mismatches, would thereby gain in overall effectiveness.

As someone whose value judgements entail special concern for the less privileged members of our societies, I wish at the same time to see an improvement in the employment prospects of the less skilled fringe of our labour force. That is a difficult project, because persistent unemployment invariably results in a high concentration of the unemployment in the less skilled group. Remedial measures should include special employment programs, which seem to entail lower net costs per job than most alternatives. Our experience with work-sharing is by and large sobering, except for early retirement schemes; but there remains scope for more part-time work – see Drèze (1986b). Given the low levels of disposable income associated with unskilled work, I would favour a restructuring of wage costs through exemption of social security contributions on the part of earnings corresponding to minimum wages, and a funding of the corresponding social security expenditures (which reflect citizen's rights rather than worker's rights) through general taxation.[7]

5.3

All the issues touched so briefly in my conclusions, from two-handed policies through investment stimulation to incomes policies and social security financing, deserve further analysis. I have tried to convince you that General Equilibrium Macroeconomics provide an appropriate theoretical framework for such analysis, including the indispensable econometric verifications and quantifications. Our mastery of that framework is still fragmentary, but avenues of research are open, and I hope that many of you will explore them. That hope seems justified, in view of the liveliness and inventiveness of European economists, as witnessed by the program of this Congress. The developments reviewed this morning, which reflect European efforts of the past fifteen years, provide another testimony. Contributions, to which time did not allow me to devote proper attention, have come from Scandinavia and the Mediterranean as well as from continental Europe and the British Isles. And the proposed framework is apt to promote intellectual exchanges between East and West. The quantity and quality of the European research efforts in economics are undeniable. There remains scope for increasing the effectiveness of these efforts, through more intimate cooperation between specialists of different fields, of different countries, of different ages, of different ways of life. It is the aim of the European Economic Association to promote such cooperation. I wish you much success in realising that aim, and making my dream come true.

---

[7] That suggestion, and its ethical basis, are presented in Drèze (1985b).

Appendix. Streamlined GEM econometric model

(A.1)   Notional output (supply) Y_t^*, unobserved, is equal to the capital stock K_t times the desired output/capital ratio B_t, estimated as a function of the relative prices of labour W_t and of capital V_t, shifted by technological progress.

$$Y_t^* = K_t \cdot e^{a_0 + a_1 t} \left(\frac{W_t}{V_t}\right)^{-a_2} := K_t \cdot B_t \left(\frac{W_t}{V_t}\right).$$

(A.2)   Full employment output $Y(LS_t)$, unobserved, is equal to the labour force LS_t times the desired output/labour ratio A_t

$$Y(LS_t) = LS_t \cdot e^{a_3 + a_1 t} \left(\frac{W_t}{V_t}\right)^{1-a_2} := LS_t \cdot A_t \left(\frac{W_t}{V_t}\right).$$

(A.3)   Consumption demand CD_t is equal to actual consumption C_t and is a function of labour incomes $W_t L_t$, transfers, gross profits $P_t Y_t - W_t L_t \ldots$; $UR = (LS - L)/LS$ is the unemployment rate

$$CD_t = C(W_t L_t, LS_t - L_t, P_t Y_t = W_t L_t, \ldots) = C(Y_t, UR_t, \ldots).$$

(A.4)   Import demand MD_t, unobserved, is a proportion μ_t of final demand YD_t, where μ_t depends upon import prices PM_t (exogenous), domestic prices $P_t, \ldots$

$$MD_t = YD_t \cdot \mu(PM_t, P_t, \ldots).$$

(A.5) $$YD_t := CD_t + I_t + G_t + X_t - MD_t = \frac{C_t + I_t + G_t + X_t}{1 + \mu(PM_t, P_t, \ldots)}.$$

(A.6) $$Y_t := C_t + I_t + G_t + X_t - M_t$$

(A.7) $$= \{(YD_t)^{-\rho} + (Y_t^*)^{-\rho} + [Y(LS_t)]^{-\rho}\}^{-1/\rho}$$

(A.8) $$= \left\{ \left[\frac{C_t + I_t + G_t + X_t}{1 + \mu(PM_t, P_t, \ldots)}\right]^{-\rho} + \left[K_t \cdot e^{a_0 + a_1 t}\left(\frac{W_t}{V_t}\right)^{-a_2}\right]^{-\rho} \right.$$
$$\left. + \left[LS_t \cdot e^{a_3 + a_1 t}\left(\frac{W_t}{V_t}\right)^{1-a_2}\right]^{-\rho} \right\}^{-1/\rho}.$$

(A.9) $$L_t = \{[L(YD_t)]^{-\rho} + (L_t^*)^{-\rho} + (LS_t)^{-\rho}\}^{-1/\rho} = A_t^{-1} Y_t.$$

(A.10)   Price inflation reflects demand pull YD_t/Y_t and cost-push, where average production cost is equal to $A^{-1}W + B^{-1}V$

$$\Delta \ln P_t = \Delta \ln P\left(\ln \frac{YD_t}{Y_t}, \Delta \ln [A_t^{-1}W_t + B_t^{-1}V_t] \right).$$

(A.11)   Wage inflation reflects price indexation, changes in labour productivity A and the rate of unemployment

$$\Delta \ln W_t = \Delta \ln W(\Delta \ln P_t, \Delta \ln A_t, UR_t).$$

(A.12)   An investment equation, to be added, should combine the effects of potential demand and excess capacities with those of factor prices and profitability

$$I_t = I\left(\frac{YD_t}{Y_t}, \frac{Y_t^*}{Y_t}, \frac{W_t}{V_t}, \frac{A_t^{-1}W_t + B_t^{-1}V_t}{P_t}, \ldots \right).$$

The capital stock becomes then endogenous.

(A.13)   An exports equation, to be added, should combine the effects of world demand, export prices,..., with those of excess demand and excess capacities

$$X_t = X\left(\frac{YD_t}{Y_t}, \frac{Y_t^*}{Y_t}, \ldots \right).$$

Eq. (A.5) is to be modified when (A.12) and (A.13) are added.

II Equilibria with price rigidities

2 Existence of an exchange equilibrium under price rigidities*

1. Introduction and contents

In this paper, we study an exchange economy where allocation of resources is guided by a price mechanism, but prices are subject to inequality constraints. An equilibrium is obtained by introducing quantity constraints on the net trades of those commodities for which the price constraints are binding. The set of admissible quantity constraints is defined in a way which avoids trivial equilibria.

Two kinds of price rigidities are considered in turn, namely constraints on nominal prices in an economy with a numeraire (Sections 4 and 5) and constraints on relative or real prices in an economy without a numeraire (Section 6). The two kinds are then considered simultaneously (Section 7). In each case, we find that inequality constraints on net trades may be substituted for price adjustments, one-to-one, as devices to equate supply and demand. (Clearly, this is a statement about feasibility, not about efficiency.)

Some background remarks on price rigidities and quantity rationing (Section 2) precede the description of the model (Section 3). The results are so organized that the basic technique of proof is introduced first on a simple problem (constraints on all nominal prices); the technique is then extended in two directions (constraints on some but not all nominal prices, constraints on all real prices); these extensions are combined in a final theorem, of which the first three are special cases (constraints on some nominal and/or some real prices).

* *International Economic Review*, 16, 2 (1975), 301–320. I wish to thank Gérard Debreu, Jean Jaskold Gabzewicz, Jean-Michel Grandmont, Birgit Grodal, Werner Hildenbrand and Karl Vind for interesting discussions and helpful suggestions; I am particularly grateful to Pierre Dehez and Dieter Sondermann who discovered mistakes in earlier versions of this paper; responsibility for remaining errors is mine.

2. Price rigidities and quantity rationing

The phenomenon of price rigidity, i.e. the persistence of prices at which supply and demand are not equal, is frequently observed, and plays an important role in some macro-economic models. Downward wage rigidity in the presence of underemployment, with or without minimum wage laws, is the foremost example.[1] Rent controls, price controls aimed at curbing inflationary pressures, usury laws, price uniformity over time or space, provide other examples.

In most cases, price rigidities may be described as inequality constraints on individual prices – either absolute or relative.[2] Absolute limits are usually expressed in monetary units. The first model considered in this paper uses a 'numeraire' commodity, always desired, whose price is set equal to 1. The other prices are constrained by absolute limits. This asymmetrical treatment is natural, when money is used as a numeraire. In a model without money, this asymmetry is no longer natural, but then price rigidities are more naturally expressed in relative, or 'real' terms. Such rigidities take the form of price limits tied to certain index numbers. In existing price-guided economies, both types of rigidities are observed simultaneously. That case is also considered below.

The imbalance between supply and demand, which may result from price rigidities, is typically absorbed by some kind of quantity rationing. The 'kind' varies from market to market. It may consist in inequality constraints on consumption (for instance, housing consumption) or on net trades (for instance, labour supply). Constraints on net trades may be absolute (i.e., an upper limit on individual demands, as under point rationing) or relative (i.e. the same fraction of all individual demands is satisfied, as under many bond issues). The rationing may also be random (as in the case of overloaded telephone exchanges) or involve priorities (e.g. workers are laid off in order of increasing seniority).

In this paper, only the simplest form of quantity rationing will be considered, namely *absolute constraints on net trades*. The reasoning applies, with minimal modifications, to absolute constraints on consumption. Other schemes (proportional or random rationing, priorities, ...) would require independent study.

---

[1] The present note was motivated by research in progress on the rational aspects of wage rigidities and unemployment compensation, viewed as a form of income insurance for which market opportunities offer no substitute.

[2] Price uniformity over time or space takes the different form of equality constraints among several prices.

In order to avoid trivial equilibria (e.g. all net trades constrained to vanish), two conditions are imposed: (i) rationing may affect either supply or demand, but it may not affect simultaneously both supply and demand; (ii) upward (downward) price rigidity must be binding if there is quantity rationing of demand (supply). The existence theorems below confirm the intuitive expectation that this simple form of rationing adequately absorbs the excess demands that may result from price rigidities.

The extension of the theorems to economies with production presents no new difficulties. However, absolute limits on individual net trades seem more natural in the case of consumers, than in the case of firms of arbitrary sizes. Absolute limits that vary from individual to individual, according to fixed quotas, could easily be accommodated.

The converse problem, namely existence of an equilibrium under quantity rationing of either consumptions or net trades (by means of absolute constraints), is covered by the standard theory. Indeed, the constraints may be included in the definition of the consumption sets (or the production sets), so long as convexity of these sets is preserved.[3]

3. The model and a lemma

Consider an exchange economy with n commodities indexed $j = 1, 2, \cdots n$ and N consumers indexed $i = 1 \cdots N$.

Consumer i is defined by $(X^i, \succcurlyeq_i, w^i)$. $x \geq y$ means $x_j \geq y_j \forall j$ and $x \neq y$; $x > y$ means $x_j > y_j \forall j$.

Throughout this paper, we shall make the following assumptions:

ASSUMPTION 1. The consumption set $X^i \subset R^n_+$, with elements x^i, is closed, convex and satisfies: $x \in X^i$ implies $\{x\} + R^n_+ \subset X_i$.

ASSUMPTION 2. The preference ordering $\succcurlyeq_i$ on X^i is complete, continuous and convex; $x \geq y$ implies $x \succcurlyeq_i y$; there is an index set $I \subset \{1, 2, \ldots n\}$ such that $x \geq y$ and $x_j > y_j \forall j \in I$ imply $x \succ_i y$.

ASSUMPTION 3. The initial resources w^i belong to the interior of X^i.

The index set I in Assumption 2 will consist of that commodity (numeraire) or those commodities (base of an index number) in terms of whose price the constraints are expressed. Clearly, it would be meaningless to use a worthless commodity as numeraire.... .

---

[3] This would not be the case if the consumer had the choice of 'consuming' either nothing, or else a minimum quantity, of some good.

Define $w = \sum_i w^i$, the total resources of the economy; and $z^i = x^i - w^i$, the net trade of consumer i.

A *price system* p is a vector of R^n. The price constraints will require that p should belong to some set

$$P = \{p \in R^n_+ \mid f(p) = 1, \bar{p} \geq p \geq \underline{p}\}.$$

Alternative definitions of the normalization rule $f(p)$ and of the bounds $(\bar{p}, \underline{p})$ will be considered below. In some cases (when the bounds are tied to index numbers), $\bar{p} = \bar{p}(p)$.

A *rationing scheme* is a pair of vectors $(L, l) \in R^n \times R^n$, with $L \geq 0 \geq l$.

Given a price vector p and a rationing scheme (L, l), the budget set of consumer i is defined by

$$\gamma^i(p, L, l) = \{x \in X^i \mid p(x - w^i) \leq 0, L \geq x - w^i \geq l\}.$$

$w^i \in X^i$ implies $\gamma^i(p, L, l) \neq \phi$ for all admissible p and (L, l).

An *exchange economy with price rigidities* is here defined as

$$\mathscr{E} = \{(X^i, \succcurlyeq_i, w^i), P\}.$$

An *equilibrium under price rigidities and rationing*, or 'equilibrium for $\mathscr{E}$', is here defined as an N-tuple of consumption vectors $\{x^i\}$, a price system $p \in P$ and a rationing scheme (L, l) such that

(i)   for all i, x^i is a maximal element for $\succcurlyeq_i$ of $\gamma^i(p, L, l)$;

(ii) $\sum_i(x^i - w^i) = 0$;

(iii) $\forall j, L_j = x^i_j - w^i_j$ for some i implies $x^h_j - w^h_j > l_j \forall h$

$\qquad l_j = x^i_j - w^i_j$ for some i implies $x^h_j - w^h_j < L_j \forall h$;

(iv) $\forall j, \bar{p}_j > p_j$ implies $L_j > x^i_j - w^i_j \forall i$

$\qquad p_j > \underline{p}_j$ implies $l_j < x^i_j - w^i_j \forall i$.

Condition (ii) is stated in equality form because quantity rationing may be used to eliminate excess supply. Condition (iii) states that rationing may affect either supply or demand, but may not affect simultaneously both supply and demand. Condition (iv) states that no quantity rationing is allowed unless price rigidities are binding.

The continuity properties of the budget set correspondence γ^i, from $R^n_+ \times R^n_+ \times R^n_-$ to X^i, play an important role in the technical derivations below. In the usual model, where

$$P = R^n_+, \quad L = +\infty, \quad l = -\infty,$$

$\gamma^i(p)$ is continuous, under Assumptions 1 and 3, at every $p \geq 0$;[4] that is, whenever γ^i owns some $\bar{x}$ such that $p(\bar{x} - w^i) < 0$. A similar result holds in the present model; however, the existence of the required $\bar{x}$ depends not only on $p \geq 0$ but also on $l \leq 0$, $p \cdot l < 0$.

LEMMA. *The correspondence* $\gamma^i(p, L, l)$ *from* $R^n_+ \times R^n_+ \times R^n_-$ *to* X^i *is continuous at every point* (p^0, L^0, l^0) *where for some* $j, p^0_j > 0$ *and* $l^0_j < 0$.

PROOF. Define

$$\alpha^i(p) = \{x \mid x \in R^n, \, p(x - w^i) \leq 0\}$$
$$\beta^i(L, l) = \{x \mid x \in X^i, \, L \geq x - w^i \geq l\}.$$

$\alpha^i(p)$ and $\beta^i(L, l)$ are convex; α^i is continuous at every $p \geq 0$; we first prove that β^i is continuous as well.

$$\beta^i(L, l) = \beta^i(L) \cap \beta^i(l),$$

where

$$\beta^i(L) = \{x \mid x \in X^i, \, L \geq x - w^i\}$$
$$\beta^i(l) = \{x \mid x \in X^i, \, x - w^i \geq l\}.$$

Because $w^i \in \text{int } X^i$, $\beta^i(L)$ and $\beta^i(l)$ have non-empty interiors for all

$$(L, l) \in R^n_+ \times R^n_-$$

and are continuous. $\beta^i(L, l)$ is upper hemicontinuous, as an intersection of continuous correspondence.

To prove lower hemicontinuity, let

$$(L^s, l^s) \to (L^0, l^0)$$

and let

$$x^0 \in \beta^i(L^0, l^0).$$

Define

$$J_1 = \{j \mid j = 1 \cdots n, \, L^0_j = 0 = l^0_j\},$$
$$J_2 = \{j \mid j = 1 \cdots n, \, L^0_j > l^0_j\};$$

---

[4] See e.g. Debreu (1959) (proposition (i) of 4.8.).

by appropriate reindexing, let

$$J_1 = \{1 \cdots m\},$$
$$J_2 = \{m + 1, \cdots n\}$$

and write

$$L^0 = (L_1^0, L_2^0),\ l^0 = (l_1^0, l_2^0),\ x^0 = (x_1^0, x_2^0),\ w^i = (w_1^i, w_2^i)$$

with

$$L_1^0 = l_1^0 = x_1^0 = 0 \text{ and } L_2^0 \geq x_2^0 \geq l_2^0.$$

The set

$$\{x_2\,|\,(0, x_2) \in X^i, L_2^0 \geq x_2 - w_2^i\} \cap \{x_2\,|\,(0, x_2) \in X^i, x_2 - w_2^i \geq l_2^0\}$$

in R^{n-m} has a nonempty interior; therefore, there exists a sequence

$$x^s = (0, x_2^s),\ x^s \to x^0,\ x^s \in \beta^i(L^s, l^s)\,\forall\,s.$$

Accordingly, β^i is continuous for all

$$(L, l) \in R_+^n \times R_-^n.$$

Now, γ^i is upper hemicontinuous, as an intersection of continuous correspondences.

To prove lower hemicontinuity, let

$$(p^s, L^s, l^s) \to (p^0, L^0, l^0), \qquad\qquad p_j^0 > 0,\ l_j^0 < 0,$$

and let

$$x^0 \in \gamma^i(p^0, L^0, l^0).$$

Because β^i is continuous, there exists a sequence $\{\hat{x}^s\}$,

$$\hat{x}^s \in \beta^i(p^s, L^s, l^s), \qquad\qquad \hat{x}^s \to x^0.$$

If

$$x^0 \in \text{int } \gamma^i(p^0, L^0, l^0),$$

there exists s' such that

$$\hat{x}^s \in \alpha^i(p^s, L^s, l^s)$$

for all $s \geq s'$; indeed,

$$p^0(x^0 - w^i) < 0$$

implies

$$p^s(\hat{x}^s - w^i) < 0, \qquad\qquad s \geq s'.$$

Let then

$$p^0(x^0 - w^i) = 0.$$

There exists

$$\bar{x} \in \alpha^i(p^0), \qquad\qquad \bar{x}_j < w^i_j, \ \bar{x}_k = w^i_k, \ k \neq j,$$

with

$$\bar{x} \in \beta^i(L^0, l^0), \ p^s(\bar{x} - w^i) < 0, \qquad\qquad s \geq s'.$$

Define $\{x^s\}$ by:

$$\left.\begin{array}{l} p^s(x^s - w^i) = 0 \\ x^s = \lambda^s \hat{x}^s + (1 - \lambda^s)\bar{x} \end{array}\right\} \text{ for all } s \text{ such that } \hat{x}^s \notin \alpha^i(p^s)$$

$$x^s = \hat{x}^s \qquad\qquad \text{otherwise.}$$

x^s exists and is unique.

$$x^s \in \gamma^i(p^s, L^s, l^s).$$

Also, $x^s \to x^0$; indeed, when $p^s \to p^0$,

$$p^s(\hat{x}^s - w^i) \to p^0(x^0 - w^i) = 0$$

but

$$p^s(\bar{x} - w^i) \to p^0(\bar{x} - w^i) < 0,$$

so that $p^s(x^s - w^i) = 0$ implies that $\lambda^s \to 1$, $x^s \to x^0$. The sequence x^s has all the required properties to complete the proof of lower hemicontinuity.

QED

4. Limited flexibility of all nominal prices

In this section, we prove the existence of an equilibrium when there exists a numeraire (money) and prices are subject to constraints in terms of that numeraire. It simplifies exposition to assume the existence of an upper limit on every price. Proceeding under that assumption, we introduce a technique of proof that will be used again in later sections. The assumption that every price is bounded upward is relaxed in Section 5.

THEOREM 1. *Let*

$$\mathscr{E} = \{(X^i, \succcurlyeq_i, w^i), P\}$$

satisfy Assumptions 1, 2 with index set $I = \{1\}$, *and 3; let*

$$P = \{p \in R^n \mid p_1 = 1, +\infty > \bar{p} \geq p \geq \underline{p} \geq 0\};$$

there exists an equilibrium for $\mathscr{E}$.

The proof of the theorem rests upon a definition and a remark.
Consider the pair of vectors $(M, m) \in R^n \times R^n$ defined by

$$M_j = \bar{p}_j + w_j, m_j = \underline{p}_j - w_j, \qquad\qquad j = 1 \cdots n,$$

and the compact, convex set

$$Q = \{q \in R^n \mid M \geq q \geq m\}.$$

DEFINITION. For every $q \in Q$ define the price system $p(q)$ and the
rationing scheme $(L(q), l(q))$ by:

$$\text{(D)} \begin{cases} p_j(q) = \min\left[\bar{p}_j, \max\left(q_j, \underline{p}_j\right)\right] = \max\left(\underline{p}_j, \min\left(q_j, \bar{p}_j\right)\right), \\ L_j(q) = M_j - \max\left(\bar{p}_j, q_j\right), \\ l_j(q) = m_j - \min\left(\underline{p}_j, q_j\right), \qquad\qquad j = 1 \cdots n. \end{cases}$$

This definition is illustrated in figure 2.1, which is drawn for a case

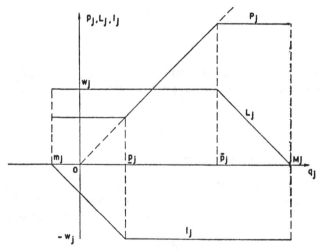

Figure 2.1

where $\bar{p}_j > w_j > \underline{p}_j > 0$. The figure reveals that, given $(w_j, \bar{p}_j, \underline{p}_j)$, there exists a one-to-one relation between q_j and the triplet (p_j, L_j, l_j).

Obviously, for all

$$q \in Q, \ \bar{p} \geq p(q) \geq \underline{p}, \ w \geq L(q) \geq 0, \ 0 \geq l(q) \geq -w;$$

and (p, L, l) is a continuous vector-valued function of q, $\forall q \in Q$.

Remark. Let $x^i \in \gamma^i(q)$; it then follows from (D) that

$$(q + x^i - w^i) = \mathrm{def}\,(q + z^i) \in Q.$$

Indeed:

$$q + z^i \leq q + L(q) = q + M - \max(\bar{p}, q) \leq M$$

$$q + z^i \geq q + l(q) = q + m - \min(q, \underline{p}) \geq m.$$

PROOF OF THEOREM 1. The proof will establish the existence of an equilibrium for $\mathcal{E}$ with $p = p(q)$, $L = L(q)$, $l = l(q)$, for some $q \in Q$ with $q_1 = 1$. Let

$$Q_1 = \{q \in Q \mid q_1 = 1\}, \ _1q = (q_2 \cdots q_n),$$

$$Q' = \{_1q \in R^{n-1} \mid (1, _1q) \in Q_1 \subset Q\}.$$

Let $\xi^i(q)$ be the subset of $\gamma^i(q)$ consisting of those elements which are maximal for $\succcurlyeq_i$. When $q_1 = 1$, $l_1(q) < 0$ and $p_1 = 1$. Therefore (lemma in Section 3), γ^i is continuous at $[p(q), L(q), l(q)]$, ξ^i is upper hemicontinuous there, and the correspondence $\xi^i(q)$, from Q_1 to X^i, is upper hemicontinuous on Q_1. Because commodity 1 is always desired, $p(q)\,(x^i - w^i) = 0$ for all $x^i \in \xi^i(b)$. Because $\gamma^i(q)$ is compact and $\succcurlyeq_i$ is continuous and convex, $\xi^i(q)$ is nonempty and convex.

Define

$$\zeta(q) = \{z \mid z \in R^n, z + w \in \sum_i \xi^i(q)\},$$

the aggregate excess demand correspondence (from Q_1 to R^n).

Let $_1z = \mathrm{def}(z_2 \cdots z_n)$ and define a correspondence μ from Q' to Q' by:

$$\mu(_1q) = \{_1q' \in R^{n-1} \mid _1q' = _1q + \frac{_1z}{N}, z \in \zeta(q)\}.$$

$\mu(_1q)$ is convex, because $\zeta(q)$ is convex. μ is upper hemicontinuous, because ζ is upper hemicontinuous, $\mu(_1q) \subset Q'$, because $_1q + _1z^i \in Q'$ for all $x^i \in \gamma^i(q)$ by the remark above, and Q' is convex. Also, Q' is nonempty and compact.

All the conditions of Kakutani's theorem are satisfied, and μ has a fixed point $_1q^*$. There exist $q^* \in Q_1$ and $z^* \in \zeta(q^*)$ with $_1z^* = 0$. Because $p(q)z^i = 0$ for all $z^i \in \zeta^i(q)$, $_1z^* = 0$ implies $z^* = 0$. There exist $\{x^{*i}\}$, $p^* = p(q^*)$, $L^* = L(q^*)$, $l^* = l(q^*)$, such that conditions (i) and (ii) in the definition of an equilibrium for $\mathcal{E}$ are satisfied. We now verify that conditions (iii) and (iv) are satisfied as well.

To begin with (iv), $\bar{p}_j > p_j$ implies

$$L_j = M_j - \bar{p}_j = w_j$$

and

$$w_j - z_j^i = w_j - x_j^i + w_j^i = \sum_h x_j^h - x_j^i + w_j^i > \sum_h x_j^h - x_j^i \geq 0.$$

Hence $\bar{p}_j > p_j$ implies

$$L_j - z_j^i > 0 \,\forall\, i,$$

and $L_j - z_j^i = 0$ for some i implies $p_j = \bar{p}_j$. The reasoning for $p_j > \underline{p}_j$ is similar.

To prove (iii), note first that $L_1 > x_1^i - w_1^i > l_1$. For some j, $2 \leq j \leq n$, let $p_j = \bar{p}_j$; then

$$l_j = m_j - \underline{p}_j = -w_j$$

and

$$z_j^i + w_j = x_j^i + w_j - w_j^i > 0$$

because $x_j^i \geq 0$ and $\sum_{h \neq i} w_j^h > 0$. Hence, if $L_j - z_j^i = 0$ for some i, then $p_j = \bar{p}_j$ by the proof of (iv) and $z_j^h - l_j > 0 \,\forall\, h$. The reasoning for $p_j = \underline{p}_j$ is similar.   QED

5. Limited flexibility of some nominal prices

To relax the assumption that P is compact is a straightforward technical task. In view of Assumption (2), we may assume without loss of generality that $p \geq 0$. Let us now allow $\bar{p}_j = +\infty$ for some, possibly all $j = 2 \cdots n$. (In particular, when $\bar{p}_j = +\infty$ and $\underline{p}_j = 0$, $j = 2 \cdots n$, we have a traditional exchange economy without price rigidities.)

THEOREM 2. *Let*

$$\mathcal{E} = \{(X^i, \succcurlyeq_i, w^i), P\}$$

satisfy Assumptions 1, 2 with index set $I = \{1\}$, and 3; let

$$P = \{p \in R^n \,|\, p_1 = 1, \, +\infty \geq \bar{p} \geq p \geq \underline{p} \geq 0\};$$

there exists an equilibrium for $\mathscr{E}$.

PROOF. Consider a sequence of economies

$$\mathscr{E}^k = \{(X^i, \succcurlyeq_i, w^i), p^k\},$$

where

$$P^k = \{p \in R^n \,|\, p_1 = 1, \, +\infty > \bar{p}^k \geq p \geq \underline{p}\}$$

with $\bar{p}_j^k = \bar{p}_j$ whenever

$$\bar{p}_j < +\infty, \, \bar{p}_j^k \to +\infty$$

otherwise. For every $k = 1, 2, \cdots$, there exists an equilibrium for $\mathscr{E}^k$, say $\{(x^i)^k, p^k, L^k, l^k\}$, with

$$p^k \in P^k \quad \text{and} \quad w \geq L^k \geq 0 \geq l^k \geq -w.$$

For all i, the sequences $(x^i)^k$ are bounded and there exists a converging subsequence, say

$$(x^i)^k \to \hat{x}^i, \quad i = 1 \cdots N, \, L^k \to \hat{L}, \, l^k \to \hat{l}.$$

To show that the sequence p^k is bounded, assume on the contrary that

$$\|p^k\| \to +\infty.$$

Let

$$\Pi^k = \operatorname{def} \frac{p^k}{\|p^k\|}; \quad \|\Pi^k\| = 1$$

and there exists a converging subsequence, say $\Pi^k \to \hat{\Pi}$, with $\|\hat{\Pi}\| = 1$, $\hat{\Pi}_1 = 0$ and $\hat{\Pi}_j > 0$ for some j. For that j, $p_j^k \to +\infty$ and there exists k' such that

$$p_j^k > \underline{p}_j, \, l_j^k = -w_j < 0, \, \forall k \geq k';$$

hence, $\hat{l}_j < 0$, γ^i is continuous at $(\hat{\Pi}, \hat{L}, l)$, ξ^i (compact-valued, since $M \geq L \geq 0 \geq l \geq m$) is upper hemicontinuous and closed there, and $\hat{x}^i \in \xi^i(\hat{\Pi}, \hat{L}, \hat{l})$. But this contradicts Assumption 2 with $I = \{1\}$, since $\hat{\Pi}_1 = 0$. Therefore, p^k is bounded and there exists a subsequence with

$$\{(x^i)^k, p^k, L^k, l^k\} \to \{(\hat{x}^i), \hat{p}, \hat{L}, \hat{l}\},$$

an equilibrium for $\mathscr{E}$. Indeed,

$$\hat{x}^i \in \xi^i(\hat{p}, \hat{L}, \hat{l}) \subset X^i, \hat{p} \in P,$$

and conditions (ii)–(iv) in the definition of an equilibrium are satisfied for all k. The verification that these conditions also hold in the limit is straightforward.   QED

COROLLARY. *Under the assumptions of Theorem 2, let* $\{(\hat{x}^i), \hat{p}, L, \hat{l}\}$ *be an equilibrium for* $\mathscr{E}$; *for all j such that*

$$\bar{p}_j = +\infty, \; L_j > \hat{x}^i_j - w^i_j, \qquad\qquad\qquad i = 1 \cdots N.$$

PROOF. Follows from condition (iv) and $+\infty > \hat{p}$.   QED

6. Limited flexibility of some or all real prices

We will now consider rigidities of real prices, instead of nominal prices. To that effect, let Π be a price index defined by

$$\Pi = \sum_{i=1}^{n} \alpha_i p_i,$$

and consider constraints of the type

$$\bar{k}_j \Pi \geq p_j \geq \underline{k}_j \Pi.$$

To simplify exposition, we assume in this section that $\alpha_i > 0$ for *all* $i = 1 \cdots n$. The more general case is treated in Section 7.

Because the physical units in which we measure quantities of the commodities are arbitrary, we may multiply these units by α_i, $i = 1 \cdots n$. The individual prices being similarly multiplied by α_i, the price index becomes

$$\Pi = \sum_{i=1}^{n} p_i.$$

It is now convenient to normalize prices on the unit simplex by setting

$$\Pi = \sum_{i=1}^{n} p_i = 1.$$

The constraints then become

$$\bar{p}_j = \bar{k}_j \Pi \geq p_j \geq \underline{k}_j \Pi = \underline{p}_j, \qquad\qquad\qquad j = 1 \cdots n.$$

With this normalization, it suffices to assume weak monotonicity of preferences: $x > y$ implies $x \succ_i y$. That is, the index set I in Assumption 2 is the full set $\{1, 2, \cdots n\}$. Under monotonicity of preferences, there is no loss of generality in assuming

$$1 = \sum_{i=1}^{n} p_i \ge p_j \ge 0, \qquad\qquad\qquad j = 1 \cdots n.$$

Let ι denote the n-vector $\{1, 1, \cdots 1\}$.

THEOREM 3. *Let*

$$\mathscr{E} = \{(X^i, \succcurlyeq_i, w^i), P\}$$

satisfy Assumptions 1, 2 with index set $I = \{1, 2, \cdots n\}$, *and 3; let*

$$P = \{p \in R^n \mid \sum_{i=1}^{n} p_i = 1, \iota \ge \bar{p} \ge p \ge \underline{p} \ge 0\}$$

with

$$\sum_{i=1}^{n} \bar{p}_i \ge 1 > \sum_{i=1}^{n} \underline{p}_i;$$

there exists an equilibrium for $\mathscr{E}$.

PROOF. Let again

$$Q = \{q \in R^n \mid \bar{p} + w = M \ge q \ge m = \underline{p} - w\}$$

and let $p(q)$, $L(q)$, $l(q)$ be defined as per (D) in Section 4 above. $\sum_{i=1}^{n} p_i(q)$ is a monotonic non-decreasing function of q. Because

$$\sum_{i=1}^{n} \bar{p}_i \ge 1 > \sum_{i=1}^{n} \underline{p}_i,$$

there exists q such that

$$\sum_{i=1}^{n} p_i(q) \ge (\le) 1.$$

For arbitrary $q \in Q$, define

$$q'_j(q) = \min(M_j, \max(q_j + \alpha, m_j)), \qquad\qquad j = 1 \cdots n,$$

α such that

$$\sum_{i=1}^{n} p_i(q') = 1.$$

$q'(q)$ is an always defined, single-valued, continuous function from Q to Q. Let then

$$p'(q) = p(q'(q)),$$

$$L'(q) = L(q'(q)),$$

$$l'(q) = l(q'(q)),$$

$$\gamma'^i(q) = \gamma^i(q'(q)),$$

and

$$\xi'^i(q) = \xi^i(q'(q)).$$

Because

$$\sum_{i=1}^{n} p'_i(q) \equiv 1 > \sum_{i=1}^{n} \underline{p}_i,$$

there exists for every $q \in Q$ some j such that

$$p'_j(q) > \underline{p}_j \geq 0, l'_j(q) < 0.$$

Accordingly (lemma above), $\gamma'^i(q)$ is continuous at

$$(p'(q), L'(q), l'(q)) \ \forall \, q \in Q,$$

and $\xi^i(q)$ is upper hemicontinuous (as well as nonempty and convex).
Let

$$\zeta'(q) = \{z \in R^n \,|\, z + w \in \sum_{i=1}^{n} \xi'^i(q)\}$$

and define a correspondence μ' from Q to Q by:

$$\mu'(q) = \{q'' \,|\, q'' = q' + \frac{z}{N}, z \in \zeta'(q)\}.$$

$\mu'(q) \subset Q$ because $q' + z^i \in Q$ for all $x^i \in \gamma^i(q') = \gamma'^i(q)$ and Q is convex. $\mu'(q)$ is convex, because $\zeta'(q)$ is convex. μ' is upper hemicontinuous, because q' is continuous, ζ' is upper hemicontinuous and Q is compact. All the conditions of Kakutani's theorem are satisfied, and μ' has a fixed point

$$q^* = q'(q^*) + \frac{z^*}{N}, \qquad\qquad z^* \in \zeta'(q^*),$$

where

$$q'_j(q^*) = \min\,(M_j, \max\,(q^*_j + \alpha^*, m_j))$$

and $p'(q^*) \cdot z^* \leq 0$. If $\alpha^* < 0$, then

$$\forall j \frac{z^*_j}{N} = \min\,(q^*_j - m_j, -\alpha^*) \geq 0, \ p'_j(q^*)z^*_j \geq 0;$$

hence

$$p'(q^*) \cdot z^* \le 0 \text{ implies } p'_j(q^*)z^*_j = 0.$$

There exists j such that $p'_j(q^*) > p_j \ge 0$ and $l'_j(q^*) < 0$, so that $q^*_j + \alpha^* > m_j$, $z^*_j > 0$. This contradicts $p'_j(q^*)z^*_j = 0$, therefore $\alpha^* \ge 0$. If $\alpha^* = 0$, then $q'(q^*) = q^*$ and $z^* = 0$. If $\alpha^* > 0$, then

$$\forall j \frac{z^*_j}{N} = \max(q^*_j - M_j, -\alpha^*) \le 0, \ p'_j(q^*)z^*_j \le 0.$$

Let

$$J_1 = \text{def}\{j \mid j = 1 \cdots n, \ z^*_j = 0\},$$
$$J_2 = \text{def}\{j \mid j = 1 \cdots n, \ z^*_j < 0\}.$$

We know that there exist

$$x^i \in \zeta'^i(q^*), \qquad\qquad\qquad i = 1 \cdots N,$$

such that

$$z^* = \sum_{i=1}^{n} (x^i - w^i) \le 0.$$

In view of Assumption 2, there must exist

$$y^i \in \zeta'^i(q^*), \qquad\qquad\qquad i = 1 \cdots N,$$

with

$$y^i_j = x^i_j \ \forall j \in J_1, \ y^i_j \ge x^i_j \ \forall j \in J_2$$

and

$$\sum_{i=1}^{n} (y^i - w^i) = 0.$$

We may thus conclude that $\alpha^* \ge 0$ implies $0 \in \zeta'(q^*)$.

Accordingly, there exist $\{x^{*i}\}$,

$$p^* = p'(q^*) = p(q'(q^*)),$$
$$L^* = L'(q^*) = L(q'(q^*)),$$
$$l^* = l'(q^*) = l(q'(q^*)),$$

$x^{*i} \in X^i$, $p^* \in P$, such that conditions (i) and (ii) in the definition of an equilibrium for $\mathscr{E}$ are satisfied. To verify that conditions (iii) and (iv) are satisfied as well, note that $p(q')$, $L(q')$, $l(q')$ satisfy definition (D), so that the reasoning in the proof of Theorem 1 applies again without modification.

QED

7. Limited flexibility of some nominal and some real prices

We will now finally consider simultaneously rigidities of some real prices and of some nominal prices – still restricting attention, for each commodity, to either type of rigidity but not both. At the same time, we will generalize the assumption of Theorem 3 to the effect that all commodities enter with positive weight in the definition of the relevant price index. Theorem 4 below includes as special cases Theorems 1, 2 and 3 above. The technique of proof combines the reasoning in these three simpler cases.

The basic structure of the model in this section is as follows. There are n commodities, indexed $j = 1 \cdots n$. Commodity 1, with price $p_1 = 1$, is an always desired numeraire. Commodities $2, 3, \cdots m \leq n$ are subject to price constraints in terms of the numeraire:

$$\bar{p}_j \geq p_j \geq \underline{p}_j, \qquad\qquad j = 2 \cdots m.$$

We admit $\bar{p}_j = +\infty$ for some (all) j. There exists a price index

$$\Pi = \sum_{j \in J} \alpha_j p_j, \qquad\qquad J \subset \{1, 2, \cdots n\},$$

where J is an arbitrary (nonempty) index set. Commodities $m + 1 \cdots n$ are subject to price constraints in terms of the index

$$\Pi : \bar{k}_j \Pi \geq p_j \geq \underline{k}_j \Pi, \qquad\qquad j = m + 1 \cdots n.$$

The following monotonicity assumptions on preferences are made:

ASSUMPTION 4. $x \geq y$ and $x_1 > y_1 \Rightarrow x \succ_i y$.

ASSUMPTION 5. $x \geq y$ and $x_j > y_j$ for some $j \in J \Rightarrow x \succ_i y$.

That is, we assume Assumption 2 with $I = \{1\}$ *and* with $I = \{j\}$ for each j in J.

Assumptions 4 and 5 will guarantee that no constraints are expressed with reference to a worthless numeraire or commodity basket, and specifically that $+\infty > \Pi > 0$ in equilibrium.

Technically, it will prove more convenient to normalize prices by the rule

$$\sum_{j \in J} p_j = 1 = \Pi$$

(under rescaling by α_j of the physical units and prices of commodity j, $\forall j \in J$) and to define the admissible set P as follows (where $\bar{p}_j \equiv \bar{k}_j$, $\underline{p}_j \equiv \underline{k}_j$, $j = m + 1 \cdots n$):

$$P = \{p \in R^n \mid \sum_{j \in J} p_j = 1, p_1 \geq 0, \bar{p}_j p_1 \geq p_j \geq \underline{p}_j p_1, \quad j = 2 \cdots m,$$

$$\bar{p}_j \geq p_j \geq \underline{p}_j, \quad j = m + 1 \cdots n\}.$$

$P \neq \phi$ whenever

$$\sum_{\substack{j \in J \\ j > m}} \bar{p}_j \geq 1 > \sum_{\substack{j \in J \\ j > m}} \underline{p}_j.$$

Given some $p^0 \in P$ with $p_1^0 > 0$, there exists $p^* = p^0/p_1^0$ with

$$p_1^* = 1, \bar{p}_j \geq p_j^* \geq \underline{p}_j, \qquad\qquad j = 2 \cdots m,$$

$$\bar{p}_j \sum_{j \in J} p_j^* = \bar{k}_j \Pi^* \geq p_j^* \geq \underline{k}_j \Pi^* = \underline{p}_j \sum_{j \in J} p_j^*, \qquad j = m + 1 \cdots n.$$

THEOREM 4. Let

$$\mathscr{E} = \{(X^i, \succcurlyeq_i, w^i), P\}$$

satisfy Assumptions 1, 2 with $I = \{1\}$ *and with* $I = \{j\}$ $\forall j \in J \subset \{1, 2, \cdots n\}$, and 3; let

$$P = \{p \in R^n \mid \sum_{j \in J} p_j = 1, p_1 \geq 0, \bar{p}_j p_1 \geq p_j \geq \underline{p}_j p_1, \qquad j = 2 \cdots m,$$

$$\bar{p}_j \geq p_j \geq \underline{p}_j, \quad j = m + 1 \cdots n\}$$

with

$$\sum_{\substack{j \in J \\ j > m}} \bar{p}_j \geq 1 > \sum_{\substack{j \in J \\ j > m}} \underline{p}_j;$$

there exists an equilibrium for $\mathscr{E}$, with $p_1 > 0$.[5]

PROOF. Let

$$\mathscr{E}^k = \{(X^i, \succcurlyeq_i w^i), P^k\}$$

---

[5] For $j = 2 \cdots m$, condition (iv) in the definition of an equilibrium for $\mathscr{E}$ should obviously be read as:

$$\bar{p}_j p_1 > p_j \text{ implies } L_j > x_j^i - w_j^i \forall i$$
$$p_j > \underline{p}_j p_1 \text{ implies } l_j < x_j^i - w_j^i \forall i.$$

where

$$P^k = \{p \in P \mid \bar{p}_1^k \geq p_1 \geq \underline{p}_1 = 0, \bar{p}_j^k p_1 \geq p_j \geq \underline{p}_j p_1, \qquad j = 2 \cdots m,$$
$$\bar{p}_j^k \geq p_j \geq \underline{p}_j, \quad j = m + 1 \cdots n\},$$

with $\bar{p}_1^k < \infty, \bar{p}_j^k = \bar{p}_j$ whenever $\bar{p}_j < \infty, \bar{p}_j^k \to +\infty$ otherwise. $P \neq \phi$ implies $P^k \neq \phi$, for $\bar{p}_j^k$ large enough. We first prove the existence of an equilibrium for $\mathcal{E}^k$. In this part of the proof, the superscript k is omitted, for notational convenience.

Define

$$M_j = w_j + \bar{p}_j, m_j = \underline{p}_j - w_j, \qquad\qquad j = 1, m + 1 \cdots n;$$
$$M_j(q_1) = w_j + \bar{p}_j w_1 + \bar{p}_j \min(\bar{p}_1, q_1),$$
$$m_j(q_1) = \underline{p}_j \max(\underline{p}_1, q_1) - w_j - \underline{p}_j(w_1 + \bar{p}_1), \qquad j = 2 \cdots m;$$
$$Q = \{q \in R^n \mid M \geq q \geq m\},$$

a convex, compact set

The convexity of Q is illustrated in figure 2.2 for the subspace (q_1, q_2).

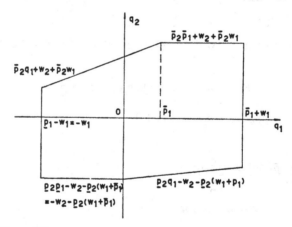

Figure 2.2

For every $q \in Q$, define:

$$\text{(D)} \quad \begin{cases} p_j(q) = \min(\bar{p}_j, \max(q_j, \underline{p}_j)) \\ L_j(q) = M_j - \max(\bar{p}_j, q_j) \\ l_j(q) = m_j - \min(q_j, \underline{p}_j) \end{cases} \qquad j = 1, m + 1 \cdots n$$

$$\text{(D')} \begin{cases} p_j(q) = \min(\bar{p}_j p_1(q), \max\{q_j, \underline{p}_j p_1(q)\}) \\ L_j(q) = M_j(q_1) - \max\{\bar{p}_j p_1(q), q_j\} \\ l_j(q) = m_j(q_1) - \min\{q_j, \underline{p}_j p_1(q)\} \end{cases} \qquad j = 2 \cdots m.$$

We remark the following implications of this definition:

(i) $\forall q \in Q, p(q) \in P$

(ii) $\forall q \in Q, w + w_1 \bar{p} \geq L(q) \geq 0$

$$0 \geq l(q) \geq -w - (w_1 + \bar{p}_1)\underline{p}.$$

These inequalities are obviously enough for $j = 1, m + 1 \cdots n$.
For $j = 2 \cdots m$, they may be verified as follows:

$$\begin{aligned} L_j(q) &= M_j(q_1) - \max(\bar{p}_j p_1(q), q_j) \\ &= M_j(q_1) - \max(\bar{p}_j \min\{\bar{p}_1, \max(q_1, \underline{p}_1)\}, q_j) \\ &\leq M_j(q_1) - \max(\bar{p}_j \min(\bar{p}_1, q_1), q_j) \\ &= w_j + \bar{p}_j w_1 + \bar{p}_j \min(\bar{p}_1, q_1) - \max(\bar{p}_j \min(\bar{p}_1 q_1), q_j) \\ &\leq w_j + \bar{p}_j w_1. \end{aligned}$$

$$\begin{aligned} L_j(q) &= M_j(q_1) - \max(\bar{p}_j p_1(q), q_j) \\ &= \min(M_j(q_1) - q_j, M_j(q_1) - \bar{p}_j p_1(q)) \\ &\geq \min(M_j(q_1) - \max_Q q_j, M_j(q_1) - \bar{p}_j p_1(q)) = 0 \end{aligned}$$

$$\begin{aligned} l_j(q) &= m_j(q_1) - \min(q_j, \underline{p}_j p_1(q)) \\ &= m_j(q_1) - \min(q_j, \underline{p}_j \min\{\bar{p}_1, \max(q_1, \underline{p}_1)\}) \\ &\geq m_j(q_1) - \min(q_j, \underline{p}_j \max(q_1, \underline{p}_1)) \\ &= \underline{p}_j \max(\underline{p}_1, q_1) - w_j - \underline{p}_j(w_1 + \bar{p}_1) - \min(q_j, \underline{p}_j \max(\underline{p}_1, q_1)) \\ &\geq -w_j - \underline{p}_j(w_1 + \bar{p}_1). \end{aligned}$$

$$\begin{aligned} l_j(q) &= m_j(q_1) - \min(q_j, \underline{p}_j p_1(q)) \\ &= \max(m_j(q_1) - q_j, m_j(q_1) - \underline{p}_j p_1(q)) \\ &\leq \max(m_j(q_1) - \min_Q q_j, m_j(q_1) - \underline{p}_j p_1(q)) = 0 \end{aligned}$$

(iii)   Accordingly, the budget set correspondence

$$\begin{aligned} \gamma^i(q) &= \gamma^i(p(q), L(q), l(q)) \\ &= \{x \mid x \in X^i, p(q)(x - w^i) \leq 0, L(q) \geq x - w^i \geq l(q)\} \end{aligned}$$

is compact-valued; *a fortiori*, $\xi^i(q) \subset \gamma^i(q)$ is compact-valued.

(iv)   for all $x^i \in \gamma^i(q)$,

$$M_j \geq q_j + L_j(q) \geq q_j + z_j^i \geq q_j + l_j(q) \geq m_j, \qquad\qquad j = 1 \cdots n.$$

(v) $\sum_{j \in J} p_j(q)$ is a monotonic, non-decreasing function of q.

Define

$$q_j'(q) = \text{Max} \, [M_j(q_1'), \min \{q_j + \alpha, m_j(q_1')\}], \qquad\qquad j = 1 \cdots n,$$

α such that $\sum_{j \in J} p_j(q') = 1$. [Of course,

$$M_j(q_1') = M_j, m_j(q_1') = m_j, j = 1, m + 1 \cdots n.]$$

$q'(q)$ is an always defined, single-valued, continuous function from Q to Q.
Define

$$p'(q) = p(q'(q)),$$
$$L'(q) = L(q'(q)),$$
$$l'(q) = l(q'(q)),$$
$$\gamma'^i(q) = \gamma^i(q'(q)),$$
$$\xi'^i(q) = \xi^i(q'(q)), \qquad\qquad\qquad i = 1 \cdots N.$$

There exists $j \in \{1 \cdots n\}$ such that $p_j'(q) > 0$ and $l_j'(q) < 0$. Indeed, if $p_1'(q) > 0$, then $l_1'(q) < 0$ and the result obtains with $j = 1$. If $p_1'(q) = 0$, then

$$\sum_{\substack{j \in J}} p_j'(q) = 1 > \sum_{\substack{j \in J \\ j < m}} p_j$$

implies

$$p_j'(q) > p_j(q) \geq 0$$

for some $i \in J, j > m$, or

$$p_j'(q) > p_j p_1'(q) = 0$$

for some $j \in J, m \geq j > 1$.[6] In either case, $l_j'(q) < 0$ for that same j, as desired. Consequently (lemma above), $\gamma'^i(q)$ is continuous at $p'(q)$, $L'(q)$, $l'(q)$ and $\xi'^i(q)$ is upper hemicontinuous (as well as nonempty and convex). We may now repeat the reasoning in the proof of Theorem 3. Letting

$$\zeta'(q) = \{z \in R^n \mid z + w \in \sum_{i=1}^{N} \xi'^i(q)\},$$

---

[6] Actually, when $\bar{p}_j^* < \infty$, $p = 0$ implies $p_j = 0 \, \forall j = 2 \cdots m$; the more general statement in the text avoids the use of $\bar{p}_j^* < \infty$ in preparation for the last part of the proof.

we define

$$\mu'(q) = \{q'' \mid q'' = q' + \frac{z}{N}, z \in \zeta'(q)\}.$$

$\mu'(q)$ has a fixed point

$$q^* = q'(q^*) + \frac{z^*}{N},$$

$$z^* \in \zeta'(q^*),$$

$$q'_j(q^*) = \min(M_j, \max(q^*_j + \alpha^*, m_j))$$

where

$$M_j = M_j(q'_1(q^*)),$$
$$m_j = m_j(q'_1(q^*)), \qquad\qquad j = 2 \cdots m,$$

and

$$p'(q^*)z^* \leq 0.$$

One verifies that $\alpha^* \geq 0$, and $\alpha^* \geq 0$ implies $0 \in \zeta'(q^*)$. There exist $\{x^{*i}\}$, $p^* = p'(q^*)$, $L^* = L'(q^*)$, $l^* = l'(q^*)$ defining an equilibrium for $\mathscr{E}^k$.

We may now repeat the reasoning in the proof of Theorem 2. That is, we consider a sequence of economies

$$\mathscr{E}^k = \{(X^i, \succcurlyeq_i, w^i), P^k\}$$

with $\bar{p}^k_1 \to \infty$, $\bar{p}^k_j \to \infty$, whenever $\bar{p}_j = +\infty$. For every $k = 1, 2, \cdots$, there exists an equilibrium for $\mathscr{E}^k$, say $\{(x^i)^k, p^k, L^k, l^k\}$, with $p^k \in P^k$ and

$$w + w_1 \bar{p}^k \geq L^k \geq 0 \geq l^k \geq -w - (w_1 + \bar{p}^k_1)p - \text{see remark (ii) } supra.$$

At an equilibrium for $\mathscr{E}^k$, we may replace L^k by

$$\underline{L}^k = \min\{w, L^k\},$$

and we may replace l_k by

$$\bar{l}^k = \max\{l_k, -w\},$$

without affecting the allocation or its equilibrium property. Thus, $\{(x^i)^k, p^k, \underline{L}^k, \bar{l}^k\}$ is an equilibrium for $\mathscr{E}^k$, with

$$w \geq \underline{L}^k \geq 0 \geq \bar{l}^k \geq -w,$$

and there exists a subsequence with $(x^i)^k \to \hat{x}^i$, $\underline{L}^k \to \hat{L}$, $\bar{l}^k \to \hat{l}$. To show that the sequence p^k is bounded, assume on the contrary that $\| p^k \| \to \infty$ and define

$$\Pi^k = \frac{p^k}{\| p^k \|};$$

$$\Pi^k \to \hat{\Pi} \quad \text{with} \quad \| \hat{\Pi} \| = 1,$$

$$\sum_{j \in J} \hat{\Pi}_j = 0$$

and $\hat{\Pi}_j > 0$ for some $j \notin J$. The fact that $\hat{x}^i \in \xi^i(\hat{\Pi}, \hat{L}, \hat{l})$ contradicts Assumption 2 with $I = \{j\} \; \forall j \in J$, since $\sum_{j \in J} \hat{\Pi}_j = 0$. Hence, p^k is bounded and there exists a subsequence with

$$\{(x^i)^k, p^k, \underline{l}^k, \bar{l}^k\} \to \{(\hat{x}^i), \hat{p}, \hat{L}, \hat{l}\}.$$

Furthermore, $\hat{x}^i \in \xi^i(\hat{p}, \hat{L}, \hat{l})$ implies $\hat{p}_1 > 0$ in view of Assumption 2 with $I = \{1\}$. Finally, we note that

$$\hat{x}^i \in \xi^i(\hat{p}, \hat{L}, \hat{l}) \subset X^i,$$

$\hat{p} \in P$ and conditions (ii)–(iv) in the definition of an equilibrium are satisfied for all k. They also hold in the limit, and $\{(\hat{x}^i), \hat{p}, \hat{L}, \hat{l}\}$ defines an equilibrium for $\mathscr{E}$, with $\hat{p}_1 > 0$. QED

8. Concluding remarks

The lengthy proof of Theorem 4 suggests that a more powerful technique might be required to handle more complicated cases – for instance, cases where constraints on different prices are tied to different index numbers.

One might also wish to consider at once the more general case, where the set of admissible prices P is an arbitrary (convex) set in R^n. The difficulty with this more general approach is that one would loose the one-to-one correspondence between price rigidities and quantity rationing.

Before exploring these formal generalisations, it might be wise to gain further insight in the meaningfulness and implications of the equilibrium concept used in this paper. Such insight will hopefully be gained through detailed analysis of specific models (for instance, models of temporary equilibrium with downwards rigidities of real wages, or with money and price controls aimed at curbing inflation).[7]

---

[7] Instances of such analysis may already be found in unpublished papers of Jean-Pascal Bénassy (1975, 1982).

One normative implication of the equilibrium concept used here is immediate. Let $(\{\bar{x}^i\}, \bar{p}, \bar{L}, \bar{l})$ be an equilibrium for the economy

$$\mathscr{E} = \{(X^i, \succcurlyeq_i, w^i), P\}.$$

Consider then the economy defined by the same agents *and the constraints on net trades*

$$\bar{L} \geq x^i - w^i \geq \bar{l}.$$

The allocation $\{\bar{x}^i\}$ is Pareto efficient for the economy, and sustained by the price system $\bar{p}$.[8]

The relative efficiency of alternative rationing schemes (absolute, relative, random, ...) designed to cope with the same rigidities is another open question – a much more difficult question, however.

---

[8] *Proof.* Replace X^i by $\{x \mid x \in X^i, \bar{L} + w^i \geq x \geq \bar{l} + w^i\} = \bar{X}^i$; $(\{\bar{x}^i\}, \bar{p})$ defines a competitive equilibrium for the economy $\{(\bar{X}^i, \succcurlyeq_i, w^i), R^n_+\}$.

3   On supply-constrained equilibria*

1. Introduction

1.1.

In the microeconomic literature on equilibrium under price rigidities and
quantity rationing, starting with the work of Bénassy (1975), Drèze (1975)
and Younès (1975), it has been customary to impose as part of the
definition of equilibrium that a given numeraire commodity should not
be rationed. This practice has two distinct motivations. On the one hand,
it guarantees that at least one commodity is not rationed, thereby ruling
out the trivial equilibrium enforced by rationing to zero the supply of all
commodities or, alternatively, their demand.[1] On the other hand, this
practice provides a more realistic treatment of money as a numeraire,
since quantity constraints on *net* trades of money are very rarely observed.
This second motivation, unlike the first, requires that the never-constrained
commodity be chosen *a priori*.

For the remaining commodities, rationing may affect either supply or
demand but not both sides of a same market simultaneously. This
requirement of 'orderly rationing' (Hahn, 1978) seems generally accepted, at
least to study systematic imbalance as distinct from frictional imbalance.[2] It

* *Journal of Economic Theory*, 33 (1984), 172–182. With Pierre Dehez. Support from the
Projet d'Action Concertée financed by the Belgian government (Contract 80/85–12) is
gratefully acknowledged. The authors wish to thank T. Andersen, P. Champsaur and a
referee for interesting comments.

[1] If in addition, the unrationed numeraire always has a positive price, then consumers'
constrained demands are upper hemi-continuous in prices and quantity constraints whenever
initial endowment of the numeraire is positive (see Drèze (1975), p. 304).

[2] Although this point has not been investigated systematically, it would seem possible to
relax the usual requirement, allowing instead for a limited amount of frictional rationing
on the short side of a market; see also Henin (1980).

is supported by casual observations as well as theoretical arguments; see Malinvaud and Younès (1977b) and Grandmont *et al.* (1978). For a commodity with a predetermined price, the rationing may affect either side of the market. For a commodity with downward (resp. upward) price rigidity, rationing is limited to supply (resp. demand). When the price of a given commodity is constrained to lie in a given interval, possibly consisting of a single point, it is not possible to rule out *a priori* that a given side of the market be constrained.

This feature has sometimes been regarded as unsatisfactory, on grounds of realism again. For experience suggests that certain types of market imbalances are more common than others. Broadly speaking, there seems to be a tacit concensus that rationing of supply occurs more frequently than rationing of demand, outside exceptional situations (like wartime rationing or accidental power shortages). This view has been defended explicitly by two authors, van der Laan (1980) and Kurz (1982), whose seminal work on supply-constrained equilibria has inspired the present contribution.

Thus, van der Laan (1980, p. 63) writes:

> In our opinion constraints on the supply side can often more easily be realized than constraints on the demand side, for in most cases the number of sellers is less than the number of buyers. On the labor market, the reverse is true, but a restriction on the number of working hours is easily implemented.

Accordingly, van der Laan introduces a concept of equilibrium where demand is never rationed (even when prices are upward rigid) and supply is rationed only if prices are downward rigid. Under assumptions similar to those of Drèze (1975), he proves existence of an exchange equilibrium where *not all* net supplies are constrained to zero. He thereupon proves the existence of an equilibrium, where the net supply of some commodity is not rationed.[3] But it is not possible to choose a priori the commodity whose supply is not rationed.

Kurz introduces a different equilibrium concept where supply rationing takes the form of 'unemployment probabilities' and demand is never rationed. His motivation is similar and is stated as follows (1982, p. 102):

> Since in practice it is difficult to implement rationing of demand it appears to us as a very satisfactory result that the markets of an economy with distorted price structure can be cleared with a supplementary mechanism of endogenous

---

[3] This result can be found in another paper by van der Laan (1982). In his first paper (1980), he proves the existence of an equilibrium where the supply constraint is positive for at least one commodity.

probabilities of resource unemployment which are uniformly perceived... This conclusion is reinforced by the fact that demand rationings rarely occur in market economies while resource unemployments are very common.

For a pure exchange economy where price rigidities take the form of '*linkages*', i.e. functional relations between the prices of different commodities, he shows that: '*Markets can be made to clear with unemployment only and with one of the commodities being fully employed*' (p. 107, his italics). Suppliers of the fully employed commodity are not rationed but again it is not possible to choose *a priori* the commodity which is to remain unconstrained

1.2.

The present paper has the modest goal of providing sufficient conditions for the existence of an equilibrium with price rigidities and quantity rationing, where:

(i)   demand is never rationed;

(ii)   net trades of an *a priori* chosen always desired numeraire (hereafter called 'money') are never rationed;

(iii) supply is rationed only when *real* prices are downward rigid, real prices being defined by money prices deflated by some given price index.

The justification for stating (iii) in terms of real prices is twofold. This is the appropriate formulation when rigidities affect real prices (e.g. downward rigidity of real wages). It is equivalent to rigidity of money prices when the relevant price index is itself constrained (e.g. money prices historically non-decreasing).

A set of sufficient conditions appears in the statement of the existence theorem. The simplest case where they are satisfied is that of an economy where the relative prices of all commodities other than the numeraire are fixed (i.e. real prices are fixed) and the general level of money prices is flexible upwards.[4] More generally, our theorem allows for a partition of the set of commodities other than the numeraire into two groups; namely, a first group used to define the price index, with real prices fixed and money prices flexible upwards, and a second group of commodities whose real prices are subject to arbitrary upper and lower bounds.

---

[4] A symmetrical result for demand-constrained equilibria would require the general level of money prices to be flexible downwards, with weak desirability for commodities.

When the real prices of the commodities used to define the price index (hereafter called 'index commodities') are not all fixed but some are constrained by upper and lower bounds, it still follows from our theorem that an equilibrium exists if property (iii) is relaxed to allow supply constraints for all commodities used to define the price index. We show that this relaxation is consistent with the definition of equilibrium proposed by Chetty and Nayak (1978) for a similar situation.[5] And we show by means of an example that this relaxation is unavoidable.

1.3.

We deal with a private ownership production economy. The model and the basic assumptions are introduced in Section 2. The concept of supply-constrained equilibrium is defined in Section 3. The statement and proof of the existence theorem are given in Section 4. In Section 5, we discuss the possibility of extending our result. A speculative concluding remark is offered in Section 6.

2. The model

Let us consider a private ownership economy with m consumers, n producers and $l + 1$ commodities, indexed respectively $i = 1 \ldots m$, $j = 1 \ldots n$ and $h = 0, 1 \cdots l$. Commodity $h = 0$ is used as numeraire and its price is set equal to one. For convenience, we call it '*money*' and refer to the other commodities as '*real*' commodities.

A price system is a vector $p \in R_+^{l+1}$ with $p_0 = 1$. Rationing of the agents takes the form of absolute constraints on individual net supplies. A rationing scheme is a set of $m + n$ constraints[6] $(l_1 \cdots l_m, s_1 \cdots s_n)$, where $l_i, s_j \in R_+^{l+1}$.

Consumer i is characterized by a consumption set $X_i \subset R^{l+1}$ on which his preferences are defined, a vector $\omega_i \in R_+^{l+1}$ of initial resources and a vector of shares $\theta_i \in R_+^n$, with $\sum_i \theta_{ij} = 1$, $j = 1 \cdots n$. The following assumptions hold for all consumers:

A.1. X_i is a non-empty closed and convex subset of R_+^{l+1};

A.2. $\succsim_i$ is a complete, continuous and convex preorder on X_i;

[5] The authors prove the existence of an exchange equilibrium when prices are constrained to belong to a convex polyhedron or to a (strictly) convex set.
[6] The rationing constraints are therefore allowed to vary from one agent to another (although, in the existence proof, we restrict ourselves to a uniform rationing scheme). But each agent's constraint must be independent of his actions.

A.3.   money is desirable, i.e. $x_i \in X_i$, $x_i' \in R_+^{l+1}$, $x_{ih}' = x_{ih}$ for all $h \neq 0$ and $x_{i0}' > x_{i0}$ imply $x_i' \in X_i$ and $x_i' \succ_i x_i$;

A.4. $\omega_i \in \text{int } X_i$.

Producer j is characterised by a production set $Y_j \subset R^{l+1}$ and the following assumptions hold for all producers:

A.5. Y_j is a non-empty, closed and convex subset of R^{l+1};

A.6. $0 \in Y_j$.

Furthermore, the following assumptions[7] hold for the total production set $Y = \sum Y_j$:

A.7. Y is a closed subset of R^{l+1};

A.8. $Y \cap (-Y) \subset \{0\}$;

A.9. $R_-^{l+1} \subset Y$.

A price index is defined as a function $f : R_+^{l+1} \to R_+$; for a given price system p, $f(p)$ represents the general price level. The following assumptions hold for the price index:

A.10.   the function f is homogeneous of degree one;

A.11.   there exists a non-empty subset $I \subset \{1 \cdots l\}$ such that $f(p) = f((p_h)_{h \in I})$ for all $p \in R_+^{l+1}$.

The set of admissible price systems is defined by

$$P = \{p \in R_+^{l+1} \mid p_0 = 1, \underline{p}_h \leqslant \frac{p_h}{f(p)} \leqslant \bar{p}_h (h = 1 \cdots l), f(p) \geqslant b\}$$

where the constraints $(\underline{p}_h, \bar{p}_h)_{h=1}^l$ and b satisfy the following assumptions:

A.12. $0 \leqslant \underline{p}_h \leqslant \bar{p}_h < +\infty$, $\bar{p}_h > 0$ for all $h = 1 \cdots l$ and $b > 0$;

A.13. $f((\underline{p}_h)_{h \in I}) \leqslant 1 \leqslant f((\bar{p}_h)_{h \in I})$.

These assumptions ensure that P is a non-empty set.

---

[7] For a discussion of these assumptions, see Debreu (1959). Notice that these assumptions ensure that $Y \cap R_+^{l+1} = \{0\}$ and $(Y + R_-^{l+1}) \subset Y$. As in Debreu, the assumptions of closedness and convexity made on the *individual* production sets could have been made on the *total* production set instead. In the process of proving the existence of an equilibrium, the individual production sets would then have to be replaced by their closed convex hull.

3. Supply-constrained equilibrium

A *supply-constrained equilibrium* is defined by a set of consumption plans
$(x_1^* \cdots x_m^*)$, a set of production plans $(y_1^* \cdots y_n^*)$, a price system $p \in P$ and a
rationing scheme $(l_1 \cdots l_m, s_1 \cdots s_n)$ satisfying the following conditions:

E.1. $\sum x_i^* = \sum \omega_i + \sum y_j^*$;

E.2. for all i, x_i^* is $\succsim_i$-maximal on the budget set

$$\{x_i \in X_i \mid p(x_i - \omega_i) \leqslant \sum_j \theta_{ij} p y_j^*, \omega_i - x_i \leqslant l_i\};$$

E.3. for all j, y_j^* maximizes $p y_j$ on the set $\{y_j \in Y_j \mid y_j \leqslant s_j\}$;

E.4. $l_{ih} = s_{jh} = +\infty$ for all i and all j whenever $h = 0$, or h is such that
$\underline{p}_h = 0$ or $\underline{p}_h < p_h/f(p)$.

Condition E.1 is consistent with the assumption A.9 of free disposal.
Condition E.4 excludes the rationing of money and of the commodities
for which either the real price is downward flexible or the lower bound
on the real price is not binding.

4. Existence of a supply-constrained equilibrium

We prove the existence of a supply-constrained equilibrium when *the real
prices of the index commodities are fixed* using a technique introduced by
van der Laan (1980).

THEOREM. *Under the assumptions A.1 to A.13, there exists a supply-
constrained equilibrium if $\underline{p}_h = \bar{p}_h$ for all $h \in I$.*

PROOF. Let us define $\underline{p}_0 = 0$ and $\bar{p}_0 = 1/b$. For our convenience, we
shall work with the following admissible price set:

$$P' = \{p \in R_+^{l+1} \mid \underline{p} \leqslant p \leqslant \bar{p}, f(p) = 1\}.$$

This set is 'equivalent' to P given that the agents' behaviour is invariant
under any proportional change in the price system. Indeed, on the one
hand, $p \in P'$, $p_0 > 0$, implies $(1/p_0) p \in P$ and, on the other hand, $p \in P$
implies $(1/f(p)) p \in P'$.

We will actually prove the existence of an equilibrium where supply is
uniformly rationed, i.e. $l_i = s_j = s$ for all i and all j.

Let us define $\omega = \sum \omega_i$ and $M = \{h \mid p_h = 0\}$. Thus $0 \in M$; furthermore,
the assumptions of the theorem require that $f(\underline{p}) = f(\bar{p}) = 1$ and $I \subset M^c$,
$M^c = \{0, 1 \cdots l\} \backslash M$.

Following Debreu (1959, p. 76), we define the set $A \subset R^{(l+1)(m+n)}$ of attainable states by $(x_1 \cdots x_m, y_1 \cdots y_n) \in A$ if and only if $x_i \in X_i$ for all $i = 1 \cdots m$, $y_j \in Y_j$ for all $j = 1 \cdots n$ and $\sum x_i = \omega + \sum y_j$. We then define the set $\hat{X}_i$ of attainable consumption plans for consumer i, i.e., the projection of A on X_i. Similarly, we define the set $\hat{Y}_j$ of attainable production plans for producer j.

The assumptions on the consumption sets and on the production sets ensure that A is a compact set (Debreu (1959, p. 77)). Let K be a closed cube of R^{l+1} with centre 0 and containing *in its interior* the $\hat{X}_i$'s and the $\hat{Y}_j$'s. Let $2a$ be the length of one of its sides. We then define $\bar{X}_i = X_i \cap K$ $(i = 1 \cdots m)$ and $\bar{Y}_j = Y_j \cap K$ $(j = 1 \cdots n)$. These sets are compact. By construction, $x_i \in \bar{X}_i$ for all i, with $x_{i0} = a$ for some i, and $y_j \in \bar{Y}_j$ for all j imply $\sum x_{i0} > \omega_0 + \sum y_{j0}$. This property is used later to prove (i) and (iii).

The set of admissible rationing constraints is defined by

$$S = \{s \in R_+^{l+1} \mid s_h = a \text{ for all } h \in M, 0 \leqslant s_h \leqslant a \text{ for all } h \in M^c\}.$$

Following van der Laan (1980, p. 66) we consider the set

$$Q = \{q \in R_+^{l+1} \mid \lambda_h \bar{p}_h \leqslant q_h \leqslant \bar{p}_h, y_h \geqslant 0 \ (h = 0, 1 \cdots l), \sum_{h=0}^{l} \lambda_h = 1\}$$

on which we define the functions $p(\cdot)$ and $s(\cdot)$ by

$$p_h(q) = \max(\underline{p}_h, q_h) \qquad (h = 0, 1 \cdots l)$$

and

$$s_h(q) = a \qquad (h \in M)$$
$$= \min(1, q_h/\underline{p}_h)a \qquad (h \in M^c).$$

These functions are continuous on Q and satisfy $p(q) \in P'$ and $s(q) \in S$ for all $q \in Q$. Indeed, $h \in I$ implies $p_h(q) = \bar{p}_h$ by hypothesis; hence $f(p(q)) = f(\bar{p}) = 1$. Furthermore, $p(q)s(q) > 0$ for all $q \in Q$. Indeed, $0 \notin Q$, i.e. for all $q \in Q$, there exists h such that $q_h > 0$. Either $h \in M$, in which case $p_h(q) = q_h > 0$ and $s_h(q) = a > 0$ or $h \in M^c$, in which case $p_h(q) \geqslant \underline{p}_h > 0$ and $s_h(q) > 0$.

We define successively the set $\eta_j(q)$ of production plans which maximize $p(q)y_j$ on the set $\{y_j \in \bar{Y}_j \mid y_j \leqslant s(q)\}$, the corresponding level of profit $\pi_j(q)$ and the set $\xi_i(q)$ of consumption plans which are $\succsim_i$-maximal on the set

$$\gamma_i(q) = \{x_i \in X_i \mid p(q)(x_i - \omega_i) \leqslant \sum_j \theta_{ij} \pi_j(q), \omega_i - x_i \leqslant s(q)\}.$$

The assumptions A.5 and A.6 on Y_j ensure that the correspondence defined on R_+^{l+1} by $\{y_j \in \bar{Y}_j \mid y_j \leqslant s\}$ is continuous.[8] By continuity of the function $s(\cdot)$, the correspondence defined on Q by $\{y_j \in \bar{Y}_j \mid y_j \leqslant s(q)\}$ is itself continuous. Thus, the correspondence η_j is u.h.c. on Q and the function π_j is continuous on Q. Furthermore, $\eta_j(q)$ is non-empty and convex for all $q \in Q$.

The correspondence defined by $\{x_i \in X_i \mid p(x_i - \omega_i) \leqslant r, \omega_i - x_i \leqslant s\}$ is continuous in (p, r, s) whenever $p \cdot s > 0$ and $r \geqslant 0$; see Drèze (1975, p. 304). Therefore, by continuity of the functions $p(\cdot)$, $s(\cdot)$ and $\pi_j(\cdot)$, the correspondence γ_i is itself continuous on Q. Thus, the correspondence ξ_i is u.h.c. on Q. Furthermore, $\xi_i(q)$ is non-empty and convex for all $q \in Q$.

Let us now consider the correspondence μ defined on $Z = \Pi \bar{X}_i \times \Pi \bar{Y}_j$ by

$$\mu(x_1 \cdots x_m, y_1 \cdots y_n)$$
$$= \{q' \in Q \mid q' \text{ maximizes } q(\textstyle\sum x_i - \omega - \sum y_j) \text{ on } Q\}.$$

Consider finally the correspondence $\varphi = \mu \times \Pi \xi_i \times \Pi \eta_i$ from $Z \times Q$ into itself. It is u.h.c. and non-empty and convex-valued. Furthermore, the set $Z \times Q$ is non-empty, convex and compact. Thus, by Kakutani's theorem, the correspondence φ has a fixed point. Let us denote by $(x_1^* \cdots x_m^*, y_1 \cdots y_n, q^*)$ such a fixed point, i.e. $x_i^* \in \xi_i(q^*)$ for all $i = 1 \cdots m$, $y_j \in \eta_j(q^*)$ for all $j = 1 \cdots n$, $q^* \in Q$ and $q^* z \geqslant qz$ for all $q \in Q$, where $z = \sum x_i^* - \omega - \sum y_j$.

(i) $q_0^* > 0$. Assume on the contrary that $q_0^* = 0$. Then $p_0(q^*) = 0$ and therefore, by A.3, $x_{i0}^* = a$ for all i. As we have seen before, this implies $z_0 > 0$, and hence $q_0^* = \bar{p}_0 > 0$ by definition of μ, a contradiction.

This ensures that the price system $p^* = (1/q_0^*) p(q^*)$ is well defined and belongs to P. Summing over all budget constraints, we get $p^* z \leqslant 0$. Let us define $s^* = s(q^*)$.

(ii) $z \leqslant 0$. Assume on the contrary that $z_k > 0$ for some k. Then $q_k^* = \bar{p}_k$, implying $p_k^* > 0$. Hence, $p^* z \leqslant 0$ requires the existence of some $h \neq k$ such that $p_h^* > 0$ and $z_h < 0$. By definition of Q, the intersection of this set with $\{q \in R_+^{l+1} \mid q_k = \bar{p}_k\}$ contains the point where $q_h = 0$ for all $h \neq k$. Therefore $z_h < 0$ implies $q_h^* = 0$. If $h \in M$, we have $p_h^* = 0$, a contradiction to $p_h^* > 0$; if $h \notin M$, we have $s_h^* = 0$, a contradiction to $z_h < 0$.

[8] If $Y_j = \{0\}$, it is trivial; if not, Proposition 2 (p. 23) and Problem 6 (p. 35) in Hildenbrand (1974) can be used to prove continuity, taking the assumptions A.5 and A.6 into account.

(iii) $p^*z = 0$.   Assume on the contrary that $p^*z < 0$. There must exist a consumer, say, i, whose budget constraint is not binding. By A.3, this is possible only if $x^*_{i0} = a$. But $z_0 \leqslant 0$ which implies $x^*_{i0} < a$, a contradiction.

Together (ii) and (iii) imply $p^*_h z_h = 0$ for all h. Hence, by A.9, there exists $(y^*_1 \cdots y^*_n)$ such that $\sum y^*_j = z + \sum y_j$ and $y^*_j \in \eta_j(q^*)$ for all j. Condition E.1 is therefore fulfilled.

Using a standard argument, one shows that the x^*_i's and the y^*_j's actually satisfy the conditions E.2 and E.3 (see Debreu (1959, p. 87)).

On the one hand, $y^*_{jh} < a$ for all j and all h; on the other hand, by A.4, $\omega_{ih} < a$ for all i and h, implying $\omega_{ih} - x^*_{ih} < a$ for all i and all h. Condition E.4 is then automatically satisfied given the definition of the functions $p(\cdot)$ and $s(\cdot)$. Indeed if $h \in M$, $s^*_h = a$; if $h \notin M$, $p^*_h > \bar{p}_h f(p)$ is equivalent to $q^*_h > p_h$, implying $s^*_h = a$.   QED

It is to be noted that the equilibrium defined in the above proof satisfies the following additional condition:

E.5. $s_h = 0$ for all $h \notin M$ and $p_h = 0$ for all $h \in M$, $h \neq 0$, implies $f(p) = b$.

Indeed, $s^*_h = 0$ for all $h \notin M$ and $p_h = 0$ for all $h \in M$, $h \neq 0$, is equivalent to $q^*_h = 0$ for all $h \neq 0$ which implies $q^*_0 = \bar{p}_0$, i.e., $p_0(q^*) = \bar{p}_0$ and $f(p^*) = b$.

Let us consider the case where $p_h > 0$ for all $h \neq 0$, i.e., $M = \{0\}$. In that case, condition E.5 rules out the situation where no supply of real commodities is allowed while the general price level is not at its lower bound. It therefore allows for the case where the lower bound imposed on the general price level is so high that it is necessary to constrain to zero the net supply of all real commodities. But it excludes the case where an equilibrium would be obtained by constraining to zero all net supplies while increasing sufficiently the general price level. This argument shows that if the preferences of at least one consumer are monotone on a subset of real commodities, then $s^*_h > 0$ for some $h \neq 0$, whenever b is sufficiently small. In other words, complete flexibility of the general price level ensures existence of an equilibrium where the supply of at least one real commodity is allowed.[9]

---

[9] One would have preferred $s_h = +\infty$ for some $h \neq 0$. This has been proved (under different assumptions) by van der Laan in a recent paper (1984) using the technique of simplicial approximation.

5. Extension of the existence theorem: a counterexample

For our convenience, we still work with price systems in the equivalent set P′.

5.1.

When the prices of the index commodities are not all fixed but some are allowed to vary between given bounds,[10] it may be necessary to constrain the supply of some index commodity, the price of which exceeds its lower bound. Indeed, a price index function is typically monotone increasing. Accordingly, lowering the price of that commodity would require raising the price of some other index commodity k in order to keep $f(p)$ equal to one; and raising some other price may bring about the very situation one is trying to avoid, namely, the necessity to constrain the supply of commodity k, the price of which now exceeds its lower bound.

The following example illustrates this point. It concerns a pure exchange economy with four commodities. Let $f(p) = p_2 + p_3$, the set P' being given by

$$P' = \{p \in R_+^4 \mid 0 \leqslant p_0 \leqslant 1; 0 \leqslant p_1 \leqslant 0.3; 0.4 \leqslant p_2, p_3 \leqslant 1;$$
$$p_2 + p_3 = 1\}.$$

There is a single consumer with initial endowment $(1, 1, 1, 1)$ and preferences represented by the utility function $x_0 x_1 x_2 x_3$.

A supply-constrained equilibrium must have net trades equal to zero, no constraints on demands and no constraint on commodity 0. Under the assumed preferences, this means $s_h = 0$ whenever $p_h > p_k$ for some $k \neq h$; for otherwise, the consumer will wish to sell commodity h to buy commodity k. And P' imposes that $p_2, p_3 > p_1$. Hence $s_2 = s_3 = 0$. But P' also imposes that $p_2 + p_3 = 1 > \underline{p}_2 + \underline{p}_3$. Hence, either $p_2 > \underline{p}_2$ with $s_2 = 0$, or $p_3 > \underline{p}_3$ with $s_3 = 0$, or both.[11]

5.2.

The equilibrium concept introduced by Chetty and Nayak (1978) for the case where P is a convex polyhedron or a strictly convex set stipulates:

---

[10] In such a case, the index set I contains at least two commodities and there exist h and k in I, $h \neq k$, such that $p_h < \bar{p}_h$ and $p_k < \bar{p}_k$.

[11] Situation of this kind could be avoided if no upper bound on prices were ever effective, in which case existence of a supply-constrained equilibrium would immediately follow from the results in Drèze (1975).

'If a selling restriction is binding for some agent, for some commodity, one cannot decrease the price of the concerned commodity *keeping the price of all other commodities fixed*' (p. 4, our italics). For any commodity $h \in I$, the condition $f(p) = 1$ has precisely that connotation. Hence, the equilibrium concept of Chetty and Nayak authorizes supply constraints on all the index commodities. Therefore, if one allows every index commodity to be supply-constrained, existence follows from our theorem since we have proved existence for *every* admissible $(p_h)_{h \in I}$.

6. Concluding remark

Altogether, the situations covered by our existence theorem are of some speculative interest. If real prices are subject to exogenous constraints (as they would, for instance, under mark-up pricing, at least in the short run), and if prices do not adjust immediately downwards to eliminate excess supply but do adjust upwards to eliminate excess demand, then a supply-constrained equilibrium as defined here would have some claim to realism *in the short run*. Also, it would be partially self-fulfilling because a built-in bias toward increases in the general price level strengthens reluctance to lower money prices in response to excess supply: better to let the price level rise and keep your money prices unchanged, thereby saving the costs of two successive price changes.[12]

[12] The convergence toward a supply-constrained equilibrium along an adjustment process of that general type is being investigated and will be the subject of another paper.

4 Competitive equilibria with quantity-taking producers and increasing returns to scale[*]

1. Introduction

In the competitive model, where production sets are convex, firms are assumed to maximise profit at given prices. In the non-convex case, this assumption is known to be inadequate. Profit maximisation may lead to unbounded outputs and, more generally, the supply correspondence which assigns profit-maximising production plans to prices may be neither convex valued nor upper hemicontinuous. Beyond these problems, even in the convex case, this behaviour often lacks in realism: many producers announce prices and satisfy the demand which materialises at these prices,[1] instead of choosing optimal quantities in reaction to prices (formed on commodity exchange for instance).

In the present paper, we introduce axiomatically a concept of equilibrium, which combines the following two properties: (i) producers announce prices for their outputs and satisfy the demand which materialises at these prices and (ii) these output prices are 'competitive'. We first prove that under the assumption of convexity, these equilibria coincide with the usual competitive equilibria, thus deserving the label of the 'competitive equilibria with price-taking agents'. In the general case, allowing for non-convex

[*] *Journal of Mathematical Economics*, 17 (1988), 209–30. With Pierre Dehez. This is a revised version of a paper which has appeared as CORE Discussion paper 8623 and EUI Working paper 86/243. The initial motivation for this work came from a remark by Jean Dermine. Early progress owes much to discussions with Bernard Cornet and Jean-Philippe Vial. At a later stage, important technical arguments and continued interest came from Bernard Cornet. We express our thanks to them, to Martin Hellwig and referees who read the manuscript carefully, as well as to colleagues or seminar participants who over the years provided an inspiring mixture of criticisms and encouragements.

[1] Under convexity, when supply is defined by a correspondence rather than by a function, meeting demand naturally determines output levels.

technologies, we then prove the existence of competitive equilibria with quantity-taking producers where conditions (i) and (ii) are satisfied for each producer.

Condition (i) is a condition of *voluntary trading* on prices and quantities: the output must be such that, at the given prices, it is not more profitable for the producers to produce less. Thus, at an equilibrium, producers maximise profit subject to a sales constraint.[2] The competitive property for output prices referred to in condition (ii) is a condition of minimality. For a convex production set with a smooth boundary, output prices coincide with marginal costs if and only if they satisfy voluntary trading and are the lowest prices which satisfy that condition: output prices could not be lowered without violating voluntary trading. We also show that minimality of output prices is the only complement to voluntary trading which retrieves competitive prices in the convex case. Applied to the general case, this definition is analogous to that of '*supply price*' introduced by Marshall: '... the price, the expectation of which will *just* suffice to maintain the existing aggregate amount of production...' (Marshall (1920, p. 343, our emphasis)), and used by Pigou (1928) and by Keynes (1936, p. 24).

To formalise these conditions, we shall in this introduction consider a single producer with a technology described by a production set Y, a closed subset of $\mathbb{R}^l$ containing the origin and satisfying free disposal and absence of free production. To simplify further our presentation, we shall consider the case where inputs are distinguished from outputs and the associated cost function is differentiable, so that marginal costs are well defined. Production plans are then decomposed as $y = (a, b)$, where $a \leq 0$ denotes the vector of inputs and b the vector of outputs.[3] Price systems are decomposed accordingly as $p = (p_a, p_b)$ and the cost function is defined by

$$c(b, p_a) = \min_{(a, b) \in Y} (-p_a \cdot a).$$

A price system $p = (p_a, p_b)$ and a production plan $\bar{y} = (\bar{a}, \bar{b})$ satisfy the condition of voluntary trading if the following inequalities are satisfied:

$$p_a \cdot \bar{a} + p_b \cdot \bar{b} \geq p_a \cdot a + p_b \cdot b \quad \text{for all} \quad (a, b) \in Y, b \leq \bar{b}. \tag{*}$$

---

[2] This is to be contrasted with the work of Scarf (1986) who considers an economy with a production sector described by an aggregate production set displaying a form of increasing returns. At an equilibrium, profits are zero but maximum subject to an input constraint. For a detailed comparison, see our paper on distributive production sets (Dehez and Drèze, 1988b).

[3] For vector inequalities, we adopt the following sequence of symbols: $\geq$, $>$, $\gg$.

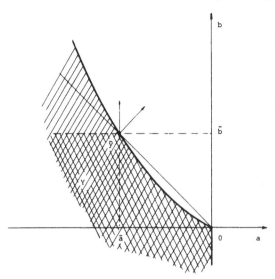

Figure 4.1

This condition says that at prices p, no smaller output yields higher profits, although the producer may be eager to sell more at these prices (as would be the case under diminishing marginal costs, a situation illustrated in fig. 4.1). Voluntary trading clearly implies that production costs are minimised. Furthermore, because inactivity is feasible, voluntary trading implies non-negative profits.

The condition (*) can equivalently be written as $p_b \in \psi(\bar{b}, p_a)$, where ψ is the correspondence defined by

$$\psi(\bar{b}, p_a) = \{p_b \geq 0 \mid p_b \cdot \bar{b} - c(\bar{b}, p_a) \geq p_b \cdot b - c(b, p_a), \ \forall b \leq \bar{b}\}.$$

In fig. 4.2, $\psi(\bar{b}, p_a)$ is the set of all prices p_b greater than or equal to average cost at $\bar{b}$, given p_a. More generally, it may happen that all prices satisfying voluntary trading exceed average cost and therefore entail positive profits, as in fig. 4.3.

To understand the content of condition (ii), it is useful to refer to the convex case first in which voluntary trading alone allows for output prices which exceed competitive levels by an arbitrary margin. Indeed, if marginal costs are well defined at $\bar{b}$, hence equal to the gradient vector $\nabla_b c(\bar{b}, p_a)$, we have

$$\psi(\bar{b}, p_a) = \{p_b \mid p_b \geq \nabla_b c(\bar{b}, p_a)\},$$

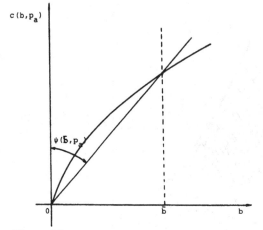

Figure 4.2

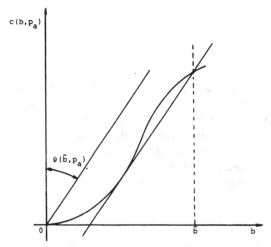

Figure 4.3

as illustrated in fig. 4.4. Competitive prices are then extracted from that set by the straightforward condition that output prices should be minimal in that set. This additional condition can be written as $p_b \in \psi^*(\bar{b}, p_a)$, where ψ^* is the correspondence defined by

$$\psi^*(\bar{b}, p_a) = \{p_b \in \psi(\bar{b}, p_a) \mid \nexists\, p_b' \in \psi(\bar{b}, p_a), p_b' < p_b\}.$$

In the differentiable and convex case, we then have $\psi^*(\bar{b}, p_a) = \nabla_b c(\bar{b}, p_a)$. Consequently, competitive outputs are characterized indifferently by the

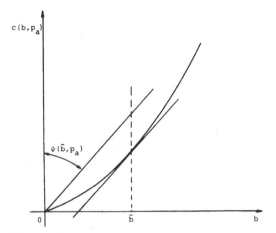

Figure 4.4

property that profit is maximised at given prices or by the property that output prices satisfy voluntary trading and are minimal.

Let us now review the economic arguments which suggest that 'minimal output prices under voluntary trading' is a competitive-like property, in the light of the arguments put forward to justify the concept of competitive equilibrium in the convex case. We shall treat positive and normative aspects separately.

From a positive viewpoint, competitive equilibria have predictive appeal in a convex economy at two distinct logical levels. In the case of a constant returns technology freely accessible to all, a deep argument says that profits will be eliminated by entry of new producers or by spontaneous coalition formation. As shown in a companion paper (Dehez and Drèze (1988b)), the argument of elimination of profit by the entry of new producers carries over to the case of increasing returns for a particular class of technologies, called *output-distributive*, which thus appear as non-convex counterparts to convex cones.

When some (convex) producers use non-reproducible resources to which potential contestants do not have access and to which a rent accrues in the form of profits, this argument no longer applies. In such situations, where returns are strictly diminishing, a competitive equilibrium will emerge only if producers follow certain rules of behaviour, like profit maximisation at given prices; or if the economic organisation privileges competitive outcomes, for instance through auction markets; or if a substitute to free entry exists, for instance through close substitutes.

Beyond the special case of output-distributive production sets, not treated here explicitly, the positive appeal (if any...) of our equilibrium concept is of this second kind. It will emerge, for instance, if producers quote prices, meet whatever demand materialises at these prices, and revise output prices downward when demand falls short of supply, whenever these lower prices remain compatible with voluntary trading. Alternatively, if markets are organised by auctioneers or regulators who adjust prices in the direction of excess supply subject to the downward rigidities induced by voluntary trading, then an equilibrium will be characterised by minimal output prices under voluntary trading. The example of fig. 4.1 should convince anyone that excess supply at given prices is a natural byproduct of increasing returns. Once that conclusion is accepted, it seems natural to require that sales constraints only set in when prices become downward rigid,[4] and prices have no reason to be downward rigid if they are not minimal, barring monopolistic elements. Of course, increasing returns provide a natural invitation to model monopolistic competition along the lines suggested by Negishi (1961); like a number of others, we are currently investigating that possibility.

Short of being able to model the tâtonnement process leading to a competitive equilibrium with quantity-taking producers,[5] we prove existence of an equilibrium by a fixed point argument involving a correspondence under which:

– market prices respond to excess demand,
– consumers announce their (excess) demands given market prices and given incomes which incorporate the profits computed at market prices,
– for given production plans, producers announce prices such that output prices are minimal subject to voluntary trading at the given input prices,
– *producers revise their production plans in the direction of discrepancies between market prices and the prices which they announce.*

From a normative viewpoint, competitive equilibria have the compelling appeal of Pareto optimality. Our equilibria formalise the natural tendency of regulators to impose minimal output prices, a tendency presumably based on the idea that lower prices compatible with voluntary trading (hence covering marginal costs) are better from a welfare point of view.[6]

---

[4] This corresponds to the concept of equilibrium with price rigidities and quantity rationing introduced by Drèze (1975).

[5] See, however, Drèze (1990) for an example of a process which leads to a supply-constrained equilibrium as defined in Dehez and Drèze (1984).

[6] Regulation often takes the related, yet distinct, form of imposing 'competitive' (i.e. minimal subject to voluntary trading) rates of return on investment. However, we shall show that imposing minimum profit under voluntary trading is not competitive in the sense that this condition, when added to voluntary trading, does not necessarily reproduce marginal costs in the convex case.

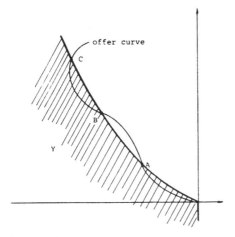

Figure 4.5

However, in the example of fig. 4.5, our definition of equilibrium admits three equilibria, labelled *A*, *B* and *C* respectively, where *C* Pareto dominates *B* which Pareto dominates *A*. We are unwilling to introduce further conditions which would privilege the global optimum *C*, because they would require more sophisticated information.[7] Furthermore, simple examples, like the one illustrated in fig. 4.6, show that second-best Pareto

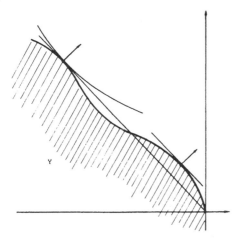

Figure 4.6

[7] Note that, in the absence of convexity, marginal cost pricing is necessary, but not sufficient, for Pareto efficiency (see Guesnerie, 1975b).

optimality may require the violation of voluntary trading. Our equilibria may thus be viewed as *third-best*, the additional constraint beyond voluntary trading being that only minimal information be used, namely prices and quantities. However, our work is best viewed as complementary to that inspired by normative considerations, like marginal cost pricing equilibria; see the important literature on this subject, starting with Guesnerie (1975b), in particular the recent contributions by Brown *et al.* (1986) and Dierker *et al.* (1985), and the papers in *Journal of Mathematical Economics*, 17 (1988). Our emphasis instead is on *decentralisation* through simple signals and incentive compatible mechanisms, i.e. on *equilibrium analysis*.

The paper is organized as follows. The private ownership is described in Section 2 where the basic assumptions are introduced. The behaviour of producers is then analysed in Section 3 where voluntary trading and minimality of output prices are combined. The equilibrium concept is then defined and existence is proved in Section 4.

2. Description of the economy

The model we shall consider is the private ownership economy as described in Debreu's *Theory of Value* (1959). There are l commodities, n producers and m consumers. Producer j is characterised by a production set Y_j. Consumer i is characterised by a consumption set X_i, a preference relation $\succeq_i$, an initial endowment ω_i and shares in profits $(\theta_{i1}, \ldots, \theta_{in})$. By definition, the latter satisfy $0 \leq \theta_{ij} \leq 1$ for all i and j, and $\sum_i \theta_{ij} = 1$ for all j. We make the following assumptions on consumer's characteristics:

C.1. X_i is a closed subset of $\mathbb{R}^l$, convex and bounded below.

C.2. $\succeq_i$ is a complete, continuous, convex[8] and non-satiated preordering of X_i.

C.3.   There exists $\hat{x}_i \in X_i$ such that $\hat{x}_i \ll \omega_i$.

These are the assumptions used in *Theory of Value*. Although they could be weakened through more specific assumptions on preferences and endowments, our focus is here on the production side. We make the following assumptions on the production sets:

P.1.   For all j, Y_j is a closed subset of $\mathbb{R}^l$.

P.2.   For all j, $Y_j + \mathbb{R}^l_- \subset Y_j$.

P.3.   For all j, $Y_j \cap \mathbb{R}^l_+ = \{0\}$.

[8] By *convex*, we mean: $x \succ \bar{x}$ implies $\lambda x + (1 - \lambda)\bar{x} \succ \bar{x}$ for all λ, $0 < \lambda < 1$.

These are again usual assumptions, except that the aggregate production set $\sum Y_j$ is not assumed to be convex. Furthermore, *free disposal* (P.2) and *absence of free production* (P.3) are assumed to hold at the individual level. Note that P.3 implies that *inactivity is feasible*: $0 \in Y_j$ for all j. The set of feasible allocations, $A = \{(x_1, \ldots, x_m, \ y_1, \ldots, y_n) \in \Pi X_i \times \Pi Y_j \mid \sum x_i \leq \sum \omega_i + \sum y_j\}$ is non-empty as a consequence of the assumptions C.3 and P.3. The following assumption[9] is introduced in addition to C.1 to ensure that A is a bounded set in $\mathbb{R}^{l(m+n)}$:

> *P.4.*   For all $z \in \mathbb{R}^l$, the set $\{(y_1, \ldots, y_n) \in \Pi Y_j \mid \sum y_j \geq z\}$ is bounded in $\mathbb{R}^{ln}$.

Altogether, our assumptions ensure the existence of a competitive equilibrium in the case where the aggregate production set is convex [see Debreu (1959)].

The behaviour of the consumers is the usual one: they take the prices and profits as given when choosing the consumption plans which are best with respect to their preferences in their budget sets. As stressed in the introduction, the behaviour of the producers differs from the usual one; it is the object of the next section.

3.   Behaviour of the producers

In this section, we shall be concerned with a given producer characterised by a production set Y which satisfies P.1 and P.2. It is therefore a closed and comprehensive[10] set, and consequently its boundary coincides with the set of weakly efficient production plans:

$$\partial Y = \{y^* \in Y \mid \not\exists \, y \in Y, y \gg y^*\}.$$

In the standard competitive model, the production sets are convex and the behaviour of producers is summarized by their supply correspondences which define profit-maximising production plans at given prices. Here instead, we proceed along the lines initiated by Dierker *et al.* (1985) who use the concept of 'pricing rule' defining 'acceptable' prices associated with production plans. More precisely, a pricing rule is a correspondence $\phi \colon \partial Y \to \mathbb{R}^l_+$, and a price system $\bar{p} \in \mathbb{R}^l_+$ and a production plan $\bar{y} \in \partial Y$ are said to be 'in equilibrium' (from the point of view of the producer) if and only if $\bar{p} \in \phi(\bar{y})$. When Y is convex, profit maximisation is obtained when

---

[9] This assumption has been preferred to the usual assumptions on the asymptotic cone of the aggregate production set because it is less restrictive.

[10] A set X is *comprehensive* if it satisfies free disposal: $X + \mathbb{R}^l_- \subset X$.

the pricing rule is the normal cone, i.e. $\phi(\bar{y}) = \mathbb{N}_Y(\bar{y})$.[11] Indeed, in that case, the condition $\bar{p} \in \phi(\bar{y})$ reads $\bar{p} \cdot \bar{y} \geq \bar{p} \cdot y$ for all $y \in Y$.

To prove existence of an equilibrium for given pricing rules, one assumes that the latter are correspondences which, when intersected with the unit simplex, are upper hemicontinuous with non-empty, compact and convex values.

The subject of the present section is precisely to construct a pricing rule ϕ which embodies the idea of voluntary trading and minimality of output prices, while satisfying these requirements. That pricing rule is obtained after a sequence of intermediate definitions - ψ, ψ^* and ψ^{**} - which generalise the reasoning made in the introduction. As we proceed, we shall use systematically the convex case as a benchmark.

To formalise voluntary trading, we define the set of price systems which are compatible with it:[12]

$$\psi(\bar{y}) = \{p \in \mathbb{R}^l_+ \mid p \cdot \bar{y} \geq p \cdot y \text{ for all } y \in Y, y \leq \bar{y}^+\}. \tag{1}$$

Thus, at any price $p \in \psi(\bar{y})$, it is profitable for the producer to meet the demand as given by $\bar{y}^+$, instead of producing less.

REMARK 1.   The set $\psi(\bar{y})$ can equivalently be defined as the normal cone to the convex set co $\{y \in Y \mid y \leq \bar{y}^+\}$ at $\bar{y}$.[13]

REMARK 2.   If $\bar{y} \in \partial Y \cap \mathbb{R}^l_-$, then $\psi(\bar{y})$ coincides with the normal cone of $\mathbb{R}^l_-$ at $\bar{y}$ which is given by $\{p \in \mathbb{R}^l_+ \mid p \cdot \bar{y} = 0\}$. Furthermore, $\psi(0) = \mathbb{R}^l_+$.

The following Lemma establishes the basic properties of the associated correspondence ψ:

LEMMA 1   *If Y satisfies P.1 to P.3, the correspondence $\psi: \partial Y \to \mathbb{R}^l_+$ is closed*[14] *and its values are non-degenerate,*[15] *closed and convex cones with vertex zero.*

(The proofs of the lemmata are given in the appendix.)

---

[11] Formally, the *normal cone* to a convex set X at a point $\bar{x} \in X$ is defined by $\mathbb{N}_X(\bar{x}) = \{p \in \mathbb{R}^l \mid p \cdot \bar{x} \geq p \cdot x \text{ for all } x \in X\}$; for more details on the concepts of convex analysis, see Rockafellar (1970).

[12] For any vector $x \in \mathbb{R}^l$, x^+ denotes the vector with coordinates $\max(0, x_h)$.

[13] Here, co denotes the convex hull and $\overline{\text{co}}$ will denote its closure.

[14] As pointed out to us by Bernard Cornet, closedness of the correspondence ψ follows also from the continuity of the correspondence $\mu(\bar{y}) = \{y \in Y \mid y \leq \bar{y}^+\}$. It is interesting to note that this correspondence is lower hemicontinuous while the isoquant correspondence does not generally have this property. See Hildenbrand (1974) for the definitions of the various concepts of continuity of correspondence.

[15] A closed cone is *non-degenerate* if it differs from its vertex.

As we do not want to make an *a priori* distinction between inputs and outputs, we must identify the inputs and outputs for every production plan. The *set of inputs* at $\bar{y} \in Y$ is the subset of $\{1,\ldots,l\}$ defined by

$$I(\bar{y}) = \{h \mid \bar{y}_h < 0 \quad \text{or} \quad y_h \leqq 0 \text{ for all } y \in Y\}.$$

It is the index set of the commodities which are either effectively used as inputs at $\bar{y}$ or never appear as outputs. It therefore includes the commodities which are not related to the production process. Its complement in $\{1,\ldots,l\}$, $I^c(\bar{y})$, defines the set of outputs, effective and potential, at $\bar{y}$: Commodity h is an output at $\bar{y}$ if $\bar{y}_h \geqq 0$ and $y_h > 0$ for some $y \in Y$.

REMARK 3. Under P.3, the set $I(\bar{y})$ is non-empty except possibly at $\bar{y} = 0$.

The following lemma provides a simple characterisation of $\psi(\bar{y})$ in the convex case:

LEMMA 2. *Let Y be a convex set satisfying P.1 to P.3. Then, for all $\bar{y} \in \partial Y$,*

$$\psi(\bar{y}) = \mathbb{N}_Y(\bar{y}) + C(\bar{y}),\qquad(2)$$

where $C(\bar{y}) = \{p \in \mathbb{R}^l_+ \mid p_h = 0 \text{ for all } h \in I(\bar{y})\}$.

As an immediate consequence of Lemma 2, the normal cone, $\mathbb{N}_Y(\bar{y})$ is seen to be a subset of $\psi(\bar{y})$ in the convex case. Furthermore, the lemma indicates that to retrieve competitive prices from voluntary trading in the convex case, one should lower the output prices. We then approach the general case by considering first the set of prices whose output components are minimal subject to voluntary trading:

$$\psi^*(\bar{y}) = \{p \in \psi(\bar{y}) \mid \nexists\, p \in \psi(\bar{y}), p < \bar{p}, p_h = \bar{p}_h \,\forall\, h \in I(\bar{y})\}.\qquad(3)$$

This is a cone with vertex zero which is generally not convex when several outputs are involved, and which is possibly degenerate. The conditions under which it is degenerate are given in the following lemma:

LEMMA 3. *Let Y satisfy P.1 to P.3. Then, $\psi^*(\bar{y}) = \{0\}$ if and only if $p \in \psi(\bar{y})$ implies $p_h = 0$ for all $h \in I(\bar{y})$.*

In words, $\psi^*(\bar{y})$ is degenerate *if and only if* voluntary trading imposes zero input prices.

REMARK 4. If $\bar{y} \neq 0$ and $\psi^*(\bar{y}) = \{0\}$ then $\bar{y} \notin \mathbb{R}^l_-$ and all inputs must be in use at $\bar{y}$, i.e. $\bar{y}_h < 0$ for all $h \in I(\bar{y})$.

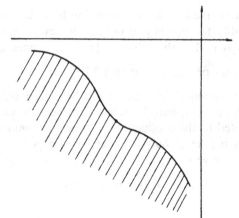

Figure 4.7

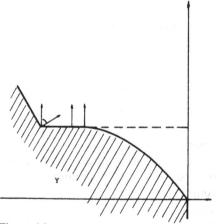

Figure 4.8

Such a situation may occur at points where isoquants are not convex or at inefficient boundary points. This condition follows from the fact that production costs are minimised under voluntary trading. Such a situation may also occur at efficient points where the normal cone – *generalised*[16] in the sense of Clarke – contains non-zero elements with zero coordinates for all inputs. These cases are illustrated in figs. 4.7 and 4.8. It should be noticed that $\psi^*(\bar{y}) = \{0\}$ may occur in the convex case as well.

[16] Clarke (1975) has proposed the definition of a generalised normal cone for the boundary of closed sets, which coincides with the standard normal cone in the convex case and is always different from $\{0\}$ (see also Clarke (1983) and Rockafellar (1979)).

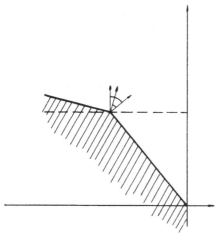

Figure 4.9

From Lemma 2, we can immediately conclude that, in the convex case, the following sequence of inclusions holds for all $\bar{y} \in \partial Y$:

$$\psi^*(\bar{y}) \subset \mathbb{N}_Y(\bar{y}) \subset \psi(\bar{y}), \tag{4}$$

and, as a corollary, we get the following result:

LEMMA 4. *Let Y be a convex set satisfying P.1 to P.3, and consider a point $\bar{y} \in \partial Y$ at which $\psi^*(\bar{y}) \neq \{0\}$ and $\mathbb{N}_Y(\bar{y})$ is a half-line. Then, $\psi^*(\bar{y}) \equiv \mathbb{N}_Y(\bar{y})$.*

Hence, when Y is convex and has a 'smooth' boundary, minimality of output prices subject to voluntary trading is equivalent to profit maximization, except in the extreme situation where all inputs are in use and voluntary trading imposes zero input prices.

As can be seen from the proof of Lemma 2, $C(\bar{y})$ in (2) is the smallest set which, when added to the normal cone, yields $\psi(\bar{y})$. Therefore, minimizing the prices of all outputs, potential and effective, is the only way to retrieve competitive prices from voluntary trading in the convex and smooth case. At points where the boundary is not smooth, $\mathbb{N}_Y(\bar{y})$ is typically larger than $\psi^*(\bar{y})$, as shown in fig. 4.9.

To study the general case, we shall distinguish three possibilities:

Case 1. $\psi^*(\bar{y}) \neq \{0\}$,

Case 2. $\psi^*(\bar{y}) = \{0\}$ and $\psi(\bar{y}) \cap \mathbb{N}_Y(\bar{y}) \neq \{0\}$,

Case 3. $\psi^*(\bar{y}) = \{0\}$ and $\psi(\bar{y}) \cap \mathbb{N}_Y(\bar{y}) = \{0\}$.

While the second case may arise with convex production sets, the third does not. Indeed, from Lemma 2, $\psi(\bar{y}) \cap N_Y(\bar{y}) = N_Y(\bar{y})$ for all $\bar{y} \in \partial Y$, where $N_Y(\bar{y}) \neq \{0\}$. We conjecture that actually the third case does not arise if isoquants are convex:

CONJECTURE   Assume that the set $\{y \in Y \mid y^+ = \bar{y}^+\}$ is convex. Then, if $\psi^*(\bar{y}) = \{0\}$, there exists $p \in N_Y(\bar{y})$, $p \neq 0$, such that $p_h = 0$ for all $h \in I(\bar{y})$.

Let us consider the correspondence $\psi^{**}: \partial Y \to \mathbb{R}^l_+$ defined by

$$
\begin{aligned}
\psi^{**}(\bar{y}) &= \psi^*(\bar{y}) && \text{in Case 1,} \\
&= \psi(\bar{y}) \cap N_Y(\bar{y}) && \text{in Case 2,} \qquad (5) \\
&= \psi(\bar{y}) && \text{in Case 3.}
\end{aligned}
$$

Then Lemma 5 suggests the following definition for our pricing rule:

$$
\phi(\bar{y}) = \overline{\text{co}} \left\{ p \in \mathbb{R}^l_+ \mid \exists (p^\tau, y^\tau) \to (p, \bar{y}), y^\tau \in \partial Y, p^\tau \in \psi^{**}(y^\tau) \forall \tau \right\} \qquad (6)
$$

where ψ^{**} is defined in (5). By construction, $\phi(\bar{y})$ is a non-degenerate closed convex cone with vertex zero. However, because the convex hull of a closed correspondence is not necessarily a closed correspondence, we must prove the following:

LEMMA 5.   *The correspondence* $\phi: \partial Y \to \mathbb{R}^l_+$ *is closed.*

Hence ϕ is the smallest closed and convex-valued correspondence containing ψ^{**}, and it satisfies the technical requirements necessary to qualify as a pricing rule: when intersected with the unit simplex, it defines a correspondence $\bar{\phi}: \partial Y \to S$ which has non-empty, convex and compact values and is upper hemicontinuous.

As an immediate consequence of the fact that ψ is a closed correspondence with convex values, the following result holds:

LEMMA 6.   *For all* $\bar{y} \in \partial Y$, $\phi(\bar{y}) \subset \psi(\bar{y})$.

Hence, prices in $\phi(\bar{y})$ are compatible with voluntary trading. Therefore, production costs are minimized and, if $0 \in Y$, profit is non-negative.

THEOREM 1.   *Let* Y *be a set satisfying P.1 to P.3. If* Y *is convex, then* $\phi(\bar{y}) \equiv N_Y(\bar{y})$ *for all* $\bar{y} \in \partial Y$.

PROOF.   Because Y is convex, Case 3 does not arise and, by Lemma 2, we have:

$$
\begin{aligned}
\psi^{**}(\bar{y}) &= \psi^*(\bar{y}) && \text{in Case 1,} \\
&= N_Y(\bar{y}) && \text{in Case 2.}
\end{aligned}
$$

Hence, $\psi^{**}(\bar{y}) \subset \mathbb{N}_Y(\bar{y})$ for all $\bar{y} \in \partial Y$. Because the normal cone defines a closed correspondence with convex values [see Rockafellar (1970)], we have

$$\overline{\mathrm{co}}\,\{p \in \mathbb{R}^l_+ \mid \exists\,(p^v, y^v) \to (p, \bar{y}),\, y^v \in \partial Y,\, p^v \in \psi^{**}(y^v)\,\forall\, v\} \subset \mathbb{N}_Y(\bar{y}).$$

The converse inclusion follows from a result which has been communicated to us by Bernard Cornet, according to which *the boundary of a convex set is almost everywhere 'smooth'*:

LEMMA 7. *Let Y be a non-empty, closed, convex and comprehensive subset of $\mathbb{R}^l$, $Y \ne \mathbb{R}^l$. Then there exists a dense subset $E \subset \partial Y$ such that the normal cone is a half-line at every point in E and can be defined for all $\bar{y} \in \partial Y$ as*

$$\mathbb{N}_Y(\bar{y}) = \overline{\mathrm{co}}\,\{p \in \mathbb{R}^l_+ \mid \exists\,(p^v, y^v) \to (p, \bar{y}),\, y^v \in E,\, p^v \in \mathbb{N}_Y(y^v)\,\forall\, v\}.$$

Then, by Lemma 4, $\psi^{**}(\bar{y}) = \mathbb{N}_Y(\bar{y})$ for all $\bar{y} \in E$, and

$$\overline{\mathrm{co}}\,\{p \in \mathbb{R}^l_+ \mid \exists\,(p^v, y^v) \to (p, \bar{y}),\, y^v \in E,\, p^v \in \psi^{**}(y^v)\,\forall\, v\} \equiv \mathbb{N}_Y(\bar{y}).$$

The desired inclusion then follows when the sequences are taken in $\partial Y \backslash E$ as well.

REMARK 5. Under our definition of inputs, choosing output prices which minimise profits under voluntary trading does generally not select a subset of $\psi^*(\bar{y})$: $\hat{\psi}(\bar{y}) \not\subset \psi^*(\bar{y})$ for all $\bar{y} \in \partial Y$, where

$$\hat{\psi}(\bar{y}) = \{\bar{p} \in \psi(\bar{y}) \mid \not\exists\, p \in \psi(\bar{y}),\, p \cdot \bar{y} < \bar{p} \cdot \bar{y},\, p_h = \bar{p}_h\,\forall\, h \in I(\bar{y})\}.$$

This inclusion would hold if an alternative definition of output had been adopted, restricting attention to effectively produced commodities. But in that case, one would loose the equivalence result in the convex case as the latter requires the minimisation of the prices of potential outputs as well.

REMARK 6. The pricing rule ϕ defined in (6) does not yield minimal output prices, properly speaking, outside of Case 1. Continuity of the voluntary trading correspondence defined in the introduction has been established for the case of a continuously differentiable cost function. In that case, minimal output prices can be obtained by minimising a convex norm, yielding a closed correspondence, and existence of an equilibrium at which output prices are minimal could then be proved. Moreover, proving that the correspondence ψ is lower hemicontinuous when the boundary of Y is 'smooth' (in the sense that the cone of Clarke is a half-line everywhere except possibly at the origin) remains an open problem.

4. The equilibrium concept

In this section, we shall formally define what we mean by a 'competitive equilibrium with quantity-taking producers' and prove its existence under the assumptions listed in section 2.

A competitive equilibrium with quantity-taking producers is defined by a price system $\bar{p} \neq 0$, a list of production plans $(\bar{y}_1, \ldots, \bar{y}_n)$ and a list of consumption plans $(\bar{x}_1, \ldots, \bar{x}_m)$ satisfying the following properties:

E.1.   It is a feasible allocation, up to free disposal:

$$\sum \bar{x}_i \leq \sum \bar{y}_j + \sum \omega_i, \quad \text{with equality for the commodities whose} \\ \text{price is positive.}$$

E.2.   It is a best choice for the consumers given the prices and profits:

For all i, $\bar{x}_i$ is $\succeq_i$-maximal in

$$\{x_i \in X_i \,|\, \bar{p} \cdot x_i \leq \bar{p} \cdot \omega_i + \sum_j \theta_{ij}\bar{p} \cdot \bar{y}_j\}.$$

E.3.   It is a best choice for the producers given the prices and demand levels:

For all j, $\bar{p} \cdot \bar{y}_j \geq \bar{p} \cdot y_j$ for all $y_j \in Y_j, y_j \leq \bar{y}_j^+$.

E.4.   For every producer, output prices are minimal under voluntary trading:

For all j, $\bar{y}_j \in \partial Y_j$ and $\bar{p} \in \phi_j(\bar{y}_j)$.

The first two conditions are standard.[17] The third condition imposes voluntary trading: at the going prices, every producer chooses to satisfy the demand fully. As a consequence, production costs are minimised at $\bar{p}$ and $\bar{y}_j \in \partial Y_j$ for all j. In terms of the correspondence defined in (1), this condition simply reads: $\bar{p} \in \psi_j(\bar{y}_j)$ for all j. The pricing rule ϕ_j which appears in E.4 is as defined in (6) and prices are therefore convex combinations of limits of prices whose output components are minimal. By Lemma 6, condition E.4 actually embodies E.3.

THEOREM 2.   *Under the assumptions C.1 to C.3 and P.1 to P.4, an equilibrium exists.*

This theorem follows from the general existence theorem in Bonnisseau and Cornet (1988) which covers pricing rules with bounded losses. Our

---

[17] If there was a producer with a convex production set satisfying free disposal, condition E.1 could be written with equality.

special case, where profits are non-negative by construction, permits, however, a comparatively simple proof which is given in the appendix.[18]

REMARK 7. It is well known that the condition $\sum \bar{y}_j \in \partial \sum Y_j$ cannot be expected to hold when non-convexities prevail in production; see, for instance, Beato and Mas-Colell (1985). Accordingly, our equilibrium is in general not production efficient in the aggregate.

REMARK 8. Following Theorem 1, at an equilibrium, convex producers actually maximise their profit at given prices. As a consequence, for a convex economy, our equilibrium concept coincides with the standard notion of competitive equilibrium.

REMARK 9. Our definition allows for a trivial existence proof when $\phi_j(0) = \mathbb{R}^l_+$ for all non-convex producers, a case where they all face set-up costs. The proof would consist in constraining the non-convex producers to inactivity and in noting the existence of a competitive equilibrium in the resulting convex economy.

Appendix

PROOF OF LEMMA 1

For any given $\bar{y} \in \partial Y$, $\psi(\bar{y})$ is clearly a convex cone with vertex zero. The assumptions P.1 to P.3 ensure that $\bar{y}$ belongs to the boundary of the convex set co $\{y \in Y \mid y \leqq \bar{y}^+\}$. Because $\psi(\bar{y})$ is equivalently defined as the normal cone to that set at $\bar{y}$ (cf. Remark 1), it is non-degenerate. To prove closedness, let us fix some $\bar{y} \in \partial Y$ and consider a sequence (p^v, y^v) converging to $(\bar{p}, \bar{y})$ such that $y^v \in \partial Y$ and $p^v \in \psi(y^v)$ for all v. Assume that $\bar{p} \notin \psi(\bar{y})$, i.e. $\bar{p} \cdot \hat{y} > \bar{p} \cdot \bar{y}$ for some $\hat{y} \in Y$, $\hat{y} \leqq \bar{y}^+$. For v large enough, (p^v, y^v) is close to $(\bar{p}, \bar{y})$ and we then have successively: $\bar{p} \cdot \hat{y} > \bar{p} \cdot y^v$ and $p^v \cdot \hat{y} > p^v \cdot y^v$. If $\hat{y} \leqq (y^v)^+$, the last inequality would contradict $p^v \in \psi(y^v)$. If not, let us consider the sequence $(\hat{y}^v)$ defined by $\hat{y}^v_h = y^v_h$ if h satisfies $\hat{y}_h > \max(0, y^v_h)$, and by $\hat{y}^v_h = \hat{y}_h$ if h satisfies $\hat{y}_h \leqq \max(0, y^v_h)$. By construction, $\hat{y}^v \leqq \hat{y}$. Therefore $\hat{y}^v \in Y$ because Y is comprehensive. Also by construction, $\hat{y}^v \leqq (y^v)^+$. Furthermore, if h satisfies $\hat{y}_h > \max(0, y^v_h)$, we have $\hat{y}^v_h = y^v_h < \hat{y}_h \leqq \bar{y}_h$. Hence, for v large enough, $\hat{y}^v$ is arbitrarily close to $\hat{y}$ and we have: $p^v \cdot \hat{y}^v > p^v \cdot y^v$, contradicting $p^v \in \psi(y^v)$.

[18] The proof supplied in the appendix is inspired by the existence proof in Vohra (1988). Our proof can be viewed as the proof of existence of an equilibrium for pricing rules entailing no loss (like, for instance, average cost pricing) and could be generalised to pricing rules depending on all production and consumption plans and on 'market' prices. We are grateful to the Editors for publishing this proof, thereby making our paper self-contained.

PROOF OF LEMMA 2

When Y is convex, $\psi(\bar{y})$ is the normal cone to the intersection of Y with the set $\{y \in \mathbb{R}^l \,|\, y \leq \bar{y}^+\}$. Following Rockafellar (1970, p. 233), $\psi(\bar{y})$ can then be written as $\psi(\bar{y}) = \mathbb{N}_Y(\bar{y}) + \{p \in \mathbb{R}^l_+ \,|\, p_h = 0$ for all h such that $y_h < 0\}$, where the last term is the normal cone to $\{y \in \mathbb{R}^l \,|\, y \leq \bar{y}^+\}$ at $\bar{y}$. Let us now fix some $\bar{p} \in \mathbb{N}_Y(\bar{y})$ and assume that for some h, $\bar{y}_h = 0$ and $y_h \leq 0$ for all $y \in Y$. Then the vector p obtained from $\bar{p}$ by adding a positive quantity δ to its hth coordinate is again an element of $\mathbb{N}_Y(\bar{y})$. Indeed, we then have $p \cdot \bar{y} = \bar{p} \cdot \bar{y} \geq \bar{p} \cdot y$ for all $y \in Y$ and $\bar{p} \cdot y \geq \bar{p} \cdot y + \delta y_h = p \cdot y$ for all $y \in Y$. Hence, $p \in \mathbb{N}_Y(\bar{y})$.

PROOF OF LEMMA 3

It is immediate that $\psi^*(\bar{y}) = \{0\}$ can occur only if for all $p \in \psi(\bar{y})$, $p_h = 0$ for all $h \in I(\bar{y})$. To prove the converse, let us fix some $\bar{y} \in \partial Y$ and assume that this condition holds. Then, the vectors in $\psi(\bar{y})$ have arbitrary coordinates in $\mathbb{R}_+$ for the non-negative outputs, and $\psi^*(\bar{y}) = \{0\}$ follows.

PROOF OF LEMMA 4

$\psi^*(\bar{y})$ is a cone contained in $\mathbb{N}_Y(\bar{y})$. Hence, if $\psi^*(\bar{y})$ is non-degenerate and $\mathbb{N}_Y(\bar{y})$ is a half-line, the equality follows.

PROOF OF LEMMA 5

Let S be the unit simplex of $\mathbb{R}^l_+$. The correspondence γ defined on ∂Y by $\gamma(\bar{y}) = \mathrm{co}(S \cap \{p \in \mathbb{R}^l_+ \,|\, \exists\, (p^v \cdot y^v) \to (p, \bar{y}), \, y^v \in \partial Y, \, p^v \in \phi^{**}(y^v) \,\forall\, v\})$ is upper hemicontinuous (see Hildenbrand (1974, pp. 23 and 26)). We first show that, for any non-degenerate cone of $\mathbb{R}^l_+$ with vertex zero, $\mathrm{co}\, C \equiv \mathrm{cone}$ $(\mathrm{co}(C \cap S))$, where the right-hand side is the cone with vertex zero generated by $\mathrm{co}(C \cap S)$. Because $C \cap S \subset C$, a first inclusion follows. To establish the converse inclusion, let us take some $\bar{p} \in \mathrm{co}\, C$, $\bar{p} \neq 0$. Then, there exists (p^i, λ^i) such that $\bar{p} = \sum_i \lambda^i p^i$, $\sum_i \lambda^i = 1$, $p^i \in C$ and $\lambda^i \geq 0$ for all i. The p^i's can be taken all different from zero and we define the vectors $q^i = (1/\sum_h p^i_h) p^i$; $q^i \in S$ by construction and $q^i \in C$ because C is a cone. Hence, $q^i \in C \cap S$ for all i. We then define $\beta = 1/(\sum_i \lambda^i \sum_h p^i_h)$ and $\mu^i = (\lambda^i/\beta) \sum_h p^i_h$. By construction, $\beta \sum_i \mu^i q^i = \sum_i \lambda^i p^i = \bar{p}$, $\sum_i \mu^i = 1$ and $\mu^i \geq 0$ for all i and $\beta > 0$. Hence, $\bar{p} \in \mathrm{cone}(\mathrm{co}(C \cap S))$ and $\phi(\bar{y}) = \mathrm{cone}$ $(\gamma(\bar{y}))$. Let us now consider a sequence $(p^v, y^v) \to (\bar{p}, \bar{y})$ such that $p^v \in \phi(y^v)$ for all v. Then there exist sequences (λ^v) and (q^v) such that $p^v = \lambda^v q^v$ and

$q^r \in \gamma(y^r)$ for all v. Because $\gamma(\bar{y}) \subset S$, we have $\lambda^r = \sum p_h^r \to \sum \bar{p}_h = \bar{\lambda}$. Because γ is upper hemicontinuous, there exists a subsequence (q^r) converging to some $\bar{q}$, such that $\bar{q} \in \gamma(\bar{y})$ [see Hildenbrand (1974, p. 24)]. Hence, $\lambda \bar{q} = \bar{p}$ and $\bar{p} \in \phi(\bar{y})$.

PROOF OF LEMMA 6

Let $\bar{p} \in \{p \in \mathbb{R}_+^l \mid \exists (p^r, y^r) \to (p, \bar{y}), \ y^r \in \partial Y, \ p^r \in \psi^{**}(y^r) \forall v\}$ for some $\bar{y} \in \partial Y$, $\bar{p} \neq 0$. Using the inclusion $\psi^*(\bar{y}) \subset \psi(\bar{y})$ and applying the definition, $(\bar{p}, \bar{y}) = \lim (p^r, y^r)$ with $p^r \in \psi(y^r)$ for all v. Because ψ is a closed correspondence, $\bar{p} \in \psi(\bar{y})$, and because it has convex values, the result follows.

PROOF OF LEMMA 7 (Cornet)

Let us consider $e^\perp = \{y \in \mathbb{R}^l \mid e \cdot y = 0\}$, the space orthogonal to e, the vector of $\mathbb{R}^l$ with all coordinates equal to 1. From Lemma 5.1 in Bonnisseau and Cornet (1988), we know that there exists a continuous function λ: $e^\perp \to \mathbb{R}$ such that for all $s \in e^\perp$, $\lambda(s)$ is the unique real number satisfying $(s - \lambda(s)e) \in \partial Y$. Moreover, the mapping Λ defined by $\Lambda(s) = s - \lambda(s)e$ is a homeomorphism from $e^\perp$ onto ∂Y. Consequently, the boundary of Y can be written as $\partial Y = \{y \in \mathbb{R}^l \mid y = s - \lambda(s)e, \ s \in e^\perp\}$ and, because Y is comprehensive, we also have $Y = \{y \in \mathbb{R}^l \mid y = s - \lambda e, \ \lambda \geq \lambda(s), \ s \in e^\perp\}$. Hence, Y coincides with $a(\text{epi } \lambda)$ where epi λ denotes the epigraph of λ and $a: e^\perp \times \mathbb{R} \to \mathbb{R}^l$ is the linear isomorphism defined by $a(s, \lambda) = s - \lambda e$. Hence, Y being a convex set, epi λ is itself convex, implying that λ is a convex function.

Let $\partial \lambda$ denote the subdifferential of λ. As an intermediary result, we shall prove that $\mathbb{N}_Y(s - \lambda(s)e) \cap S = \partial \lambda(s) + \{(1/l)e\}$ for all $s \in e^\perp$. Let us define $\bar{y} = \bar{s} - \lambda(\bar{s})e$, for some $\bar{s} \in e^-$. Then, $\bar{y} \in \partial Y$. We first fix some $\bar{p} \in \mathbb{N}_Y(\bar{y})$. Then $\bar{p} = \bar{q} + (1/l)e$, where $\bar{q} \in \text{proj}_{e^\perp} \bar{p}$. Since $\bar{p} \in S$, we have $\bar{q} \in e^\perp$. Applying the definition of the normal cone, we get $\bar{p} \cdot \bar{y} = \bar{p} \cdot (\bar{s} - \lambda(\bar{s})e) \geq \bar{p} \cdot (s - \lambda(s)e)$ for all $s \in e^-$. Then, by definition of $e^\perp$, $\bar{q} \cdot \bar{s} - \lambda(\bar{s})e \geq \bar{q} \cdot s - \lambda(s)e$ for all $s \in e^\perp$, i.e. $\bar{q} \in \partial \lambda(\bar{s})$. Conversely, let us fix some $\bar{p} \in \bar{q} + (1/l)e$, with $\bar{q} \in \partial \lambda(\bar{s})$. Applying the definition of the subdifferential, we get $\bar{p} \cdot \bar{y} = \bar{q} \cdot \bar{s} - \lambda(\bar{s})e \geq \bar{q} \cdot s - \lambda(s)e \geq \bar{q} \cdot s - \lambda e$ for all $\lambda \geq \lambda(s)$ and $s \in e^\perp$. Hence, $\bar{p} \cdot \bar{y} \geq \bar{p} \cdot y$ for all $y \in Y$, i.e. $\bar{p} \in \mathbb{N}_Y(\bar{y})$.

Let D denote the set of points in $e^\perp$ where λ is differentiable. By Rockafellar (1970, Theorems 25.1, 25.5 and 25.6), we have $\partial \lambda(s) = \{\nabla \lambda(s)\}$ for all $s \in D$, D is a dense subset of e^- and $\partial \lambda(s) = \overline{\text{co}} \{q \in e^\perp \mid \exists (s^r) \to s, \ s^r \in D \forall v, \ q = \lim \nabla \lambda(s^r)\}$ for all $s \in e^\perp$. Let us finally define

$E = \{y \in \mathbb{R}^l \mid y = s - \lambda(s), s \in D\}$. Because Λ is a homeomorphism, E is a dense subset of ∂Y. Furthermore, using our intermediary result, $\mathbb{N}_Y(y)$ is a half-line for all $y \in E$, and we have $\mathbb{N}_Y(y) \cap S = \overline{co}\,\{p \in S \mid \exists\,(p^v, y^v) \to (p, y), y^v \in E, p^v \in \mathbb{N}_Y(y^v) \cap S\,\forall\,v\}$. Because $\mathbb{N}_Y$ defines a closed correspondence, the conclusion of the lemma then follows.

PROOF OF THEOREM 2

Because the set of feasible allocations is non-empty and bounded, the attainable consumption and production sets, defined as the projections on A of X_i and Y_j respectively, are bounded. Therefore, there exists a closed cube K in $\mathbb{R}^l$ with length k, centered at the origin and containing in its interior the attainable consumption and production sets [see Debreu (1959, p. 85)]. We define $\bar{X}_i = X_i \cap K$ and $\bar{Y}_j = \{y' \in Y_j' \mid \not\exists\, y \in Y_j, y \geqq y'$, with strict inequality if $y_h' > 0\}$, where $Y_j' = \partial(Y_j + \{ke\}) \cap \mathbb{R}_+^l$ and $e = (1, \ldots, 1) \in \mathbb{R}_+^l$. Let f_j denote the projection of points in $\mathbb{R}_+^l \setminus \{0\}$ on the unit simplex $S = \{x \in \mathbb{R}_+^l \mid \sum x_h = 1\}$. It is well known that under P.1 to P.4, as a function from $\bar{Y}_j$ into S, f_j defines a homeomorphism which satisfies

(a) $f_j(y_j) \gg 0$ if and only if $y_j \gg 0$.

(See for instance Brown et al. (1986).) Let us then define the function g_j on S by $g_j(s) = f_j^{-1}(s) - ke$. The assumption P.2 ensures that $g_j(s) \in \partial Y_j$ for all $s \in S$.

The *demand correspondence* of consumer i, $\xi_i \colon S^{n+1} \to \bar{X}_i$, is defined by $\xi_i(p, s_1, \ldots, s_n)$, the set of $\succeq_i$-maximisers on $\{x \in \bar{X}_i \mid p \cdot x \leqq p \cdot \omega_i + \sum_j \theta_{ij} p \cdot g_j(s_j)\}$ if the right-hand side of the budget constraint exceeds $\min p \cdot \bar{X}_i$, and by $\arg \min p \cdot \bar{X}_i$ if not. This (quasi) demand correspondence is upper hemicontinuous and has non-empty, compact and convex values [see Debreu (1962, p. 261)].

The *supply correspondence* of producer j is a function $\beta_j \colon S^3 \to S$ defined by

$$\beta_j(p, q_j, s_j) = \frac{1}{\lambda_j(\cdot)} F_j(\cdot)$$

where $F_{jh}(\cdot) = \max(0, s_{jh} + p_h - q_{jh})$ and $\lambda_j(\cdot) = \sum_h F_{jh}(\cdot)$. Clearly, $\lambda_j(\cdot) \geq 1$ on S^3, ensuring the continuity of β_j. Here p denotes 'market prices' as opposed to the q_j which denote 'producer prices'.

Market prices are determined through the standard 'market' correspondence $\mu \colon \Pi \bar{X}_i \times S^n \to S$ defined by $\mu(x_1, \ldots, x_m, s_1, \ldots, s_n) = \arg$

$\max_{p \in S} p \cdot (\sum x_i - \sum \omega_i - \sum g_j(s_j))$. The continuity of the g_j's ensures that this correspondence is upper hemicontinuous with non-empty, convex and compact values.

The prices of producer j are determined through the correspondence $\bar{\phi}_j: S \to S$ defined by $\bar{\phi}_j(s_j) = \phi_j(g_j(s_j)) \cap S$. Because the correspondences ϕ_j are closed (by Lemma 5) with values which are non-degenerate convex cones with vertex zero, and the g_j's are continuous functions, the correspondences $\bar{\phi}_j$ are upper hemicontinuous with non-empty, convex and compact values [see Hildenbrand (1974, p. 23)].

We are now in a position to construct a correspondence Φ from $S^{2n+1} \times \Pi X_i$ into itself whose fixed points are equilibria:

$$\Phi(p, q_1, \ldots, q_n, s_1, \ldots, s_n, x_1, \ldots, x_m)$$
$$= \mu(\cdot) \times \Pi \beta_j(\cdot) \times \Pi \bar{\phi}_j(\cdot) \times \Pi \xi_i(\cdot).$$

By Kakutani's theorem, Φ has a fixed point $(\bar{p}, \bar{q}_1, \ldots, \bar{q}_n, \bar{s}_1, \ldots, \bar{s}_n, \bar{x}_1, \ldots, \bar{x}_m)$ and we define $\bar{y}_j = g_j(\bar{s}_j)$ and $\bar{z} = \sum \bar{x}_i - \sum \bar{y}_j - \sum \omega_i$. Then $\bar{y}_j \in \partial Y_j$ for all j and the following conditions are satisfied:

(b)　$\bar{s}_j = \beta_j(\bar{p}, \bar{q}_j, \bar{s}_j)$.

(c)　$\bar{x}_i \in \xi_i(\bar{p}, \bar{s}_1, \ldots, \bar{s}_n)$　for all　i.

(d)　$p \cdot \bar{z} \leq \bar{p} \cdot \bar{z}$　for all　$p \in S$.

(e)　$\bar{q}_j \in \phi_j(\bar{y}_j) \cap S$　for all　j.

Let us define $\bar{\lambda}_j = \lambda_j(\bar{p}, \bar{q}_j, \bar{s}_j)$. Then, (b) implies

(f)　$\bar{\lambda}_j \bar{s}_{jh} \geq \bar{s}_{jh} + \bar{p}_h - \bar{q}_{jh}$,

with equality whenever $\bar{s}_{jh} > 0$. Multiplying both sides of (f) by $\bar{s}_{jh}$ and summing over all h, we get $(\bar{\lambda}_j - 1)\bar{s}_j \cdot \bar{s}_j = (\bar{p} - \bar{q}_j) \cdot \bar{s}_j$ where $\bar{\lambda}_j \geq 1$ and $\bar{s}_j \cdot \bar{s}_j \geq 1/l$. We therefore have the following set of inequalities:

(g)　$(\bar{p} - \bar{q}_j) \cdot \bar{s}_j \geq 0$　for all　j.

By definition of f_j, there exists $\bar{\mu}_j > 0$ such that $\bar{s}_j = \bar{\mu}_j(\bar{y}_j + ke)$. Using the fact that $(\bar{p} - \bar{q}_j) \cdot e = 0$, we then have $(\bar{p} - \bar{q}_j) \cdot \bar{s}_j = \bar{\mu}_j(\bar{p} - \bar{q}_j) \cdot \bar{y}_j$ which, combined with (g), gives

(h)　$\bar{p} \cdot \bar{y}_j \geq \bar{q}_j \cdot \bar{y}_j$　for all　j.

By (e) $\bar{q}_j \cdot \bar{y}_j \geq 0$ and therefore $\bar{p} \cdot \bar{y}_j \geq 0$ for all j and C.3 ensures that for all i, $\bar{p} \cdot \omega_i + \sum_j \theta_{ij} \bar{p} \cdot \bar{y}_j > \min p \cdot \bar{X}_i$. Combined with (c), this implies that the budget constraints apply. Summing over all budget constraints, we get $\bar{p} \cdot \bar{z} \leq 0$ which, combined with (d), gives $\bar{z} \leq 0$. The fixed point therefore defines an attainable state and consequently $f_j^{-1}(\bar{s}_j) \gg 0$ for all j. Hence, by (a), $\bar{s}_j \gg 0$ for all j; and by (f), $\bar{\lambda}_j = 1$ and $\bar{q}_j = \bar{p}$ for all j. Conditions E.3 and E.4 are therefore established. Condition E.2 follows from (c) by a standard argument (see Debreu (1959, p. 87)). On the other hand, C.2. implies local non-satiation. As a consequence, the budget constraints hold with equality, and condition E.1 follows from $\bar{p} \cdot \bar{z} = 0$.

III Efficiency of constrained equilibria

5 Optimality properties of rationing schemes[*]

1. Introduction and summary

1.1.

General equilibrium theory has recently been enlarged with a formal analysis of equilibrium under price rigidities and quantity rationing – see, e.g., the survey paper by Grandmont (1977). Although the relevant concepts are at least as old as Keynes' 'General Theory', the formal analysis within the general equilibrium methodology is still young. So far, theorists have devoted much of their attention to very simple models, starting with a pure exchange economy. On the price side, they have privileged the case of fixed prices, and to a lesser extent the case of prices subject to inequality constraints, defined independently for each commodity. On the quantity side, they have privileged the case of inequality constraints on net trades defined independently for each commodity; this case is sometimes described as 'market-by-market rationing'. An always desired numeraire with unit price is never rationed, however.

Under standard assumptions (initial resources interior to a convex consumption set; complete, continuous, convex preferences), there exist equilibria where for each commodity either supply or demand is rationed, or neither, but not both simultaneously; and where supply (resp. demand) is rationed only in case of downward (resp. upward) price rigidity.[1] Here

[*]*Journal of Economic Theory*, 23, 2 (1980), 131–49. With Heinz Müller. The authors are grateful to Pierre Dehez for many helpful comments.
[1] This last feature is somewhat surprising, considering the possibility of excess demand for a Giffen good – a point that has been discussed orally, but not in the literature, to the best of our knowledge. The problems connected with Giffen goods are clearly recognized in the literature on the stability of tâtonnement processes—see, e.g. Arrow and Hahn (1971, p. 300).

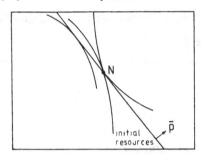

Figure 5.1.   Examples of efficient non-Walrasian equilibrium

'equilibrium' means that each consumer attains a best point, for his preferences, over the intersection of his budget set with the quantity constraints.

The efficiency of such equilibria may be considered at three levels, namely (i) relative to the set of all physically feasible allocations; (ii) relative to the set of physically feasible allocations for which the net trades of all consumers have zero value at an admissible price vector; (iii) relative to the set of allocations sustained as equilibria by an admissible price vector and by admissible quantity constraints. Allocations that are efficient at the first level are called 'unconstrained Pareto optima'; allocations that are efficient at the second or third level are 'constrained Pareto optima'.

Clearly, efficiency at one level implies efficiency at the next level, and inefficiency at one level implies inefficiency at the previous level, but not conversely.

Walrasian equilibria are always efficient at the first level. Non-Walrasian equilibria may be efficient at that level. An example is given in the Edgeworth box of fig. 5.1 (for the fixed prices $\bar{p}$, at the point N, where the preferred sets of the two consumers can be separated). But this is the exception rather than the rule.[2] The inefficiency at the first level of non-Walrasian equilibria is due to the constraint that all net trades must have zero value at prices belonging to a predetermined set.[3]

---

[2] It cannot happen under convex smooth preferences. Indeed, in that case, a non-Walrasian equilibrium (as defined above in the text) which is also an unconstrained Pareto optimum must involve 'forced trading' and therefore cannot be sustained by market-by-market rationing. Here 'forced trading' means that a proportional reduction of the net trades on all commodities would be preferred; feasible sets that are convex and contain the initial endowment rule out forced trading in equilibrium. See also Theorem 3 in Madden (1978).

[3] A recent paper by Balasko (1978) shows that, under an asumption of smooth preferences, there always exists an unconstrained Pareto optimum, where all net trades have zero value at arbitrary predetermined prices. But that particular Pareto optimum is usually not an equilibrium. It may also fail to be individually rational, as can easily be verified in an Edgeworth box.

Non-Walrasian equilibria may, or again may not, be efficient at the second level. The relative inefficiency is now due to the constraint that quantity rationing must operate 'market-by-market'. In contrast, efficiency may require, say, that some individuals *increase their trading on the short side of one market in exchange for less rationing on the long side of another market*. In other words, efficiency may require some form of interdependent rationing. Examples are given in Younès (1975) or Böhm and Müller (1977).

The inefficiency of non-Walrasian equilibria at the third level is at the heart of Keynesian theory. It is often referred to as 'spillover effects' – see Bénassy (1975). Given a non-Walrasian equilibrium, a Pareto improvement could result if *the quantity constraints on several markets were relaxed simultaneously*; see, for instance, the example in Grandmont (1978).

1.2.

It is not generally possible to achieve efficiency at the first level without restoring price flexibility. But efficiency at the second level can be achieved through more sophisticated rationing schemes. For a fixed-price vector, the characterisation of allocations that are efficient at the second level (Section 4) is an immediate application of standard optimality theory – as presented for instance in Chapter 6 of Debreu's *Theory of Value* (1959).

Indeed, when the numeraire has a price of unity and is always desired but never rationed, the quantity of numeraire consumed by an individual subject to a budget constraint and an arbitrary rationing scheme is always equal to his initial endowment minus the value of his net trades on other commodities. Using this identity to eliminate the numeraire and the budget constraints, one may define a new exchange economy on the remaining goods. The initial endowments for these goods are unchanged. The consumption sets and preferences among these goods are derived from those of the original economy by associating with each consumption vector the corresponding consumption of numeraire (as defined above), and then referring to the original consumption set and preferences. The new exchange economy satisfies (in the reduced commodity space) the same standard assumptions as the original economy (initial resources interior to a convex consumption set; complete, continuous, convex preferences). Accordingly, one may apply to the new economy the second theorem of welfare economics: *An optimum is an equilibrium relative to a price system* – see Debreu (1959, Sect. 6.4).

The interpretation in a fixed-price exchange economy is the following:

With every allocation that is efficient at the second level, one can associate a vector of *coupon prices* for commodities other than the numeraire; the (relatively) efficient allocation assigns to every individual a consumption preferred by him to any other element of his budget set with smaller coupon value.

Going back to our remark about the inefficiency of 'market-by-market' rationing, we note that coupon prices express the trade-offs that characterise, explicitly or implicitly, any form of interdependent rationing. Efficiency requires identical trade-offs (marginal rates of substitution among commodities other than the numeraire) for all individuals.

The name 'coupon prices' evokes the coupon rationing schemes sometimes implemented to cope with scarcities. It should prevent confusion with the fixed prices in terms of the numeraire, to which we shall refer as 'money prices'. We call '*coupons equilibrium*' an allocation sustained by coupon prices, in the above sense (Definition 1).

The coupon values of the net trades at such an equilibrium sum up to zero (for market clearing), but are of arbitrary sign for a given consumer. A coupons equilibrium may thus fail to be individually rational, and may involve 'forced trading.'

The same remark applies to unconstrained Pareto optima – but not to competitive equilibria, which involve individual net trades of zero value; and competitive equilibria exist, under standard assumptions. An example (Appendix 5.1) shows that coupons equilibria where all net trades have a coupon value of zero may fail to exist. On the other hand, there always exist coupons equilibria where each consumer realizes the net trade which he prefers among those in his budget set whose coupon value *does not exceed* a given, nonnegative constant (the same for all individuals). We reserve the name '*uniform coupons equilibrium*' for those allocations, and we call '*coupons endowment*' the upper-limit set on the coupon value of individual net trades. It is positive when some individuals attain the best point of their budget set through a net trade of negative coupon value; it is zero otherwise.

Uniform coupons equilibria may be regarded as counterparts of competitive equilibria. The existence theorem is proved by similar techniques. The implied net trades are always 'fair' (remark at the end of Section 4). Also (Section 3), there always exist uniform coupons equilibria with coupon prices that are *positive* in case of *upward* price rigidity, *negative* in case of *downward* price rigidity, and zero otherwise.[4] A

---

[4] An example (Appendix 5.2) shows, unfortunately, that this particular set of coupons equilibria may fail to contain any allocation which is Pareto optimal relative to the set of admissible prices.

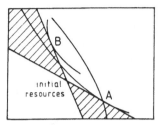

Figure 5.2. Example of Pareto-inefficient coupons equilibrium

companion paper by Aumann and Drèze (1986) relates uniform coupons equilibria to Shapley value allocations in large economies.

The characterisation of allocations that are efficient at the second level as coupons equilibria has three immediate extensions, namely:

(i)   an allocation which is efficient relative to an arbitrary *set of admissible prices* must *a fortiori* be efficient relative to the particular prices at which its net trades have zero value,[5] hence it must be a coupons equilibrium;

(ii) every coupons equilibrium is efficient relative to all the other allocations compatible with the *same* money prices (Proposition 1);

(iii) a coupons equilibrium at which no pair of consumers could profitably exchange coupons against the numeraire is an unconstrained Pareto optimum (Section 5).

1.3.

This discussion reveals that optimality of rationing schemes does not raise new problems when prices are fixed. When individual money prices are only subject to inequality constraints, much deeper issues arise. First, the set of feasible allocations is not convex, as the Edgeworth box of fig. 5.2 illustrates. (When prices p are restricted to the interval $\bar{p} \geqslant p \geqslant \underline{p}$, the set of feasible allocations is the shaded 'bow-tie' area.) Second, a coupons equilibrium may fail to be efficient relative to the set of feasible allocations. Indeed, there may exist, *at different prices* (belonging to the admissible set), another coupons equilibrium which is Pareto superior, i.e., better from the viewpoint of all consumers (compare points A and B in fig. 5.2).

---

[5] Such prices exist, by the definition of 'efficiency at the second level'.

The present paper addresses itself (Section 6) to the following question. Suppose that an allocation x is efficient relative to a given vector of money prices p. It is then a coupons equilibrium, say with coupon prices a. Consider an alternative price system $\hat{p} \neq p$. We would like to know whether or not there exists an allocation compatible with $\hat{p}$ which is preferred by all consumers to the given allocation x. In the affirmative, one could conclude that the allocation x is inefficient with respect to any set of admissible prices containing $\hat{p}$; under a slight misuse of terminology, one could also say that '$\hat{p}$ is Pareto superior to p'. The question studied here is: Do the coupon prices a contain any information about the set of prices $\hat{p}$ (possibly empty) which are Pareto superior to p?

One could have hoped that positive (respectively negative) coupon prices provide an unambiguous signal that higher (respectively lower) prices could sustain Pareto superior allocations. This is unfortunately not true.[6] However, a necessary condition for the prices $\hat{p}$ to be Pareto superior to p can be stated as follows. We still consider the allocation x, efficient relative to the prices p. We ask each consumer what minimal coupons endowment would be required in order for him to attain, at the alternative money prices $\hat{p}$ and *at the prevailing coupon prices a*, a consumption at least as good as his consumption under the allocation x. The sum over all consumers of the required endowments must be *negative* in order for $\hat{p}$ to be Pareto superior to p (Proposition 3). Unfortunately, this necessary condition is not sufficient. Also, in order to verify that a given allocation x, compatible with prices p, is Pareto optimal relative to some set of admissible prices P, one should verify that the necessary condition is violated for *every* $\hat{p}$ in P.

Sufficient conditions of constructive interest can be defined, for $\hat{p}$ in a neighbourhood of p. We ask each consumer how much numeraire he would be just willing to forego in order to increase his coupons endowment by one (infinitesimal) unit; that is, we elicit the (marginal) money value of coupons to consumers. If that value is the same for all consumers, we already know that the prevailing allocation is an unconstrained Pareto optimum, so that no $\hat{p}$ Pareto superior to p exists. If that value is zero for some consumers, any (respectively some) $\hat{p}$ close to p at which the prevailing net trades of all these consumers have negative (respectively nonpositive) money values is Pareto superior to p. If that value is positive for all consumers, call its reciprocal the coupon value of money, and calculate the vector of covariances (over the consumers) of net trades with

---

[6] See also footnotes 2, 4.

the coupon value of money. Infinitesimal price changes with signs *opposite* to those of the respective covariances define a Pareto superior price vector. These sufficient conditions are not necessary, however.

In view of the nonconvexity of the set of allocations that are feasible relative to a convex set of admissible prices (fig. 5.2), it seems unlikely that these results could be strengthened substantially.

2. The model

An exchange economy with price rigidity $\mathscr{E}$ is defined by:

$M = \{0 \ldots m\}$ the set of commodities:

$\varDelta = \{p \in R_+^{m+1} \mid p_0 = 1, -\infty < \underline{p}_h \leqslant p_h \leqslant \bar{p}_h < \infty, h = 1 \ldots m\}$ the set of admissible prices:

$N = \{1 \ldots n\}$ the set of consumers, where each consumer i is characterized by his consumption set, $X^i \subseteq R_+^{m+1}$, his initial endowment, $w^i \in R_+^{m+1}$ and his preferences.

For the optimality analysis of Sections 4–6, we make the standard assumption that i's preferences are defined by a complete preordering $\succcurlyeq_i$ on X^i. For the existence theorem in Section 3, we allow more generality. Let $S = \{a \in R^{m+1} \mid a_0 = 0\}$ and $c^i \in R$ define, respectively, the set of coupon prices and the coupons endowment of consumer i; for $p \in \varDelta$, $a \in S$, $c^i \in R$, the budget set of consumer i is

$$B^i(p, a, c^i) = \{w^i + z^i \in X^i \mid pz^i = 0, az^i \leqslant c^i\}. \tag{1}$$

The preferences of consumer i are given by the correspondence $D^i: X \times \varDelta \times S \times R^n \to R^{m+1}$, where $X = \Pi_{i \in N} X^i$. Thus, $D^i(x, p, a, (c^j)_{j \in N}) \cap X^i$ is the set of all $\bar{x}^i \in X^i$ which consumer i prefers to x^i, when all other individuals $h \neq i$ consume x^h, the price system is p, the vector of coupon prices is a and the vector of coupons endowments is $(c^j)_{j \in N}$.[7] The set of feasible net trades relative to $\varDelta$ is defined for later reference by

$$Z(\varDelta) := \left\{ (z^1 \ldots z^n) \in R^{n(m+1)} \left| \begin{array}{l} w^i + z^i \in X^i \, \forall i \in N, \sum_{i \in N} z^i = 0, \\ \\ \exists \, p \in \varDelta \text{ s.t. } \forall i \in N, pz^i = 0 \end{array} \right. \right\}. \tag{2}$$

We shall also need

$$Z^i(p) := \{z^i \mid pz^i = 0, w^i + z^i \in X^i\}; \quad Y^i = X^i - \{w^i\}. \tag{3}$$

---

[7] This allows for noncomplete and nontransitive preferences.

DEFINITION 1.   For the economy $\mathscr{E}$ a *coupons equilibrium* is a list of net trades $(z^i)_{i\in N}$, coupons endowments $(c^i)_{i\in N}$, a price $p\in\Delta$, and a coupon price $a\in S$ such that

$$\sum_{i\in N} z^i = 0 \tag{4}$$

$$w^i + z^i \in B^i(p,a,c^i) \quad \text{and}$$
$$D^i(w+z,p,a,(c^j)_{j\in N}) \cap B^i(p,a,c^i) = \phi \,\forall\, i\in N. \tag{5}$$

A coupons equilibrium $\{(z^i,c^i)_{i\in N}, p, a\}$ is called *uniform* if $c^i = c\,\forall\, i\in N$.

Note.   Equations (4) and (5) imply $\sum_{i\in N} c^i \geqslant 0$.

In the sequel, we shall have occasion to use the following assumptions, for all $i\in N$:[8]

A.1 X^i is a closed convex subset of R^{m+1} with $X^i \supseteq X^i + R^{m+1}_+$.

A.2 $w^i \in \text{Int } X^i$.

A.3 D^i has a relative open graph, is convex valued and is irreflexive, i.e., $x^i \notin D^i(x,p,a,(c^j)_{j\in N})$.

A.3′ $\succcurlyeq_i$ is continuous; if $x^1, x^2 \in X^i$, and $t\in(0,1)$ then $x^2 \succ_i x^1 \Rightarrow tx^2 + (1-t)x^1 \succ_i x^1$.

A.3″ $\succcurlyeq_i$ is representable by a strictly quasi-concave, twice continuously differentiable utility function

$$u^i: Y^i \to R \quad \text{with} \quad \frac{\partial u^i}{\partial z_0} > 0 \,\forall\, z\in Y^i.$$

A.4   Strict desirability for commodity 0.

3.   Existence of coupons equilibria

THEOREM.   *For every economy $\mathscr{E}$ which satisfies A.1, A.2, A.3, and A.4 there exists a uniform coupons equilibrium $\{(z^i,c)_{i\in N}, p, a\}$ such that for $h = 1\ldots m$,*

$$a_h > 0 \Rightarrow p_h = \bar{p}_h$$
$$a_h < 0 \Rightarrow p_h = \underline{p}_h. \tag{6}$$

---

[8] For the preference relation on net trades and on consumption bundles the same symbol $\succcurlyeq_i$ is used. No confusion should arise. Of course, $z^1 \succcurlyeq_i z^2$ iff $w^i + z^1 \succcurlyeq_i w^i + z^2$.

Under the additional assumption that Δ contains no Walrasian equilibrium price, there exists a uniform coupons equilibrium satisfying (6) with $a \neq 0$.

REMARK: An example in Appendix 5.1 shows that a coupons equilibrium with $c^i = 0$ $\forall i \in N$ may fail to exist. On the other hand, if $x \in X$ satisfies $\sum_i z^i = 0$ and for some $p \in \Delta$, $pz^i = 0$ $\forall i \in N$, there always exists a coupons equilibrium $\{(\hat{z}^i, c^i)_{i \in N}, p, a\}$ such that $x^i \in B^i(p, a, c^i) \forall i \in N$. More specifically, define continuous functions $t^i \colon \Delta \to R^{m+1}, i \in N$ s.t.

$$pt^i(p) = 0 \,\forall i \in N$$
$$\sum_{i \in N} t^i(p) = 0, \tag{7}$$

and replace A.2 by

A.2′ $w^i + t^i(p) \in \text{int } X^i \, \forall \, i \in N, \forall \, p \in \Delta$.

Then under A.1, A.2′, A.3′, and A.4 there exist a coupons equilibrium $\{(z^i, c^i)_{i \in N}, p, a\}$ and a nonnegative number k such that $c^i = at^i(p) + k$.

The functions t^i are introduced to determine the distribution of coupons. $t^i(p)$ is always a feasible net trade for consumer $i \in N$. Therefore, we have in equilibrium $w^i + z^i \succcurlyeq_i w^i + t^i(p) \,\forall i \in N$. For the special case $t^i(p) \equiv 0$ $\forall \, i \in N$ a uniform coupons equilibrium is obtained.

Note that A.2′ is a generalization of A.2.

PROOF OF THE THEOREM. First we convert $\mathscr{E}$ into an abstract economy Γ with $n + 2$ players (see Greenberg and Müller (1979); Shafer and Sonnenschein (1975)). After defining the abstract economy Γ, we show (Lemma 1) that it has an equilibrium. Next, we show (Lemma 2) that an equilibrium for Γ defines a coupons equilibrium for $\mathscr{E}$, which satisfies (6). Finally, we prove the last statement in the theorem.

Since $\mathscr{E}$ is an exchange economy, by using standard techniques one can replace $X^i i \in N$ by the compact sets.

$$\hat{X}^i \colon X^i \cap [-\alpha, \alpha]^{m+1}, \qquad i \in N, \ \alpha \text{ sufficiently large}.$$

Let $\Gamma = (\hat{X}^i, \mathscr{A}^i, \hat{D}^i)_{i=1}^{n+2}$ be the abstract economy defined by:[9]

$\hat{X}^i i \in N$, the consumption sets;

$\hat{X}^{n+1} := \Delta$;

$\hat{X}^{n+2} := \hat{S} := \{(e, f) \mid e \in R_+^{m+1}, f \in R_-^{m+1}, e_0 = f_0 = 0, \|(e, f)\| \leq 1\}$;

---

[9] For $b \in R^l, \|b\| = \sum_{h=1}^l |b_h|$. The definition of $\mathscr{A}^i, i \in N$, follows Bergström (1976).

$$\mathscr{A}^i(p,e,f) := \{x^i \in \hat{X}^i \mid p(x^i - w^i) \leqslant 0, (e+f)(x^i - w^i)$$

$$\leqslant 1 - \|e+f\|\} i \in N;$$

$$\mathscr{A}^i = \hat{X}^i, i = n+1, n+2;$$

$$\hat{D}^i(p,x,e,f) = D^i(x,p,e+f,(1-\|e+f\|)_{j\in N}), i\in N;$$

$$\hat{D}^{n+1}(p,x,e,f) := \{\hat{p}\in \varDelta \mid \hat{p}z > pz\}, z := \sum_{i\in N}(x^i - w^i);$$

$$\hat{D}^{n+2}(p,x,e,f) := \{(\hat{e},\hat{f})\in \hat{S} \mid \hat{e}(z+p-\bar{p}) + \hat{f}(z+p-\underline{p})$$

$$> e(z+p-\bar{p}) + f(z+p-\underline{p})\}.$$

LEMMA 1. $\varGamma$ *has an equilibrium* $(x,p,e,f)\in \hat{X} := \Pi_{i=1}^{n+2}\hat{X}^i$, *i.e.*,

$$(x,p,e,f)\in \prod_{i=1}^{n+2} \mathscr{A}^i(p,e,f) \tag{8}$$

and

$$\mathscr{A}^i(p,e,f) \cap \hat{D}^i(x,p,e,f) = \phi, \qquad i = 1 \dots n+2. \tag{9}$$

Proof.   1. $\mathscr{A}^i(p,e,f)$ is continuous.

a.   Upper-hemicontinuity follows from A.2.

b.   We want to show that $\mathscr{A}^i$ is lower hemicontinuous at (p^0,e^0,f^0) if $p^0\in \varDelta$, $(e^0,f^0)\in \hat{S}$.

b.1   If $\|e^0+f^0\| < 1$ the lower-hemicontinuity of $\mathscr{A}^i$ is obtained by a standard argument from A.2.

b.2   If $\|e^0+f^0\| = 1$ then (i) $w^i\in \mathscr{A}^i(p^0,e^0,f^0)$; (ii) from $w^i\in \text{Int } X^i$ and the linear independence of p^0 and $e^0+f^0(e_0^0+f_0^0 = 0, p_0^0 = 1)$, one concludes: $\exists \hat{x}^i\in \text{Int } \mathscr{A}^i(p^0,e^0,f^0)$.

Again lower-hemicontinuity follows from a standard argument.

2.   For $i = 1 \dots n+2$, $\hat{X}^i$ is a nonempty compact and convex subset of R^{m+1}.

3.   For $i = 1 \dots n+2$, $\mathscr{A}^i(p,e,f)$ is nonempty, compact, and convex if $p\in \varDelta, (e,f)\in \hat{S}$.

Therefore by the theorem in Shafer and Sonnenschein (1975), $\varGamma$ has an equilibrium (x,p,e,f).   QED

LEMMA 2. $\{(z^i,c)_{i\in N}, p, e+f\}$ *with* $c := 1 - \|e+f\|$, $z^i := x^i - w^i$, *is a coupons equilibrium for* $\mathscr{E}$, *which satisfies* (6).

PROOF. Denote

$$\bar{R} := \{j \in M \setminus \{0\} \mid z_j = \max_{h \in M \cdot \{0\}} |z_h|\},$$

$$\underline{R} := \{j \in M \setminus \{0\} \mid -z_j = \max_{h \in M \cdot \{0\}} |z_h|\}.$$

Assume $\max_{h \in M \cdot \{0\}} |z_h| > 0$. Then, using (9) for $i = n + 1$, $j \in \bar{R} \Rightarrow p_j = \bar{p}_j, j \in \underline{R} \Rightarrow p_j = \underline{p}_j$.

For $h \in M \setminus \{0\}, p_h - \bar{p}_h \leqslant 0$ and $p_h - \underline{p}_h \geqslant 0$; hence, using (9) for $i = n + 2$, we have $\sum_{j \in \bar{R} \cup \underline{R}} (e_j + |f_j|) = 1$, and $\|e + f\| = 1$. Also, $(e + f)z = \sum_{j \in \bar{R} \cup \underline{R}} (e_j + f_j)z_j = \max_{h \in M \cdot \{0\}} |z_h| > 0.$

This leads to a contradiction with $(e + f)(x^i - w^i) \leqslant 0$. Hence $z_h = 0 \, \forall h \in M \setminus \{0\}$ and $z_0 = 0$ by Walras law and A.1, A.4. Therefore, we have $pz^i = 0 \, \forall i \in N$.

Obviously $\{(z^i, c)_{i \in N}, p, e + f\}$ with $c = 1 - \|e + f\|$ satisfies (4) and (5) in the definition of a coupons equilibrium. Equation (6) follows from (9) with $i = n + 2$.   QED

Turning to the last statement in the theorem, assume $a = e + f = 0$. Then $\mathscr{A}^i(p, e, f) = \{x^i \in \hat{X}^i \mid p(x^i - w^i) \leqslant 0\} \, \forall i \in N$. Therefore p is a Walrasian equilibrium price contrary to assumption and the theorem is proved.
                                                                            QED

4. Coupons equilibria and optimality

DEFINITION 2. $(z^1 \ldots z^n) \in Z(\Delta)$ is a constrained Pareto optimum if there exists no $(\hat{z}^1 \ldots \hat{z}^n) \in Z(\Delta)$ such that

$$\hat{z}^i \succcurlyeq_i z^i \qquad \forall i \in N$$

$$\hat{z}^j \succ_j z^j \qquad \text{for some } j \in N.$$

It is a weak constrained Pareto optimum if there exists no $(\hat{z}^1 \ldots \hat{z}^n) \in Z(\Delta)$ such that $\hat{z}^i \succ_i z^i \, \forall i \in N$.

PROPOSITION 1.[10] *Assume*[11]

1. X^i *is convex for all* $i \in N$;

2. *the preferences* $\succcurlyeq_i$ *are strictly convex* $(i \in N)$, *i.e., if* $y \succcurlyeq_i x$ *then* $\lambda x + (1 - \lambda)y \succ_i x \, \forall \lambda \in (0, 1)$.

[10] This proposition already appears in Hahn (1978) for the case where $c_i = 0 \, \forall i \in N$; the example in Appendix A shows that coupons equilibria may fail to exist, in that case.

[11] Without any assumption we obtain weak constrained Pareto optimality of coupons equilibria if $\Delta = \{p\}$.

Then every coupons equilibrium with prices p is a Pareto optimum relative to $\Delta = \{p\}$.

PROOF. Let $\{(z^i, c^i)_{i \in N}, p, a\}$ be a coupons equilibrium. Assume there exists $(\hat{z}^1 \ldots \hat{z}^n) \in Z(p)$ with $\hat{z}^i \succcurlyeq_i z^i \, \forall i \in N$ and $\hat{z}^j \succ_j z^j$ for some $j \in N$. Then $a\hat{z}^i \geqslant az^i \, \forall i \in N$ and $a\hat{z}^j > c^j \geqslant az^j$. Hence $\sum_{i \in N} a\hat{z}^i > 0$. But this contradicts $\sum_{i \in N} \hat{z}^i = 0$.   QED

The example in Appendix 5.1 shows that this result cannot be extended to the general case (where Δ is not a singleton).

On the other hand, a constrained Pareto optimum can be represented as a coupons equilibrium. By reformulating a theorem in Debreu (1959) one obtains

PROPOSITION 2. *Assume A.1 and A.3'. If $(z^{*i})_{i \in N}$ is Pareto optimal relative to $\Delta = \{p\}$, where some $z^{*j}(j \in N)$ is not a satiation point in $Z^j(p)$,[12] there exist a coupons price $a \in S, a \neq 0$, and real numbers $(c^i)_{i \in N}$ such that*

1. $\sum_{i \in N} c^i = 0, az^{*i} = c^i$;

2. $c^i = \min \{az^i \mid z^i \in Z^i(p), z^i \succcurlyeq_i z^{*i}\} \, i \in N$.

Remarks. 1. If there exists $z^i \in Z^i(p)$ with $az^i < c^i$ then A.3' and 2 imply $z^{*i} \succcurlyeq_i z^i \, \forall z^i \in \{z^i \in Z^i(p) \mid az^i \leqslant c^i\}$. See Debreu (1959, pp. 68–69).

2. The example in Appendix C shows that one cannot impose (6) if Δ is not a singleton.

PROOF OF PROPOSITION 2. $(z^{*i})_{i \in N}$ is Pareto optimal on $Z(\{p\})$. Replacing X^i by $Z^i(p)$, the assumptions in the theorem on pp. 95–96 of Debreu (1959) are verified and there exists $\hat{a} \in R^{m+1} \setminus \{0\}$ and $c^i \in R(i \in N)$ satisfying 1 and 2. But $\hat{a}_0 \neq 0$ is not ruled out. However, one can choose $\hat{a}$ s.t. $p\hat{a} = 0$. This implies that $\hat{a}$ and p are linearly independent. Therefore one checks easily that $a = \hat{a} - \hat{a}_0 p \neq 0$ is the coupons price we are looking for.   QED

REMARKS. 1. Δ is of the form $\{p \in R^{m+1}_+ \mid p_0 = 1, \; \underline{p}_h \leqslant p_h \leqslant \bar{p}_h, h = 1 \ldots m\}$ and $a_0 = 0$ is imposed in the definition of a coupons equilibrium. Therefore, commodity 0 has some properties which are typical of money. Usually the positive value of money is guaranteed by a price dependent expected utility index and special assumptions. Pareto optimality should then be redefined in that broader context. This remark does not apply to the case where Δ is a singleton.

---

[12] If z^{*i} is a satiation point for all $i \in N$, then $(z^{*i})_{i \in N}$ can be represented as a coupons equilibrium with $a = 0, c^i = 0$ for all i.

2. Referring to the paper by Schmeidler and Vind (1972) on 'Fair Net Trades', we note that, when $X^i = R_+^{m+1}$, then:

(i) the net trades implied by a *uniform* coupons equilibrium are fair, but not necessarily strongly fair;

(ii) the net trades implied by a coupons equilibrium are not necessarily fair.

5. Trading of coupons against the numeraire

When coupons may be traded like commodities, the budget set for consumer $i \in N$ is given by

$$pz^i - \mu r^i \leqslant 0, \quad z^i \in Y^i \tag{10}$$

$$az^i + r^i \leqslant c^i, \tag{11}$$

where $\mu \in R_+$ is the price of coupons in units of the numeraire and $r^i \in R$ is the number of coupons sold by i. Equations (10) and (11) can be reduced to

$$(p + \mu a) z^i \leqslant \mu c^i, \quad z^i \in Y^i$$

and we are in the Walrasian framework with prices $(p + \mu a)$ and lump-sum transfers $(\mu c^i)_{i \in N}, \mu \sum_{i \in N} c^i = 0$.

6. Coupons equilibria and Pareto improving price changes

We mentioned already that in general a coupons equilibrium is not Pareto optimal relative to Δ, if Δ is not a singleton. This section consists of two propositions. Starting from a coupons equilibrium $\{(z^i, c^i)_{i \in N}, p, a\}$ the first proposition gives a necessary condition for the existence of a Pareto-superior allocation at prices $\hat{p} \in \Delta$. The second proposition provides us with conditions which are sufficient to find a Pareto-superior coupons equilibrium in the neighbourhood of the first equilibrium.

If $a = 0$, then the coupons equilibrium $\{(z^i, c^i)_{i \in N}, p, a\}$ is a Walrasian equilibrium and therefore is Pareto optimal. Therefore, we shall assume $a \neq 0$.

PROPOSITION 3. *Assume A.1, A.2 and A.3′.*

Let $((z^i, c^i)_{i \in N}, p, a)$ *be a coupons equilibrium, with* $a \neq 0$ *and* $\forall i \in N$
$c^i = \min \{az^i \,|\, \hat{z}^i \in Z^i(p), \hat{z}^i \succcurlyeq_i z^i\}$.

If there exists $\hat{p}$ *and* $(\hat{z}^1 \dots \hat{z}^n) \in Z(\{\hat{p}\})$ *with* $\hat{z}^i \succ_i z^i \,\forall i \in N$, *then*

(I)   *there exist* $(\hat{c}^i)_{i\in N}$ *and* $(\tilde{x}^i)_{i\in N}$, $\tilde{x}^i \in B^i(\hat{p}, a, \hat{c}^i)$ *such that* $\sum_i \hat{c}^i < 0$ *and* $\tilde{x}^i \succ_i w^i + z^i \,\forall i \in N$.[13]

PROOF.   Using A.1, A.2, and A.3', there exists λ in $(0,1)$ such that $\forall i \in N, \bar{z}^i := \lambda \hat{z}^i$ belongs to the relative interior of $Z^i(\hat{p})$ with $\bar{z}^i \succ_i z^i$. Let $\bar{c}^i := a\bar{z}^i$, $\sum_{i\in N} \bar{z}^i = 0$ implies $\sum_{i\in N} \bar{c}^i = 0$. Let $c^{*i} := \text{Min}\{a\hat{z}^i \mid \hat{z}^i \in Z^i(\hat{p}), \hat{z}^i \succcurlyeq_i z^i\}$. Then $c^{*i} < \bar{c}^i$; indeed, $a_0 = 0$, $a \neq 0$, and $\hat{p}_0 = 1$ implies that a and $\hat{p}$ are linearly independent; A.3' and $\bar{z}^i \in$ rel. int. $Z^i(\hat{p})$ imply the inequality. Consequently, $\sum_i c^{*i} < \sum_i \bar{c}^i = 0$ and because of A.3', (I) is satisfied by taking, say

$$\hat{c}^i = \frac{\bar{c}^i + c^{*i}}{2}, \quad \forall i \in N. \qquad\qquad \text{QED}$$

Our last proposition uses the following definition. The marginal value of coupons in terms of the numeraire, abbreviated as '*money value of coupons*', is defined for individual i at a best point $w^i + z^i$ of the budget set $B^i(p, a, c^i)$, as the following limit $\bar{\mu}^i$, when it exists and is unique:

$$\bar{\mu}^i = \lim_{\Delta c^i \to 0} \left\{ \min \frac{\Delta w_0^i}{\Delta c^i} \,\middle|\, \exists \hat{z}^i, p\hat{z}^i = -\Delta w_0^i, a\hat{z}^i = c^i + \Delta c^i, \hat{z}^i \succcurlyeq_i z^i \right\}.$$

(12)

PROPOSITION 4.   *Assume A.1 and A.3''.*

Let $((z^i, c^i)_{i\in N}, p, a)$. $a \neq 0$, *be a coupons equilibrium with* $\forall i \in N$ $z^i \in$ *int* Y^i. *Then* $\bar{\mu}^i$, *the money value of coupons to* i, *is well defined. Let* $I = \{i \in N \mid \bar{\mu}^i = 0\}$.
If either
  (i) $I = \phi$ *and* $\exists l \in \{1\dots m\}$ *such that* $\sum_{i\in N} z_l^i / \bar{\mu}^i \neq 0$, *or*
  (ii) $I \neq \phi$, $I \neq N$ *and* $Q = \{q \in R^m \mid \sum_{l=1}^m q_l z_l^i \leqslant 0 \,\forall i \in I\} \neq \{0\}$, *then there exists a coupons equilibrium* $((\hat{z}^i, \hat{c}^i)_{i\in N}, \hat{p}, \hat{a})$, *with* $\hat{p}$ *in a neighborhood of* p *and with* $\hat{z}^i \succcurlyeq_i z^i \,\forall i \in N$, $\hat{z}^h \succ_h z^h$ *some* $h \in N$.

PROOF.   1.   Under the assumptions of the proposition, $\forall i \in n, z^i$ is the unique optimal solution of the problem max $U^i(z)$ subject to $z \in Y^i$, $pz = 0$, $az - c^i \leqslant 0$. By part (iii) of the 'Kuhn–Tucker stationary-point necessary optimality theorem' in Mangasarian (1969, p. 173), there exist $v^i \in R$, $\mu^i \in R_+$ such that grad $U^i(z) - v^i p - \mu^i a = 0$. Furthermore A.3'' implies $v^i > 0$. The ratio μ^i/v^i is unique and equal to the limit in (12).

---

[13]See also the interpretation on p. 96. One checks easily that condition (I) is not sufficient.

2. The notation $p = (1, \bar{p})$, $a = (0, \bar{a})$, $z = (z_0, \bar{z})$ is used. First we are looking for Δp, $(\Delta z^i)_{i \in N}$ s.t.

$$z^i + \Delta z^i \in Y^i, \quad (p + \Delta p)(z^i + \Delta z^i) = 0, \quad \sum_{i \in N} \Delta z^i = 0 \tag{13}$$

and

$$U^i(z^i + \Delta z^i) \geqslant U^i(z^i) \quad \text{for all } i \in N$$
$$U^h(z^h + \Delta z^h) > U^h(z^h) \quad \text{for some } h \in N.$$

From (13), one obtains

$$\Delta z_0^i + \bar{p} \, \Delta \bar{z}^i + \bar{z}^i \, \Delta \bar{p} + \Delta \bar{p} \, \Delta \bar{z}^i = 0. \tag{14}$$

On the other hand,

$$U^i(z^i + \Delta z^i) - U^i(z^i)$$

$$= \Delta z^i \cdot \operatorname{grad} U^i(z^i) + R^i(\Delta z^i) \tag{15}$$

$$= \Delta z^i \cdot (v^i p + \mu^i a) + R^i(\Delta z^i) \quad \text{by 1} \tag{16}$$

$$= v^i \, \Delta z_0^i + v^i \, \Delta \bar{z}^i \cdot \bar{p} + \mu^i \, \Delta \bar{z}^i \cdot \bar{a} + R^i(\Delta z^i). \tag{17}$$

In order to obtain

$$U^i(z^i + \Delta z^i) - U^i(z^i) > 0 \tag{18}$$

we need by (14), (17)

$$\mu^i \, \Delta \bar{z}^i \cdot \bar{a} - v^i \, \Delta \bar{p} \cdot \bar{z}^i + R^i(\Delta z^i) - v^i \, \Delta \bar{p} \cdot \Delta \bar{z}^i > 0. \tag{19}$$

3. If $\bar{\mu}^i > 0 \, \forall \, i \in N$ take

$$k, l \in \{1 \dots m\} \quad \text{s.t.} \quad \frac{1}{n} \sum_{i \in N} \frac{z_l^i}{\bar{\mu}^i} := \operatorname{cov}\left(z_l^i, \frac{1}{\bar{\mu}^i}\right) \neq 0, a_k \neq 0$$

and define

$$\Delta p_h = -\varepsilon \operatorname{cov}(z_l^i, 1/\bar{\mu}^i) \quad \text{if } h = l$$
$$= 0 \quad \text{if } h \neq l$$

$$\Delta z_h^i = -\frac{\varepsilon z_l^i \operatorname{cov}(z_l^i, 1/\bar{\mu}^i)}{a_k \bar{\mu}^i} + \frac{\varepsilon \left[\operatorname{cov}(z_l^i, 1/\bar{\mu}^i)\right]^2}{a_k} \quad \text{if } h = k,$$
$$= 0 \quad \text{if } h \neq k, h \in \{1 \dots m\}.$$

For $\varepsilon > 0$ small enough, (19) is satisfied since

$$\mu^i a_k \frac{- \varepsilon z_l^i \operatorname{cov}(z_l^i, 1/\bar{\mu}^i)}{a_k \bar{\mu}^i} + \mu^i \varepsilon \left[\operatorname{cov}\left(z_l^i, \frac{1}{\bar{\mu}^i} \right) \right]^2 > - \varepsilon v^i z_l^i \operatorname{cov}\left(z_l^i, \frac{1}{\bar{\mu}^i} \right) + o(\varepsilon)$$

and (14), (18) are satisfied, too, by a proper choice of Δz_0^i.

Also for ε small enough, $z^i + \Delta z^i \in \operatorname{int} Y^i, i \in N$.

4. If $\bar{\mu}^i = 0$ for some but not all $i \in N$, then we distinguish two cases, namely:

(1) $\hat{Q} := \{ q \in Q \mid q \bar{z}^i < 0 \text{ for some } i \in I \} \neq \phi$

(2) $\hat{Q} = \phi$.

4.1. If $\hat{Q} \neq \phi$ take $q \in \hat{Q}$ and $j \in I$ s.t. $q \bar{z}^j < 0$. Choose, $\forall i \in N \backslash I, y^i$ such that $\bar{\mu}^i \bar{y}^i \cdot \bar{a} > q \bar{z}^i$.

Then there exists $\varepsilon > 0$ s.t.

$$\bar{\mu}^i \Delta \bar{z}^i \cdot \bar{a} > \Delta \bar{p} \cdot \bar{z}^i - \frac{1}{v^i} R^i(\Delta z^i) + \Delta \bar{p} \cdot \Delta \bar{z}^i \, \forall i \in N \backslash I$$

$$\text{with } \Delta \bar{z}^i = \varepsilon \bar{y}^i, \Delta \bar{p} = \varepsilon q$$

and

$$0 > \Delta \bar{p} \cdot \bar{z}^j - \frac{1}{v^j} R^j(\Delta z^j) + \Delta \bar{p} \cdot \Delta \bar{z}^j \text{ with } \Delta \bar{z}^j = - \sum_{i \in N \backslash I} \Delta \bar{z}^i.$$

In addition we define $\Delta z^i = 0 \, \forall i \in I \backslash \{j\}$.

For ε small enough, $z^i + \Delta z^i \in \operatorname{int} Y^i$ and $z^i + \Delta z^i \succcurlyeq_i z^i \forall i \in N$, $z^h + \Delta z^h \succ_h z^h$ for some $h \in N$.

4.2. If $\hat{Q} = \phi$ then define

$$P := \{ q \in R^m \mid q \bar{z}^i = 0 \, \forall i \in I \} \neq \{0\}; \quad P \text{ is a linear subspace.}$$

We shall look for $\Delta \bar{p} \in P$ such that

$$0 \geqslant - \frac{1}{v^i} R^i(\Delta z^i) + \Delta \bar{p} \cdot \Delta \bar{z}^i \, \forall i \in I \tag{20}$$

$$\bar{a} \cdot \Delta \bar{z}^j > \Delta \bar{p} \cdot \left(\frac{1}{\bar{\mu}^j} \bar{z}^j \right) - \frac{1}{\mu^j} R^j (\Delta z^j) + \frac{1}{\bar{\mu}^j} \Delta \bar{p} \cdot \Delta \bar{z}^j \, \forall \, j \in N \backslash I. \tag{21}$$

A necessary condition for (21) is

$$\bar{a} \cdot \left(\sum_{j \in N \backslash I} \Delta \bar{z}^j \right) > \Delta \bar{p} \cdot \left(\sum_{j \in N \backslash I} \frac{1}{\bar{\mu}^j} \bar{z}^j \right)$$

$$- \sum_{j \in N \backslash I} \frac{1}{\mu^j} R^j (\Delta z^j) + \Delta \bar{p} \cdot \left(\sum_{j \in N \backslash I} \frac{1}{\bar{\mu}^j} \Delta \bar{z}^j \right).$$

(a) If there exists $q \in P$ s.t. $q \cdot (\sum_{j \in N \backslash I} \bar{z}^j / \bar{\mu}^j) < 0$, then by choosing $\Delta \bar{z}^i = 0 \, \forall \, i \in I, \Delta p = \varepsilon q$ with $\varepsilon > 0$, (20) is fulfilled. Furthermore, choose $y \in R^m$ s.t. $\bar{a} \cdot y > 0$. Then there exist $\alpha_j \in R, j \in N \backslash I$, with $\sum_{j \in N \backslash I} \alpha_j = 0$ s.t. (21) holds for $\Delta \bar{z}^j := \alpha_j \varepsilon y$, $\varepsilon > 0$ small enough.

(b) Finally, let

$$q \left(\sum_{j \in N \backslash I} \frac{1}{\bar{\mu}^j} \bar{z}^j \right) = 0 \, \forall \, q \in P. \tag{22}$$

Since there exist $y \in R^m$ and $q \in P$ with $\bar{a}y > 0, qy > 0$, we can, in view of A.3'', find $M > 0$ and $\bar{\varepsilon} > 0$ s.t. (20) holds $\forall \, i \in I$ when $\Delta \bar{p} := M \varepsilon q$, $\Delta \bar{z}^i := - (\varepsilon / \# I) y$ and $0 < \varepsilon \leqslant \bar{\varepsilon}$.

Furthermore by (22), there exist $\alpha^j \in R \, (j \in N \backslash I)$ with $\sum_{j \in N \backslash I} \alpha^j = 1$, and $\bar{\varepsilon} > 0$ s.t. (21) holds $\forall \, j \in N \backslash I$ at $\Delta \bar{p} = M \varepsilon q$, when $\Delta \bar{z}^j := \alpha^j \varepsilon y$ and $0 < \varepsilon \leqslant \bar{\varepsilon}$.

Under either (a) or (b) for ε small enough, $z^i + \Delta z^i \in \text{int } Y^i$ and $z^i + \Delta z^i \succcurlyeq_i z^i \, \forall \, i \in N, z^h + \Delta z^h \succ_h z^h$ some $h \in N$.

5. With $\Delta p, (\Delta z^i)_{i \in N}$ introduced in 3 or 4, as the case may be, we define an economy $\hat{\mathscr{E}}$ for which $\hat{\Lambda} := \{p + \Delta p\} = \{\hat{p}\}$, and the other elements are as before; and we define $t^i(\hat{p}) = z^i + \Delta z^i, i \in N$. By the theorem and remark of Section 3, there exists a coupons equilibrium $((\hat{z}^i, \hat{c}^i)_{i \in N}, \hat{p}, \hat{a})$, where $\hat{c}^i = \hat{a}t^i(\hat{p}) + \hat{k} \geqslant 0$ and $\hat{z}^i \succcurlyeq_i z^i + \Delta z^i \, \forall \, i \in N$. By construction, $z^i + \Delta z^i \succcurlyeq_i z^i \, \forall \, i \in N$ and $z^h + \Delta^h \succ_h z^h$ some $h \in N$.   QED

Appendix 5.1

The first example shows that, for the coupons endowment $c^i = 0 \, \forall \, i \in N$, coupons equilibria may fail to exist.

EXAMPLE. $N = \{i, j\}, M = \{0, 1\}$.

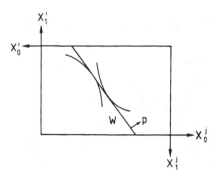

Figure 5.3.   Example of an economy for which no coupons
equilibrium exists when $c^i = 0 \, \forall \, i$

Obviously for the coupons endowments $c^i = c^j = 0$ (i.e., coupons endowments corresponding to zero net trades) no coupons equilibrium exists. The nonexistence of equilibria in the example is related to satiation. If one consumer wants to throw away some of his coupons the market clearing condition $\sum_{i \in N} z^i = 0$ can no longer be satisfied. This leads to nonexistence.

Appendix 5.2

The next example shows that the set of uniform coupons equilibria satisfying condition (6) may fail to contain any constrained Pareto optimum.

EXAMPLE.

$$N = \{i, j\}, \quad M = \{0, 1, 2\}, \quad X^i = X^j = R_+^3, \quad w^i = (6, 5, 4),$$

$$w^j = (6, 1, 1)$$

$$\Delta = \{(1, \bar{p}) \mid 0 \leqslant \bar{p} \leqslant (2, 3)\}.$$

The preferences are given by

$$U^i(x_0, x_1, x_2) = x_0 + 10x_1 + 5x_2$$

$$U^j(x_0, x_1, x_2) = x_0 + 10x_1 + 10x_2.$$

Only $p = (1, 2, 3)$ can be an equilibrium price. Otherwise there would be excess supply for good 0. By condition (6), a uniform coupons equilibrium then entails $a_1 > 0, a_2 > 0$. Figure 5.4 is drawn on that basis, in the space

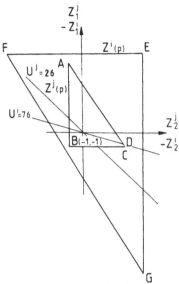

Figure 5.4. Example of an economy for which the uniform coupons equilibria are Pareto inefficient

of net trades for goods 1 and 2. The set $Z^j(p)$ is the triangle ABC. The set $Z^i(p)$ is the bigger triangle EFG with vertices parallel to those of ABC. The indifference curves of i and j are straight lines, parallel, respectively, to the line $U^i = 76$ or $8z_1 + 2z_2 = 0$ and to the line $U^j = 26$ or $8z_1 + 7z_2 = 0$. When $c^i = c^j = 0$ and $a_1/a_2 = 4$, individual i is indifferent among all the net trades z^i with $z_1^i = -(1/4)z_2^i$; whereas the best point of $B^j(p, a, c^j)$ takes z^j to D on the boundary of $Z^j(p)$, with coordinates $z_1 = -3/5, z_2 = 12/5$. Accordingly, the prices $(1, 2, 3)$; the coupon prices $(0, .8, .2)$; the coupons endowments $(0, 0)$; and the net trades $z^i = (6, 3/5, -12/5), z^j = (-6, -3/5, 12/5)$ define a uniform coupons equilibrium with utility levels $U^i = 76$, $U^j = 38$.

When $c^i \geqslant 0$ and $a_1/a_2 \neq 4$, the best point of $B^i(p, a, c^i)$ takes z_i to the boundary of $Z^i(p)$, so that $-z^i$ lies outside of $Z^j(p)$ and no coupons equilibrium exists. Furthermore one verifies easily that there are no uniform coupons equilibria with $c^i = c^j > 0$. We have thus exhibited the only uniform coupons equilibrium satisfying (6). Its inefficiency is revealed by considering the price vector $\hat{p} = (1, 1/2, 2) \in \varDelta$ and the net trades $\hat{z}^i = (5.5, 1, -3)$, $\hat{z}^j = (-5.5, -1, 3)$ which entail the utility levels $U^i = 76.5$, $U^j = 40.5$.

Appendix 5.3

From Proposition 2 we know that a constrained Pareto optimum can be represented as a coupons equilibrium. The last example shows, however, that condition (6) cannot be imposed.

EXAMPLE.

$$N = \{i, j, k\}, \quad M = \{0, 1\}, \quad X^i = X^j = X^k = R^2_+,$$

$$w^i = (0, 4), \quad w^j = (2, 0), \quad w^k = (5, 1)$$

$$\Delta = \{(1, p_1) \,|\, 0.5 \leqslant p_1 \leqslant 2\}$$

$$U^h(x_0, x_1) = x_0 x_1 \quad h = i, j, k.$$

Obviously $(z^i, z^j, z^k) = ((2, -2), (-1, 1), (-1, 1))$ is a constrained Pareto optimum $(p = (1, 1))$.

It can be represented as a coupons equilibrium but condition (6) cannot be imposed. This can be seen easily. $p_1 = 1$ would imply $a = 0$. But then consumer k would choose $\hat{z}^k = (-2, 2)$.

6 Values of markets with satiation or fixed prices*

1. Introduction

Pure exchange economies, or *markets*, in which the preferences satisfy conditions of monotonicity and nonsatiation have been studied thoroughly in the past. In this paper we investigate the opposite situation: the utility functions need not be monotonic, and do have absolute maxima. The resulting theory has significant new qualitative features.

This study is not motivated by an abstract desire to remove as many assumptions as possible. It originated in the analysis of *fixed price* economies, which have been used extensively in the past decade[1] to model market failures such as unemployment. In such economies, all trade is restricted to take place at exogenously fixed prices $\bar{p}$. In effect, this limits each trader t to his *fixed price hyperplane*, i.e. the set of all bundles x in his original consumption set for which $\bar{p} \cdot x = \bar{p} \cdot e(t)$, where $e(t)$ is t's endowment; under the usual assumptions, t's utility has an absolute maximum on this set, and is not monotonic there.[2]

* *Econometrica*, 54, 6 (1986), 1271–1318. With Robert Aumann. Sections 7, 8, 9, 12, 13 and appendices A, B, C and D are not reproduced here. The work of R. J. Aumann was supported by CORE at Université Catholique de Louvain, by the Institute for Advanced Studies at the Hebrew University of Jerusalem, and by the Institute for Mathematical Studies in the Social Sciences (Economics) at Stanford University under a grant from the U.S. National Science Foundation. This work is part of the Projet d'Action Concertée on 'Applications of Economic Decision Theory' sponsored by the Belgian Government under Contract No. 80/85-12. We are grateful to Jean-François Mertens for carefully reading the manuscript and suggesting significant improvements.

[1] See, e.g., the survey by Drazen (1980).

[2] Indeed, monontonicity is meaningless in this context, since there is no natural partial order on the fixed price hyperplane.

In general, price rigidities prevent a market from 'clearing' (i.e., supply from matching demand); various quantity constraints or rationing schemes have been proposed to bring the situation back into equilibrium. In the more traditional markets, without fixed prices, there is a close relationship between competitive equilibria and game theoretic concepts such as the core[3] and the Shapley value;[4] thus one may expect game theory also to be helpful in suggesting equilibria for fixed price economies. It turns out that the core is not well suited to this purpose (see Section 8). But we shall find that the Shapley value allocations in fixed price economies correspond to a natural extension of competitive equilibria, closely related to the concept of coupons equilibria defined by Drèze and Müller (1980).

To describe our results, let us return to the more general context of markets with satiation. The reason that competitive equilibria may fail to exist in such markets is that no matter what the prices[5] are, the satiation points of some traders may be in the interiors of their budget sets.[6] Thus some traders will be using less than the maximum budget available to them, creating a total budget excess. This suggests a revision of the equilibrium concept that allows the budget excess to be divided among all the traders, say as *dividends*: Each trader's budget is then the sum of his dividend and the market value of his endowment at the market prices. A given system of dividends and prices is in equilibrium if it generates equal supply and demand.

This in itself is not satisfactory because it is too broad: Drèze and Müller showed that the fundamental proposition of welfare economics continues to apply here, i.e., that *every* Pareto optimal allocation is generated by some system of dividends and prices. However, the Shapley value yields much more specific information. Our main result says that when there are many individually insignificant agents, every Shapley value allocation is generated by a system of dividends and prices in which all dividends are nonnegative and depend only on the net trade sets[7] of the agents, not on their utilities. Thus the income allocated to each agent – over and above the market value of his endowment – depends only on his trading *opportunities*; on what he is *able* to offer, not on what he wants

[3] Cf., e.g., Hildenbrand (1982).

[4] Cf., e.g., Aumann (1975) or Hart (1977b).

[5] We are here discussing endogenous market prices q, which should not be confused with the exogenous prices $\bar{p}$ in fixed price economies. See Section 7.

[6] See Section 3 for an example.

[7] The net trade set of agent t is $C(t) - e(t)$, where $C(t)$ is his consumption set, and $e(t)$ his endowment.

to offer. Moreover, the dependence is monotonic; the larger the net trade set, the higher the dividend.

Two brief illustrations may clarify this point. When a bond issue is over-subscribed, bonds are normally rationed to the subscribers in proportion to the amount requested. Under complete information, this procedure has no equilibrium; the subscribers will always request more than they really want, this will be taken into account by the other subscribers, and so on. But in the rationing scheme implied by the Shapley value, the maximum that a subscriber may buy is based not on what he requests, which is subject to manipulation, but on what he *could* buy; on his net worth, say.

The second illustration deals with unemployment in a fixed wage context. Various rationing schemes that involve cutting down on working hours have been proposed. In the scheme suggested by the Shapley value, the maximum work week for any particular worker would depend on how much time he has. Thus a youngster who must by law attend school, or a kidney patient undergoing time-consuming dialysis, would be assigned a quota smaller than the average, *even though he might be able to fill the average quota.*

Economic models have two basic components, the objective and the subjective. The first consists of the physical opportunities or *abilities* of the agents: resources, technologies, constraints on consumption, and so on. The second consists of the utilities or *preferences*. In a market, the objective component is completely described by the net trade sets of the agents. Outcomes of economic models usually depend on both components, often quite intricately.

Competitive equilibria 'decouple' the two components. Each agent optimizes over an endogenous choice set, his budget set; in equilibrium, the choices mesh, they 'clear' the market. The optimisation, of course, is subjective; it depends on the agent's preferences. But the choice set itself does not; it depends only on his net trade set, i.e., on purely objective factors. Our result implies that the dividend equilibria to which the Shapley value leads also decouple in this way.

On a more technical level, our analysis has several unusual features. Though we are dealing with a large number of individually insignificant agents, we do not model it with a nonatomic continuum; rather, we use a finite-type asymptotic model of the Debreu and Scarf (1963) genre. Asymptotic and continuous results may differ in various ways,[8] but

---

[8] E.g. in ease and transparency of the formulation, in the generality of the results, in the methods of proof, and in the discussion of errors and rates of convergence. Compare Aumann and Shapley (1974, Section 34, 208–210).

usually, the results are qualitatively similar. Here they are not. The continuum is too rough a tool; it obliterates the fine structure of the problem, and so leads to inconclusive results. The matter will be discussed further in Section 8.2.

Another unusual feature, related to the first, is the critical importance of small coalitions. The Shapley value of a player is the expectation of his 'contribution to Society' when the players are ordered at random; the probability that he is second or third in the order is small, and is usually ignored. Here, we are led to equations in which the first-order terms cancel, and the second-order terms, which take events of small probability into account, become decisive. When there is an excess supply of labour, the length of the work week allocated to a given worker depends on his expected contribution when he arrives on the scene; unless he is very early, this is negligible.

The plan of the paper is as follows. In Sections 2–5, we present the model and state our main result. Since the proof of that result is quite complex, we do not reproduce it here, but refer readers to the original article in *Econometrica*, 54, 6 (1986), 1282–92 and 1305–10. Section 7 contains the application to fixed prices, and Section 8 is devoted to a discussion of some alternative approaches. Finally, Section 9 summarises some additional results of a more quantitative nature and discusses open problems. For a formal statement, proofs and illustration of the additional results, readers are again referred to the original article in *Econometrica*, 54, 6 (1986), 1299–1304 and 1311–17.[9]

2. Markets with satiation

A (finite) *market with satiation* is defined by:

(2.1)   a finite set T (the *trader space*);

(2.2)   a positive integer d (the number of *commodities*);

(2.3)   for each trader, t, a compact convex subset X_t of R^d, whose interior is nonempty and contains the origin 0 (t's *net trade set*); and

(2.4)   for each trader t, a concave continuous function u_t on X_t (t's *utility function*).

Because X_t is compact, the continuous functions u_t must attain its maximum; denote by B_t the set of all points in X_t at which the maximum is attained (the *satiation* or *bliss* set of trader t), and note that it is compact and convex. To avoid trivialities, assume $0 \notin B_t$, i.e., the initial bundle never satiates.

---

[9] Sections 7, 8, 9 here correspond to sections 10, 11 and 14 respectively in the original article.

A few matters of terminology and notation: the inner product of two vectors q and x is denoted $q \cdot x$; 'w.r.t.' means 'with respect to' and 'w.l.o.g.' means 'without loss of generality'; R^k, R^k_+, and R^k_{++} denote, respectively, Euclidean k-space, its (closed) nonnegative orthant, and its (open) strictly positive orthant; int and bd denote 'interior' and 'boundary' respectively.

3. Dividend equilibria

An *allocation* in a market with satiation is a vector $x = (x_t)_{t \in T}$, where x_t is a feasible net trade for trader t (i.e., $x_t \in X_t$), and $\sum_{t \in T} x_t = 0$. A *price vector* is any member of R^d other than 0; since utilities need not be monotonic, one cannot confine oneself to nonnegative prices. The classical notion of *competitive equilibrium* is defined for markets with satiation just as it is for ordinary markets: it consists of a price vector q and an allocation x such that for all t, x_t maximizes u_t over the *budget set* $\{x \in X_t : q \cdot x \leqslant 0\}$.

Competitive equilibria do not in general exist in markets with satiation. Consider, for example,[10] a market with two agents, 1 and 2, and one commodity; suppose that the satiation points are on opposite sides of the origin, e.g., $u_1(x) = -(x-1)^2$, $u_2(x) = -(x+2)^2$. W.l.o.g. the price vector is ± 1; in either case one agent receives 0 and the other his satiation point, and these do not sum to 0.

The example is not due to any pathologies associated with the low dimension.[11] Consider a market with two commodities and three agents having the same net trade set, and with indifference maps as illustrated in figure 6.1. No matter what the price vector is, the satiation point of at least one trader must be in the interior of the budget set,[12] so that his utility will be maximised there over the budget set; whereas the utilities of the remaining agents will be maximised on the budget line. The resulting three points cannot sum to 0.

What is happening is that at least one trader creates a surplus by refusing to make use of his entire budget; but the definition of competitive equilibrium does not permit the other agents to use this surplus, so an imbalance results.[13]

---

[10] This example appears in Drèze and Müller (1980).

[11] Such as the disconnectedness of the set of price vectors.

[12] This holds as long as 0 is in the interior of the convex hull of the three satiation points.

[13] If free disposal were permitted, the example would go away; but this is not a reasonable assumption in the absence of monotonicity. Moreover, 'disposal' is not really possible in the fixed-price application (Section 7).

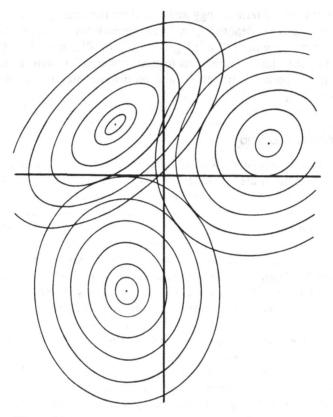

Figure 6.1

To overcome this problem, define a *dividend* to be a vector $c = (c_t)_{t \in T}$ whose components c_t are real numbers. A *dividend equilibrium* consists of a price vector q, a dividend c, and an allocation x, such that for all t, x_t maximizes u_t over the *dividend budget set*

$$\{x \in X_t : q \cdot x \leqslant c_t\}.$$

A dividend may be thought of as a cash allowance added to the budget of each trader; its function is to distribute among the unsatiated agents the surplus created by the failure of the satiated agents to use their entire budget.

A dividend c is *nonnegative* if all the c_t are nonnegative; *monotonic in the net trade sets*, if $X_t \supset X_s$ implies $c_t \geqslant c_s$. Occasionally, the word dividend will also be used for a component c_t of c.

4. Value allocations

A *comparison vector* on the trader space T is a vector $\lambda = (\lambda_t)_{t \in T}$, where each λ_t is a positive real number. For each comparison vector λ and coalition[14] S, define

$$v_\lambda(S) := \max \left\{ \sum_{t \in S} \lambda_t u_t(x_t) : \sum_{t \in S} x_t = 0 \text{ and } x_t \in X_t \text{ for all } t \text{ in } S \right\}. \quad (4.1)$$

In words, $v_\lambda(S)$ is the maximum total utility that S can get for itself by redistributing its endowment among its members, when the utilities u_t are weighted by the λ_t. A *value allocation* (in a given market with satiation) is an allocation x for which there exists a comparison vector λ such that for all traders t,

$$(\phi v_\lambda)(t) = \lambda_t u_t(x_t), \quad (4.2)$$

where ϕv_λ denotes the Shapley value of the game v_λ; we say that λ and x are *associated* with each other. (Recall that

$$(\phi v_\lambda)(t) = E(v_\lambda(S \cup t) - v_\lambda(S)), \quad (4.3)$$

where E denotes 'expectation', and S is the set of traders preceding t in a random order on all traders.[15])

At a value allocation, the weighted utility each player receives is equal to his Shapley value in the game v_λ. In other words, if transfers of utility are permitted with exchange rates λ_t, then the Shapley value of the resulting game is achieved, *without transfers of utility*, at the allocation x. Compare Shapley (1969) and Aumann (1975).

5. The main theorem

Let M^1 be a market with satiation; denote the traders by $1, \dots, k$, the utility functions by $u_1, \dots, u_k$, the net trade sets by $X_1, \dots, X_k$, and the satiation sets by $B_1, \dots, B_k$. The *n-fold replication* M^n of M^1 is the market with satiation in which there are nk traders, n of each of the k 'types' in M^1; i.e. the trader space T^n in M^n is the union of k disjoint sets $T^n_1, \dots, T^n_k$ (the *types*), such that $u_t = u_i$ and $X_t = X_i$ whenever $t \in T^n_i$. We assume as follows:

---

[14] A *coalition* is a subset of T.
[15] Shapley's definition (1953) of ϕ is in terms of a set of axioms, from which (4.3) is derived. See Roth (1977) for an interesting discussion of Shapley's axioms.

ELBOW ROOM ASSUMPTION: *For each* $J \subset \{1, \ldots, k\}$,

$$0 \notin \mathrm{bd} \left[\sum_{i \in J} B_i + \sum_{i \notin J} X_i \right]. \tag{5.1}$$

In words, for any coalition J in M^1, if it is at all possible simultaneously to satiate all agents in J, then this can also be done 'with room to spare', i.e. when all other agents are restricted to the interiors of their net trade sets.[16]

This assumption holds generically in a certain very natural sense. The left side of (5.1) represents the total endowment of the market, whereas its right side is the boundary of a convex set in R^d, hence at most $(d-1)$-dimensional. Since there are only finitely many J, the assumption holds for all but a $(d-1)$-dimensional set of total endowments. A formal genericity statement can be made in terms of translates of the X_i; translating the net trade set is equivalent to varying the endowment. For details, see Section 8.3.

Note also that since the J's are sets of types, the number of conditions (5.1) is fixed at 2^k, and does not vary with n.

Call an allocation $\hat{x}$ in M^n *equal treatment* if it assigns the same net trade to traders of the same type. Such an allocation $\hat{x}$ defines a k-tuple x of net trades, one for each type; x is an allocation in M^1, which is said to *correspond* to $\hat{x}$.

MAIN THEOREM: *For each n, let x^n be an allocation in the unreplicated market M^1, corresponding to an equal treatment value allocation in the n-fold replication M^n. Let x^∞ be a limit point[17] of $\{x^n\}$. Then there is a nonnegative dividend c that is monotonic in the net trade sets, and a price vector q, such that (q, c, x^∞) is a dividend equilibrium in M^1.*

From the monotonicity it follows that the dividends are determined by the net trade sets, i.e., $X_i = X_j$ implies $c_i = c_j$. Thus, the theorem says that all value allocations in large markets with satiation approximate dividend equilibrium allocations, where the dividends depend only on the net trade sets, and monotonically so.[18] In particular, call a dividend

---

[16] See Section 7 for an interpretation in the fixed price case.

[17] Limit of a subsequence.

[18] Of course, the dividends are endogenously determined by all the data of the market, including all the utilities. Yet, in any given market, traders with the same net trade set have the same dividend.

equilibrium (q, c, x) *uniform*[19] if all the c_t are the same. Then we have the following:

COROLLARY 5.3:   *Under the conditions of the theorem, assume that all traders have the same net trade set. Then (q, c, x^∞) is a uniform dividend equilibrium.*

The following existence result, for which (5.1) is not needed, gives substance to the main theorem:

PROPOSITION 5.4:   *For every n, there is an equal treatment value allocation in the n-fold replication M^n.*

Further results will be stated in Section 9.

6.   An informal demonstration of the main theorem

Let $\lambda^n = (\lambda_1^n, \ldots, \lambda_k^n)$ be a comparison vector associated[20] with x^n. Normalize λ^n so that the sum of its coordinates is 1. For simplicity,[21] assume for each i that x_i^n and λ_i^n converge as $n \to \infty$; that each of the x_i^n as well as their limit x_i^∞ is interior to the net trade set X_i; and that the utility function u_i is strictly convex and continuously differentiable on X_i.

In the classical context of monotonicity and nonsatiation, λ_i tends to a positive limit for all types i (Champsaur, 1975). But as we shall see below, in our context some of the λ_i^n may tend to 0. This is the crucial difference between the two contexts, and it is this that leads to the positive dividends.

The situation may in fact be quite complicated; there may be differences in order of magnitude even between those λ_i^n that tend to 0. In this section, though, we will assume for simplicity that those λ_i^n that do tend to 0 all have the same order of magnitude.[22] If there are such types, they are called *lightweight*, the others *heavyweight*.[23]

By definition, the allocation x^n is optimal[24] for the all-trader set T^n. This implies that all the (weighted) utility gradients $\lambda_i^n u_i'(x_i^n)$ are equal;

[19] This concept is due to Drèze and Müller (1980), who showed, using fixed point methods, that uniform dividend equilibria always exist. They worked in a fixed price context, using 'uniform coupons equilibrium' for what we call 'uniform dividend equilibrium'.

[20] More precisely λ^n is a k-dimensional vector corresponding to an nk-dimensional equal treatment comparison vector $\hat{\lambda}^n$ associated with the equal treatment allocation $\hat{x}^n$ corresponding to x^n. There must always be such a $\hat{\lambda}^n$.

[21] Use of the phrase 'for simplicity' means that the restriction involved is for purposes of the informal demonstration in this section only, and is not needed for the rigorous treatment in the omitted sections.

[22] More precisely, $\lim_{n \to \infty} \lambda_i^n / \lambda_j^n$ exists and is positive whenever both λ_i^n and λ_j^n tend to 0.

[23] The formal definition of 'lightweight' is slightly different, but yields the same result.

[24] An allocation is called *optimal* for a coalition S if it achieves the maximum total utility for S when the utilities u_i are multiplied by the weights λ_i^n.

otherwise transfers could lead to gains in total utility. Denote the common value of all these gradients by q^n; thus

$$\lambda_i^n u_i'(x_i^n) = \lambda_j^n u_j'(x_j^n) = q^n \tag{6.1}$$

for all i and j. If we let $n \to \infty$ and set $\lambda_i^\infty := \lim_{n \to \infty} \lambda_i^n$, $q^\infty := \lim_{n \to \infty} q^n$, we get

$$\lambda_i^\infty u_i'(x_i^\infty) = \lambda_j^\infty u_j'(x_j^\infty) = q^\infty. \tag{6.2}$$

Our demonstration is based on (4.3), which says that the Shapley value of a given trader t is his expected contribution to a randomly chosen coalition; more precisely, to the coalition S of traders before t in a randomly chosen order on all traders.

If S is large, it is very likely to be a good sample of all the traders, i.e. to have approximately equal numbers of traders of each type. The allocation that is optimal for S is then approximately the same as the allocation x^n that is optimal for the all-trader coalition T^n.

Adding t to S will not change this optimal allocation by much; each trader will be allocated approximately the same net trade as before. In particular, if t is of type i, he will be allocated approximately x_i^n. Since all the net trades must sum to 0, the net trade of t must somehow be divided among all the traders, with each trader subtracting a small part of x_i^n from his net trade. Since all the utility gradients are q^n, the utility of each trader is decreased by q^n times that small part. Altogether, this causes a change in total utility of $-q^n \cdot x_i^n$. To this must be added the utility $\lambda_i^n u_i(x_i^n)$ that t himself now enjoys. Thus t's contribution to S (the worth of $S \cup t$ less the worth of S) is given approximately by

$$\Delta := \lambda_i^n u_i(x_i^n) - q^n \cdot x_i^n. \tag{6.3}$$

All this is valid only when S is reasonably large. Otherwise – e.g. when S has no more than a fixed finite number of traders (such as one or a hundred or a thousand) – the reasoning breaks down. Denote by P^n the probability that S is 'small', so that t's contribution is not measured by Δ. This event is perhaps not very well defined, but in this section we are making no attempt at precision. It is in any case clear that $P^n \to 0$ as $n \to \infty$, and that the order of P^n is at least $1/n$ (obtained already when S has only one trader).

Letting δ denote the conditional expectation of t's contribution given that S is small,[25] we conclude that

[25] Both Δ and δ depend on n; we suppress the corresponding superscript to keep our notation as uncluttered as possible.

$$(\phi v_i^n)((t) \approx (1 - P^n)\varDelta + P^n \delta. \tag{6.4}$$

Note that we are ignoring the probability that S is large but nevertheless not a good sample of the entire population; this probability is very small indeed, much smaller than P^n, and in fact has no influence on the value. Note that δ is uniformly bounded; this follows, e.g., from the continuous differentiability of the utilities u_i on the compact sets X_i.

The definition (4.2) of the value stipulates that

$$(\phi v_i^n)(t) = \lambda_i^n u_i(x_i^n).$$

Together with (6.4) and the definition of $\varDelta$, this yields

$$q^n \cdot x_i^n \approx \varepsilon^n (\delta - \lambda_i^n u_i(x_i^n)), \tag{6.5}$$

where $\varepsilon^n := P^n/(1 - P^n) \to 0$.

The case in which none of the λ_i^n tend to 0 is the simplest, and we dispose of it first. With strict convexity, the elbow room assumption (5.1) rules out the possibility of simultaneously satiating all traders, a situation that is in any case rather uninteresting. Hence $u_i'(x_i^\infty) \neq 0$ for at least one i; and since $\lambda_i^\infty > 0$ for all i, it follows from (6.2) that x^∞ satiates no one, that $q^\infty \neq 0$, and that for all i, the gradient of u_i at x_i^∞ is in the direction of q^∞. Letting $n \to \infty$ in (6.5), we obtain $q^\infty \cdot x_i^\infty = 0$; hence the net trade x_i^∞ maximises u_i over the budget set $\{x \in X_i : q \cdot x \leqslant 0\}$. Thus x^∞ is an ordinary competitive allocation, and hence trivially part of a dividend equilibrium that satisfies the appropriate conditions.

Up to now the analysis has been as in the classical context of monotonicity and nonsatiation, where limits of value allocations are always competitive (Champsaur, 1975). But as we saw in Section 3, in our context there are situations in which competitive allocations need not even exist. By the above analysis, then, there must be some lightweights; of course there must also be heavyweights, since the sum of the k weights λ_i^n is normalised to be 1. This is the case of central interest in this paper, to which we now turn.

If we take i lightweight in (6.2), we find $q^\infty = 0$; hence $u_j'(x_j^\infty) = 0$ for heavyweight j, and hence x^∞ satiates all heavyweights. Suppose now that t is a lightweight trader of type i. Since $q^\infty = 0$, letting $n \to \infty$ in (6.5) as before would simply yield $0 = 0$. For something more informative, we must look at the fine structure, at the second order effects. This is done by dividing (6.5) by $\|q^n\|$ which, like q^n, tends to 0 as $n \to \infty$.

Assume for simplicity that $q^n/\|q_n\|$ actually tends to a limit q; note that $\|q\| = 1$. We shall see below that t's expected contribution δ to small coalitions is of larger order of magnitude than the term $\lambda_i^n u_i(x_i^n)$ on the right side of (6.5). Hence dividing (6.5) by $\|q^n\|$ and letting $n \to \infty$, we find

$$q \cdot x_i = \lim_{n \to \infty} (\varepsilon^n / \|q^n\|) \delta =: c_i; \tag{6.6}$$

the limit exists on the right because it exists on the left.

By definition, q^n is proportional to the unweighted utility gradient $u'_i(x^n_i)$; therefore its direction $q^n / \|q^n\|$ is equal to the direction of $u'_i(x^n_i)$. Letting $n \to \infty$, we deduce that q is the direction of $u'_i(x^\infty_i)$ whenever x^∞_i does not satiate t. In that case, therefore, (6.6) says that x^∞_i maximises t's utility over the dividend budget set defined by prices q and dividend c_i. Of course, when x^∞_i *does* satiate t, his utility is maximised globally, and *a fortiori* over his dividend budget set.

For lightweight i, it remains therefore only to show that c_i depends monotonically on the net trade set X_i, and in particular is independent of the utility u_i. To see this, let us examine the contribution of t when joining a fixed small coalition S. This may be divided into three components:

(i) t's own utility after joining;

(ii) the change in the total utility of the lightweight traders in S due to t's joining; and

(iii) the change in the total utility of the heavyweight traders in S due to t's joining.

In the first two of these three components, the utilities have weights tending to 0; in the third they do not. Thus for large n, the contribution of t to himself and to other lightweights is negligible; the importance of his contribution to S comes from what he can do to improve the lot of the heavyweights in S. Therefore he should distribute his resources so as to maximise the heavyweights' gain in utility, paying no attention to his own. His ability to do this is limited only by his net trade set, and has nothing to do with his utility. Moreover, the larger his net trade set, the more he can do, and this yields the monotonicity.

The reasoning works only when S is a fixed coalition of relatively small size. In that case the heavyweights in S cannot, in general, be simultaneously satiated; since S is small, they will then be a significant distance from satiation.[26] When t joins, he brings in resources (not utility!) that could

[26] In principle, the equality of marginal utilities expressed by (6.1) should still hold when x^n_i and x^n_j are replaced by y^n_i and y^n_j, where y^n is optimal for an arbitrary (fixed) S. In fact, when S is small and n large, y^n_i is very likely to be on the boundary of X_i, so that we have a corner situation, in which marginal utilities need not be equal. We therefore cannot deduce that y^n_j is close to satiation for heavyweight j, and indeed it will usually not be.

be used significantly to improve the lot of at least one heavyweight trader, perhaps even to bring that one all the way to satiation; that would be a good deal more worthwhile than using the resources for himself or for other lightweight traders, whose utilities have weights tending to 0. A more even handed distribution of the resources among the heavyweights would yield still more, but giving it all to one gives us a lower bound on t's contribution, and indicates that it is of larger order than λ_i^n.

If, however, S is large, it is probably a good sample of all agents, and then all types j will be close to x_j^∞; in particular, the heavyweights will already be satiated, even before t joins. Thus by joining, t cannot improve the heavyweights by much. The upshot is that no matter how t uses his resources – whether for himself, for his lightweight colleagues, or for the heavyweights – the increment in total utility will be the same; in the first two cases the utilities are weighted by small weights of the order λ_i^n, and in the last, the increase in the utility u_j is small.

We come finally to the case in which the type i of the additional trader t is heavyweight. In calculating the contribution δ to small coalitions, the significant components are now (i) and (iii), rather than just (iii); component (ii) remains negligible. Note, though, that on the right side of (6.5) we now have not δ, but something close to $\delta - \lambda_i^\infty u_i(x_i^\infty)$. Since $\lambda_i^\infty u_i(x_i^\infty)$ is the absolute maximum that t can get, component (i) of δ is certainly at least cancelled out, and very likely more than cancelled out. Thus what is left is at most component (iii). The rest of the argument is as before, with (6.6) modified to read:[27]

$$q \cdot x_i^\infty \leqslant \lim_{n \to \infty} (\varepsilon^n/\|q^n\|)[\text{component (iii) of } \delta] =: c_i. \tag{6.7}$$

Since i is heavyweight, x_i^∞ satiates; hence we must only show that it satisfies the budget inequality, which (6.7) indeed shows.

We end with a word of caution. The argument in this section is meant only to be indicative, and cannot easily be made rigorous. The difficulties we encounter in the rigorous treatment are intrinsic; they are not due to the generality of the treatment. Assuming differentiability, strict concavity, and so on enabled a simplified presentation in this section, but it would not help appreciably in the formal treatment.

---

[27] For technical reasons, the definition of the dividend c_i for heavyweight types i that we use in the formal proof is a little different from (6.7). Since x_i^∞ is generally in the interior of the dividend budget set when i is heavyweight, there is sometimes a little leeway in defining the dividend. Of course, if $X_i = X_j$ for some lightweight j, then we must have $c_i = c_j$, so the leeway disappears.

7. Fixed price markets

A (finite) fixed price market is defined by:

(7.1)   a finite set T (the *trader space*);

(7.2)   an integer $d + 1$ that is at least 2 (the *number of commodities*);

(7.3)   for each trader t, a point e_t in R_{++}^{d+1} (t's *endowment*);

(7.4)   for each trader t, a concave continuous function u_t^* on R_+^{d+1} (t's *utility function*); and

(7.5)   a point $\bar{p}$ in R_{++}^{d+1} (the *fixed price vector*).

A fixed price market is just like an ordinary market (without satiation), except that all trade is constrained to take place at the exogenously given prices $\bar{p}$. In effect, this means that each trader t can only consume bundles in his *fixed price hyperplane*

$$H_t := \{y \in R_+^{d+1} : \bar{p} \cdot y = \bar{p} \cdot e_t\}.$$

The utility u_t^* is defined on the entire orthant R_+^{d+1} only for convenience; all that is actually used is its restriction to H_t.

An *allocation* in a fixed price market is a vector $y = (y_t)_{t \in T}$, where $y_t \in H_t$ for each t (trading takes place at prices $\bar{p}$ and all consumptions are nonnegative), and $\sum_{t \in T} y_t = \sum_{t \in T} e_t$ (trading does not affect the total quantity of each good). A *coupons price vector* is a member q^* of R^{d+1} not proportional to $\bar{p}$ (i.e., unequal to $\alpha \bar{p}$ for any real α). A *coupons endowment* for agent t is a real number c_t. A *coupons equilibrium* consists of a coupons price vector q^*, a vector $c = (c_t)_{t \in T}$ of coupons endowments, and an allocation y, such that for all traders t, y_t maximises u_t^* over the *coupons budget set*

$$\{y \in R_+^{d+1} : \bar{p} \cdot y = \bar{p} \cdot e_t \text{ and } q^* \cdot y \leqslant q^* \cdot e_t + c_t\}.$$

The notion of coupons equilibrium is due to Drèze and Müller (1980). If the traders maximise their utilities subject only to the fixed prices $\bar{p}$, then in general the market will not clear. To obtain market clearing, one introduces an auxiliary currency, *in addition* to the ordinary currency in which the fixed prices $\bar{p}$ are stated. This auxiliary currency may be thought of as rationing 'coupons'; each transfer of commodities must be paid for both in ordinary money, at prices $\bar{p}$, and in coupons, at prices q^*. Coupons may not be exchanged for ordinary money.

The coupons endowments c_t are called *monotonic in the commodity endowments* if $e_t \geqslant e_s$ (coordinatewise) implies $c_t \geqslant c_s$; and *uniform* if all the c_t are the same.

In a $(d + 1)$-commodity fixed price market M^*, the spaces $H_t - e_t =: X_t$ of net trades are compact convex subsets of the d-dimensional subspace Q of R^{m+1} that is orthogonal to $\bar{p}$; M^* may be viewed as a d-commodity market M with satiation. If (q, c, x) is a dividend equilibrium in this market, then q is a linear functional on Q, and x is in Q^k; extending q in an arbitrary way to a linear functional q^* on all of R^{d+1} yields a coupons equilibrium $(q^*, c, x + e)$ in M^*, where e is the initial allocation in M^*. In brief, dividend equilibria in M correspond naturally to coupons equilibria in M^* (cf. Drèze and Müller, 1980, p. 133). Hence our main theorem implies that in fixed price markets with k types, limiting value allocations are associated with coupons equilibria enjoying the appropriate monotonicity properties.

Clearly, monotonicity in the net trade sets is equivalent to monotonicity in the endowments:

$$X_t \supset X_s \text{ if and only if } e_t \geqslant e_s \text{ (coordinatewise).} \tag{7.6}$$

Thus, *all value allocations in large fixed price markets approximate coupons equilibrium allocations, where the coupons endowments depend only on the commodity endowments, and monotonically so.* In particular, if all commodity endowments are the same, we are led to uniform coupons equilibria.

Note that in the context of fixed prices, the elbow room assumption is satisfied if there is no set J of types whose aggregate demand for some good h precisely exhausts the total supply of that good.[28]

So much for the technical treatment. We end this section with some remarks of a more conceptual nature, which relate this work to other work on fixed prices.

As mentioned in the introduction, our interest in markets with satiation arose from the desire to discover what kind of allocations the Shapley value would generate, in markets with fixed prices. The study of these markets in economic theory has been mostly oriented towards equilibria with one-sided, market-by-market rationing. The specific features of the equilibrium concept are either imposed directly, as in Drèze (1975), or derived from more basic assumptions (no involuntary trading, efficient recourse to a set of admissible trades,...), as in Malinvaud and Younès (1977a). By contrast, the analysis presented here imposes no conditions on the problem or its solution, beyond the constraint that all trading should take place at exogenously given prices.[29] Rather, we apply a general

---

[28] That is, $\sum_{i \in J} y_i^h = \sum e_i^h$, where y_i maximizes u_i^* over H_i.

[29] This is not the place to discuss the rationale for studying markets with fixed prices.

solution concept (the Shapley value) to the problem. The equilibrium concept (coupons equilibrium) and its specific features (nonnegative coupons endowments monotonically geared to initial resources) are an output of the analysis, not an input.

Whatever further properties Shapley value allocations may be found to possess, these properties will also emerge from the problem formulation, kept here to essentials. By this we mean in particular keeping out of the problem formulation elements like 'market-by-market rationing', which make the solution set depend upon inessentials like the definition of commodities.[30]

To clarify this point, note that the formal description of a market specifies for each trader a set (the consumption set), a real function on it (the utility function), and a point in it (the endowment). The set must also be endowed with an additive structure (to enable us to describe transfers between traders). Nothing more is required to describe a market from the economic viewpoint; the above structure completely specifies the opportunities as well as the incentives.

This suggests that one might want an economic 'solution' (such as an equilibrium concept) to depend only on this structure, to be invariant under 'inessential' changes, changes in the specification of the situation that leave this basic structure invariant. Familiar examples of such 'inessential' changes are changing the units of the commodities, or using different commodities that are utility substitutes, or permuting the commodities. But the principle of invariance under inessential changes applies equally well in less familiar cases, e.g. for rotations or other affine transformations.[31]

The Walras equilibrium is invariant in this sense; so are the kinds of dividend equilibrium and coupons equilibrium defined in this paper.[32] But the 'market-by-market' rationing equilibria mentioned above are not; they depend on identifying specific 'commodities', which are not present in the opportunities or the incentives.

All this is reflected in the game-theoretic treatment. Game theory gets at the essence; it separates the intrinsic from the conventional. Thus it is

---

[30] Indeed, in applied work, identifying specific 'commodities' is often quite difficult.

[31] For example, suppose that each of two mutual funds is composed of stock in the same two companies, but in different proportions. Suppose that the companies themselves are not public, but that the funds are; in essence, therefore, one can buy into the companies in any proportion between those offered by the two funds. Then it should make no difference whether the 'commodities' are defined to be company stock or fund stock.

[32] The monotonicity conditions for coupons equilibria ostensibly involves the commodities, but (7.6) shows that it is merely a restatement of an 'invariant' condition.

not surprising that the game-theoretic analysis leads to a 'commodity-free' solution.

When institutional aspects (like market-by-market rationing) are deemed important, they should perhaps be introduced exogenously into the problem formulation. This brings us to the basic methodological dichotomy, whether economic theory should be concerned with 'explaining' the genesis of institutions, or with 'predicting' their consequences. In the end, each of these activities has its own validity.

8. Alternative approaches

8.1. The core

The core of a market is the set of all allocations that cannot be improved upon by any coalition S. 'Improved upon' has two possible meanings:

(a) Some members of S are better off and none worse off.

(b) All members of S are better off.

In classical markets these two meanings lead to the same core, but here they do not. Neither core is very interesting; the first is too small, the second is too large.

Let M^1 be a market with satiation, M^n its n-fold replication. For simplicity we assume that the utilities are strictly convex and that not all traders can be simultaneously satiated; the elbow room assumption (5.1) is, however, unnecessary here.

Under (a), the Debreu-Scarf Theorem (1963) applies; the proof goes through without difficulty. Specifically, the a-core of M^n enjoys the equal treatment property. Hence it may be represented by a set C_a^n of allocations in the unreplicated market M^1. Then $C_a^{n+1} \subset C_a^n$, and the limiting a-core, $C_a^\infty := \cap_{n=1}^\infty C_a^n$, coincides with the set of competitive allocations.

As we saw in Section 3, markets with satiation often have no competitive allocations; the limiting a-core is then empty. This is what we meant by 'too small'.

Under (b), the core M^n may be very large, and does not even enjoy the equal treatment property. If we nevertheless confine ourselves to equal treatment allocations, we are, as above, led to a set C_b^n of allocations in M^1, where again $C_b^{n+1} \subset C_b^n$. We are interested in $C_b^\infty := \cap_{n=1}^\infty C_b^n$.

For each allocation x in M^1, let $G_i(x) := \{x \in X_i : u_i(x) > u_i(x_i)\}$ be the set of net trades preferred by i to x. Then C_b^∞ consists precisely of those allocations x for which 0 is not in the convex hull of the union of the preferred sets $G_i(x)$; since the preferred set is empty for satiated traders, we may take the union over unsatiated i only. For example, any dividend equilibrium allocation with nonnegative dividends is in the limiting b-core, even if the dividends are not in any sense monotonic; they may even be different for identical[33] types. Any individually rational allocation x at which only one type is unsatiated will also be in the limiting b-core. What is happening is that the satiated traders are useless as partners in an improving scheme; the unsatiated must fend for themselves, and they may well lack the resources for this. This makes the b-core very large.

We note for the record that the limiting value allocations are in the limiting b-core; but in general they constitute only a small subset. This fits in well with our experience in other market contexts with cores. For example, in large transferable utility markets with nondifferentiable utilities the core may be quite big, but if it has a centre of symmetry, then the value is that centre of symmetry (Hart, 1977a). More generally (asymmetric core, nontransferable utility), the value allocations in a large nondifferentiable market often constitute a small 'central' subset of a relatively big core (Hart, 1977b, 1980; Mertens, 1988; Tauman, 1981).

8.2.   *The continuum approach*

There is no difficulty in defining nonatomic markets with satiation. One simply replaces the trader space T by a nonatomic measure space $(T, \mathscr{C}, \mu)$ with $\mu(T) = 1$, and requires that the net trade sets X_t and the utility functions u_t be measurable in an appropriate sense, and the u_t uniformly bounded. An *allocation* is now a measurable function x from T to R^d with $x(t) \in X_t$ for all t and $\int_T x = 0$. As before, we assume that no allocation satiates all traders, but do not require anything like the 'elbow room' assumption (5.1). The definition of competitive equilibrium remains literally unchanged.

A *generalized comparison function* is an integrable function from T to R^1_+ with a positive integral; if it is to R^1_{++}, it is a *comparison function*. A *coalition* is a measurable subset of T (i.e. a member of $\mathscr{C}$). Given a generalized comparison function λ, define a nonatomic game v_λ by

$$v_\lambda(S) := \max\left(\int_S \lambda(t)u_t(x(t))\mu(dt) : \int_S x = 0 \quad \text{and} \quad x(t) \in X_t \text{ for all } t \in S\right)$$

---

[33] Having the same utilities and net trade sets. Confining ourselves to equal treatment allocations in M^n does not mean that identical types get the same net trade; it only means that in M^n, different replicas of the same trader in M^1 get the same net trade.

for each coalition S. A (*generalised*) *value allocation* is an allocation x for which there exists a (generalised) comparison function λ such that

$$(\phi v_\lambda)(dt) = \lambda(t)u_t(x(t))\mu(dt) \tag{8.1}$$

for all 'infinitesimal' agents dt, where ϕ is an appropriate[34] value operator. (A more formal statement of (8.1) is that $(\phi v_\lambda)(S) = \int_S \lambda(t)u_t(x(t))\mu(dt)$ for all coalitions S.)

So much for the definitions. Unfortunately, the results are rather disappointing. All we can say is:

(8.2) *Every value allocation is competitive.*

(8.3) *An allocation is a generalised value allocation if and only if it is competitive or satiates some agents.*

We have already noted that markets with satiation often have no competitive equilibria; in that case there are *no* value allocations in the continuum approach. The *generalised* value allocations, on the other hand, constitute a very large set even then, consisting of all allocations satiating at least one agent. There is no restriction at all on what nonsatiated agents get; they may even be assigned individually irrational net trades.

To demonstrate these results, assume for simplicity that the u_t are continuously differentiable and strictly convex, and that the allocations in question are interior (i.e., $x(t) \in$ int X_t for all t). Let x be a generalised value allocation. As at (6.1), there is a vector q such that

$$\lambda(t)u_t'(x(t)) = q, \tag{8.4}$$

for all t. Moreover, the value $(\phi v_\lambda)(dt)$ is the average contribution of dt to a coalition S. In the continuum case, 'almost all' coalitions are large; hence as at (6.3),

$$(\phi v_\lambda)(dt) = \lambda(t)u_t(x(t))\mu(dt) = q \cdot x(t)\mu(dt),$$

and together with (8.1), we obtain that for all t,

$$q \cdot x(t) = 0. \tag{8.5}$$

If x is a value allocation, i.e., $\lambda(t) > 0$ for all t, then $u_t'(x(t))$ is either equal to 0 for all t or is unequal to 0 for all t. If it is equal to 0 for all t, then all traders are simultaneously satiated, which we have ruled out. Hence

---

[34] See, e.g., Kannai (1966), Aumann and Shapley (1974), Hart (1980), Mertens (1980, 1988), or Neyman and Tauman (1979). What is needed here is a value with the 'diagonal' property.

it is unequal to 0 for all t, whence $q \neq 0$; together, (8.4) and (8.5) then assert precisely that (q, x) is a competitive equilibrium, whence x is a competitive allocation.

If x is not a value allocation, i.e., $\lambda(t) = 0$ for some t, then $q = 0$. Hence for those t for which $\lambda(t) \neq 0$, we must have $u'_t(x(t)) = 0$, and hence these t are satiated. Conversely, if x is any allocation that satiates some traders, let λ be a generalised comparison function that assigns weight 0 to all traders unsatiated at x. The value $(\phi v_\lambda)(dt)$ is the average contribution of dt to a diagonal[35] coalition θT, where θ ranges from 0 to 1. The case $\theta = 0$ has no effect on the average and may be ignored. As soon as $\theta > 0$, there are enough unsatiated traders in θT to supply all the resources desired by the satiated traders in θT. Thus dt contributes nothing if he is unsatiated, and only his own utility $\lambda(t) u_t(x(t)) \mu(dt)$ if he is satiated, which means that (8.1) is satisfied. Thus any such x is a generalised value allocation.

The reader will have realised that what prevents the continuum approach from achieving a more satisfactory result is that 'small' coalitions play no role. Coalitions either have positive measure, in which case they behave like 'large' coalitions, or have measure 0, in which case they are ignored. The crucial coalitions in the limit approach[36] (the one used in this paper) are those whose size is positive but of smaller order of magnitude than that of the all-trader set; the continuum approach is not equipped to take account of such coalitions.

8.3. *The elbow room assumption in a model with explicit endowments*

To show that (5.1) holds generically, we must reformulate the definition of a market with satiation so that the endowments appear explicitly. Accordingly, define a *market with satiation and explicit endowments* to consist of a finite set T (the *trader space*), a positive integer d (the number of *commodities*), and for each trader t,

a compact convex subset X_t^0 of R^d (t's *consumption set*);

a concave continuous function u_t^0 on X_t^0 (t's *utility function*); and

a point e_t in the interior of X_t^0 (t's *endowment*).

To regain from this a market with satiation as in Section 2, simply define

---

[35] See Aumann and Shapley (1974, Chapter III).

[36] Of course, the value operator ϕ may itself be defined by a limit approach, even when it is applied to nonatonic games. Nevertheless, the kind of second-order effect that is crucial in the proof of the main theorem does not obtain then.

$X_t := X_t^0 - e_t$ (algebraic subtraction!) and $u_t(x) := u_t^0(x + e_t)$. The remainder of the treatment is then exactly as before.

In this formulation, the elbow room assumption is equivalent to the following: for each $J \subset \{1, \ldots, k\}$,

$$\sum_{i=1}^k e_i \notin \mathrm{bd} \left[\sum_{i \in J} B_i^0 + \sum_{i \notin J} X_i^0 \right], \tag{8.6}$$

where e_i is the endowment of a type i trader, and B_i^0 is the set of points in X_i^0 at which u_i^0 is maximised. Note that for each J, the right side of (8.6) represents the boundary of a compact convex set in R^d that is independent of the endowments; such sets are closed and of measure 0. The left side is simply the total endowment. Since there are only finitely many different possible choices of J, it follows that the elbow room assumption holds for all total endowment vectors except for a closed set of measure 0 in R^d; hence also for all k-tuples $(e_1, \ldots, e_k)$ of endowments except for a closed set of measure 0 in R^{dk}.

Conceptually, the situation here is perhaps a little different from that of other generic theorems in the literature. The exceptional set is entirely explicit and has transparent geometric and economic meanings; in any given market one can, so to speak, 'see at a glance' whether or not the elbow room assumption is satisfied.

9.   Further results and open problems

The main theorem (Section 5) shows that the dividends depend only on the net trade sets, and monotonically so. In fact, we know much more about them both qualitatively and quantitatively.

The competitive case is from our point of view less interesting, and it is convenient to exclude it. A summary of additional results is then as follows.

The dividends c_i are all strictly positive (rather than just nonnegative); in addition to monotonicity, they satisfy a concavity condition; and there is an 'explicit' formula for them. The order of magnitude of the weights λ_i^n of each lightweight type i is exactly $1/n$. Lightweight types whose utilities are differentiable, and whose maxima are interior, are unsatiated; hence if all utilities are differentiable and all maxima interior, then the heavyweights are precisely the satiated types, the lightweights precisely the unsatiated. In the case of one commodity ($d = 1$), all traders on the 'short' side are satiated.

All these results are stated formally and proved in Section 12 and Appendix C of the original *Econometrica* paper; some illustrations are also given in Section 13 there.

Foremost among the open problems is that of the converse. To what extent are the necessary conditions that we have found for limiting value allocations also sufficient? In the case of ordinary markets, without satiation, this is related to smoothness: see Mas-Colell (1977) and Hart (1977b). It is quite likely that smoothness is relevant here too.

Another interesting task is to dispense with the finite type assumption. As we have seen, one cannot simply use a continuum; what is called for is a limiting approach, in which the limit is a continuum of different types. There is a large literature on this type of model in connection with the core equivalence principle; cf. Hildenbrand's book (1974) and survey article (1982). Another approach that could conceivably be helpful for this purpose is that of nonstandard analysis (cf. Brown and Robinson, 1972).

One might also like to explore the consequences of dispensing with the equal treatment restriction, the elbow room assumption, or the assumption that 0 is in the interior of each net trade set.

Perhaps most interesting at this stage would be to derive additional qualitative properties of the solution in particular contexts. In the case $d = 1$ (one commodity), for example, what happens to the dividends when the capacity of the long side is much larger than the supply of the short side? When they are almost equal? Can this kind of result, once obtained, be generalised to $d > 1$? The 'explicit formula' gives us a powerful tool for investigating these and other questions arising in particular contexts.

IV Public goods and the public sector

7 Public goods with exclusion*

1. Introduction

Equilibrium concepts for public goods discussed in the literature rely upon 'individualised prices', i.e. upon unlimited price discrimination between consumers. Such is the case, notably, for Lindahl equilibria, pseudo-equilibria and subscription equilibria; see, for example, Malinvaud (1972). In practice, however, price discrimination is either nonexistent or limited to a few broad categories of consumers. There are many good reasons for this practice, in particular: the lack of incentives for correct revelation of the preferences to which 'individualised prices' are related; the costs of administering and policing tariffs, of collecting and processing the necessary information, etc.; and the political and ethical constraints imposed on public services or licensed private monopolies, on grounds of equal treatment for instance.

Concepts of equilibrium with price rigidities and quantity constraints recently introduced for private goods (see, for example, Bénassy (1975), Drèze (1975) or the survey article by Grandmont (1977)) are susceptible of application to public goods. This idea underlies some work of de Carvalho (1979) on tâtonnement processes for public goods of the type defined by Malinvaud (1971) and Drèze and de la Vallée Poussin (1971). de Carvalho introduces (chapter 5) the additional constraint that individual contributions towards financing the public goods must be kept equal over predetermined groups of consumers. The properties of the constrained

*Journal of Public Economics, 13 (1980), 5–24. Helpful comments by Peter Hammond, Claude Henry, Guy Laroque, Maurice Marchand, Jean-Philippe Vial and Claus Weddepohl are gratefully acknowledged. Part of the work on this manuscript was done during visits to the University of Essex, and to the Institute for Mathematical Studies in Social Sciences at Stanford University under support from National Science Foundation Grant SOC 75-21820-A01.

processes are analysed, with the help of an appropriate concept of second-best Pareto optimality.

The present paper investigates a parallel application for public goods with exclusion. Public goods with exclusion are public goods (physical feasibility requires only that no single individual should consume more than total output), the consumption of which by individuals can be controlled, measured and subjected to payment or other contractual limitations. A nearly perfect example is provided by cable television with coin-operated unscramblers or with meters. Public facilities with controlled access and excess capacity (trains, parks, theatres, etc.) also provide good examples. Some information services (weather reports, credit rating, etc.) or intellectual services (computer programs, copyrights, musical authorship, etc.) fall in the same category. The services of fire or police departments provide another extreme example.[1]

The simple idea underlying the present paper is that public goods with exclusion are typically made available at fixed prices *up to the total quantity produced.* Individual consumers may thus buy at given prices an amount of their choice, not exceeding total output.[2] This may be contrasted with the concept of Lindahl equilibrium, where each consumer buys the total output at a price of his own.

The theory of demand under quantity rationing (see, for example, Tobin (1952)) provides an adequate tool to develop the demand side of our model. We find it convenient to work with demand *functions*; accordingly, we assume that preferences are strictly convex. Constrained demand functions then define the single most preferred element from those in the budget set which satisfy the quantity constraints. We assume that constrained demand functions are Lipschitz continuous (differentiability would not be a reasonable requirement, in the presence of quantity constraints). (A few details are given in Section 3 below.)

On the supply side, we assume that each public good is produced by a single firm. This seems empirically realistic, and saves us the trouble of specifying how individual purchases are distributed among producers. And we consider alternative institutional arrangements.

---

[1] In some of these examples, congestion phenomena occur, and the quality of the public goods varies with the number of users – a feature analysed in Lévy-Lambert (1968). The model and results presented here apply to the variable quality case as well, even though that case is not treated explicitly.

[2] More generally, a limited amount of price discrimination could be introduced, either between consumers or according to quantities purchased. The model and results presented here lend themselves to natural extensions in these directions.

Thus, an individual producer could be a public monopoly, aiming at welfare maximisation, with or without a budget constraint (as in Boiteux (1956)); it could be a profit-maximising private monopoly; or it could be a licensed private monopoly, pursuing profit maximisation within statutory regulations. Two types of regulations will be considered here, namely price regulation (the prices of public goods are set by the regulatory agency, the quantities are set for profit maximisation at these fixed prices); and quantity regulation (the quantities of public goods are set by the regulatory agency, the prices are set for profit maximisation at these quantities). The not uncommon practice of price regulation for licensed private monopolies (railroads, urban transportation companies, cable television networks, etc.) lends particular relevance to that arrangement, which is singled out for the existence theorem in Section 4 below.

Our equilibrium concept thus combines consumer equilibrium, under given prices and quantity constraints, with producer equilibrium of one type or another. When producer behaviour reflects welfare maximisation (either constrained or unconstrained), equilibrium is defined by the Pareto principle, and the existence of equilibrium is not an issue if the set of feasible allocations is compact. In the case of private monopolies, one must first define precisely what is meant by 'profit maximisation'. After introducing the model in Section 2, we define our concept of profit maximisation in Section 3. It assumes that producers of public goods know the constrained demand functions for their output. (In particular, they know the marginal revenue associated with an increase in output.) We argue that such an assumption is needed to avoid trivial solutions. Unfortunately, the resulting profit function generally is not concave.

A *market equilibrium* is characterised by physical feasibility, consumer equilibrium and profit maximisation. The existence of a market equilibrium is proved in section 4 for the special case where each producer of public goods supplies a single commodity, at a regulated price. It is shown in section 5 that output of public goods at a market equilibrium is then generically *less* than required for second-best Pareto efficiency (given the prices).

In general, market equilibria may fail to exist, owing to nonconcavity of the profit functions. The profit-maximisation problem may then be difficult to solve, and a 'bounded rationality' approach may be more realistic. As a first step in that direction, we define a *market stationary point* by the properties of physical feasibility, consumer equilibrium, and stationarity of the profit functions. The existence of a market stationary point, under price regulation, is proved in Section 4. The technique of proof is readily adapted to other cases as well, under appropriate assumptions. But we emphasise that stationary points of the profit functions need not be local maxima.

An important issue raised, but not treated, in Section 4, concerns the properties of the correspondence relating market stationary points to the prices of public goods, under price regulation. Treating that issue properly would require mathematical developments lying beyond the scope of the present paper.

Finally, some efficiency issues are discussed in Section 5. It is first recalled that a welfare-maximising public utility, capable of financing its deficit by lump-sum taxes, should set the public good prices at a level sufficiently low that each consumer demands the entire output. This is neither surprising nor very interesting. Attention is therefore focussed on situations where a budget constraint is imposed on the producer. Four sets of first-order conditions are then contrasted, namely those of the public monopoly and of the private monopoly successively unregulated, price regulated and quantity regulated. Although a general case can be made in favour of the public monopoly and against the unregulated private monopoly, it is not possible to rank the intermediate alternatives of price versus quantity regulation. A rigorous comparison of these alternatives would also require further progress with the unanswered question raised at the end of Section 4.

Because the present paper is meant to be suggestive rather than exhaustive, the choice of assumptions is dictated by convenience rather than generality.

2. The model

We consider an economy with:

n private goods, indexed $j = 1 \ldots n$, with $N = \{1 \ldots n\}$;

m public goods, indexed $i = 1 \ldots m$, with $M = \{1 \ldots m\}$;

l consumers, indexed $h = 1 \ldots l$, with $L = \{1 \ldots l\}$;

k producers of private goods or private producers, indexed $g = 1 \ldots k$, with $K = \{1 \ldots k\}$;

f producers of public goods or public producers, indexed $e = 1 \ldots f$, with $F = \{1 \ldots f\}$.

The set M is *partitioned* into subsets $M^1 \ldots M^e \ldots M^f$, with cardinality $m^1 \ldots m^e \ldots m^f$. For $i \in M^e$ and $i' \in M^{e'}, i < i'$ implies $e \leqq e'$; and $e < e'$ implies $i < i'$. (That is, the public producers specialise in disjoint sets of goods; and the indices of public producers are monotonic nondecreasing in the indices of goods.) If ζ is a vector of R^m, we denote by ζ^e the subvector with indices in M^e; and by $^e\zeta$ its complement, with indices in $M \backslash M^e$.

For the private goods, we denote by:[3]

$p \in \varDelta \subset R^n_+$ their prices; $\varDelta = \{p \in R^n_+ \mid \sum_j p_j = 1\}$;

$x^h \in X^h \subset R^n$ the consumption of consumer h; X^h is closed, convex and bounded below;

$w^h \in \operatorname{int} X^h$ the initial resources of consumer h;

$y^g \in Y^g \subset R^n$ the production of private producer g; Y^g is closed and convex;

$Y^g \cap R^n_+ = \{0\}; (\sum_g Y^g) \cap -(\sum_g Y^g) = \{0\}$;

$y^e \in R^n_-$ the imputs of public producer e.

For the public goods, we denote by:

$q \in R^m_+$ their prices; $q = (q^1 \ldots q^e \ldots q^f)$;

$z^h \in R^m_+$ the consumption of consumer h; $z^h = (z^{h1} \ldots z^{he} \ldots z^{hf})$;

$Q \in R^m_+$ their production; $Q = (Q^1 \ldots Q^e \ldots Q^f)$.

The public producer e chooses a production plan (y^e, Q^e) $\in Y^e \subset R^n_- \times R^{m^e}_+$; Y^e is closed, convex, and $R^n_- \times \{0\} \subset Y^e$. Furthermore, it is assumed that for every y^e, the section of Y^e in R^m_+, i.e. the set $\{Q^e \mid (y^e, Q^e) \in Y^e\}$, is bounded; it will be denoted $S_{y^e}(Y^e)$. This condition is automatically satisfied when the asymptotic cone of Y^e does not contain any nonnegative element other than zero.

Physical feasibility requires:

$$\sum_h (x^h - w^h) \leqq \sum_g y^g + \sum_e y^e; \tag{1}$$

$$z^h \leqq Q, \text{ for all } h \in L. \tag{2}$$

A feasible allocation, a, is an $(l + k + f)$-tuple of vectors

$$(x^h, z^h) \in X^h \times R^m_+, h = 1 \ldots l,$$

$$y^g \in Y^g, g = 1 \ldots k,$$

$$(y^e, Q^e) \in Y^e, e = 1 \ldots f,$$

satisfying (1) and (2). The set of feasible allocations is A.

LEMMA. A is bounded.

[3] $\leqq$ means $\leqq$ coordinate-wise; $<$ means $\leqq$ and $\neq$; $R^n_+ = \{x \in R^n \mid x \geqq 0\}$; $R^n_- = \{x \in R^n \mid x \leqq 0\}$.

PROOF. In so far as private goods are concerned, see proposition (2) on p. 77 of Debreu (1959). This also implies that $\sum_e y^e$ is bounded, hence that $y^e \leq 0$ is bounded for each e. The lemma then follows from our assumption that $S_{y^e}(Y^e)$ is bounded for every y^e.   QED

The profits of private producers, $v^g = py^g$, belong to the consumers according to the ownership fractions $\theta_{hg} \geq 0$, $\sum_h \theta_{hg} = 1$.

The profits of the public producers are defined by

$$v^e = py^e + q^e \sum_h \min(z^{he}, Q^e),\tag{3}$$

an expression that simplifies somewhat when (2) is taken into account, and that is discussed extensively in section 3 below.

These profits belong to the consumers according to the ownership fractions $\theta_{he} \geq 0$, $\sum_h \theta_{he} = 1$.

A *budgeted allocation* consists of a feasible allocation a and price vectors $(p, q) \in \Delta \times R^m_+$ such that, for all h, the budget constraint

$$p(x^h - w^h) + qz^h \leq \sum_g \theta_{hg} v^g + \sum_e \theta_{he} v^e = _{\text{def}} r^h\tag{4}$$

is satisfied. Define $r = (r^1 \ldots r^h \ldots r^l) \in R^l_+$.

For each $h \in L$, there exists a preference ordering $\succsim_h$ defined on $X^h \times R^m_+$; $\succsim_h$ is complete, continuous and strictly convex; $(x, z) \geq (x', z')$ implies $(x, z) \succsim_h (x', z')$; $x > x'$ implies $(x, z) \succ_h (x', z)$.

Natural conditions for $(a, p, q) \in A \times \Delta \times R^m_+$ to define a *market equilibrium* include:

> $\forall h \in L$, (x^h, z^h) is the best element[4] for $\succsim_h$ over the set of vectors satisfying (2) and (4);   (5)

> $\forall g \in K$, y^g maximises v^g on Y^g.   (6)

To these conditions must be added a specification of the behaviour of the public producers. In the case of a public monopoly aiming at welfare maximisation, this specification will involve the standard concept of Pareto optimality.

In the case of a private monopoly aiming at profit maximisation, it would seem natural to impose

$$(q^e, y^e, Q^e) \text{ maximise } v^e \text{ on } Y^e,\tag{7}$$

---

[4] In view of our assumption of strict convexity of preferences, that element is unique, and we work with demand *functions*.

subject possibly to $q^e = \bar{q}^e$ under price regulation or to $Q^e = \bar{Q}^e$ under quantity regulation. We now turn to a discussion of condition (7).

3. Behaviour of the public producers

3.1.

Whereas conditions (5) and (6) are standard and well understood, conditions (7) raise some difficulties. Going back to expression (3), we see that the profits v^e of public producer e depend upon p, y^e, q^e, the demand levels z^{he}, and Q^e. We must now specify which among these variables enter as decision variables, as functions of the decision variables, and as parameters, in the maximisation problem.

The list of decision variables will depend upon the institutional arrangements. Under price regulation, the decision variables will be y^e and Q^e, with $q^e = \bar{q}^e$ entering as a parameter. Under quantity regulation, the decision variables will be y^e and q^e, with $Q^e = \bar{Q}^e$ entering as a parameter. In the absence of regulation, the decision variables will be y^e, q^e and Q^e.

Let us consider first, and in some detail, the case of a price-regulated public producer who maximises profits with respect to y^e and Q^e. Three different specifications of the maximisation problem are possible.

(i)   First, one could treat p and z^{he}, $h \in L$, as parameters. Then, condition (7) becomes: (y^e, Q^e) maximise $\bar{p} y^e + \bar{q}^e \sum_h \min(\bar{z}^{he}, Q^e)$ on Y^e (where all parameters are identified by overbars). The drawback of this approach is that (5) and (7) will hold trivially with $z^{he} = Q^e = 0$ and $y^e = 0$;[5] our economy then reduces to a standard private goods economy, with well-known properties.

(ii)   Going to the other extreme, one could treat p and $z^{he}, h \in L$, as jointly determined endogenous variables, the levels of which would depend upon y^e and Q^e. Under this approach the public producer would be assumed capable of tracing the influence of his decisions (y^e, Q^e), not only on the demands for public goods z^{he} through the constraints (2), but also on the prices of private goods p (both directly via y^e and indirectly via the influence of Q^e on the private demands x^{he}) and on the other determinants of z^{he} (namely p, r^h and ^eQ, all of which are jointly determined in equilibrium). This approach is technically difficult, because the market

---

[5] Indeed, if $\bar{z}^{he} = 0$, then $\min(\bar{z}^{he}, Q^e)$ is equal to zero identically in Q^e; hence $v^e = py^e \leq 0$ is maximal at $y^e = 0$, $Q^e = 0$; but when $Q^e = 0$, then $z^{he} = 0$ by (2); accordingly, the trivial solution $z^{he} = Q^e = 0$ satisfies simultaneously (5) and (7).

clearing prices p need not be unique; it is quite unrealistic because it endows the public producer with too much information and computing abilities; and it is not in the spirit of competitive analysis, which aims at modelling price-taking behaviour.

(iii) More realistically, one should treat p, r and ^eQ as parameters, and assume that the public producer recognises only the *direct* influence of his output decisions Q^e on the demand levels $z^{he}(Q^e; \bar{p}, \bar{q}, \bar{r}^h, {}^e\bar{Q})$. This middle course seems natural and still consistent with the spirit of competitive analysis. Indeed, we noted under (i) that it would be illogical for the public producer to assume that an increase in his output would leave sales unchanged. It would be equally unsatisfactory for him to assume that the additional output would be bought by *all* consumers, including those currently buying quantities $z_i^h < Q_i$. Barring these two extremes leads to recognise the direct influence of Q^e on $z^{he}(Q^e; \bar{p}, \bar{q}, \bar{r}^h, {}^e\bar{Q})$, neither more nor less.[6]

3.2.

Under this third approach, retained here, the next issue to be settled is *how* the public producer perceives the influence of Q^e on z^{he}, $h \in L$. One possibility would be to use the concept of *effective demand* as defined by Clower (1965) or Bénassy (1975). Let $\zeta_i^h = z_i^h(Q_1 \ldots Q_{i-1}, + \infty, Q_{i+1} \ldots Q_m; p, q, r^h)$, $\zeta^h = (\zeta_1^h \ldots \zeta_m^h) = (\zeta^{h1} \ldots \zeta^{he} \ldots \zeta^{hf})$; one could then rewrite (7) as follows:

$$(y^e, Q^e) \text{ maximise } \bar{p}\, y^e + \bar{q}^e \sum_h \min(\bar{\zeta}^{he}, Q^e) \text{ on } Y^e. \tag{8}$$

This formulation is adequate when $m^e = 1$ (each public producer supplies a single good), but not when $m^e = 1$, *because it implies that the public producer ignores the relationships of substitution or complementarity among the public goods which he supplies.*

Indeed, if goods i and $i + 1$ in M^e are strongly complementary, with $z_i^h = Q_i$ and $z_{i+1}^h = Q_{i+1}$, it could be that simultaneous increases of Q_i and Q_{i+1} by δ bring about increases in both z_i^h and z_{i+1}^h by δ; whereas $\zeta_i^h < z_i^h + \delta$, and $\zeta_{i+1}^h < z_{i+1}^h + \delta$, owing to the limited appeal of increasing the consumption of either good when its complement remains constrained.[7]

---

[6] As a technical side remark, we note that the public producer could indifferently recognise, or ignore as we assume here, the influence of his own profits v^e on individual incomes r^h. At a point where the profit function is stationary, the two formulations are identical to the first order.

[7] More frequent service on a local bus route may fail to stimulate demand if the connecting railroad service is not improved simultaneously...

Conversely, if the two goods are close substitutes, it could be that simultaneous increases of Q_i and Q_{i+1} by δ bring about smaller increases in z_i^h and z_{i+1}^h than suggested by ζ^h.[8]

When simultaneous modifications of several quantities are contemplated, the relevant concept is the vector-valued *constrained demand function* $z^{he}(Q^e; p, q, r^h, {}^eQ)$ defined by (5) for alternative values of Q^e. We shall assume here that, with the aid of his econometric and marketing consultants, the public producer knows the aggregate demand functions

$$z^e(Q^e; \bar{p}, \bar{q}, \bar{r}, {}^e\bar{Q}) = \sum_h z^{he}(Q^e; \bar{p}, \bar{q}, \bar{r}^h, {}^e\bar{Q}).$$

Since these functions satisfy (2), we may now rewrite (7) as

$$(y^e, Q^e) \text{ maximize } \bar{p}\, y^e + \bar{q}^e \sum_h z^{he}(Q^e; \bar{p}, \bar{q}, \bar{r}^h, {}^e\bar{Q})$$

$$= {}_{\text{def}}\, v^e(y^e, Q^e; \bar{p}, \bar{q}, \bar{r}, {}^e\bar{Q}), \text{ on } Y^e. \tag{9}$$

We shall then say that a budgeted allocation (a, p, q) is a *market equilibrium, under price regulation,* if it satisfies (5), (6) and (9). We prove in Section 4, the existence of such a market equilibrium, with arbitrary q, for the special case where M^e is a singleton for all e in F. And we show in Section 5 that output of public goods, at such an equilibrium, is generically less than required for second-best Pareto efficiency, given q.

3.3.

The optimization problem faced by public producer e, namely (9), is in general neither differentiable nor concave. Indeed, conditions (2) imply that demand functions cannot be everywhere differentiable. And the constrained demand functions $z^{he}(Q^e; \cdot)$ need not be concave, as an example in the appendix illustrates.

The fact that problem (9) is not concave has two important implications.

First, a market equilibrium may fail to exist. An example in the appendix illustrates the point. In that example, public goods are demanded by a single consumer, and are therefore not different from private goods. The existence problem lies with the behaviour of the public producer, who takes into account the influence of his output decisions on demand levels. Similar

---

[8] The prospective audiences for additional coverage by a TV network of domestic soccer games and foreign soccer games cannot be evaluated independently...

problems are encountered in general equilibrium models with imperfect competition – see, for example, Arrow and Hahn (1971, ch. 6.4). Still, it should be noted that lack of existence follows here from the absence of market-clearing prices *for the private goods*, owing to a discontinuity in the behaviour (here the demand for inputs) of the public producers. In most practical situations this problem should be of secondary importance, given sufficiently well-behaved markets for private goods. The purpose of the example in the appendix is thus to orient, not to discourage, the search for reasonable assumptions implying the existence of market equilibria, under price regulation.

The fact that problem (9) is not concave has another implication, namely that public producer *e* may find it difficult to solve that problem. Operational sufficient conditions for a maximum are not available, except in special cases; and the development of algorithms for nondifferentiable, nonconvex optimisation is still in an early stage – see, for example, Mifflin (1976). It may seem unnatural to impose on the behaviour of public producers a requirement (ability to solve problem (9)) that could be very hard to meet. Some kind of 'bounded rationality' approach may seem more natural.

As a modest step in that direction, we note that *necessary conditions* for a solution of problem (9) are available, provided only the relevant functions be Lipschitz – see Clarke (1975, 1976). These necessary conditions define stationary points of the optimization problem. To impose that these conditions be satisfied is to impose a minimal requirement upon the behaviour of public producers. We shall verify that this requirement is consistent with general equilibrium. But we recognise that this is only a first step towards a satisfactory 'bounded rationality' approach, because public producers may typically do better than simply finding a stationary point of their profit function; they may for instance be able to find a local maximum, in which case continuity problems arise once again.

Sufficient conditions for preferences to yield Lipschitz demand functions satisfying (2) can be defined. Because these conditions are somewhat technical and may not have received a definitive formulation, we shall not reproduce them here. Instead, we shall stipulate directly in the statement of our existence theorem below that individual demand functions are locally Lipschitz. We note from Cornet and Laroque (1980) that assumptions under which unconstrained demand functions are differentiable imply that constrained demand functions satisfying (2) are Lipschitz. And we note for further reference that Lipschitz functions are almost everywhere differentiable. At points where they are not differentiable one can, following Clarke (1975, 1976), define generalised gradients.

DEFINITIONS.

(i)   The demand functions $z^h(p, q, r^h, Q)$, which associate with every point $(p, q, r^h, Q) \in \Delta \times R_+^{2m+1}$ the best element for $\succ_h$ over (2) and (4), are Lipschitz if, for every compact set B in $\Delta \times R_+^{2m+1}$, there is a constant k_B^h such that, for all (p, q, r^h, Q) and $(\hat{p}, \hat{q}, \hat{r}^h, \hat{Q})$ in B,

$$\| z^h(p, q, r^h, Q) - z^h(\hat{p}, \hat{q}, \hat{r}^h, \hat{Q}) \| \leq k_B^h \| (p, q, r^h, Q) - (\hat{p}, \hat{q}, \hat{r}^h, \hat{Q}) \|,$$

where $\| \cdot \|$ denotes the Euclidean norm.

(ii)   The generalized gradient of the Lipschitz function $f: R^n \to R$ at x, denoted $\partial f(x)$, is the convex hull of all points ζ of the form $\zeta = \lim_{s \to \infty} \nabla f(x_s)$, where $\{x_s\}$ is a sequence converging to x such that f is differentiable at each x_s and where $\nabla f(x)$ is the gradient (vector of partial derivatives) of f at x_s.

(iii)   For $C \in R^n$ convex, the normal cone to C at $x \in C$ is

$$N_C(x) = \{ w \in R^n : (x' - x)w \leq 0, \quad \forall x' \in C \}.$$

First-order necessary conditions for problem (9) can be defined by means of theorem 1 in Clarke (1976), if the decision variables are restricted to a compact convex set. For convenience, we eliminate y^e from problem (9), and solve the problem in Q^e over an arbitrary compact convex set – to be defined in section 4. To that end, define:

$$\gamma^e(p, Q^e) = \min \{ -py^e \mid (y^e, Q^e) \in Y^e \}$$
$$= \min \{ -py^e \mid y^e \in S_{Q^e}(Y^e) \}; \tag{10}$$

$$v^e(Q^e; \bar{p}, \bar{q}, \bar{r}, {}^e\bar{Q}) = \bar{q}^e \sum_h z^{he}(Q^e; \bar{p}, \bar{q}, \bar{r}^h, {}^e\bar{Q})$$
$$- \gamma^e(Q^e; \bar{p}), Q^e \in \mathrm{Pr}_{M^e}(Y^e), \quad e = 1 \ldots f. \tag{11}$$

When Y^e is convex, then γ^e is a convex function of Q^e for given p, hence a Lipschitz function of Q^e – see theorem 10.4 in Rockafellar (1970).

PROPOSITION.

If Q^{e*} maximises the Lipschitz function $v^e(Q^e; \cdot)$ over the compact convex set $Z^e \subset R_+^{m^e}$, then

$$0 \in - \partial v^e(Q^{e*}; \bar{p}, \bar{q}, \bar{r}, {}^e\bar{Q}) + N_{Z^e}(Q^{e*})$$
$$\subset - \bar{q}^e \sum_h \partial z^{he}(Q^{e*}; \bar{p}, \bar{q}, \bar{r}^h, {}^e\bar{Q}) + \partial \gamma^e(Q^{e*}; \bar{p}) + N_{Z^e}(Q^{e*}). \tag{12}$$

[The inclusion follows from proposition 8 in Clarke (1976).]

We shall then say that a budgeted allocation (a, p, q) is *a market stationary point, under price regulation*, if it satisfies conditions (5), (6) and (12). We prove in section 4 the existence of market stationary points, under price regulation, with the mild assumption that demand functions are Lipschitz. The terms 'stationary point' reflect the property that conditions (12) are not *sufficient* for (y^{e*}, Q^{e*}) to define a maximum for problem (9), not even locally.

3.4.

Applying a similar reasoning to the quantity-regulated public producer would lead us to reformulate (7) as

$$(y^e, q^e) \text{ maximise } \bar{p}y^e + q^e \sum_h z^{he}(q^e; \bar{Q}, \bar{p}, {}^e\bar{q}, \bar{r}^h)$$
$$= {}_{\text{def}} v^e(y^e, q^e; \bar{Q}, \bar{p}, {}^e\bar{q}, \bar{r}) \text{ subject to } (y^e, \bar{Q}^e) \in Y^e, \tag{13}$$

for which a necessary first-order condition is

$$0 \in -\partial v^e(y^{e*}, q^{e*}; \bar{p}, {}^e\bar{q}, \bar{r}, \bar{Q}) + N_{Z^e}(y^{e*}, q^{e*}). \tag{14}$$

Finally, for the unregulated public producer, (7) would become

$$(y^e, Q^e, q^e) \text{ maximise } py^e + q^e \sum_h z^{he}(q^e, Q^e; {}^e\bar{Q}, \bar{p}, {}^e\bar{q}, \bar{r}^h)$$
$$= {}_{\text{def}} v^e(q^e, y^e, Q^e; {}^e\bar{Q}, \bar{p}, {}^e\bar{q}, \bar{r}) \text{ subject to } (y^e, Q^e) \in Y^e, \tag{15}$$

with first-order condition

$$0 \in -\partial v^e(q^{e*}, y^{e*}, Q^{e*}; \bar{p}, {}^e\bar{q}, \bar{r}, {}^e\bar{Q}) + N_{Z^e}(q^{e*}, y^{e*}, Q^{e*}). \tag{16}$$

In both cases Z^e is an arbitrary convex set in the relevant space; and the argument for recognising the influence of q^e on z^{he} is that we want to avoid the trivial solutions $q_i = +\infty$, which could obtain if z_i^h were treated as a parameter.

4. Existence of market stationary points or equilibria, under price regulation

THEOREM. *For the economy described in section 2, if the demand functions are Lipschitz, then given any $q \in R_+^m$:*

(i)   *there exists $a \in A$ and $p \in \Delta$ such that (a, p, q) is a market stationary point, under price regulation; and*

(ii)   *when each public producer supplies a single public good, every market stationary point is a market equilibrium, under price regulation.*

PROOF

(i) The proof is an application of Kakutani's theorem.

In view of the lemma in Section 2 we may, for α and α' in R_+ sufficiently large, replace the consumption set $X^h \times R^m_+$ by the compact set $\hat{X}^h = (X^h \cap [-\alpha, \alpha]^n) \times [0, \alpha]^m$, $\forall h \in L$; replace the production set Y^g by the compact set $\hat{Y}^g = Y^g \cap [-\alpha, \alpha]^n$, $\forall g \in K$; and replace the production set Y^e by the compact set $\hat{Y}^e = Y^e \cap ([-\alpha', 0]^n \times [0, \alpha]^{m^e})$, $\forall e \in F$.

Let $Z^e = _{\text{def}} [0, \alpha]^{m^e}$, and let $\text{Pr}_{M^e}(\hat{Y}^e)$ denote the projection of Y^e on $R^{m^e}_+$, i.e. the set $\{Q^e \mid \exists \, y^e \text{ s.t.} (y^e, Q^e) \in \hat{Y}^e\}$. If $\text{Pr}_{M^e}(\hat{Y}^e) \neq Z^e$, then using the assumptions that $\hat{Y}^e$ is closed and that the demand functions are Lipschitz, we can extend $\hat{Y}^e$ to a larger set $\tilde{Y}^e$ with $\text{Pr}_{M^e}(\tilde{Y}^e) = Z^e$, in such a way that the sets of solutions to (12) on Z^e are thereby unaffected, for given $q \in R^m_+$, identically in $p \in \Delta, r \in R^l_+$ and $Q \in [0, \alpha]^m$.

To that end let $\tilde{Q}^e(Q^e)$ be the unique element in the closed convex set $\text{Pr}_{M^e}(\hat{Y}^e)$ such that

$$\| \tilde{Q}^e(Q^e) - Q^e \| \leqq \| \hat{Q}^e - Q^e \|, \text{ for all } \hat{Q}^e \in \text{Pr}_{M^e}(\hat{Y}^e).$$

We may then define, for all e in F:

$$\tilde{Y}^e = \hat{Y}^e \cup \{ (y^e, Q^e) \in R^n_- \times Z^e \mid y^e \in S_{\tilde{Q}^e(Q^e)}(\hat{Y}^e)$$
$$- \{ T \| \tilde{Q}^e(Q^e) - Q^e \| i^n \} \}, \tag{17}$$

where $i^n = (1 \ldots 1) \in R^n$ and T is a suitable constant.[9]

Then, for $p \in \Delta$,

$$\tilde{\gamma}^e(Q^e; p) = _{\text{def}} \min \{ -py^e \mid (y^e, Q^e) \in \tilde{Y}^e \}$$
$$= \gamma^e(\tilde{Q}^e(Q^e); p) + T \cdot \| \tilde{Q}^e(Q^e) - Q^e \|, Q^e \in Z^e;$$
$$\tilde{v}^e(Q^e; p, q, r, {}^eQ) = _{\text{def}} q^e \sum_h z^{he}(Q^e; p, q, r^h, {}^eQ) - \tilde{\gamma}^e(Q^e; p). \tag{18}$$

That is, we have extended $\hat{Y}^e$ in such a way that the (hypothetical) cost of an unfeasible output Q^e increases, at an arbitrarily large but finite rate T, with the distance of Q^e from the set of feasible outputs $\text{Pr}_{M^e}(\hat{Y}^e)$. By the Lipschitz property, T may be chosen such that $\partial \tilde{v}^e(Q^e; p, q, r, {}^eQ) < 0$ for

---

[9] The constant T implicitly defines α' and must be chosen so as to preserve convexity of the function $\tilde{\gamma}^e(Q^e; p)$ in (18).

all $Q^e \in Z^e \backslash \text{Pr}_{M^e}(\hat{Y}^e)$, identically in $p \in \Delta, r \in R^l_+$ and $Q \in [0,\alpha]^m$. This construction has the further property that

$$\partial \hat{\gamma}^e(Q^e; p) + N_{Z^e}(Q^e) \subset \partial \gamma^e(Q^e; p)$$
$$+ N_{\text{Pr}_{M^e}(Y^e)}(Q^e) \forall Q^e \in \text{Pr}_{M^e}(Y^e). \tag{19}$$

(See proposition 11 in Clarke (1976).) It follows that the sets of solutions to (12) are unaffected by our extension.

We shall accordingly proceed on the assumption that $\text{Pr}_{M^e}(\hat{Y}^e) = Z^e$.

In order to apply Kakutani's theorem, we define functions x^h, z^h and correspondences $\eta^g, \eta^e, \phi^e, \psi$ as follows:

Let $B = {}_{\text{def}}(\Pi_h \hat{X}^h) \times (\Pi_g \hat{Y}^g) \times (\Pi_e \hat{Y}^e) \times \Delta$, a compact set with elements b, b', etc.

For each h, let $\beta^h(b)$ be the subset of $\hat{X}^h$ satisfying (2) and (4), and let $(x^h(b), z^h(b))$ be the best point in $\beta^h(b)$ for $\succ_h$; β^h is a continuous correspondence (see the lemma in Drèze (1975)); $(x^h(b), z^h(b))$ are continuous vector-valued functions.

For each g, let

$$\eta^g(b) = \eta^g(p) = \{y^g \in \hat{Y}^g \mid py^g \geqq py \forall y \in \hat{Y}^g\}.$$

For each e, let

$$\eta^e(b) = \eta^e(p, Q^e) = \{y^e \in S_{Q^e}(\hat{Y}^e) \mid -py^e = \gamma^e(p, Q^e)\},$$
$$\phi^e(b) = \{Q^e \in R^{m^e}_+ \mid \exists \chi^e \in \partial v^e(Q^e; p, q, r, {}^eQ),$$
$$Q_i = \max[0, \min(Q_i + \chi_i, \alpha)], \forall i \in M^e\}.$$

Let

$$\psi(b) = \left\{ p \in \Delta \mid (p - p')\left(\sum_h x^h - \sum_h w^h - \sum_g y^g - \sum_e y^e \right) \geqq 0 \forall p' \in \Delta \right\};$$

the correspondences η^g, η^e, ϕ^e and ψ are nonempty, compact-valued, convex-valued and upper hemicontinuous (for ϕ^e, see propositions 1 and 7 in Clarke (1976)).

All the conditions of Kakutani's theorem being verified, the correspondence from B to B defined by $(x^h, z^h, \eta^g, \eta^e, \phi^e, \psi)$ has a fixed point – say b^*. That b^* is a market stationary point is verified as follows.

For the private goods, standard arguments imply that $p_j^* > 0 \forall j \in N$. Therefore, $b^* = (a^*, p^*)$ with $a^* \in A, p^* \in \text{int } \Delta$. This implies $Q_i^* < \alpha \forall i \in M$.

Consider the vector ϕ^{e*}. By definition, there exists $\chi^{e*} \in \partial v^e(Q^{e*} \mid p^*, q, r^*, {}^eQ^*)$ such that $\forall i \in M^e$, either $\chi_i^* = 0$, or $Q_i^* = 0$

with $\chi_i^* \leqq 0$. In both cases, $0 \in - \partial v^e(Q^{e*} \mid p^*, q, r^*, {}^eQ^*) + N_{Z^e}(Q^{e*})$, with $Q_i^* < \alpha \, \forall \, i \in M^e$, and (12) is satisfied.

(ii) There remains to show that, when M^e is a singleton, then any (y^{e*}, Q^{e*}) satisfying (12) at (p^*, q, r^*, Q^*) also solve (9) there. To that end, we remark that $v^e(Q^e; p^*, q, r^*, {}^eQ^*)$ is a concave function of $Q^e \in R_+$. Indeed, each demand function $z^{he}(Q^e; p^*, q, r^{h*}, {}^eQ^*)$ is of the form $z^{he} = \min(\zeta^{he}, Q^e)$, and $\gamma^e(Q^e; p^*)$ is a convex function of Q^e.[10]   QED

REMARK

In order to prove (i), it is not necessary to assume that Y^e is convex; it would suffice to assume that $\mathrm{Pr}_{M^e}(Y^e)$ is convex; that, for every Q^e in $\mathrm{Pr}_{M^e}(Y^e)$, the section of Y^e in $R_-^n, S_{Q^e}(Y^e)$, is convex; and that $\gamma^e(Q; \cdot)$ is Lipschitz. These assumptions are still restrictive, but they are definitely less restrictive than the convexity of Y^e. In particular, they allow for production by means of a single process with fixed relative coefficients and increasing returns to scale; but not for a mixture of several such processes.

Similar techniques could be used to prove the existence of market stationary points under quantity-regulation, or in the absence of regulation. Additional precautions are needed, however, to rule out situations where arbitrarily small quantities would be sold at arbitrarily large prices.

The interpretation of the conditions (12) defining the supply of public goods under price regulation is straightforward. If the individual demand functions z^h and the cost function γ^e are differentiable at b^* (implying $Q_i > 0, \forall \, i \in M^e$), then (12) reduces to

$$q^e \sum_h \frac{\partial z^{he}}{\partial Q_i} = \frac{\partial \gamma^e}{\partial Q_i}, \quad \forall \, i \in M^e. \tag{20}$$

These conditions assert that the marginal cost of each public good is equal to the marginal revenue associated with its production. At a point of differentiability, either $z_i^h < Q_i$, in which case $\partial z^{he}/\partial Q_i = 0$; or $z_i^h = Q_i$, in which case $\partial z_i^h/\partial Q_i = 1$ and $\partial z_j^h/\partial Q_i$ is arbitrary as to sign (being equal to zero when $z_j^h = Q_j$). Total differentiation of (20) could then yield the partial derivatives of the supply of public goods with respect to their own prices, to the prices of private goods and to the individual incomes. More generally, however, one must recognise the possibility that demand or cost functions may fail to be differentiable. The equality (20) among partial

---

[10] Of course, a simple existence proof can be presented directly for this special case.

derivatives is then replaced by an inclusion relation among generalised gradients. Although the interpretation is basically unchanged, total differentiation is no longer well defined, and another approach should (and undoubtedly could) be devised to study the dependence of public good supply on their own prices and on other parameters.

5. Some efficiency considerations

Leaving aside questions of incentives and of technological efficiency, the best institutional arrangements for the provision of public goods with exclusion is a public monopoly operating without a budget constraint and financing its deficit by means of lump-sum taxes. Such a monopoly may indeed choose public good prices low enough to generate from each consumer a demand equal to the entire supply – for instance zero price. A Pareto optimum may then be achieved, but the 'exclusion' feature is lost. In order to obtain more relevant and more interesting results, one must introduce a budget constraint and resort to a second-best optimum. The presence of a budget constraint is probably the main reason why a public agency would price public goods in the first place.

The rules of behaviour of a public monopoly aiming at welfare maximisation under a budget constraint will depend upon the degree of sophistication with which the welfare objective is pursued. In a refined analysis, where the effects of the supply and pricing of public goods on private goods prices and consumer incomes are taken into account, rather complex – and unrealistic – rules of behaviour emerge. When these indirect effects are ignored, the rules of behavior are easier to understand and less unrealistic.[11] A simple formulation of the second-best Pareto-optimisation problem for producer e[12] is the following:

$$\max_{q^e, Q^e} \sum_h \lambda^h U^h(x^h, z^h) \text{ subject to } q^e \sum_h z^{he}(q^e, Q^e; p, {}^eq, r^h, {}^eQ)$$

$$- \gamma^e(Q^e; p) \geqq t^e, \tag{21}$$

where

U^h is a utility function representing the preferences of consumer h,
λ^h is a weight assigned to consumer h, to be eliminated from the efficiency conditions,

[11] Similar comments were made in section 3 regarding the degree of sophistication with which the profit-maximisation objective is pursued.

[12] The additional complexities of a simultaneous analysis for several public producers are illustrated in Boiteux (1956).

(x^h, z^h) are functions of (p, q, Q, r^h), and
t^e is a preassigned budget.

The prices p of private goods, the incomes r^h, and the prices and quantities of the remaining public goods $(^e q, {^e Q})$ are treated as parameters.

For ease of interpretation, first-order conditions will be stated at a point of differentiability; under the further assumption that the public monopoly accepts the prevailing income distribution and does not itself attempt to correct it, the weights λ^h may be eliminated, and the first-order efficiency conditions may be written as follows:

$$\sum_h [(1 - v^e) \pi^{he} + v^e q^e] \frac{\partial z^{he}}{\partial Q^e} = \frac{\partial \gamma^e}{\partial Q^e}, \tag{22}$$

$$\sum_h \left(v^e z^{he} + q^e \frac{\partial z^{he}}{\partial q^e} \right) = 0, \tag{23}$$

where v^e is a parameter set at the smallest value in $(0, 1)$ such that the budget constraint is satisfied, and where π^h is the vector of marginal rates of substitution between public goods and income, measuring the marginal willingness to pay for public goods, of consumer h. Of course, $\pi^h \geqq q$; $\pi_i^h = q_i$ whenever $z_i^h < Q_i$; and $z_i^h = Q_i$ whenever $\pi_i^h > q_i, i = 1 \ldots m$.

The interpretation of conditions (22) and (23) is quite straightforward. If the budget constraint were not binding (t^e large negative), then $v^e = 0$ and a first-best solution in (22)–(23) is given by $z^{he} = Q^e, \forall h$,

$$\frac{\partial \gamma^e}{\partial Q^e} = \sum_h \pi^{he} \frac{\partial z^{he}}{\partial Q^e} = \sum_h \pi^{he}.$$

Every consumer buys the whole supply of public goods; and each public good is produced in such a quantity that its marginal cost is equal to the sum over all consumers of their marginal willingness to pay for it (i.e. the so-called 'Lindahl–Samuelson' conditions are satisfied).

At the other extreme, if the public monopoly could only meet its budget constraint by maximising profits, then $v^e = 1$ and the solution to (22)–(23) is the same as that which would prevail under an unregulated private monopoly: Prices of public goods are set at such levels that marginal revenue is equal to zero; and quantities of public goods are such that marginal revenue (measured in terms of q^e, not of π^{he}) is equal to marginal cost.

Between these two extremes we find intermediate solutions. Thus, in (23) with $1 > v^e > 0$, marginal revenues are set equal to zero after 'inflating' the price elasticities by a factor $1/v^e$; in (22), marginal revenues and marginal willingnesses to pay are combined (in the proportions v^e and $1 - v^e$, respectively).

The information required to implement these conditions is substantial, but not unreasonable. It combines the information needed for welfare maximization, namely the vectors π^{he}; and the information needed for profit maximization, namely the demand derivatives $\{\partial z^{he}/\partial Q^e, \partial z^{he}/\partial q^e\}$. In addition, the parameter v^e must be evaluated somehow – probably by trial and error. The general picture is reminiscent of that obtained for telephone services, where the quality of service obeys a 'public good' condition like (22) whereas tariffs geared to a budget constraint obey conditions like (23) – see, for example, Marchand (1973) or Deschamps (1976). The telephone industry also offers a good illustration of the difficulties associated with implementation of these formulae.

In the case of regulated private monopolies, price regulation would lead to quantities set according to formula (22) with $v^e = 1$, i.e. according to formula (20); and quantity regulation would lead to prices set according to formula (23) with $v^e = 1$.

In the special case where each public producer supplies a single commodity, under price regulation, we may conclude from (20) and (22) that output of each public good is generically less than the output required for Pareto efficiency, at the given prices q. This is so because

$$\frac{\partial z_i^h}{\partial Q_i} \geqq 0 \text{ and } \pi_i^h \geqq q_i,$$

as remarked earlier. Consequently,

$$\frac{\partial \gamma^e}{\partial Q_i} = q_i \sum_h \frac{\partial z_i^h}{\partial Q_i} \leqq \sum_h [(1 - v^e) \pi^{he} + v^e q^e] \frac{\partial z^{he}}{\partial Q^e}, \qquad (24)$$

identically in $v^e < 1$, with equality obtaining only in the limiting case where $\pi_i^h = q_i$ for all h such that $\partial z_i^h/\partial Q_i = 1 > 0$. The willingness of consumers to pay for an additional unit of public good generically exceeds the marginal cost of that unit. Output geared to equality of marginal cost and marginal revenue is inefficient by default, never by excess.

An interesting question concerns the regulation mechanism. Thus, under price regulation, what levels should be chosen for the public good prices q^e, given that quantities will be determined by formula (20)? Two remarks are in order here. *First*, a satisfactory answer to that question requires knowledge of the way in which the supply of public goods Q^e will react to the prices q^e. This is the question raised – but not answered – at the end of Section 4. *Second*, a realistic view of the problem must again reckon with a budget constraint, that is with the possibility that a private producer would discontinue its operation (set $Q^e = 0$) if it could not obtain a satisfactory profit level at the imposed prices q^e.

If the regulatory agency ignores the influence of public good prices on the supply of public goods, but recognizes that prices must be high enough to guarantee a given level of profits to the private monopoly, then prices will be set according to formula (23), with v^e taking the smallest value in (0, 1) such that the required profit level is attained, when quantities are determined by (20), i.e. by (22) with $v^e = 1$.

Similarly, an agency setting quantities would apply formula (22), and the private monopoly would set prices according to formula (23) with $v^e = 1$. Although these solutions are not 'optimal', they would seem to provide reasonable, realistic goals. Note that under price regulation the only information required consists in the price elasticities of demand, and the parameter v^e. Under quantity regulation, the required information bears on willingness to pay for public goods, on quantity elasticities of demand, and on v^e. (The need to collect information about willingness to pay for public goods may be regarded as a drawback of quantity regulation.)

From the foregoing discussions it seems safe to conclude that a public monopoly could be more efficient than a regulated private monopoly, and a regulated private monopoly could be more efficient than an unregulated private monopoly. The reasoning is simply that under the more efficient arrangement it is possible to bring about exactly the same solution as under the less efficient one, but it is also possible to do better. This conclusion is hardly surprising. More interesting would be a comparison of the efficiency levels achievable under price regulation and quantity regulation, respectively. Such a comparison is of a global, not of a local nature and therefore difficult to make. Even locally (say for small departures from either the public monopoly solution or the unregulated private monopoly solution), the comparison is difficult because it involves the response of public good supply to a change in their prices, under price regulation; or the response of public good prices to a change in their quantities, under quantity regulation. We must again conclude to the need of further research on these topics.

Appendix

A.1. Example of preferences yielding nonconcave constrained demand functions

There is a single private good, with price $p = 1$. There are two public goods, with prices $q_1 = 1$ and $q_2 = \frac{1}{2}$. The preferences of consumer h (superscript omitted) are representable by the strictly quasiconcave utility function

$$u = \tfrac{1}{2}x + \min\{\sqrt{z_1} + \sqrt{z_2}, \tfrac{1}{3}(\sqrt{z_1} + \sqrt{z_2} + 2)\}. \tag{A.1}$$

Maximising u subject to

$$x + z_1 + \tfrac{1}{2}z_2 \leqq r, z_1 \leqq Q_1, z_2 \leqq Q_2, \tag{A.2}$$

yields the solutions given in table A.1 for alternative values of Q_1 and Q_2.

Table A.1

$Q = (Q_1, Q_2)$	$z = (z_1, z_2)$	$qz = z_1 + (z_2/2)$
$(1, 0)$	$(1, 0)$	1
$(0, 1)$	$(0, 1)$	$\frac{1}{2}$
$(\frac{1}{2}, \frac{1}{2})$	$(\frac{1}{9}, \frac{4}{9})$	$\frac{1}{3}$

A.2. Example of an economy for which a market equilibrium may fail to exist

In order to simplify exposition and aid intuition, we use utility functions which are not *strictly* quasiconcave and increasing. There is no difficulty in extending the example to strictly convex and monotone preferences.

There are two private goods, with prices $p_1 \geqq 0$ and $p_2 = 1 - p_1 \geqq 0$. There are two public goods, with prices $q_1 = 1$ and $q_2 = \frac{1}{2}$. There are two consumers, g and h. Their preferences are representable by the concave utility functions:

$$u^h = \tfrac{1}{2}\min(x_1^h, x_2^h) + \min\{\sqrt{z_1^h} + \sqrt{z_2^h}, \tfrac{1}{3}(\sqrt{z_1^h} + \sqrt{z_2^h} + 2)\},$$

$$u^g = \min(x_1^g + 4x_2^g, 4x_1^g + x_2^g). \tag{A.3}$$

The initial resources are defined by $w_1^h = w_2^h = w_1^g = w_2^g = 2$.

There are no private producers. There is a single public producer (superscript omitted) with production set

$$Y = \{y, Q \mid y_1 + Q_1 \leqq 0, y_2 + Q_2 \leqq 0\}. \tag{A.4}$$

The profits of the public producer belong to consumer h (i.e. $\theta_h = 1, \theta_g = 0$).

The preferences of consumer h and the production technology imply that profits are maximised at the point $Q = (1,0) = -y$ when $p_1 \leq \frac{3}{4}$; at the point $Q' = (0,1) = -y'$ when $p_1 \geq \frac{3}{4}$. The preferences of consumer h also imply $x_1^h = x_2^h$ identically in p. Under these conditions, and given the levels of initial resources, physical feasibility requires $x_1^g = x_2^g - 1$ if $p_1 \leq \frac{3}{4}$ and $x_1^g = x_2^g + 1$ when $p_1 \geq \frac{3}{4}$. But equilibrium of consumer g requires $p_1 = \frac{4}{5}$ when $x_1^g = x_2^g - 1 > 0$ and $p_1 = \frac{1}{3}$ when $x_1^g = x_2^g + 1 > 1$. Accordingly, no market equilibrium exists at the assumed prices q.

In this particular example, market equilibria will exist at other prices q — like $q_1 = q_2 = 1$. Trivial equilibria will always exist at $q = 0, Q = 0$. We have not attempted to construct an example where only trivial equilibria exist.

8 Second-best analysis with markets in disequilibrium: public sector pricing in a Keynesian regime*

1. Introduction

In second-best models, attention is typically focussed on a particular source of departure from economic efficiency (like taxes, a budget constraint, monopoly power, an externality, incomplete markets ...).[1] The analysis aims at defining optimal policies to cope with this source of inefficiency. It is usually assumed that the economy is otherwise competitive. This makes the problem well defined, and amenable to analysis with the powerful tools of microeconomics and general equilibrium theory. In some cases, this assumption is justified. In other cases, it is clearly inappropriate, as when imperfect competition or quantity rationing (especially of labour supply) prevail. The practical problems of defining second-best public policies in an environment where prices do not reflect economic scarcities are particularly challenging in Western Europe today.[2]

* In *The Performance of Public Enterprises: Concepts and Measurements*, M. Marchand, P. Pestieau and H. Tulkens, eds. (North-Holland, 1984); and in *European Economic Review*, 29, 3, pp. 263–301. This is a revised version of a paper prepared for the Symposium on 'Price and Quantity Controls' held in New Delhi, February 1981, on the occasion of the Golden Jubilee of the Indian Statistical Institute and presented at the Conference on the Concept and the Measurement of the Performance of Public Enterprises held at Université de Liège in September 1982. I have benefited from constructive suggestions by Paul Champsaur, V. K. Chetty, Jean P. Drèze, Maurice Marchand, Knud Munk, Pierre Pestieau and Henry Tulkens; and I am particularly indebted to Christophe Chamley and Roger Guesnerie for pointing out deficiencies in the earlier version and suggesting improvements. Responsibility for remaining errors is entirely mine. This work is part of Projet d'Action Concertée on 'Applications of Economic Decisions Theory' sponsored by the Belgian Government under contract no 80/85–12.

[1] See e.g. Guesnerie (1975a) for a survey and references.
[2] See Dermine and Drèze (1981) for an example.

To some extent, macroeconomic theory is concerned with welfare-improving public policies in non-competitive environments. And recent contributions have developed some links between macroeconomics and general equilibrium theory.[3] These developments are conducive to sharper statements of welfare objectives in macroeconomic analysis.

A beginning has also been made at extending the traditional second-best methodology to more general assumptions about the regime prevailing in the rest of the economy; see Bronsard and Wagneur (1982), Jean P. Drèze (1982), Picard (1982) or Roberts (1982).[4] Obviously, concepts are now available to pose well-defined problems, tools and techniques are available to analyse them.

The present paper studies a simple and well-known problem, namely second-best pricing by a public sector operating under a binding budget constraint;[5] the private sector is not assumed to be in competitive equilibrium, but rather in a regime of Keynesian underemployment (excess supply of labour and of commodities, quantity rationing). The purpose of the paper is twofold. First, I wished to investigate the possibility of defining operational policies, and the nature of economic information required to implement them. (Operational implementation has been of less concern in the references given above.) Second, I wished to investigate whether and how elements of both microeconomic and macroeconomic reasoning fitted into the definition of such policies.

For the simple problem under discussion, these two questions were answered unequivocally. Operational rules can be defined, both for second-best policies and locally for welfare-improving policies. In special cases, they are even relatively simple. In general, they tend to be complex, but not more complex than similar rules in otherwise competitive environments. The informational requirements are different, however. On the one hand, welfare analysis involves reservation prices, which differ from market prices when there is quantity rationing. Reservation prices are not directly observable from market data. On the other hand, the welfare implications of price adjustments cannot be retrieved from supply and demand functions alone. Multiplier effects through aggregate income and employment must be assessed as well. General equilibrium macroeconomic model building appears indispensable for second-best analysis.

---

[3] See e.g. Malinvaud (1977) or the survey paper by Drazen (1980).

[4] A complementary problem has also been treated recently by Guesnerie and Roberts (1984), namely the role of quantity constraints as instruments towards achieving second-best optimality; an example of this role is found in Section 3 below.

[5] See Boiteux (1956), Drèze (1964), pp. 27–34, or Drèze and Marchand (1976) for the neoclassical treatment of the problem.

This brings me to the second question. It was revealing for me to discover progressively how these macroeconomic multiplier effects emerged naturally from the general equilibrium analysis of the reactions by individual agents. There was no need to introduce elements of macroeconomic reasoning specifically, as they were definitely present to start with. In this context, the quest for microeconomic foundations of macroeconomics is replaced by the discovery of macroeconomic implications of microeconomics!

These answers to my two queries seemed sufficiently instructive to justify presentation of a very simple analysis. The model and main result are contained in Section 3, methodological conclusions are given in Section 5. These two sections are self-contained, and form the core of the paper. Section 2 restates the neo-classical analysis of Boiteux [1956]. Additional results and elements of comparison are presented in Section 4.

2. The Boiteux model

2.1.

Boiteux (1956) considers the problem of optimal pricing policies for a public firm, or public sector, operating under a budget constraint.[6] In order to facilitate comparisons with the next section, I specialise his model to the case of a single type of labour. There are l physical commodities, indexed $i = 1, \ldots, l$ with prices $p = (p_1, \ldots, p_l)$. The price of labour is w, and serves as a numeraire (w is fixed).

There are m households, indexed $h = 1, \ldots, m$. Household h consumes a vector x^h in R^l and supplies a quantity of labour l^h in R_+. Its preferences are represented by the strongly quasi-concave, twice continuously differentiable utility function $U^h(x^h, l^h)$. The budget constraint of household h is

$$px^h \leqslant r^h + wl^h, \tag{2.1}$$

where r^h is an 'income' resulting from transfers and shares in private profits. It is convenient to represent household preferences by means of the indirect utility function $V^h(p, w, r^h)$, written simply as $V^h(p, r^h)$ under

---

[6] The motivation for the work of Boiteux came from the problem of defining pricing policies in a nationalised firm, the French railroads, operating under increasing returns to scale. A first-best optimum, with prices equal to marginal costs, would result in a budget deficit, to be covered by taxes. The budget constraint is supposed to provide incentives for cost minimisation. See Drèze [1964], pp. 27–8, for a brief review of the issues and a few references. The same analysis applies when the budget constraint arises from the need to finance the production of public goods; see Drèze and Marchand (1976).

fixed w, and defined by

$$V^h(p, r^h) = \max_{x^h, l^h} [U^h(x^h, l^h) \mid px^h = r^h + wl^h]. \tag{2.2}$$

In (2.2), the budget constraint is written as an equality, reflecting a monotonicity assumption. The indirect utility function is then endowed with the useful property

$$\frac{\partial V^h}{\partial p} \Big/ \frac{\partial V^h}{\partial r^h} = -x^h = \frac{\partial r^h}{\partial p}\bigg|_{V^h}. \tag{2.3}$$

See Roy (1942) or Phlips (1974) for details.

The commodity demand and labour supply functions implied by (2.2) are denoted $x^h(p, r^h)$, $l^h(p, r^h)$ respectively, and assumed differentiable for convenience.[7]

There are n private firms, indexed $j = 1, \ldots, n$. Firm j produces a vector of commodities y^j in R^l, using a quantity of labour l^j in R_+. Its technology is defined by a strongly convex production set $Y^j \subset R^l \times R_+$, containing the origin. The efficient boundary of that set is implicitly defined by a differentiable, convex function expressing the minimal labour requirement l^j as a function of the output vector y^j, namely $l^j(y^j)$. The profits of firm j are

$$\Pi^j = py^j - wl^j(y^j). \tag{2.4}$$

Profit maximisation at given prices defines the supply functions $y^j(p)$ and the labour demand function $l^j(y^j(p)) = l^j(p)$. They are assumed differentiable[7] and satisfy

$$p\frac{\partial y^j}{\partial p} - w\frac{\partial l^j}{\partial p} = 0. \tag{2.5}$$

The public sector produces a vector of commodities z in R^l, using a quantity of labour l^z in R_+. No convexity assumption is made on the production set of the public sector. The efficient boundary of that set is implicitly defined by the differentiable function $l^z(z)$ defining the minimal labour requirement l^z as a function of the output vector z.

The public sector is subject to the budget constraint

$$\Phi =_{\text{def}} pz - wl^z(z) \geq b, \tag{2.6}$$

where b is some given number.

---

[7] See the comments on this assumption in Section 4.3.

The model is closed by imposing the market clearing conditions

$$\sum_h x^h(p, r^h) - \sum_j y^j(p) - z \leqslant 0 \qquad (2.7)$$

$$\sum_h l^h(p, r^h) - \sum_j l^j(p) - l^z(z) = 0 \qquad (2.8)$$

and by relating the household incomes to profits in the private firms and the public sector. Note that conditions (2.7)–(2.8) imply by aggregation

$$\sum_h r^h - \sum_j (py^j - wl^j) - (pz - wl^z) \leqslant 0. \qquad (2.9)$$

In a private ownership economy, business profits are redistributed to households according to given ownership fractions $\theta^{hj} \geqslant 0$, $h = 1, \ldots, m$, $j = 1, \ldots, n$, satisfying $\sum_h \theta^{hj} = 1$ for all j. It is natural to specify similarly that the public budget (positive or negative) is shared among households according to given fractions β^h, $\sum_h \beta^h = 1$. One may think of β^h as defining the marginal share of household h in the public budget; indeed, it would make no difference to the analysis if the contribution of household h were defined as $b_0^h + \beta^h(pz - wl^z - b_0)$ where $b_0 = \sum_h b_0^h$ is some arbitrary number.

On this basis, r^h is defined by

$$r^h = \sum_j \theta^{hj}[py^j(p) - wl^j(p)] + \beta^h[pz - wl^z(z)], \quad h = 1, \ldots, m.$$
$$(2.10)$$

Adding the conditions (2.10) over h yields (2.9). Also when the conditions (2.7) hold with equality, then (2.7) and (2.10) together imply (2.8) – as could be expected from Walras' law.

The problem of defining a Pareto-optimal public policy may then be stated as

(P1) $\max\limits_{p,z} \sum_h \lambda^h V^h(p, r^h)$ subject to (2.6), (2.7) and (2.10)

where the non-negative vector $\lambda = (\lambda^1, \ldots, \lambda^m)$ reflects distributive goals (together with some chosen representation of household preferences in the functions V^h).

2.2

First-order necessary conditions for problem (P1) are summarized in the following:

PROPOSITION 1

At an interior solution of Problem (P1), there exists a multiplier $\rho \geqslant 0$, such that

$$\sum_h \lambda^h \frac{\partial V^h}{\partial r^h}\left[x^h - \sum_j \theta^{hj}\frac{d\Pi^j}{dp} - \beta^h\frac{d\Phi}{dp}\right] = \rho\frac{d\Phi}{dp}, \tag{2.11}$$

where $\dfrac{d\Pi^j}{dp} = y^j$ *and*

$$\frac{d\Phi}{dp} = \frac{z + \left(p - w\frac{\partial l^z}{\partial z}\right)\left[\sum_h\left(\frac{\partial x^h}{\partial p} + \frac{\partial x^h}{\partial r^h}\sum_j\theta^{hj}y^j\right) - \sum_j\frac{\partial y^j}{\partial p}\right]}{1 - \left(p - w\frac{\partial l^z}{\partial z}\right)\sum_h\beta^h\frac{\partial x^h}{\partial r^h}}; \tag{2.12}$$

if $\Phi > b$ at the solution, then $\rho = 0$.

PROOF

Substituting from (2.10) for r^h in the maximand, the Lagrangean of problem (P1) is

$$\Lambda = \sum_h \lambda^h V^h(p, \sum_j \theta^{hj}(py^j(p) - wl^j(p)) + \beta^h(pz - wl^z(z)))$$

$$- \mu(\sum_h x^h(p, \sum_j \theta^{hj}(py^j(p) - wl^j(p)) + \beta^h(pz - wl^z(z))) - \sum_j(y^j(p)) - z)$$

$$- \rho(b - pz - wl^z(z)). \tag{2.13}$$

The first-order conditions are – using (2.3) and (2.5) –

$$\frac{\partial \Lambda}{\partial p} = \sum_h \lambda^h \frac{\partial V^h}{\partial r^h}(-x^h + \sum_j \theta^{hj}y^j + \beta^h z)$$

$$- \mu\left[\sum_h\left(\frac{\partial x^h}{\partial p} + \frac{\partial x^h}{\partial r^h}(\sum_j \theta^{hj}y^j + \beta^h z)\right) - \sum_j\frac{\partial y^j}{\partial p}\right] + \rho z = 0; \tag{2.14}$$

$$\frac{\partial \Lambda}{\partial z} = \sum_h \lambda^h \frac{\partial V^h}{\partial r^h}\beta^h\left(p - w\frac{\partial l^z}{\partial z}\right)$$

$$+ \mu\left[1 - \sum_h \frac{\partial x^h}{\partial r^h}\beta^h\left(p - w\frac{\partial l^z}{\partial z}\right)\right] + \rho\left(p - w\frac{\partial l^z}{\partial z}\right) = 0. \tag{2.15}$$

Conditions (2.15) can be solved explicitly for

$$
\mu = - \frac{\left[\sum_h \lambda^h \frac{\partial V^h}{\partial r^h} \beta^h + \rho\right]\left(p - w\frac{\partial l^z}{\partial z}\right)}{1 - \left(p - w\frac{\partial l^z}{\partial z}\right)\sum_h \beta^h \frac{\partial x^h}{\partial r^h}}.
\tag{2.16}
$$

Substituting from (2.16) into (2.14) and collecting terms yields

$$
\sum_h \lambda^h \frac{\partial V^h}{\partial r^h}\left(x^h - \sum_j \theta^{hj}y^j\right) = z\left[\rho + \sum_h \beta^h\left(\lambda^h \frac{\partial V^h}{\partial r^h} - \mu\frac{\partial x^h}{\partial r^h}\right)\right]
$$

$$
- \mu\left[\sum_h\left(\frac{\partial x^h}{\partial p} + \frac{\partial x^h}{\partial r^h}\sum_j \theta^{hj}y^j\right) - \sum_j \frac{\partial y^j}{\partial p}\right]
$$

$$
= \frac{\left[\sum_h \lambda^h \frac{\partial V^h}{\partial r^h} \beta^h + \rho\right]\left[z + \left(p - w\frac{\partial l^z}{\partial z}\right)\left(\sum_h \frac{\partial x^h}{\partial p} + \sum_h \frac{\partial x^h}{\partial r^h}\sum_j \theta^{hj}y^j - \sum_j \frac{\partial y^j}{\partial p}\right)\right]}{1 - \left(p - w\frac{\partial l^z}{\partial z}\right)\sum_h \beta^h \frac{\partial x^h}{\partial r^h}},
\tag{2.17}
$$

which is the same as (2.11)–(2.12). That $\rho = 0$ when $\Phi > b$ at the solution reflects complementary slackness.   QED

When the budget constraint of the public sector is not binding ($\rho = 0$), the left-hand side of (2.11) should be equal to zero. These conditions then state that the net effect on the real income of households of a small change in p should vanish, when real incomes are weighted by the terms $\lambda^h \partial V^h/\partial r^h$ reflecting distributive goals. Indeed, a change in p affects the real income of household h directly through the price level – a unit increase in p_i being equivalent to a loss of nominal income in the amount x_i^h – and indirectly through the 'property and transfer income' $\sum_j \theta^{hj}\Pi^j + \beta^h\Phi$. The effects of a change in p on Π^j and on Φ are asymmetrical, because $p - w\,\partial l^j/\partial y^j = 0$ for all j. It is noteworthy that the effect of a change in p on Φ in (2.12) is a 'final' effect, taking into account the income effects through the Π^j's (in the numerator) and the multiplier effect through Φ itself (via the denominator).[8]

When $\rho = 0$, conditions (2.11) depart from marginal cost pricing on distributive grounds alone. Indeed, if the weights $\lambda^h \partial V^h / \partial r^h$ were equal, reflecting a form of endorsement of the resulting income distribution,[9] then (2.11) would reduce to

$$\sum_h x^h - \sum_j y^j - \frac{d\Phi}{dp} = z - \frac{d\Phi}{dp} = 0. \tag{2.18}$$

Setting $p = w \, \partial l^z / \partial z$ in (2.12) would entail $d\Phi/dp = z$, satisfying (2.18).

When the budget constraint of the public sector is binding ($\rho > 0$), conditions (2.11) assert that the (marginal) costs to households of an increase in p (as measured by the left-hand side) should be proportional to the (marginal) benefits to the public sector, $d\Phi/dp$; the factor of proportionality (ρ) being adjusted so as to satisfy the constraint.[10]

2.3.

When lump-sum transfers of income among households are introduced as a policy option in problem (P1), first-order conditions are simplified on two grounds. First, distributive goals are pursued through transfers, so that first-order conditions are freed from that aspect. Second, the transfers implicitly redistribute all business profits as well as the public budget. As a consequence, the income effects associated with private

---

[8] This multiplier effect is not mentioned in the literature, because conditions (2.11) may be stated alternatively as

$$\sum_h \lambda^h \frac{\partial V^h}{\partial r^h} \left(x^h - \sum_j \theta^{hj} \frac{d\Pi^j}{dp} \right) = \hat{\rho} \frac{d\Phi}{dp}$$

with

$$\hat{\rho} = \left(\sum_h \lambda^h \frac{\partial V^h}{\partial r^h} \beta^h + \rho \right) \Big/ \left[1 - \left(p - w \frac{\partial l^z}{\partial z} \right) \sum_h \beta^h \frac{\partial x^h}{\partial r^h} \right].$$

When interest is centred on situations where the budget constraint is binding, it suffices to find $\hat{\rho}$ such that $\Phi = b$.

[9] The endorsement consists in not favouring further transfers of consumption, under unchanged production levels; as distinct from transfers of disposable incomes, which would affect demand, hence production and prices.

[10] It is readily verified that formula (2.11) is the same as formula (5.21) in Drèze and Marchand (1976), where the Boiteux results using lump-sum transfers are also recorded. The cost-benefit interpretation of second-best results is stressed and discussed in Jean P. Drèze (1982).

profits and the multiplier effects associated with the public budget no longer appear in the first-order conditions, but the price derivatives $\partial x^h/\partial p$ are replaced by the *compensated* price derivatives $\partial x^h/\partial p + x^h \, \partial x^h/\partial r^h =_{\text{def}} \partial \hat{x}^h/\partial p$.

Denoting the transfers by t^h, $h = 1, \dots, m$, the new problem is:

(P2) $\displaystyle \max_{p, z, t^h} \sum_h \lambda^h V^h(p, r^h + t^h)$

subject to (2.6), (2.7), (2.10) and

$$\sum_h t^h = 0 \qquad (\tau). \tag{2.19}$$

PROPOSITION 2

At an interior solution of problem (P2), there exists a multiplier $\hat{\rho} \geqslant 0$ such that

$$x - \frac{d\Pi}{dp} - \frac{d\hat{\Phi}}{dp} = \hat{\rho} \frac{d\hat{\Phi}}{dp}, \tag{2.20}$$

where $\dfrac{d\hat{\Phi}}{dp} = z + \left(p - w \dfrac{\partial l^z}{\partial z} \right) \dfrac{\partial \hat{z}}{\partial p}$; *if* $\Phi > b$ *at the solution, then* $\hat{\rho} = 0$.

PROOF

The first-order conditions (2.14)–(2.15) of problem (P1) are not modified by the addition of constraints (2.19). The first-order condition for t^h is

$$\frac{\partial \Lambda}{\partial t^h} = \lambda^h \frac{\partial V^h}{\partial r^h} - \mu \frac{\partial x^h}{\partial r^h} - \tau = 0. \tag{2.21}$$

(Note that $\tau > 0$ by monotonicity of preferences.)

Substituting from (2.21) into (2.15), then into (2.14), yields

$$\frac{\partial \Lambda}{\partial z} = (\tau + \rho)\left(p - w \frac{\partial l^z}{\partial z} \right) + \mu = 0, \quad \mu = -(\tau + \rho)\left(p - w \frac{\partial l^z}{\partial z} \right);$$

$$\tag{2.22}$$

$$\frac{\partial \Lambda}{\partial p} = -\sum_h \lambda^h \frac{\partial V^h}{\partial r^h} x^h + \tau x - \mu\left(\sum_h \frac{\partial x^h}{\partial p} - \sum_j \frac{\partial y^j}{\partial p}\right) + \rho z = 0$$

$$= -\left(\tau x + \mu \sum_h \frac{\partial x^h}{\partial r^h} x^h\right) + \tau x - \mu\left(\sum_h \frac{\partial x^h}{\partial p} - \sum_j \frac{\partial y^j}{\partial p}\right) + \rho z$$

$$= (\tau + \rho)\left(p - w\frac{\partial l^z}{\partial z}\right)\left[\sum_h \left(\frac{\partial x^h}{\partial p} + x^h \frac{\partial x^h}{\partial r^h}\right) - \sum_j \frac{\partial y^j}{\partial p}\right] + \rho z = 0.$$
$$(2.23)$$

Noting that $x - \dfrac{d\Pi}{dp} = x - y = z$, this last condition is equivalent to (2.20) with $\hat{\rho} = \rho/\tau$, under the obvious definition of $\partial \hat{z}/\partial p$. That $\rho = 0$ when $\Phi > b$ at the solution reflects complementary slackness.   QED

An alternative statement of conditions (2.20), after cancelling z between $x - d\Pi/dp$ and $d\hat{\Phi}/dp$, is

$$-\left(p - w\frac{\partial l^z}{\partial z}\right)\frac{\partial \hat{z}}{\partial p} = \hat{\rho}\frac{d\hat{\Phi}}{dp}.$$
$$(2.20')$$

The left-hand side of (2.20') measures the *cost* to households of a *compensated* change in p, account being taken of the fact that the compensation (x) is paid out of private profits ($d\Pi/dp$) and the part of the public budget reflecting the direct effect of the price change (z). That cost is then simply minus the change in Φ net of the direct effect of the price change, i.e. *the cost is minus the change in household incomes net of the compensation*. This seems to provide a slightly contrived, but still natural, interpretation of proposition 2 in cost-benefit terms.

2.4.

More recently, welfare economists have become interested in the related problem of defining, for an arbitrary initial position satisfying all the constraints, *directions of policy adjustments*, along which infinitesimal moves are *welfare improving*, see in particular Guesnerie (1977) and Guesnerie and Tirole (1981), where this problem is labelled 'the reform problem'.

In the case of problem (P1) the reform problem is easily stated: find dp such that

$$\Phi + \frac{d\Phi}{dp}dp \geqslant b,$$
$$(2.24)$$

$$\sum_h \lambda^h \frac{\partial V^h}{\partial r^h}\left(x^h - \sum_j \theta^{hj}y^j - \beta^h\frac{d\Phi}{dp}\right)dp < 0. \tag{2.25}$$

Condition (2.24) corresponds to budgetary feasibility and condition (2.25) to welfare improvement. Technological feasibility is not an issue here, because the marginal cost of the change in z associated with dp is included in the term $(d\Phi/dp)dp$.

If $\Phi > b$ at the initial position, then condition (2.24) is redundant. For each $i = 1, \ldots, l$, considered separately, one may ascertain the sign of

$$\sum_h \lambda^h \frac{\partial V^h}{\partial r^h}\left(x_i^h - \sum_j \theta^{hj}y_i^j - \beta\frac{d\Phi}{dp_i}\right) =_{\text{def}} -\frac{d\Lambda}{dp_i}. \tag{2.26}$$

If these terms are equal to zero for all i, the initial position is an optimum. Otherwise, directions of welfare improvement are readily identified (choose dp_i with a sign opposite to that of $-d\Lambda/dp_i$).

If $\Phi = b$ at the initial position, then attention is restricted to adjustments dp such that $(d\Phi/dp)dp \geq 0$. Directions of welfare improvement are again readily identified, unless the terms (2.26) were collinear with $d\Phi/dp$, in which case the initial position is an optimum.

A direction of welfare improvement is naturally interpreted as a direction along which the cost to households of price inflation $x^h\,dp$ is more than offset by the income effect $\left(\sum_j \theta^{hj}y^j + \beta^h\,d\Phi/dp\right)dp$, on the (weighted) average; i.e. the change in income is more than sufficient to permit an unchanged consumption, at the new prices.

When $\Phi = b$ and $(d\Phi/dp)dp = 0$ along a direction of welfare improvement, then the cost to households of price inflation should be more than offset by the income effect through private profits. If distributional aspects were neglected, the condition for welfare improvement would reduce to

$$\left(\sum_h x^h - \sum_j y^j\right)dp = zdp < 0. \tag{2.27}$$

Since $d\Phi/dp \propto z + (p - w\,\partial l^z/\partial z)\,dz/dp$, the conditions $(d\Phi/dp)dp = 0$ and $z\,dp < 0$ together imply

$$\left(p - w\frac{\partial l^z}{\partial z}\right)\frac{dz}{dp}dp > 0, \tag{2.28}$$

which says that the market value of the induced change in public production exceeds its marginal cost. This interpretation is also applicable to (2.20').

3. A simple Keynesian model

3.1.

For ease of exposition, I consider a very simple Keynesian model, where:

(i)   the private and public sectors supply disjoint sets of consumption goods, using a single type of labour as their only variable primary input;

(ii)   labour and privately produced goods are traded at given fixed prices, and excess supply prevails on these markets;

(iii)   the numeraire, in terms of which prices are defined, is a non-produced, always desired, never rationed commodity (a 'money'). The extension to other regime specifications is briefly discussed in Section 4.3. In Section 3.1, I introduce the notation, and discuss the assumptions on market clearing, consumer decisions and the budget constraint. In Section 3.2, I discuss existence of Keynesian equilibria and I give a simple example. Second-best pricing rules without lump-sum transfers of income are derived in Section 3.3. Local welfare improvements are discussed in Section 3.4.

There are $1 + l + k + 1$ commodities. The first commodity is the non-produced numeraire, with price $p_0 \equiv 1$. The next l commodities are supplied by the private sector. Their prices $p_y = (p_{y1}, \ldots, p_{yl})$ are exogenously given and fixed. The next k commodities are supplied by the public sector, which sets their prices $p_z = (p_{z1}, \ldots, p_{zk})$. The last commodity is homogeneous labour. The wage rate w is exogenously given and fixed. I also write $p = (1, p_y, p_z, w)$ for the price system.

Household h consumes a quantity m^h of the numeraire commodity, a vector of privately produced commodities y^h in R^l_+ and a vector of publicly produced commodities z^h in R^k_+; it supplies a quantity of labour l^h in R_+. I also write $x^h = (m^h, y^h, z^h, -l^h)$ for the consumption (and labour supply) of household h. The preferences of household h are represented by the twice continuously differentiable utility function $U^h(x^h)$, monotonic and strongly quasi-concave in m^h, y^h and z^h. The budget constraint of household h is

$$px^h = m^h + p_y y^h + p_z z^h - wl^h \leqslant r^h. \tag{3.1}$$

The corresponding indirect utility function is $V^h(p, r^h)$.

The private sector is treated as an aggregate, in order to avoid the complication of specifying how the aggregate supply constraint is projected on individual firms. The private sector supplies a demand-determined vector of goods y in R_+^l, using a technology-determined quantity of labour l^y in R_+, where

$$y = \sum_h y^h, \quad l^y = l^y(y). \tag{3.2}$$

The function l^y is convex and twice continuously differentiable. Private profits are

$$\Pi = p_y y - w l^y. \tag{3.3}$$

The vector of marginal costs is denoted $m_y = w \dfrac{\partial l^y}{\partial y}$. The assumption of excess supply is equivalent to

$$p_y - m_y(y) \geq 0. \tag{3.4}$$

This assumption is understood as holding: (i) at an arbitrary starting point, where one seeks to define directions of welfare improvement; or (ii) at a second-best optimum, which one seeks to characterise. Of course, one would also like to treat a deeper question, namely: given an arbitrary starting point where excess supply prevails, and given optimal feasible policies, will the resulting second-best optimum still be characterised by excess supply (of labour and privately produced commodities)? That deeper question, treated in Guesnerie (1981), is not taken up here – except for the peripheral comments in Sections 3.2 and 4.3.[11]

The public sector supplies a vector of goods z in R_+^k, using a technology-determined quantity of labour l^z in R_+, where

$$z = \sum_h z^h, \quad l^z = l^z(z). \tag{3.5}$$

The function l^z is twice continuously differentiable. No convexity assumption is made. The vector of marginal costs is denoted $m_z = w\, \partial l^z/\partial z$. The public sector is subject to the budget constraint

$$\Phi = p_z z - w l^z \geq b, \tag{3.6}$$

where Φ denotes net public revenue.

---

[11] Under a constant returns technology, (3.4) holds globally whenever it holds locally. But constant returns is a long-run phenomenon, whereas rigid prices are a short-run phenomenon.

Aggregate labour demand L is defined by

$$L = l^y(y) + l^z(z). \tag{3.7}$$

The supply of labour by household h is subject to the quantity constraint

$$l^h \leqslant \bar{l}^h(L). \tag{3.8}$$

This constraint is understood to reflect both (i) underemployment arising from imbalance between labour demand and labour supply; and (ii) institutional rigidities preventing an employed person from choosing freely the number of hours worked.

Household h maximises $U^h(x^h)$ subject to (3.1) and (3.8). It simplifies exposition drastically, at very little cost in realism, if we assume that the constraint (3.8) is strictly binding for all h.[12] In particular, this preserves the differentiability of individual demand functions, thereby avoiding the need to use the heavier formalism of generalised gradients. The more general case is reviewed in Section 4.3.

The approach taken here consists in assuming that the individual constraints $\bar{l}^h(L)$ are adjusted in a continuously differentiable way, with

$$\sum_h l^h = \sum_h \bar{l}^h(L) = L, \quad \sum_h \frac{\partial l^h}{\partial L} = \sum_h \frac{\partial \bar{l}^h}{\partial L} = 1. \tag{3.9}$$

No precise specification of the individual constraints is introduced, and the individual decision x^h is written directly as a function of aggregate employment L:

$$x^h = x^h(p, r^h, L). \tag{3.10}$$

The function x^h consists of a constrained labour supply $l^h = \bar{l}^h(L)$, inelastic to (p, r^h), and a consumption demand $m^h(p, r^h; \bar{l}^h)$, $y^h(p, r^h; \bar{l}^h)$, $z^h(p, r^h; \bar{l}^h)$ endowed with standard properties. Indeed, consumption demand maximises U^h subject to (3.1), with l^h fixed. In particular, it satisfies

$$\frac{\partial m^h}{\partial r^h} + p_y \frac{\partial y^h}{\partial r^h} + p_z \frac{\partial z^h}{\partial r^h} = 1;$$

$$\frac{\partial m^h}{\partial p_z} + p_y \frac{\partial y^h}{\partial p_z} + p_z \frac{\partial z^h}{\partial p_z} + z^h = 0. \tag{3.11}$$

---

[12] Strictly, in the sense that

$$l^h = \bar{l}^h \quad \text{and} \quad \frac{\partial l^h}{\partial \bar{l}^h} = 1, \quad \frac{\partial l^h}{\partial p} = 0, \quad \frac{\partial l^h}{\partial r^h} = 0.$$

Also, m^h, y^h and z^h are differentiable with respect to $l^h = \bar{l}^h(L)$, hence with respect to L, with

$$\frac{\partial m^h}{\partial L} + p_y \frac{\partial y^h}{\partial L} + p_z \frac{\partial z^h}{\partial L} = w \frac{\partial l^h}{\partial L}. \tag{3.12}$$

The assumption of excess supply of labour is conveniently stated, if one defines

$$\frac{\partial U^h}{\partial r^h} = \frac{\partial U^h}{\partial x^h} \frac{\partial x^h}{\partial r^h} \geqslant 0, \quad w_R^h = - \frac{\partial U^h}{\partial l^h} \Big/ \frac{\partial U^h}{\partial r^h}. \tag{3.13}$$

Thus, w_R^h is the 'reservation wage' of household h. Since no assumption is made about the sign of $\partial U^h / \partial l^h$, the sign of w_R^h is also indeterminate. This allows for the possibility that an unemployed person would prefer to work, even at no gain in disposable income. Excess supply of labour means

$$w \geqslant w_R^h. \tag{3.14}$$

A *compensated* change in the constraint $\bar{l}^h$ is a change $d\bar{l}^h$ accompanied by an income transfer $(w_R^h - w)d\bar{l}^h$, resulting in an unchanged utility level. Using the symbol $\hat{x}^h$ for compensated demand functions, I define[13]

$$\frac{\partial \hat{m}^h}{\partial L} = \frac{\partial m^h}{\partial \bar{l}^h} \frac{\partial \bar{l}^h}{\partial L} + (w_R^h - w) \frac{\partial \bar{l}^h}{\partial L} \frac{\partial m^h}{\partial r^h} = _{\text{def}} \frac{\partial m^h}{\partial L} + (w_R^h - w) \frac{\partial \bar{l}^h}{\partial L} \frac{\partial m^h}{\partial r^h};$$

$$\frac{\partial \hat{y}^h}{\partial L} = \frac{\partial y^h}{\partial L} + (w_R^h - w) \frac{\partial \bar{l}^h}{\partial L} \frac{\partial y^h}{\partial r^h}, \quad \frac{\partial \hat{z}^h}{\partial L} = \frac{\partial z^h}{\partial L} + (w_R^h - w) \frac{\partial \bar{l}^h}{\partial L} \frac{\partial z^h}{\partial r^h};$$

$$\frac{\partial \hat{y}}{\partial L} = \sum_h \frac{\partial \hat{y}^h}{\partial L}, \quad \frac{\partial \hat{z}}{\partial L} = \sum_h \frac{\partial \hat{z}^h}{\partial L}. \tag{3.15}$$

Finally, I define

$$\bar{w}_R = \sum_h w_R^h \frac{\partial \bar{l}^h}{\partial L}, \tag{3.16}$$

---

[13] If preferences were additive between l^h on the one hand, (m^h, y^h, z^h) on the other hand, then

$$\frac{\partial \hat{m}^h}{\partial L} = w_R^h \frac{\partial \bar{l}^h}{\partial L} \frac{\partial m^h}{\partial r^h}, \quad \frac{\partial \hat{y}^h}{\partial L} = w_R^h \frac{\partial \bar{l}^h}{\partial L} \frac{\partial y^h}{\partial r^h}, \quad \frac{\partial \hat{z}^h}{\partial L} = w_R^h \frac{\partial \bar{l}^h}{\partial L} \frac{\partial z^h}{\partial r^h} \quad \text{and}$$

$$\frac{\partial \hat{m}^h}{\partial L} + p_y \frac{\partial \hat{y}^h}{\partial L} + p_z \frac{\partial \hat{z}^h}{\partial L} = w_R^h \frac{\partial \bar{l}^h}{\partial L}.$$

the aggregate, or average 'reservation wage'; it reflects both the individual reservation wages and the projection on individual households of the changes in overall employment.

The indirect utility function should now be written as $V^h(p, r^h, \bar{l}^h(L))$ $=_{\text{def}} V^h(p, r^h, L)$, with

$$\frac{\partial V^h}{\partial L} = \frac{\partial U^h}{\partial l^h}\frac{\partial \bar{l}^h}{\partial L} + w\frac{\partial V^h}{\partial r^h}\frac{\partial \bar{l}^h}{\partial L} = (w - w_R^h)\frac{\partial V^h}{\partial r^h}\frac{\partial \bar{l}^h}{\partial L}. \tag{3.17}$$

As for r^h, it is here defined as

$$r^h = m_0^h + \theta^h\Pi + \beta^h\Phi, \tag{3.18}$$

where $m_0^h > 0$ is the initial holding of the numeraire commodity.

3.2.

For a given wage w, vector of private sector prices p_y, and rationing scheme $\bar{l}(L)$ satisfying (3.9), a *Keynesian equilibrium* for the economy just described is defined by a vector of public sector prices p_z and an m-tuple of consumption vectors $x^h = (m^h, y^h, z^h, l^h)$ such that, if we define r^h as in (3.18) and Π, Φ and L as in (3.3), (3.6) and (3.7):

$$\Pi = p_y\sum_h y^h - wl^y(\sum_h y^h) \tag{3.3'}$$

$$\Phi = p_z\sum_h z^h - wl^z(\sum_h z^h) \tag{3.6'}$$

$$L = l^y(\sum_h y^h) + l^z(\sum_h z^h) \tag{3.7'}$$

then

(i) $\quad x^h = x^h(p, r^h, L) = x^h(p, m_0^h + \theta^h\Pi + \beta^h\Phi, L)$ with $l^h = \bar{l}^h(L)$;

(ii) $\quad \sum_h m^h = \sum_h m_0^h$ and $\sum_h l^h = L$;

(iii) $\quad$ the inequality constraints (3.4), (3.6) and (3.14) are satisfied:

$$p_y - w\frac{\partial l^y}{\partial y} \geq 0, \quad \Phi \geq b \quad \text{and, for all } h, \quad w - w_R^h \geq 0.$$

It may be noted that condition (ii) is implied by the other conditions, since (3.9) implies $\sum_h l^h = L$ and (3.18) then implies

$$\sum_h m^h + p_y \sum_h y^h + p_z \sum_h z^h - w \sum_h l^h = \sum_h m^h + \Pi + \Phi$$

$$= \sum_h r^h = \sum_h m_0^h + \Pi + \Phi. \tag{3.19}$$

Does such an equilibrium exist? This question is of course far from trivial. Even in the absence of a public sector, it is a difficult question, to which a partial answer only can be given. The partial answer comes from the theory of 'supply-constrained equilibria', as developed initially by van der Laan (1980) and extended more recently by van der Laan (1982, 1984), Kurz (1982) and Dehez and Drèze (1984).

A 'supply-constrained equilibrium' is an equilibrium with quantity rationing of supply only. For the private sector of the economy described in Section 3.1, a supply-constrained equilibrium is almost the same as a Keynesian equilibrium. The main difference is that, under the original definition by van der Laan (1980), supply of the numeraire commodity 0 could be rationed (in which case $p_{yj} = m_{yj}$ for some produced commodity j). Under this proviso, and under the additional assumption that each household initially holds a strictly positive quantity of every commodity, van der Laan (1980) proves the existence of a supply-constrained equilibrium for any given (fixed) price vector.[14] Without additional assumptions,[15] Dehez and Drèze (1984) prove that, for an arbitrary fixed vector of relative prices p_y/w, and for an arbitrary positive lower bound w_0 on w, there exists a supply-constrained equilibrium with $w \geqslant w_0$ and no rationing of the numeraire – i.e. there exists a Keynesian equilibrium with $w \geqslant w_0$.

Both of these results can be extended to the economy with a public sector described in Section 3.1, under the additional assumptions that $l(z)$

---

[14] The analysis of van der Laan (1980) is confined to a pure exchange economy, but the extension to production raises no difficulty, as can be inferred from the treatment in Dehez and Drèze (1984). Also, the theorem in van der Laan (1980) asserts only that supply of some commodity is not constrained to zero; that supply of some commodity is actually unconstrained was established later by van der Laan (1982).

[15] Although Dehez and Drèze assume strictly positive initial holdings of all commodities, that assumption is used only to guarantee the continuity of demand functions, which results here from positive holdings of the numeraire ($m_0^h > 0$) and positive prices p_y.

is convex and $b = 0$.[16] The result of van der Laan will then imply existence of a supply-constrained equilibrium, for given p_y and w, at *all* prices p_z of the public sector. The result of Dehez and Drèze on the other hand will imply that, for an arbitrary fixed vector of relative prices p_y/w and p_z/w, and an arbitrary $w_0 > 0$, there exists a Keynesian equilibrium with $w \geqslant w_0$.

These extensions remain incompletely satisfactory, however. Using van der Laan's approach, one needs to assume strictly positive initial holdings of all commodities, and it could be that households are rationed in their supplies of some commodity other than labour – contrary to the spirit of a Keynesian equilibrium. Using the approach of Dehez and Drèze, one cannot conclude that there exists a Keynesian equilibrium at *all* prices p_z of the public sector, for some *fixed* $w \geqslant w_0$.

It seems likely that further research will overcome these shortcomings. In the meantime, some comfort is derived from the observation that a Keynesian equilibrium exists, at some w, for the private sector of the economy described in Section 3.1.[17] If the public sector forms a 'small' part of the economy, the presumption that a Keynesian equilibrium will also exist at all prices p_z is not unreasonable.

Finally, it should be noted that a supply-constrained equilibrium could possibly be competitive – with either Walrasian or non-Walrasian prices.

Being unable to present satisfactory existence results at this stage, I shall motivate the sequel by giving a very simple example, where an equilibrium with involuntary unemployment exists, at *all* admissible public sector prices.

Consider an economy with a single household, a numeraire, one good produced by the public sector and labour. Household preferences are

---

[16] The extension consists in treating the public sector as a firm which maximises $p_z z$ subject to the constraints $z \in Z$, $p_z z - wl^z(z) \geqslant b$ and $z \leqslant \sum_h z^h(.)$. Convexity of Z is required for the continuity (with respect to $\sum_h z^h$) of the constraint set. It is not surprising that reliance on a standard existence proof requires convexity of the production set. For a new approach to the existence problem, see Dierker, Guesnerie and Neuefeind (1985). The condition $b = 0$ guarantees that a feasible z exists (which might fail to be the case when $b > 0$); for the approach followed by Dehez and Drèze it implies that the constraint set depends only on p_z/w and is independent of w. Although the assumption that Z is convex runs against the initial motivation of the problem, the presence of excess supply in the private sector introduces other distortions under which second-best pricing by the public sector still poses an interesting problem, even under convexity – as the example below clearly reveals.

[17] That is also the reason for introducing explicitly a numeraire, which is never rationed, and of which households hold positive endowments. (That it is not produced is unimportant, since it would not be produced anyhow at high values of w.) I am grateful to Christophe Chamley for pointing out the shortcomings of my earlier formulation, where I had neglected that precaution.

represented by the utility function

$$U = m + 2z^{1/2} - \frac{l^2}{2}.$$ (3.20)

Given the price vector $p = (1, p_z, w)$, the endowment m_0 and the income r, the unconstrained demand and supply functions are given by

$$l = w, \quad z = \frac{1}{p_z^2}, \quad m = m_0 + w^2 + r - \frac{1}{p_z},$$ (3.21)

for all parameter values at which non-negativity constraints are not binding. Then,

$$V(p, r) = m_0 + r + \frac{w^2}{2} + \frac{1}{p_z}.$$ (3.22)

The production set of the public sector is defined by

$$l^z(z) = z.$$ (3.23)

Substituting for l from (3.23) into (3.20), a first-best optimum is obtained by solving

$$\max_z m_0 + 2z^{1/2} - \frac{z^2}{2}, \quad z = 1.$$ (3.24)

Suppose now that the wage level is set at $w = 2$. If no budget constraint is imposed on the public sector, then

$$\Phi = p_z z - w l^z(z) = (p_z - 2)z.$$ (3.25)

The first best can still be achieved at $z = 1$ by setting $p_z = 1$ and letting the household choose z and l, subject to $l \leqslant \bar{l} = 1$ and $r = \Phi = -1$; the solution is $z = 1/p_z^2 = 1$, $l = \bar{l} = 1$, $m = m_0 + wl + r - p_z z = m_0 + 2 - 1 - 1 = m_0$. This is an instance of a Walrasian allocation sustained by non-Walrasian prices and a quantity constraint.

Suppose next that $w = 2$ and $b = 0$, so that the public sector must satisfy the constraint

$$\Phi = p_z z - w l^z(z) = (p_z - 2)z \geqslant 0, p_z \geqslant 2.$$ (3.26)

Recognising that $p_z \geqslant 2$ implies $z = 1/p_z^2 \leqslant 1/4$, it follows that the labour supply will be constrained by $l \leqslant \bar{l} = 1/p_z^2$, so that a second-best optimum is obtained by solving

$$\max_{z \leqslant 1/4} m_0 + 2z^{1/2} - \frac{z^2}{2}, \quad z = \frac{1}{4}.$$ (3.27)

This allocation is achieved by setting $p_z = 2$, and letting the household choose z and l, subject to $l \leqslant \bar{l} = 1/4$, $r = \Phi = 0$; the solution is $z = 1/p_z^2 = 1/4$, $\quad l = \bar{l} = 1/4$, $\quad m = m_0 + wl + r - p_z z = m_0 + 1/2 + 0 - 1/2 = m_0$.

3.3.

The problem of second-best public sector pricing in the Keynesian environment of Section 3.1 is[18]:

(P3) $\qquad \max_{p_z, \Pi, \Phi, L} \sum_h \lambda^h V^h[p, m_0^h + \theta^h \Pi + \beta^h \Phi, L] = \sum_h \lambda^h V^h[p, \Pi, \Phi, L]$

subject to

$$\Pi - p_y \sum_h y^h(p, \Pi, \Phi, L) + w l^y(\sum_h y^h(p, \Pi, \Phi, L)) = 0 \quad (\pi) \quad (3.3)$$

$$\Phi - p_z \sum_h z^h(p, \Pi, \Phi, L) + w l^z(\sum_h z^h(p, \Pi, \Phi, L)) = 0 \quad (\phi) \quad (3.6)$$

$$L - l^y(\sum_h y^h(p, \Pi, \Phi, L)) - l^z(\sum_h z^h(p, \Pi, \Phi, L)) = 0 \quad (v) \quad (3.7)$$

$$b - \Phi \leqslant 0 \qquad\qquad\qquad\qquad\qquad\qquad (\rho). \quad (3.6')$$

PROPOSITION 3

At an interior solution of problem (P3), there exists a multiplier $\rho \geqslant 0$, *such that*

$$\sum_h \lambda^h \frac{\partial V^h}{\partial r^h} \left[z^h - \theta^h \frac{d\Pi}{dp_z} - \beta^h \frac{d\Phi}{dp_z} - (w - w_R^h) \frac{\partial \bar{l}^h}{\partial L} \frac{dL}{dp_z} \right] = \rho \frac{d\Phi}{dp_z},$$

where

(3.28)

$$\begin{bmatrix} \dfrac{d\Pi}{dp_z} \\[2mm] \dfrac{d\Phi}{dp_z} \\[2mm] \dfrac{dL}{dp_z} \end{bmatrix} = (I - M)^{-1} \begin{bmatrix} (p_y - m_y)\dfrac{\partial y}{\partial p_z} \\[2mm] z + (p_z - m_z)\dfrac{\partial z}{\partial p_z} \\[2mm] \dfrac{\partial l^y}{\partial y}\dfrac{\partial y}{\partial p_z} + \dfrac{\partial l^z}{\partial z}\dfrac{\partial z}{\partial p_z} \end{bmatrix}, \qquad (3.29)$$

---

[18] The formulation of the problem with Π, Φ and L as arguments, but subject to equality constraints, is a matter of technical convenience.

$$
M = \begin{bmatrix}
(p_y - m_y)\sum_h \dfrac{\partial y^h}{\partial r^h}\theta^h & (p_y - m_y)\sum_h \dfrac{\partial y^h}{\partial r^h}\beta^h & (p_y - m_y)\sum_h \dfrac{\partial y^h}{\partial \bar{l}^h}\dfrac{\partial \bar{l}^h}{\partial L} \\[2ex]
(p_z - m_z)\sum_h \dfrac{\partial z^h}{\partial r^h}\theta^h & (p_z - m_z)\sum_h \dfrac{\partial z^h}{\partial r^h}\beta^h & (p_z - m_z)\sum_h \dfrac{\partial z^h}{\partial \bar{l}^h}\dfrac{\partial \bar{l}^h}{\partial L} \\[2ex]
\dfrac{\partial l^y}{\partial y}\sum_h \dfrac{\partial y^h}{\partial r^h}\theta^h & \dfrac{\partial l^y}{\partial y}\sum_h \dfrac{\partial y^h}{\partial r^h}\beta^h & \dfrac{\partial l^y}{\partial y}\sum_h \dfrac{\partial y^h}{\partial \bar{l}^h}\dfrac{\partial \bar{l}^h}{\partial L} \\[2ex]
+\dfrac{\partial l^z}{\partial z}\sum_h \dfrac{\partial z^h}{\partial r^h}\theta^h & +\dfrac{\partial l^z}{\partial z}\sum_h \dfrac{\partial z^h}{\partial r^h}\beta^h & +\dfrac{\partial l^z}{\partial z}\sum_h \dfrac{\partial z^h}{\partial \bar{l}^h}\dfrac{\partial \bar{l}^h}{\partial L}
\end{bmatrix} ;
$$

if $\Phi > b$ at the solution, then $\rho = 0$.

PROOF

The proof consists in differentiating the Lagrangean Λ of problem (P3) and eliminating unknowns by substitution.

$$
\frac{\partial \Lambda}{\partial \Pi} = \sum_h \lambda^h \frac{\partial V^h}{\partial r^h}\theta^h - \pi\left[1 - \left(p_y - w\frac{\partial l^y}{\partial y}\right)\sum_h \frac{\partial y^h}{\partial r^h}\theta^h\right]
$$

$$
+ \phi\left(p_z - w\frac{\partial l^z}{\partial z}\right)\sum_h \frac{\partial z^h}{\partial r^h}\theta^h
$$

$$
+ v\left(\frac{\partial l^y}{\partial y}\sum_h \frac{\partial y^h}{\partial r^h}\theta^h + \frac{\partial l^z}{\partial z}\sum_h \frac{\partial z^h}{\partial r^h}\theta^h\right) = 0. \tag{3.30}
$$

$$
\frac{\partial \Lambda}{\partial \Phi} = \sum_h \lambda^h \frac{\partial V^h}{\partial r^h}\beta^h + \pi\left(p_y - w\frac{\partial l^y}{\partial y}\right)\sum_h \frac{\partial y^h}{\partial r^h}\beta^h
$$

$$
- \phi\left[1 - \left(p_z - w\frac{\partial l^z}{\partial z}\right)\sum_h \frac{\partial z^h}{\partial r^h}\beta^h\right]
$$

$$
+ v\left(\frac{\partial l^y}{\partial y}\sum_h \frac{\partial y^h}{\partial r^h}\beta^h + \frac{\partial l^z}{\partial z}\sum_h \frac{\partial z^h}{\partial r^h}\beta^h\right) + \rho = 0. \tag{3.31}
$$

$$
\frac{\partial \Lambda}{\partial L} = \sum_h \lambda^h \frac{\partial V^h}{\partial L} + \pi\left(p_y - w\frac{\partial l^y}{\partial y}\right)\sum_h \frac{\partial y^h}{\partial L} + \phi\left(p_z - w\frac{\partial l^z}{\partial z}\right)\sum_h \frac{\partial z^h}{\partial L}
$$

$$
- v\left(1 - \frac{\partial l^y}{\partial y}\sum_h \frac{\partial y^h}{\partial L} - \frac{\partial l^z}{\partial z}\sum_h \frac{\partial z^h}{\partial L}\right) = 0. \tag{3.32}
$$

$$
(I - M') \begin{bmatrix} \pi \\[6pt] \phi \\[6pt] v \end{bmatrix} = \begin{bmatrix} \displaystyle\sum_h \lambda^h \frac{\partial V^h}{\partial r^h} \theta^h \\[10pt] \displaystyle\sum_h \lambda^h \frac{\partial V^h}{\partial r^h} \beta^h + \rho \\[10pt] \displaystyle\sum_h \lambda^h \frac{\partial V^h}{\partial L} \end{bmatrix} = \begin{bmatrix} \displaystyle\sum_h \lambda^h \frac{\partial V^h}{\partial r^h} \theta^h \\[10pt] \displaystyle\sum_h \lambda^h \frac{\partial V^h}{\partial r^h} \beta^h + \rho \\[10pt] \displaystyle\sum_h \lambda^h \frac{\partial V^h}{\partial r^h}(w - w_R^h)\frac{\partial \bar{l}^h}{\partial L} \end{bmatrix}.
$$

$$(3.33)$$

$$
(\pi, \phi, v) = \left(\sum_h \lambda^h \frac{\partial V^h}{\partial r^h} \theta^h, \sum_h \lambda^h \frac{\partial V^h}{\partial r^h} \beta^h + \rho, \right.
$$

$$
\left. \sum_h \lambda^h \frac{\partial V^h}{\partial r^h}(w - w_R^h)\frac{\partial \bar{l}^h}{\partial L} \right) \cdot (I - M)^{-1}. \tag{3.34}
$$

$$
\frac{\partial \Lambda}{\partial p_z} = \sum_h \lambda^h \frac{\partial V^h}{\partial p_z} + \pi \left(p_y - w \frac{\partial l^y}{\partial y} \right) \sum_h \frac{\partial y^h}{\partial p_z} \tag{3.35}
$$

$$
+ \phi \left[z + \left(p_z - w \frac{\partial l^z}{\partial z} \right) \sum_h \frac{\partial z^h}{\partial p_z} \right]
$$

$$
+ v \left(\frac{\partial l^y}{\partial y} \sum_h \frac{\partial y^h}{\partial p_z} + \frac{\partial l^z}{\partial z} \sum_h \frac{\partial z^h}{\partial p_z} \right) = 0
$$

$$
= -\sum_h \lambda^h \frac{\partial V^h}{\partial r^h} z^h + (\pi, \phi, v) \begin{bmatrix} (p_y - m_y)\dfrac{\partial y}{\partial p_z} \\[10pt] z + (p_z - m_z)\dfrac{\partial z}{\partial p_z} \\[10pt] \dfrac{\partial l^y}{\partial y}\dfrac{\partial y}{\partial p_z} + \dfrac{\partial l^z}{\partial z}\dfrac{\partial z}{\partial p_z} \end{bmatrix}
$$

$$
= -\sum_h \lambda^h \frac{\partial V^h}{\partial r^h} z^h + \begin{bmatrix} \displaystyle\sum_h \lambda^h \frac{\partial V^h}{\partial r^h} \theta^h \\[10pt] \displaystyle\sum_h \lambda^h \frac{\partial V^h}{\partial r^h} \beta^h + \rho \\[10pt] \displaystyle\sum_h \lambda^h \frac{\partial V^h}{\partial r^h}(w - w_R^h)\frac{\partial \bar{l}^h}{\partial L} \end{bmatrix} \cdot (I - M)^{-1} \begin{bmatrix} (p_y - m_y)\dfrac{\partial y}{\partial p_z} \\[10pt] z + (p_z - m_z)\dfrac{\partial z}{\partial p_z} \\[10pt] \dfrac{\partial l^y}{\partial y}\dfrac{\partial y}{\partial p_z} + \dfrac{\partial l^z}{\partial z}\dfrac{\partial z}{\partial p_z} \end{bmatrix}
$$

$$
= -\sum_h \lambda^h \frac{\partial V^h}{\partial r^h} z^h + \left(\sum_h \lambda^h \frac{\partial V^h}{\partial r^h} \theta^h, \sum_h \lambda^h \frac{\partial V^h}{\partial r^h} \beta^h + \rho, \sum_h \lambda^h \frac{\partial V^h}{\partial r^h} (w - w_R^h) \frac{\partial \bar{l}^h}{\partial L} \right) \begin{bmatrix} \dfrac{d\Pi}{dp_z} \\[2mm] \dfrac{d\Phi}{dp_z} \\[2mm] \dfrac{dL}{dp_z} \end{bmatrix},
$$

which is the same as (3.28).

The justification for the notation $(d\Pi/dp_z, \ d\Phi/dp_z, \ dL/dp_z)$ is provided by differentiating totally the system (3.3), (3.6), (3.7):

$$
(I - M) \begin{bmatrix} d\Pi \\[2mm] d\Phi \\[2mm] dL \end{bmatrix} - \begin{bmatrix} (p_y - m_y)\dfrac{\partial y}{\partial p_z} \\[3mm] z + (p_z - m_z)\dfrac{\partial z}{\partial p_z} \\[3mm] \dfrac{\partial l^y}{\partial y}\dfrac{\partial y}{\partial p_z} + \dfrac{\partial l^z}{\partial z}\dfrac{\partial z}{\partial p_z} \end{bmatrix} dp_z = 0, \quad (3.36)
$$

which yields (3.29). That $\rho = 0$ when $\Phi > b$ at the solution reflects complementary slackness.   QED

Let us first interpret formula (3.28) in cost-benefit terms and compare it with formula (2.11). The marginal revenue to the public sector of, say, increasing p_z still appears on the right-hand side. The difference lies in the formulae for evaluating appropriately that marginal revenue, (3.29) instead of (2.12). The left-hand side of (3.28) still measures the total marginal cost to consumers of an increase in p_z. That cost now consists of four components, reflecting the four capacities in which a household is affected by adjustments in public sector prices; namely, qua consumer (z^h), qua asset holder $(\theta^h \, d\Pi/dp_z)$, qua taxpayer $(\beta^h \, d\Phi/dp_z)$ and qua constrained supplier of labour $((w - w_R^h)\,(\partial \bar{l}^h/\partial L)(dL/dp_z))$. The first three terms appeared already in (2.11); the only difference concerns again the evaluation of $d\Pi/dp_z$ and of $d\Phi/dp_z$, which is discussed below. The fourth term on the right-hand side of (3.28) is more novel; it evaluates the welfare implications of a change in aggregate employment. If increasing p_z leads to less employment $(dL/dp_z < 0)$, some households see their labour supply further constrained $((\partial \bar{l}^h/\partial L)(dL/dp_z) < 0)$, at a loss of welfare (per unit of labour time) equal to the difference between the forgone market wage w and the reservation wage w_R^h. This kind of effect had no place in (2.11), since in the Boiteux framework market wage and reservation wage are equal, for each household. Here is thus a term whose *raison d'être* lies in the presence of market disequilibrium. Note that quantitative evaluation of this term raises a new problem, to the extent that w_R^h is not directly observable, or measurable from market data.

In order to understand formula (3.29), a word of comment on the nature of 'multiplier effects' in problem (P3) is in order. When public sector prices p_z are adjusted, household demands react, due to the price derivatives $\partial y/\partial p_z$, $\partial z/\partial p_z$. This primary reaction entails adjustments in employment given by

$$\frac{\partial L}{\partial p_z} dp_z = \left(\frac{\partial l^y}{\partial y} \frac{\partial y}{\partial p_z} + \frac{\partial l^z}{\partial z} \frac{\partial z}{\partial p_z} \right) dp_z$$

and in private profits given by

$$\frac{\partial \Pi}{\partial p_z} dp_z = (p_y - m_y) \frac{\partial y}{\partial p_z} dp_z;$$

as for the public budget, it is adjusted by

$$\frac{\partial \Phi}{\partial p_z} dp_z = \left[z + (p_z - m_z) \frac{\partial z}{\partial p_z} \right] dp_z.$$

These adjustments in employment, profits and the public budget affect households via the employment constraints $\bar{l}^h(L)$ and the incomes $\theta^h \Pi + \beta^h \Phi$; this induces further reactions of demand, due to the derivatives $\partial x^h/\partial L$ and $\partial x^h/\partial r^h$. The matrix M describes the direct impact on Π (first row), Φ (second row) and L (third row) of unitary adjustments in Π (first column), Φ (second column) and L (third column) respectively. Multiplying M into the vector of adjustments

$$\left(\frac{\partial \Pi}{\partial p_z} dp_z, \frac{\partial \Phi}{\partial p_z} dp_z, \frac{\partial L}{\partial p_z} dp_z \right)'$$

defines the next round of adjustments in Π, Φ, and L; multiplying M into this second round defines the third round; and so on. The familiar matrix-multiplier process operates, and the final outcome is

$$
\begin{bmatrix} \dfrac{d\Pi}{dp_z} \\[2mm] \dfrac{d\Phi}{dp_z} \\[2mm] \dfrac{dL}{dp_z} \end{bmatrix} = (I + M + M^2 + M^3 + \ldots) \begin{bmatrix} (p_y - m_y)\dfrac{\partial y}{\partial p_z} \\[2mm] z + (p_z - m_z)\dfrac{\partial z}{\partial p_z} \\[2mm] \dfrac{\partial l^y}{\partial y}\dfrac{\partial y}{\partial p_z} + \dfrac{\partial l^z}{\partial z}\dfrac{\partial z}{\partial p_z} \end{bmatrix}
$$

$$
= (I - M)^{-1} \begin{bmatrix} (p_y - m_y)\dfrac{\partial y}{\partial p_z} \\[2mm] z + (p_z - m_z)\dfrac{\partial z}{\partial p_z} \\[2mm] \dfrac{\partial l^y}{\partial y}\dfrac{\partial y}{\partial p_z} + \dfrac{\partial l^z}{\partial z}\dfrac{\partial z}{\partial p_z} \end{bmatrix}. \tag{3.37}
$$

Thus, *conditions (3.28)* reduce to a cost-benefit analysis of adjustments in public sector prices, where costs and benefits are evaluated by means of the 'comparative statics' approach of macroeconomics, taking all multiplier effects into account. This is the Keynesian counterpart to the cost-benefit analysis appropriate for (2.11), where price effects had the leading role. Although the computations underlying (3.28) look much more forbidding than those underlying (2.11), the added complexity is to a large extent apparent rather than real, as I will show in Section 4.2 below. A basic principle is common to both results, namely the 'comparative statics' evaluation of the relevant costs and benefits. How the comparative statics analysis should be conducted is dictated by the assumptions made about market clearing in the private sector – either through price flexibility or through quantity rationing (in the short run).

3.4.

The result stated in proposition 3 is directly applicable to the 'reform problem' of Section 2.4.

Starting from a situation where the budget constraint is not binding ($\Phi > b$), the reform problem is: find dp_z such that

$$
\sum_h \lambda^h \frac{\partial V^h}{\partial r^h}\left[z^h - \theta^h \frac{d\Pi}{dp_z} - \beta^h \frac{d\Phi}{dp_z} - (w - w_R^h)\frac{\partial \bar{l}^h}{\partial L}\frac{dL}{dp_z}\right] dp_z < 0.
$$
$$\tag{3.38}$$

Starting instead from a situation where $\Phi = b$, and $\rho > 0$, the reform problem becomes: find dp_z such that[19]

$$\frac{d\Phi}{dp_z} dp_z = 0, \quad \sum_h \lambda^h \frac{\partial V^h}{\partial r^h} \left[z^h - \theta^h \frac{d\Pi}{dp_z} - (w - w_R^h) \frac{\partial \bar{l}^h}{\partial L} \frac{dL}{dp_z} \right] dp_z < 0.$$

(3.39)

These conditions are easily checked, provided one can estimate the final impact of dp_z on Π, Φ and L; and provided the coefficients of these impact terms be somehow available. To gain insight, consider the special case where the distributive weights $\lambda^h \dfrac{\partial V^h}{\partial r^h}$ are taken equal for all h. Then, (3.39) reduces to

$$\frac{d\Phi}{dp_z} dp_z = 0, \quad \left[z - \frac{d\Pi}{dp_z} - (w - \bar{w}_R) \frac{dL}{dp_z} \right] dp_z < 0.$$

(3.40)

The welfare-improvement condition for price increases is that the cost of inflation, zdp_z, be more than offset by the gains associated with private profits, $d\Pi$, and employment, $(w - \bar{w}_R)dL$. It is interesting to bring out how these three aspects are combined in (3.40). In the present model, aggregate value added is equal to $p_y y + p_z z$. Dividing through by that quantity, we may rewrite the welfare-improvement condition as

$$\frac{zdp_z}{p_y y + p_z z} - \frac{\Pi}{p_y y + p_z z} \frac{d\Pi}{\Pi} - \frac{wL}{p_y y + p_z z} \frac{w - \bar{w}_R}{w} \frac{dL}{L} < 0. \quad (3.41)$$

The first term is a rate of inflation (relative increase in the cost of an unchanged aggregate consumption); the second term weighs the rate of increase in profits $d\Pi/\Pi$, by the share of profits in value added; the third terms weighs the rate of increase in employment, dL/L, by the share of wages in value added *times* one minus the ratio of the reservation wage to the nominal wage. Even if the reservation wage were zero, and if private profits were unaffected by a change in p_z, then one percentage point of inflation would still carry more weight than an increase in employment by one percentage point – unless value added consisted of wages alone. A negative reservation wage (which is not to be ruled out) is needed before employment carries more weight than inflation. This somewhat

---

[19] The condition $d\Phi/dp_z = 0$ is imposed to keep the public budget unchanged; $d\Phi/dp_z > 0$ would be acceptable, but would modify the condition for welfare improvement.

counterintuitive conclusion rests on the special assumptions that distributive aspects may be ignored, and that nominal wage rates remain constant. Clearly, more realistic assumptions would be required to reach substantive conclusions, in particular about the welfare cost of inflation; but the methodological path is clearly delineated.

More generally, the welfare-improvement condition in (3.39) could be approached by treating the problem of income redistribution at the functional rather than at the personal level. Defining

$$\lambda_{zi} = \sum_h \lambda^h \frac{\partial U^h}{\partial r^h} z_i^h / z_i, \quad \lambda_{\Pi} = \sum_h \lambda^h \frac{\partial U^h}{\partial r^h} \theta^h,$$

$$\lambda_w = \sum_h \lambda^h \frac{\partial U^h}{\partial r^h} \frac{\partial l^h}{\partial L}, \quad \bar{w}_R = \sum_h \lambda^h \frac{\partial U^h}{\partial r^h} w_R^h \frac{\partial l^h}{\partial L} / \lambda_w, \qquad (3.42)$$

one would express (3.39) as

$$\frac{d\Phi}{dp_z} dp_z = 0, \quad \left[\lambda_z z - \lambda_{\Pi} \frac{d\Pi}{dp_z} - \lambda_w (w - \bar{w}_R) \frac{dL}{dp_z} \right] dp_z < 0. \qquad (3.43)$$

This condition could be verified, once the relative weights λ_z/λ_w (consumers versus workers) and λ_z/λ_{Π} (consumers versus business shareholders) are evaluated. A further simplification would result if λ_z were not evaluated for each commodity separately, as suggested by (3.42), but only for a few groups of commodities. A broad value judgement of that kind seems inherent in any realistic policy analysis.

4. Some comparisons and extensions

Proposition 3 states the main result on which the methodological comments of Section 5 are based. These comments do not rely significantly on the contents of the present section, which may thus be skipped without loss of continuity.

The comparisons bear successively on the simple Keynesian model with lump-sum transfers of income (Section 4.1) and on a neoclassical analogue to this model (Section 4.2). Some extensions are taken up in Section 4.3.

4.1.

When lump-sum transfers of income among households are introduced as a policy option in problem (P3), simplifications comparable to those mentioned in Section 2.3 for problem (P1) are achieved: The first-order conditions are freed from distributive aspects; income multipliers no longer appear in the first-order conditions, but derivatives of the demand functions are *compensated* derivatives. This remark applies both to price derivatives $(\partial y^h/\partial p_z, \partial z^h/\partial p_z)$ and to derivatives with respect to the employment constraint $(\partial y^h/\partial L, \partial z^h/\partial L)$, for which the relevant expressions were given in (3.15). Note that these expressions involve the reservation wages w_R^h, which are not directly observable. For this reason, the result given below in proposition 4 has less operational usefulness than its counterpart in proposition 2, which involves only the familiar compensated price derivatives. One may think about proposition 4 as giving the second-best pricing rule for an economy with exact price indexation of *individual* incomes and with 100% unemployment insurance (that is, with unemployment compensations offsetting exactly the *individual* utility losses due to unemployment).

An employment multiplier still appears in proposition 4, in spite of the unemployment compensation, because the employment constraint is an argument of the compensated demand functions. If that were not the case,[20] then the employment multiplier could be eliminated from the formulae in proposition 4, as revealed by the alternative formulation (4.4').

There are two equally natural ways of introducing lump-sum transfers (of the numeraire) into problem (P3). The first consists in treating the initial holdings m_0^h as policy variables, subject to a constraint on their sum:

$$\sum_h m_0^h \leqslant m_0 \qquad\qquad (\mu). \qquad (4.1)$$

One then solves problem (P4) with these additional variables. This is equivalent to the procedure followed in proposition 2. Alternatively, one can treat the incomes r^h as policy variables, subject to a single constraint on their sum, i.e.

(P4) $\displaystyle \max_{p_z, r^h, L} \sum_h \lambda^h V^h(p, r^h, L)$

subject to (3.7) and

---

[20] In terms of footnote 13 above, additive preferences between labour and physical commodities lead to derivatives of the compensated demand functions with respect to the employment constraint equal to the income effects of the reservation wages; these derivatives would vanish if in addition reservation wages were equal to zero.

$$\sum_h r^h - p_y \sum_h y^h(p, r^h, L)$$

$$+ wl^y(\sum_h y^h(p, r^h, L)) - p_z \sum_h z^h(p, r^h, L)$$

$$+ wl^z(\sum_h z^h(p, r^h, L)) \leqslant 0 \qquad\qquad (\sigma) \quad (4.2)$$

$$b - p_z \sum_h z^h(p, r^h, L) + wl^z(\sum_h z^h(p, r^h, L)) \leqslant 0 \qquad\qquad (\rho). \quad (4.3)$$

PROPOSITION 4

At an interior solution of problem (P4), *there exists a multiplier* $\hat{\rho} \geqslant 0$ *such that*

$$z - (p_y - m_y)\left(\frac{\partial \hat{y}}{\partial p_z} + \frac{\partial \hat{y}}{\partial L}\frac{d\hat{L}}{dp_z}\right) - \left[z + (p_z - m_z)\left(\frac{\partial \hat{z}}{\partial p_z} + \frac{\partial \hat{z}}{\partial L}\frac{d\hat{L}}{dp_z}\right)\right]$$

$$- (w - \bar{w}_R)\frac{d\hat{L}}{dp_z} = \hat{\rho}\left[z + (p_z - m_z)\left(\frac{\partial \hat{z}}{\partial p_z} + \frac{\partial \hat{z}}{\partial L}\frac{d\hat{L}}{dp_z}\right)\right] \qquad (4.4)$$

where $(\hat{y}, \hat{z})$ *denote compensated demand functions and*

$$\frac{d\hat{L}}{dp_z} = \left(\frac{\partial l^y}{\partial y}\frac{\partial \hat{y}}{\partial p_z} + \frac{\partial l^z}{\partial z}\frac{\partial \hat{z}}{\partial p_z}\right)\left(1 - \frac{\partial l^y}{\partial y}\frac{\partial \hat{y}}{\partial L} - \frac{\partial l^z}{\partial z}\frac{\partial \hat{z}}{\partial L}\right)^{-1}; \qquad (4.5)$$

if $\Phi > b$ *at the solution, then* $\hat{\rho} = 0$.

PROOF

Instead of solving problem (P4) directly, I solve problem (P3) with m_0^h a policy variable, subject to constraints (4.1). (The interested reader may verify that the direct solution is indeed given by (4.4)–(4.5).) The first-order conditions (3.30)–(3.32), (3.35) of problem (P3) are not modified by the addition of constraint (4.1). The first-order condition for m_0^h is

$$\frac{\partial \Lambda}{\partial m_0^h} = \lambda^h \frac{\partial V^h}{\partial r^h} + \pi\left(p_y - w\frac{\partial l^y}{\partial y}\right)\frac{\partial y^h}{\partial r^h} + \phi\left(p_z - w\frac{\partial l^z}{\partial z}\right)\frac{\partial z^h}{\partial r^h}$$

$$+ v\left(\frac{\partial l^y}{\partial y}\frac{\partial y^h}{\partial r^h} + \frac{\partial l^z}{\partial z}\frac{\partial z^h}{\partial r^h}\right) - \mu = 0. \qquad (4.6)$$

Combining this new condition successively with (3.30), (3.31) and (3.32), we obtain – using (3.15) and (3.18) –

$$\frac{\partial A}{\partial \Pi} - \sum_h \frac{\partial A}{\partial m_0^h} \theta^h = -\pi + \mu = 0; \tag{4.7}$$

$$\frac{\partial A}{\partial \Phi} - \sum_h \frac{\partial A}{\partial m_0^h} \beta^h = -\phi + \rho + \mu = 0; \tag{4.8}$$

$$\frac{\partial A}{\partial L} - \sum_h \frac{\partial A}{\partial m_0^h} (w - w_R^h) \frac{\partial \bar{l}^h}{\partial L} = \pi \left(p_y - w \frac{\partial l^y}{\partial y} \right) \sum_h \frac{\partial \hat{y}^h}{\partial L}$$

$$+ \phi \left(p_z - w \frac{\partial l^z}{\partial z} \right) \sum_h \frac{\partial \hat{z}^h}{\partial L} - v \left[1 - \frac{\partial l^y}{\partial y} \sum_h \frac{\partial \hat{y}^h}{\partial L} - \frac{\partial l^z}{\partial z} \sum_h \frac{\partial \hat{z}^h}{\partial L} \right]$$

$$+ \mu(w - \bar{w}_R) = 0. \tag{4.9}$$

Substituting from (4.7)–(4.8) into (4.9) and solving for v/μ yields:

$$\frac{v}{\mu} = \left[\left(p_y - w \frac{\partial l^y}{\partial y} \right) \frac{\partial \hat{y}}{\partial L} + \left(1 + \frac{\rho}{\mu} \right) \left(p_z - w \frac{\partial l^z}{\partial z} \right) \frac{\partial \hat{z}}{\partial L} + (w - \bar{w}_R) \right]$$

$$\left(1 - \frac{\partial l^y}{\partial y} \frac{\partial \hat{y}}{\partial L} - \frac{\partial l^z}{\partial z} \frac{\partial \hat{z}}{\partial z} \right)^{-1}. \tag{4.10}$$

(Note that $\mu > 0$ by desirability of the numeraire commodity.)

Combining finally (4.6) with (3.35), we obtain

$$\frac{\partial A}{\partial p_z} + \sum_h \frac{\partial A}{\partial m_0^h} z^h = \pi \left(p_y - w \frac{\partial l^y}{\partial y} \right) \sum_h \frac{\partial \hat{y}^h}{\partial p_z}$$

$$+ \phi \left[z + \left(p_z - w \frac{\partial l^z}{\partial z} \right) \sum_h \frac{\partial \hat{z}^h}{\partial p_z} \right]$$

$$+ v \left(\frac{\partial l^y}{\partial y} \sum_h \frac{\partial \hat{y}^h}{\partial p_z} + \frac{\partial l^z}{\partial z} \sum_h \frac{\partial \hat{z}^h}{\partial p_z} \right) - \mu z = 0. \tag{4.11}$$

Defining $d\hat{L}/dp_z$ as per (4.5), and substituting from (4.7), (4.8) and (4.10) into (4.11) yields

$$\left(p_y - w\frac{\partial l^y}{\partial y}\right)\left(\frac{\partial \hat{y}}{\partial p_z} + \frac{\partial \hat{y}}{\partial L}\frac{d\hat{L}}{dp_z}\right)$$

$$+ \left(1 + \frac{\rho}{\mu}\right)\left[z + \left(p_z - w\frac{\partial l^z}{\partial z}\right)\left(\frac{\partial \hat{z}}{\partial p_z} + \frac{\partial \hat{z}}{\partial L}\frac{d\hat{L}}{dp_z}\right)\right]$$

$$+ (w - \bar{w}_R)\frac{d\hat{L}}{dp_z} - z = 0. \tag{4.12}$$

which is the same as (4.4), with $\hat{\rho} = \rho/\mu$. That $\hat{\rho} = 0$ when $\Phi > b$ at the solution reflects complementary slackness. QED

An alternative statement of conditions (4.4), after cancelling the compensation terms, is

$$-\left(p_y - \bar{w}_R\frac{\partial l^y}{\partial y}\right)\left(\frac{\partial \hat{y}}{\partial p_z} + \frac{\partial \hat{y}}{\partial L}\frac{d\hat{L}}{dp_z}\right)$$

$$+ \left(p_z - \bar{w}_R\frac{\partial l^z}{\partial z}\right)\left(\frac{\partial \hat{z}}{\partial p_z} + \frac{\partial \hat{z}}{\partial L}\frac{d\hat{L}}{dp_z}\right)$$

$$= \hat{\rho}\left[z + \left(p_z - w\frac{\partial l^z}{\partial z}\right)\left(\frac{\partial \hat{z}}{\partial p_z} + \frac{\partial \hat{z}}{\partial L}\frac{d\hat{L}}{dp_z}\right)\right]. \tag{4.4'}$$

PROOF OF FORMULA (4.4′)

Remembering that $m_y = w\ \partial l^y/\partial y$, $m_z = w\ dl^z/\partial z$, we collect and rearrange the terms involving w in (4.4), obtaining

$$w\left[\frac{\partial l^y}{\partial y}\frac{\partial \hat{y}}{\partial p_z} + \frac{\partial l^z}{\partial z}\frac{\partial \hat{z}}{\partial p_z} + \left(\frac{\partial l^y}{\partial y}\frac{\partial \hat{y}}{\partial L} + \frac{\partial l^z}{\partial z}\frac{\partial \hat{z}}{\partial L} - 1\right)\frac{d\hat{L}}{dp_z}\right]$$

which is equal to zero in view of (4.5). Collecting similarly the terms involving $\bar{w}_R$ in (4.4′), we obtain

$$\bar{w}_R\left[\frac{\partial l^y}{\partial y}\frac{\partial \hat{y}}{\partial p_z} + \frac{\partial l^z}{\partial z}\frac{\partial \hat{z}}{\partial p_z} + \left(\frac{\partial l^y}{\partial y}\frac{\partial \hat{y}}{\partial L} + \frac{\partial l^z}{\partial z}\frac{\partial \hat{z}}{\partial L}\right)\frac{d\hat{L}}{dp_z}\right]$$

which is equal to $\bar{w}_R\, d\hat{L}/dp_z$, as required by (4.4). QED

The interpretation of (4.4′) is similar to that of (2.20′). The left-hand side measures the cost to households of a change in p_z, under exact compensation for both the price effects (z) and the employment effects $(\bar{w}_R - w)d\hat{L}/dp_z$; that cost is equal to minus the change in household incomes net of the compensation; this corresponds to the change in private profits and the public budget, computed at the reservation wage and net of the direct effect of price changes (z). (The right-hand side still measures the 'monetary' benefit to the public sector of the price change, i.e. its contribution towards meeting the budget constraint.)

Formula (4.4′) is directly applicable to the reform problem. Starting from a situation where $\Phi = b$ and imposing $d\Phi = (d\phi/dp_z)dp_z = 0$, we obtain:

PROPOSITION 5

Under suitable lump-sum transfers of income among households and 100% unemployment compensation, compensated price adjustments that leave unchanged the public budget are welfare improving if and only if they lead to adjustments in private and public productions whose market value exceeds their marginal cost evaluated at the reservation wage.

In proposition 5, reservation wages correspond to a 'shadow price for labour', in terms of which definite conclusions are reached. This is in contrast to proposition 3, where altogether different computations are required.

4.2.

Lest the reader be misled about the relative complexity of welfare pricing rules in Keynesian and neoclassical models, I sketch the counterpart to proposition 3, under the assumption that the wage rate w and the private sector prices p_y adjust to clear markets competitively. It will be seen that the first-order conditions, albeit different, are just as complex as in proposition 3.

In comparison with the model of Section 2, the different feature is that w and p_y are no longer policy instruments, but adjust to clear markets. The problem of second-best public sector pricing now becomes:

$$x^h = x^h(p, r^h), \quad l^y = l^y(p), \quad y = y(p). \tag{4.13}$$

In comparison with the model of Section 2, the different feature is that w and p_y are no longer policy instruments, but adjust to clear markets. The problem of second-best public sector pricing now becomes:

(P6) $\quad \max\limits_{p,\,\Phi} \sum\limits_h \lambda^h V^h(p, m_0^h + \theta^h(p_y y(p) - wl^y(p)) + \beta^h \Phi)$

subject to

$$Y(p, \Phi) =_{\text{def}} \sum_h y^h(p, m_0^h + \theta^h(p_y y(p) - wl^y(p)) + \beta^h \Phi)$$

$$- y(p) = 0 \qquad\qquad (\eta) \quad (4.14)$$

$$L(p, \Phi) =_{\text{def}} \sum_h l^h(p, m_0^h + \theta^h(p_y y(p) - wl^y(p)) + \beta^h \Phi)$$

$$- l^y(p) - l^z \left(\sum_h z^h(p, m_0^h + \theta^h(p_y y(p) - wl^y(p)) \right.$$

$$\left. + \beta^h \Phi) \right) = 0 \qquad\qquad (\nu) \quad (4.15)$$

$$\Phi - p_z \sum_h z^h(p, m_0^h + \theta^h(p_y y(p) - wl^y(p)) + \beta^h \Phi)$$

$$+ wl^z \left(\sum_h z^h(p, m_0^h + \theta^h(p_y y(p) - wl^y(p)) + \beta^h \Phi) \right) = 0 \ (\phi) \quad (3.6)$$

$$b - \Phi \leqslant 0 \qquad\qquad (\rho). \quad (3.6')$$

PROPOSITION 6

At an interior solution of problem (P6) *there exists a multiplier* $\rho \geqslant 0$ *such that*

$$\sum_h \lambda^h \frac{\partial V^h}{\partial r^h} \left[z^h + y^h \frac{dp_y}{dp_z} - l^h \frac{dw}{dp_z} - \theta^h \frac{d\Pi}{dp_z} - \beta^h \frac{d\Phi}{dp_z} \right] = \rho \frac{d\Phi}{dp_z} \quad (4.16)$$

where

$$\frac{d\Pi}{dp_z} = y \frac{dp_y}{dp_z} - l^y \frac{dw}{dp_z}$$

and

$$\begin{bmatrix} \dfrac{dp_y}{dp_z} \\[2mm] \dfrac{dw}{dp_z} \\[2mm] \dfrac{d\Phi}{dp_z} \end{bmatrix} = D^{-1} \begin{bmatrix} -\dfrac{\partial Y}{\partial p_z} \\[2mm] -\dfrac{\partial L}{\partial p_z} \\[2mm] z + (p_z - m_z)\dfrac{\partial z}{\partial p_z} \end{bmatrix}, \qquad (4.17)$$

$$D = \begin{bmatrix} \dfrac{\partial Y}{\partial p_y} & \dfrac{\partial Y}{\partial w} & \dfrac{\partial Y}{\partial \Phi} \\[2mm] \dfrac{\partial L}{\partial p_y} & \dfrac{\partial L}{\partial w} & \dfrac{\partial L}{\partial \Phi} \\[2mm] -(p_z - m_z)\left(\dfrac{\partial z}{\partial p_y} + \dfrac{\partial z}{\partial \Pi}\dfrac{\partial \Pi}{\partial p_y}\right) & -(p_z - m_z)\left(\dfrac{\partial z}{\partial w} + \dfrac{\partial z}{\partial \Pi}\dfrac{\partial \Pi}{\partial w}\right) & 1 - (p_z - m_z)\dfrac{\partial z}{\partial \Phi} \end{bmatrix};$$

if $\Phi > b$ at the solution, then $\rho = 0$.[21]

PROOF

As before, we differentiate the Lagrangean Λ of problem (P6) and eliminate unknowns by substitution.

$$\frac{\partial \Lambda}{\partial p_y} = \sum_h \lambda^h \left(\frac{\partial V^h}{\partial p_y} + \frac{\partial V^h}{\partial r^h}\theta^h y\right) - \eta\left(\sum_h \frac{\partial y^h}{\partial p_y} + \sum_h \frac{\partial y^h}{\partial r^h}\theta^h y - \frac{\partial y}{\partial p_y}\right)$$

$$- \nu\left[\sum_h \frac{\partial l^h}{\partial p_y} + \sum_h \frac{\partial l^h}{\partial r^h}\theta^h y - \frac{\partial l^y}{\partial p_y} - \frac{\partial l^z}{\partial z}\left(\sum_h \frac{\partial z^h}{\partial p_y} + \sum_h \frac{\partial z^h}{\partial r^h}\theta^h y\right)\right]$$

$$+ \phi\left(p_z - w\frac{\partial l^z}{\partial z}\right)\left(\sum_h \frac{\partial z^h}{\partial p_y} + \sum_h \frac{\partial z^h}{\partial r^h}\theta^h y\right) = 0. \tag{4.18}$$

$$\frac{\partial \Lambda}{\partial w} = \sum_h \lambda^h \left(\frac{\partial V^h}{\partial w} - \frac{\partial V^h}{\partial r^h}\theta^h l^y\right) - \eta\left(\sum_h \frac{\partial y^h}{\partial w} - \sum_h \frac{\partial y^h}{\partial r^h}\theta^h l^y - \frac{\partial y}{\partial w}\right)$$

$$- \nu\left[\sum_h \frac{\partial l^h}{\partial w} - \sum_h \frac{\partial l^h}{\partial r^h}\theta^h l^y - \frac{\partial l^y}{\partial w} - \frac{\partial l^z}{\partial z}\left(\sum_h \frac{\partial z^h}{\partial w} - \sum_h \frac{\partial z^h}{\partial r^h}\theta^h l^y\right)\right]$$

$$+ \phi\left(p_z - w\frac{\partial l^z}{\partial z}\right)\left(\sum_h \frac{\partial z^h}{\partial w} - \sum_h \frac{\partial z^h}{\partial r^h}\theta^h l^y\right) = 0. \tag{4.19}$$

$$\frac{\partial \Lambda}{\partial \Phi} = \sum_h \lambda^h \frac{\partial V^h}{\partial r^h}\beta^h - \eta\sum_h \frac{\partial y^h}{\partial r^h}\beta^h - \nu\left(\sum_h \frac{\partial l^h}{\partial r^h}\beta^h - \frac{\partial l^z}{\partial z}\sum_h \frac{\partial z^h}{\partial r^h}\beta^h\right)$$

$$- \phi\left[1 - \left(p_z - w\frac{\partial l^z}{\partial z}\right)\sum_h \frac{\partial z^h}{\partial r^h}\beta^h\right] + \rho = 0. \tag{4.20}$$

---

[21] These conditions could undoubtedly be reconciled explicitly with (2.11), by introducing in the statement of problem (P1) the condition that z^h is equal to zero for a subset of commodities.

Adopting a more concise notation, we may solve these equations for (η, v, ϕ):

$$
D' \begin{bmatrix} \eta \\ v \\ \phi \end{bmatrix} = \begin{bmatrix} \dfrac{\partial Y}{\partial p_y} & \dfrac{\partial L}{\partial p_y} & -(p_z - m_z)\left(\dfrac{\partial z}{\partial p_y} + \dfrac{\partial z}{\partial \Pi}\dfrac{\partial \Pi}{\partial p_y}\right) \\[2ex] \dfrac{\partial Y}{\partial w} & \dfrac{\partial L}{\partial w} & -(p_z - m_z)\left(\dfrac{\partial z}{\partial w} + \dfrac{\partial z}{\partial \Pi}\dfrac{\partial \Pi}{\partial w}\right) \\[2ex] \dfrac{\partial Y}{\partial \Phi} & \dfrac{\partial L}{\partial \Phi} & 1-(p_z - m_z)\dfrac{\partial z}{\partial \Phi} \end{bmatrix} \begin{bmatrix} \eta \\ v \\ \phi \end{bmatrix}
$$

$$
= \begin{bmatrix} \sum_h \lambda^h \dfrac{\partial V^h}{\partial r^h}(-y^h + \theta^h y) \\[2ex] \sum_h \lambda^h \dfrac{\partial V^h}{\partial r^h}(l^h - \theta^h l^y) \\[2ex] \sum_h \lambda^h \dfrac{\partial V^h}{\partial r^h}\beta^h + \rho \end{bmatrix}. \tag{4.21}
$$

$$
(\eta, v, \phi) = \left(\sum_h \lambda^h \dfrac{\partial V^h}{\partial r^h}(-y^h + \theta^h y),\ \sum_h \lambda^h \dfrac{\partial V^h}{\partial r^h}(l^h - \theta^h l^y),\right.
$$

$$
\left. \sum_h \lambda^h \dfrac{\partial V^h}{\partial r^h}\beta^h + \rho\right). D^{-1}. \tag{4.22}
$$

$$
\frac{\partial \Lambda}{\partial p_z} = \sum_h \lambda^h \frac{\partial V^h}{\partial p_z} - \eta \sum_h \frac{\partial y^h}{\partial p_z} - v\left(\sum_h \frac{\partial l^h}{\partial p_z} - \frac{\partial l^z}{\partial z}\sum_h \frac{\partial z^h}{\partial p_z}\right)
$$

$$
+ \phi\left[z + \left(p_z - w\frac{\partial l^z}{\partial z}\right)\sum_h \frac{\partial z^h}{\partial p_z}\right] = 0
$$

$$
= -\sum_h \lambda^h \frac{\partial V^h}{\partial r^h}z^h + (\eta, v, \phi) \begin{bmatrix} -\dfrac{\partial Y}{\partial p_z} \\[2ex] -\dfrac{\partial L}{\partial p_z} \\[2ex] z + (p_z - m_z)\dfrac{\partial z}{\partial p_z} \end{bmatrix} \tag{4.23}
$$

$$
= -\sum_h \lambda^h \frac{\partial V^h}{\partial r^h} z^h + \begin{bmatrix} \sum_h \lambda^h \frac{\partial V^h}{\partial r^h}(-y^h + \theta^h y) \\[2mm] \sum_h \lambda^h \frac{\partial V^h}{\partial r^h}(l^h - \theta^h l^y) \\[2mm] \sum_h \lambda^h \frac{\partial V^h}{\partial r^h}\beta^h + \rho \end{bmatrix}' D^{-1} \begin{bmatrix} -\dfrac{\partial Y}{\partial p_z} \\[2mm] -\dfrac{\partial L}{\partial p_z} \\[2mm] z + (p_z - m_z)\dfrac{\partial z}{\partial p_z} \end{bmatrix}
$$

$$
= -\sum_h \lambda^h \frac{\partial V^h}{\partial r^h} z^h
$$

$$
+ \left(\sum_h \lambda^h \frac{\partial V^h}{\partial r^h}(-y^h + \theta^h y), \sum_h \lambda^h \frac{\partial V^h}{\partial r_h}(l^h - \theta^h l^y), \sum_h \lambda^h \frac{\partial V^h}{\partial r^h}\beta^h + \rho \right) \begin{bmatrix} \dfrac{dp_y}{dp_z} \\[2mm] \dfrac{dw}{dp_z} \\[2mm] \dfrac{d\Phi}{dp_z} \end{bmatrix} = 0,
$$

which is the same as (4.16).

The justification for the notation $(dp_y/dp_z, dw/dp_z, d\Phi/dp_z)$ is provided by differentiating totally the system (4.14), (4.15), (3.6):

$$
D \begin{bmatrix} dp_y \\ dw \\ d\Phi \end{bmatrix} + \begin{bmatrix} \dfrac{\partial Y}{\partial p_z} \\[2mm] \dfrac{\partial L}{\partial p_z} \\[2mm] -z - (p_z - m_z)\dfrac{\partial z}{\partial p_z} \end{bmatrix} dp_z = 0, \tag{4.24}
$$

which yields (4.17). That $\rho = 0$ when $\Phi > b$ at the solution reflects complementary slackness. QED

It is an easy exercise to combine the approaches of propositions 3 and 6 to cover the case where markets for privately produced commodities clear through price adjustments whereas the labour market 'clears' through quantity rationing (involuntary unemployment) at a fixed nominal wage w.

The main modification to problem (P6) consists of reintroducing L as an argument of V^h, y^h and z^h while replacing (4.15) by (3.7) with $l^y = l^y(p_y)$. This leads to the problem:

(P7) $$\max_{p,\,\Phi,\,L} \sum_h \lambda^h V^h(p, m_0^h + \theta^h(p_y y(p_y) - wl^y(p_y)) + \beta^h \Phi, L)$$

subject to:

$$Y(p, \Phi, L) =_{\text{def}} \sum_h y^h(p, m_0^h + \theta^h(p_y y(p_y)$$

$$- wl^y(p_y)) + \beta^h \Phi, L) - y(p_y) = 0 \qquad (\eta) \quad (4.14')$$

$$L - l^y(p_y) - l^z(\sum_h z^h(p, m_0^h + \theta^h(p_y y(p_y) - wl^y(p_y))$$

$$+ \beta^h \Phi, L)) = 0 \qquad (v) \quad (4.15')$$

$$\Phi - p_z \sum_h z^h(p, m_0^h + \theta^h(p_y y(p_y) - wl^y(p_y)) + \beta^h \Phi, L)$$

$$+ wl^z(\sum_h z^h(p, m_0^h + \theta^h(p_y y(p_y) - wl^y(p_y)) + \beta^h \Phi, L))$$

$$= 0 \qquad (\phi) \quad (3.6)$$

$$b - \Phi \leqslant 0 \qquad (\rho). \quad (3.6')$$

PROPOSITION 7

At an interior solution of problem (P7), there exists a multiplier $\rho \geqslant 0$ such that

$$\sum_h \lambda^h \frac{\partial V^h}{\partial r^h}\left[z^h + y^h\frac{dp_y}{dp_z} - \theta^h\frac{d\Pi}{dp_z} - \beta^h\frac{d\Phi}{dp_z} - (w - w_R^h)\frac{\partial \bar{l}^h}{\partial L}\frac{dL}{dp_z}\right] = \rho\frac{d\Phi}{dp_z},$$

$$(4.25)$$

where

$$\frac{d\Pi}{dp_z} = y\frac{dp_y}{dp_z}$$

and

$$
\begin{bmatrix} \dfrac{dp_y}{dp_z} \\[2ex] \dfrac{d\Phi}{dp_z} \\[2ex] \dfrac{dL}{dp_z} \end{bmatrix} = Q^{-1} \begin{bmatrix} -\dfrac{\partial Y}{\partial p_z} \\[2ex] z + (p_z - m_z)\dfrac{\partial z}{\partial p_z} \\[2ex] \dfrac{\partial l^z}{\partial z}\dfrac{\partial z}{\partial p_z} \end{bmatrix}, \tag{4.26}
$$

$$
Q = \begin{bmatrix} \dfrac{\partial Y}{\partial p_y} & \dfrac{\partial Y}{\partial \Phi} & \dfrac{\partial Y}{\partial L} \\[2ex] -\dfrac{\partial l^y}{\partial p_y} - \dfrac{\partial l^z}{\partial z}\left(\dfrac{\partial z}{\partial p_y} + \dfrac{\partial z}{\partial \Pi}y\right) & -\dfrac{\partial l^z}{\partial z}\dfrac{\partial z}{\partial \Phi} & 1 - \dfrac{\partial l^z}{\partial z}\dfrac{\partial z}{\partial L} \\[2ex] -(p_z - m_z)\left(\dfrac{\partial z}{\partial p_y} + \dfrac{\partial z}{\partial \Pi}y\right) & 1 - (p_z - m_z)\dfrac{\partial z}{\partial \Phi} & -(p_z - m_z)\dfrac{\partial z}{\partial L} \end{bmatrix};
$$

if $\Phi > b$ *at the solution, then* $\rho = 0$.

The proof follows the same lines as that of proposition 6 and is left to the reader. The interpretation of proposition 7 is analogous to that of proposition 3.

4.3.

I conclude this section with three remarks about extensions of the results recorded here.

First, the analytics of the present paper lack in either rigour or realism, where differentiability is concerned. As is well known, the conditions required to obtain differentiability of household demand functions at all prices and incomes are severe and unrealistic;[22] they imply strictly positive consumption of *all* commodities at *all* prices and incomes. And in the present context, the differentiability problem is compounded by the presence of quantity rationing, as recognised in Section 3.1.

The appropriate remedy to this deficiency will be to free the analysis of differentiability assumptions, relying instead upon the property of Lipschitz continuity. Under assumptions much more reasonable than those required for differentiability of ordinary demand functions, constrained

---

[22] See, e.g. Debreu (1972).

demand functions are Lipschitz continuous in prices, income and quantity constraints.[23] I thus feel confident that a rigorous extension to the more realistic non-differentiable case is possible, and will be forthcoming as soon as the required mathematical talent is mobilised.

Second, the Keynesian model introduced in Section 3 is very simple, and calls in particular for a generalisation to several types of labour, and arbitrary sets of inputs in private and public production. I have attempted that extension and found that it lay beyond the scope (and length!) of the present paper. Yet, a neat characterisation (in cost-benefit terms) of second-best input decisions in the public sector will have its place on the record.

Third, the kind of analysis presented here for a Keynesian environment can be replicated for alternative regimes, and it would seem natural to work out general formulae allowing for some markets to be in excess demand, others in excess supply and others still in equilibrium.[24] These formulae will combine elements of the multiplier analysis in Section 3.3 and the price adjustments analysis in Section 4.2. No logical difficulties are involved in the study of local welfare improvements. For second-best optimality, *a priori* identification of the regime that will prevail on each market at the solution is problematic, from a theoretical as well as an empirical viewpoint. One must go back to a more basic approach, like that of Guesnerie (1981) to study this problem in theory and discover the associated empirical requirements (like measures of excess supplies and demands...). This difficulty does not arise in the reform problem, however.

5. Methodological conclusions

Although the model used in this paper is very simple and special, the answers which it has provided to the questions raised in the introduction seem endowed with broader methodological validity. Here are the main conclusions which I have drawn for myself.

(i) It is possible to exhibit operational solutions to second-best or reform problems in non-competitive environments; where the term 'operational' refers to solutions involving well-defined quantities, directly amenable to empirical evaluation, as distinct from quantities defined only conceptually, in terms of other quantities themselves defined only

[23] See Cornet and Laroque (1980).
[24] The general formulae obtained by Bronsard and Wagneur (1982), Jean P. Drèze (1982), Picard (1982), ... provide the starting point for this extension.

conceptually ... The methodology of general equilibrium with quantity rationing has been found adequate to our task. Hopefully, further extensions of general equilibrium theory (imperfect competition, increasing returns to scale...) will eventually enlarge our research potential in directions of greater realism. For the kind of problems studied here, the main difficulties do not seem to lie with the theoretical definition of solutions, but rather with their empirical implementation.

(ii) In situations involving quantity rationing, second-best or welfare-improving policies will typically depend upon quantities which, though amenable to empirical evaluation, are not directly observable and cannot be inferred from currently available economic data. In our example, reservation wages and marginal costs in supply constrained private firms were found relevant. In general, reservation prices for commodities subject to quantity constraints will be relevant. These vary from one agent to the next, and are not revealed through their choices. Special programs of data collection (like sample surveys) will be needed in order to evaluate these quantities.

(iii) The information needed to implement second-best or welfare-improving policies will typically be the kind of information which macroeconometric models seek to summarize. In our example, traditional quantities like price and income elasticities of demand need to be supplemented with such quantities as elasticities of employment with respect to output, separate demand estimates for employed and unemployed consumers, or for wage earners and property holders... To a particular second-best problem will correspond particular information needs, which the agency faced with the problem[25] cannot be expected to meet by itself. Some coordination of econometric investigations, or access to general information services, will typically be called for. If the demand for econometric information of the kind needed in my example develops, it may exert an influence on the design of econometric models, in order to make them fully consistent with the theoretical framework used to define second-best or welfare-improving policies.

(iv) Precision of the econometric estimates used for implementing second-best policies is apt to be limited. Special attention should be given to the compounding of errors in formulae – like (3.29) – involving non-linear functions of many estimated coefficients.

(v) The theoretical framework of general equilibrium analysis, based upon choices of individual economic agents, is adequate to study second-

---

[25] Like the French railroads, in the instance which motivated Boiteux.

best policy problems; there is no need to appeal specifically to macro-economic reasoning. The link with macroeconomic thinking comes from reconciling concepts which are new to microeconomics with those traditionally used in macroeconomics; and from reconciling the quantities defined by aggregation over individuals or commodities[26] with the quantities entering traditional macroeconomic models. To repeat a concise introductory statement, the rediscovery of the macroeconomic implications of microeconomics may well be a more fruitful research agenda than the exhibition of the microeconomic foundations of macroeconomics.

(vi) No comments of a substantive nature about the contents of propositions 3–5 will be offered here. The main point about the contents of my results is that welfare implications of public policies are ultimately derived from their impact on the welfare of individual agents, in their quadruple capacity as consumers, asset-holders, taxpayers and suppliers of labour. General equilibrium analysis is the natural tool to bring out the exact nature of these individual impacts. If the example discussed here is not misleading, the same approach will eventually be reconciled with macroeconomic policy models involving global objectives like increased employment with a more stable price level. There is of course a long way to go, before a satisfactory second-best analysis of models with dynamics and money is available. An immediate goal may be to explore more realistic and more general models than my simple Keynesian example, allowing for aggregation of markets in different regimes. A canonical formulation of such models, difficult as it may still seem, would justify a systematic search for substantive characterisation of second-best and welfare-improving policies.

---

[26] As in the calculations involving profits.

V   Price adjustments

9   Demand estimation, risk aversion and sticky prices*

1. Introduction and summary

The purpose of this chapter is to point out that uncertainty about the price elasticity of demand has an effect comparable to that of a kink in the demand curve, for a risk-averse firm; the kink being located at the prevailing price and quantity. The reason for this effect, namely estimation uncertainty, is entirely distinct from the standard reason invoked in the literature on kinky demand curves, since Sweezy (1939), namely asymmetrical reactions of competitors. Thus symmetrical, but imperfectly known reactions would produce asymmetrical effects. And asymmetrical, but imperfectly known, reactions would produce doubly asymmetrical effects – the asymmetry generated by uncertainty being compounded with that generated by the reactions themselves.

The effect of uncertainty in the context considered here is analogous to the effect of uncertainty about rates of return on savings decisions by consumers. Variance of rates of return affects these decisions in the same way as *adverse* changes in expected returns – see Drèze and Modigliani (1972) or Sandmo (1974). Thus, uncertainty about rates of return has an effect comparable to that of a kink in the budget line constraining present and future consumption; the kink being located at the endowment point. (The reason for that kink is again distinct from the standard reason, namely a difference between lending and borrowing rates; both asymmetries must again be compounded.)

We first illustrate our point for the special case of a linear demand curve, a linear cost curve, and a 'truncated minimax' decision criterion – see Van Moeseke (1965) for a discussion of that criterion, which calls for maximising expected value minus a multiple of standard deviation. In

*Economics Letters, 4 (1979), 1–6; © North-Holland Publishing Co.

that special case, the effect of uncertainty about the price elasticities of demand is precisely equivalent to that of a kink in the demand curve. We then extend our argument to local analysis of a general situation.

Whether firms are risk averse or not is a sometimes debated issue, which is not taken up here. The author's current views on that issue are summarised by Drèze (1979a).

A number of possible extensions (uncertainty about the level of demand at the prevailing price, uncertainty about costs, price decisions aimed at gathering information about the demand elasticity, costs associated with price changes, multiperiod problems ...) seem to raise unrewarding analytical difficulties and are therefore left as exercises for the readers!

2. A special case

We consider first the linear demand and cost functions

$$q = a - bp, \tag{2.1}$$

$$C(q) = cq + d, \tag{2.2}$$

where q denotes quantity, p denotes price, and (a, b, c, d) are positive scalars. Starting from a point (q_0, p_0) on the demand function, we may express profits Π as a function of price,

$$
\begin{aligned}
\Pi(p) = pq - C(q) &= (p - c)[q_0 + b(p_0 - p)] - [C(q_0) - cq_0] \\
&= \Pi(p_0) + (p - p_0)[q_0 - b(p - c)]. \tag{2.3}
\end{aligned}
$$

If b is unknown, but estimated by means of a probability density, then $\Pi(p)$ is a random variable with moments

$$E[\Pi(p)] = (p - c)[q_0 + E(b)(p_0 - p)] - [C(q_0) - cq_0], \tag{2.4}$$

$$V[\Pi(p)] = V(b)(p - c)^2(p_0 - p)^2, \tag{2.5}$$

and standard deviation

$$\sigma[\Pi(p)] = \sigma(b)(p - c)|p_0 - p|, \tag{2.6}$$

over the relevant range where $p > c$.

The 'truncated minimax' criterion calls for maximising the linear homogeneous function of Π,

$$E[\Pi(p)] - \alpha\sigma[\Pi(p)]$$

$$= (p - c)[q_0 + E(b)(p_0 - p) - \alpha\sigma(b)|p_0 - p|] - [C(q_0) - cq_0]$$

$$= (p - c)\left[q_0 + \left\{ E(b) + \alpha\sigma(b)\frac{|p_0 - p|}{p - p_0} \right\}(p_0 - p) \right]$$

$$- [C(q_0) - cq_0]$$

$$= (p - c)[q_0 + \beta(p)\cdot(p_0 - p)] - [C(q_0) - cq_0]$$

$$= \Pi(p_0) + (p - p_0)[q_0 - \beta(p)\cdot(p - c)], \qquad (2.7)$$

where

$$\beta(p) = E(b) + \alpha\sigma(b)\cdot s(p - p_0),$$

$$s(x) = \text{sign of } x = 1 \qquad \text{if } x > 0$$

$$= -1 \quad \text{if } x < 0$$

$$= 0 \qquad \text{if } x = 0.$$

We thus verify that, in this special case, uncertainty about b is equivalent to an *adverse* change in $E(b)$; indeed, the term in $\sigma(b)$ works like an increase in the response of demand to price increases, and a decrease in the response of demand to price decreases, i.e. it is equivalent to a kink in the demand function at (q_0, p_0), see figure 9.1.

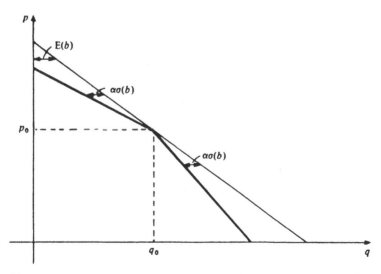

Figure 9.1

3. The general case (local analysis)

For a local analysis of the general case, we write

$$\Pi(p) = p \cdot q(p) - C(q), \qquad (3.1)$$

with

$$q(p_0) = q_0, \quad \left.\frac{dq}{dp}\right|_{p_0} = -b, \quad \left.\frac{dC}{dq}\right|_{q_0} = c,$$

and expand the utility function of the firm, $u[\Pi(p)]$, in a Taylor series around $u[\Pi(p_0)]$,

$$u[\Pi(p)] \simeq u[\Pi(p_0)] + (p - p_0)\frac{du}{d\Pi}\frac{d\Pi}{dp}\bigg|_{p_0}$$

$$+ \frac{(p - p_0)^2}{2}\left[\frac{d^2u}{d\Pi^2}\left(\frac{d\Pi}{dp}\right)^2\bigg|_{p_0} + \frac{du}{d\Pi}\frac{d^2\Pi}{dp^2}\bigg|_{p_0}\right]$$

$$\simeq u[\Pi(p_0)] + \frac{du}{d\Pi}\bigg|_{p_0}\{(p - p_0)[q_0 - b(p_0 - c)]$$

$$- (p - p_0)^2 b\}$$

$$+ \frac{d^2u}{d\Pi^2}\bigg|_{p_0}\frac{(p - p_0)^2}{2}[q_0 - b(p_0 - c)]^2. \qquad (3.2)$$

Expression (3.2) is meant to hold for p close to p_0. Accordingly, the fourth-order terms $(p - p_0)^2(d^2q/dp^2)$ and $(p - p_0)^2(d^2c/dq^2)$ have been dropped.

Uncertainty about the demand elasticity means uncertainty about b in (3.2). The expected utility associated with a given p is then

$$Eu[\Pi(p)] \simeq u[\Pi(p_0)] + \frac{du}{d\Pi}\bigg|_{p_0}(p - p_0)[q_0 - E(b)(p - c)]$$

$$+ \frac{d^2u}{d\Pi^2}\bigg|_{p_0}\frac{(p - p_0)^2}{2}E[q_0 - b(p_0 - c)]^2. \qquad (3.3)$$

Let $\phi[\Pi(p_0)] = \phi_0$ denote the absolute risk-aversion function of the firm evaluated at $\Pi(p_0)$, i.e.

$$\phi_0 = -\frac{d^2u}{d\Pi^2}\bigg|_{\Pi(p_0)}\bigg/\frac{du}{d\Pi}\bigg|_{\Pi(p_0)} \geq 0. \tag{3.4}$$

Under risk aversion, $\phi_0 > 0$, under risk neutrality, $\phi_0 = 0$, see Pratt (1964) or Arrow (1965). We may then rewrite (3.3) as

$$\frac{Eu[\Pi(p)] - u[\Pi(p_0)]}{du/d\Pi|_{\Pi(p_0)}} \simeq (p - p_0)[q_0 - E(b)(p - c)]$$

$$- \frac{\phi_0}{2}(p - p_0)^2 E[q_0 - b(p_0 - c)]^2, \tag{3.5}$$

or equivalently as

$$\frac{Eu[\Pi(p)] - u[\Pi(p_0)]}{du/d\Pi|_{\Pi(p_0)}} \simeq (p - p_0)\bigg\{q_0 - (p - c)\bigg[E(b)$$

$$+ \frac{\phi_0}{2}\frac{p - p_0}{p - c}\{(p_0 - c)^2 V(b)$$

$$+ [q_0 - E(b)(p_0 - c)]^2\}\bigg]\bigg\}$$

$$= (p - p_0)\{q_0 - (p - c)\beta(p)\}, \tag{3.6}$$

where $\beta(p) \gtrless E(b)$ as $p \gtrless p_0$, when $\phi_0 > 0$.

The expression for $\beta(p)$ plays the same role in (3.6) as in (2.7). In both cases, the sign of $\beta(p) - E(b)$ is the sign of $(p - p_0)$. Unfortunately, the expression for $\beta(p)$ is much more complicated in (3.6) than in (2.7). (This is of course the reason for considering the special case first.) In (2.7), the difference $\beta(p) - E(b)$ is equal to a constant times the sign of the difference $p - p_0$; in (3.6), the difference $\beta(p) - E(b)$ is a non-linear function of $(p - p_0)$. In other words, the 'certainty equivalent' demand derivative $\beta(p)$ is not constant over half lines but moves away from $E(b)$ in a non-linear way as p moves away from p_0; see Figure 9.2.[1]

If changes in p (away from p_0) must take place in multiples of a certain 'unit' δ, this non-linearity implies that $\beta(p_0 + \delta) - \beta(p_0) \neq \beta(p_0) - \beta(p_0 - \delta)$; finite differences will be evaluated as if the 'certainty equivalent' demand function had a kink at (p_0, q_0).

Maximisation of the left-hand side of (3.5) or (3.6) with respect to p is

---

[1] It is readily verified that $\beta(p)$ is a concave function of $p - p_0$. A few printing errors have been corrected in this section.

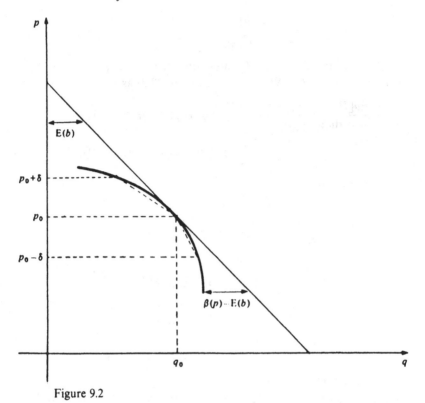

Figure 9.2

equivalent to maximisation of expected utility. A risk-neutral firm would simply maximise the first term on the right-hand side. This would also maximise $(p - p_0)[q_0 - E(b)(p - c)] - (\phi_0/2)(p - p_0)^2[q_0 - E(b)(p - c)]^2$, over the range where the quadratic approximation is valid. The remaining term,[2] $- (\phi_0/2)(p - p_0)^2(p_0 - c)^2 V(b)$, is maximal at $p = p_0$ and therefore pulls the optimal p towards p_0 in the case of a risk-averse firm. (This justifies the reference to sticky prices in the title of this note.)

[2] Omitting third and higher powers of $(p - p_0)$.

10 Stability of a Keynesian adjustment process*

1. Introduction

1.1. Outline

In this paper, I study the stability of an adjustment process on prices and quantities that converges in finitely many steps to an equilibrium admitting excess supply of (some) factors of production. The finite convergence results from the fact that the leading adjustments are finite, and the equilibrium concept allows for ε-discrepancies between transacted *input* levels and those required by technology. The excess supply of factors of production at the equilibrium is associated with downward rigidities of nominal factor prices. Such an equilibrium is a special case of the so-called 'supply-constrained equilibria' studied by Dehez and Drèze (1984), following a seminal contribution of van der Laan (1980). These rigidities are best understood as reflecting non-competitive supply behaviour by owners of the production factors. (Here, the supply of factors by individual households is modelled as totally inelastic to prices, whose downward rigidity may be viewed as a form of collective income protection.)

The modelling of the economy embodies a distinction between primary inputs and other commodities. The leading adjustments concern the prices and quantities of primary inputs; quantity adjustments reflect the profit seeking decisions of producers (firms) and price increases take place under the pressure of excess demand. Thus, the quantity adjustments are decentralised firm by firm, and the price adjustments are decentralised market by market.

* In *Equilibrium Theory and Applications*, W. Barnett, B. Cornet, C. d'Aspremont, J. Jaskold-Gabsewicz and A. Mas-Colell, eds., Cambridge University Press, Cambridge, forthcoming. Helpful suggestions from Paul Champsaur, Pierre Dehez, Henry Tulkens and Gerd Weinrich are gratefully acknowledged.

205

A tâtonnement process is studied first, to clear the ground on a simpler case. My main interest, however, goes to a non-tâtonnement process, with production and consumption activities carried out in continuous time out of equilibrium. Feasibility of these activities is ensured by inventories, and it is shown that bounded inventory levels are sufficient for feasibility.

To establish finite convergence of a simple decentralised non-tâtonnement adjustment process, with ongoing production and consumption, is a major step towards realism. The equilibrium concept also has claims to realism. The empirical record clearly supports the view that non-storable factors of production, in particular labour and the services of capital, are not fully used all the time; see figure 10.1 for European data, 1973–89. It thus seems meaningful to study the stability properties of equilibria with that property. (The ε-feature I regard as entirely innocuous; some might claim that it adds to realism; to me, it is a convenience – neither more nor less.)

Of course, a price has to be paid for these results, in the form of assumptions. These come at three distinct levels.

(i) Most basic are the behavioural assumptions about consumers and producers. Consumers are, as usual, price takers and preference maximisers. They hold endowments of the primary factors of production and supply these inelastically – an assumption that is not quite realistic for (female) labour services, but could be relaxed. Producers are modelled implicitly as setting prices of commodities through a mark-up on production costs (where the mark-up rates may reflect perceived demand elasticities or fixed costs); their demand for factors is derived from their input needs to meet the demand for commodities at these prices. As suggested in Section 1.2, these behavioural assumptions seem consistent with empirical findings. I regard them as specific, but not particularly restrictive.

(ii) A major difficulty arising in non-tâtonnement processes with ongoing production and consumption concerns the modelling of expectations and intertemporal optimisation under uncertainty. That difficulty is completely eschewed here, to concentrate on stability. Both firms and consumers are assumed to hold static point expectations, that is to anticipate that prices and quantity constraints observed today will continue to prevail forever after. That assumption is very crude, and motivated exclusively by the understandable desire to split difficulties. It is accompanied by an assumption of stationary preferences for consumers and by an equally crude assumption about inventory decisions by firms. I regard these (standard) assumptions as very strong, but provisional.

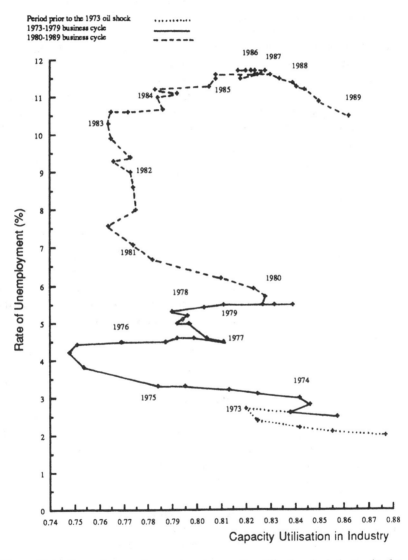

Figure 10.1   Rate of unemployment and capacity utilisation in industry in the European Community. Quarterly observations are shown, with the years marked against the first quarter. *Source: European Economy*

(iii) At a third level, I will introduce two assumptions – one on technology and the other on consumer preferences – which are clearly restrictive, but are needed for my stability proofs. The assumption on technology is absence of joint production and constant returns. This permits choosing input coefficients on the basis of input prices alone, without reference to output levels. It would complicate matters to dispense with that simplifying assumption. The assumption on consumer preferences is absence of inferior goods – an assumption that is clearly unrealistic,[1] but which plays for quantity adjustments a role similar to that played by gross substituability (not assumed here) for price adjustments. I do not know to what extent these two assumptions, which permit a reasonably straightforward derivation of strong results, could be generalised. Here lies a natural topic for further research.

1.2. Origins and organisation

The intellectual origins of this paper are twofold. On the one hand, there was a theoretical inspiration, arising from my work with Pierre Dehez on supply-constrained equilibria. This led me in 1983 to study the stability of a tâtonnement process, for an economy with a Leontief technology (no joint production, constant returns and fixed coefficients); see Drèze (1983). The motivation was to obtain a supply-constrained equilibrium as the outcome of a decentralised adjustment process on prices and quantity constraints, without assuming outright such properties as 'orderly' (one-sided) rationing. As a by-product, I wanted to investigate the presumptions that constrained demands could guide an adjustment process just as effectively as notional demands, whereas quantity constraints could make a useful contribution to stability. Both presumptions were verified on a simple but suggestive example, borrowed without modifications from Chapter 7 of Morishima's book *The Economic Theory of Modern Society* (1976). That paper, which forms the core of Sections 2 and 3 below, was never published, because I wanted to extend my analysis to non-tâtonnement; my intellectual wanderings in real time kept postponing the task.

The second source of inspiration was empirical. In the years 1984–89, I was involved in the European Unemployment Program (EUP), a (successful) joint effort by researchers in ten countries to analyse the determination of aggregate output and employment by means of a small

---

[1] See however Section 8.5.

macroeconometric model, the specification of which would be the same in each country but flexible enough to encompass equilibrium as well as disequilibrium situations; see Drèze *et al.* (1991). That methodology led to the verification of a number of empirical regularities, in which I recognised interesting similitudes with the structure of Morishima's model. These regularities include econometric results compatible with the following specifications: (i) pricing at average cost plus a mark-up; (ii) no rationing of final demand; (iii) downwards rigidity of nominal wages; (iv) persistent unemployment; (v) CES-Leontief technology with constant returns; see Drèze and Bean (1990).

These findings provided the motivation to extend my earlier analysis in two directions, namely: a more general technology encompassing the CES-Leontief specification (general convex production sets, subject only to the twin restrictions of constant returns and absence of joint production); and non-tâtonnement. These extensions are included in the present paper. In the process of carrying out the extensions, I also realised that my 1983 stability proof could be simplified significantly.

The paper is divided in two parts. Part I presents the tâtonnement process corresponding to Morishima's model (Sections 2 and 3), with a simple illustration for the Barro and Grossman (1971)–Malinvaud (1977) Macroeconomic Model (Section 4) and the extension to variable input coefficients (Section 5). Part II presents the extension to non-tâtonnement (Sections 6 and 7). Some comments and concluding remarks are offered in Section 8.

PART I: TÂTONNEMENT

2.   The economy and the process

2.1.   *The economy*

The tâtonnement process studied in Part I may be viewed as a formalisation of the system described in Chapter 7 of Morishima's book *The Economic Theory of Modern Society* (1976), and summarised as follows by the author:

The Keynesian system we have described above has the following system of transmission between its parts. First, suppose that prices of factors of production are given arbitrarily or historically. The prices of products are determined so that they satisfy the equation: prices = costs + normal profits. Now all prices are given, and therefore the income of workers and capitalists per unit of product is determined, and we can determine the remaining unknowns, l individual outputs, by the equations of the theory of effective demand ... since we take the gross investment in capital goods as given. Outputs thus determined decide the demand for labour and the services of capital goods. When these demands do not exceed the existing quantities of capital goods and the supplies of various kinds of labour corresponding to given prices and wages, then there is no excess demand for producer goods. Therefore ... prices are stationary because of the downward rigidity of wages and the prices of capital services, and we have an underemployment equilibrium accompanied by idle capital or unemployment.

In contrast to this, if excess demand exists for capital services or for labour, the prices of producer goods will change ... . The change spreads in turn to product prices, the outputs of each good and the excess demands for producer goods, and then back once again to the point of departure, namely the prices of producer goods. The process of price adjustment is repeated until full-employment equilibrium or underemployment equilibrium is eventually established.

The structure of the economy is summarised in the upper half of table 10.1 (p. 213).

There are $1 + m + n$ commodities. Commodity 0 is 'money', commodities $1 \ldots m$ are inputs, commodities $m + 1 \ldots m + n$ are consumer goods. The price of money is equal to 1. The prices of inputs are denoted $p \in R^m$, the prices of outputs are denoted $q \in R^n$.

An $m \times n$ technology matrix A describes the net input requirements for producing consumer goods. Thus, A_{kj} is the quantity of input k consumed per unit of consumer good j. It is a net quantity, in the sense that intermediate commodities are not recognised explicitly but instead are represented by their own input requirements. This assumes that the economy is 'productive' (no A_{kj} is infinite). Inputs are of three types: labour services, natural resources (land, minerals, ...) and 'machines'. The availability of inputs is fixed in the short run and is the only limiting factor in the production of consumer goods.[2]

There are N consumers indexed $i = 1 \ldots N$. Consumer i initially holds a positive quantity of money m_0^i and a non-negative vector of input

[2] It is suggestive, although not necessary, to think about each consumer good as being produced on a specific 'machine', the capacity of which sets an upper limit to the production of that good. In this interpretation, a 'machine' is typically a shop or plant (e.g. a weaving plant with many looms, rather than a single loom). All the facilities which permit production of a given consumer good with the same unit requirements in labour and natural resources may thus be lumped into a single 'machine'. When the input requirements differ, variable coefficients and diminishing returns fit into the linear technology – but at the cost of handling perfect substitutes in consumption, hence demand correspondences.

endowments $z^i \in R^m$. Typically, each consumer will supply one type of labour services, up to a maximal amount corresponding to his or her endowment. Ownership of natural resources and 'machines' is shared among consumers, possibly reflecting their fixed ownership fractions in firms controlling these inputs.

The (nominal) prices of inputs are initially set at given levels $p(0)$ and are eventually adjusted *upwards* along the process in response to excess demand; they are never adjusted downwards. At these prices, consumers supply their total endowments z^i. Excess supply of an input is accompanied by quantity rationing. I denote by $\zeta_k^i(t)$ the upper bound on the net sales of input k by consumer i at stage t of the process. By construction, $z_k^i \geq \zeta_k^i(t) \geq 0$. (Under an alternative interpretation, the ζ^i's denote input levels for which household i has contracted with the production sector.) I also define the *effective aggregate supply* of inputs by

$$z_k^S(t) = \sum_i \zeta_k^i(t). \tag{2.1}$$

The corresponding vectors are

$$\zeta^i(t) = (\zeta_1^i(t) \ldots \zeta_m^i(t))', \; z^S(t) = (z_1^S(t) \ldots z_m^S(t))'. \tag{2.2}$$

The prices of consumer goods are derived from the prices of inputs through the mark-up formula

$$q'(t) = p'(t)A\mathcal{M}, \tag{2.3}$$

where $\mathcal{M}$ is an $n \times n$ diagonal matrix such that $\mathcal{M}_{jj} - 1 \geq 0$ is the mark-up factor for commodity j, $j = 1 \ldots n$.

Under the price formula (2.3), consumer goods are supplied inelastically to meet consumer demand. That is, output of consumer goods is determined by effective demand, say $y(t)$, generating a factor demand

$$z^D(t) = Ay(t). \tag{2.4}$$

Comparison of the demand $z_k^D(t)$ and the supply $z_k^S(t)$ for factor k leads to the adjustments in price $p_k(t)$ and quantity constraints $\zeta_k^i(t)$ described below.

The effective demands of consumer goods depend upon their prices $q(t)$ and upon the consumer incomes $r^i(t)$, defined by

$$r^i(t) = m_0^i + \sum_k p_k(t)\zeta_k^i(t) = m_0^i + p'(t)\zeta^i(t). \tag{2.5}$$

In this formulation consumers collect income only for the quantities of factors which they can sell, at a given stage of the process. They do not, *along the process*, collect their shares of current profits arising from the mark-up factor. This formulation is somewhat hybrid; greater realism would suggest distribution of profits with explicit lags. The chosen simplification seems unimportant, for my purposes here.

Assuming strictly convex preferences for money and consumer goods, I shall use the demand *functions*

$$y_0^i(q(t), r^i(t)) \in R, \; y^i(q(t), r^i(t)) \in R^n.$$

Thus, demand for consumer goods depends upon input prices and quantity constraints only through the incomes $r^i(t)$. (A more general formulation is used in Part II.)

Two assumptions about individual demand functions will be used below, namely:

ASSUMPTION NI

For all i, for all q, r^i and $\hat{r}^i \geq r^i$, $y^i(q, \hat{r}^i) \geq y^i(q, r^i)$.

ASSUMPTION MPC

For each i, there exists $\gamma^i > 0$ (independent of q and r^i) such that, for all q, r^i and $\hat{r}^i \leq r^i$, $y_0^i(q, \hat{r}^i) \geq y_0^i(q, r^i) + \gamma^i(\hat{r}^i - r^i)$.

Assumption NI (Non Inferiority) rules out inferior goods, which is very unfortunate, since there is nothing pathological about such goods (see however Section 8.5). Assumption MPC (Marginal Propensity to Consume) states that the marginal propensity to spend is bounded away from unity.

The description of the economy is now complete, and may be summarised as follows (see also table 10.1):

(i) Given a vector of input prices $p(t)$ and a matrix of quantity constraints $[\zeta_k^i(t)]$, individual incomes are defined by

$$r^i(t) = m_0^i + \sum_k p_k(t)\zeta_k^i(t) = m_0^i + p'(t)\zeta^i(t) \qquad (2.5)$$

and prices for consumer goods are defined by:

$$q(t) = p'(t)A\mathcal{M}; \qquad (2.3)$$

(ii) Demand for consumer goods is defined by:

$$y(t) = \sum_i y^i(t) = \sum_i y^i(q(t), r^i(t)); \qquad (2.6)$$

Table 10.1

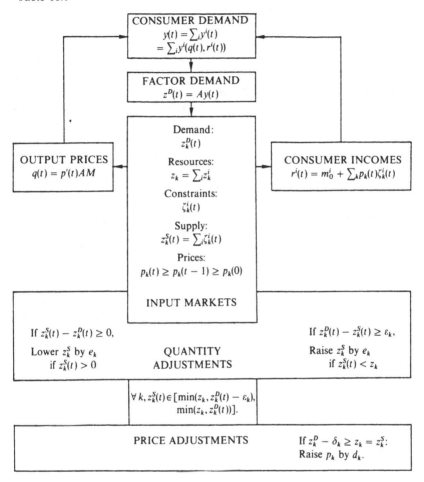

that demand implies a demand for inputs

$$z^D(t) = Ay(t). \tag{2.4}$$

2.2. The process

Upon comparing the demand vector for inputs $z^D(t)$ with the supply vector $z^S(t) = \Sigma_i \zeta^i(t)$, adjustments in prices and quantity constraints can be defined. I shall consider a *hierarchical process*, under which *prices are adjusted only after all justified adjustments in quantity constraints have been realised*; in other words, quantities move faster than prices, in agreement with the Clower–Leijonhufvud reappraisal of Keynesian economics.[3]

The process is *discrete*. For each input k, there is a quantity unit e_k, of which all initial endowments are treated as integer multiples. Quantity constraints $\zeta_k^i(t)$ are adjusted by discrete steps of fixed, constant size e_k. And there is a price unit d_k. Prices $p_k(t)$ are similarly adjusted by discrete steps of fixed, constant size d_k.

The adjustment rules involve *thresholds*. No adjustment in input levels, hence in quantity constraints, takes place unless the excess demand or supply for an input, $|z_k^D(t) - z_k^S(t)|$, reaches some *a priori* given minimal level ε_k (at least one quantity unit, possibly more). And no adjustment in price takes place unless the excess *demand* for an input, $z_k^D(t) - z_k^S(t)$, is at least equal to some *a priori* given minimal level δ_k ($\geq \varepsilon_k$).

This approach has two consequences. First, it leads to a finite convergence theorem, under rather weak assumptions. Second, it leads only to an *approximate equilibrium*, where a small discrepancy between supply and demand (at most δ_k) is tolerated.

The idea that prices are not adjusted unless demand exceeds supply by at least some given (but arbitrarily small) δ_k is definitely appealing, considering the fixed costs of changing prices. An arbitrarily small discrepancy between supply and demand of an *input* seems tolerable, as it can be absorbed by a commensurate adjustment in productivity, product quality or inventories.[4] In my definition of equilibrium, the discrepancy is of arbitrary sign. In the adjustment process, I assume that firms always get rid of excess inputs, and rely on productivity or inventory adjustments to achieve feasibility. That formulation is geared to the non-tâtonnement analysis, where it is technically more convenient and logically more congruent with the notion that excess demand for final commodities is absorbed by inventories.

---

[3] 'In the Keynesian macro-system the Marshallian ranking of price – and quantity – adjustment speeds is reversed: in the shortest period flow quantities are freely variable, but one or more prices are given, and the admissible range of variation for the rest of the prices is thereby limited': Leijonhufvud (1968), p. 52.

[4] Note that, if profits are defined as $\pi = q'y - p'\sum_i \zeta^i$, so that any discrepancy between supply and demand of inputs is absorbed by the production sector, then automatically $\sum_i y_0^i + \pi = \sum_i m_0^i$ in equilibrium. Indeed, $\sum_i y_0^i + \pi = \sum_i (r^i - q'y^i) + \pi = \sum_i (m_0^i + p'\zeta^i) - q'y + q'y - p'\sum_i \zeta^i = \sum_i m_0^i$, which corresponds to Walras law in this model.

DEFINITION

An *ε-equilibrium with excess supply* consists of a vector of input prices $p \in R^m$, a matrix of quantity constraints $[\zeta_k^i] \in R^{Nm}$, a vector of inputs $z^D \in R^m$, a vector of outputs $y \in R^n$, a vector of prices $q \in R^n$ with $q' = p'A\mathcal{M}$ and an N-tuple of vectors $(y_0^i, y^i) \in R \times R^n$ such that:

(i) (z^D, y) maximises $q'y - p'z^D$ subject to $z^D \geq Ay$, $y \leq \sum_i y^i$;

(ii) (y_0^i, y^i) maximises i's preferences, subject to $y_0^i + q'y^i \leq m_0^i + p'\zeta^i$;

(iii) $[0] \leq [\zeta_k^i] \leq [z_k^i]$, $\sum_i y^i \leq y$;

(iv) for all $k = 1 \ldots m$, $|z_k^D - \sum_i \zeta_k^i| \leq \varepsilon$.

DESCRIPTION OF THE PROCESS P

The process is defined in terms of the sequence $(p(t), [\zeta_k^i(t)])$, $t = 0, 1, 2 \ldots$. The other parameters are at all stages defined through (2.3)–(2.6).

(*P i*) *Initiation.* Initial input prices $p(0)$ are historically given, with $p_k(0) > 0$ for all k.

Initial quantity constraints are historically set at $\zeta_k^i(0)$, an integer multiple of e_k, with $z_k^i \geq \zeta_k^i(0) \geq 0$ for all i and k.

(*P ii*) *General Step – Adjustment of a Quantity Constraint.* At stage t, a single quantity constraint is adjusted, provided there exists an input k for which such an adjustment is justified. (The order in which markets are visited is immaterial.)

Two situations are distinguished:

(a) $z_k^S(t) - z_k^D(t) > 0$.

Then necessarily $z_k^S(t) > 0$, and there exists i such that $\zeta_k^i(t) > 0$. For some (any) such i, set

$$\zeta_k^i(t + 1) = \zeta_k^i(t) - e_k. \tag{2.7}$$

(That is, the constraint on net sales of input k by consumer i is lowered by one unit e_k. Because $\zeta_k^i(t)$ results from the operation of the process, starting from an integer multiple of e_k, $\zeta_k^i(t) > 0$ implies $\zeta_k^i(t + 1) \geq 0$.)

(b) $z_k^D(t) - z_k^S(t) \geq \varepsilon_k$ with $z_k^S(t) < z_k$.

Then necessarily there exists i such that $\zeta_k^i(t) < z_k^i$. For some (any) such i, set

$$\zeta_k^i(t + 1) = \zeta_k^i(t) + e_k. \tag{2.8}$$

(That is, the constraint on net sales of input k by consumer i is raised by one unit e_k. Because both $\zeta_k^i(t)$ and z_k^i are integer multiples of e_k, $\zeta_k^i(t) < z_k^i$ implies $\zeta_k^i(t + 1) \leq z_k^i$.)

(*P iii*) *General Step – Adjustment of a Price.* If, at stage t, no adjustment of quantity constraints is justified, then it must be the case, that for all k,

$$z_k^S(t) \in [\min(z_k, z_k^D(t) - \varepsilon_k), \min(z_k, z_k^D(t))], z_k^S(t) \leq z_k^D(t). \tag{2.9}$$

If there exists k such that $z_k^D(t) - \delta_k \geq z_k^S(t) = z_k$, set

$$p_k(t + 1) = p_k(t) + d_k. \tag{2.10}$$

(That is, if input k is in excess demand by at least δ_k, with no binding constraints on net sales, the price of that input is raised by a fixed amount d_k.)

(*P iv*) *Termination.* If, for all k, (2.9) holds with $z_k^D(t) < z_k + \delta_k$, the process terminates.

A state of the economy where the process terminates is an *ε-equilibrium with excess supply*, where

$$\varepsilon \leq \max_k \delta_k, \tag{2.11}$$

an arbitrarily small quantity.

Indeed, conditions (i)–(iii) in the above definition are always satisfied along process P. Conditions (iv) are satisfied when the process terminates, since (2.9) implies $z_k^S(t) - z_k^D(t) \leq 0$ and (P iv) implies $z_k^S(t) - z_k^D(t) > -\delta_k$, so that $|z_k^D(t) - z_k^S(t)| \leq \delta_k$ as desired.

3. Stability

The proof of the stability theorem below rests upon the following lemma, which establishes that *all prices are bounded along the process* P.

LEMMA I

Under process P, for all k, for all t,

$$p_k(t) \leq \max\left(\frac{\sum_i m_0^i}{\delta_k} + d_k, p_k(0)\right) \stackrel{\text{def}}{=} \bar{p}_k.$$

PROOF

From the definition of the process, $p_k(t + 1) = p_k(t)$ unless

$$z_l^D(t) - z_l^S(t) \geq 0 \text{ for all } l, \; z_k^D(t) - z_k^S(t) \geq \delta_k. \tag{3.1}$$

Moreover,

$$\sum_l p_l(t)z_l^D(t) = \sum_l p_l(t) \sum_{j=1}^n A_{lj}y_j(t) \qquad \text{by (2.4)}$$

$$= \sum_{j=1}^n \frac{1}{\mu_{jj}} q_j(t)y_j(t) \leq \sum_{j=1}^n q_j(t)y_j(t) \qquad \text{by (2.3)}$$

$$= \sum_i (r^i(t) - y_0^i(t)) \qquad \text{by (2.6)}$$

$$= \sum_i \left[\sum_l p_l(t)\zeta_l^i(t) + m_0^i - y_0^i(t) \right] \qquad \text{by (2.5)}$$

$$= \sum_l p_l(t)z_l^S(t) + \sum_i (m_0^i - y_0^i(t)).$$

Thus

$$\sum_{\substack{l=1 \\ l \neq k}}^m p_l(t)[z_l^D(t) - z_l^S(t)] + p_k(t)[z_k^D(t) - z_k^S(t)] \leq \sum_i (m_0^i - y_0^i(t)).$$

If $p_k(t + 1) > p_k(t)$, then

$$\delta_k p_k(t) \leq p_k(t)[z_k^D(t) - z_k^S(t)] \leq \sum_i (m_0^i - y_0^i(t))$$

$$- \sum_{\substack{l=1 \\ l \neq k}}^m p_l(t)[z_l^D(t) - z_l^S(t)]$$

$$\leq \sum_i m_0^i,$$

where the last inequalities follow from (3.1), and $y_0^i(t) \geq 0$. Thus, $p_k(t + 1)$ will not rise above $p_k(t)$ unless $p_k(t) \leq \sum_i m_0^i/\delta_k$, which proves the lemma.

QED

The logic of the above proof is straightforward. If the demand for input k exceeds its supply by the finite amount δ_k, *and no input is in excess supply*, then even with zero mark-up the value of aggregate demand must exceed the revenue from the sale of factors by at least $\delta_k p_k(t)$; that discrepancy must be financed from initial money holdings, so that $\delta_k p_k(t) \leq \sum_i m_0^i(t)$.

The lemma has a very important implication, namely that *only a finite bounded number of price adjustments can occur under process* P. Indeed, each such adjustment calls for increasing some price p_k by the constant finite amount d_k, and each p_k has a finite upper bound $\bar{p}_k$. In order to establish finite convergence of the process, it will thus suffice to establish that only a finite, *uniformly* bounded number of quantity adjustments can take place between two price adjustments. The overall process will thus consist of a bounded number of uniformly bounded numbers of steps, i.e. of a bounded number of steps.

THEOREM I

Under assumptions NI and MPC, provided for all $k = 1 \ldots m$, e_k is small enough $(e_k \leq \frac{1}{2}\varepsilon_k)$, the process P is stable, and converges in a bounded number of steps to an ε-equilibrium with excess supply.

PROOF

We only need to prove that at most a finite uniformly bounded number of quantity adjustments can take place between two price adjustments. Let p denote the price vector resulting from either initiation or some price adjustment, and let $t + 1$ denote a general quantity adjustment step. The process P is best viewed, over the set of quantity adjustment steps between two successive price adjustments, as associating with $(p, [\zeta_k^i(t)])$ $\in R^m \times R^{Nm}$ the set of solutions $(p, [\zeta_k^i(t + 1)]) \in R^m \times R^{Nm}$ compatible with the description of the process. This is a finite set, with elements generated by alternative choices of k or i, where alternative choices exist. Hence, it is closed, and compact because the solutions are bounded: $z_k^i \geq \zeta_k^i(t) \geq 0$ for all i, k and t. The proof is a simplified version of the proof of theorem 6.2, pp. 290–291 in Champsaur, Drèze and Henry (1977), using the Lyapunov function

$$L(t) = \sum_{l=1}^{m} p_l \max \left[z_l^D(t) - \varepsilon_l - z_l^S(t), z_l^S(t) - z_l^D(t) \right]$$

$$\leq \sum_{l=1}^{m} p_l \max \left[z_l^D(t), z_l^S(t) \right]. \tag{3.2}$$

That function is uniformly bounded above, because p_l is bounded (by $\bar{p}_l$ in the lemma), $z_l^S(t) \leq \sum_i z_i^l$ and $p_l z_l^D(t) \leq \sum_j p_j z_j^D(t) \leq \sum_j p_j \sum_i z_j^i + \sum_i m_0^i$ as verified in the proof of the lemma. Also, $L(t) \geq -\sum_{l=1}^{m} p_l \varepsilon_l \geq -\sum_{l=1}^{m} \bar{p}_l \varepsilon_l$. Thus, $L(t)$ is uniformly bounded, both above and below. The proof consists in showing that there exists a positive constant $c = \min_{k=1\ldots m} c_k$, *bounded away from zero*, such that $L(t) - L(t+1) \geq c$, unless no further quantity adjustment is possible at $(t+1)$. The two possibilities corresponding to (P ii) (a) and (P ii) (b) are considered successively.

Case (P ii) (a)

In this case, for all $l = 1 \ldots m$, $p_l(t+1) = p_l(t) = p_l$, so that $q(t+1) = q(t)$ as well. Also, for all $h = 1 \ldots N$, $h \neq i$, $\zeta^h(t+1) = \zeta^h(t)$, so that $r^h(t+1) = r^h(t)$ and $y^h(t+1) = y^h(q(t), r^h(t)) = y^h(t)$. For all $l = 1 \ldots m$, $l \neq k$, $\zeta_l^i(t+1) = \zeta_l^i(t)$, so that $z_l^S(t+1) = z_l^S(t)$. On the other hand $\zeta_k^i(t+1) = \zeta_k^i(t) - e_k$, so that $z_k^S(t+1) = z_k^S(t) - e_k$. Finally, $r^i(t+1) = r^i(t) + p_k [\zeta_k^i(t+1) - \zeta_k^i(t)] = r^i(t) - e_k p_k < r^i(t)$. In view of assumption NI, $y^i(t+1) = y^i(q(t), r^i(t+1)) \leq y^i(q(t), r^i(t)) = y^i(t)$, so that $y(t+1) \leq y(t)$ and $z^D(t+1) \leq z^D(t)$.

For all $l = 1 \ldots m$, $l \neq k$,

$$\max \left[z_l^D(t+1) - \varepsilon_l - z_l^S(t+1), z_l^S(t+1) - z_l^D(t+1) \right]$$
$$= \max \left[z_l^D(t+1) - \varepsilon_l - z_l^S(t), z_l^S(t) - z_l^D(t+1) \right]$$
$$\leq z_l^D(t) - z_l^D(t+1)$$
$$\quad + \max \left[z_l^D(t) - \varepsilon_l - z_l^S(t), z_l^S(t) - z_l^D(t) \right].$$

Also, $z_k^D(t+1) \leq z_k^D(t) < z_k^S(t) = z_k^S(t+1) + e_k$, and for e_k small enough $(e_k \leq \frac{1}{2}\varepsilon_k)$,

$$z_k^D(t+1) - \varepsilon_k - z_k^S(t+1) = z_k^D(t+1) - \varepsilon_k - z_k^S(t) + e_k$$
$$\leq z_k^D(t+1) - e_k - z_k^S(t) \leq z_k^D(t) - e_k - z_k^S(t) < -e_k$$

$$< z_k^S(t) - e_k - z_k^D(t)$$
$$= z_k^S(t + 1) - z_k^D(t) \le z_k^S(t + 1) - z_k^D(t + 1),$$

so that

$$\max\left[z_k^D(t + 1) - \varepsilon_k - z_k^S(t + 1), z_k^S(t + 1) - z_k^D(t + 1) \right]$$
$$= z_k^S(t + 1) - z_k^D(t + 1)$$
$$= z_k^S(t) - z_k^D(t) - e_k + z_k^D(t) - z_k^D(t + 1)$$
$$= \max\left[z_k^D(t) - \varepsilon_k - z_k^S(t), z_k^S(t) - z_k^D(t) \right]$$
$$+ z_k^D(t) - z_k^D(t + 1) - e_k.$$

Consequently,

$$L(t + 1) - L(t) \le \sum_{l=1}^{m} p_l[z_l^D(t) - z_l^D(t + 1)] - e_k p_k.$$

Furthermore,

$$z_l^D(t) - z_l^D(t + 1) = \sum_{j=1}^{n} A_{lj}[y_j^i(t) - y_j^i(t + 1)]$$

and $\sum_{l=1}^{m} p_l A_{lj} = \dfrac{1}{\mu_{jj}} q_j,$

so that

$$\sum_{l=1}^{m} p_l[z_l^D(t) - z_l^D(t + 1)] = \sum_j \frac{1}{\mu_{jj}} q_j(t)[y_j^i(t) - y_j^i(t + 1)]$$
$$\le \sum_j q_j(t)[y_j^i(t) - y_j^i(t + 1)]$$
$$= [r^i(t) - y_0^i(t) - r^i(t + 1) + y_0^i(t + 1)]$$
$$= [e_k p_k + y_0^i(t + 1) - y_0^i(t)] \le e_k p_k(1 - \gamma^i),$$

where the last inequality follows from assumption MPC. Hence,

$$L(t + 1) - L(t) \le e_k p_k(1 - \gamma^i - 1) \le -e_k p_k \gamma^i \le -c_k < 0,$$

where the existence of $c_k > 0$ follows from $p_k \ge p_k(0) > 0$.

Case (P ii) (b)

This case is entirely symmetrical to the previous one, and the same reasoning applies, with $\zeta_k^i(t + 1) = \zeta_k^i(t) + e_k$, $r^i(t + 1) = r^i(t) + e_k p_k$ and $z^D(t + 1) \ge z^D(t)$.

For all $l = 1 \ldots m$, $l \neq k$, we have $z_l^S(t + 1) = z_l^S(t)$ and

$$\max \left[z_l^D(t + 1) - \varepsilon_l - z_l^S(t + 1), \; z_l^S(t + 1) - z_l^D(t + 1) \right]$$
$$\leq \max \left[z_l^D(t + 1) - \varepsilon_l - z_l^S(t), \; z_l^S(t) - z_l^D(t) \right]$$
$$\leq z_l^D(t + 1) - z_l^D(t) + \max \left[z_l^D - \varepsilon_l - z_l^S(t), \; z_l^S(t) - z_l^D(t) \right].$$

Also, for $e_k \leq \dfrac{\varepsilon_k}{2}$,

$$z_k^D(t + 1) - \varepsilon_k - z_k^S(t + 1) \geq z_k^D(t) - \varepsilon_k - z_k^S(t) - e_k \geq -e_k$$
$$\geq e_k - \varepsilon_k \geq z_k^S(t) + e_k - z_k^D(t) \geq z_k^S(t + 1) - z_k^D(t + 1),$$

so that

$$\max \left[z_k^D(t + 1) - \varepsilon_k - z_k^S(t + 1), \; z_k^S(t + 1) - z_k^D(t + 1) \right]$$
$$= z_k^D(t + 1) - \varepsilon_k - z_k^S(t + 1)$$
$$= z_k^D(t + 1) - z_k^D(t) - e_k + z_k^D(t) - \varepsilon_k - z_k^S(t)$$
$$= z_k^D(t + 1) - z_k^D(t) - e_k + \max \left[z_k^D(t) - \varepsilon_k - z_k^S(t), \; z_k^S(t) - z_k^D(t) \right].$$

By the reasoning of the previous case,

$$\sum_{l=1}^{m} p_l[z_l^D(t + 1) - z_l^D(t)] \leq r^i(t + 1) - y_0^i(t + 1) - r^i(t) + y_0^i(t)$$

$$\leq e_k p_k(1 - \gamma^i),$$

$$L(t + 1) - L(t) \leq -e_k p_k \gamma^i \leq -c_k < 0.$$

Combining the two cases, and writing c for $\min_k c_k$, we have shown that $L(t + 1) - L(t) \leq -c < 0$ unless (2.9) holds and no further quantity adjustment is possible. Since $L(t)$ is uniformly bounded above and below for all t, only a finite number of successive quantity adjustments is possible. The condition $e_k p_k(t)\gamma^i \geq c_k > 0$ may be imposed in the form $e_k p_k(t)\gamma^i \geq e_k p_k(0)\, \gamma^i \geq c_k > 0$, so that c_k is independent of the stage of the process, and the number of successive quantity adjustments is uniformly bounded, as desired. QED

The logic of the second part of the proof is again straightforward. Each quantity adjustment on z_k^S reduces the absolute money value of excess demand for input k by $e_k p_k(t)$ at unchanged demand for commodities, and affects only the disposable income of a single consumer by that same amount. By MPC, the money value of effective demand for commodities will adjust by at most $(1 - \gamma^i)e_k p_k(t)$, leaving a positively bounded margin of $e_k p_k(t)\gamma^i \geq c$ by which the absolute money value of excess demand for inputs must fall.

4. Illustration

The so-called 'three goods economy' dear to macro-theorists has money, a single input labour ($m = 1$), and a single produced commodity ($n = 1$). In the specification of Malinvaud (1977), the N consumers are identical. At a given money wage $p(t)$ and commodity price $q(t) = p(t) a \mu$, the economy is conveniently described by figure 10.2. The horizontal axis corresponds to labour, the vertical axis to the commodity. The ray OA describes the Leontief technology. Let each household supply a single unit of labour – the e_k of Section 2 being here renormalised to unity; hence, its labour supply constraint (ζ_k^i) can take two values: 0 or 1. To these two values correspond the incomes $r^i = m_0^i$ and $r^i = m_0^i + p(t)$, respectively, with associated demand levels $y^i(m_0^i, q(t))$ and $y^i(m_0^i + p(t), q(t))$. Aggregate demand is thus a linear function of employment, for which the relevant measure during the tâtonnement is $z^S(t) = \sum_i \zeta^i(t)$; namely:

$$y(t) = z^S(t) y^i(m_0^i + p(t), q(t)) + [N - z^S(t)] y^i(m_0^i, q(t)). \qquad (4.1)$$

That linear function, defined over the domain $[0, N]$, is plotted in figure 10.2. If the upper end of that line segment (point B) belonged to the line OA, reflecting equality of supply and demand for the commodity at full employment of labour, one could conclude that $(p(t), q(t))$ are competitive prices. In figure 10.2a, point B lies below the line OA, whereas in figure 10.2b, point B lies above the line OA.

To start with figure 10.2a, let $t = 0$ and $\sum_i \zeta^i(0) = z^S(0)$ be a relatively small number, as drawn. One can then read from the graph $z^D(0) \gg z^S(0)$, which calls for a quantity adjustment step (P ii) (b), i.e. for a unit increase in employment: $z^S(1) = z^S(0) + 1$. This reasoning will continue to hold so long as $z^D(t) - z^S(t) > \varepsilon$; it will cease to hold when $y(t)$ is close enough to the point K so that an ε-equilibrium with excess supply has been reached.

The same reasoning applies with a starting point $z^S(0)$ relatively large (close to N), the only difference being that the quantity adjustment steps are of the type (P ii) (a). Thus, in the case of figure 10.2a, process P converges through a sequence of quantity adjustments to the vicinity of a Keynesian equilibrium (point K) at the original wage and price $(p(0), q(0))$.

Turning to figure 10.2b, we note that $z^D(0) \gg z^S(0)$ for all $z^S(0) \in [0, N]$. This leads to a sequence of quantity adjustment steps (P ii) (b) until eventually $z^S(t) = N = z \ll z^D(t)$. Because $z^S(t) = z$, no further quantity adjustment is possible, and the process triggers a price adjustment (P iii): the excess demand for labour leads to a nominal wage increase, so that $p(t + 1) = p(t) + d \; (= p(0) + d)$. The commodity price q is immediately

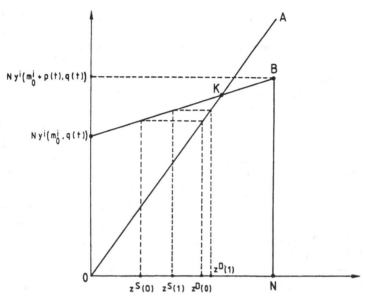

Figure 10.2a

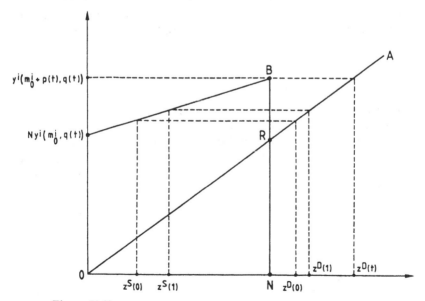

Figure 10.2b

raised from $q(t) = q(0) = p(0)a\mu$ to $q(t + 1) = p(t + 1)a\mu$ – leading to the new demand level $y(t + 1) = Ny^i(m_0^i + p(t + 1), q(t + 1))$. If $y(t + 1) \gg \overline{NR} = N/a$, i.e. if commodity demand still exceeds appreciably full employment output, we remain in the case of figure 10.2b and a further wage-price increase is triggered by the process. The reasoning in the proof of lemma I shows that this cannot happen infinitely many times, so that eventually point B falls back to the vicinity of line OA (at R) and an allocation close to a competitive equilibrium is attained. That reasoning says that, when prices cover wage costs, wage income can at best purchase produced output; thus, excess demand is financed entirely by initial money holdings, and must become negligible as the price level keeps rising. (That compelling argument does not assert that excess demand falls *monotonically* – only that it falls *eventually*.) Thus, in the case of figure 10.2b, process P converges, through a sequence of quantity adjustments followed by a sequence of wage-price increases, to the vicinity of a competitive equilibrium.

A further complication arises when existing equipment permits employing only $M < N$ workers. In order to fit that complication into process P, one must treat equipment as another input, with a price (rent) that will rise under the pressure of excess demand, eventually bringing the economy to the vicinity of a point with a clearing commodity market and unemployment – at the original wage and at a commodity price inflated by the rent on capital equipment.[5] Details are left to the reader.

5. Variable coefficients

The description of the technology in the model of Sections 2–3 is very specific. The *a priori* distinction between primary inputs and final commodities is perhaps acceptable at the economy-wide level. But the Leontief technology is extreme. The standard approach in general equilibrium economics would introduce a convex aggregate production set Y, then rewrite condition (i) in the definition of an ε-equilibrium as

$$(z^D, y) \text{ maximises } q'y - p'z^D \text{ subject to } (z^D, y) \in Y, y \leq \sum_i y^i. \qquad \text{(i*)}$$

[5] In the standard terminology of equilibria with quantity rationing, the process terminates at the intersection of the Keynesian and classical regimes – as suggested in Keynes' *General Theory*.

The Leontief specification says that '$(z^D, y) \in Y$ if and only if $z^D \geq Ay$', where A is a given matrix.

There is no difficulty in extending the definition of process P to a general specification of the technology. For instance, one could define $z^D(t)$ at each step through cost minimisation at given input prices and output levels:

$$(z^D, y) \text{ minimises } p'(t)z^D(t) \text{ subject to } (z^D(t), y(t)) \in Y. \qquad (5.1)$$

It would be interesting to know whether the extended process converges. My conjecture is that it would – possibly under some mild conditions; but the technique of proof would be more complicated. Short of having investigated the matter, I can at least give an example of a variable coefficients technology under which the extended process has the same properties as the original process – namely a convex technology with constant returns and no joint production.

In that case, the aggregate production set Y is the sum of n distinct production sets Y^j, one for each commodity $j = 1 \ldots n$, and Y^i is a convex cone with vertex zero (constant returns), such that, for all $(z^D, y) \in Y^j$, $y_l = 0$, $l = 1 \ldots n$, $l \neq j$ (no joint production). The important implication of such a technology, for my purposes, is that *technological choices are fully determined by input prices and do not depend upon output levels*. If either cuts of Y^j in z^D-space for given y_j are strictly convex, or an appropriate selection is made when (5.1) has multiple solutions,[6] then *we are back to the Leontief technology so long as input prices do not change*.

For process P, this means that we can work with the Leontief specification along sequences of quantity adjustment steps (P ii), and update the input-output matrix at (within) price adjustment steps (P iii) only. Consequently, the proof of theorem I remains valid without modification. This establishes the following:

COROLLARY

If the Leontief technology of Section 2 is extended to a general convex technology with constant returns and no joint production, theorem I still holds, wording unchanged.

Some econometricians – including Sneessens and Drèze (1986a) or Drèze and Bean (1991) – would argue that technical coefficients are revised infrequently anyhow; accordingly a more realistic extension of process P

---

[6]For instance, minimise $|z^D(t) - z^D(t - 1)|$.

would retain the hierarchical structure, and introduce revisions of technical coefficients only when the process terminates. This would lead to consider a sequence of processes, each of which converges in finitely many steps, with technical coefficients for the v-th process minimising cost for the input prices and output levels at the termination of process $v - 1$. I would again conjecture that convergence of such a sequence would follow from mild conditions.

PART II: NON-TÂTONNEMENT

6.   A non-tâtonnement process

6.1.   Principles

It is not difficult to suggest a guiding principle towards one extension of theorem I to a non-tâtonnement process, with production and consumption activities carried out in continuous time out of equilibrium. Suppose that firms hold inventories of consumer goods, out of which consumer demand can be satisfied *temporarily* when it exceeds production. Such an assumption is not as general as one would like, because it rules out non-storable commodities, like electricity, opera seats or labour services (which are occasionally subject to demand rationing). This is an exploratory paper, and storable commodities will do. If consumer demand is never rationed, and the production sector is still treated as an aggregate, then activities 'out of equilibrium' differ from activities 'at equilibrium' (of the process) in a single respect, namely that the quantities of inputs stipulated by the process may differ from those needed to satisfy demand. That households may experience excess supply of inputs, along the process, is not a novel feature, since that possibility is already accepted at equilibrium. But firms realise their input demands at equilibrium, whereas that may not be possible out of equilibrium. Still, excess demand for some inputs should not prevent firms from making use of whatever production possibilities they have, in order to satisfy at least partially the demand for their outputs, while drawing *temporarily* on inventories for the balance. And hoarding some inputs *temporarily* is common place, when firms adjust progressively to a demand shortfall or are prevented from using some input k because the complementary input l is in short supply. Modelling production activities out of equilibrium is a natural task, as those who have worked on dynamic planning of production, inventories and workforce know.

A key word in my tale so far is 'temporarily'. Clearly, inventory depletion cannot go on forever, nor will firms hoard factors of production forever. Regarding the first point, adjustment in either production levels or prices (to choke off demand) should be fast enough that the drain on inventories comes to a halt before the warehouse, or the shelves, are empty.[7] A reasonable assignment for non-tâtonnement stability analysis is thus to investigate *sufficient conditions* on the adjustment process under which *a form of equilibrium is reached, in real time, before reasonable levels of initial inventories are depleted.* This is where the finite convergence property established in theorem I pays off! If that property can be extended to a non-tâtonnement framework, with production and consumption activities out of equilibrium, then it will suffice to show that the amount of inventory depletion between two steps of the process is uniformly bounded; one will then conclude that bounded initial inventories are sufficient to guarantee feasibility of the non-tâtonnement process. That is precisely the approach followed here, and the nature of the result established by theorem II.

The second point, namely that hoarding of factors of production should also be temporary, has two aspects. One aspect concerns the optimising behaviour of firms with respect to hiring and firing of inputs given their anticipations regarding input prices and product demand. This is a topic in the difficult area of stochastic optimisation. Another aspect concerns the drain on liquidities associated with temporary hoarding of factors of production. Bankruptcies present genuine modelling difficulties. Again, these can be avoided if initial cash holdings plus proceeds from the sale of inventories suffice to finance factor hoardings out of equilibrium.

In this paper, stochastic optimisation will be bypassed altogether, through assumptions on (static and deterministic) expectations. And the idea that quantities move faster than prices will be carried to the extreme, so that disequilibrium during the real time devoted to quantity adjustments (hiring and firing of primary factors of production) will not have destabilising consequences. (This is explained in Section 6.5.) Under these conditions, the key to the stability analysis will still be provided by a lemma establishing that input prices are bounded above, so that finitely many upward price adjustments need be considered.

6.2.   Time

In reality, firms make decisions about prices and input levels at arbitrary

---

[7]This property is *assumed*, not demonstrated, in the imaginative, and rather unique, analysis of non-tâtonnement stability by Fisher (1983).

points in time, whereas production and consumption activities are carried out as continuous flows. I will model the non-tâtonnement counterpart of the adjustment process introduced in Part I in terms of *rates of flow per unit of calendar time* of input uses, incomes, consumption and production; and in terms of *steps of the process*, i.e., adjustments of prices or input flows, occurring at *finitely spaced points of calendar time*. It is natural to think of these steps as taking place in quick succession, and to ignore the variations of the rates of flow (of consumption or production) inside the short intervals separating two steps. Accordingly, *the points in calendar time corresponding to the steps of the process are also the decision points for the agents.* Stock variables – like money or inventories – are then easily updated (integrals of flows are obtained as the product of a constant rate of flow by the length of a time span).

The basic notation for Part II consists in using the integers $\dots t, t + 1,$ $\dots$ to number the steps of the process; and in using the symbol $\tau(t)$ to denote the span of calendar time separating steps t and $t + 1$, with the natural normalisation $\tau(t) \leq 1$. Furthermore, the symbols z, ζ, y used with appropriate indices in Part I to denote the supply and demand of inputs or commodities, retain the same definition; they are now interpreted as rates of flow per unit of calendar time. Production and consumption decisions concern these rates of flow. Equilibrium requires equality (up to ε, in so far as inputs are concerned) of the demand *rates* and supply *rates*.

6.3. Consumer demand

In so far as consumers are concerned, I shall now use *stationary demand functions* with three arguments: $m^i(t)$, $p'(t)\zeta^i(t)$ and $q(t)$. Thus, the income $r^i(t) = m_0^i + p'(t)\zeta^i(t)$ of (2.5) is split into two components: a stock of money balances $m^i(t)$ and a flow of income from the sale of inputs $p'(t)\zeta^i(t)$. The reason for separating out these two components is of course that the intertemporal budget constraint recognises the repetitive nature of the income flow associated with the input sales. I shall assume that the endowments of inputs are perpetual flows at the constant rates $[z_k^i]$, and that consumers hold *static point expectations* about p, q and ζ^i.[8] Thus, after observing $p(t), q(t), \zeta^i(t)$, household i expects $p(t') = p(t), q(t') = q(t)$ and $\zeta^i(t') = \zeta^i(t)$ for all $t' > t$; and it solves the problem of optimally

---

[8] If consumers are infinitely lived and have stationary additive consumption tastes (so that past consumption is irrelevant to current decisions), the stationarity of demand should follow; I have not investigated that question in detail.

allocating its resources – consisting of the stock $m^i(t)$ and the perpetual constant flow $p'(t)\zeta^i(t)$ – to consumption over time. The solution of that problem is an infinite sequence of flows of consumption per unit of calendar time, the first component of which, to be denoted $y^i(t)$, is implemented. Because $\tau(t) \leq 1$, a new step of the process will take place before the unit of calendar time covered by $y^i(t)$ is exhausted; at that point, the household will observe $p(t + 1)$, $q(t + 1)$, $\zeta^i(t + 1)$ and choose $y^i(t + 1)$ in the same way. The stationarity of the demand functions says that, if $m^i(t + 1) = m^i(t)$, $p'(t + 1)\zeta^i(t + 1) = p'(t)\zeta^i(t)$ and $q(t + 1) = q(t)$, then $y^i(t + 1) = y^i(t)$.

Money balances are defined recursively by

$$m^i(t + 1) = m^i(t) + \tau(t)[p'(t)\zeta^i(t) - q'(t)y^i(t)] \geq 0. \tag{6.1}$$

That is, money balances are updated by the flow of receipts minus expenditures since the previous step and they are not allowed to become negative. With static expectations and stationary demand functions, households typically plan to deplete gradually their money balances; in that case $m^i(t + 1) < m^i(t)$ and, when $p'(t + 1)\zeta^i(t + 1) = p'(t)\zeta^i(t)$ and $q'(t + 1) = q'(t)$, then $y^i(t + 1) < y^i(t)$.

At the date of step t of the process, the rate of consumption flow per unit of calendar time chosen by household i is thus

$$y^i(t) = y^i(m^i(t), p'(t)\zeta^i(t), q(t)) \in R^n. \tag{6.2}$$

It satisfies suitable extensions of assumptions NI and MPC, namely:

ASSUMPTION NI'

> For all i, for all q, m^i, $p'\zeta^i$ and $\hat{m}^i \geq m^i$, $\hat{p}'\hat{\zeta}^i \geq p'\zeta^i$, $y^i(\hat{m}^i, \hat{p}'\hat{\zeta}^i, q) \geq y^i(m^i, p'\zeta^i, q)$.

ASSUMPTION MPC'

> For each i, there exist $\beta^i > 0$ and $\gamma^i > 0$ (independent of q, m^i and $p'\zeta^i$) such that, for all q, m^i, $p'\zeta^i$ and $\hat{m}^i \geq m^i$, $\hat{p}'\hat{\zeta}^i \geq p'\zeta^i$, $\hat{p}'\hat{\zeta}^i - q' y^i(\hat{m}^i, \hat{p}'\hat{\zeta}^i, q) \geq p'\zeta^i - q'y^i(m, p'\zeta^i, q) + \gamma^i(\hat{m}^i - m^i) + \beta^i(\hat{p}'\hat{\zeta}^i - p'\zeta^i)$.

6.4. *Production and factor demand*

In the non-tâtonnement process, it is suggestive to think about the ζ's as *levels of contracts between consumers and producers*. This is most transparent for labour services: $\zeta^i_k(t)$ measures the flow of labour service k for which household i is engaged in a labour contract at the date of step t. To say that $\zeta^i_k(t+1) = \zeta^i(t) + (-)e_k$, is to say that employment of household i goes up (down) by e_k, i.e. by one elementary unit of labour type k. Similarly, if good k is a plot of land owned by household i, then $\zeta^i_k \le z^i_k$ is the acreage rented out at the date of step t. In a more contrived way perhaps, if good k is an oil refinery belonging to a firm in which household i holds a fraction z^i_k of the shares, and if the refinery operates at 60% of capacity, earning an imputed rent equal to 60% of p_k, then $\zeta^i_k = .6\,z^i_k$ is the *share* of the rent accruing to household i.

The behaviour of producers (or 'implicit firms') at the date of step t will then be defined by the solution of the following problem, where $\hat{y}(t)$ denotes the flow of production at that date:

$$\max_{y(t)} q'(t)\hat{y}(t) \text{ subject to } \hat{y}(t) \le y(t) = \sum_i y^i(t)$$

$$A\hat{y}(t) \le \sum_i \zeta^i(t) \tag{6.3}$$

where $q'(t) = p'(t)A\mathcal{M}$ as per (2.3). This formulation reflects revenue maximising production decisions under two constraints: production should not exceed demand $y(t)$; production cannot use more inputs than currently under contract. (Treating the cost of inputs as given by the extant contracts, revenue maximisation is equivalent to profit maximisation.)

The first constraint is introduced as a shortcut, to eschew the more complex issue of inventory accumulation, that should be faced in a further elaboration of the model introduced here. (It is indeed inelegant to assume that firms withdraw from inventories to fill the gap between sales and production, but never replenish inventories during the time span covered by the adjustment process; the saving grace is of course the finiteness of that time span, established in theorem II below.) The second constraint is transparent. Note however the implicit efficiency in the use of inputs. Because production is here modelled in aggregate terms, it will not be the case that some inputs are idle in one firm whilst another firm has to forego profitable production due to lack of the same inputs. There would be no difficulty whatever, and some gain of realism, in treating subsets of commodities as the outputs of different firms, say $f = 1 \dots F$, and denoting by $\zeta^i_{k,f}(t)$ the amount of input k sold by household i to firm f at t.

As another related shortcut, I shall assume that firms hire (fire) inputs when the quantity contracted is inferior (superior) to the level *needed to meet final effective demand* $y(t)$. In that way, step (P ii) of process P is kept unchanged. This formulation remains somewhat unsatisfactory, because it implies for instance that an airline will react to an increase in demand by hiring pilots and stewards, even though its planes are used to capacity. Under a more realistic formulation, these quantity adjustments should depend upon information regarding the *potential* availability of *all* inputs, $\sum_i (z^i - \zeta^i)$. (Thus, the airline might hire personnel if it knows that there exist idle planes for sale or hire.) It should be possible to develop such an approach.

I shall introduce a simplification that reduces drastically the extent to which firms keep under contract (and remunerate) idle inputs. The simplification consists in carrying to the limit the idea (introduced in Section 2.2) that quantity adjustments are faster than price adjustments. A natural way to implement that idea consists in imposing that the span of calendar time separating a quantity adjustment from the previous step is much shorter than the corresponding span separating a price adjustment from the previous step. Since the latter time span is finite, the limit of 'much shorter' is zero, and I shall assume that *stocks do not change* (the integral of the flows vanishes) *between a quantity adjustment and the previous step of the process.* That is, I will suppress the calendar time required to make quantity adjustments; only between successive price adjustments will there elapse sufficient time to justify updating stocks. (Boundedness of all rates of flow is not an issue.)

An important implication of this specification is that, provided the finite convergence properties are preserved, conditions (2.9) will hold all the time, except for a set of measure zero (the finite set of time spans, themselves each of measure zero, preceding quantity adjustments). Accordingly, the quantities of inputs hired by firms will never exceed those needed to satisfy commodity demand, except over a set of measure zero in calendar time. This does not mean that firms never retain idle inputs. But the reason for idleness will then be always the same (except again over the null set just defined), namely that *other* inputs are not currently available. Inputs in excess of the requirements associated with commodity demand are assumed to be 'fired' instantaneously. (Similarly, inputs corresponding to these requirements are 'hired' instantaneously, *if available* in idle supply.) This is a major simplification, which could eventually be relaxed in an attempt at greater realism.

Under that specification, the receipts of firms from the sale of commodities always cover their outlays for payment of inputs, when $\mathcal{M} - I \geq [0]$. This is because the quantities of inputs contracted do not exceed the requirements corresponding to the sales: given that output prices cover (possibly with a margin) input costs, sales receipts cover outlays for inputs. It does not follow that the margin exceeds the value of inventory depletion; only that net cash flows are non-negative, outside of the null set. Liquidity is thus never an issue for the firms (for the production sector). Moreover, *the stock of money held by households is non-increasing over calendar time.* Indeed, net cash flows of households and producers sum to zero and the set of measure zero in calendar time does not affect moneys stocks.

7. Stability

7.1. *Formal definitions*

Putting together the elements introduced in Section 6, we may describe the state of the economy at the time of step t by the triple $(p(t), \zeta^i(t), m^i(t))_{i=1\ldots N}$. From these variables, we may compute successively

(i) output prices $q(t)$, via (2.3)
(ii) demand for consumer goods, via (6.2)
(iii) demand for inputs, via (2.4).

The evolution of the economy is governed by the process P', defined in terms of the sequences $(p(t), \zeta^i(t), m^i(t), \tau(t))$, $t = 0, 1, 2, \ldots$ and of the conditions (2.3), (2.4), (6.1) and (6.2).

DESCRIPTION OF PROCESS P

($P'i$) *Initiation.*   Initial input prices $p(0) > 0$, quantity constraints $[\zeta^i_k(0)]$, $[z^i_k] \geq [\zeta^i_k(0)] \geq [0]$, and money stocks $m^i(0) > 0$ are historically given.

($P'\,ii$) *General Step – Adjustment of a Quantity Constraint.*   Such a step is carried out if there exists k such that either

$$z^S_k(t) - z^D_k(t) > 0 \tag{7.1}$$

or

$$z^D_k(t) - z^S_k(t) \geq \varepsilon_k \text{ with } z^S_k(t) < z_k. \tag{7.2}$$

Let then $p(t + 1) = p(t)$, $\tau(t) = 0$, and $m^i(t + 1) = m^i(t)$ for all i. Two situations are distinguished.

(a) If some (any) k is such that (7.1) holds, then necessarily $z_k^S(t) > 0$ and there exists i such that $\zeta_k^i(t) > 0$. For some (any) such i, set

$$\zeta_k^i(t + 1) = \zeta_k^i(t) - e_k. \tag{2.7}$$

Then,

$$y^i(t + 1) = y^i(m^i(t), p'(t)\zeta^i(t) - p_k(t)e_k, q(t))$$

and, for all $h \neq i$,

$$y^h(t + 1) = y^h(t) = y^h(m^i(t), p'(t)\zeta^h(t), q(t)).$$

(b) If some (any) k is such that (7.2) holds, then necessarily there exists i such that $\zeta_k^i(t) < z_k^i$. For some (any) such i, set

$$\zeta_k^i(t + 1) = \zeta_k^i(t) + e_k. \tag{2.8}$$

Then,

$$y^i(t + 1) = y^i(m^i(t), p'(t)\zeta^i(t) + p_k(t)e_k, q(t))$$

and for all $h \neq i$,

$$y^h(t + 1) = y^h(t) = y^h(m^h(t), p'(t)\zeta^h(t), q(t)).$$

(*P' iii*) *General Step – Adjustment of a Price.* Such a step is carried out if there exists no k for which either (7.1) or (7.2) holds. It must then be the case that, for all k,

$$z_k^S(t) \in [\min(z_k, z_k^D(t) - \varepsilon_k), \min(z_k, z_k^D(t))], \ z_k^S(t) \leq z_k^D(t). \tag{2.9}$$

If there exists k such that $z_k^D(t) - \delta_k \geq z_k^S(t) = z_k$, set

$$p_k(t + 1) = p_k(t) + d_k; \tag{7.3}$$

for all $j \neq k$, set $p_j(t + 1) = p_j(t)$; and set $[\zeta^i(t + 1)] = [\zeta^i(t)]$. Also, for some $1 \geq \tau(t) > 0$, let

$$m^i(t + 1) = m^i(t) + \tau(t) [p'(t)\zeta^i(t) - q'(t)y^i(t)] \tag{6.1}$$

$$y^i(t + 1) = y^i(m^i(t + 1), p'(t)\zeta^i(t) + d_k\zeta_k^i(t), q(t + 1)) \tag{6.2}$$

where $q_j(t + 1) = q_j(t) + A_{kj}d_k$.

(*P' iv*) *Termination.* If for all k, (2.9) holds with $z_k^D(t) < z_k + \delta_k$, the process terminates.

DEFINITION

An *ε-equilibrium with excess supply* consists of a state (p, ζ^i, m^i), a vector of inputs $z^D \in R^m$, a vector of outputs $\hat{y} \in R^n$, a vector of prices $q \in R^n$, with $q' = p'A\mathcal{M}$, and an N-tuple of vectors $y^i \in R^n$ such that

(i) $(z^D, \hat{y})$ maximises $q'\hat{y} - p'z^D$ subject to $z^D \geq A\hat{y}$, $\hat{y} \leq \sum_i y^i$;

(ii) $y^i = y^i(m^i, p'\zeta^i, q)$

(iii) $0 \leq \zeta_i \leq z_i$, $\sum_i y_i \leq \hat{y}$;

(iv) for all $k = 1 \ldots m$, $|z_k^D - \sum_i \zeta_k^i| \leq \varepsilon$.

As before, a state of the economy where the process terminates defines an ε-equilibrium with excess supply, where ε satisfies (2.11). The equilibrium is defined by the terminal values of (p, ζ^i, m^i) together with $\hat{y} = \sum_i y^i$ $z^D = A\hat{y}$, $q' = p'A\mathcal{M}$ and $y^i = y^i(m^i, p'\zeta^{i\prime}, q)$. These values satisfy conditions (i)–(iii) in the definition. (2.9) and (P' iv) still imply that condition (iv) holds as well.

7.2. Theorem

The proof of stability theorem II below rests upon the analogue of lemma I, proved here in two easy steps.

LEMMA II

Under process P', for all $t = 0, 1, 2 \ldots$, $\sum_i m^i(t + 1) \leq \sum_i m^i(t) \leq \sum_i m^i(0)$.

PROOF

From the definition of the process, $\tau(t) = 0$ unless $z_l^S(t) \leq z_l^D(t)$ for all l. Thus, $\tau(t) > 0$ implies

$$p'(t)z^S(t) \leq p'(t)z^D(t) = p'(t)Ay(t)$$
$$\leq p'(t)A\mathcal{M}y(t) = q'(t)y(t). \tag{7.4}$$

Consequently, for all t:

$$\tau(t)[p'(t)z^S(t) - q'(t)y(t)] \leq 0. \tag{7.5}$$

Aggregating (6.1) over i, then using (7.5):

$$\sum_i m^i(t + 1) = \sum_i m^i(t) + \tau(t)[p'(t)z^S(t) - q'(t)y(t)]$$

$$\leq \sum_i m^i(t), \tag{7.6}$$

which proves the lemma.

QED

LEMMA III

Under process P', for all k, for all t,

$$p_k(t) \leq \max\left(\frac{\sum_i m^i(0)}{\delta_k} + d_k, p_k(0)\right) \stackrel{\text{def}}{=} \bar{p}_k.$$

PROOF

From the definition of the process, $p_k(t + 1) = p_k(t)$ unless $z_l^S(t) \leq z_l^D(t)$ for all l; and $p'(t)z^D(t) \leq q'(t)y(t)$ by (7.4). The condition that $m^i(t + 1) \geq 0$ for all $\tau(t) \in [0, 1]$ implies – see (6.1) with $\tau(t) = 1$ – that:

$$q'(t)y^i(t) \leq m^i(t) + p'(t)\zeta^i(t). \tag{7.7}$$

Summing over i, and using (7.4), then lemma II:

$$p'(t)z^D(t) \leq \sum_i m^i(t) + p'(t)z^S(t)$$

$$\leq \sum_i m^i(0) + p'(t)z^S(t). \tag{7.8}$$

Proceeding as in the proof of lemma I,

$$\delta_k p_k(t) \leq p_k(t)[z_k^D(t) - z_k^S(t)]$$
$$\leq \sum_i m^i(0) - \sum_{l \neq k} p_l(t)[z_l^D(t) - z_l^S(t)] \leq \sum_i m^i(0)$$

and the proof of the lemma follows.

QED

THEOREM II

Under assumptions NI' and MPC', provided for all $k = 1 \ldots m$, e_k is small enough ($e_k \leq \varepsilon_k/2$) and provided initial inventories are high enough (meaning

at least equal to a finite lower bound related to the data of the economy),
the process P′ is feasible, is stable and converges in a bounded number of
steps to an ε-equilibrium with excess supply.

PROOF

The proof is entirely parallel to that of theorem I.

It follows from lemma III that the number of price adjustments is bounded. Let *their* number be $T \le \bar{T}$ and number them $\theta = 1 \ldots T$. Also, because the quantity adjustments are treated as instantaneous, the aggregate withdrawals from inventories are given by:

$$\sum_{\theta=1}^{T} \tau(\theta)[y(\theta) - \hat{y}(\theta)] \le \sum_{\theta=1}^{T} [y(\theta) - \hat{y}(\theta)] \le \sum_{\theta=1}^{T} y(\theta). \tag{7.9}$$

For each θ, $y(\theta)$ is a uniformly bounded quantity, because

$$q'(\theta)y(\theta) \le \sum_{i} m^i(\theta) + p'(\theta)z^S(\theta)$$

$$\le \sum_{i} m^i(0) + \bar{p}'z \tag{7.10}$$

and $q'(\theta)$ is bounded below by $q'(0) = p'(0)A\mathcal{M} > 0$. This establishes the boundedness of the initial inventory levels that are required in order for process P′ to be feasible at all steps (without any need for quantity rationing of consumer demand).

To complete the proof, there remains only to verify that the number of quantity adjustment steps (P′ ii) between any pair of price adjustment steps (P′ iii) is uniformly bounded. The reasoning used in the proof of theorem I to establish that property is readily extended to the present case. Indeed, if t denotes a price adjustment step and $p(t + v) = p(t)$, $v > 0$, then $t + v$ is a general quantity adjustment step, and $\tau(t + v) = 0$. For all $v > 1$, it follows that $m^i(t + v) = m^i(t + v - 1)$. We may accordingly use that property in the proof (adding the single step corresponding to $v = 1$ does not affect the boundedness property). We may then repeat the reasoning in the proof of theorem I, substituting $m^i(t + 1)$ for $m^i(0)$ and $p'(t)\zeta^i(t + v)$ for $r^i(t)$. In the discussion of case (P ii)(a), the equality $r^i(t + 1) = r^i(t) - e_k p_k$ is then replaced by

$$p'(t)\zeta^i(t + v + 1) = p'(t)\zeta^i(t + v) - e_k p_k; \tag{7.11}$$

and assumption NI′ implies $y^i(t + v + 1) \le y^i(t + v)$. The discussion of that case then proceeds without modification, until assumption MPC is used. That specific step is now replaced by:

$$\sum_l p_l[z_l^D(t + v) - z_l^D(t + v + 1)]$$

$$\leq \sum_j q_j(t)[y_j^i(t + v) - y_j^i(t + v + 1)]$$

$$\leq e_k p_k(1 - \beta^i) \tag{7.12}$$

where the last inequality follows directly from MPC$'$ and (7.11). Similar remarks apply to the discussion of case (P ii)(b), and the proof of theorem II is complete. QED

8. Comments and conclusions

8.1. *Summary*

In the broadest outline, this paper gives content to a very simple idea: if nominal prices are downwards rigid, and if they are prevented by some nominal rigidity from rising indefinitely, then price dynamics are apt to converge. A realistic feature of this paper, inspired by the work of Morishima (1976), is to trace back all downwards price rigidities to primary factors of production. As for the upper bound on inflation, it comes from the combination of a nonvanishing demand for, and an exogenous stock of, nominal balances. These two aspects deserve some discussion, provided in Sections 8.2 and 8.3.

The downwards price rigidities impose an equilibrium concept allowing for excess supply. Some claim to the realism of such a concept was made in the introduction. At any rate, it is a necessary corollary to price rigidities. Still, I discuss in Section 8.4 the two main avenues towards a competitive equilibrium, namely price flexibility and fiscal expansion.

These specifications contribute some novel features to stability analysis. They have enabled me to prove stability of a tâtonnement process from the minimal assumption of non-inferiority (further discussed in Section 8.5); then to define a rather realistic non-tâtonnement process, and to prove its feasibility and stability under a reasonable condition on inventory holdings.

The non-tâtonnement process allows for production and consumption activities out of equilibrium. But I do not take here the crucial step of modelling explicitly the uncertainty surrounding future prices and quantity constraints, then the stochastic optimisation problems faced by consumers and producers. That step deserves priority on the research agenda. It is related to the issue of money demand, taken up in Section 8.2.

The specific formulation of the processes P and P', the assumptions and methods of proof used in this paper are quite crude. No doubt, the presentation could be improved substantially through further technical work. One comment in that direction is offered in Section 8.6.

8.2. *Temporary equilibrium and money demand*

The uncertainty about future prices (and quantity constraints) is modelled explicitly in the theory of temporary equilibrium – see Grandmont (1974, 1977) – where much attention has been given to the conditions (on expectations) under which inflation remains bounded. Clearly, that is the proper way to study price dynamics; but it is a hard way.

The notion that money supply has something to do with inflation is familiar to many. But it needs to be spelled out in microeconomic models of price making, of which one example is offered here.

The assumption MPC, putting a floor to money demand, is rather crude and should be generalised, both by deriving money demand explicitly from consumer behaviour, and by including assets and their prices (e.g. interest rate) in the analysis.

An intriguing question is whether the supply of money, or direct controls on the prices of primary inputs, are the only conceivable instruments to check inflation in models of the type studied here (in models with downward price rigidities and mark-up pricing).

8.3. *Downward price rigidities*

Why some prices remain downwards rigid in the face of excess supply is an intriguing question, revived in particular by the persistence of European unemployment.

In the case of labour services, the protection by trade unions of workers' incomes is undoubtedly an important element of the answer. The extent to which that protection should be regarded as inefficient use of monopoly power, or as a second-best efficient arrangement in the absence of contingent or forward markets for jobs, remains to be ascertained; see Drèze (1989b), Gollier (1988), and Drèze and Gollier (1989) for a theoretical second-best analysis.

The issue concerns other inputs as well, in particular plant and equipment. When excess capacity prevails, the prices of commodities (e.g. automobiles) are not automatically geared to short-run marginal cost. This is probably a mixture once again of monopolistic profit maximisation and of second-best efficient arrangements under incomplete markets. Price fluctuations are costly for consumers, and are apt to generate erratic patterns of intertemporal substitution, compounding the difficulty of investment decisions under incomplete markets. Our understanding of these issues is still limited: the combination of non convex technology, monopolistic competition and incomplete markets remains forbidding ...

One clearcut difference between labour on the one hand and plant or equipment on the other is the ease with which excess physical capacities can be eliminated through scrapping and postponement of investment; whereas excess demand for physical capacities can be eliminated through investment. There lies probably the reason for the differences in the evolution of unemployment and excess capacities in Figure 10.1.

In the model presented here, physical capacities are treated as primary inputs. It would be natural to put an upper bound on their real prices, reflecting the cost of additional investment; and to introduce a scrapping or investment postponement feature, to eliminate progressively the excess capacities. The model would gain in realism, probably at little technical complication. And the role of wages in explaining downwards price rigidities would stand out all the more sharply.

8.4.   *Towards competitive equilibria*

The quantity adjustment steps of processes P or P′ bring about 'orderly' (one-sided) rationing; the price adjustment steps eliminate all forms of excess demand. What sort of additional steps could eliminate the excess supplies?

Price flexibility is a first answer – even though I have just argued that some form of downwards rigidity makes sense. Since the process is governed by input prices, it seems plausible that an assumption of gross substitutability for inputs would pave the way to convergence of a process with flexible prices towards competitive equilibria. And most econometricians would find the substitutability assumption for inputs quite acceptable. Eventually this issue should be investigated.

It is appropriate to remind ourselves, at this point, that Keynes regarded wage flexibility as the hard way, and thought that demand stimulation through monetary policy provided an easier way. (On pp. 267–9 of *The General Theory*, he argues that 'it can only be a foolish ... an unjust ... an inexperienced person who would prefer a flexible wage policy to a flexible money policy'.) The model of the present paper lends itself to study the effect of increasing the money balances of the households –

which amounts to a fiscal expansion through income transfers, with accommodating money supply.

It is easy to construct examples where no finite amount of fiscal expansion will eliminate excess supplies altogether. (Thus, if two inputs are always used in the ratio one to two, but are supplied inelastically in the ratio one to one, so that the competitive price of the first is zero; then a competitive equilibrium could only be obtained in the limit, with *infinite* fiscal expansion *cum* inflation.)[9] But it is also easy to think about assumptions under which fiscal policy would be effective. (Some degree of input substitutability would help ...) A serious attack on these problems again requires explicit treatment of the uncertainties associated with fiscal policy (whether it will ultimately be financed by taxes or monetised, for instance). So I must refer back to Section 8.2 ...

8.5. *The non-inferiority assumption*

Of all the undesirable assumptions used in this paper, none is more *blatantly* unrealistic than absence of inferior goods (NI). That assumption is used only once, in the proof of theorem I, to show that lower (higher) household incomes lead to lower (higher) demand for *all primary inputs*. In that sense, the relevant assumption is one of 'non-inferior factors' – and is perhaps less blatantly unrealistic ... Still, if potatoes are an inferior good, and a plot of land is good only for growing potatoes, we have an instance of 'inferior factor'. I have accordingly used assumption NI, because I could not think of any other primitive assumption ruling out inferior factors.

It is plausible that further research may permit weakening even the 'non-inferior factors' assumptions; perhaps I have convinced myself too quickly that it was a natural requirement for the problem at hand ... Otherwise, it would be a matter of empirical research to discover how significant the problem is.[10]

8.6. *Farewell*

As intimated above, I regard the basic idea of this paper as sound and useful, but the formulation as technically crude. In particular, the technical

---

[9] More technically: at full use of the second input, fiscal expansion would create excess demand, hence an increase in the price of that input, passed into output prices; but the price of the first input (in excess supply) remains fixed, so that its relative (real) price tends to zero as fiscal expansion keeps feeding inflation.

[10] The more relevant empirical question is probably whether some broad types of labour (like unskilled physical labour) are inferior factors.

formulation is more extreme than common sense and casual empiricism would suggest. Thus, not all output prices are set by producers as a mark-up on costs; not all primary inputs have downwards rigid prices; increases in input prices are apt to be passed into output prices only if they are viewed as permanent; and so on. I can only hope that the crude formulation does not obliterate the useful ideas.

Among the improvements that seem easiest to achieve, I should mention first explicit disaggregation of production into the activities of a number of producers, each endowed with its own production set, hiring its own factors, setting its own prices and possibly distributing its profits. Readers are invited to interpret the paper as if that improvement had already been achieved – it would have, had more time been available ...

Also, suppressing altogether the calendar time needed for quantity adjustments, or the redistribution of profits during the time span covered by the process, are convenient simplifications that do not seem essential.

The lasting usefulness of the contribution attempted in this paper is apt to stand or fall on the realism of widespread downwards factor price rigidities and widespread mark-up pricing of produced commodities. And the major challenge to all *students* of price dynamics remains that of *modelling* non-deterministic expectations and stochastic sequential decision-making by consumers and firms.

VI Wage policies

11 The role of securities and labour contracts in the optimal allocation of risk-bearing*

1. In memoriam

1.1.

The economics of uncertainty should some day inspire students of economic thought. Developments over the past few decades provide a vivid illustration of the interplay between abstract theorising and applied interests. In any account of these developments, the specific early contribution of Karl Borch (1960) is bound to stand out. The circumstances are noteworthy. In 1959, Karl Borch (then forty years old) came to Bergen from a succession of jobs for international organisations. He writes:[1] 'When in 1959 I got a research post which gave me almost complete freedom, as long as my work was relevant to insurance, I naturally set out to develop an economic theory of insurance.' That he should *within a year*[2] have made a decisive step in that direction is amazing.

The nature of the step is also noteworthy. Borch knew the recent theoretical papers of Allais (1953) and especially of Arrow (1953). He understood perfectly their significance as well as their limitations, at a time when very few economists had taken notice. As he explained more explicitly in 1962,[3] he attributed that lack of recognition to the fact that these 'relatively simple models appear too remote from any really

* In *Risk, Information and Insurance*: *Essays in the Memory of Karl Borch*, H. Loubergé, ed., Kluwer Academic Publishers, Boston, 1989.
[1] See Blaug (1986), p. 103.
[2] The chronology is a bit uncertain, since the publication in *Skandinavisk Aktuarietidskrift*, 1960, pp. 163–84, mentions 'Received January 1961'.
[3] Borch (1962), p. 425.

interesting practical economic situation'. 'However, the model they consider gives a fairly accurate description of a *reinsurance market*.' The
contribution of Karl Borch in 1960 was to give empirical content to the
abstract model of general equilibrium with markets for contingent claims.
In this way, he brought economic theory to bear on insurance problems,
thereby opening up that field considerably; and he brought the experience
of reinsurance contracts to bear on the interpretation of economic theory,
thereby enlivening considerably the interest for that theory. In his
subsequent publications, Karl Borch often related advanced theoretical
results to casual observations – sometimes in a genuinely entertaining
manner, which transmits to younger generations a glimpse of the wit and
personal charm of our late friend.[4]

1.2.

Several papers by Karl Borch follow a simple lucid pattern: after a brief
problem-oriented introduction, the first-order conditions for efficient risk-
sharing are recalled, then applied to the problem at hand; the paper ends
with a discussion of applicability and confrontation with stylised facts.
And the author prefers a succession of light touches, in numbered
subsections, to formal theorems and lengthy discussions.

Borch helped establish, and travelled repeatedly, the bridge linking the
theory of (re)insurance markets and the 'Capital Asset Pricing Model',
developed by his student Jan Mossin (1966) among others. Although
Borch was keenly conscious of the restrictive nature of the assumptions
underlying the CAPM,[5] he often used that model as an illustration,
stressing that 'the applications of CAPM have led to deeper insight into
the functioning of financial markets'.[6] The purpose of this paper is to
introduce labour incomes in an asset pricing model, and to show that the
assumptions underlying CAPM lead to a simple operational characterisation of Pareto-efficient risk-sharing through capital markets *and labour
contracts*. The characterisation of efficient labour contracts takes the form
of a simple wage indexation scheme, to which Karl Borch might have
recognised the merit of bringing abstract theory to bear on an interesting
practical economic situation. The integrated treatment of capital markets
and labour contracts bears some analogy to the integrated treatment of

---

[4] See e.g. Borch (1976).
[5] See e.g. Borch (1968a).
[6] Quoted from Borch (1985).

insurance markets and capital markets. It also has some implications for private insurance and reinsurance contracts.

2. Efficient and linear-sharing rules

2.1.

A simple form of risk-sharing problem arises when n agents, indexed $i = 1 \ldots n$ and endowed with (differentiable, concave monotone increasing) cardinal utility functions for wealth $u^i(y^i)$, have to share an aggregate wealth level Y, which depends upon exogenous circumstances. Let there be S alternative 'states' indexed $s = 1 \ldots S$, with associated aggregate wealth levels Y_s. Feasible sharing arrangements must satisfy

$$\sum_i y_s^i = Y_s, s = 1 \ldots S, \tag{1}$$

where y_s^i is the wealth of agent i in state s. Write $y^i = (y_1^i \ldots y_S^i)$, an S-vector; $y_s = (y_s^1, \ldots y_s^n)$, an n-vector; $y = (y^1 \ldots y^n)$, an nS-vector and assume that the n agents agree about the probabilities $\phi_1 \ldots \phi_S$ of the S states. A Pareto-efficient sharing arrangement y is defined by the property that there exists no $\hat{y}$ satisfying (1) with $E_s u^i(\hat{y}_s^i) = \sum_s \phi_s u^i(\hat{y}_s^i) \geq \sum_s \phi_s u^i(y_s^i) = E_s u^i(y_s^i)$ for all i, $\sum_i E_s u^i(\hat{y}_s^i) > \sum_i E_s u^i(y_s^i)$. As shown by Borch (1960), if y is Pareto efficient, then there exist n positive constants $k_1, k_2 \ldots k_n$, normalised by $k_1 = 1$, such that

$$\frac{du^1}{dy_s^1} = k_i \frac{du^i}{dy_s^i}, \quad s = 1 \ldots S, \quad i = 2 \ldots n. \tag{2}$$

There also exist S non-negative prices for contingent claims $q_1 \ldots q_S$, normalised by $\sum_s q_s = 1$, such that

$$\frac{q_s}{q_1} = \frac{\phi_s}{\phi_1} \frac{\dfrac{du^i}{dy_s^i}}{\dfrac{du^i}{dy_1^i}}, \quad s = 2 \ldots S, \quad i = 1 \ldots n. \tag{3}$$

The constants k_i may reflect the initial wealth endowments of agents reaching an efficient sharing arrangement through trade in contingent claims; or they may reflect the bargaining strengths of agents reaching that arrangement through cooperative negociations; or they may reflect the distributive ethics of a central authority responsible for implementing the arrangement; or again they may remain undetermined and be used for analytical convenience alone. In every case, it is true that y solves problem (P 1):

$$\max_{y} \sum_{i} k_i E_s u^i(y_s^i) \qquad (P1)$$

subject to (1).

It follows from (2) and our assumptions that

$$\frac{dy_s^i}{dY_s} > 0, \quad i = 1 \ldots n, \quad s = 1 \ldots S. \qquad (4)$$

More specifically, define the absolute risk tolerance of agent i, T_A^i by[7]

$$T_A^i(y_s^i) = -\frac{\dfrac{du^i}{dy_s^i}}{\dfrac{d^2 u^i}{d(y_s^i)^2}}; \qquad (5)$$

and define similarly the aggregate relative risk tolerance of the group of agents, T_A, by

$$T_A(y_s) = \sum_{i} T_A^i(y_s^i) = -\sum_{i} \frac{\dfrac{du^i}{dy_s^i}}{\dfrac{d^2 u^i}{d(y_s^i)^2}}. \qquad (6)$$

Then, as shown in Borch (1960, p. 169)

$$\frac{dy_s^i}{dY_s} = \frac{T_A^i(y_s^i)}{T_A(y_s)}. \qquad (7)$$

Defining similarly the relative risk tolerances T_R^i, T_R by

$$T_R^i(y_s^i) = \frac{T_A^i(y^i)}{y_s^i}, \quad T_R(y_s) = \sum_{i} \frac{y_s^i}{Y_s} T_R^i(y_s^i) = \frac{1}{Y_s} T_A(y_s), \qquad (8)$$

we may write

$$\frac{Y_s}{y_s^i} \frac{dy_s^i}{dY_s} = \eta_{y_s^i Y_s} = \frac{T_R^i(y_s^i)}{T_R(y_s)}. \qquad (9)$$

[7] T_A^i is the reciprocal of the absolute risk aversion introduced by Arrow (1965) and Pratt (1964).

2.2.

For application purposes, it is of interest to consider the special case of *linear sharing rules* where dy_s^i/dY_s is a constant, say β_i, independent of s. In such cases,

$$y_s^i = \alpha_i + \beta_i Y_s, \quad s = 1 \dots S; \quad \sum_i \alpha_i = 0, \quad \sum_i \beta_i = 1. \tag{10}$$

It is readily verified, and shown for instance in Borch (1968b, p. 253) or Wilson (1968), that Pareto-efficient sharing rules are linear if and only if all agents have utility functions belonging to one and the same of the following classes (up to monotone linear transformations):[8]

$$u^i(y_s^i) = |c_i|^\gamma - |c_i - y_s^i|^\gamma, \quad \gamma > 1, c_i \geq y_s^i \geq 0, \quad \text{or}$$
$$\gamma < 0, y_s^i \geq 0 \geq c_i; \tag{11}$$

$$u^i(y_s^i) = (y_s^i - c_i)^\gamma, \quad \gamma < 1, \quad y_s^i \geq 0 \geq c_i; \tag{12}$$

$$u^i(y_s^i) = \log(y_s^i - c_i), \quad y_s^i \geq 0 \geq c_i; \tag{13}$$

$$u^i(y_s^i) = 1 - e^{-\gamma_i(y_s^i - c_i)}$$

or equivalently

$$u^i(y_s^i) = 1 - e^{-\gamma_i y_s^i}, \quad \gamma_i > 0, \quad y_s^i \geq 0. \tag{14}$$

The values of β_i in (10) and of the expressions for T_A^i corresponding to (11)–(14) are given by:

$$\beta^i = k_i^{\frac{1}{1-\gamma}} / \sum_j k_j^{\frac{1}{1-\gamma}}, \quad T_A^i(y_s^i) = \frac{|y_s^i - c_i|}{|\gamma - 1|} \quad \text{under (11)–(13)} \tag{15}$$

$$\beta_i = \gamma_i^{-1} / \sum_j \gamma_j^{-1}, \quad T_A^i(y_s^i) = \gamma_i^{-1} \quad \text{under (14).} \tag{16}$$

The linearity of the sharing rules follows from the linearity of the absolute risk tolerance – a property usually referred to as 'hyperbolic absolute risk aversion' (HARA).

---

[8] (13) is a special case of (12) with $\gamma = 0$; c_i is introduced in (14) for the sake of symmetry but plays no role there.

3. Capital asset pricing

3.1.

The special case of (11) corresponding to $\gamma = 2$ (quadratic utility) leads to a particularly elegant treatment of portfolio choices and capital asset pricing. The simplest model involves m assets indexed $j = 1 \ldots m$ with (non-negative) random payoffs π_s^j, so that $Y_s = \sum_j \pi_s^j$. The n agents are initially endowed with shares $\bar{\theta}_{ij} \geq 0$, $\sum_i \bar{\theta}_{ij} = 1$ for all j, of the m assets. The assets are traded on a stock exchange at prices $p_j, j = 1 \ldots m$, leading to terminal shares $\theta_{ij} \geq 0$, $\sum_i \theta_{ij} = 1$ for all j. In addition, the agents may stipulate deterministic side-payments a_i, $\sum_i a_i = 0$. Accordingly, the budget constraints and terminal wealths of the agents are

$$\sum_j p_j \theta_{ij} + a_i = \sum_j p_j \bar{\theta}_{ij} \tag{17}$$

$$y_s^i = a_i + \sum_j \theta_{ij} \pi_s^j, \quad i = 1 \ldots n, \quad s = 1 \ldots S. \tag{18}$$

From section 2, it follows that efficient portfolios will satisfy (10) with $\alpha_i = a_i$, $\beta_i = \theta_{ij} \equiv \theta_i$ (identically in j), $\sum_i \theta_i = 1$, so that

$$y_s^i = a_i + \theta_i \sum_j \pi_s^j, \quad i = 1 \ldots n, \quad s = 1 \ldots S. \tag{19}$$

The CAPM theory consists in showing that competitive clearing of the markets for assets (of the stock market) leads to asset prices at which all individuals (maximising expected utility subject to (17) with given p_j's) choose to hold fully diversified portfolios ($\theta_{ij} \equiv \theta_i$), with

$$\theta_i = \frac{T_A^i(\bar{Y})}{T_A(\bar{Y})}, \quad i = 1 \ldots n; \tag{20}$$

$$p_j = E\pi^j - \frac{1}{T_A(\bar{Y})} \text{cov}(\pi^j, Y), \quad j = 1 \ldots m. \tag{21}$$

In expression (21), the market price of asset j is obtained as equal to its expected payoff minus a risk premium, computed as the product of that asset's contribution to the variance of the aggregate payoff $Y = \sum_j \pi^j$ times a market price of risk (per unit of variance), namely $1/T_A(\bar{Y})$.

3.2.

An important byproduct of the CAPM is the existence of an S-vector q of prices for contingent claims, with[9]

$$q_s = \phi_s \left[1 - \frac{1}{T_A(\bar{Y})}(Y_s - \bar{Y}) \right], s = 1 \ldots S, \sum_s q_s = 1; \tag{22}$$

$$p_j = \sum_s q_s \pi_s^j, \quad j = 1 \ldots m. \tag{23}$$

If the payoffs π_s^j to the different assets result from some parallel choice, say from a set $\Pi^j \subset R^S$ of feasible payoffs, then efficient choices should satisfy

$$\sum_s q_s \pi_s^j \geq \sum_s q_s \hat{\pi}_s^j \, \forall \, (\hat{\pi}_1^j \ldots \hat{\pi}_S^j) \in \Pi^j, \quad j = 1 \ldots m. \tag{24}$$

Conditions (24) give operational content to the familiar notion that (production) choices by firms maximise their market value. In general, that decision criterion is ill-defined; see, e.g. Drèze (1974b, section 6.3). It takes a specific framework, like that of CAPM, to make it operational.

I also note for further reference that the CAPM formulas remain valid if the agents hold in addition state-dependent endowments so long as the endowment vectors lie in the span of the $m + 1$ vectors $(\iota, \pi^1 \ldots \pi^m)$ where $\iota = (1 \ldots 1)'$ and $\pi^j = (\pi_1^j \ldots \pi_S^j)$; see Geanakopolos in Duffie et al. (1988).

3.3.

Under the formulation of the CAPM outlined here, it is not imposed that $y_s^i \geq 0$ for all i and s. These natural non-negativity constraints complicate the presentation considerably, and are often ignored in analytical work. A possible justification for that practice goes as follows.

Under (11) with $\gamma = 2$, $T_A^i(\bar{Y}) = c_i - \bar{y}^i$ and $T_A(\bar{Y}) = \sum_i c_i - \bar{Y} := C - \bar{Y}$. Inserting these expressions in (20) and noting from (19) that $\bar{y}^i = a_i + \theta_i \bar{Y}$, we may relate a_i to θ_i as follows:

$$\theta_i = \frac{c_i - a_i - \theta_i \bar{Y}}{C - \bar{Y}}, a_i = c_i - \theta_i C. \tag{25}$$

---

[9] See e.g. Drèze (1982, formula (2.21)).

Write v_i for $\sum_i \bar{\theta}_{ij} p_j$ and define $V = \sum_i v_i = \sum_j p_j$. It also follows from (21) and (8) that

$$V = \bar{Y} - \frac{\sigma_Y^2}{T_A(\bar{Y})} = \bar{Y} - \frac{\sigma^2 Y}{\bar{Y} T_R(\bar{Y})} = \bar{Y}\left(1 - \frac{\sigma_Y^2}{\bar{Y}^2 T_R(\bar{Y})}\right). \tag{26}$$

The budget equation (17), with $\theta_{ij} = \theta_i$ for all j, becomes in that notation

$$\theta_i V + c_i - \theta_i C = v_i, \quad \theta_i = \frac{c_i - v_i}{C - V}. \tag{27}$$

Using (25) and (27), the non-negativity condition on y_s^i takes the form

$$y_s^i = a_i + \theta_i Y_s = c_i - \theta_i C + \theta_i Y_s = c_i - \theta_i (C - Y_s)$$

$$= c_i - (C - Y_s)\frac{c_i - v_i}{C - V} = v_i - (c_i - v_i)\frac{V - Y_s}{C - V} \geq 0; \tag{28}$$

$$\frac{v_i}{V}\frac{C - V}{c_i - v_i} = \frac{T_R(V)}{T_R^i(v_i)} \geq \frac{V - Y_s}{V} = 1 - \frac{Y_s}{\bar{Y}\left(1 - \frac{\sigma_Y^2}{\bar{Y}^2 T_R(\bar{Y})}\right)}, \tag{29}$$

where use has been made of the definition (8) to obtain a relationship among dimensionless ratios. In order for the inequality (29) to hold for all i and s, it must be the case that

$$\frac{\sum_i \frac{v_i}{V} T_R^i(v_i)}{\max_i T_R^i(v_i)} \geq 1 - \frac{\min_s Y_s}{\bar{Y}\left(1 - \frac{\sigma_Y^2}{\bar{Y}^2 T_R(\bar{Y})}\right)} = \frac{\sum_j p_j - \min_s Y_s}{\sum_j p_j}. \tag{30}$$

In words: the maximal (over states) relative loss on the market portfolio should not exceed the ratio of the average to the maximal (over agents) relative risk–tolerance index (evaluated at the initial wealth).

In an economy with many heterogeneous agents and many states, condition (30) is unlikely to be verified. On the other hand, in applications where Y_s stands for national income, the quantity

$$\frac{\bar{Y} - \min_s Y_s}{\bar{Y}} \geq 1 - \frac{Y_s}{\bar{Y}\left(1 - \frac{\sigma_Y^2}{\bar{Y}^2 T_R(\bar{Y})}\right)}$$

is apt to be quite small in the short run – like 3 or 4 per cent – and condition

(30) is quite likely to be fulfilled. Also, in an economy with many agents, it will be of limited relevance to the equilibrium and efficiency of asset markets that a few agents are prevented by non-negativity constraints from holding a portfolio satisfying the tangential first-order conditions. I shall accordingly follow in the sequel the standard practice of ignoring the non-negativity constraints on y_s^i. And I shall similarly ignore the conditions $c_i \geq y_s^i$ which define the range over which representation of preferences by a quadratic utility is meaningful.

4. A model of asset pricing and labour contracts

4.1.

The CAPM has provided a useful framework to analyse a number of problems related to financial markets. From a practical viewpoint, that model has helped private investors or investment services understand and implement better the principles of asset diversification; it has also supplied financial intermediaries with a theoretical underpinning for their autonomous discovery of the merits of mutual funds. Yet, for most families, human wealth is the major component of total wealth, and uncertainties about labour income are of greater concern than uncertainties about portfolio returns.

Taking labour incomes into account raises two questions about the CAPM, a positive one and a normative one. From a positive viewpoint, is the model still valid when the endowment of agents includes uncertain labour incomes? That question has been taken up by Mayers (1973) and his followers – in particular Fama and Schwert (1977) at the empirical level.[10]

The normative issue is broader. In capitalist economies, tradeable assets are typically shares of stock in business firms that engage in the production of goods and services; labour incomes consist mostly of wages and salaries paid out by these firms. Profits are equal to value added minus wages, and constitute the basic element of the payoffs which enter as elementary data in the CAPM. The question of efficient risk-sharing should accordingly be raised simultaneously for the division of value added between profits and wages, for the portfolio choices of agents earning wages as well as returns on their portfolios, and for the resulting capital market equilibria.

---

[10] Of related interest is the so-called 'consumption-based CAPM' of Breeden (1979), Cornell (1981) and Grossman-Shiller (1982).

4.2.

In a simple model, each asset j corresponds to a business firm employing, in state s, a (homogeneous) labour force l_s^j to produce an output $f_s^j(l_s^j)$. The state-dependent production function f_s^j is assumed differentiable monotone concave. If the total wage bill paid by firm j in state s is denoted t_s^j then profits π_s^j are given by

$$\pi_s^j = f_s^j(l_s^j) - t_s^j. \tag{31}$$

The theory of implicit (labour) contracts, as initially developed by Azariadis (1975), Baily (1974) and Gordon (1974) – see Rosen (1985) or Hart and Holmström (1987) for recent surveys – has been concerned with a characterisation of efficient production as well as risk-sharing between firms and employees, through *ex ante* agreements regarding t_s^j and l_s^j.

The *ex ante* aspect is important. It means that employees are hired, and contractual agreements are reached, prior to observing the true state. This feature is essential to permit risk-sharing, i.e. transfers of income across states. Typically, these transfers take the form of wages above the marginal product of labour in some states, below it in other states.

Up to incentive compatibility and institutional feasibility, efficient contracts are characterised by two sets of conditions:

(i) l_s^j should be such that the marginal value product of labour, df_s^j/dl_s^j, is equal to the reservation wage of employees;
(ii) t_s^j, the wage bill of the firm in state s, should be such that the division of income between capital and labour corresponds to efficient risk-sharing.

In order to give empirical content to these conditions, it is typically assumed that the reservation wages and utility functions of all employees are identical, and that the firm has well-defined risk preferences, represented by some 'utility function of the firm'.

Under the assumptions of the CAPM, suitably extended, sharper conclusions are possible.

4.3.

An important practical issue raised by labour contracts is the extent to which labour times and wages are allowed to vary (across individuals and across states). Clearly, the answer to that question varies from firm to firm, depending upon technological and economic constraints. Thus, team work requires close coordination of individual labour times; some processes admit more readily part-time work than others; and so on. A simple formulation allows labour times to vary across individuals (thus allowing part-time work) while requiring that variations across states be in the same proportions for all members of a given firm. I shall retain that formulation. And I shall follow the standard practice in the theory of implicit contracts of imposing that, for all s, $l_s^j \leq l^j$, where l^j is the quantity of labour (the number of full-time equivalent workers) covered by the contract.

On the other hand, I shall not at this stage impose specific restrictions on the individual wages beyond the natural requirement that wage costs per unit of labour to the firm be the same for all its employees. As we shall see, it is easy to express that requirement in operational terms, under the CAPM framework.

To formalise these ideas, let there be n agents (households) $i = 1 \ldots n$, each supplying inelastically a quantity of labour $\bar{l}^i$ and owning initially a fraction $\bar{\theta}_{ij} \geq 0$ of the capital of firm j, with $\sum_i \bar{\theta}_{ij} = 1$ for each j.

Let each agent i supply a fraction $\zeta_{ij} \geq 0$ of the labour inputs of firm j, with $\sum_j \zeta_{ij} l^j \leq \bar{l}^i$ and $\sum_i \zeta_{ij} = 1$ in equilibrium. Write w_s^{ij} for the wage rate paid by firm j to agent i in state s. Then, the wage bill t_s^j and the profits π_s^j are defined by

$$t_s^j = l_s^j \sum_i \zeta_{ij} w_s^{ij}, \quad \pi_s^j = f_s^j(l_s^j) - l_s^j \sum_i \zeta_{ij} w_s^{ij}. \tag{32}$$

To simplify exposition, I shall *not* impose the limited liability conditions $\pi_s^j \geq 0$.

Wages and dividends (profit shares) are paid out *after* observing the state. Shares of stock are traded, at prices p_j, *before* observing the state. If terminal holdings of agent i are denoted θ_{ij}, then the budget constraints of the agents are still given by (17), but their terminal wealths are now given by

$$y_s^i = a_i + \sum_j \theta_{ij} \pi_s^j + \sum_j \zeta_{ij} l_s^j w_s^{ij}, \quad i = 1 \ldots n, \quad s = 1 \ldots S. \tag{33}$$

4.4.

The decisions of the firms concern the employment levels l_s^j and the wage rates w_s^{ij}. In a world of uncertainty, it is not easy to specify decision criteria for business firms when markets are incomplete; see Drèze (1982, 1985a, 1989a). However, it was noted above that there exists under the CAPM a vector q of prices for contingent claims such that $p_j = \sum_s q_s \pi_s^j$; see (23). In that case, the criterion of *maximising the market value of the firm* becomes unambiguous. It is then consistent with market-value maximisation for the firm to contract with agent i for a positive fraction ζ_{ij} of the firm's employment if and only if

$$\zeta_{ij} \sum_s q_s \left(\frac{df_s^j}{dl_s^j} - w_s^{ij} \right) = 0, \quad i = 1 \ldots n, \quad j = 1 \ldots m. \tag{34}$$

Conditions (34) are a specific illustration of the general conditions (24) characterising market-value maximisation. They also imply that wage costs per unit of labour be the same for all the employees of a given firm.

Conditions (34) are of course predicated upon the existence (and observability) of a vector q of prices for contingent claims, which is verified in the CAPM and will need to be established for the generalised framework under discussion.

4.5.

To close the model, there remains only to consider the joint decisions of the agents (households) about labour supply to firms and portfolios of assets.

The decision problem of a representative agent is:

$$\max_{a_i, \theta_{ij}, \zeta_{ij}} \sum_s \phi_s u^i (a_i + \sum_j \theta_{ij} \pi_s^j + \sum_j \zeta_{ij} l_s^j w_s^{ij}) \tag{P2}$$

subject to (17) and $\sum_j \zeta_{ij} l_s^j \le \bar{l}^i$, $s = 1 \ldots S$.

The first-order conditions for a solution of problem (P 2) are

$$\theta_{ij} \sum_s \phi_s \frac{du^i}{dy_s^i} (\pi_s^j - p_j) = 0, \quad a_i = \sum_j p_j (\bar{\theta}_{ij} - \theta_{ij}), \tag{35}$$

$$\zeta_{ij} \left[\sum_s \phi_s \frac{du^i}{dy_s^i} l_s^j w_s^{ij} - \lambda^i \right] = 0, \exists s : \sum_j \zeta_{ij} l_s^j = \bar{l}^i \tag{36}$$

where $\lambda^i \ge 0$ is the dual variable associated with the constraint $\sum_j \zeta_{ij} l_s^j \le \bar{l}^i$.

4.6.

In short, a *feasible arrangement* for the economy consists of m employment vectors $l^j = (l_1^j \ldots l_S^j)$ in R_+^S and n decision vectors $d^i = (a_i, \theta_{i1} \ldots \theta_{im}, \zeta_{i1} \ldots \zeta_{im})$ in $R \times R_+^{2m}$, satisfying $\sum_i a_i = 0$, $\sum_i \theta_{ij} = \sum_i \zeta_{ij} = 1$ for all $j = 1 \ldots m$ and $\sum_j \zeta_{ij} l_s^j \leq \bar{l}^i$ for all $i = 1 \ldots n$, $s = 1 \ldots S$. Denote a feasible arrangement by $z \in Z$.

A feasible arrangement does not specify the terminal wealth levels of the agents, until the personalised wages w_s^{ij} are also specified. Let then a *feasible allocation* for the economy be defined by a feasible arrangement z and an m-tuple W of matrices of personalised wages $W^j = [w_s^{ij}]$ in R_+^{nS}, $j = 1 \ldots m$. The associated terminal wealth levels are then defined by (33), with π_s^j as defined in (32).

A feasible allocation (z, W) is *Pareto efficient* if there exists no alternative feasible allocation $(\hat{z}, \hat{W})$ such that the alternative wealth vectors

$$\hat{y}^i = (\hat{y}_1^i \ldots \hat{y}_S^i), \hat{y}_s^i = \hat{a}_i + \sum_j \hat{\theta}_{ij} \hat{\pi}_s^j + \sum_j \hat{\zeta}_{ij} \hat{l}_s^j \hat{w}_s^{ij},$$

$$i = 1 \ldots n, \quad s = 1 \ldots S,$$

satisfy

$$E_s u^i(\hat{y}_s^i) = \sum_s \phi_s u^i(\hat{y}_s^i) \geq \sum_s \phi_s u^i(y_s^i) = E_s u^i(y_s^i),$$

$$\sum_i E_s u^i(\hat{y}_s^i) > \sum_i E_s u^i(y_s^i). \tag{37}$$

A feasible allocation (z, W) is *decentralised* by the asset prices p in R_+^m and the prices for contingent claims q in R_+^S if it satisfies (17), (34), (35) and (36).

5. Efficiency and equilibrium

5.1.

Let the preferences of the n agents be represented by the quadratic utility functions

$$u^i(y_s^i) = c_i^2 - (c_i - y_s^i)^2, \quad E_s u^i(y_s^i) = \sum_s \phi_s u^i(y_s^i), \quad i = 1 \ldots n. \tag{38}$$

Then, necessary and sufficient conditions for the Pareto efficiency of a feasible allocation (z, W), at which $c_i > y_s^i > 0$ for all i and s, and $\sum_s \frac{df_s^j}{dl_s^j} > 0$ for all j, are

(i) for each j, let $l^j = \max_t l_t^i$; then, for each s, $(l^j - l_s^j)\frac{df_s^j}{dl_s^j} = 0$; and $\sum_j l^j = \sum_i \bar{l}^i$;

(ii) there exists a vector q in R_+^S of prices for contingent claims and a risk premium R such that, for each $j, k = 1 \ldots m$,

$$l^{jk}\sum_s q_s \left[\frac{df_s^j}{dl_s^j} - \frac{df_s^k}{dl_s^k}\right] = 0; \tag{39}$$

for each $i = 1 \ldots n$, for each $s = 1 \ldots S$:

$$q_s = \phi_s \frac{c_i - y_s^i}{c_i - E_s y_s^i} \tag{40a}$$

$$= \phi_s \left[1 - R\left\{\sum_j f_s^j(l_s^j) - E_s \sum_j f_s^j(l_s^j)\right\}\right] := \phi_s[1 - R(Y_s - \bar{Y})]; \tag{40b}$$

(iii) for each i, there exists a pair (α_i, β_i) in $R \times R_+$ such that, for all $s = 1 \ldots S$,

$$y_s^i = \alpha_i + \beta_i \sum_j f_s^j(l_s^j), \quad \alpha_i = c_i - \beta_i \sum_h c_h, \quad \beta_i = \frac{c_i - E_s y_s^i}{\sum_h c_h - E_s \sum_h y_s^h}.$$

Properties (i) and (ii) characterise efficient employment levels, property (iii) efficient risk-sharing. The remainder of section 5.1 is devoted to establish these properties.

Let $(k_1 \ldots k_n)$ be a vector of positive constants, and consider the problem

$$\max_{l^j, l_s^j, y_s^i, \zeta_{ij}} \Lambda = \sum_i k_i E_s u^i(y_s^i)$$

subject to

$$\sum_i y_s^i \le \sum_j f_s^j(l_s^j) \quad s = 1 \ldots S$$

$$l_s^j \le l^j \quad s = 1 \ldots S, \quad j = 1 \ldots m \qquad (P3)$$

$$\sum_j \zeta_{ij} l^j \le \bar{l}^i \quad i = 1 \ldots n$$

$$1 \le \sum_i \zeta_{ij} \quad j = 1 \ldots m.$$

It follows from $du^i/dy_s^i > 0$, $df_s^j/dl_s^j \ge 0$ and $\sum_s df_s^j/dl_s^j > 0$ that all constraints may be imposed with equality, establishing (i). The problem is then reduced to:

$$\max_{l^j, y_s^i} \Lambda = \sum_i k_i E_s u^i(y_s^i) \qquad (P4)$$

subject to

$$\sum_i y_s^i = \sum_j f_s^j(l^j) \quad s = 1 \ldots S \quad (\mu_s)$$

$$\sum_j l^j = \sum_i \bar{l}^i \qquad (v)$$

where (μ_s, v) denote the Lagrange multipliers associated with the constraints.

The first-order conditions for problem (P4) are

$$\frac{\partial \Lambda}{\partial y_s^i} = k_i \phi_s \frac{du^i}{dy_s^i} - \mu_s = k_i \phi_s(c_i - y_s^i) - \mu_s = 0, \qquad (41)$$

$$\frac{\partial \Lambda}{\partial l^j} = \sum_s \mu_s \frac{df_s^j}{dl^j} - v = 0. \qquad (42)$$

Because problem (P4) calls for maximising a concave function over a convex set, the first-order conditions are both necessary and sufficient. Defining $q_s := \mu_s / \sum_t \mu_t > 0$, (39) follows from (42) and (40a) follows from (41). To verify (40b) write (40a) as $q_s = \phi_s[1 - y_s^i - E_s y_s^i/c_i - E_s y_s^i]$ and sum over i both the numerator and denominator of the fraction. Letting $R := [\sum_t c_i - \sum_t E_s y_s^i]^{-1}$ and using $Y_s = \sum_i y_s^i = \sum_j f_s^j(l^j)$, the equality in (40b) follows, and (ii) is verified.

In order to verify (iii), let $Y_s = \sum_i y_s^i = \sum_i c_i - \dfrac{\mu_s}{\phi_s} \sum_i \dfrac{1}{k_i}$ from (41). Hence,

$$\frac{\mu_s}{\phi_s} = \frac{\sum_i c_i - Y_s}{\sum_i \dfrac{1}{k_i}} \quad \text{and}$$

$$y_s^i = c_i - \frac{1}{k_i} \frac{\sum_h c_h - Y_s}{\sum_h \dfrac{1}{k_h}} = \alpha_i + \beta_i Y_s$$

with

$$\beta_i = \frac{\dfrac{1}{k_i}}{\sum_h \dfrac{1}{k_h}} = \frac{c_i - y_s^i}{\sum_h c_h - Y_s}, \quad \alpha_i = c_i - \beta_i \sum_h c_h$$

as desired. This completes the proof.

To reconcile property (iii) with (22), one simply notes that

$$T_A(\bar{Y}) = \sum_i T_A^i(\bar{Y}) = \sum_i [c_i - E_s y_s^i], \tag{43}$$

so that β_i in property (iii) is indeed equal to $\dfrac{T_A^i(\bar{Y})}{T_A(\bar{Y})}$.

5.2.

The characterisation of Pareto efficiency in section 5.1 is helpful to define personalised wages which, together with competitive asset markets and with employment levels that maximise market value, sustain a Pareto-efficient allocation as a decentralised equilibrium. From property (iii), we learn that linear sharing rules remain optimal, in the extended setting with endogenous output and employment levels.[11] Two conclusions follow immediately. First, for an agent supplying no labour and interested in portfolio returns alone, a diversified portfolio ($\theta_{ij} = \theta_i$ for all j) remains optimal if and only if aggregate profits $\sum_j \pi_s^j$ are linearly related to aggregate wealth (output) $\sum_j f_s^j(l^j)$. Aggregate profits are equal to aggregate

---

[11] For examples of related situations where the linearity of optimal rules is violated, see Drèze (1989b) or Drèze and Gollier (1989).

output minus the aggregate wage bill. Accordingly, aggregate profits are linearly related to aggregate output if and only if wages are linearly related to aggregate output. Second, for an agent supplying labour but owning no assets, Pareto efficiency requires that wage income be linearly related to aggregate output. These two conclusions thus converge to suggest that wages should be linearly related to aggregate output. In particular, this confirms that adjusting wages to the marginal product of labour in each state is not consistent with efficient risk-sharing, outside of the special case where the marginal product of labour is linearly related to its average product. In general, *ex post* competitive clearing of the labour market is *ex ante* inefficient! A simple approach to efficiency would consist in setting a fixed wage $\bar{w}$, independent of the state, and relying entirely on the stock market to generate efficient risk-sharing (through diversified portfolios). This, however, would typically require that wage earners not endowed with initial assets borrow in order to hold risky assets. In practice, such borrowing is impractical, costly and subject to moral hazard. A natural alternative is to specify personalised wages consisting of a fixed part and a part indexed on aggregate wealth, with individual wage earners free to choose the respective magnitudes of the constant and variable parts of their wages. If these two parts satisfy (34), the allocation will be decentralised under the criterion of market value maximisation; it will then automatically satisfy (i) and (ii) of section 5.1.

To implement these ideas, consider a fixed wage $\bar{w}$, an indexed wage $w_s = \delta Y_s$ and personalised wages $w_s^{ij} = \eta_i \bar{w} + (1 - \eta_i)w_s$, $i = 1 \ldots n$, $j = 1 \ldots m, s = 1 \ldots S$. The following definition embodies a natural concept of decentralised equilibrium.

An *equilibrium with flexible wage indexation* consists of a feasible arrangement $z \in Z$, a vector of asset prices $p \in R_+^m$, a fixed wage $\bar{w}$ and an indexed wage $w_s = \delta Y_s = \delta \sum_j f_s^j(l^j)$, $s = 1 \ldots S$, n individual indexing weights $\eta_i \in [0, 1]$, and a risk premium R such that:

(a) for each agent $i = 1 \ldots n$, the portfolio $(\theta_{ij})_{j=1 \ldots m}$ and the indexing weight η_i solve

$$\max_{\theta_{ij}, \eta_i} \sum_s \phi_s u^i(y_s^i)$$

where   (P5)

$$y_s^i = \bar{l}^i[\eta_i \bar{w} + (1 - \eta_i)\delta Y_s] + \sum_j p_j(\bar{\theta}_{ij} - \theta_{ij}) + \sum_j \theta_{ij}\pi_s^j$$

(b) for each firm $j = 1 \ldots m$, the employment level l^j solves

$$\max_{l_j} \sum_s \phi_s [1 - R(Y_s - \bar{Y})][f_s^j(l^j) - \bar{w}l^j]$$

$$= \sum_s \phi_s [1 - R(Y_s - \bar{Y})][f_s^j(l^j) - w_s l_j]$$

$$= \sum_s \phi_s [1 - R(Y_s - \bar{Y})]\pi_s^j;$$

(c) $\sum_i \theta_{ij} = 1, \quad \sum_i \bar{l}^i = \sum_j l^j.$

5.3.

When the preferences of the n agents are represented by the quadratic utility functions (38), then

(i) There exists an equilibrium with flexible wage indexation, where $\theta_{ij} = \theta_i$, $j = 1 \ldots m$, $i = 1 \ldots n$, $R^{-1} = T_A(\bar{Y}) = \sum_i T_A^i(\bar{Y})$ and $\bar{w} = \delta(\bar{Y} - R\sigma_Y^2)$.

(ii) Every equilibrium with flexible wage indexation is Pareto efficient.

The remainder of this section is devoted to a proof of these two propositions, starting with (i).

The simplest approach to prove existence is to introduce explicitly the prices for contingent claims q_s and to consider the production economy with a single type of labour and S contingent commodities, of respective prices $(\bar{w}, q_1 \ldots q_s)$. The initial ownership fractions $\bar{\theta}_{ij}$ are treated as fixed, and the individual budget constraints are replaced by

$$\sum_s q_s y_s^i - \bar{w}\bar{l}^i - \sum_j \bar{\theta}_{ij} \sum_s q_s [f_s^j(l^j) - \bar{w}l^j] \leq 0. \tag{44}$$

The resulting economy is a particular case of that considered in chapter 7 of *Theory of Value* (Debreu, 1959), so that there exists a competitive equilibrium where for each j

$$\sum_s q_s \frac{df_s^j}{dl^j} - \bar{w} = 0 \tag{45}$$

(profit maximisation) and for each i

$$\frac{q_s}{\sum_t q_t} = \frac{\phi_s \dfrac{du^i}{dy_s^i}}{\sum_t \phi_t \dfrac{du^i}{dy_t^i}} = \phi_s \frac{c_i - y_s^i}{c_i - \sum_t \phi_t y_t^i} \tag{46}$$

(expected utility maximisation). Because that competitive equilibrium is Pareto efficient, it must have the properties listed in section 5.1. Thus, there exists for each i a pair (α_i, β_i) as defined in property (iii) there; and there exists a risk premium $R = 1/T_A(\bar{Y})$ such that, for each $s, q_s = \phi_s[1 - R(Y_s - \bar{Y})]$. At the competitive equilibrium, l^j maximises

$$\sum_s q_s[f^j_s(l_s) - \bar{w}l^j] = \sum_s \phi_s[1 - R(Y_s - \bar{Y})][f^j_s(l^j) - \bar{w}l^j],$$

as required.

In order to implement the competitive equilibrium as an equilibrium with flexible wage indexation, we need to define the share prices p and the flexible wage parameter δ; and we need to specify for each individual i the 'market' portfolio $\theta_{ij} = \theta_i, j = 1 \ldots m$, the lump-sum transfer a_i and the indexing weight η_i. The portfolio and indexing weight must satisfy $1 \geq \theta_{ij} \geq 0, 1 \geq \eta_i \geq 0, i = 1 \ldots n$ and $\sum_i \theta_{ij} = 1, j = 1 \ldots m$.

I first choose δ such that $\sum_s q_s w_s = \delta \sum_s q_s Y_s = \bar{w}$; i.e.

$$\delta = \frac{\bar{w}}{[\bar{Y} - R\sigma_Y^2]}, \tag{47}$$

as required. Defining next as usual $p_j = \sum_s q_s \pi^j_s$, we verify at once

$$p_j = \sum_s q_s[f^j_s(l^j) - \bar{w}l^j] = \sum_s q_s[f^j_s(l^j) - \delta Y_s l^j]. \tag{48}$$

If each agent i earns a labour income equal to $\bar{l}^i[\eta_i \bar{w} + (1 - \eta_i)\delta Y_s]$, then we may define the aggregate wage bill as

$$\sum_i \bar{l}^i[\eta_i \bar{w} + (1 - \eta_i)\delta Y_s] = \bar{w}\sum_i \bar{l}^i\eta_i + \delta\left[\sum_i \bar{l}^i(1 - \eta_i)\right]Y_s$$

$$:= F + DY_s \tag{49}$$

thereby defining the fixed component F and the variable (indexed) component DY_s of the aggregate wage bill. (That $1 \geq D \geq 0$ is verified below.) It then follows that, for each s

$$\sum_j \pi^j_s = \sum_j f^j_s(l^j) - \sum_i \bar{l}^i[\eta_i \bar{w} + (1 - \eta_i)\delta Y_s]$$

$$= Y_s(1 - D) - F. \tag{50}$$

A portfolio consisting of a constant share $\theta_{ij} = \theta_i$ of all firms will then yield $\theta_i \sum_j \pi_s^j = \theta_i [Y_s(1 - D) - F]$ in state s. Under such a portfolio, the expression for y_s^i in (a) of the definition becomes

$$y_s^i = \bar{l}^i \eta_i \bar{w} + \sum_j p_j(\bar{\theta}_{ij} - \theta_i) - \theta_i F$$

$$+ \bar{l}^i(1 - \eta_i)\delta Y_s + \theta_i(1 - D)Y_s \qquad (51)$$

which is of the form $y_s^i = \alpha_i + \beta_i Y_s$ with

$$\alpha_i = \bar{l}^i \eta_i \bar{w} + \sum_j p_j(\bar{\theta}_{ij} - \theta_i) - \theta_i F,$$

$$\beta_i = \bar{l}^i(1 - \eta_i)\delta + \theta_i(1 - D). \qquad (52)$$

A solution to (52) with $1 \geq \eta_i \geq 0$ and $1 \geq \theta_i \geq 0$ is obtained as follows. For any D, $1 \geq D \geq 0$, start with $\theta_i = \beta_i$ and $\bar{l}^i(1 - \eta_i)\delta = \beta_i D$. Then, $\delta \sum_i \bar{l}^i(1 - \eta_i) = D$ and for each i, $\beta_i = \beta_i D + \beta_i(1 - D)$, $\theta_i \in [0, 1]$ and $1 - \eta_i > 0$. Also, $\beta_i - \bar{l}^i(1 - \eta_i)\delta \geq 0$, since $\beta_i \geq 0$ and $1 - D \geq 0$. If it were the case that $\eta_i < 0$, then set $\hat{\eta}_i = 0$, $\hat{\theta}_i(1 - \hat{D}) = \beta_i - \bar{l}^i\delta \geq \beta_i \hat{D}$, where $\hat{D} = \delta \sum_i \bar{l}^i(1 - \hat{\eta}_i)$. It is still true that $\beta_h - \bar{l}^h(1 - \hat{\eta}_h)\delta \geq 0$ for all h; hence, $1 > D \geq \hat{D} \geq 0$ and $1 \geq \hat{\theta}_i \geq 0$ since

$$\hat{\theta}_i = \frac{\beta_i - \bar{l}^i(1 - \hat{\eta}_i)\delta}{\sum_h \beta_h - \delta \sum_h \bar{l}_h(1 - \hat{\eta}_h)} \leq 1.$$

In this way we construct a solution with $1 \geq \eta_i \geq 0$ and $1 \geq \theta_i \geq 0$ for all i, $1 \geq D \geq 0$ as desired. It is fully defined by $1 - \eta_i = \min(\beta_i D / \bar{l}^i \delta, 1)$ and $\theta_i = [\beta_i - \bar{l}^i(1 - \eta_i)\delta]/(1 - D)$.

To verify that the solution just defined solves problem (P 5) in condition (a) of the definition, write the first-order conditions, which are necessary and sufficient since the maximand is concave and the feasible set convex:

$$\frac{\partial E_s u^i(y_s^i)}{\partial \theta_{ij}} = E_s \frac{du^i}{dy_s^i}(\pi_s^j - p_j) = 0 = \sum_s \phi_s(c^i - y_s^i)(\pi_s^j - p_j) \qquad (53)$$

$$\frac{\partial E_s u^i(y_s^i)}{\partial \eta_i} = \bar{l}^i E_s \frac{du^i}{dy_s^i}(\bar{w} - \delta Y_s) = 0$$

$$= \sum_s \phi_s(c_i - y_s^i)(\bar{w} - \delta Y_s). \qquad (54)$$

Using the definition of y_s^i, and writing Θ_i for the vector $(\theta_{i1} \ldots \theta_{im})'$, conditions (53)–(54) may be written in an obvious matrix notation as

$$(c_i - \bar{y}_i) \begin{pmatrix} \bar{\pi} - p \\ \bar{Y} - \dfrac{\bar{w}}{\delta} \end{pmatrix} + \begin{bmatrix} \sum_{\pi Y} & \sum_{\pi\pi} \\ \sum_{YY} & \sum_{Y\pi} \end{bmatrix} \begin{pmatrix} \bar{l}^i(1 - \eta_i)\delta \\ \Theta_i \end{pmatrix} = 0. \tag{55}$$

Summing these conditions over i, using the definition of D and $\sum_i \theta_{ij} = 1$,

$$\sum_i (c_i - \bar{y}_i) \begin{pmatrix} \bar{\pi} - p \\ \bar{Y} - \dfrac{\bar{w}}{\delta} \end{pmatrix} + \begin{bmatrix} \sum_{\pi Y} & \sum_{\pi\pi} \\ \sum_{YY} & \sum_{Y\pi} \end{bmatrix} \begin{pmatrix} D \\ \iota \end{pmatrix} = 0. \tag{56}$$

Inserting (56) into (55),

$$\begin{bmatrix} \sum_{\pi Y} & \sum_{\pi\pi} \\ \sum_{YY} & \sum_{Y\pi} \end{bmatrix} \left[\frac{c_i - \bar{y}_i}{\sum_h c_h - \bar{Y}} \begin{pmatrix} D \\ \iota \end{pmatrix} - \begin{pmatrix} \bar{l}^i(1 - \eta_i)\delta \\ \Theta_i \end{pmatrix} \right] = 0 \tag{57}$$

which always admit the solution $\bar{l}^i(1 - \eta_i)\delta = \beta_i D$, $\Theta_i = \beta_i \iota$, where $\beta_i = (c_i - \bar{y}_i)/(\sum_h c_h - \bar{Y}) = T_A^i(\bar{Y})/T_A(\bar{Y})$. Since furthermore y^i is constant over all pairs $(\hat{\eta}_i, \hat{\theta}_i)$ such that $\beta_i = \bar{l}^i(1 - \hat{\eta}_i)\delta + \hat{\theta}_i(1 - D)$, the modifications introduced in the previous paragraph do not violate the first-order conditions (57). This completes the proof of proposition (i).

To show next that an equilibrium with flexible wage indexation is Pareto efficient, one notes from (56) that, in equilibrium, $p = \bar{\pi} - R \sum_{\pi Y}$, $\bar{w} = \delta[\bar{Y} - R\sigma_Y^2]$, where $R^{-1} = \sum_i c_i - \bar{Y}$. (Indeed, $\sum_{\pi Y} D + \sum_{\pi\pi} \iota = \sum_{\pi Y}$ and $\sum_{YY} D + \sum_{Y\pi} \iota = \sum_{YY} = \sigma_Y^2$.) Therefore, maximisation of market value by firms is equivalent to maximisation of profits $\sum_s q_s \pi_s^j$ at prices $q_s = \phi_s[1 - R(Y_s - \bar{Y})]$. And one notes from (57) that $y_s^i = \alpha_i + \beta_i Y_s$, with $\beta_i = \bar{l}^i(1 - \eta_i)\delta + \theta_i(1 - D) = T_A^i(\bar{Y})/T_A(\bar{Y})$. The verification of the conditions listed at the beginning of section 5.1 is then immediate.

6. Concluding comments

6.1.

The results presented in section 5 may be summarised as follows. I have studied an economy consisting of a given set of firms, which hire labour to produce a state-dependent output, and whose shares are traded on a stock market. Efficient risk-sharing among all the agents in the economy calls for individual incomes related to aggregate output (or wealth). In the simple special case of quadratic utilities, efficiency requires that individual incomes be linearly related to aggregate wealth, i.e. consist of a fixed part and a variable part, proportional to aggregate wealth. The variable part should distribute the random fluctuations of aggregate wealth over individuals in proportion to their risk tolerances – independently of the extent to which the individual incomes come from wages or from profit shares.

If wages were fixed (state independent), an efficient allocation of risk would require that workers buy shares of stock on credit, using their wage earnings as collateral. Such arrangements are impractical, costly and subject to moral hazard. If wages were set after observing the state and equal to the marginal value product of labour, an efficient allocation of risks would require that workers insure their wage uncertainty, either by selling short a portfolio perfectly positively correlated with their wages or by buying on credit a portfolio perfectly negatively correlated with their wages. Such portfolios may not exist; at best, the arrangements are impractical, costly and subject to moral hazard.

Flexible wage indexation is a more practical alternative. It calls for setting wages that consist of two parts, namely a fixed part (indexed on consumer prices, in practice) and a variable part, indexed on aggregate output (wealth). Each individual chooses freely the relative importance of the two parts of his or her wage income, as well as the composition of his or her portfolio. Efficient risk-sharing emerges naturally, without recourse to short sales or credit. The only requirement is that the risk premium by which the expected value of a variable wage exceeds the fixed wage should be consistent with the risk premium by which the expected value of a firm's profits differs from the market price of its shares. That is, a single price of risk determines simultaneously the trade-off between the fixed and variable wage, and the prices of shares on the stock market. And the efficient allocation is sustained as a decentralised equilibrium.

Although the results were established for quadratic utilities, they can be extended to the 'hyperbolic absolute risk aversion' class at a small technical cost. The implicit property on which the results rest is the extended validity of the CAPM to situations where the endowments (here, the labour incomes) of the agents lie in the span of the vectors of returns to the marketed assets – see Geanakoplos in Duffie *et al.* (1988). The fact that all firms have the same shareholders leads them to offer the same labour contracts – see Drèze (1989a).

6.2.

The nature of the result should be properly understood. It applies to the compensation of *workers under contract*, not directly to the wages of new entrants to the labour market in state *s*. The presentation is timeless, but it should be remembered that two 'dates' are involved: an initial date, at which firms hire employees, the labour market clears, and asset markets clear; and a future date, at which production materialises, wages and dividends are paid out. The 'state' is unknown at the initial date, but will be known at the future date.

The market clearing fixed wage at the initial date is $\bar{w}$. But labour contracts offer the prospect of stipulating state-dependent wages that bring about efficient risk-sharing between firms and their employees. The results of section 5 give a simple operational content to the abstract model of labour contracts. But it should be understood that the *level* of all wages is determined by the condition of market clearing at the initial date – that is, by the condition $\sum_i \bar{l}^i = \sum_j l^j$, which determines $\bar{w}$ and affects w_s which is proportional to $\bar{w}$ (as well as to Y_s) according to formula (47). Should the labour market reopen at the future date in state *s*, with new entrants to the labour market, then a new market clearing wage for new contracts, $\bar{w}_s$, will prevail. Since $\bar{w}_s$ will be determined by the supply and demand for new contracts, whereas w_s is predetermined as part of the initial contracts, one should not expect that $\bar{w}_s = w_s$ identically in *s*. Wage differentiation between successive cohorts of workers will generally be required for efficiency. That topic goes beyond the scope of the present paper. It is treated in Drèze and Gollier (1989).

6.3.

In the model of section 5, firms hire labour at the initial date, and are constrained not to use additional labour in any state. Because the opportunity cost of labour is equal to zero in every state, no layoffs ever occur. This feature calls for two remarks.

First, when the labour market clears, the weighted expected marginal product of labour (adjusted for risk), $\sum_s q_s \, df_s^j/dl^j$, is the same in all firms and equal to the fixed wage. It may still be the case that the marginal product of labour differs across firms in specific states. In such states, a more efficient use of labour could be achieved if some labour were transferred from the low productivity to the high productivity firms. Such arrangements are sometimes observed (for instance, fishermen may find casual employment on shore on days of sea storm or boat maintenance), but they are the exception rather than the rule. A smooth organisation of such arrangements would require *ex ante* evaluation of the marginal product of labour in every state. That kind of contingent information is typically unavailable.

Second, under a more general specification, where labour supply would reflect the disutility or opportunity cost of labour, it may no longer be efficient to set $l_s^j = l^j$ for all s. In particular, under a high opportunity cost of labour (due for instance to generous unemployment benefits), it would be natural to set $l_s^j < l^j$ in those states s where the marginal product of labour is low ('bad' states). In order for the analysis to go through, it would then be required that (cardinal) individual preferences for leisure and wealth be representable by separable functions:

$$U^i(l^i, y^i) = v^i(l^i) + u^i(y^i), \quad i = 1 \ldots n. \tag{58}$$

That assumption, under which risk tolerance remains independent of leisure time or work effort, is rather restrictive when U^i is defined up to an affine transformation.

6.4.

The superiority of flexible wage indexation over fixed wages comes from the reduction in the risk premium $R = 1/T_A(\bar{Y}) = 1/\sum_i T_A^i(\bar{y}^i)$. Consider an economy with two types of agents, n_1 asset owners with $\sum_{i=1}^{n_1} \theta_{ij} = 1$ for all j and n_2 workers with no endowment of initial assets. The firms could hire the available labour at a fixed wage $\bar{w}_1$ such that

$$\bar{w}_1 = \sum_s \frac{df_s^j}{dl^j} \phi_s [1 - R_1(Y_s - \bar{Y})] \tag{59}$$

where R_1 is the risk premium incorporated in the asset prices and verifying $R_1^{-1} = \sum_{i=1}^{n_1} T_A^i(\bar{y}^i)$. The risk premium R_1 exceeds the risk premium R of section 5, which verifies instead $R^{-1} = \sum_{i=1}^{n_1+n_2} T_A^i(\bar{y}^i)$. In order to assess the reduction in the risk premium, it is useful to write it in terms of the relative risk tolerances defined in (8):

$$R^{-1} = \sum_{i=1}^{n_1+n_2} \frac{T_A^i(\bar{y}^i)}{\bar{y}^i} \cdot \bar{y}^i = \bar{Y} \sum_{i=1}^{n_1+n_2} \frac{\bar{y}^i}{\bar{Y}} T_R^i(\bar{y}^i) = \bar{Y} T_R(\bar{Y}) \tag{60}$$

$$R_1^{-1} = \sum_{i=1}^{n_1} \frac{T_A^i(\bar{y}^i)}{\bar{y}^i} \cdot \bar{y}^i = \bar{Y}_1 \sum_{i=1}^{n_1} \frac{\bar{y}^i}{\bar{Y}_1} T_R^i(\bar{y}^i)$$

$$= \bar{Y}_1 T_R(\bar{Y}_1), \quad \bar{Y}_1 = \sum_{i=1}^{n_1} \bar{y}^i. \tag{61}$$

If it were the case that the average relative risk tolerance for all the agents, $T_R(\bar{Y})$, is equal to the average risk tolerance for the asset owners, $T_R(\bar{Y}_1)$; then it would follow from (60)–(61) that

$$\frac{R_1}{R} = \frac{\bar{Y}}{\bar{Y}_1} \tag{62}$$

where $\bar{Y}/\bar{Y}_1$ is the ratio of total wealth to non-human wealth (of national income to capital income). That ratio should be approximately equal to the reciprocal of the capital share in income and wealth (one minus the labour share), hence it should fall in the range from 3 to 4. The reduction in the risk premium resulting from flexible wage indexation versus fixed wages would be dramatic. The calculation is probably an overestimation, to the extent that the average risk tolerance of asset owners may exceed that of wage earners. Unfortunately, the logical arguments to that effect are ambiguous, and the empirical evidence is very limited.

It should be noted that the reduction in the risk premium benefits the wage earners, because

$$\bar{w} = \sum_s \phi_s \frac{df_s^j}{dl^j} - R \sum_s \phi_s \frac{df_s^j}{dl^j}(Y_s - \bar{Y}) > \bar{w}_1$$

$$= \sum_s \phi_s \frac{df_s^j}{dl^j} - R_1 \sum_s \phi_s \frac{df_s^j}{dl_s^j}(Y_s - \bar{Y}). \tag{63}$$

6.5.

The main difficulty in applying a flexible indexation scheme lies with the measurement of the 'aggregate wealth' variable Y_s. That difficulty has a logical side and a practical side.

The logical issue concerns the wealth *concept*. A static (timeless) framework was used here for simplicity of exposition. In reality, one would need to choose between a flow concept like national income, justified for instance by the argument that wealth is the present value of income; or a stock concept combining asset values and some evaluation of human wealth. The former approach is definitely the more practical. Although the period over which the flow should be measured is arbitrary, the year seems inescapable ... Another issue concerns the geographical area over which the aggregate income flow should be measured. A national measure again seems inescapable. Yet, capital markets are linked internationally. To the extent that national incomes are imperfectly correlated across countries, the international linkage should reduce the national risk premia.

The practical issue concerns the speed and objectivity with which national income is measured. Up-to-date information about labour incomes and wage costs is part of our system, and is forthcoming when wages are geared to a monthly index of consumer prices. National income is measured less frequently, less accurately and with longer delay.

6.6.

From the standpoint of individual firms, the proposed indexation scheme should be a matter of indifference, so long as they accept the market risk-premium as a guideline and attempt to maximise market value. That principle does not apply to small firms which are not traded on a stock exchange. Thus, a private entrepreneur who owns an independent firm typically invests in that firm most of his (her) wealth, instead of holding a diversified portfolio. The relevant risk premium for that firm should then reflect the owner's risk tolerance rather than the market price of risk. Being unable to shed risks on the market, that entrepreneur could benefit from sharing risks with his (her) employees, through profit-sharing at the firm level. In a small firm, productivity may also be enhanced by the incentive effects of profit-sharing.

On the other hand, many contracts, like house rental or life insurance, could embody partial indexation on national income as a further step towards more efficient risk-sharing at the economy-wide level.

12 Wages, employment and the equity–efficiency trade-off*

1. Introduction

In a decentralised market economy, prices play two roles: an *economic* role, as prices guide production and consumption decisions; and a *financial* role, as prices determine the receipts of the seller and the expenditure (hence the real income) of the buyer.[1] The first role is geared to *efficiency* of resource allocation; the second is related to *equity* of the personal distribution of real incomes...

The dual role of prices is obvious in the case of *wages*. In a market economy, the level and hierarchy of wages guide the labour demand by firms; and wages determine the real incomes of workers.[2] An economically efficient use of human labour, free of involuntary unemployment as well as unfilled job offers, may lead to an 'inequitable' income distribution. (The meaning of 'inequitable' is explained below.) This may be linked to the functional distribution between capital and labour, or to the wage disparities by skills. In this paper, I use a streamlined model, with identical workers and a single wage rate; but I consider the spread between wages and unemployment benefits.

The second theorem of welfare economics[3] *suggests* a general solution to the potential conflict between efficiency and equity. Under the conditions

* Expository Paper written for the session on 'Equity–Efficiency Trade-Off' at the 9th Meeting of French-Speaking Belgian Economists, Liège, November 1988 and published in *Recherches Economiques de Louvain*, 55, 1, 1–31; translated from the French by the author.
[1] Cf. Lévy-Lambert (1969) for a systematic discussion of that theme.
[2] The same duality remains present in a labour-managed economy: see Drèze (1984a, 1989a).
[3] See e.g. Koopmans (1957).

of the theorem, every Pareto-efficient allocation of resources[4] corresponds to competitive clearing of all markets, under an appropriate redistribution of wealth (i.e. under a proper set of individualised lump-sum taxes and transfers). Economic policy thus boils down to two specific tasks: bring about competitive clearing of all markets, and implement the lump-sum transfers suggested by equity considerations.

Without reviewing here the conditions of the theorem,[5] I will mention the two main difficulties surrounding its applicability.

(i) The argument rests on existence of a complete set of markets, and does not apply to an economy with incomplete markets. In a temporal economy with uncertain future, this calls for existence of an insurance market for each good at each date conditionally on each possible 'state' of the economic environment (as defined by demography, natural resources, technology, tastes, institutions ...). In real economies, markets are incomplete – due to many reasons, one of which is close to my subject matter. *In a temporal economy, some agents concerned with markets at future dates are unable to trade today.* This applies in particular to labour markets. Each year, a new generation of young workers enters the labour market. The future generations (whose members are in school today) do not sell their labour services forward and contingently (on graduation, on the state of the economy ...). To that extent, markets are incomplete, and the second welfare theorem is not applicable. In particular, it is not demonstrated, and *it is in general not the case, that sequential competitive clearing of labour markets is Pareto efficient.* (In other words, the alleged efficiency of fully flexible wages is not to be taken for granted; I show in Section 3 that full flexibility can be inefficient.)

The nature of the inefficiency is the following. Economic fluctuations may cause substantial wages fluctuations (due to inelastic labour supply), hence substantial uncertainty of workers' incomes. It is inefficient to let workers bear that uncertainty, which could be shared better. (As shown in Section 3, a suitable degree of wage rigidity, combined with unemployment benefits, provides income insurance and is more efficient than full wage flexibility.)

(ii) The argument of the second welfare theorem also rests on the possibility of implementing lump-sum transfers among households, at

---

[4] I.e., such that no household could be made better off without some other household being made worse off.

[5] The most restrictive assumption concerns convexity of production sets. That assumption is definitely unrealistic, but unfortunately essential for decentralisation of efficient decisions through prices. See Dehez and Drèze (1988a) for a concept of decentralised *equilibrium* with increasing returns to scale.

no real cost. This has two aspects. First, individualised transfers, or discriminatory taxes, must be ethically acceptable. (Which house of representatives would vote a special tax on eyesight accuracy or knowledge of foreign languages, on grounds of measured correlation with high productivity?) Second, the transfers and taxes must be 'neutral' (non-distorting); for instance, they should not affect labour supply, entrepreneurship, savings, investment, consumer or technological choices, a.s.o.

In reality, taxes and transfers are always based on simple, objective characteristics, that keep discrimination to a minimum; and they always entail some loss of efficiency, due to administrative costs, incentive effects and distortions. That real cost must be taken into account. *It is sometimes less inefficient to tamper with prices, in order to modify directly the income distribution, than to correct that distribution through taxes and transfers.* Wages are a good example. To modify the distribution of income between property owners and workers, wage setting and income taxes provide alternative instruments, whose real costs should be contrasted.

In this paper, I use a very simple model to characterise the efficiency–equity trade-off, when wage setting is used to correct the income distribution (Section 2) or improve risk-sharing (Section 3), in a market economy where firms hire and fire labour so as to maximise market value. Some implications and extensions are mentioned briefly at the end (Section 4).

2. Wages, transfers and distortions

2.1.

In this section, I bring out the role of wages and unemployment benefits to correct the income distribution, when taxes are distorting and thus entail a real cost.

The simplest relevant model involves n identical workers, who either work (sell one unit of labour) for a wage w, or do not work and collect unemployment benefits t. (Working time is not a variable here.) Moreover, workers may have to pay a lump-sum tax $a < 0$ or may receive a lump-sum transfer $a > 0$ (sometimes called 'universal grant' or 'negative income tax', but here specific to workers). The income of a worker is thus $w + a \geq 0$ if employed, $t + a \geq 0$ if unemployed. I write m for the monetary equivalent of the utility or disutility of work, here assumed for convenience invariant with income. The utility of a worker is therefore $u(w - m + a)$ if employed, $u(t + a)$ if unemployed. The function u is concave (diminishing marginal utility) and differentiable, with $u' > 0$, $u'' < 0$. Its (cardinal) interpretation is discussed below.

Workers are employed in the production sector, here treated as an aggregate; value added is defined through a concave production function (diminishing returns) $f(l)$, where l denotes employment, determined by the first-order condition for profit maximisation $f'(l) = w$ (the marginal value product of labour is equal to the wage rate). I write $l(w)$ for 'l such that $f'(l) = w$'.[6] A wage cost w thus implies gross profits in the amount $f(l(w)) - wl(w)$.

Profits are distributed to shareholders, a group distinct from the workers. (Shareholders' preferences are taken into account in Section 3, but play no role in Section 2.) Profits are subject to a lump-sum tax $T < 0$ or subsidy $T > 0$.[7]

Budgetary equilibrium requires that taxes, transfers and unemployment benefits sum to zero, i.e. $T + na + (n - l)t = 0$. I wish to take into account the real cost of (distorting) taxes. In order to study the choice between wages and transfers, without being specific about the nature of tax distortions, I will impute a real cost $d \geq 0$ to each dollar of tax or subsidy on profits. The total real cost of taxation is thus $d|T| = d|na + (n - l)t| \geq 0$. The *net* profits associated with wages w, benefits t and transfers a are thus defined by

$$\Pi(w, t, a) = f(l(w)) - wl(w) - [na + (n - l(w))t]$$
$$- d|na + (n - l(w))t|. \tag{1}$$

When $t = 0$, the competitive wage w^* is equal to the maximum of $f'(n)$ and m. When $f'(n) \geq m$, then $w^* = f'(n)$ and $l(w^*) = n$. When $f'(n) < m$, then $w^* = m$ and $l(w^*) < n$. Unemployment $n - l(w^*)$ is 'voluntary' since $u(w - m + a) = u(a) = u(t + a)$. The two cases are illustrated in figure 12.1, with the marginal value product of labour given respectively by curve $\bar{f}'(l)$ and by curve $\hat{f}'(l)$.

More generally, when $t > 0$, wages must be such that $w - m \geq t$, because otherwise the labour supply would vanish.

2.2.

Competitive wages might induce a distribution of income among workers and shareholders which the government wishes to correct, which amounts

---

[6] Technically, labour demand is defined by the inverse function $l(w) = (f')^{-1}(w)$.

[7] That convenient formulation is realistic when profits are taxed at a flat rate, independent of personal income. (Such is by and large the case in Belgium.)

to say that the income distribution is judged 'inequitable'. Thus, if $w^* = m$ and $a = 0$, the government would typically wish to raise the income of workers. More generally, $w^* > m$ may be judged intolerably low, or high, relatively to profits (to shareholders' income).

In such a model, the government has the choice of two instruments to correct the income distribution, a or t. (At full employment, or when $t = 0$, nobody collects benefits and the only instrument available to *reduce* workers' income is a.)

Assume that the government wishes to raise workers' income, starting from a situation where $w - m + a = t + a$ (unemployment nonexistent or voluntary). *The best instrument is that which permits a given increment of workers' income at the least cost in terms of net profits.* ('Best' means here 'second-best'; the income distribution condition and the real cost of transfers rule out the 'first-best'.)

The choice of the better instrument is given by the solution of the following problem:

PROBLEM P.1

$\max\limits_{w,a,t} \Pi(w, t, a)$ subject to

$$u(w - m + a) = u(t + a) \geq u(b),$$
$$0 \leq t \leq w - m, \; l(w) \leq n, f'(l) = w.$$

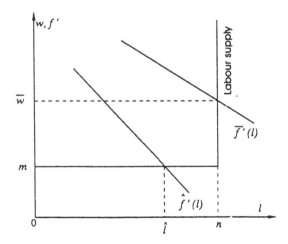

Figure 12.1

From the definition (1), when $na + (n - l)t \geq 0$, we may compute:

$$\frac{d\Pi(w, t, a)}{da} = \frac{\partial \Pi(w, t, a)}{\partial a} = -(1 + d)n; \tag{2}$$

$$\frac{d\Pi(w, t, a)}{dt} = \frac{\partial \Pi(w, t, a)}{\partial t} + \frac{\partial \Pi(w, t, a)}{\partial w} \frac{dw}{dt}$$

$$= \frac{\partial \Pi(w, t, a)}{\partial t} + \frac{\partial \Pi(w, t, a)}{\partial w}$$

$$= -(1 + d)(n - l) + f' \cdot \frac{dl}{dw} - w \frac{dl}{dw}$$

$$- l + (1 + d)t \frac{dl}{dw}$$

$$= -(1 + d)(n - l) - l + (1 + d)t \frac{dl}{dw}; \tag{3}$$

$$\frac{d\Pi(w, t, a)}{dt} - \frac{d\Pi(w, t, a)}{da} = ld + (1 + d)t \frac{dl}{dw}$$

$$= (1 + d)l \left[\frac{d}{1 + d} + \frac{t}{l} \frac{dl}{dw} \right]$$

$$= (1 + d)l \left[\frac{d}{1 + d} + \frac{t}{w} \eta_{lw} \right] \tag{4}$$

where $\eta_{lw} = \frac{w}{l} \frac{dl}{dw} < 0$ denotes the wage elasticity of employment.

The necessary and sufficient condition under which higher wages and unemployment benefits dominate lump-sum transfers to all workers[8] is

$$\frac{d}{1 + d} \geq \frac{t}{w} |\eta_{lw}| = \frac{w - m}{w} |\eta_{lw}| = \frac{w - m}{l} \left| \frac{dl}{dw} \right|. \tag{5}$$

Condition (5) lends itself to a natural interpretation in terms of the real costs (distortions) associated with the two instruments. The left-hand side measures the real cost per dollar of taxes levied on profits. (Indeed, the cost is d for one dollar of net revenue, i.e. for $1 + d$ dollars of gross

---

[8] If the lump-sum transfers were granted to a broader group than workers alone, the real cost of transfers would increase proportionately, and the relative efficiency of wages to raise workers' income would be enhanced. This remark applies in particular to 'universal grants' available to all.

revenue.) The right-hand side measures the real cost per dollar of incremental wage bill. (A unit increase of w increases the wage bill by l and reduces employment by $dl/dw < 0$, at a loss of output $f' \, dl/dw = w \, dl/dw$; but the employment change contributes directly $-m \, dl/dw$ to the real income of workers; the real cost is thus $(w - m) \, dl/dw$ per unit increase of w or $(w - m)/l \cdot (dl/dw)$ per dollar of wage bill.) Thus condition (5) reads: *wages are a more efficient instrument of income redistribution than lump-sum transfers when wages induce less costly distortions than taxes, dollar for dollar.*

Looking at the limiting cases $d = 0$ and $t \, dl/dw = 0$, one concludes from (5) that either instrument might qualify: *when taxes are non-distorting* $(d = 0)$, lump-sum transfers are a more efficient instrument of income redistribution than wages; on the other hand, *when wages cover exactly the real opportunity cost of work* $(w - m = 0)$, *or when the wage elasticity of employment is non-negative, then wages are a more efficient instrument of income redistribution than lump-sum transfers financed by non-neutral taxes.*

The use of both instruments is balanced, and problem P.1 is solved, when (5) holds as equality, i.e. when

$$\frac{w - m}{w} = \frac{\dfrac{d}{1 + d}}{|\eta_{lw}|}. \tag{6}$$

Readers familiar with second-best tax theory will interpret (6) as a 'Boiteux–Ramsey rule' or 'inverse elasticity rule' for the relative spread between the market price (w) and the social cost (m) of a factor of production. (The same readers will interpret (5) in terms of 'direction of improvement' for the 'reform' problem.)

I will discuss in Section 2.4 the measurement of the parameters (m, d, η) of (5)–(6), and the practical circumstances under which condition (5) is apt to hold.

2.3.

I turn now to a more sophisticated point. *When condition (5) holds at less than full employment* $(n > l)$, *raising wages at unchanged unemployment benefits is less distortionary, per dollar of labour income, than raising simultaneously wages and benefits.* That conclusion follows directly from the fact that unemployment benefits are financed by taxes which entail more distortions than wage increases, when (5) holds. Yet the proposed policy would induce *involuntary* unemployment, because it would eventually result in $w - m > t$, i.e. a real income disparity between employed and unemployed workers. Is that a desirable component of income redistribution policies?

We encounter here the difficult choice between *ex post* and *ex ante* policies. To clarify the nature of that choice, it helps to reason with fixed transfers, and to investigate whether it would be desirable to simultaneously reduce benefits and raise wages. Could one in this way reduce the deadweight loss of distortions, at unchanged expected utility for a worker? If so, one could also raise net profits at unchanged workers' (expected) utility, *a Pareto improvement.*

Since all workers are identical, it is natural to stipulate that they are hired randomly, so that each individual worker is employed with probability l/n, unemployed with probability $(n - l)/n$. A worker's expected utility is then computed as

$$Eu = \frac{l}{n}u(w - m + a) + \frac{n - l}{n}u(t + a). \tag{7}$$

When $w - m = t$, unemployment is voluntary and $Eu(w - m + a) = u(t + a)$. On the other hand, under involuntary unemployment $(w - m > t)$, expected utility is a weighted average of the two different levels $u(w - m + a)$ and $u(t + a)$. Formula (7) then takes on its full meaning, based on the axiomatic decision theory underpinning the definition of cardinal, or von Neumann-Morgenstern utility.[9] The interpretation, also illustrated in figure 12.2, goes as follows: the uncertain prospect promising the net incomes $w - m + a$ and $t + a$ with respective probabilities l/n and $(n - l)/n$ is indifferent to the sure income y, such that

$$u(y) = \frac{l}{n}u(w - m + a) + \frac{n - l}{n}u(t + a) = Eu. \tag{8}$$

The utility function u is calibrated on the basis of such indifference

---

[9] For an elementary presentation of that theory, see Drèze (1974a).

relations. Decision theory tells us that such a calibration is always possible, provided preferences are 'consistent', according to the axioms.

We are here faced with the question: precisely what are we trying to achieve through income redistribution? If we wish to correct the income distribution on behalf of workers, in order to raise their real income to *b*, should we impose the twin conditions

$$u(w - m + a) \geq u(b), \quad u(t + a) \geq b; \tag{9}$$

or should we impose the single condition

$$Eu = \frac{l(w)}{n} u(w - m + a) + \frac{n - l(w)}{n} u(t + a) \geq u(b)? \tag{10}$$

The first formulation (9) implies directly the solution $w - m + a = t + a = b$; unemployment is voluntary, with benefits dictated by income distribution targets. When inequality (5) holds, the second formulation (10) leads to a different solution, with $w - m + a > t + a$ and $Eu = u(b)$. That solution is inegalitarian *ex post*, but egalitarian *ex ante* (before it is known who is hired and who remains unemployed), in terms of expected utility. It preserves equal chances for all workers, and grants to them acceptable income 'expectations' – but at the cost of an *ex post* disparity between the real incomes of employed and unemployed workers. That solution is less attractive in terms of *equity*, but with undeniable merits in terms of *efficiency*.

In order to understand the nature of the trade-off, it is helpful to look at the properties of the solution induced by the *ex ante* criterion when (5) holds. At given transfers $\bar{a}$, the first-order condition for efficient values of w and t corresponds to maximisation of $\Pi(w, t; \bar{a})$ *under the constraint* (10); i.e. it corresponds to a solution of the following problem:

PROBLEM P.2

$$\max_{w,t} \Pi(w, t; \bar{a}) \text{ subject to}$$

$$\frac{l(w)}{n} u(w - m + \bar{a}) + \frac{n - l(w)}{n} u(t + \bar{a}) \geq u(b),$$

$$0 \leq t \leq w - m, \quad l(w) \leq n, \quad f'(l) = w.$$

In order to solve that problem, one may differentiate condition (10), to compute by how much unemployment benefits could be cut, at unchanged expected utility, when wages are raised:

$$\frac{dt}{dw}\bigg|_{Eu} = -\frac{\dfrac{\partial Eu}{\partial w}}{\dfrac{\partial Eu}{\partial t}}$$

$$= -\frac{lu'(w - m + \bar{a}) + [u(w - m + \bar{a}) - u(t + \bar{a})]\dfrac{dl}{dw}}{(n - l)u'(t + \bar{a})}. \qquad (11)$$

Using (1), one obtains the first-order condition:

$$0 = \frac{d\Pi(w, t; \bar{a})}{dw} = \frac{\partial\Pi(w, t; \bar{a})}{\partial w} + \frac{\partial\Pi(w, t; \bar{a})}{\partial t}\frac{dt}{dw}\bigg|_{Eu}$$

$$= -l + (1 + d)t\frac{dl}{dw} \qquad (12)$$

$$+ \frac{(1 + d)}{u'(t + \bar{a})}\left\{lu'(w - m + \bar{a}) + \frac{dl}{dw}[u(w - m + \bar{a}) - u(t + \bar{a})]\right\}.$$

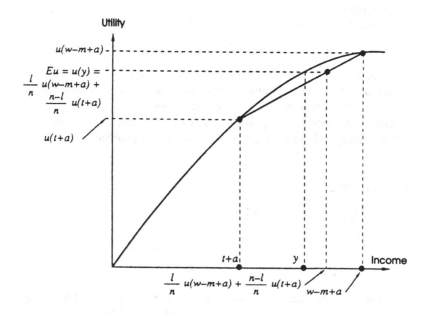

Figure 12.2

In order to interpret that condition, it is helpful to use the linear approximation:

$$u(w - m + \bar{a}) \approx u(t + \bar{a}) + (w - m - t)u'(t + \bar{a}). \tag{13}$$

Inserting (13) into (12), we obtain the equality

$$\frac{u'(w - m + \bar{a})}{u'(t + \bar{a})} = \frac{1}{1 + d} - \frac{w - m}{l}\frac{dl}{dw}. \tag{14}$$

In order to translate that condition on marginal utilities into a condition on real income disparities, one may use a further linear approximation:

$$u'(w - m + \bar{a}) \approx u'(t + \bar{a}) + (w - m - t)u''(t + \bar{a})$$

$$= u'(t + \bar{a})\left[1 + (w - m - t)\frac{u''(t + \bar{a})}{u'(t + \bar{a})}\right]$$

$$= u'(t + \bar{a})\left[1 - \frac{w - m - t}{t + \bar{a}}\left\{ -(t + \bar{a})\frac{u''(t + \bar{a})}{u'(t + \bar{a})}\right\}\right]$$

$$= u'(t + \bar{a})\left[1 - \frac{w - m - t}{t + \bar{a}} R_R(t + \bar{a})\right] \tag{15}$$

where $R_R(t + \bar{a}) = -(t + \bar{a})\dfrac{u''(t + \bar{a})}{u'(t + \bar{a})} > 0$ denotes the Arrow (1965) and Pratt (1964) relative risk-aversion measure. That quantity corresponds to a risk premium per unit of coefficient of variation (variance/expectation). It comes into the picture here, because our distributive target is the expected utility of an uncertain prospect between $w - m + \bar{a}$ and $t + \bar{a}$. The curvature of utility over that interval, as measured by R_R, defines the spread between the slopes (marginal utilities) at $w - m + \bar{a}$ and $t + \bar{a}$, respectively. Although marginal utilities are not identified, R_R is a pure number, and can be estimated from choices among uncertain prospects.

Combining (14) and (15), we can solve for the relative spread between $w - m + \bar{a}$ and $t + \bar{a}$:

$$\frac{(w - m + \bar{a}) - (t + \bar{a})}{t + \bar{a}} = \frac{\dfrac{d}{1 + d} - \dfrac{w - m}{l}\left|\dfrac{dl}{dw}\right|}{R_R(t + \bar{a})}. \tag{16}$$

The ex ante criterion recommends a relative spread between the real incomes of employed and unemployed workers equal to the ratio between the efficiency gain due to the use of wages rather than tax-financed benefits (numerator), on the one hand, and the cost of income disparity as measured by R_R, on the other hand. That ratio is thus a cost (denominator)–benefit (numerator) ratio. Accepting the *ex ante* criterion amounts to accepting a trade-off between equity and efficiency; in contrast, the *ex post* criterion imposes an egalitarian norm (for employed and unemployed workers) as an absolute equity requirement, without regard for its efficiency cost.

2.4.

It will be seen in Section 3 that the *ex ante* criterion is the only meaningful one, when one considers prospectively the situation that will prevail *in the future*. Section 2.3 was meant to introduce the *ex ante* criterion in a simpler context, to bring out its logic. The idea of an equity-efficiency trade-off just outlined strikes me as reasonable, and congruent with the general methodology of the second-best.

The *ex ante* criterion is used by several authors to model union behaviour, in the framework of the so-called 'union wage model'. That model[10] rests precisely on the assumption that unions attempt to set wages so as to maximise expected utility, namely (10), taking into account the wage elasticity of labour demand. The repeated use of a model does not make it realistic, but suggests at least that it is not meaningless.

In order to bring out explicitly the circumstances under which condition (5) is apt to hold, one should spell out the nature of tax-induced distortions. Such a task lies outside the scope of the present paper, and I will limit myself to one remark. At the time of writing (1988), the Belgian Government, keen on reducing the public deficit, has been known to reduce the number of public servants, in particular teachers or social workers, at a significant welfare loss per frank ultimately saved. That loss is comparable to a distortion cost of taxation, since it defines the 'opportunity cost' of public expenditures. The magnitude of that loss is probably such that we cannot dismiss the possibility of more severe distortions for transfers than for wages.[11]

Yet, I must admit that such formulae as (6) or (16) are not easily implemented, due to our econometric uncertainties. The real cost of tax distortions d, the real opportunity cost of labour m, the wage elasticity of

[10] See Oswald (1985) or Pencavel (1985) for a survey presentation. McDonald and Solow (1981), who use that model for purposes different from mine, quote Cartter (1959) among their forerunners.

[11] With reference to 'universal grants' or negative income taxes, one must remember that the number of beneficiaries exceeds the number of wage earners.

labour demand η_{lw} or the relative risk aversion of workers R_R are unknown parameters, estimated with sizeable standard errors. The need to take into account our econometric uncertainty is another reason to work with an *ex ante* criterion. When the effects of economic policies are uncertain, it is impossible to optimise *ex post*. Even if one adopts a *strategy* under which policies are revised after observing their effects, the time series of consequences is stochastic, and calls for *ex ante* assessment of costs and benefits. One convenient byproduct of decision theory is that it provides a justification and method for compounding econometric uncertainties with real uncertainties.

There is also scope for disagreement regarding the estimation of the relevant parameters. What model specification should we adopt, to estimate the wage elasticity of employment? Are the effects symmetrical for positive and negative shocks? Should we use estimates of a short-run, or a long-run elasticity? (The orders of magnitudes differ by a factor of 1 to 5 or more ... .)[12] We know even less about risk aversion, and the underlying decision theory is not unanimously accepted.[13] Much remains to be done, if we want to tackle rigorously even the simplest problems of income policies. It is not surprising that a pragmatic approach remains prevalent ...

3. Wages, profits and risk-sharing

3.1.

I now wish to consider prospectively, from an *ex ante* viewpoint, the pros and cons of wage flexibility. I shall again use the simplest relevant model.

In Section 2, labour demand was deduced from the production function $f(l)$, and the first-order condition $f'(l) = w$. But labour demand *tomorrow* is not known exactly today. It will depend upon economic conditions, unknown today, described tomorrow by any one of S mutually exclusive 'states', indexed $s = 1 \ldots S$, with probabilities $\phi_s > 0$. I now write $f_s(l_s)$ for the production function and $f'_s(l_s) = w_s$ for the first-order condition fixing employment l_s in state s. The other variables of the model will be indexed similarly.

According to that formulation, tomorrow's employment will be determined, in each state s, by the equality of labour's marginal value

---

[12] See Drèze and Modigliani (1981).
[13] See Drèze (1974a) and Machina (1987) for contrasting viewpoints.

product and wage cost. That is, employment will be determined *ex post*, conditionally on the state of the economy, by profit maximisation. But the economist investigates *ex ante* (today) the Pareto efficiency of the wage formation mechanism.

The *ex ante* efficiency analysis runs per force in terms of expected utilities – a natural approach, if one relies upon decision theory to represent preferences among uncertain prospects. In so far as workers are concerned, that representation has already been introduced in Section 2. For a worker seeking employment tomorrow, the hiring probability will be $l_s(w_s)/n$ if state s occurs.[14] Expected utility *conditionally on s* is

$$E(u \mid s) = \frac{l_s(w_s)}{n} u(w_s - m + a_s) + \frac{n - l_s(w_s)}{n} u(t_s + a_s). \qquad (17)$$

Unconditional expected utility is then given today by

$$Eu = \sum_s \phi_s \left\{ \frac{l_s(w_s)}{n} u(w_s - m + a_s) + \frac{n - l_s(w_s)}{n} u(t + a_s) \right\}, \qquad (18)$$

where Eu is a function of the vectors $(w_s, a_s, t_s)_{s=1...S}$. As noted above, one convenient byproduct of decision theory is the compounding of uncertainties through probabilities. An *ex ante* incomes policy is then formulated simply by

$$Eu \geq u(b). \qquad (19)$$

The profits side is less transparent. In the deterministic framework of Section 2, Pareto efficiency could be achieved by maximising profits Π under a constraint on workers' utility like (9) or (10). In a prospective framework with uncertainty, profits will depend upon the state that occurs. There is a *vector* of profits $(\Pi_1 \dots \Pi_s \dots \Pi_S)$; *ex ante* efficiency analysis must reckon with uncertainty, and *perform with profits some form of expected utility calculations*.

Net profits of business firms are typically distributed to shareholders according to their ownership fractions – say $\theta_i \geq 0$, $\sum_i \theta_i = 1$. There exist alternative interpretations of the expected utility of profits calculation

$$EV = \sum_s \phi_s V(\Pi_s). \qquad (20)$$

---

[14] I could have written n_s for the sake of generality – but that would make little difference.

One could interpret V as the outcome of a linear aggregation of shareholders' utilities

$$V(\Pi_s) = \sum_i \lambda_i u_i(\theta_i \Pi_s), \lambda_i > 0. \tag{21}$$

Harsanyi (1955) has proposed axiomatic foundations for that approach. One could interpret V as the outcome of aggregation by the stock market of the risk preferences of investors holding equilibrium portfolios. The 'Capital Asset Pricing Model' (CAPM) provides a justification of that approach,[15] see e.g., Mossin (1977). Finally, one could interpret V as a direct representation of social preferences for private profits (taking into account, inter alia, the influence of profits on investment ...). A more detailed discussion of these alternative approaches lies beyond the scope of this paper; it can be found in Drèze (1987a) for instance.

I will thus introduce a function $V(\Pi)$, $V' > 0$, $V'' < 0$, characterised in particular by the relative risk-aversion measure $R_R(\Pi) = -\Pi V''(\Pi)/V'(\Pi)$. (In the CAPM framework, $R_R(\Pi)$ can be computed from asset prices.) One can then formulate as follows the problem of finding an *ex ante* efficient policy regarding wages, unemployment benefits and transfers $(w_s, t_s, a_s)_{s=1...S}$:

PROBLEM P.3

$$\max_{(w_s, a_s, t_s)_{s=1...S}} \sum_s \phi_s V(f_s(l_s(w_s)) - w_s l_s(w_s) - [na_s + (n - l_s(w_s))t_s]$$

$$- d\,|na_s + (n - l_s(w_s))t_s|)$$

subject to $Eu \geq u(b)$.

3.2.

Problem P.3 is technically more complex than those of Section 2. It is closely related to problems analysed in Drèze (1986b, 1989a), Gollier (1988) and Drèze and Gollier (1989). A slight modification (simplification) reduces problem P.3 to a case treated in these references. The modification calls for imposing $a_s \leq 0$ (wages can be taxed, but not directly subsidised)

---

[15] Because all individual investors hold market portfolios, under the CAPM assumptions, the aggregation of all business firms into a single productive sector is warranted.

and $d = 0$ (there exist neutral taxes). Using the results of Section 2, one can see how that modification affects the solution. The condition $a_s \leq 0$ imposes wages and benefits as the single instrument for boosting workers' incomes. (Yet, $a_s < 0$ allows transfers from wages towards profits.) The condition $d = 0$ implies that unemployment is always voluntary, at a solution (at a second-best optimum). These remarks will help us reconsider the solution of P.3, after looking at the solution of the simplified version.

The simplified problem is as follows:

PROBLEM P.4

$$\max_{(w_s, a_s, t_s)_s = 1 \ldots S} \sum_s \phi_s V(f_s(l_s(w_s))) - w_s l_s(w_s) - [na_s + (n - l_s(w_s))t_s])$$

subject to

$$\sum_s \phi_s \left\{ \frac{l_s(w_s)}{n} u(w_s - m + a_s) + \frac{n - l_s(w_s)}{n} u(t_s + a_s) \right\} \geq u(b),$$

$$a_s \leq 0, \quad 0 \leq t_s \leq w_s - m, \quad l_s(w_s) \leq n,$$

$l_s(w_s)$ such that $f'_s(l_s) = w_s$.

Using Lagrange multipliers, problem P.4 may also be written as

$$\max_{(w_s, a_s, t_s)_s = 1 \ldots S} \sum_s \phi_s V(f_s(l_s(w_s))) - w_s l_s(w_s) - [na_s + (n - l_s(w_s))t_s])$$

$$+ \lambda \left\{ \sum_s \phi_s \left[\frac{l_s(w_s)}{n} u(w_s - m + a_s) \right. \right.$$

$$\left. \left. + \frac{n - l_s(w_s)}{n} u(t_s + a_s) \right] - u(b) \right\}, \tag{22}$$

subject to

$$a_s \leq 0, \quad 0 \leq t_s \leq w_s - m, \quad l_s(w_s) \leq n, \quad f'_s(l_s) = w_s.$$

In that formulation, $\lambda \geq 0$ is an undetermined multiplier, such that $\lambda[Eu - u(b)] = 0$ and $\lambda > 0$ when the condition $Eu \geq u(b)$ is binding. I shall restrict my attention to the case where $\lambda > 0$, which holds whenever $b > 0$.

In order to characterise the solutions to problem P.4, I write w_s^* for the competitive wages, defined as explained in Section 2.1 by

$$w_s^* = \max (f'_s(n), m). \tag{23}$$

PROPOSITION 1 (Drèze–Gollier)

For all $b > 0$, a solution to problem P.4 is characterised by the existence of a multiplier $\lambda > 0$ and, for each $s = 1 \ldots S$, by $w_s \geq w_s^*$, $t_s = w_s - m$, and one of the following conditions:[16]

(i) $l_s(w_s) = n$, $w_s = w_s^*$, $a_s < 0$ and $\lambda u'(w_s - m + a_s) = V'(\Pi_s)$

(full employment with taxes on wages);

(ii) $l_s(w_s) = n$, $w_s = w_s^*$, $a_s = 0$ and

$$\left(1 - \frac{w_s - m}{n} \frac{dl_s}{dw_s}\right) V'(\Pi_s) > \lambda u'(w_s - m) > V'(\Pi_s)$$

(full employment, no taxes);

(iii) $l_s(w_s) < n$, $w_s > w_s^*$, $a_s = 0$ and

$$\lambda u'(t_s) = \lambda u'(w_s - m) = V'(\Pi_s) \cdot \left[1 - \frac{w_s - m}{n} \frac{dl_s}{dw_s}\right]$$

(voluntary unemployment with unemployment benefits financed by a tax on profits).

That proposition is straightforward, yet complex … Here is an attempt at intuitive unravelling.

A pure risk-sharing problem calls for allocating efficiently among several agents a state-dependent aggregate income – say Y_s, $s = 1 \ldots S$. Let there be n identical agents, with utility functions u, each receiving the same amounts y_s; and one agent with utility function V, receiving $Y_s - n y_s$. It is well known, from the work of Borch (1960), Arrow (1965) or Wilson (1968), that efficient risk-sharing is characterised by existence of a parameter $\lambda > 0$ such that the following conditions hold:

$$\lambda u'(y_s) = V'(Y_s - n y_s), \quad \frac{u'(y_s)}{u'(y_t)} = \frac{V'(Y_s - n y_s)}{V'(Y_t - n y_t)}, \quad s, t = 1 \ldots S. \quad (24)$$

These conditions impose that all agents have identical marginal rates of substitution (between income in state s and income in state t). Accordingly, if aggregate income $Y_s = f_s(l_s)$ were given independently of the policy

---

[16] These three conditions are mutually exclusive and collectively exhaustive.

(w_s, a_s, t_s), then *ex ante* efficiency would be attained in problem P.4 when

$$\lambda u'(w_s - m + a_s) = \lambda u'(t_s + a_s) = V'(\Pi_s), s = 1 \ldots S, \tag{25}$$

with parameter λ chosen so that $Eu = u(b)$. If the transfer variables a_s were free (unconstrained and non-distorting), one could set them at levels (positive or negative) such that conditions (25) hold. Setting simultaneously $w_s = w_s^*$, aggregate real income would be maximal in each state.

In problem P.4, the transfers a_s are constrained ($a_s \leq 0$). Accordingly, conditions (25) can only be implemented in those states where competitive wages are high enough that implementation requires $a_s < 0$. These states correspond to case (i) of proposition 1; in these states, the solution is that of a pure risk-sharing problem.

On the other hand, in states where condition (25) would require positive transfers $a_s > 0$, it cannot be implemented in that way. Correcting the income distribution in favour of workers requires raising wages. But raising wages above their competitive level entails a distortion, the real cost of which per dollar of wages is equal to $(w - m)\,dl/dw < 0$ – i.e. the net marginal product times the fall in employment, as explained in Section 2.3. In our model, where benefits are adjusted to keep unemployment voluntary, a wage increase goes to n workers, so that the real cost of the distortion per dollar of foregone profits is equal to $(w - m)/n \cdot dl/dw$.

The first-order condition for efficient risk-sharing *when aggregate income is influenced by the allocation parameter* y[17] becomes

$$\lambda u'(y) = V'(Y - ny) \cdot \left(1 - \frac{1}{n}\frac{dY}{dy}\right); \tag{26}$$

see e.g. Holmström (1979). Applied to problem P.4, that condition takes the form

$$\lambda u'(w_s - m + a_s) = \lambda u'(t_s + a_s) = V'(\Pi_s) \cdot \left(1 - \frac{w_s - m}{n}\frac{dl_s}{dw_s}\right), \tag{27}$$

which is precisely the characterisation of case (iii) in proposition 1.

---

[17] The first-order condition for $\max_y \ V(Y(y) - ny) + \lambda n u(y)$ is indeed $V' \cdot \left(\dfrac{dY}{dy} - n\right)$ $+ \lambda n u' = 0; \ \lambda u' = V' \cdot \left(1 - \dfrac{1}{n}\dfrac{dY}{dy}\right).$

Thus, cases (i) and (iii) correspond to risk-sharing: pure in case (i), modified by a distortion cost in case (iii). As for (ii), it brings about a smooth transition between (i) and (iii). That case occurs when competitive wages fall below the level corresponding to the desired distribution of income – but not enough to warrant the distortion cost $(w - m)\,dl/dw$ associated with a wage increase. It is more efficient to accept the competitive income distribution *in those states* – while lowering wage taxes in other states, so as to keep a worker's expected utility at the required level $u(b)$. The undetermined multiplier λ, associated with the constraint $Eu \geq u(b)$, sees to that.

Combining the three cases, proposition 1 can be summarised as stating that wages w_s are equal to the minimum of two quantities: competitive wages and risk-sharing wages, where the latter are defined with due allowance for the distortion cost of underemployment. Risk-sharing between workers and shareholders calls for taxing wages when they are too high, for taxing profits to finance unemployment benefits when competitive wages are too low. 'Too high' and 'too low' should here be understood 'relatively to the requirements of efficient risk-sharing, given the average level of workers' income (b) suggested by incomes policy'. That is, once b is chosen, the risk aversion of the two groups (workers and shareholders) decides when wages should be taxed and when they should be kept above the competitive level.

3.3.

After presenting in Section 3.2 the basic features of an *ex ante* efficient wage policy, corresponding to a given distributive target, I can now bring out more directly the potential contribution of wage rigidities to economic efficiency.

In an economy where efficient risk-sharing between shareholders and workers is not implemented through state-dependent taxes and transfers, it is generally not efficient to let wages fluctuate to clear the labour market in each state; a more efficient policy generally calls for limited wage flexibility, ruling out excessive increases as well as excessive reductions, even though in unfavourable states that policy entails some unemployment, kept voluntary through adequate benefits; that conclusion rests on efficiency arguments, and is free of distributive arguments.

The conclusion follows directly from proposition 1. Indeed, with w_s^*

denoting competitive wages, one may define b^* implicitly by

$$u(b^*) = Eu(w_s^*, a_s = 0, t_s = 0)$$

$$= \sum_s \phi_s \left\{ \frac{l_s(w_s^*)}{n} u(w_s^* - m) + \frac{n - l_s(w_s^*)}{n} u(0) \right\}. \qquad (28)$$

That is, b^* is the sure net income regarded by a worker equivalent (utilitywise) to the random prospect defined by competitive wages and no transfers. One may then solve problem P.4 for $b = b^*$, i.e. subject to $Eu \geq u(b^*)$. The solution is characterised by proposition 1. In general, the solution will not allow $w_s = w_s^*$ for all $s = 1 \ldots S$; in general, the solution will involve case (iii), where $w_s > w_s^*$ – and that solution Pareto-dominates competitive market clearing ($w_s^* = w_s$ for all s). That solution leads to a higher expected utility, or present market value, for profits, at unchanged expected utility for workers.)

It is easy to give a *sufficient* condition under which case (iii) appears non-trivially in the solution of problem P.4; namely that there should exist two states s and t such that

$$\frac{u'(w_t^* - m)}{u'(w_s^* - m)} > \frac{V'(\Pi_t)}{V'(\Pi_s)} \left(1 - \frac{w_t^* - m}{n} \frac{dl_t}{dw_t} \right). \qquad (29)$$

(The proof is given in the Appendix.) Because the marginal rates of substitution $\dfrac{u'(w_t^* - m)}{u'(w_s^* - m)}$ and $\dfrac{V'(\Pi_t)}{V'(\Pi_s)}$ are not directly observable (in the absence of insurance markets specific to states s and t), it is helpful to use the linear approximation (15) and to rewrite (29) in the alternative form (derived in the Appendix)

$$\left[1 + \frac{w_s^* - w_t^*}{w_s^* - m} R_R(w_s^* - m) \right]$$

$$> \left[1 + \frac{\Pi_s - \Pi_t}{\Pi_s} R_R(\Pi_s) \right] \left(1 - \frac{w_t^* - m}{n} \frac{dl_t}{dw_t} \right). \qquad (30)$$

That condition holds when state s entails high competitive wages, which are taxed at the solution to P.4 – case (i) – whereas state t entails low competitive wages, which are raised at the solution – case (iii).

In condition (30), the terms $(w_s^* - w_t^*)/(w_s^* - m)$ and $(\Pi_s - \Pi_t)/\Pi_s$ measure the relative spread of wages, and of profits, between states s and t. The parameters $R_R(w_s^* - m)$ and $R_R(\Pi_s)$ translate these relative spreads into risk premia (uncertainty costs) or 'income disparity penalties'. According to condition (30), *it is efficient to intervene on the labour market and to organise risk-sharing between wages and profits, whenever the disparity penalty for wages exceeds the disparity penalty for profits by a factor high enough to cover the distortion costs caused by a wage increase* (in state *t*). That condition is the more likely to hold, the more (1) wages disparities (between states) are high, relative to profits disparities; (2) the risk aversion of workers is high, relative to that of shareholders; (3) the wage elasticity of employment is low (in absolute value). When condition (30) holds, competitive wage flexibility is Pareto-dominated by limited flexibility (with upward as well as downward rigidity).

3.4.

In concluding this section, I wish to return briefly to problem P.3, which differs from P.4 in that it allows for wage subsidies ($a_s > 0$) and takes into account the distortion cost of taxes ($d > 0$). (This section is more technical and may be skipped at no breach of continuity.)

With a_s unrestricted as to sign, but $d = 0$, the solution to the (modified) problem P.4 would generalise case (i) of proposition 1 and satisfy

(i') $w_s = w_s^*, \lambda u'(w_s - m + a_s) = V'(\Pi_s)$

(competitive wages, efficient risk-sharing through either wages taxes or transfers to workers). Cases (ii) and (iii) would drop out, and so would Section 3.3. Condition (i') includes (25) and solves a pure risk-sharing problem.

As soon as one brings in a distortion cost of taxation, that appealing simplicity evaporates. Instead of seeing the three cases of proposition 1 boil down to the single case (i'), we must now distinguish *five* cases, and their respective properties become more intricate as well! The five cases emerge from combining the three-way partition ($a_s < 0$, $a_s = 0$, $a_s > 0$) with the two-way partition ($w_s = w_s^*, w_s > w_s^*$). One of the six possibilities, namely ($a_s < 0, w_s > w_s^*$) drops out, because it would be inefficient.[18] The whole difficulty arises from the distortion cost d.

---

[18] The three cases of proposition 1 similarly emerged from combining the two-way partition ($a_s < 0, a_s = 0$) with ($w_s = w_s^*, w_s > w_s^*$), and ignoring the inefficient pair ($a_s < 0, w_s > w_s^*$).

PROPOSITION 2

For all $b > 0$, a solution to problem P.3 is characterised by the existence of a multiplier $\lambda > 0$ and, for each $s = 1\ldots S$, by one of the following conditions:

(i) $l_s(w_s) = n$, $w_s = w_s^*$, $a_s < 0$ and $\lambda u'(w_s - m + a_s) = V'(\Pi_s)(1 - d)$
(full employment with taxes on wages);

(ii) $l_s(w_s) = n$, $w_s = w_s^*$, $a_s = 0$ and

$$\min\left\{1 + d, 1 - (1 + d)\frac{w_s^* - m}{w_s^*}\eta_{l_s w_s}\right\}V'(\Pi_s)$$

$$\geq \lambda u'(w_s - m) \geq V'(\Pi_s)(1 - d)$$
(full employment, no taxes);

(iii) $l_s(w_s) = n$, $w_s = w_s^*$, $a_s > 0$ and

$$\left[1 - (1 + d)\frac{w_s - m}{w_s}\eta_{l_s w_s}\right]V'(\Pi_s) > \lambda u'(w_s - m + a_s)$$

$$= V'(\Pi_s)(1 + d)$$

(full employment and transfers to all workers financed by a tax on profits);

(iv) $l_s(w_s) < n$, $w_s > w_s^*$, $a_s = 0$,

$$\frac{w_s - m - t_s}{t_s} = \frac{\dfrac{d}{1 + d} - \dfrac{w_s - m}{l_s}\left|\dfrac{dl_s}{dw_s}\right|}{R_R(t_s)} = \frac{\dfrac{d}{1 + d} + \dfrac{w_s - m}{w_s}\eta_{l_s w_s}}{R_R(t_s)} \quad \text{and}$$

$$V'(\Pi_s)(1 + d) > \lambda u'(w_s - m) = V'(\Pi_s)\left[1 - (1 + d)\frac{w_s - m}{w_s}\eta_{l_s w_s}\right]$$

(involuntary unemployment with benefits financed by a tax on profits);

(v) $l_s(w_s) < n$, $w_s > w_s^*$, $a_s > 0$, $w_s - m = t_s$ and

$$\lambda u'(w_s - m + a_s) = \lambda u'(t_s + a_s)$$

$$= V'(\Pi_s)(1 + d)$$

$$= V'(\Pi_s)\left[1 - (1 + d)\frac{w_s - m}{w_s}\eta_{l_s w_s}\right]$$

(voluntary unemployment with unemployment benefits and transfers to all workers financed by a tax on profits).

That proposition is rather complex, so I will save the proof and full discussion for a separate occasion, and provide only a general guideline. Case (i) of proposition 2 differs from case (i) of proposition 1 by the cost of taxation; therefore, taxes on wages are lower, in order to save on that cost; the ratio of the marginal utility of wages to that of profits is reduced by a factor $1 - d$. Case (ii) admits the same interpretation here as under proposition 1, but holds under wider conditions (the case for no taxation is strengthened by the distortion cost). The distinction between case (iii) and case (iv) corresponds to the selection of the less costly (distortionwise) instrument to boost workers' incomes – either transfers, in case (iii), or wages and unemployment benefits, in case (iv). Eventually, both instruments are used simultaneously, in case (v), at rates that equate their respective efficiencies at the margin, as per equation (6) above.

The arguments adduced in Section 3.3 to the effect that limited wage flexibility (with upward as well as downward rigidities) typically Pareto-dominates competitive flexibility remain valid in this broader framework; that conclusion also remains free of distributive arguments.

4. Conclusion

4.1.

The model of Sections 2 and 3 is in many respects too crude; yet, its analysis has carried us through increasingly sophisticated arguments, culminating with proposition 2. It is not easy to relate the formal analysis to our daily experience: real world problems are more complex, yet receive less sophisticated solutions ...

Among the more important aspects of reality which are ignored here, I would stress worker heterogeneity. One major source of heterogeneity concerns workers under contract versus job seekers. In the prospective analysis, that distinction is crucial. Indeed, long-term labour contracts permit relaxing the condition equating labour's marginal value product to wage cost: that condition only needs to hold *in expectation*, i.e. *ex ante* – instead of *ex post*, i.e. state by state. The theory of (implicit) labour contracts[19] has spelled out the main characteristics of efficient contracts. Gollier (1988) has analysed a model with overlapping generations of workers. He obtains simultaneous first-order efficiency conditions for the wages and transfers applicable to future generations, and for the wages

---

[19] Cf. Rosen (1985) for a survey.

stipulated in today's contracts. One important conclusion of his analysis concerns wage discrimination between generations. Efficiency arguments go against the equity principle 'equal pay for equal work' – but to an extent limited by conditions analogous to (16) above, defining second-best efficient income disparities (here, between employed and unemployed workers).

Another important source of heterogeneity relates to the individual circumstances of workers and firms. I have focussed here exclusively on macroeconomic aspects of the labour market, on the general level of wages and on national income. There also exist individual risks, which are by and large uncorrelated with aggregate risks. The implications of that distinction have been investigated more carefully for capital markets than for wages and social security. Important issues remain open in this area and should challenge imaginative young researchers.

4.2.

The subject matter of this paper is the equity–efficiency trade-off for wages and employment. I hope to have illustrated the relevance as well as the difficulty of the subject. When taxes and transfers do not bring about the desired income distribution, wages provide another instrument worthy of attention. But non-competitive wages always entail a deadweight efficiency loss, that should be weighed against the equity gain on the one hand, against the real costs of alternative policies on the other hand. The complexity of the trade-off also means that formal analysis can suggest ways to improve upon established practice.

In practice, taxes and transfers do not bring about an equitable distribution of income – between capital and labour, between employed and unemployed workers, or between workers of different skills. These shortcomings reflect both a lack of consensus about goals and the distortion costs of taxation. It should not surprise us that labour unions try to influence wage formation, in order to boost the incomes of members.

That activity is justified, but its efficiency cost cannot be ignored. One conclusion is that union militancy is the less necessary, the more effective are general incomes policies. This conclusion is sometimes applied to corporatist countries, like Austria or Sweden, about which it is claimed that wages and fiscal policy are negotiated jointly.[20] The present paper

---

[20] See e.g. Rowthorn and Glyn (1987).

stresses the complementarity of wages and transfers to implement an income policy responsive to both equity and efficiency considerations.

We are used to hybrid systems, where wages are kept up by unemployment benefits, and these are viewed as instruments of income policy, alongside other social security transfers. The system has grown through time in a haphazard way, and its overall consistency is open to question. One weakness of the system concerns sensitivity to economic fluctuations, in particular to external shocks. Section 3 is addressed to that topic, at a high level of abstraction. The message is that full flexibility of wages is inefficient, but also that full rigidity of real wages (100% indexation of nominal wages on consumer prices) is inefficient. I have presented elsewhere[21] the risk-sharing arguments suggesting to index wages partly on consumer prices and partly on nominal national income. Our understanding of these issues is still fragmentary. Policy recommendations should be voiced with restraint, but research conclusions should be analysed carefully.[22]

Appendix: Derivations of relationships (29) and (30)

Case (iii) of proposition 1 arises whenever problem P.4 does not admit any solution with $w_s = w_s^*$ for all s; that is whenever it is more efficient to set $w_t = w_t^* + \delta > w_t^*$ for at least one state t – while compensating the drain on profits Π_t by a wage tax $a_s < 0$ and a transfer towards profits $-na_s > 0$ in some state $s \neq t$. The compensation is possible, at unchanged expected utility (or market value) of profits, provided

$$dEV(\Pi) = \phi_s V'(\Pi_s) d\Pi_s + \phi_t V'(\Pi_t) d\Pi_t = 0, \qquad (31)$$

with

$$d\Pi_s = -na_s \text{ and } d\Pi_t = \left[-n + (w_t^* - m)\frac{dl_t}{dw_t} \right]\delta$$

---

[21] See Drèze (1989a), chapters 3 and 5; chapter 5 is reproduced here as chapter 13; see also chapter 11 above.

[22] One policy recommendation that strikes me as well-documented concerns the funding of social security. At times of persistent unemployment, it is desirable to reduce wage costs. This calls for lowering labour taxes and seeking other means of funding social security. That recommendation is consistent with the logic of state dependent transfers as investigated in Section 3.

as can be seen from equation (3) when $l_t = n$, $d = 0$ and $t_t = w_t^* - m$.

Substituting in (31) and solving for a_s yields

$$-a_s = \delta\left(1 - \frac{w_t^* - m}{n}\frac{dl_t}{dw_t}\right)\frac{\phi_t V'(\Pi_t)}{\phi_s V'(\Pi_s)}. \tag{32}$$

In order for that modification to increase the expected utility of a worker, it is necessary and sufficient that

$$dEu = \phi_s u'(w_s^* - m)a_s + \phi_t u'(w_t^* - m)\delta$$

$$= -\phi_s u'(w_s^* - m)\delta\left(1 - \frac{w_t^* - m}{n}\frac{dl_t}{dw_t}\right)\frac{\phi_t V'(\Pi_t)}{\phi_s V'(\Pi_s)}$$

$$+ \phi_t u'(w_t^* - m)\delta$$

$$= \delta\phi_t u'(w_s^* - m)\left\{\frac{u'(w_t^* - m)}{u'(w_s^* - m)}\right.$$

$$\left. - \frac{V'(\Pi_t)}{V'(\Pi_s)}\left(1 - \frac{w_t^* - m}{n}\frac{dl_t}{dw_t}\right)\right\} > 0. \tag{33}$$

Because $\delta\phi_t u'(w_s^* - m) > 0$, condition (33) is indeed equivalent to (29).

Using the linear approximation (15), we may write

$$u'(w_t^* - m) \approx u'(w_s^* - m) + (w_t^* - w_s^*)u''(w_s^* - m), \tag{34}$$

$$\frac{u'(w_t^* - m)}{u'(w_s^* - m)} \approx \left[1 + \frac{w_s^* - w_t^*}{w_s^* - m}R_R(w_s^* - m)\right]. \tag{35}$$

Inserting (35) into (29), yields (30).

13 Labour management, contracts and capital markets: some macroeconomic aspects, and conclusions*

1. Provisional conclusions

So far, I have considered the relationship between labour and capital at the *firm* level, while taking into account some implications of market clearing. Two main conclusions stand out. In a world of complete markets with labour mobility, no specific gains should be expected, in equilibrium, from action by labour at the firm level: labour-management equilibria correspond to competitive (wage) equilibria. In a more realistic world of uncertainty with incomplete markets, efficient risk-sharing between capital owners (holding diversified portfolios) and workers (unable to protect their human capital through diversification) is not organised by the market and requires instead sophisticated *contractual* arrangements.

In the capitalist system, labour contracts (explicit or implicit) are the institutional support of such arrangements. Under labour management, equity contracts would be needed to the same end, but do not seem to be in systematic use, either in Yugoslavia or in capitalist countries.

Uncertainty is the standard instance of incomplete markets, but it is by no means the only one. In so far as labour services are concerned, working schedules and working conditions are other significant instances.[1] As indicated already in chapter 1, these are in the nature of public goods – on a par with the investment decisions considered in chapters 2–4. These

---

* Chap. 5 and Appendix 5 in *Labour Management, Contracts and Capital Markets*, Basil Blackwell, Oxford, 1989. All references to earlier chapters, sections or equations are references to that book.

[1] The formal analogy between uncertainty and quality choices as instances of incomplete markets is brought out in Drèze and Hagen (1978).

decisions do not seem to be fully guided by market-clearing prices, and require some form of collective decision-making at the firm level.

In so far as working conditions are concerned, labour management seems to be a natural answer. Experience suggests that partnerships are most common in situations where working conditions are an important parameter, and capital requirements are low. In so far as uncertainty is concerned, capital markets are the natural answer, because they allow for efficient risk-sharing through portfolio diversification. The standard argument, to the effect that workers are unable to bear themselves the risks of capital-intensive ventures, is a valid one. But it does not preclude equity financing of labour-managed firms. To explain why that form of organisation is seldom practised, I think that one must invoke the relative difficulty of stipulating and monitoring efficient equity contracts, for labour-managed firms, in a world of uncertainty and incomplete markets. In comparison, efficient labour contracts are easier to draw. Also, the more developed are capital markets, the easier it becomes to write down efficient labour contracts.[2] In the interesting case where all firm-specific risks are diversified away through capital markets, efficient labour contracts would simply link labour incomes to national income, to a first approximation. Drawing instead an efficient equity contract would be a very difficult task, and monitoring the contract would either be very cumbersome or be equivalent to restoring indirectly a 'capital hires labour' situation.

Efficient labour contracts transfer to workers the benefits of efficient risk-sharing on capital markets. It was noted in chapter 3 that prevailing labour contracts seem to be less than fully efficient in that respect. That remark suggests scope for improvement, about which more later; it also casts additional doubts on the practical feasibility of implementing efficient equity contracts.

These considerations go a long way towards explaining why labour management remains exceptional in industrial societies, in spite of its moral appeal and of the fact (theoretically documented in chapter 1) that it could easily coexist with salaried employment. But the analysis at the firm level must still be extended on two counts, of a more macroeconomic nature.

---

[2] That point is distinct from the point illustrated in Section 4.2, to the effect that more developed capital markets may lead to better terms for labour contracts.

2. A static macroeconomic aspect

2.1. Labour's comparative advantage

It was noted in chapter 3 that efficient capital markets would, as a first approximation (at the level of approximation embodied in the capital asset pricing model), result in individual portfolios combining a safe asset with identical tiny shares of all firms. As a consequence, all firms would have the same shareholders, or at any rate shareholders with similar preferences. If risk preferences of workers in different firms were also similar, it would then follow that, to a first approximation, efficient labour contracts imply labour incomes that are perfectly correlated across firms. In other words, a single labour contract drawn for the whole economy would come close to achieving overall efficiency; negotiations over the terms of labour contracts could become centralised at the economy-wide level, at a substantial saving of time and effort in conducting the negotiations. The counterpart for that property, in so far as the equity contracts of labour-managed firms are concerned, is that efficient contracts could be based on a stipulation of labour incomes geared to a national formula, with the rest of value added going to capital. These equity contracts would thus be indistinguishable from labour contracts.

Of course, the statements just made only hold as a first approximation. Actual capital markets do not exactly operate as predicted by the CAPM. Not all firms are financed through shares traded on the stock exchange. Individual firms, including those quoted on the stock exchange, are controlled by managers and directors, whose decisions need not fully reflect shareholder preferences. Fear of bankruptcy, which typically generates significant transaction costs, leads to aversion *vis-à-vis* individual (diversifiable) risks and to greater risk aversion at the firm level than at the market level. As noted earlier, the employees of individual firms may be particularly concerned with specific risks (because their human capital is specialised). Employees of different firms may also display different degrees of risk aversion, due for instance to self-selection or to demographic characteristics.[3] But all this being said, it remains true that negotiating the terms of labour contracts at the economy-wide level is apt to capture most of the benefits associated with efficient risk-sharing, and to avoid most of the transaction costs associated with decentralised negotiations at the firm level.

---

[3] It is explained in Drèze and Modigliani (1972) that risk aversion is apt to increase with age.

The significance of that remark is enhanced by the fact that, to a large extent, labour organisations derive their strength from their ability to operate across firms, at the level of a craft, of an industrial sector or even of the whole economy. At these levels, labour unions are in a much better position to exert an influence on the terms of the labour contracts of capitalist firms than on the terms of the equity contracts of labour-managed firms. Evidently, it is within closer reach of union power to push wages up than to pull the cost of capital down! The intersectoral and international mobility of financial capital is a source of immunity from organised influences, especially by labour. The threat of strike by the employees of a capitalist firm is apt to be more effective than the threat by members of a labour-managed firm to dispense with an equity issue! Monitoring labour markets is a much more natural target for a union than monitoring capital markets. And yet, the latter target would have to receive priority in the labour-managed economy. It is thus understandable that unions devote little energy to the promotion of labour management.

2.2.   *Second-best heuristics*

It was noted in Section 3.4 that efficient labour contracts should result in a degree of stability of workers' incomes comparable with the stability of returns to a diversified portfolio. And yet, for blue-collar workers subject to temporary or part-time layoffs, the contracts tend to stipulate instead some degree of stability for hourly wages (either nominal or real). It has been part of the strategies of organised labour to strive for income protection at a national level, through unemployment benefits, rather than at the firm level. I can see three reasons for this.

The first reason, just mentioned, is that labour organisations can often operate more effectively at that level, with greater strength and smaller transaction costs. The second reason is that not all firms are financed through equity floated on the stock market. For the smaller, more closely held firms, a national scheme of unemployment compensation is a form of risk-sharing between all members of the firm (owners and employees) and the rest of the economy. The third reason is that firms face risks of bankruptcy, so that protection of the workers is more effective when based on national schemes than when based at the firm level.

The combination of efficient economy-wide labour contracts and unemployment insurance strikes me, in the end, as a reasonable first step towards efficient risk-sharing, in the presence of uncertainty, incomplete markets and transaction costs. The last element, which is central to the explanation of market incompleteness, cannot be ignored when considering labour contracts. It would be fallacious to assume without justification that a difficulty standing in the way of market organisation disappears altogether at the firm level.

Two complementary features were mentioned, which seem worth adding to that combination. In the smaller firms, not quoted on the stock exchange or otherwise included in the risk pool of capital markets, some participation of labour in the firm-specific risks makes sense; it should be accompanied with participation in managerial decisions. Limiting forms of participation include the bond-financed labour-managed firm, the partnership or the family enterprise. They flourish in the less capital-intensive sectors of our economies. In the larger firms, financed through the stock exchange and using contract labour, one would hope that the internal organisation makes room for labour-managed or participatory decisions about working conditions.

2.3. A digression on working time

It is interesting to speculate, as a brief digression, about the extent to which the argument of collective pressure applies to working conditions as well as to income formation. The issue of working time is an intriguing case in point. Is the secular reduction in working time[4] a by-product of labour-market equilibrium, reflecting the equality of the reservation wage for hours and the marginal value product of labour according to equations (1.36) or (3.18); or is it an (explicit or implicit) component of union strategies to boost hourly wages? If the latter motivation were absent, and unions were eager to promote the welfare of their members (an acceptable hypothesis, in the small world where I live), then we should witness more union support for flexibility of individual working times.

3. A dynamic macroeconomic aspect

3.1. New entrants to the labour market

One important dimension of efficient risk-sharing between capital and labour is missing from my presentation so far. It concerns new entrants into the labour market. Bringing in that dimension explains why concern

---

[4] The combination of shorter weekly hours, longer vacations and shorter careers has nearly halved lifetime working time over the past century; see for example Armstrong (1984) or Maddison (1982).

by labour organisations about the outcome of collective wage negotiations and the organisation of economy-wide unemployment insurance is well placed. It provides a suggestive explanation of downward wage rigidity and unemployment, flowing from microeconomic considerations.

In the general equilibrium analysis of chapters 3 and 4, I focussed on efficient risk-sharing through two-period labour contracts, assuming that the markets for such labour contracts cleared in the initial period. Spot markets for labour in the second period were not needed. In reality, however, a new generation of school leavers enters the market for labour contracts each year, whereas older workers go into retirement. In the streamlined models with only two explicit periods, the present and the future, there is a specific need to consider spot markets in the second period, if one wishes to include in the analysis these future entrants into the labour market. These spot markets stand in fact for markets for new labour contracts in the future.

That extension introduces an important feature, which does not seem to have received in the theoretical literature the attention which it deserves. Future entrants into the labour market are not present when multiperiod contracts are drawn, and the markets for such contracts clear, in an initial period. In other words, whereas long-term labour contracts are commonplace, we do not observe *forward labour contracts*, binding today a firm and a prospective worker on the terms of an employment relationship taking effect in the future. Consequently, future entrants into the labour market are left to bear fully the risks associated with labour-market conditions at their time of entry. They do not participate in the risk-sharing between capital and labour embodied in the extant long-term contracts.

To be more specific, think about an economy operating under conditions of technological uncertainty. Labour productivity tomorrow will depend upon the state of the environment, so that market-clearing wage levels will also depend upon that state. Labour contracts drawn today, and capital markets, organise risk-sharing among property owners and workers. If the technological developments are particularly adverse to labour (if they result in a very low marginal value product of labour at full employment), contract wages will be kept above the marginal product, in exchange for slightly lower wages today or in other states. But the future entrants, who are not covered by the terms of a forward contract, are not insured against that contingency. When contracting tomorrow, they will have to accept wages reflecting the marginal product of their labour in the state that obtains. Because market-clearing wages are apt to vary widely, and most prospective workers have no assets, that degree of income uncertainty is costly to bear, and should be alleviated through some mutually advantageous insurance supplied by property owners and workers under contract.

The absence of forward labour contracts means that such insurance is not organised at the microeconomic level of individual firms and individual workers. The difficulty of matching on a forward basis the future supply and demand of labour services at the firm level, and the even greater difficulty of organising such matching on a contingent basis,[5] explain fully why each generation of new entrants has to look for jobs when the time comes. And there is no natural motivation for individual firms (whether capitalist or labour managed) to offer insurance against wage fluctuations to the anonymous set of prospective job seekers. By its very nature, that problem must be faced at the macroeconomic level. This is another interesting instance where microeconomic reasoning leads spontaneously to macroeconomic considerations – a situation for which I have an intimate liking.[6]

At the macroeconomic level, income insurance for new job seekers could be organised in either of two ways: namely general income maintenance programmes, or downward wage rigidity coupled with unemployment insurance. Both systems entail some costs. A general income maintenance programme, financed by taxes levied on property owners and employed workers, is costly on account of the distortive incidence of the taxes. Being a general programme, it has more beneficiaries than unemployment insurance; hence it typically calls for more tax revenue, creating more inefficiency on that score. On the other hand, downward wage rigidity results in wasteful underutilisation of labour. The two sources of inefficiency must be compared, to decide which programme (or combination of programmes) is least inefficient. Also, the amounts of insurance supplied to the newcomers will have to take these costs into account.

From the viewpoint of labour, a general income maintenance programme is less attractive, because its benefits are widely distributed. Also, it is not within the power of labour to organize such a programme. But labour organisations have indeed turned their efforts towards implement-

---

[5] With how many firms would students need to contract on a contingent basis to be sure of having a job at the end of their studies? With how many students would a firm need to contract in order to cover contingent needs a few years hence?

[6] See for example Drèze (1987b, p. 20) or Drèze (1984b, pp. 282–3).

ing downward wage rigidity coupled with unemployment insurance.[7] By its very nature, downward wage rigidity is a macroeconomic phenomenon; as a form of income insurance for newcomers, it is meaningless at the firm level.

3.2. Ex-ante *efficient downward wage rigidity*

What can be said about *efficient* provision of income insurance on behalf of newcomers through downward wage rigidity and unemployment benefits? A simple model, based on Drèze (1986b), Gollier (1988) and joint work in progress by the two of us, is presented in appendix to help investigate that novel question.

That model is meant to exhibit the simplest possible structure within which the issue can be discussed. It is accordingly an aggregate model, with a single good and a single aggregate production function whose shifts introduce 'technological uncertainty'. For simplicity, employment is the only argument of the production function. Investment and demand aspects are provisionally ignored, to concentrate on the insurance problem.

There are two generations of workers: an older generation, whose members are covered by labour contracts, the terms of which are state dependent, but set before observing the state; and a younger generation, whose members are hired after observing the state. For simplicity, I assume that all the older workers are employed under all states, and earn the state-dependent wages w_{0s}. The wages $w_s \leq w_{0s}$ of the younger workers are also state dependent and set *ex ante*, but their employment level is determined *ex post* by equality between the wage and the marginal value product of labour (equal to the marginal physical product, upon normalising to unity the price of the good in every state). Unemployed younger workers receive unemployment benefits $t_s \leq w_s$. (The conditions $t_s \leq w_s \leq w_{0s}$ are introduced for incentive compatibility.)

The wages w_{0s} and w_s are net of taxes and all workers have identical preferences, represented by the twice continuously differentiable utility function $u(w)$. These workers supply inelastically one unit of labour. There are L_0 older workers and L younger workers. The unemployment benefits are subtracted from the gross profits to define the property income

$$\pi_s = f_s(L_0 + L_s) - w_{0s}L_0 - w_sL_s - t_s(L - L_s) \tag{1}$$

---

[7] Historically, unemployment insurance did not cover new entrants into the labour force until quite recently, and still does not cover them at all in many countries; see Emerson (1988).

where $L_s \leqslant L$, the employment of younger workers, is such that

$$f_s'(L_0 + L_s) = w_s. \tag{2}$$

The preferences of property owners are represented by the utility function $V(\pi)$, best understood as reflecting portfolio choices, consistent for instance with the Capital Asset Pricing Model.

Using an undetermined parameter λ to represent the distributive choices between workers and property owners, the problem of defining *ex ante* Pareto-efficient wages and unemployment benefits becomes

$$\max_{w_{0s}, w_s, t_s} \lambda E_s V[f_s(L_0 + L_s) - w_{0s}L_0 - w_s L_s - t_s(L - L_s)]$$

$$+ E_s[L_0 u(w_{0s}) + L_s u(w_s) + (L - L_s)u(t_s)]$$

subject to $f_s'(L_0 + L_s) = w_s, L_s \leqslant L, w_{0s} \geqslant w_s \geqslant t_s.$ $\tag{3}$

The solution to this problem is best understood by looking successively at its implications for the older and for the younger generation.

For older workers under contract, efficient risk-sharing with property owners requires

$$u'(w_{0s}) = \lambda V'(\pi_s). \tag{4}$$

That is also the condition obtained in equation (3.16) as a characterization of an efficient contract at the firm level. (The simplification here comes from identical workers and anonymous shareholders.) Condition (4) prevails here, as long as $f_s'(L_0 + L) \leqslant w_{0s}$; that is, as long as it implies wages w_{0s} at least as high as the market-clearing wages for the younger generation. Otherwise (in very good states), the pressure of labour demand leads to wages higher than required by risk-sharing considerations, and determined by the conditions

$$f_s'(L_0 + L) = w_{0s} \qquad u'(w_{0s}) < \lambda V'(\pi_s). \tag{5}$$

In short, the wages of older workers correspond to the maximum of a risk-sharing wage and a market-clearing wage.

Turning to the younger generation, the solution assigns to them market-clearing wages, as long as these do not fall too much below the contractual wages. There is a maximal degree of intergenerational wage discrimination, endogenously determined, at which downward wage rigidity and unemployment set in. That solution has several interesting features:

(i) Some degree of downward wage rigidity, leading to unemployment at positive wages (in bad states), is warranted on efficiency grounds.

(ii) The wages of newcomers are lower than those of workers under contract (wage discrimination by hiring date), unless there is full employment at wages higher than warranted by risk-sharing considerations for workers under contract; the degree of discrimination depends upon the wage elasticity of labour demand and upon the risk aversion of workers.

(iii) Unemployment benefits are equal to minimum wages, so that all unemployment is voluntary *ex post* from the individual viewpoint.

Some of these features reflect the specificity of the model. The more important point for my present purposes is the first, which validates the practice of downward wage rigidity as a 'second-best efficient' risk-sharing device. That conclusion seems quite robust, in models where future generations are not otherwise insured against fluctuations in market-clearing wages. It also validates the concern of labour unions about the strength of their bargaining position in collective wage settlements. The rest of the analysis does, however, confirm that prevailing wage determination schemes are not second-best efficient – a point to which I shall return later.

Looking at the first conclusion from another angle, one could say that economy-wide wage policies form an essential part of efficient risk-sharing between property owners and workers, when the interests of future generations of workers are taken into account. (When the third conclusion holds, wages and unemployment benefits are perfect substitutes as policy instruments.)

3.3.   Wage discrimination by hiring date

It is interesting that I can write down explicitly, in this simple model, the conditions under which downward wage rigidity and unemployment set in. Assuming that contractual wages automatically satisfy condition (4), and market-clearing wages condition (2), one first observes from (ii) that wage discrimination by hiring date sets in as soon as market-clearing wages fall short of contractual wages. The reason for the discrimination is simply that wages of workers under contract can be kept above the market-clearing level without adverse implications for the employment of these workers (labour hoarding), whereas wages of new workers could not exceed the market-clearing level without generating unemployment. That unemployment would be wasteful, because the marginal product of labour is higher than the disutility of work (assumed non-existent in the appendix, but easily introduced into the model, as verified in Gollier, 1988). When market-clearing wages are close to the contractual wages reflecting efficient risk-sharing between workers and property owners, the inefficiency associated with unemployment would outweigh the gain in risk-sharing efficiency associated with higher wages for newcomers. These two considerations exactly outweigh each other, in the simple model under review, when

$$u'(w_s) = u'(w_{0s})(1 - \eta_{L_s w_s}) > u'(w_{0s}) \tag{6}$$

where $\eta_{L_s w_s}$ is the elasticity of new hirings with respect to the hiring wages.

The logic behind that condition can be explained as follows. Using (4), (2) and the definition of the elasticity, (6) is equivalent, at $L_s = L$, to

$$Lu'(w_s) = \lambda V'(\pi_s)\left[L - f_s'(L_0 + L)\frac{\mathrm{d}L_s}{\mathrm{d}w_s}\right]. \tag{7}$$

In (7), the left-hand side measures the utility gains to younger workers of receiving higher wages (higher by one unit). The right-hand side measures the utility loss to property owners of paying these higher wages to younger workers (alone). That utility loss comes from lower profits, due first to the extra unit of wages going to L workers, and next to the loss of output from lower employment; that loss of output is measured by the marginal product of labour times the change in labour demand. (Thus the elasticity comes into the formula to account for the waste associated with unemployment, not to account for any form of monopolistic behaviour.)

Condition (6) is stated in terms of the marginal utilities of workers under contract and of newcomers. Assuming identical preferences for both groups, and expanding marginal utilities in a Taylor series through quadratic terms, one can approximate (6) by the more operational condition

$$w_s = w_{0s}\left[1 + \frac{\eta_{L_s w_s}}{R_R(w_{0s})}\right], \qquad \frac{w_{0s} - w_s}{w_{0s}} = \frac{|\eta_{L_s w_s}|}{R_R(w_{0s})}, \tag{8}$$

where $R_R(w_{0s})$ is the Arrow–Pratt measure of relative risk aversion for the workers, evaluated at the contractual wage.

It conforms to intuition that the loss associated with inefficient risk-sharing is a function of the degree of risk aversion of the workers. In the operational formula (8), the maximal relative wage discrimination by hiring date is directly proportional to the wage elasticity of labour demand by firms and inversely proportional to the risk aversion of workers. When that maximal discrimination separates contractual wages from market clearing wages, downward wage rigidity sets in to prevent further discrimination. The formula which applies from there on is a slight generalisation of (6), namely

$$u'(w_s) = u'(w_{0s})\left(1 - \frac{L_s}{L}\eta_{L_s w_s}\right) = u'(w_{0s})\left(1 - w_s\frac{dL_s}{dw_s}\right). \tag{9}$$

It is interesting to speculate about the order of magnitude of the implied discrimination. To that effect, I note first that η_s, the wage elasticity of new hirings, is related to the wage elasticity of employment by the formula

$$\eta_s = \frac{w_s L_s'}{L_s} = \frac{w_s L_s'}{L_0 + L_s}\frac{L_0 + L_s}{L_s}.$$

That is, η_s is equal to the wage elasticity of employment times the ratio of total employment to new hirings. This is a fortunate feature, because it dispenses with the need to decide whether we should use a short- or a long-run elasticity number. As is well known, the orders or magnitude of the short-run and long-run elasticities of employment are quite different. According to Drèze and Modigliani (1981), for instance, the long-run elasticity could easily be 6 to 10 times as high as the short-run elasticity. But the ratio of total employment to new hirings is also very different in the two cases. According again to Belgian data, it is close to 6 on a yearly basis, whereas it should tend to 1 in the long run. Thus we may for practical purposes use the long-run wage elasticity of employment as an estimate of 'the' wage elasticity of new hirings. Unity is then a reasonable order of magnitude, even if the precision of our estimates leaves much to be desired. Hoping that L_s/L is reasonably close to unity as well, we would then conclude that the margin of wage discrimination is of the same order of magnitude as the reciprocal of the Arrow–Pratt relative risk-aversion measure for workers. Here again, we face an estimation problem. Casual appraisal of insurance deductibles suggests a margin of discrimination of the order of 20 per cent (a relative risk-aversion measure of the order of 5),[8] say plus or minus 5 per cent.

Could one translate conditions (4)–(8) into operational guidelines? Attempting to do so rigorously leads to complicated formulas of doubtful applicability. There is, however, one approximation conducive to major technical as well as logical simplification, which seems commensurate with the precision of available econometric estimates of the relevant parameters

---

[8] See Drèze (1981). It would of course be improper to use here a relative risk-aversion measure based on portfolio choices of asset owners.

(namely the wage elasticity of employment and the relative risk-aversion measure). The approximation consists in treating the factor of proportionality between $u'(w_s)$ and $u'(w_{0s})$ in (9) as a constant – say $1/\mu$.[9] The solution is then entirely characterised by

$$u'(w_{0s}) = \lambda V'(\pi_s) = \mu u'(w_s) \tag{10}$$

whenever there is less than full employment. Equation (10) is of the same form as (3.21); it is simply a characterisation of efficient risk-sharing between the three groups of agents: workers under contract, property owners and new entrants to the labour market. Implementing the solution is now a matter of achieving efficient risk-sharing through the labour contracts, linking the wage of new hires (and/or the unemployment benefits) to the contractual wages by means of formula (8), and hopefully letting demand pressure reduce the extent of discrimination at full employment. The resulting heuristic guidelines are basically the following.

Let the wages of workers under contract be determined by a simple economy-wide convention (like indexation in part on consumer prices and in part on nominal national income), giving content to the conditions (4) – or (3.16) – which characterise efficient risk-sharing between workers under contract and property owners. As long as market-clearing wages for all workers (those under contract and the new entrants) are equal to or higher than these contractual wages, the pressure of labour demand will result in full employment at these higher wages. When the market-clearing wages fall below the contractual level, wage discrimination between the workers under contract and the new workers sets in, with the new workers earning market-clearing wages, while the workers under contract continue to earn their (higher) contractual wages. That situation is allowed to prevail as long as the relative discrimination remains moderate – say not exceeding 20 per cent or so. When that level of discrimination is reached, downward wage rigidity for the new workers sets in, and there results some (inefficient) unemployment, with unemployment benefits high enough to make the unemployment voluntary. The wages of the new workers, and the unemployment benefits, are then tied to the contractual wages, to which they remain proportional (though at the lower level corresponding to the maximal tolerated discrimination).

These guidelines are presented here as 'heuristic', first because they are derived within a very incomplete model, and second because they

[9] Those rigorous formulas which I could obtain suggest that the approximation introduces a bias in the elasticity of wages to national income (thus not in the wage level itself) which is definitely upward, but moderate (say of the order of 5 per cent).

correspond to approximate and not to exact formulas. They should thus be regarded as *indicative* of the general nature of desirable policies, with no weight being attached to specific details.

Much simplicity of exposition is gained from assuming that prevailing long-term contracts are efficient, and from tailoring the wages of new workers to these contractual wages. The guidelines could thus be called 'operational'. This should not be allowed to conceal the need for characterising efficient contracts as part of the policy. The simple indexation scheme proposed for illustration is indicative of desirable properties. Why it is not encountered in practice remains to be properly understood. That fact in itself is a ground for caution. Neither should one underestimate the practical difficulty of giving empirical content to the theoretical concept of market-clearing wages, a difficulty already mentioned in section 1.5. Several recent contributions to the theory of employment address that topic from different angles, like job search, efficiency wages, intertemporal labour-leisure substitution, insider-outsider differentials, and so on.[10] A common theme of these contributions is that the concept of market-clearing wages is by no means straightforward.

3.4. Complications

The analysis sketched here ignores several complications, among which the following three seem to be particularly significant.

First, the model of the appendix is a model of pure technological uncertainty, which ignores altogether demand and investment. Demand matters whenever observed unemployment has a Keynesian dimension, with output determined at least in part by aggregate demand, at a level where the marginal value product of labour exceeds the wages of marginal workers. It is then important to take into account the marginal propensities to spend wage income and property income respectively. And investment matters because the production possibilities (hence the marginal product of labour) are influenced by investments, as well as by the state of the environment. Once these considerations are introduced, the repercussions of the wage formation (and in particular of the downward wage rigidities) on employment become much more complex, and can only be spelled out in the framework of a complete macroeconomic model.[11] Such a task lies

[10] See Lindbeck and Snower (1985) for a recent survey.

[11] Of course, empirical estimates of the wage elasticity of employment hope to incorporate these repercussions. To that extent, they are implicitly incorporated here as well.

beyond the scope of this book. It is, of course, of paramount importance for policy choices.

Second, the present discussion is based entirely on a two-period model, that is on a simple dichotomy between the present and the future. In reality, history unfolds progressively: every day is part of the previous day's future, and is in turn endowed with its own future. The risk-sharing considerations introduced here must be embedded in a dynamic picture, with a view to characterise optimal paths.[12] The dynamics of intergenerational wage discrimination are an intriguing subject.

Third, the model of the appendix is an aggregate model, which ignores the diversity among firms, skills or sectors. In reality, one typically observes more diversity; some firms or sectors operate at full capacity and hire additional labour, while others experience excess capacities and hoard labour; and there are shortages of specialised skills in the midst of serious unemployment. That diversity is another source of complication, which restricts the immediate relevance of the aggregate guidelines drawn above.

3.5. *Inegalitarian cooperatives*

It is of some interest to relate, by way of a brief digression, conclusion (ii) (following (5)) regarding wage discrimination by hiring date, to a similar conclusion reached by Meade (1982) in his discussion of the promotion of employment in labour-managed cooperatives. Recognizing that labour-managed firms would not be inclined to take on new members, when the value added per member exceeds the reservation wage of outsiders, Meade advocates the principle of 'inegalitarian cooperatives', who take on new members at a lower share in value added than existing members, or possibly even at a market wage with employee status. This corresponds to the practice, witnessed in some Israeli kibbutzim and some Western cooperatives, of hiring salaried workers at wages inferior to the earnings of members. A macroeconomic justification for that practice is provided by the second conclusion just recalled. The fuller analysis here reveals under what conditions that practice is justified, and defines an upper bound on the degree of income discrimination warranted by efficiency considerations.

---

[12] See Gollier (1988, chapter 2) for a multiperiod extension of the model in the appendix.

4. Overall conclusion

Putting together the conclusions collected in earlier sections of this chapter, I feel confident in formulating an overall conclusion.

In economies operating with uncertainty and incomplete insurance markets, it is natural to find capital hiring labour, because efficient labour contracts in capitalist firms are easier to draw and monitor than efficient equity contracts for labour-managed firms. That form of organisation meets the preference of capitalists for vesting managerial authority with representatives of capital. It also meets the preference of labour organisations for acting on labour markets rather than on capital markets. It lends itself more naturally to economies of transaction costs through centralised negotiations over contracts (sectoral or economy-wide wage settlements). Finally, it lends itself naturally to the inclusion of future generations of workers in the risk-sharing arrangements between capital and labour, through downward wage rigidity and unemployment insurance.

It seems doubtful that labour contracts prevailing in capitalist economies correspond closely to efficient risk-sharing, because they fail to link labour incomes to aggregate wealth. (Constant real wages provide too much insurance, constant nominal wages potentially too little.) Improvements are possible, but may not be easy to implement. My main suggestion would be to index wages partly on consumer prices and partly on nominal national income. Smaller firms with closely held equity could be labour managed, if working conditions call for frequent and subtle adjustments, or could practise profit-sharing and participatory decision-making. The main challenge of the day, however, lies with improving the efficiency of collective wage bargaining.

Appendix

In order to investigate some of the issues raised in this chapter, I use a variant of the highly streamlined model introduced in the appendix of Drèze (1986b) and extended in Gollier (1988).

The physical model is one where aggregate production *tomorrow* is constrained by a state-dependent neoclassical production function relating output Y_s to labour input L_s in every state s:

$$Y_s = f_s(L_s) \quad f'_s(L_s) > 0 \quad f''_s(L_s) < 0 \quad s = 1, \ldots, S. \tag{A.1}$$

Thus the stock of capital available for use tomorrow is taken as given (predetermined), and is therefore not mentioned explicitly. The labour input is split between L_0 workers under contract (insiders), who are assumed to be employed in all states, and $L_s \leqslant L$ workers of a new generation, who are assumed to supply inelastically one unit of labour each. (L is the size of the new generation.) Thus the utility of leisure is ignored (for instance, on the grounds that it is offset by the positive value of having a job; more realistic specifications are possible, but introduce unnecessary complications). The wage paid to workers under contract is w_{0s}, that specified in a new contract is w_s, and the cardinal (von Neumann-Morgenstern) utility function for income of a worker (of either generation) is denoted $u(y)$; it is assumed to be strictly concave (risk aversion) and twice continuously differentiable:

$$u = u(y) \qquad u'(y) > 0 \qquad u''(y) < 0. \tag{A.2}$$

Output price is normalised to unity in every state. Hence profits associated with the employment of newcomers are simply (subsuming L_0 under f_s)

$$\hat{\pi}_s = f_s(L_s) - w_{0s}L_0 - w_sL_s \qquad s = 1,\ldots,S. \tag{A.3}$$

I assume that firms maximise these profits *ex post* in every state, by choosing L_s while taking wages as given. This calls for equating the wage rate to the marginal (value) product of labour:

$$f_s'(L_s) = w_s \qquad s = 1,\ldots,S. \tag{A.4}$$

I shall denote by $L_s(w_s)$ the labour demand function implicitly defined by (A.4). It satisfies

$$L_s'(w_s) = \frac{1}{f_s''(L_s)} < 0 \qquad \eta_{L_sw_s} := \eta_s = \frac{w_sL_s'}{L_s} = \frac{f_s'(L_s)}{L_sf_s''(L_s)} < 0 \tag{A.5}$$

where η_s denotes the wage elasticity of *new hirings* (*not* of total employment).

I assume that profit earners hold market portfolios, and that their preferences can be represented by an aggregate utility function V, with argument profits minus taxes. The latter are simply a lump-sum tax on profits, used to finance a scheme of unemployment benefits, in an amount t_s per unemployed person. The after-tax profits are thus $\hat{\pi}_s - t_s(L - L_s) = \mathrm{def}\,\pi_s$.

The characterization of *ex ante* Pareto-efficient transfer-and-wage policies is obtained from the first-order conditions for maximising a weighted sum of expected utilities, namely that of profit earners (a function of their net profits) with weight λ and that of workers with weight unity, where the expected utility of a worker is computed with probabilities of employment and unemployment equal to L_s/L and $(L - L_s)/L$ respectively. The weight λ reflects distributive ethics.

It is assumed that all agents agree about the probabilities of the states, $\phi_s > 0$, $s = 1, \ldots, S$. Expectations in terms of these probabilities are denoted E_s. Finally, it is assumed that $u'(y) \to +\infty$ as $y \to 0$, so that the conditions $(L - L_s)t_s \geq 0$ are never binding (for t_s); and that $f'_s(L_s)$ is high enough so that the conditions $L_s \geq 0$ are never binding.

These specifications lead to the following problem:

$$\max_{w_{0s}, w_s, t_s} \Lambda = \lambda E_s V[f_s(L_s) - w_{0s}L_0 - w_s L_s - t_s(L - L_s)]$$

$$+ E_s\left\{L_0 u(w_{0s}) + L\left[\frac{L_s}{L}u(w_s) + \frac{L - L_s}{L}u(t_s)\right]\right\} \quad \text{(A.6)}$$

subject to (A.4) and to

$$w_{0s} \geq w_s \qquad (\rho_s)$$
$$w_s \geq t_s \qquad (\mu_s)$$
$$L \geq L_s \qquad (v_s)$$

where ρ_s, μ_s and v_s are Lagrange multipliers.

The condition $w_s \geq t_s$ is introduced to guarantee that workers will accept employment at the wage w_s. (The implicit rate of income taxation should not exceed 100 per cent.) The condition $w_{0s} \geq w_s$ is a standard requirement (of incentive compatibility).

The first-order necessary conditions for this problem are:

$$\frac{\partial \Lambda}{\partial w_{0s}} = -\lambda \phi_s V'(\pi_s)L_0 + \phi_s u'(w_{0s})L_0 + \rho_s = 0 \quad \text{(A.7)}$$

$$\frac{\partial \Lambda}{\partial w_s} = -\lambda \phi_s V'(\pi_s)[L_s - t_s L'_s(w_s)] + \phi_s[L_s u'(w_s)$$

$$+ L'_s(w_s)\{u(w_s) - u(t_s)\}] + \mu_s - v_s L'(w_s) - \rho_s = 0 \quad \text{(A.8)}$$

$$\frac{\partial \Lambda}{\partial t_s} = -\lambda \phi_s V'(\pi_s)(L - L_s) + \phi_s u'(t_s)(L - L_s) - \mu_s = 0. \quad \text{(A.9)}$$

In order to analyse these conditions, I first show that (i) $L = L_s$ implies $\mu_s = 0$, and (ii) $L > L_s$ implies $\mu_s > 0$. I will next show that (iii) $\mu_s > 0$ implies $w_{0s} > w_s$ and $\rho_s = 0$.

Property (i) follows immediately from (A.9).

To establish property (ii), I note that $L > L_s$ with $\mu_s = 0$ would imply through (A.9) that $u'(t_s) = \lambda V'(\pi_s)$. Also, $L > L_s$ implies $v_s = 0$. Using these two properties, (A.8) could be solved for

$$\frac{\rho_s}{\phi_s} = u'(t_s)t_sL_s'(w_s) + L_s[u'(w_s) - u'(t_s)]$$

$$+ L_s'(w_s)[u(w_s) - u(t_s)] < 0, \tag{A.10}$$

contradicting $\rho_s \geqslant 0$; where the negative sign in (A.10) follows from $L_s' < 0$ and $w_s \geqslant t_s$. Hence $L > L_s$ implies $\mu_s > 0$.

To establish property (iii), I note that $\mu_s > 0$ and $w_{0s} = w_s$ would imply $w_{0s} = w_s = t_s$ with $L > L_s$. It would then follow from (A.7) that $\lambda V'(\pi_s) - u'(t_s) = \rho_s/\phi_s L_0 \geqslant 0$, and from (A.9) that $\lambda V'(\pi_s) - u'(t_s) = -\mu_s/\phi_s(L - L_s) < 0$, a contradiction. Hence $\mu_s > 0$ implies $w_{0s} > w_s$ and $\rho_s = 0$.

Using these properties, and noting that t_s is irrelevant when $L = L_s$, we may confine the analysis to three cases:

    (a) $L = L_s$ with $w_{0s} = w_s$
    (b) $L = L_s$ with $w_{0s} > w_s$
    (c) $L > L_s$ with $w_{0s} > w_s = t_s$.

The relevant characteristics for these three cases go as follows.

First, $L = L_s$ means that $w_s = f_s'(L) := w_s^*$, where w_s^* denotes the market-clearing wage; and $L > L_s$ means that $w_s > w_s^*$.

Second, when $w_{0s} > w_s$ so that $\rho_s = 0$, it follows from (A.7) that

$$u'(w_{0s}) = \lambda V'(\pi_s), \tag{A.11}$$

namely the condition for optimal sharing (of income and risks) between workers under contract and property owners. On the other hand, when $\rho_s > 0$, then $u'(w_{0s}) = \lambda V'(\pi_s) - (\rho_s/\phi_s L_0) < \lambda V'(\pi_s)$, and wages exceed the level desired on distributive grounds.

Third, when $L > L_s$ so that $\mu_s > 0$, $\rho_s = v_s = 0$, and $w_{0s} > w_s = t_s > w_s^*$, then (A.7)–(A.9) imply

$$u'(w_s) = u'(t_s) = \lambda V'(\pi_s)\left[1 - \frac{w_s}{L}L_s'(w_s)\right]$$

$$= \lambda V'(\pi_s)\left(1 - \frac{L_s}{L}\eta_s\right)$$

$$= u'(w_{0s})\left(1 - \frac{L_s}{L}\eta_s\right). \tag{A.12}$$

Condition (A.12) implies that unemployment sets in when $u'(w_s^*) = u'(w_{0s})(1 - \eta_s)$, that is when the market-clearing wage w_s^* carries a marginal utility exceeding that of the contractual wage w_{0s} by a percentage equal to $-100\,\eta_s$ (per cent).

One way to interpret (A.12) is as follows: raising $w_s(=t_s)$ yields additional utility to workers, evaluated as $Lu'(w_s)$; the cost to property owners is the higher level of payments to labour – either as wages or as unemployment benefits financed by the tax – plus the loss of output due to the reduced employment, a loss measured by $f'_s(L_s)\,L'_s(w_s) = w_s L'_s(w_s)$ $= L_s\eta_s$. Hence the first-order condition:

$$Lu'(w_s) = \lambda V'(\pi_s)[L - w_s L'_s(w_s)]. \tag{A.12'}$$

To sum up, a solution to problem (A.6), defining *ex ante efficient* wage and unemployment benefits, can take either one of three forms, depending upon the position of the technological frontier $f_s(L_s)$ and hence upon the level of the full employment wages:

(a) $\qquad w_s = w_s^* = w_{0s} \qquad u'(w_{0s}) \leqslant \lambda V'(\pi_s).$

There is full employment, wages of the two generations of workers are both equal to the marginal value product of labour, and (possibly) higher than the level corresponding to optimal risk-sharing between workers under contract and property owners.

(b) $\qquad w_s = w_s^* < w_{0s} \qquad u'(w_{0s}) = \lambda V'(\pi_s) \qquad u'(w_s) \leqslant u'(w_{0s})(1 - \eta_s).$

There is full employment, but the wages of the two generations of workers are different (though not too different), those of the workers under contract being higher than the marginal value product of labour thanks to the income insurance supplied by property owners (against lower wages in the earlier periods).

(c) $\qquad w_{0s} > w_s = t_s > w_s^* \qquad L_s < L$

$$u'(w_s) = u'(w_{0s})\left(1 - \frac{L_s}{L}\eta_s\right) = \lambda V'(\pi_s)\left(1 - \frac{L_s}{L}\eta_s\right).$$

There is less than full employment, the wages of the two generations are different, with those of the older generation exceeding the marginal value product of labour, those of the younger generation equal to that marginal product and equal to the level of the unemployment benefits; thus all the unemployment is voluntary.

These conclusions may also be put in more sanguine terms as follows: all unemployment is voluntary and necessarily accompanied by wage discrimination between the two generations.

The fact that unemployment is voluntary is a consequence of allowing $t_s = w_s$. If one imposed instead, for incentive reasons, that $t_s \leqslant \alpha w_s$, $\alpha < 1$, then unemployment would be voluntary *ex ante* for workers as a group, but involuntary *ex post* for unemployed individuals.

The practical implications of conditions (A.12) are most conveniently explored by means of the linear approximation

$$u'(w_s) = u'(w_{0s}) + (w_s - w_{0s})u''(w_{0s})$$

$$= u'(w_{0s}) \left\{ 1 + (w_{0s} - w_s) \left[-\frac{u''(w_{0s})}{u'(w_{0s})} \right] \right\}$$

$$= u'(w_{0s})[1 + (w_{0s} - w_s)R_A(w_{0s})]$$

$$= u'(w_{0s}) \left[1 + \frac{w_{0s} - w_s}{w_{0s}} R_R(w_{0s}) \right] \tag{A.13}$$

where $R_A(w_{0s})$ and $R_R(w_{0s})$ are respectively the absolute and relative risk-aversion measures of Arrow (1965) and Pratt (1964) evaluated at w_{0s}. Inserting (A.13) into (A.12) yields

$$\frac{w_{0s} - w_s}{w_{0s}} = \frac{-(L_s/L)\eta_s}{R_R(w_{0s})} \geqslant 0 \qquad w_s = w_{0s} \left[1 + \frac{(L_s/L)\eta_s}{R_R(w_{0s})} \right]. \tag{A.14}$$

Thus the margin of relative discrimination $(w_{0s} - w_s)/w_{0s}$ is inversely proportional to the relative risk aversion of the workers, and directly proportional to the absolute value of the wage elasticity of new hirings. These two properties are intuitively natural.

VII Econometrics

14 The trade-off between real wages and employment in an open economy (Belgium)*

1. Introduction and preview

1.1. Theoretical background

The purpose of this paper is twofold. First, we discuss the nature and quantitative order of magnitude of the trade-off between real wages and employment in the small open economy Belgium. Second, we draw policy conclusions from our positive analysis, and compare income policies with alternative approaches to employment stimulation (including shorter working hours and currency depreciation).

Although our analysis is very coarse and recognises sizeable uncertainties, we hope to contribute a coherent view to the debate about the nature and likely remedies of the current state of underemployment in Belgium. Opinions differ about the respective roles of effective demand versus cost and production structures in explaining that situation.[1] The unions' demand of a shorter working week without pay cut is strongly opposed by employers on grounds of international competitiveness.

Indecisiveness is sustained by the lack of a generally accepted theoretical framework bringing both Keynesian and neo-classical reasoning to bear on the problems of an open economy. Available econometric models suffer from similar limitations.[2]

* *European Economic Review*, 15, 1–40, 1981. With Franco Modigliani. The authors thank Luc Bauwens, Gonzague d'Alcantara and Jean Dermine who collected or supplied material for the empirical analysis; Hans Tompa who skilfully carried out the computations; Jean Waelbroeck and an anonymous referee who commented on the manuscript; and numerous colleagues who participated in stimulating seminar discussions at Louvain-la-Neuve.

[1] Cf., for instance, Bleeckx et al. (1978, p. 3.39 ff) versus Eyskens (1978, pp. 13–14).

[2] Our survey has covered the models ANELISE – cf. Adams et al. (1973), Blomme (1978), BREUGHEL – cf. Berckmans and Thys-Clément (1977), COMET – cf. Barten et al. (1976), DESMOS – cf. Waelbroeck and Dramais (1974), LINK – cf. Basevi (1973), and RENA – cf. Thys-Clément et al. (1973).

Our own thinking has been influenced by two recent analytical contributions which have stressed the significance of the trade-off between real wages and employment:

(i) Malinvaud's *Theory of Unemployment Reconsidered* (1977) brings out the possibility that demand stimulation policies may be ineffective in reducing unemployment, if supply is unresponsive to aggregate demand at the going wages and prices – a situation referred to by Malinvaud as 'classical unemployment'.

(ii) In a paper initially published in Italian, Modigliani and Padoa-Schioppa (1977, 1978) have argued that, in an open economy, external balance implies a constraining relationship between the levels of real wages and employment.[3]

Malinvaud's analysis is presented for a closed economy.[4] International trade has important implications for the evaluation of the wages – employment trade-off, a point brought out by the Modigliani–Padoa-Schioppa approach. Their argument is essentially dynamic, including a mechanism of price adjustments in an open economy with fully indexed wages. We shall restate their argument in elementary comparative statics terms, and extend it to a more explicit treatment of the influence of real wages on employment through capacity adjustments. The main contribution of the present paper consists however in our attempt at quantitative evaluation of the trade-off between real wages and employment. Our empirical conclusions have shaped significantly our views on policy.

1.2. *Factual background*

Wages and salaries in Belgium are almost fully indexed. Real wages have risen by some 50% between 1970 and 1976, as compared with some 30% in other EEC countries. Their absolute level is reported to be among the highest in the world.[5] Unemployment currently stands at an alarming

---

[3] These two lines of analysis have come into contact at the IEA Conference on 'Unemployment in Western Countries Today' held in Strasbourg, September 1978. See the discussion by Modigliani of Malinvaud's paper *Macroeconomic Rationing of Employment*, (1980).

[4] Dixit (1978) extends Malinvaud's model to an open economy, along lines that are different from those followed here. Indeed, Dixit assumes that the country under study faces a perfectly elastic demand for its exports; whereas we assume that it faces a perfectly elastic supply for its imports. See Section 2.2 below.

[5] See Nyssens and Wittman (1976).

level, well above the EEC average, under due allowance for heterogeneity of definitions.[6]

The interplay of effective demand and international competitiveness in accounting for the decline of employment in Belgium is clearly illustrated by the steel, textile and clothing industries. From September 1976 through December 1977, employment of wage earners in these three industries alone fell by 29,365 persons, or 51% of the total decline experienced in manufacturing. In steel, where wages represent 50% of production costs, Belgium exports 70% of its output – but the share of Japan in world exports to countries outside the EEC and Comecon had reached 45% by 1976 (coming from 15% in 1962), whereas the share of EEC exporters had fallen to 15% (coming from 35% in 1962). Over the same period, the low-wage producers from Eastern Europe and Asia had increased their share in world exports of textiles and clothing respectively by 10 and 20 percentage points. In all three cases, the new international distribution of employment had particularly severe implications for Belgium, resulting in accelerated scrapping of capacity. The names of firms closed down, or transferred to low-wage areas, are locally familiar.

Further evidence of capacity scrapping is implied by the figures on Government disbursement of severance pay to workers dismissed by bankrupt firms with at least 10 employees (and not rehired). In 1975, 1976 and 1977, respectively 21,123, 32,262 and 24,739 persons received such payments. (These numbers correspond to 13%, 14% and 10%, respectively, of the total unemployment figures in the same year.)

Over the past decade, the volume of gross capital formation in Belgian manufacturing has been stagnant (hence falling markedly in relation to output), whereas the capital–labour ratio was undoubtedly rising.[7] Both accelerated scrapping and incomplete replacement of capacity have reduced the demand for labour.

Turning to international relations, we note that Belgium has over the years maintained its balance of trade very close to equilibrium – closer, in fact, than most countries (see fig. 14.1). Since 1970, the Belgian franc has appreciated steadily relative to all currencies except the Swiss franc, the yen, the mark and the guilder – staying fairly close to these last two currencies. The rate of inflation had been brought back to less than 4% by 1978.

[6] The unemployment rate in Belgium may be evaluated at some 8 to 11% (of the total labour force), depending upon the treatment of workers temporarily employed under special government programs.

[7] The Dutch estimates by den Hartog and Tjan (1976) and the unpublished Belgian estimates by d'Alcantara (1979) and by Vandoorne and Meeusen (1978) concur in suggesting that this ratio increases at a rate of some 5% per year.

324   *Econometrics*

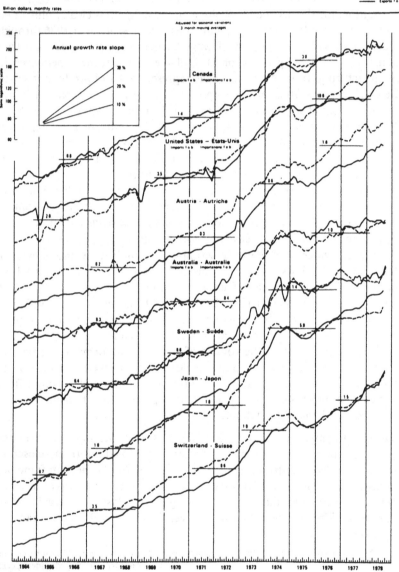

Fig. 14.1.   Organization for economic cooperation and development statistics of
foreign trade, December 1978.

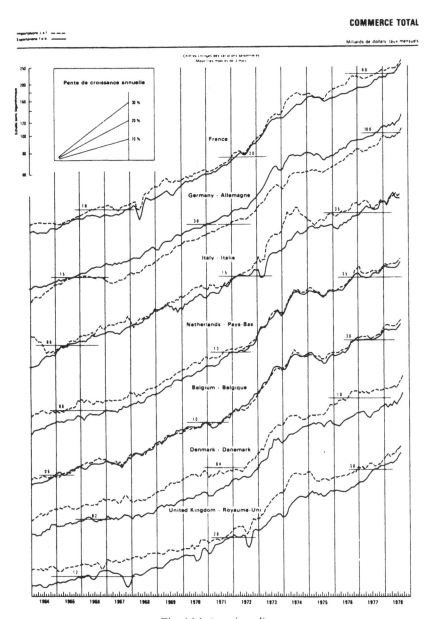

Fig. 14.1. (continued).

1.3. General approach

Against this background, we propose to study the trade-off between real wages and employment as follows. First, following Modigliani–Padoa-Schioppa, *we shall treat external balance as a binding constraint on demand management policies.*[8] Second, *we shall endeavour to assess the influence of real wages on output, hence employment, both through the rate of utilization of a given capacity and through the creation or scrapping of that capacity.* These two points are now explained briefly.

Given the Belgian experience, we find it relevant to consider initially the case of an open economy operating under a fixed (or managed) exchange rate and a tight constraint of external balance. (Exchange rate adjustments are considered briefly in Section 4.) If such an economy experiences unemployment, stimulation of domestic demand through policy measures that do not increase exports will create an external deficit, roughly equal to the imports content (direct and indirect) of the additional demand. In this way, a tight external balance constraint stands in the way of demand management policies. Similarly, if the external balance is impaired by some exogenous circumstances (like a rise in import prices or a fall in the demand for exports), one way of restoring equilibrium is to reduce imports through an appropriate reduction of domestic demand. Another example of such a circumstance would be an exogenous increase in real wages, affecting adversely the competitiveness of domestic producers on the export and import markets. If external balance implies equality of domestic demand and output, at least marginally, then *the impact of the wage increase on domestic output* (hence employment) *is measured by the reduction in domestic demand required to restore external balance.* This, in a nutshell, is our approach to evaluate the trade-off between real wages and employment in Belgium.

The assumption that external balance operates as a binding constraint is probably more natural in a long-run analysis than in a short-run analysis. Indeed, in the short run, foreign borrowing may cover temporary deficits. To that extent, our evaluation of the short-run trade-off may be biased upwards and should be understood as an upper bound – a feature that would not affect our conclusions. Moreover, it seems that the balance of payments is currently perceived by the Belgian monetary authorities as a binding constraint, because an appreciable current account deficit would make it hard to defend the desired exchange rate.

---

[8] Other previous work in the same spirit includes Oates (1966), McKinnon (1969) and Steinherr (1975).

The assumption that external balance operates as a binding constraint on demand management policies frees us from the necessity of considering these policies explicitly (or evaluating multiplier effects, and so on), at least in a first approximation where the influence of the *composition* of domestic demand on imports is ignored. For estimation purposes, the analytical burden is shifted towards estimation of the impact on external balance of domestic costs and domestic demand.

How to estimate that impact raises the second point mentioned above. The standard link between wage costs and the balance of trade goes through the behaviour of domestic producers who react to cost increases by raising their prices and/or reducing their supply (for instance by adjusting sales promotion expenditures to the new margin between price and costs). In the open economy, both measures result in a transfer of market shares from domestic toward foreign producers, and this affects the balance of trade adversely. (Price increases for exports have a positive effect, which must be subtracted.)

But it makes a difference whether a firm experiencing a rise in wage costs merely accepts some loss of sales and/or of profits, or closes down a plant altogether. The difference is twofold. In the first case, but not in the second, the reduction in employment (i) is apt to be less than proportional to the reduction in output, at least initially, and (ii) is reversible under a more favourable turn of events. Thus, capacity scrapping implies a permanent reduction in the potential demand for labour, thereby contributing an element of 'structural' or 'classical' unemployment. But *it also implies a permanent deterioration of the balance of trade* (through loss of exports or imports substitution) which, under a tight external balance constraint, requires a compensating reduction in domestic demand. The final impact on output (hence employment) is again measured by the reduction in domestic demand required to restore external balance.

We shall accordingly endeavour to evaluate separately the influence on exports and imports of domestic costs at unchanged capacity levels, and of capacity levels themselves. And we shall endeavour to evaluate the influence of real wages not only on operating costs but also on capacity levels through scrapping and investment.

1.4. Summary

Quantitative evaluation of these influences is subject to much imprecision. We have combined two approaches, both with a Bayesian inspiration, to evaluate the international trade elasticities.

First, we have collected the estimates from published econometric models of the Belgian economy, as listed in footnote 2. These estimates do not always agree, but are not too widely different either. We have averaged point estimates across models and attached to these averages subjective standard errors, reflecting the dispersion of estimates.

Second, d'Alcantara and Associates (1979) have kindly made available to us the progress report describing the international trade sector of the new model SERENA currently being estimated on behalf of the Belgian Planning Office. The specification of exports and imports functions for manufactured goods corresponds very closely to our needs. And Bauwens (1979) has conducted a Bayesian analysis of the export equations in that model. We have accordingly used as an alternative the posterior densities corresponding to the SERENA equations, with some corrections to unreasonably low standard errors.

The influence of wage costs on capacity is more difficult to quantify. Our evaluation is based on the work of den Hartog and Tjan (1976) and Kuipers and Bosch (1976), who have estimated a clay–clay vintage model for The Netherlands.[9] Simulation of that model provides an evaluation that we have treated as unbiased, but to which we have attached a substantial standard error

Making generous use of normal approximations, we obtain through a mixture of analytical and numerical integration marginal densities for the trade-off between real wages and employment in Belgium. They are reproduced as figs. 14.2–14.6 below. The variances of these densities measure the imprecision of our knowledge.

The conclusions from our empirical investigation are first that estimates of the trade-off between real wages and employment in Belgium are subject to considerable imprecision; second that the short-run elasticity of employment with respect to real wages keeping capacity constant is probably quite small (like -0.2), and definitely less than unity in absolute value; third that the corresponding medium-run elasticity taking into account capacity adjustments is probably sizeable (like -2), and definitely larger than unity in absolute value; and fourth that exchange rate adjustments might not make too much difference, in either the short or the medium run.

Turning to a discussion of policy, we shall argue that these conclusions give support to a policy of constant real labour incomes, of comprehensive efforts to redistribute work through shorter working hours or related schemes, and of selective efforts to slow down capacity scrapping.

Section 2 contains a theoretical derivation of our formulae for evaluating

[9] The research in progress by Vandoorne and Meeusen (1978) came to our attention after most of our work was completed.

the trade-off between real wages and employment in Belgium. Section 3 contains our attempt at empirical evaluation, summarized in figs. 14.2–14.6. Exchange rate adjustments are discussed in Section 4. Policy implications and recommendations are presented in Section 5 which is largely self-contained.

2. The trade-off under a fixed exchange rate and a tight external balance constraint

2.1. Notation and definitions

We use the following notation:
P_e = level of world prices (expressed in 'dollars'),
P = level of domestic prices (in domestic currency),
P_x = level of export prices (in domestic currency),
P_m = level of import prices (in domestic currency),
W = level of domestic wages (in domestic currency), a component of
C = level of domestic factor prices or costs (in domestic currency),
e = exchange rate (domestic price of 'dollars'),
L = employment (number of employed persons),
X = volume of exports,
M = volume of imports,
E = volume of aggregate world demand,
G = volume of aggregate domestic government expenditures,
H = volume of aggregate domestic private demand (consumption plus investment),
Y = volume of domestic output,
$\bar{Y}$ = volume of capacity output (defined below).

The level of import prices is immediately equated to the exogenous level of world prices, reflecting our assumption of a perfectly elastic supply of imports to the small country Belgium: $P_m/e = P_e$.[10]

Capacity output is here identified, for conceptual clarity, with notional supply. It is the volume of output that domestic producers would choose to supply, for profit maximisation, at the prevailing prices and wages, under unlimited output demand and factor supply. In the short run, $\bar{Y}$ is constrained by the existing plants and equipment; it may also be influenced by extant labour contracts (if firms would rather produce than fire workers; but would not hire new workers, even to replace voluntary leaves). In the

[10] See footnote 4. In the SERENA model, the elasticity of import prices with respect to world prices – a weighted average of the export prices of Belgium's trade partners – is estimated at 0.98 for industrial goods, which account for 80% of imports.

longer run, $\bar{Y}$ is affected by depreciation or scrapping of existing equipment and by new investment, in a manner that will be discussed further below.

In the short run, we ignore inventory adjustments and relate domestic output to final demand through an accounting identity (which also satisfies a definitional inequality),

$$Y = G + H + X - M \leqq \bar{Y}. \tag{1}$$

This formulation is used, instead of the now standard min condition,[11] because: (i) we concentrate on situations of underemployment, and ignore constraints imposed by labour supply, (ii) in the open economy, excess demand for output is absorbed by imports, (iii) formulation (1) is consistent with excess supply, absorbed by reduced output ($Y < \bar{Y}$).

2.2. The determinants of exports and imports

The trade balance, in dollars, is defined by

$$B_e = \frac{P_x}{e} X - \frac{P_m}{e} M = \frac{P_x}{e} X - P_e M. \tag{2}$$

For the purposes of this paper, what matters is not the determination of the absolute value of exports and imports, but mostly their dependence on domestic costs (wages), both directly and through capacity adjustments. The significance of capacity is obvious enough. When a plant located in Belgium is closed down and new facilities are built abroad, the exported share of that plant's output drops out of Belgian exports, and the complementary share sold domestically may reappear (at least partly) under Belgian imports. The influence of costs is also well known, but less transparent, because it may exert itself through quantity adjustments, or through prices adjustments, or through a mixture of both.

To illustrate this point with an exports-tale, one may describe two hypothetical polar cases.[12] In the first case, domestic producers accept international prices 'passively', but react to price and cost conditions by adjusting their supply (possibly by adjusting their sales promotion efforts). The volume of exports then corresponds to the volume of supply at world prices P_e, given a supply curve shaped by domestic costs C and capacity $\bar{Y}$. In the second case, the domestic producers set their own export prices,

---

[11] Actual output is the minimum of notional supply, effective demand or full employment output; se Malinvaud (1977, 1980).

[12] These two cases are also distinguished under a different approach by Ginsburgh and Zang (1978).

then meet 'passively' the demand resulting from these prices (and from their sales promotion effort). The volume of exports then corresponds to world demand at export prices P_x/e, given a demand curve shaped by world demand E and world prices P_e (the prices charged by competitors). Furthermore, export prices will depend upon domestic costs C and capacity $\bar{Y}$ as well as upon the parameters of the world's demand function. (These export prices should in principle bring about equality of marginal costs and marginal revenues.)

If we could disaggregate exports by commodities i, and if we knew the set of indices I corresponding to the first case, then we could write (using lower case letters for microeconomic variables, using superscripts to denote supply S or demand D, and doing all our accounting in 'dollars')

$$\frac{P_{x_i}}{e} = P_{e_i}, \qquad x_i = x_i^S\left(\frac{P_{x_i}}{e}, \frac{C}{e}, \bar{y}_i\right) \quad \text{for} \quad i \in I,$$

$$\frac{P_{x_i}}{e} = \frac{P_{x_i}}{e}\left(\frac{C}{e}, \bar{y}_i, E, \dots\right), \quad x_i = x_i^D\left(\frac{P_{x_i}}{e}, E, P_{e_i}\right) \quad \text{for} \quad i \notin I.$$

Aggregating over commodities within the set I and within its complement, $\bar{I}$, we could write

$$\frac{P_x}{e} = P_e, \qquad X = X^S\left(\frac{P_x}{e} = P_e, \frac{C}{e}, \bar{Y}\right) \quad \text{for } I,$$

$$\frac{P_x}{e} = \frac{P_x}{e}\left(\frac{C}{e}, \bar{Y}, E, \dots\right), \quad X = X^D\left(\frac{P_x}{e}, E, P_e\right) \qquad \text{for } \bar{I}.$$

Short of having all the relevant microeconomic information, we could still pool the arguments of both price equations, and then of both quantity equations, into single aggregate relationships of the form

$$\frac{P_x}{e} = \frac{P_x}{e}\left(P_e, \frac{C}{e}, \bar{Y}, E, \dots\right), \qquad X = X\left(P_e, \frac{P_x}{e}, \frac{C}{e}, E, \bar{Y}\right). \tag{3}$$

The burden of the analysis is then shifted to the empirical level, at which one would hope to capture the relevant influence of each variable, through appropriate functional specifications and estimation procedures.

This tale is meant as an illustration and heuristic rationale for our approach, which is dictated by the availability of empirical evidence. It consists indeed in basing our empirical evaluation on eqs. (3).

However, due to meagreness of the data base, we neglect the influence of $\bar{Y}$, E and other variables on P_x/e, which is estimated as a function of

P_e and C/e alone. That being the case, it simplifies notations and derivations to substitute in (3) for P_x/e in the quantity equation from the price equation, thereby obtaining the simpler specification,[13]

$$\frac{P_x}{e} = \frac{P_x}{e}\left(P_e, \frac{C}{e}\right), \qquad X = X\left(P_e, \frac{C}{e}, E, \bar{Y}\right). \tag{4}$$

Turning to the imports side, we could tell a similar story (somewhat less convincingly, perhaps). But it would have the disadvantage of forcing us into specification and estimation of an equation defining the domestic price level P. This complication seems largely unnecessary, because empirical analyses of the dependence of Belgian imports on domestic prices or on domestic costs give similar results. Accordingly, theoretically justified distinctions would have no empirical counterpart. We shall proceed directly to a quantity equation similar to that in (4), with either C/e or P/e as second argument.

To complete the specification, we must still define aggregate domestic demand. In principle, that variable is best represented through its individual *gross* components: G, H (possibly divided into consumption and investment), and X (on account of the share of imports in intermediate deliveries to export industries).[14] Because we neglect the possible influence of the *composition* of final demand, we retain only $G + H$ and X. And because the Belgian balance of trade is so close to equilibrium, we use (1) and replace $G + H$ by the single variable Y, to simplify notation and derivations. Accordingly, our import equation is simply

$$M = M\left(P_e, \frac{C}{e}, Y, X, \bar{Y}\right) \quad \text{or} \quad M = M\left(P_e, \frac{P}{e}, Y, X, \bar{Y}\right). \tag{5}$$

2.3. *The elasticity of employment with respect to real wages*

Substituting from (4) and (5) into (2), we obtain the external balance constraint in a form suitable for our purposes,

$$B_e = \left(\frac{P_x}{e}\left(P_e, \frac{C}{e}\right)\right)X\left(P_e, \frac{C}{e}, E, \bar{Y}\right) - P_e M\left(P_e, \frac{C}{e}, Y, X, \bar{Y}\right) \geq \bar{B}_e, \tag{6}$$

---

[13] In empirical evaluation, we shall have to remember that X depends upon C/e and P_e both directly and through P_x/e.

[14] In the import equations of SERENA, these components are weighted by import shares and aggregated into a single variable.

where $\bar{B}_e$ is some preassigned number of 'dollars' (close to zero in the Belgian historical experience). Total differentiation of (6) enables us to estimate the adjustment in domestic demand dY that should accompany an exogenous change in some other variable $d\theta$, if B_e is to *remain equal* to $\bar{B}_e$,

$$0 = dB_e = \frac{\partial B_e}{\partial \theta} d\theta + \frac{\partial B_e}{\partial Y} dY = \frac{\partial B_e}{\partial \theta} d\theta - P_e \frac{\partial M}{\partial Y} dY, \tag{7}$$

$$\frac{dY}{d\theta}\bigg|_{B_e} = \frac{\partial B_e}{\partial \theta} \bigg/ P_e \frac{\partial M}{\partial Y}. \tag{8}$$

In order to estimate the trade-off between real wages and output, then employment, under the assumptions of this section, there remains only to apply formula (8), with $\theta = W/P$ (*real* wages), then translate output changes into employment changes.

For clarity of exposition, we first keep $\bar{Y}$ fixed, and look at a change in nominal wages; thus,

$$\begin{aligned}
\frac{dY}{dW}\bigg|_{B_e,\bar{Y}} &= \left[\frac{X}{e} \frac{\partial P_x}{\partial(C/e)} \frac{\partial(C/e)}{\partial W} + \left(\frac{P_x}{e} - P_e \frac{\partial M}{\partial X} \right) \frac{\partial X}{\partial(C/e)} \frac{\partial(C/e)}{\partial W} \right. \\
&\quad \left. - P_e \frac{\partial M}{\partial(C/e)} \frac{\partial(C/e)}{\partial W} \right] \bigg/ P_e \frac{\partial M}{\partial Y} \\
&= \left[\frac{X}{e} \frac{\partial P_x}{\partial C} \frac{\partial C}{\partial W} + \left(\frac{P_x}{e} - P_e \frac{\partial M}{\partial X} \right) \frac{\partial X}{\partial C} \frac{\partial C}{\partial W} \right. \\
&\quad \left. - P_e \frac{\partial M}{\partial C} \frac{\partial C}{\partial W} \right] \bigg/ P_e \frac{\partial M}{\partial Y}.
\end{aligned} \tag{9}$$

In elasticity terms (denoting all elasticities by η),

$$\eta_{YW}|_{B_e,\bar{Y}} = \left[\frac{XP_x}{MeP_e} \eta_{P_xC} + \left(\frac{XP_x}{MeP_e} - \eta_{MX} \right) \eta_{XC} - \eta_{MC} \right] \eta_{CW}/\eta_{MY}. \tag{10}$$

Under balance of trade equilibrium, $X(P_x/e) = MP_e$, so that

$$\eta_{YW}|_{B_e=0,\bar{Y}} = [\eta_{P_xC} + (1 - \eta_{MX})\eta_{XC} - \eta_{MC}]\eta_{CW}/\eta_{MY}, \tag{11}$$

$$\begin{aligned}
\eta_{LW}|_{B_e=0,\bar{Y}} &= \eta_{LY} \cdot \eta_{YW}|_{B_e=0,\bar{Y}} \\
&= [\eta_{P_xC} + (1 - \eta_{MX})\eta_{XC} - \eta_{MC}]\eta_{CW}\eta_{LY}/\eta_{MY}.
\end{aligned} \tag{12}$$

Going on to real wages, we note that

$$\eta_{Y \cdot W/P} = \eta_{YW}\eta_{W \cdot W/P} = \eta_{YW}/\eta_{W/P \cdot W} = \eta_{YW}/(1 - \eta_{PW}), \tag{13}$$

so that

$$\eta_{L \cdot W/P}|_{B_e = 0, Y} = [\eta_{P_x C} + (1 - \eta_{MX})\eta_{XC} - \eta_{MC}]\eta_{CW}\eta_{LY}/\eta_{MY}(1 - \eta_{PW}). \tag{14}$$

We shall use eq. (14) to estimate the short-run elasticity of employment with respect to real wages, keeping capacity constant. The interpretation of this formula is easier if one starts with (11). In the numerator of (11), we find the percentage impact of a rise in wages on export prices, exports and imports, hence on the balance of trade. (The impact on imports is adjusted for the import content of exports, through the term η_{MX}.) Dividing by the income elasticity of imports gives us the percentage reduction of domestic demand needed to restore external balance. Multiplying by the elasticity of employment with respect to output, η_{LY}, yields the corresponding percentage adjustment in employment (12). Finally, a mechanical formula enables us to go from nominal wages to real wages (14).

In order to take the influence of capacity into account, we extend (9)–(14) into

$$\frac{dY}{dW}\bigg|_{B_e} = \left[\left(\frac{X}{e}\frac{\partial P_x}{\partial C} + \frac{P_x}{e}\frac{\partial X}{\partial C} - P_e\frac{\partial M}{\partial X}\frac{\partial X}{\partial C} - P_e\frac{\partial M}{\partial C}\right)\frac{\partial C}{\partial W}\right.$$
$$\left. + \left(\frac{P_x}{e}\frac{\partial X}{\partial \bar{Y}} - P_e\frac{\partial M}{\partial X}\frac{\partial X}{\partial \bar{Y}} - P_e\frac{\partial M}{\partial \bar{Y}}\right)\frac{\partial \bar{Y}}{\partial W}\right] \bigg/ P_e\frac{\partial M}{\partial Y}, \tag{15}$$

$$\eta_{L(W/P)}|_{B_e = 0} = [(\eta_{P_x C} + \eta_{XC} - \eta_{MX}\eta_{XC} - \eta_{MC})\eta_{CW}$$
$$+ (\eta_{X\bar{Y}} - \eta_{MX}\eta_{X\bar{Y}} - \eta_{M\bar{Y}})\eta_{\bar{Y}W}]\eta_{LY}/\eta_{MY}(1 - \eta_{PW}). \tag{16}$$

We shall use eq. (16) to estimate the medium-run elasticity of employment with respect to real wages, taking capacity adjustments into account.

The distinction between short and medium run is particularly relevant for the estimation of η_{LY} – a point elaborated below. Capacity adjustments through scrapping require little time and could thus take place in the short run. Being irreversible, however, they are decided on the basis of medium-run considerations. And capacity adjustments through new investment take time.

In concluding this section, we wish to remind the reader of three approximations embodied in our formulae, namely: $\eta_{P_x Y} = 0$, $\eta_{P_m W} = 0$ and $\eta_{P_m \bar{Y}} = 0$. In other empirical contexts, the corresponding terms should be reintroduced in formulae (14) and (16).

3. Empirical Evaluation

3.1. *Organization*

As announced in the introduction, our empirical analysis combines three sources of information:

(i)   the published models of the Belgian economy – ANELISE, BREUGHEL, COMET, DESMOS, LINK and RENA,

(ii)   the international trade sector of the new model SERENA,

(iii)   the simulation of the Dutch clay–clay vintage model, on which our estimation of $\eta_{\bar{Y}W}$ is based.

We first introduce our methodology by discussing the evaluation of $\eta_{Y(W/P)}|_{B_e = 0, Y}$ as defined through (11) and (13).

3.2. *Import and export elasticities*

Most of the models referred to above contain estimates of the elasticities of export prices with respect to wages, of the volume of exports with respect to export prices, and of imports with respect to domestic prices and domestic demand. In order to use these estimates, we write

$$\eta_{Y(W/P)}|_{B_e = 0, \bar{Y}} = [\eta_{P_x W} + (1 - \eta_{MX})\eta_{XW} - \eta_{MW}]/\eta_{MY}(1 - \eta_{PW}),$$

$$\eta_{XW} = \eta_{XP_x} \cdot \eta_{P_x W}, \quad \eta_{MW} = \eta_{MP} \cdot \eta_{PW}, \tag{13'}$$

$$\eta_{Y(W/P)}|_{B_e = 0, \bar{Y}} = [\eta_{P_x W} + (1 - \eta_{MX})\eta_{XP_x}\eta_{P_x W}$$
$$- \eta_{MP}\eta_{PW}]/\eta_{MY}(1 - \eta_{PW})$$
$$=_{\text{def}} \frac{\eta_{\Xi W} - \eta_{MP}\eta_{PW}}{\eta_{MY}(1 - \eta_{PW})},$$

$$\eta_{\Xi W} =_{\text{def}} \eta_{P_x W} + (1 - \eta_{MX})\eta_{XP_x}\eta_{P_x W}. \tag{13''}$$

In formula (13''), $\eta_{Y \cdot (W/P)}$ is expressed as a function of 4 elasticities, namely $\eta_{\Xi W}$ (as just defined), η_{MP}, η_{PW} and η_{MY}. In table 14.1, we present

Table 14.1

	$\eta_{P_xW} \times \eta_{XP_x} = \eta_{XW}$			$\eta_{\Xi W}$ [a]	$\eta_{MP} \times \eta_{PW} = \eta_{MW}$			η_{MY}	$\eta_{Y(W/P)}\vert_{B_r=0.5}$	η_{LY}
	η_{P_xW}	η_{XP_x}	η_{XW}		η_{MP}	η_{PW}	η_{MW}			
(1) ANELISE[b]					0.38			1.35		0.5 (0.9)[c]
(2) BREUGHEL	0.44	−0.5	−0.22	+0.31	0.36	0.56	0.20	1.67	+0.15	0.23
(3) COMET	0	−0.6	0	0	0.17	0.33	0.056	1.42	−0.06	0.3
(4) DESMOS	0.45	−1.6	−0.72	+0.02	0.32	0.3	0.10	1.26	−0.09	0.3 (0.88)[c]
(5) LINK	0.23	−2.6	−0.6	−0.13	0.44					
(6) RENA	0.58 or 0.14	−2.7	−1.57	−0.36		0.2	0.09	1.95	−0.29 or −0.08	
(7) AVERAGE	0.30	−1.6	−0.30 / −0.57	0.004 / −0.04	0.33	0.35	0.11	1.55	−0.07[d] or −0.15[e]	
(8) σ (subjective) Range				0.20	0.15	0.20 ≦0.85		0.25		
(9) SERENA	0.08		−0.64	−0.30			0.19	1.53 (1.24)[c]	−0.48	
(10) σ (adjusted)[f]				0.20			0.18	0.25		

[a] Always computed with $\eta_{MX} = 0.4$.
[b] Exports are exogenous in ANELISE.
[c] Long-term elasticities.
[d] Average of computed values in the same column.
[e] Computed from average values in the same row.
[f] Covariance $(\eta_{MW}, \eta_{MY}) = 0.00875$.

the point estimates for each of these elasticities, or its components, as reported in the various econometric models for Belgium. Subjective probability densities for $\eta_{\Xi W}$, η_{MP}, η_{PW} and η_{MY} are specified by means of independent normal densities, centred at the average values of these point estimates [line (7)], with standard deviations subjectively assessed so as to reflect (conservatively) the dispersion of the point estimates [line (8)]. The density for η_{PW} is truncated at 0.85 to avoid dividing by arbitrarily small numbers in (13″).[15]

From the four normal densities so defined one can compute a marginal density for $\eta_{Y(W/P)}$.[16] It is exhibited as fig. 14.2. The density is unimodal and moderately skewed, with a mean of -0.2, a median of -0.15, a mode of -0.12, and a standard deviation of 0.32 roughly equal to the interquartile range. The probability of a positive elasticity, corresponding to situations where the positive term $\eta_{P_x W}$ dominates the negative terms, is close to 0.25, which seems excessive.

Line (9) of table 14.1 gives the point estimates obtained for the manufacturing sector in the SERENA model. The import and export equations of that model, which correspond closely to the specification of Section 2.2, are reproduced in the appendix. The estimation is based on (annual) data for the period 1966–1976, which we regard as more directly relevant than earlier years. These points estimates are not very different from the *average* values coming from the other models. The major discrepancy concerns $\eta_{P_x W}$, and should be investigated further.[17]

A systematic Bayesian analysis of the SERENA equations for export prices and export quantities has been carried out by Bauwens (1979). His analysis includes the case of non-informative priors, which we have retained throughout. He has kindly extended his computations, to obtain the marginal posterior density for $\eta_{\Xi W}$; results and analytical details are given in the appendix. On the import side, a posterior joint density for η_{MW} and η_{MY} is easily obtained. Using again normal approximations and combining these two densities with that defined above for η_{PW}, we have computed the marginal posterior density for $\eta_{Y(W/P)}$. It is exhibited as fig. 14.3. It is again unimodal and moderately skewed, with a mean of -0.6,

[15] A similar precaution for η_{MY} was not necessary, because that variable is integrated out analytically, and zero is more than 6 standard deviations away from the mean.

[16] We thank Hans Tompa for carrying out these computations, using the bivariate numerical integration routines developed by him under the auspices of the Programme National d'Impulsion à la Recherche en Informatique of the Belgian Government.

[17] The model SERENA estimates $\eta_{P_x C}$ as ~ 0.22, leading to $\eta_{P_x W} = \eta_{P_x C} \eta_{CW} \sim 0.08$ when $\eta_{CW} \sim \frac{1}{3}$. Replacing C by W in appendix eq. (A.5) yields the direct estimate $\eta_{P_x W} \sim 0.15$, which we suspect to be biased upwards by the fact that W then serves in part as a proxy for other components of C.

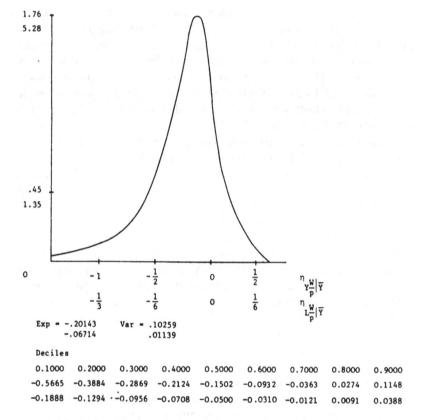

Exp = −.20143   Var = .10259
      −.06714   .01139

Deciles

0.1000	0.2000	0.3000	0.4000	0.5000	0.6000	0.7000	0.8000	0.9000
−0.5665	−0.3884	−0.2869	−0.2124	−0.1502	−0.0932	−0.0363	0.0274	0.1148
−0.1888	−0.1294	−0.0956	−0.0708	−0.0500	−0.0310	−0.0121	0.0091	0.0388

Fig. 14.2.   Short-run estimates from macromodels.

a median of −0.5, a mode of −0.36, and a standard deviation of 0.44 roughly equal to the interquartile range. The probability of a positive elasticity is now much smaller – some 7%.

To the extent that the densities in figs. 14.2 and 14.3 are derived from the same data base, it would be improper to use one of them to revise the other through Bayes theorem. But it would be legitimate to average them, with weights reflecting the subjective probabilities assigned to the alternative specifications underlying the two approaches. Because both densities ultimately lead to the same substantive conclusions, we do not pursue the matter further.

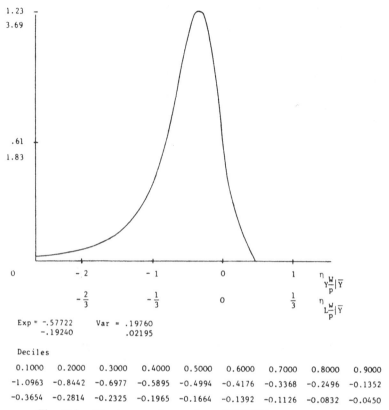

Exp = -.57722   Var = .19760
      -.19240   .02195

Deciles

0.1000	0.2000	0.3000	0.4000	0.5000	0.6000	0.7000	0.8000	0.9000
-1.0963	-0.8442	-0.6977	-0.5895	-0.4994	-0.4176	-0.3368	-0.2496	-0.1352
-0.3654	-0.2814	-0.2325	-0.1965	-0.1664	-0.1392	-0.1126	-0.0832	-0.0450

Fig. 14.3.   Short-run estimates from SERENA.

3.3.   Output elasticity of employment

As for η_{LY}, which is almost the same concept as in Okun's Law, we must distinguish carefully between the short-run elasticity and the medium-run elasticity. The models do likewise, suggesting short-run elasticities of 0.3 as in COMET and DESMOS[18] but long-run elasticities of 0.9 as in ANELISE and DESMOS. The main reason for the distinction is of course that labour is a semi-fixed factor in the short run but not in the medium or long run.

[18] The short-run estimate of η_{LY} is 0.23 in BREUGHEL and 0.5 in ANELISE. Okun's estimate is 0.33 for the U.S., where employment is less stable than in Europe, but where participation rates are also less stable, and included in Okun's estimate.

Given the high probability that $\eta_{Y(W/P)}$ is small, it did not seem important to refine the analysis of the transition from $\eta_{Y(W/P)}$ to $\eta_{L(W/P)} = \eta_{Y(W/P)} \cdot \eta_{LY}$. In principle, one should multiply $\eta_{Y(W/P)}$ by a random variable, centred around 0.3 for the short-run analysis and endowed with a suitable distribution. We have omitted that refinement and supplied an alternative scale in figs. 14.2 and 14.3; the conditional density of $\eta_{L(W/P)}$, given that $\eta_{LY} = 0.3$, is simply the density of $\eta_{Y(W/P)}$, rescaled by a factor of 0.3. The substantive conclusions to which both figures lead are the same; namely that $\eta_{L(W/P)}|_{B_e = 0, \dot{Y}}$ is small in absolute value, the order of magnitude being -0.1 to -0.2, and is contained in the interval $(-0.5, 0)$ with a probability close to 0.9.

3.4. Capacity adjustments

Turning to the role of capacity adjustments, we shall retain the SERENA point estimates of $\eta_{X\dot{Y}} = 0.77$ and $\eta_{M\dot{Y}} = 0.29$, whereby $(1 - \eta_{MX})\eta_{X\dot{Y}} - \eta_{M\dot{Y}} = 0.75$. Although capacity variables (usually a degree of utilisation) play little role in the foreign trade equations of other models, a coefficient close to unity also appears in the DESMOS model, and corresponds well to what we want to capture. The more elusive coefficient is of course $\eta_{\dot{Y}W}$. On *a priori* grounds, one would expect that elasticity to be sizeable, reflecting the spatial relocation of capacity induced by comparisons of labour costs in Belgium with those prevailing: In low-wage areas of Asia, North Africa etc., where multinational as well as domestic firms invest; in other EEC countries, where real wages have increased more slowly than in Belgium over the past decade; in industrialised countries like the U.S. or the U.K., whose competitiveness has improved through real currency depreciation.

An empirical basis appropriate for quantifying this phenomenon is obviously lacking. We do feel, however, that an *indication* about the value of $\eta_{\dot{Y}W}$ is given by the simulation results for the Dutch clay–clay vintage model, as reported by Kuipers and Bosch (1976). The model, based on earlier work of Solow (1962) or Phelps (1963), is described as follows by den Hartog and Tjan (1976, p. 37):

Equipment is classified into vintages according to the year of installation. With respect to the relation between installed equipment, production and labour for each vintage the following assumptions hold:
—Production capacity is determined by installed equipment. Capital productivity – that is, the inverse of the capital-output ratio – is equal for all vintages of equipment and, in addition, remains constant in the course of time.

—Labour requirements per unit of equipment decrease with a constant relative rate the younger a vintage of equipment is; labour requirements, however, become fixed at the moment of installation of new equipment.

The workings of the model are described as follows by the same authors (*ibid*, p. 40):

... if the revenue of a vintage covers its wage sum ... this vintage will be kept in operation. If this revenue is lower the vintage will be scrapped ... . Thus, if real labour costs either fall or remain constant this brings about a lengthening of economic life span of the oldest vintage. If the rate of increase of real labour costs, however, equals the rate of labour saving technical progress then the economic life span remains constant. A faster rate of increase causes a shortening of the economic life span of the oldest vintage in operation.

Using this model, and empirical estimates of its parameters for the Netherlands (including a rate of labour saving technical progress close to 5%), Kuipers and Bosch (1976) have simulated labour demand six years ahead under alternative assumptions about the rate of investment and the rate of increase of real wages. The differences in employment associated with differences in the level of real wages imply elasticities ranging from −1.4 in the first year to nearly −2 in the last year.[19]

These elasticities reflect accelerated scrapping of existing equipment becoming unprofitable at the higher real wages. They do not include any influence of real wages on new investment. On this score, they provide a lower bound to the elasticity of employment with respect to real wages through capacity adjustments. On the other hand, the clay–clay approach exaggerates the elasticity of capacity with respect to real wages. Some *ex post* substitution of capital for labour would slow down the scrapping process. These two sources of bias go in opposite directions, and we use the median figure of −1.7 in the case of Belgium. We realise that estimation and simulation of a similar model with Belgian data could give different results. But we are unable to guess in what direction the difference would go, and can only account for that by assigning to this estimate a substantial standard error.

[19] See the figures in table 14.2. With an initial employment level of 3,863,000 persons, a decrease of 55,000 jobs amounts to 1.42% of the total labour force.

Table 14.2[a]

Year	i = 6%				i = 5%				i = 4%			
	ω = 6%	ω = 5%	ω = 4%	ω = 3%	ω = 6%	ω = 5%	ω = 4%	ω = 3%	ω = 6%	ω = 5%	ω = 4%	ω = 3%
Predictions of capacity demand for labour in the period 1975–1980 in thousands of man-years												
1974	3863[b]	3863[b]	3863[b]	3863[b]	3863[b]	3863[b]	3863[b]	3863[b]	3863[b]	3863[b]	3863[b]	3863[b]
1975	3879	3934	3989	4045	3876	3931	3986	4042	3873	3928	3983	4039
1976	3816	3927	4036	4146	3807	3918	4027	4136	3798	3909	4017	4127
1977	3742	3919	4086	4252	3723	3900	4067	4233	3705	3882	4049	4215
1978	3669	3903	4136	4362	3638	3872	4105	4331	3607	3841	4047	4300
1979	3566	3881	4180	4468	3518	3834	4132	4420	3472	3788	4086	4374
1980	3448	3854	4227	4576	3381	3787	4161	4509	3317	3722	4096	4444
Predictions of structural unemployment in the period 1975–1980 in thousands of man-years												
1974	246[b]	246[b]	246[b]	246[b]	246[b]	246[b]	246[b]	246[b]	246[b]	246[b]	246[b]	246[b]
1975	229	174	119	63	232	177	122	66	235	181	125	69
1976	292	181	72	−38	301	190	81	−28	311	199	91	−19
1977	366	189	22	−144	385	207	41	−125	407	226	59	−107
1978	439	205	−28	−256	470	237	3	−223	501	267	34	−192
1979	542	227	−72	−360	590	274	−25	−312	636	320	21	−266
1980	660	254	−119	−468	727	321	−53	−401	792	386	11	−337

[a] i = rate of growth of investment; ω = rate of growth of real wages.
[b] Actual figures.
Source: Kuipers and Bosch (1976, p. 78, tables 4.1 and 4.2).

We have evaluated (16) as

$$
\begin{aligned}
\eta_{L(W/P)}\big|_{B_e=0} &= \frac{\eta_{\Xi W} - \eta_{MP}\eta_{PW}}{\eta_{MY}(1-\eta_{PW})}\eta_{LY} \\
&\quad + \frac{\eta_{X\bar{Y}}(1-\eta_{MX}) - \eta_{M\bar{Y}}}{\eta_{MY}}\eta_{L\bar{Y}}\eta_{\bar{Y}(W/P)} \\
&\underset{\text{def}}{=} \frac{\eta_{\Xi W} - \eta_{MP}\eta_{PW}}{\eta_{MY}(1-\eta_{PW})}(0.9) + \frac{0.75\eta_{L\bar{Y}}\eta_{\bar{Y}(W/P)}}{\eta_{MY}} \\
&= \eta_{Y(W/P)}\big|_{B_e=0,\bar{Y}}(0.9) + \frac{\eta_{L\bar{Y}}\eta_{\bar{Y}(W/P)}}{\eta_{MY}}(0.75),
\end{aligned}
\tag{16'}
$$

with the first term as already discussed in section 3.2 and with a normal density for $\eta_{L\bar{Y}}\eta_{\bar{Y}(W/P)}$ centred at -1.7 with a standard error of 0.7. The resulting densities for $\eta_{L(W/P)}\big|_{B_e=0}$ are given in fig. 14.4, using the information from published econometric models; and in fig. 14.5, using the information from SERENA.

These two densities are similar in shape – being both unimodal and moderately skewed – but their moments are not equal. On the basis of the published models, we have in fig. 14.4 an expected value of -1.12 and a standard deviation of 0.53. On the basis of SERENA, we have in fig. 14.5 an expected value of -1.82 and a standard deviation of 0.8. The difference in expectations is due in part to different densities for $\eta_{Y(W/P)|\bar{Y}}$, as already revealed by figs. 14.2 and 14.3, and in part to different densities for η_{MY} in the denominators. The expectation of η_{MY} is 1.55 in the case of fig. 14.4, but 1.24 in the case of fig. 14.5. We regard the latter figure as more reasonable.[20]

For this reason, and because we regard the export equations in SERENA as more satisfactory on theoretical grounds (specification) as well as empirical grounds (sample period and estimation method), we do not average the densities in figs. 14.4 and 14.5. We use instead the density of fig. 14.5 to estimate the medium-run elasticity of employment with respect to real wages. That density implies an elasticity greater than unity (in absolute value) with probability 0.87.[21]

[20] Import equations estimated for EEC countries with annual data for the period 1953–1976 yield estimates of η_{MY} ranging from -1.33 to -1.81, with very small standard errors; and estimates for $\eta_{M(W/P)}$ and η_{MY} which are generally insignificant or unreasonable. But income elasticities probably reflect the positive trend in the share of international trade in economic activities. Conditionally on estimates of η_{MY} adjusted downwards by 0.3 or so, the estimates of the other coefficients become much more reasonable. A value of η_{MY} close to unity would make sense in the case of Belgium.

[21] The corresponding probability in fig. 14.4 is 0.57. If the expectation of η_{MY} were lowered from 1.55 to 1.24, that probability would become 0.7.

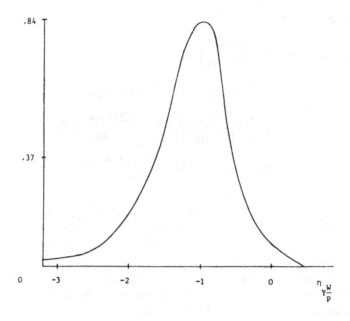

Exp = -1.1230   Var = .27454

Deciles

0.1000	0.2000	0.3000	0.4000	0.5000	0.6000	0.7000	0.8000	0.9000
-1.7834	-1.5150	-1.3411	-1.2015	-1.0775	-0.9587	-0.8361	-0.6973	-0.5106

Fig. 14.4.   Medium-run estimates from macro-models.

The results of our empirical analysis, crude as it may be, are summarised in fig. 14.6, which reproduces the densities of figs. 14.3 and 14.5 drawn to the same scale. This figure is the starting point for our policy discussion in Section 5. In order to avoid giving a spurious impression of accuracy, we do refer in Section 5 to a short-run elasticity like −0.2 and to a medium-run elasticity like −2. The reader is referred to fig. 14.6 for drawing his own sharper conclusions.

4.   Exchange rate adjustments

4.1.   Formula

Without attempting to treat the subject as extensively as it deserves, we may apply the methodology of Section 2 to evaluate the effects on

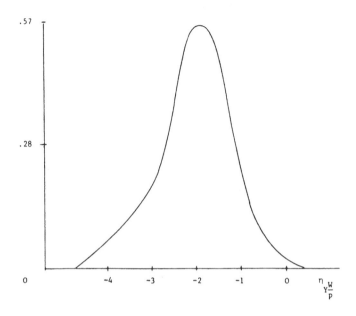

Exp = -1.8221   Var = .63052

Deciles

0.1000	0.2000	0.3000	0.4000	0.5000	0.6000	0.7000	0.8000	0.9000
-2.8210	-2.3968	-2.1270	-1.9152	-1.7298	-1.5547	-1.3769	-1.1793	-0.9202

Fig. 14.5.   Medium-run estimates from SERENA.

employment of exchange rate adjustments. We shall go quickly through the derivation, introduce some estimates borrowed from two recent Belgian studies, and conclude with a few comments.

We use formula (8) with $\theta = e$. In order to capitalize on our work in section 3 and because the published studies deal with η_{Ce} and η_{Pe}, but not directly with $\eta_{P_x e}$, we shall work through η_{XC} and η_{MP}. To that end, we note from eq. (4) that $\eta_{P_x e} = 1 + \eta_{P_x C}(-1 + \eta_{Ce})$, and use the following relationships:

$$\frac{\partial X}{\partial e} = \frac{\partial X}{\partial C}\left(\frac{\partial C}{\partial e} - \frac{C}{e}\right), \qquad \frac{\partial M}{\partial e} = \frac{\partial M}{\partial P}\left(\frac{\partial P}{\partial e} - \frac{P}{e}\right). \tag{17}$$

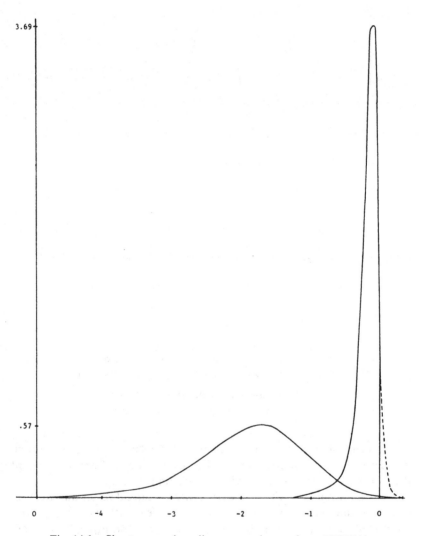

Fig. 14.6. Short-run and medium-run estimates from SERENA.

Consequently,

$$\frac{\partial B_e}{\partial e} = -\frac{P_x X}{e^2} + \frac{X}{e}\frac{\partial P_x}{\partial e} + \left(\frac{P_x}{e} - P_e\frac{\partial M}{\partial X}\right)\frac{\partial X}{\partial C}$$

$$\times \left(-\frac{C}{e} + \frac{\partial C}{\partial e}\right) - P_e\frac{\partial M}{\partial P}\left(-\frac{P}{e} + \frac{\partial P}{\partial e}\right)$$

$$= \frac{XP_x}{e^2}[-1 + \eta_{P_xe} + \eta_{XC}(-1 + \eta_{Ce})]$$

$$-\frac{P_eM}{e}[\eta_{MP}(-1 + \eta_{Pe}) + \eta_{MX}\eta_{XC}(-1 + \eta_{Ce})]$$

$$= \frac{XP_x}{e^2}(\eta_{P_xC} + \eta_{XC})(-1 + \eta_{Ce})$$

$$-\frac{PeM}{e}[\eta_{MP}(-1 + \eta_{Pe}) + \eta_{MX}\eta_{XC}(-1 + \eta_{Ce})], \tag{18}$$

$$\eta_{Ye}|_{B_e} = \left[\frac{XP_x}{MeP_e}(\eta_{P_xC} + \eta_{XC})(-1 + \eta_{Ce})\right.$$

$$\left. - \eta_{MP}(-1 + \eta_{Pe}) - \eta_{MX}\eta_{XC}(-1 + \eta_{Ce})\right]\bigg/\eta_{MY}, \tag{19}$$

$$\eta_{Le}|_{B_e=0} = [(\eta_{P_xC} + \eta_{XC} - \eta_{MX}\eta_{XC})(-1 + \eta_{Ce})$$

$$- \eta_{MP}(-1 + \eta_{Pe})]\eta_{LY}/\eta_{MY}. \tag{20}$$

4.2. Numerical evaluation

In a recent publication, the Banque Nationale de Belgique (1978) has used input–output matrices to study the impact of a devaluation on domestic prices P and on costs in export industries C. Both short-run (1 year) and medium-run (3 years) elasticities are reported, first under the assumption that wages only are indexed, next under the assumption that all costs are indexed (remain constant in real terms). The results are summarised in table 14.3, rows 1 and 2. It would seem most natural to assume that non-wage costs do not adjust in the short run, but do so in the medium run. The first and fourth columns of table 14.3 would thus seem most significant. Still, we do the computation for each column, using the figures collected in section 3, with η_{LY} equal to 0.3 in the '1 year' calculations and to 0.9 in the '3 years' calculations.

Table 14.3

| | Banque Nationale de Belgique | | | | De Grauwe–Holvoet | |
| | Only wages indexed | | All costs indexed | | | |
	1 year	3 years	1 year	3 years		
η_{P_e}	0.52	0.56	0.74	1.11	0.64	
η_{C_e}	0.64	0.66	0.73	0.88	0.80	
η_{LY}	0.3	0.9	0.3	0.9	0.3	0.9
$\eta_{Le}\vert_{B_e=0}$[a]	0.12	0.33	0.08	0.03	0.08	0.24

[a]Computed by (20′).

In an independent publication, De Grauwe and Holvoet (1978), using the so-called Scandinavian model, estimate η_{P_e} and η_{C_e} for EEC-countries. Their results appear in column 5, for the case where wages are indexed. It is assumed that export prices in 'dollars' do not change and that cost increases in the sheltered sector are passed on to domestic prices.
Using the point estimates from SERENA, our evaluation of (20) is

$$\eta_{Le}\vert_{B_e=0} \simeq [-0.92(-1 + \eta_{C_e}) - 0.56(-1 + \eta_{P_e})]\frac{\eta_{LY}}{1.53}. \qquad (20')$$

The results are given in row 4 of table 14.3.

4.3. Comments

The figures in the first two rows of table 14.3 are not all equally plausible, and some of them are difficult to fit into a consistent overall picture. We do not mean to endorse them uniformly. But they cover a broad range of hypotheses, and the calculations uniformly suggest a rather limited impact of a devaluation on employment.

With Belgian exporters behaving largely as price-takers, a devaluation would hardly stimulate employment in the short run, where the elasticity of employment to output is low. With Belgian wages fully indexed, a devaluation would not stimulate employment appreciably in the long run, where domestic prices and costs progressively adjust and restore the previous conditions of international competitiveness.

Of course, a short-run elasticity of employment with respect to the exchange rate equal to 0.12 is not really negligible, and some might suggest that a 30% devaluation would be justified if it did result in a 4% increase in employment. But there is room for argument here. Important elements are neglected – like the elusive effects of a devaluation on the non-trade items in the balance of payments or on capacity adjustments; and the distributive aspects of a sharp rise in prices cannot be ignored.

The purpose of the exercise in this section is not to claim that the present exchange rate, or exchange rate policy, of Belgium are optimal. It is rather to suggest that the analysis of Sections 2 and 3, under a fixed (managed) exchange rate, is not grossly misleading, in the short run as well as in the long run.

5. Policy Implications

5.1. *Summary of findings*

As announced in Section 1.4, 'the conclusions from our empirical investigation are first that estimates of the trade-off between real wages and employment in Belgium are subject to considerable imprecision; second that the short-run elasticity of employment with respect to real wages keeping capacity constant is probably quite small (like −0.2), and definitely less than unity in absolute value; third that the corresponding medium-run elasticity taking into account capacity adjustments is probably sizeable (like − 2), and definitely larger than unity in absolute value; and fourth that exchange rate adjustments might not make too much difference, in either the short or the medium run'. Also, it is worth emphasising that the capacity adjustments affecting employment take the form of accelerated scrapping. The simulations by Kuipers and Bosch reveal that the effects of new investment are less sizeable, in addition to being less immediate; of course, given enough time, they become dominant.

These findings are not surprising, considering on the one hand that labour has become a semi-fixed factor of production; on the other hand that an international redistribution of employment is under way. For policy purposes, our results provide, in spite of their imprecision, unequivocal answers to several questions of immediate interest to decision-makers, including labour unions.

The short-run inelasticity means that general wage policies (for instance general rebates on employer contributions to social security) are unlikely to provide an effective stimulus to employment in the short run. Measures aimed at an immediate impact must be sought in different directions – like selective wage policies or work-sharing schemes, about which more below. But the medium-run elasticity means that such measures should be designed in a way that carefully avoids increases in wage costs – for otherwise the medium-run effects could become adverse. Instead, measures promoting simultaneously work sharing and wage restraint over time could provide a much needed stimulus to employment in the short as well as the medium run.

5.2. *Wages and union policies*

Looking at these problems from the viewpoint of labour unions, the question of central interest is whether the elasticity of employment with respect to real wages is greater or smaller than unity, in absolute value. This question is of central interest because total real labour income is equal to $(W/P)L$, and

$$\frac{d(W/P)L}{d(W/P)} = L + \frac{W}{P}\frac{dL}{d(W/P)} = L(1 + \eta_{L(W/P)}). \tag{21}$$

So long as $\eta_{L(W/P)} > -1$ (or $|\eta_{L(W/P)}| < 1$), the unions have an obvious motivation to press for higher real wages, even in full awareness of a negative impact on employment. The motivation is particularly strong if the reduction in employment is distributed more or less evenly through a reduction of working hours instead of being concentrated on a smaller number of totally unemployed workers; for in this way there are no victims, and everybody enjoys additional leisure. Our findings accordingly suggest that *the unions' demand of a shorter working week without pay cut is entirely rational on short-run considerations.* Long-run considerations tell a different story, however, in which the numerical magnitude of the wage elasticity of employment plays a role.

Indeed, pursuing our line of analysis one step further, we may bring out the first-order condition for an *optimal real wage and working week, taking the utility of leisure into account.* Using the symbol L to denote total labour demand in man hours and N to denote the working population, here assumed given, we write $h = L/N$ for the amount of labour (hours) performed by one worker and $r = (W/P)(L/N)$ for the corresponding real labour income. Conceptually, the choice of a working week is a collective choice, to which public-goods theory is applicable – see Weddepohl (1979). It is still of some interest to consider the solution that would emerge, taking $\eta_{L(W/P)}$ into account, if all workers had the same utility function $u(r, h)$ with arguments real income r and hours worked h. In that case,[22]

$$u(r, h) = u\left(\frac{W}{P}\frac{L}{N}, \frac{L}{N}\right), \quad \frac{du}{d(W/P)} = \frac{\partial u}{\partial r} \cdot \left(\frac{L}{N} + \frac{W}{PN}\frac{\partial L}{\partial(W/P)}\right) + \frac{\partial u}{\partial h}\left(\frac{1}{N}\frac{\partial L}{\partial(W/P)}\right),$$

(22)

$$\frac{du}{d(W/P)} \lesseqgtr 0 \quad \text{as} \quad -\frac{\partial u/\partial h}{\partial u/\partial r} = \frac{dr}{dh}\bigg|_u \lesseqgtr \frac{W}{P}(1 + \eta_{(W/P)\cdot L}).$$

(23)

This is of course a familiar monopolistic solution[23] which requires $|\eta_{L(W/P)}| > 1$ at an optimum. If $\eta_{L(W/P)}|_{B_e} \simeq -2$, then (23) requires $dr/dh|_u \simeq \frac{1}{2}(W/P)$; and if $\eta_{L(W/P)} \simeq -1.5$, then (23) requires $dr/dh|_u \simeq \frac{1}{3}(W/P)$; that is, a real wage equal respectively to two or three times the marginal rate of substitution between leisure and income.

It is thus conceivable for labour to choose deliberately a combination of relatively high real wages and relatively low (but equally distributed) employment, at a solution of (23). For moderate values of $\eta_{L(W/P)}$, such a solution makes sense.[24] But its monopolistic nature also implies that each *individual* would prefer to work more hours at the going wage rate, to

---

[22] Formula (23) remains valid if one takes into account unemployment in an attempt to define a real wage, a working week *and an implied unemployment rate* which are *simultaneously optimal* from labour's viewpoint. If unemployment compensation is equal to U and treated as exogenously given, then a worker's utility is equal to $u((W/P)h, h)$ if employed but to $u(U, 0)$ if unemployed. The number of employed workers is $(1/h) L(W/P)$, not necessarily equal to the working population N. The implied unemployment rate is then $[1 - (1/Nh)L(W/P)]$. The expected utility of an 'anonymous' worker is given by

$$Eu = \frac{1}{Nh}L\left(\frac{W}{P}\right) \cdot u\left(\frac{W}{P}h, h\right) + \left[1 - \frac{1}{Nh}L\left(\frac{W}{P}\right)\right] \cdot u(U, 0).$$

(22')

Maximising this expression with respect to *both* W/P and h leads to first-order conditions which still imply

$$\frac{dr}{dh}\bigg|_u = \frac{W}{P}(1 + \eta_{(W/P)\cdot L})$$

at an interior solution. Whether or not unemployment compensation should be taken as given in this analysis raises further issues, that lie beyond the scope of the present paper. For a microeconomic analysis of a related issue, see Baily (1974) and the survey in Dreze (1979a).

[23] The 'public goods' aspect calls for replacing the marginal rate of substitution in (23) by an average over all workers, in the general case.

[24] As an empirical proposition, it seems more likely that union leaders underestimate the longer run elasticity of employment with respect to real wages. The imprecision of the long-run estimate may also play a role here – although expected utility theory provides a justification for using the expected value of $L(W/P)$ in (22'), hence the expected value of $\eta_{L(W/P)}$ in (23).

work overtime, to engage in moonlighting, etc. The difficulties of policing a monopolistic solution, which is rational for a syndicate but not for its individual members, are well known and confirmed by casual empiricism in our context.

5.3. Distributive aspects

When labour unions set wages at a level implying monopolistic advantages, who is the monopolist exploiting? Our approach provides a suitable vehicle for analytical discussion of that issue, but a limited basis for empirical purposes. (There comes indeed a point where there is no satisfactory substitute for numerical simulation of a complete model.)

Starting from eqs. (13)–(14) we may note the following:

(i) Labour can enforce arbitrary levels of *real* wages only to the extent that $\eta_{PW} < 1$. As η_{PW} tends to 1, the adjustments in output implied by changes in real wages tend to infinity. A feature of the Belgian economy is that η_{PW} is relatively small – like one third. This reflects the large ratio of imports to GNP (0.55 in 1976). In less open economies, η_{PW} is closer to one. If all firms were setting prices in a fixed proportion to costs (proportional mark-up), then η_{PW} would differ from unity only to the extent that the prices of imported or non-produced goods (land a.s.o.) are inelastic to domestic wages and prices.

(ii) An increase in wages has both real effects and distributive effects; the real effects recognized here concern output, and labour inputs; a wage increase brings about a reduction of output, which is a real social loss; this loss is partly offset by a reduction in labour inputs, which is a gain to the extent that it means additional desired leisure shared by all, but could be a real loss if it meant involuntary unemployment for some with unchanged hours for the others.

(iii) When $|\eta_{L(W/P)}| < 1$, an increase in real wages entails an increase in real labour income. The real income to other sectors must then fall by the sum of the loss of output and the gain to labour. How this fall is distributed over the other sectors depends upon the extent to which firms transfer the burden to buyers of goods and services, through price increases. When $\eta_{PW} < 1$, the transfer is incomplete and the fall in profits absorbs part of labour's gain in addition to the loss of output.

(iv) To whom is part of the burden transferred through higher prices? Clearly not back to labour, since wages are by assumption fully indexed. Rather, to earners of relatively fixed incomes (mostly from property or self-employment), and to the rest of the world (in the form of improved terms of trade). In the case of Belgium, the part of the burden shifted to the rest of the world is small.

(v) When $|\eta_{L(W/P)}| > 1$, an increase in real wages entails a fall in real labour income, which absorbs part of the loss of output. The real income to other sectors must then fall by the difference between the loss of output and the loss to labour. (The rest of the reasoning is unchanged.)

Empirical assessment of these real and distributive effects requires a more elaborate model of price and income formation than has been introduced here. Still, for illustrative purposes, we have computed a crude estimate, on the following premises for the short run:

$$\eta_{PW} = 0.33, \qquad \eta_{Y(W/P)} = -0.6, \qquad \eta_{L(W/P)} = -0.2, \quad \eta_{P_x W} = 0.2,$$

and

$$X/Y = M/Y = 0.5, \qquad WL/PY = 0.75.$$

A 10% autonomous increase in real wages, $\Delta(W/P) = 10\% \, (W/P)$, would then have the following implications, when evaluated marginally.[25]

Increase in
  nominal wages:

$$\frac{1}{W}\Delta W = \frac{10\%}{1 - \eta_{PW}} = 15\%,$$

prices:

$$\frac{1}{P}\Delta P = \eta_{PW} \times 15\% = 5\%,$$

export prices:

$$\frac{1}{P_x}\Delta P_x = \eta_{P_x W} \times 15\% = 3\%,$$

import prices:

$$\frac{1}{P_m}\Delta P_m = 0,$$

price of domestic product sold domestically:

$$\frac{1}{P_h}\Delta P_h = \left(\frac{1}{P}\Delta P - \frac{M}{Y}\frac{1}{P_m}\Delta P_m\right)\bigg/\left(1 - \frac{M}{Y}\right) = \frac{5\%}{0.5} = 10\%,$$

[25] That is, the calculations hold strictly for arbitrarily small wage increases; they are presented in terms of a finite change for case of interpretation.

price of value added:

$$\frac{1}{P_Y}P_Y = \frac{X}{Y}\frac{1}{P_x}\Delta P_x + \left(1 - \frac{X}{Y}\right)\frac{1}{P_h}\Delta P_h$$

$$= 0.5 \times 3\% + 0.5 \times 10\% = 6.5\%.$$

*Change in
  output:*

$$\frac{1}{Y}\Delta Y = \eta_{Y(W/P)} \times 10\% = -6\%,$$

employment:

$$\frac{1}{L}\Delta L = \eta_{L(W/P)} \times 10\% = -2\%,$$

nominal domestic income:

$$\frac{1}{P_Y Y}\Delta P_Y Y = \frac{1}{P_Y}\Delta P_y + \frac{1}{Y}\Delta Y = 6.5\% - 6\% = +0.5\%,$$

real domestic income:

$$\frac{P}{P_Y Y}\Delta\frac{P_Y Y}{P} = \frac{1}{P_Y Y}\Delta P_Y Y - \frac{1}{P}\Delta P = 0.5\% - 5\% = -4.5\%.$$

Net income effects (expressed in percentage of national income before the wage increase) *on*

domestic labour income:

$$\frac{1}{Y}\Delta L\frac{W}{P} = \frac{L(W/P)}{Y}\left(\frac{1}{L}\Delta L + \frac{P}{W}\Delta\frac{W}{P}\right) = +6\%,$$

domestic non-labour income:

$$\frac{1}{Y}\left(\Delta\frac{P_Y Y - LW}{P}\right) = -4.5\% - 6\% = -10.5\%,$$

rest of the world:

$$\frac{1}{Y}\left(\Delta Y - \Delta\frac{P_Y Y}{P}\right) = -6\% + 4.5\% = -1.5\%.$$

In the longer run, assuming $\eta_{Y(W/P)} = \eta_{L(W/P)} = -2$, these implications become

$$\frac{1}{Y}\Delta Y = \frac{1}{L}\Delta L = -20\%,$$

$$\frac{1}{P_Y Y}\Delta P_Y Y = 6.5\% - 20\% = -13.5\%,$$

$$\frac{P}{P_Y Y}\Delta \frac{P_Y Y}{P} = -13.5\% - 5\% = -18.5\%,$$

$$\frac{1}{Y}\Delta L\frac{W}{P} = 0.75(-20\% + 10\%) = -7.5\%,$$

$$\frac{1}{Y}\Delta \frac{P_Y Y - LW}{P} = -18.5\% + 7.5\% = -11\%,$$

$$\frac{1}{Y}\left(\Delta Y - \Delta \frac{P_Y Y}{P}\right) = -20\% + 18.5\% = -1.5\%.$$

The overall picture is thus the following. In both the short and the long run, a wage increase causes a fall in output and real income, of which only a minor part is shifted to the rest of the world (through export prices). In the short run, labour gains, thanks to higher real wages and inelastic employment. Domestic non-labour incomes fall by the *sum* of the loss in real national income and the gain to labour; this sum is roughly equal to 1.75 times labour's gain.

In the longer run, the losses to non-labour income and to the rest of the world are unchanged. But the larger fall in real income is absorbed by labour, whose real income falls markedly. Yet, to the extent that the decline in employment reflects additional leisure, the utility level of workers falls less sharply than their measured real income, and may even rise somewhat.[26]

5.4. Work-sharing through shorter hours

The foregoing discussion brings out the relevance of our empirical findings for the current debate about work-sharing through shorter hours.

First, it is not surprising that labour unions should press for shorter

---

[26] In our illustrative calculations, workers' utility would rise if $dr/dh|_u = \frac{1}{2}(W, P)$, but not if $dr/dh|_u = \frac{1}{2}(W/P)$.

hours, as part of a strategy designed to maximize workers' welfare at non-competitive wages. For a given level of aggregate labour input, less unemployment through shorter hours entails definite distributive advantages.

This distributive proposition has fairly general validity. If the conditions of world demand and of domestic supply at the prevailing wages entail less than full employment, work-sharing through shorter hours deserves serious consideration. Indeed, we have seen that the scope for demand management is limited by the external balance constraint, whereas wage cuts would have little short-run impact.

Second, it is understandable that unions should press for shorter hours at unchanged take-home pay. Indeed, if the wage rate exceeds the marginal rate of substitution between income and leisure, shorter hours at unchanged hourly wages entail a loss of utility for employed workers – whereas shorter hours at unchanged take-home pay entail a definite gain of utility.

Third, it is not surprising to find employers strongly opposed to shorter hours at unchanged take-home pay, since this entails a commensurate increase in hourly wage costs. Wage increases lead to a substantial fall in domestic non-labour incomes (including profits) in the short run as well as in the longer run.

Fourth, shorter hours at unchanged take-home pay could have a positive impact on employment in the short run, but would have a negative longer run impact, unless accompanied by some form of cost absorption. Indeed, if employment were determined simply as $N = (1/h)L(W/P)$, and take-home pay were given as $\bar{r} = (W/P)h$, then

$$N = \frac{1}{h}L\left(\frac{\bar{r}}{h}\right),$$

$$\frac{\mathrm{d}N}{\mathrm{d}h} = \frac{-L}{h^2} + \frac{1}{h}\frac{\mathrm{d}L}{\mathrm{d}(W/P)}\left(\frac{-\bar{r}}{h^2}\right)$$

$$= \frac{-L}{h^2}\left(1 + \frac{\bar{r}}{Lh}\frac{\mathrm{d}L}{\mathrm{d}(W/P)}\right) = \frac{-L}{h^2}(1 + \eta_{L(W/P)}), \tag{24}$$

$$\eta_{Nh} = -(1 + \eta_{L(W/P)}) \gtrless 0 \quad \text{as} \quad |\eta_{L(W/P)}| \gtrless 1. \tag{25}$$

Thus, $\eta_{Nh} < 0$ in the short run but $\eta_{Nh} > 0$ in the medium or long run, if our empirical analysis is correct.[27]

[27] Remember that shorter hours amount to reducing h; the effect on N has a sign opposite to that of η_{Nh}.

Actually, the impact of shorter hours on employment is apt to be still more unfavourable, to the extent that employment is not simply determined as $(1/h)L(W/P)$. Thus shorter hours could be absorbed without new hirings by those firms which currently hoard labour. And a gradual reduction in hours per week would in many cases accelerate capital–labour substitution instead of stimulating employment. Empirical evidence bearing on this issue is deceptively meagre, and further research is needed. But the qualitative conclusions are not apt to change. In the short run, $\eta_{L(W/P)}$ is sufficiently small, so that η_{Nh} would remain negative even if new hirings amount only to one third or even less of the reduction in labour inputs through shorter hours. In the longer run, our conclusion would be strengthened.

In summary, then, shorter hours make sense, if and only if they permit some form of cost absorption, like productivity gains, wage restraint or selective subsidies.

Productivity gains are possible when shorter hours for individual workers permit a more intensive use of capital through additional shifts. The clearest example consists in operating a plant 6 days per week instead of 5, with individuals working 4 days per week instead of 5; the number of employees can then be increased by 50% without additional investment.[28] This means a reduction in the capital–output ratio and a substitution of labour for capital. But the substitution is realised either through increased output (if there is a commensurate demand), or through concentration of production in the more efficient plants (which are apt to be the less labour intensive), or through postponement of new investments. These conditions are restrictive, and we do not know how frequently they would be satisfied.

Wage restraint may take the form of constant take-home pay (in real terms) and more leisure, as a substitute for rising take-home pay. If the shorter work schedule can be made attractive to workers, such restraint is more likely to be accepted. But it is still unlikely to emerge spontaneously, so long as the wage rate exceeds the marginal rate of substitution between income and leisure. And the cost savings arising from a break in the trend of real wages accrue only progressively over time; whereas the effectiveness of some schemes may require that major reductions in individual working hours (like 10%) be implemented at once.

Therefore, selective subsidies covering part of the incremental costs associated with shorter hours at constant take-home pay might be needed to anticipate future cost savings and to provide adequate motivation for

[28]Further examples are given in Drèze (1979c).

the needed reorganisations. Such subsidies should naturally be linked to new hirings and conditioned to wage restraint. They should be temporary, and leave incentives for productivity gains. They could hopefully be recovered over time through the savings resulting for the treasury from a higher level of employment.[29]

5.5.   *Capacity adjustments and selective wage subsidies*

The observation that capacity adjustments affect employment first and foremost through accelerated scrapping has policy implications too.

Faced with the prospect of capacity scrapping, union leaders frequently urge for (and elicit) public support of marginally unprofitable activities (for instance through rebates on employers' contributions to social security), on the grounds of a smaller final cost to the treasury.[30] This argument is correct on short-run considerations: In situations of unemployment, the private and social costs of labour differ, and corrective measures should be attempted. In the long run, this practice carries the dangers of reducing labour mobility, and of being anticipated by employers and unions, who could regard public support as a substitute for productive efficiency and wage restraint. Also, it should be judged against the alternative of investment subsidies, which have less impact on employment in the short run, but hold more long-run promise.

Appendix: Foreign trade equations from SERENA

The foreign trade sector consists of three structural equations explaining M_t, P_{xt} and X_t respectively. This system is treated as block-recursive between M_t (first block) and P_{xt}, X_t (second block). The estimates pertain to the manufacturing sector, which accounts for 80% of Belgium's foreign trade.

---

[29] A comprehensive program, calling for shorter hours, wage restraint, new hirings and rebates on employers' contributions to social security, was proposed by the Belgian Government in the Spring of 1979, as a basis for nationwide collective bargaining. The program received cautious support from some unions but was rejected by other unions and by the employers' organisations. Eventually, a more limited program, including selective subsidies to new hirings under work-sharing schemes, was started in the fall of 1979.

[30] Such is the case, at times of severe unemployment, when the required support is less than unemployment compensation plus total contributions to social security plus income taxes – or approximately U.S.$10,000 per wage-earner per year in Belgium today.

(i) *Imports of manufactured goods*

$$\ln M_t = \delta_0 + \delta_1 \ln Y_t^0 + \delta_2 \ln \frac{P_{et}}{C_t} + \delta_3 \ln \frac{\bar{Y}_t}{Y_t} + v_t, \tag{A.1}$$

where Y_t^0 is a weighted average of government expenditures on goods and services, consumption, investment, intermediate deliveries and inventory variations.

Estimation by ordinary least squares from annual data, 1966–1976, yields

$$\ln M_t = -0.45 + 1.24 \ln Y_t^0 - 0.56 \ln \frac{P_{et}}{C_t} - 0.29 \ln \frac{\bar{Y}_t}{Y_t}. \tag{A.2}$$
$$(0.11) \quad (0.07) \qquad (0.19) \qquad (0.14)$$

The elasticity of imports with respect to domestic demand has been estimated by $\delta_1 - \delta_3 = 1.53$ in the short run ($\bar{Y}$ given) and by $\delta_1 = 1.24$ in the longer run ($\bar{Y}/Y$ given). As indicated in the text, the variance and covariances from (A.2) have been multiplied by four for the purpose of evaluating the posterior density of η_{YW} in figs. 14.3 and 14.5.

(ii) *Exports of manufactured goods*

$$\ln P_{xt} = (1 - \alpha)\ln P_{et} + \alpha \ln C_t + u_{1t}, \tag{A.3}$$

$$\ln X_t = \beta_0 + \beta_1 \Delta \ln E_t$$
$$+ \alpha \left[\eta_1 \ln E_t + \eta_2 \ln \frac{P_{xt}}{P_{et}} + \eta_3 \ln \frac{P_{xt-1}}{P_{et-1}} \right]$$
$$+ (1 - \alpha)\left[\ln \bar{Y}_t + \gamma \ln \frac{P_{xt-1}}{C_{t-1}} \right] + u_{2t} \tag{A.4}$$
$$\equiv \beta_0 + \beta_1 \Delta \ln E_t + \beta_2 \ln E_t + \beta_3 \ln \frac{P_{xt}}{P_{et}} + \beta_4 \ln \frac{P_{xt-1}}{P_{et-1}}$$
$$+ (1 - \alpha)\ln \bar{Y}_t + \beta_5 \ln \frac{P_{xt-1}}{C_{t-1}} + u_{2t}.$$

Full information maximum likelihood estimation of this simultaneous system of 2 equations from annual data, 1966–1976, yields

$$\ln P_{xt} = 0.77 \ln P_{et} + 0.22 \ln C_t, \tag{A.5}$$
$$(0.09)$$

$$\ln X_t = -1.6 + 0.7 \Delta \ln E_t + 0.64 \ln E_t - 3.01 \ln \frac{P_{xt}}{P_{et}}$$

$$\qquad (0.18) \qquad (0.16) \qquad (0.07) \qquad (0.44)$$
$$\qquad [0.22] \qquad [0.29] \qquad [0.11] \qquad [2.71]$$

$$-2.12 \ln \frac{P_{xt-1}}{P_{et-1}} + 0.77 \ln \bar{Y}_t + 1.03 \ln \frac{P_{xt-1}}{C_{t-1}}. \qquad (A.6)$$

$$\quad (0.60) \qquad\qquad (0.10) \qquad\quad (0.42)$$
$$\quad [1.13] \qquad\qquad\qquad\qquad\quad [0.80]$$

The numbers in parentheses are *asymptotic* standard errors, which are definitely unreliable in our small sample case. The numbers in square brackets are posterior standard deviations computed by Bauwens (1979), conditionally on α, in his Bayesian analysis with a non-informative prior. These exact finite sample results confirm the strong downward bias of the asymptotic formulae.

The coefficients of the export equations are related to $\eta_{\Xi W}$ of formula (13") by

$$\eta_{\Xi W} = \tfrac{1}{3}\{\alpha + 0.6[\alpha(\beta_3 + \beta_4) - (1-\alpha)\beta_5]\}, \qquad (A.7)$$

when $\eta_{CW} = \tfrac{1}{3}$.

Proceeding from a non-informative prior density, the posterior joint density for the coefficients α and $\beta = (\beta_0, \beta_1, \ldots, \beta_5)$, evaluated marginally with respect to the covariance matrix of the disturbances, may be written as

$$f(\beta|\alpha, \text{data}) \cdot f(\alpha|\text{data}), \qquad (A.8)$$

with $f(\beta|\alpha, \text{data})$ taking the form of a multivariate t density with expectation $\bar{\beta}_\alpha$, covariance matrix V_α and $v = 11$ degrees of freedom[31] – say $f_t(\beta|\bar{\beta}_\alpha, V_\alpha, v)$. We may write from (A.7)

$$\eta_{\Xi W} = \alpha/3 + C'_\alpha \beta, \qquad C'_\alpha = (0, 0, 0, 0.2\alpha, 0.2\alpha, -0.2(1-\alpha)),$$
$$(A.7')$$

so that

$$f(\eta_{\Xi W}|\alpha, \text{data}) = f_t(\eta_{\Xi W}|\alpha/3 + C'_\alpha \bar{\beta}_\alpha, C'_\alpha V_\alpha C_\alpha, v). \qquad (A.8)$$

---

[31] There is some arbitrariness in the choice of the 'degress of freedom' parameter in the (non-informative) prior density. We have experimented with alternative values. They only affect the posterior variances, which are inflated anyhow, as indicated below.

Integrating (A.8) with respect to the posterior density $f(\alpha|\text{data})$ by numerical methods yields the density in fig. 14.7, with expected value -0.31 and standard deviation 0.11. This density has been approximated by the normal density with that same mean and twice that standard deviation for the purpose of evaluating the posterior density of η_{YW} in figs. 14.3 and 14.5.

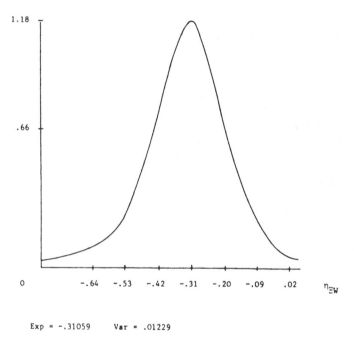

Exp = -.31059   Var = .01229

Fig. 14.7. Estimate of $\eta_{\Xi W}$ from SERENA.

15 A discussion of Belgian unemployment, combining traditional concepts and disequilibrium econometrics*

The sorest ill that Heaven hath
Sent on this lower world in wrath—
Unemployment (to call it by its name)
Waged war on economics,
Sparing no country from the plague.
They died not all, but all were sick.
No jobs were left;
So hope and therefore joy were dead.
Richard the Lion-hearted council held and said:
'Let us all turn eyes within
And ferret out the hidden sin.'
Himself let no one spare nor flatter,
But make clean conscience in the matter.
'I Yield myself', concluded he;
'And yet I think, in equity,
Each should confess his sins with me.'
Belgians, confessing in their turn,
Thus spoke in tones of deep concern:
'We have little to say
That you do not know anyway.
Without claiming to be exhaustive
We put a few facts in perspective.
Then turn to summarising

* *Economica*, 53 (1986), S89–S119. With Henri Sneessens. We wish to acknowledge gratefully the collaboration of Robert Leroy and Serge Wibaut in collecting and organising data, of Fati Mehta in estimating the model of Section 4, and of Yves Leruth in preparing auxiliary computations. Responsibility for all the views expressed or omitted here is our own. We also acknowledge the financial support of the Belgian Government under Projet d'Action Concertée, no. 80/85-12.

362

Scanty results on manufacturing.
Next we illustrate a methodology
That was pioneered in our country.
By way of conclusions
We share our interrogations.'

1. Factual perspectives

With a GDP of less than $100 billion and exports of more than $60 billion, Belgium comes perhaps closer than any other country to being a 'small open economy'. Consequently, trends in world trade and export performance have a major impact on domestic activity, whereas the impact of domestic fiscal policy is damped by import leakages. Table 15.1 presents a few figures confirming these observations.

The rise in Belgian unemployment since 1974 has been appalling. Figure 15.1 compares the unemployment rate in Belgium with that of the European Community (EC9) since 1960. It displays clearly the sharper take-off of Belgian unemployment since 1974.

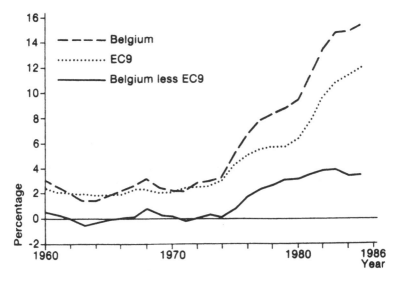

Fig. 15.1.   Unemployment rate, Belgium, 1960–84.

Table 15.1. *GDP, Belgium 1975–83, at 1980 prices*

	% of GDP, 1975	% change, 1975–80	% change, 1980–83	% change, 1975–83	% of GDP, 1983
Private consumption	63	17	−1	16	63
Public consumption	18	18	0	18	18
Gross fixed investment	22	9	−22	−15	16
Exports	47	48	7	58	63
Imports	48	50	−3	45	60
GDP	100	15	0	15	100
Public deficit	6	67	32	119	14

Source: OECD National Accounts (1984).

Additional facts about employment and unemployment over the period 1974–83 are collected in table 15.2. The salient features are as follows.

1. Male employment has gone down by 10 per cent while female employment has gone up by 3 per cent; the sharper increase in female unemployment is thus due to the increase in active population.
2. The increase in female employment is equal to the number of women in special employment programmes; otherwise, there are offsetting movements in public employment (+ 69,200) and private employment (− 71,000) of women.
3. The decline in private employment (15.3 per cent altogether) is concentrated (up to 88 per cent) in manufacturing, where the decline is staggering: 29.8 per cent!

The evolution of total employment (private and public) in five sectors is given in figure 15.2.

Another useful piece of information concerns hours worked and the evolution of labour inputs in man-hours. In the manufacturing sector, average hours went down by 11 per cent in 10 years (1973–83), so that labour inputs went down by 37.3 per cent.[1] Taking into account a 15 per cent increase in value added at constant prices, the apparent increase in gross hourly productivity is nearly 85 per cent. In services, average hours went down by 9 per cent and gross hourly productivity went up by 27 per cent.

That enormous apparent increase in gross hourly productivity in manufacturing accounts for much of the differential rise in Belgian unemployment; it is one of the main facts to be explained if anything is to be learned from the rise in Belgian unemployment.

[1] Indeed, 70.2 × 0.89 = 62.5. The figures in this paragraph come from Sonnet (1985).

Table 15.2. *Belgian population and employment, by sex and status, 1974–83*

	Men			Women			Total		
	1974 ('000)	1974–83 ('000)	(%)	1974 ('000)	1974–83 ('000)	(%)	1974 ('000)	1974–83 ('000)	(%)
(1) Population of working age (men: 15–64, women: 15–59)	3103.1	+225.9	+7.3	2827.6	+199.8	+7.3	5930.7	+425.7	+7.2
(2) Active population	2625.1	−45.9	−1.8	1354.2	+279.9	+20.7	3979.3	+233.0	+5.9
(3) Participation rates	84.6		−7.1	47.9		+6.1	67.1		−0.8
(4) Early retirements	0	+99.8		0	+26.4		0	+126.2	
(5) Unemployment	45.7	+207.1	+8.1	51.2	+241.1	+14.1	96.9	+448.2	+10.5
(6) Unemployment rates	1.7		−9.8	3.8		+3.0	2.4		−5.5
(7) Total employment	2579.4	−253.0		1302.9	+38.9		3882.3	−214.1	
(8) of which: special programmes	7.6	+35.4		1.4	+40.5		9.0	+75.9	
(9) Public servants	537.4	+57.9	+10.8	262.0	+109.7	+41.9	799.4	+167.6	+21.0
(10) Self-employed	405.8	−9.1	−2.2	228.5	+1.5	+0.7	634.3	−7.6	−1.2
(11) Wage-earners	1636.0	−301.6	−18.4	812.5	72.5	−8.9	2448.5	−374.1	−15.3
(12) of which: manufacturing	805.2	−213.7	−26.5	295.9	−114.8	−38.8	1101.1	−328.5	−29.8

Source: Official statistics and calculations at ECOS and IRES, Université Catholique de Louvain.

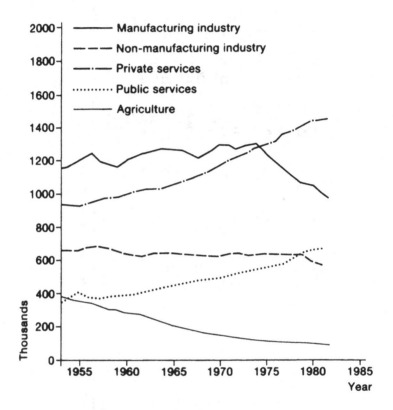

Fig. 15.2.   Belgian employment in five sectors, 1953–81.

A broader picture of the Belgian economy is given by figure 15.3, which presents time-series for the income share of labour, unemployment, budget deficits and balance of payments deficits. The striking (though not unexpected) aspect of these series is the concomitant break in trends in the early 1970s. At that time Belgium underwent a deep and swift transformation: the country, previously one of relatively stable prices and labour share, with low unemployment and low deficits, thereafter came to be characterized by significant inflation, including real wage inflation, high unemployment and sizeable deficits.

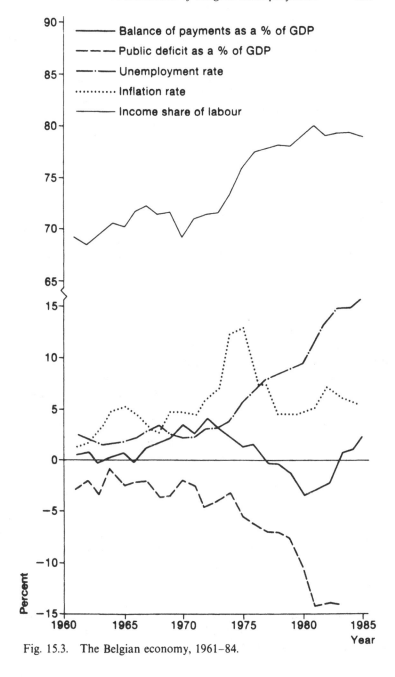

Fig. 15.3. The Belgian economy, 1961–84.

Table 15.3. *Growth rates of real wages and income shares of labour, 1971–80*

	Growth of real compensation per employee, total economy, 1971–80		Adjusted share of labour income total economy		
	Ave. rate	Cumulative percentage	1971	1980	1980–71
Belgium	4.6	57	70.9	79	8.1
Japan	4.2	51	73.4	80.6	7.2
France	4.1	49	70.9	75.7	4.8
Italy	3.4	40	80.7	81.7	1
EC9	**3.2**	**37**	**74.6**	**76.3**	**1.7**
W. Germany	3.1	36	73.2	73	−0.2
Netherlands	2.8	32	74.2	73.9	−0.3
UK	2.3	26	73.2	75.4	2.2
Denmark	1.4	15	79.4	79.4	0
USA	1.0	11	74.1	74.1	0

Source: European Economy (1984, Tables 23 and 24). The deflator of compensation per employee is the consumer price index.

The percentage change in real wages for the period 1971–80 amounts to 57 per cent for Belgium as against 37 per cent for the rest of the European Community (EC9). The third and fourth columns of table 15.3 give the income share of labour in 1971 and 1980. The picture emerging from the table is by no means clear-cut. There is a mild suggestion that real wages rose more rapidly in countries where the income share of labour was initially lower, and typically rose quickly enough there to bring about, by 1980, a labour share exceeding the average (with Italy and Denmark the more obvious exceptions). The more solid fact, in so far as Belgium is concerned, is the exceptionally high rate of increase of real wages in the 1970s – a fact that one would like to explain, and the consequences of which one would like to evaluate.

A similar picture of rapid transition from balanced growth to pronounced disequilibrium is conveyed by figure 15.4. This figure, which is discussed at greater length in Section 4, presents estimates of labour supply (*LS*), 'potential employment' (*LP* – defined as the employment corresponding to the desired utilization of productive capacities) and 'Keynesian labour demand' (*LK* – defined as the employment needed to meet effective demand for domestic output). Three distinct time periods stand out clearly on that figure: 1955–62, 1963–74 and 1975 onward. In the first subperiod, structural unemployment was progressively eliminated

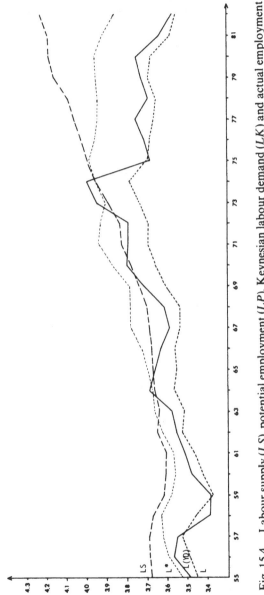

Fig. 15.4. Labour supply (*LS*), potential employment (*LP*), Keynesian labour demand (*LK*) and actual employment (*LT*), Belgium, 1955–82.

by industrialisation in Flanders – see Leroy (1962). The development of new industrial activities there had by 1963 led to a situation of near equilibrium $(LS \simeq LP \simeq LK)$. That situation prevailed until 1974. The 'golden sixties' give an almost perfect picture of balanced growth: the three series move on parallel trends, with cyclical fluctuations superimposed on the demand series (LK). Since 1975, however, the three series diverge markedly: labour supply keeps growing (owing to the growth of female population and participation rates); potential employment stagnates until 1979 and then falls off (owing to the decline in investment), and Keynesian labour demand declines sharply in 1975 and again in 1981 (owing to insufficient effective demand). The behaviour of LP and LK is also influenced by labour-saving investment and technological progress (see below).

On the policy side, three points seem worth mentioning.

1. Ever since unemployment became a major issue in the mid-1970s, Belgium has actively developed a number of special programmes: early retirement, apprenticeships for the young, the fully subsidised hiring of unemployed persons in non-profit organisations, etc. Without these programmes, the unemployment rate would be another 5 percentage points higher (table 15.2, rows (4), (5) and (8)).

2. Until 1981, Belgium tried to maintain the stability of its exchange rate *vis-à-vis* the German mark and Dutch guilder; by 1981 a substantial current deficit had developed. In February 1982 the Belgian franc devalued by 8 per cent. This measure was accompanied by an incomes policy which has been continued until now. Whereas almost all wages and salaries had previously been fully indexed, the government has imposed real wage reductions of some 2 to 3 per cent per year since then.

3. Business investments have for many years benefited from interest rate subsidies. Over the past three years, tax advantages have been granted to individuals investing in stocks and to individuals or institutions subscribing new equity issues.

2. Some tightrope exercises over manufacturing

In this section, we report briefly on three empirical studies of the Belgian manufacturing sector, which hopefully bear some relevance to the decline of employment there. Our reports are brief because these studies proceed from a very thin data base; their results are suggestive, but not conducive to precise quantitative conclusions. Accordingly, we simply quote a few relevant results, with a minimum of explanations.

d'Alcantara (1983) has estimated a seven-sector model of the Belgian economy, with a putty–clay vintage production model for each sector. There are four inputs (capital, labour, energy and materials). The model is estimated from 14 annual observations (1963–76). As of 1977, the estimated output elasticity of manufacturing labour demand was 2.5 times higher when computed for scrapping old equipment than when computed for new investment. In other words, when replacing old equipment by new at unchanged capacity, three out of every five workers concerned could be dispensed with. The loss of some 150,000 jobs in manufacturing from 1973 to 1977 is explained by d'Alcantara as the net outcome of 'destroying' 340,000 jobs by scrapping old equipment, while 'creating' 190,000 jobs through new investment (of which some 135,000 correspond to modernisation and some 55,000 correspond only to capacity expansion).

Lambert (1988) has estimated a streamlined model of the Belgian manufacturing sector, defined by aggregation of micro-markets in disequilibrium. On specific micro-markets, transactions correspond to the minimum of supply and demand. Assuming lognormality of the distribution over micro-markets of the ratio of supply to demand, one obtains an approximate expression for aggregate transactions as a *CES* function of aggregate supply and aggregate demand. The exponent of the ·*CES* function can be estimated from business survey data, namely from the proportion of firms reporting excess supply of goods and or excess demand for labour.

The model is estimated from 18 annual observations (1963–80). The estimation results permit a decomposition of the observed decline in manufacturing employment from 1974 to 1980 (namely, 23.5 per cent) into four components: the change in frictional unemployment (negligible), the change in demand (accounting for 4.5 out of 23.5 per cent), the change in the stock of capital (negligible), and the substitution of capital for labour induced by relative prices (accounting for 19 out of 23.5 per cent).

A related approach is followed by Gérard and Vanden Berghe (1984) in their analysis of manufacturing investment. These authors recognise that at any point in time some firms operate on competitive product markets and gear investment to a desired capital stock reflecting relative prices, whereas other firms operate on imperfectly competitive product markets and gear investment to a desired capital stock reflecting effective demand. An aggregation procedure comparable to that of Lambert (1988) leads again to an approximate expression for the desired stock of capital as a *CES* function of two expressions, one of which involves relative prices and the other effective demand. Estimates of the parameters of that expression imply estimates of the elasticity of desired capital with respect to relative prices (here, the ratio of the cost of capital to the price of output) and with respect to effective demand (here, actual output). These two elasticities vary over time. The former is positively related to the proportion of firms constrained by sales expectations; the latter, negatively related. Estimates derived from annual observations for the period 1956–82 (without reliance on business survey data) suggest a rapidly growing influence of effective demand on investment after 1974. Tentative as it may still be, that finding is worth keeping in mind when speculating about the determinants of investment.

When considering the share of exports in the final demand for Belgian manufactures, it is also important to treat exports endogenously, and to investigate the influence on exports of domestic costs and production capacities. Bauwens and d'Alcantara (1983) have estimated a two-equation model (price and quantities) for Belgian exports of manufactures. Their results are consistent with an elasticity of export quantities with respect to domestic production capacities equal to unity and suggest an elasticity of the value of exports with respect to domestic wages of the order of −0.3. As for export prices, they seem to be determined largely by world prices (elasticity 0.8) and less so by domestic costs (elasticity 0.2).

Before drawing a tentative conclusion from the material collected in this section, we wish to introduce an additional bit of evidence. It concerns the number of (blue- and white-collar) workers laid off as a result of their employers' bankruptcy. The exact coverage of the statistic is not entirely clear; bankruptcies involving less than 20 employees are not included, and there may be other omissions. On the other hand, some of the bankrupt firms continued under new ownership (typically with a much smaller workforce). Be that as it may, it is striking to find an annual average (1976–83) of at least 30,000 workers laid off because of bankruptcy. It was noted in table 15.2 that, over the period 1974–83, an average of 37,400 jobs a year were destroyed in the private sector. The rate of attrition suggested by bankruptcies is thus not far from the actual overall rate!

We conclude that all the findings reported in this section are consistent with, and give empirical content to, the frequently heard diagnostic that the Belgian manufacturing sector was choked by the *combination* of domestic labour costs growing faster than those of competitors and effective demand slackening off in a context of world recession. That *combination* was particularly damaging for two reasons. First, high costs and low output resulted in a severe loss of profitability, leading some firms to scrap capacity and lay off workers, while other firms simply went bankrupt. Second, slack demand at the world level prevented Belgian producers from passing on wage costs into prices and enabled foreign competitors to take over the market share thus abandoned. (From 1975 to 1979, wholesale prices of manufactures showed no trend, whereas retail and service prices went up 40 per cent.)

If one adds the observation that those firms that survived could do so only thanks to major gains in productivity, one has come a long way towards explaining the exceptional increase in apparent gross labour productivity of Belgian manufacturing industries. It would be hazardous to attempt to impute the overall increase back to individual causes, as there was much interaction. But it seems clear that wage behaviour has played a significant role; without that additional complication, the impact of the recession on manufacturing employment (down by 29.8 per cent from 1974 to 1983) would have been less severe. The differential rise of unemployment in Belgium relative to EC9 since 1974 corresponds to some 10 per cent of the employment in manufacturing; with a differential rise in real wages of some 20 percentage points in Belgium relative to EC9 over the period 1971–80, a moderate wage elasticity of employment of -0.5 would account for the differential rise in unemployment.

3. A macroeconomic rationing model

This section is devoted to the presentation and estimation of a two-market macroeconomic rationing (or disequilibrium) model of the Belgian economy. The background is thus a Barro–Grossman–Benassy–Malinvaud model, i.e. a situation in which price and wage adjustments are not sufficient to clear the goods and labour markets at each moment of time, so that employment can be, broadly speaking, determined by a sales constraint (Keynesian unemployment), by a capacity constraint (classical unemployment), or by a labour supply constraint (repressed inflation and underconsumption).[2] The model that will be developed rests on previous work on Belgian data by Sneessens (1981, 1983) and Lambert (1988). The

---

[2] For the sake of simplicity, we shall not make explicit the distinction between the repressed inflation and underconsumption regimes, although this distinction will be taken into account in estimation via the labour hoarding phenomenon.

first subsection below will be devoted to the discussion of production constraints. These are the cornerstone of the model, around which the rest is organised. The first part of the model describes the determination of production and employment, given the production constraints just mentioned. The second part describes the formation of prices and wages. Prices are represented by a mark-up on costs, plus a positive demand pressure effect. Wages are determined by productivity gains plus a negative unemployment effect. These specifications are rather crude, and we do not claim that they reflect a fully satisfactory theory of price and wage formation. Rather, they reflect minimal influences taken into account in most empirical studies. The simplicity of these specifications is convenient to bring out the properties of the whole model, which are considered in the second subsection below. We pay special attention to the inflation-unemployment trade-off and to the meaning of the non-inflationary rate of unemployment (*NIRU*) in a quantity rationing model. Empirical results are presented in Section 4.

Production constraints

Traditional macroeconomic models typically contain production relationships appearing indirectly in the form of factor demand functions. In a rationing context, production constraints will furthermore be used to determine the highest production level at which firms can reasonably aim, given the availability of production factors (capital and labour) and the prevailing production technology. The determination of these upper bounds on production is crucial for the distinction between the three regimes alluded to above, namely Keynesian unemployment, classical unemployment and repressed inflation. These upper bounds can be modelled in several ways. We shall use an extended version of the Leontief–Cobb–Douglas model already used in Sneessens (1981).

Optimal factor proportions (or technical coefficients) are chosen so as to minimise production costs. Let us assume that changing these technical coefficients is costly. When these costs are high, transitory stimuli (such as a sales constraint) will not induce a firm to modify its production technique. Consequently, labour and capital appear as complementary inputs in the short run although they are substitutes in the longer run. This seems realistic enough.

If long-run cost considerations only are taken into account and temporary disturbances such as sales constraints are neglected, a Cobb–

Douglas production function is readily shown to imply a capital–labour ratio that remains proportional to relative labour costs:

$$\ln \frac{K}{L} = C_0 + \Theta(\Lambda) \ln \frac{W}{V} \tag{1}$$

where W and V stand for labour and capital usage costs, respectively, and Λ is the lag operator. The lag polynomial function $\Theta(\Lambda)$ represents the slow adjustment of the capital–labour ratio to relative cost changes. By substitution into the Cobb–Douglas function itself, one can derive expressions for the output–labour and output–capital ratios:

$$\ln \frac{Y}{L} = C_1 + a_1(t) + (1 - a_2)\Theta(\Lambda) \ln \frac{W}{V}$$

$$\ln \frac{Y}{K} = C_2 + a_1(t) - a_2\Theta(\Lambda) \ln \frac{W}{V} \tag{2}$$

where $a_1(t)$ allows for exogenous technical progress and a_2 is the coefficient of labour in the Cobb–Douglas function. Constant returns to scale are implicitly assumed. Equation (2) can be written more compactly as

$$\frac{Y}{L} = A\left(t, \frac{W}{V}\right)$$

$$\frac{Y}{K} = B\left(t, \frac{W}{V}\right). \tag{3}$$

In the very short run, the technical coefficients A and B are fairly rigid, as in a Leontief production model. The limits imposed on production by the availability of production factors are $A \times LS$ and $B \times KA$, where LS and KA stand for the supply of labour and the available capital stock, respectively. *Repressed inflation* occurs when the labour constraint is operative, *classical unemployment* when the capital constraint is operative. *Keynesian unemployment* occurs when the demand for goods remains below these two upper bounds, so that the production level is determined by the demand for goods.

When production capacities are fully utilised, the production level is $YP \equiv B \times KA$. The corresponding 'potential' employment level is $LP = A^{-1} \times YP = A^{-1} \times B \times KA$. After substitution for A and B and first-differencing, one obtains

$$\Delta \ln LP = -\Theta(\Lambda)(\Delta \ln W - \Delta \ln V) + \Delta \ln KA. \tag{4}$$

The rate of growth of potential employment is equal to minus the rate of growth of relative labour costs plus the investment rate ($\Delta \ln KA \simeq I/KA$). Notice that the lag polynomial $\Theta(\Lambda)$ implies that the effects of a wage change will be slow to appear, while the effects of changes in the investment rate are more immediate. Figure 15.5 reproduces the evolution of the two series $\Theta(\Lambda) (\Delta \ln W - \Delta \ln V)$ and $\Delta \ln KA$ from 1955 to 1982. The values of the lag polynomial are those obtained by ML estimation (see Section 4). The potential employment level declines whenever the investment rate falls below the rate of growth of relative labour costs, that is, whenever the rate of growth of the economy does not induce the creation of enough new jobs to replace those lost by productivity gains. This situation has been observed in every year since 1975, except for 1979. The investment slack has become especially important in 1981–82. It is responsible for the fall in the potential employment level indicated in figure 15.4.

Potential employment is not a constraint that can be relaxed overnight through wage adjustments. Technical adjustment costs imply that changes in relative factor costs are only progressively translated into capital–labour substitution. It is even likely that the adjustment to a wage fall is slower than the adjustment to a rise, because there is little incentive to get rid of capital-intensive equipment once it has been paid for. More precisely, wage moderation in the short run is likely to have a larger impact on the demand for goods than on supply and potential employment. This point has already been stressed forcefully by Malinvaud (1982b).

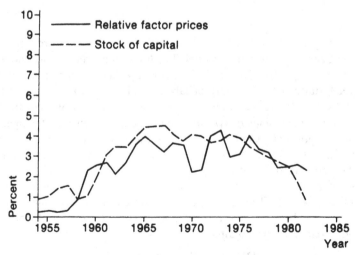

Fig. 15.5.   Rates of change in the stock of capital and relative factor prices.

Properties of the model

Our definition in the previous section of the Keynesian, classical and inflation regimes applies to individual firms only. What we observe at the aggregate level is a time-varying mixture of the three regimes. This point has been illustrated by Muellbauer (1978) and Malinvaud (1980). It is taken into account by aggregating explicitly over 'micro-markets', as in Lambert (1988). For expository reasons, we first consider an homogeneous economy and analyse each polar case separately; that is, we proceed as though all firms were always at the same time in the same regime. The consequences of aggregation and of structural imbalances are then reintroduced.

Specification details will not be given until Section 4. Moreover, because investment is kept exogenous, we take as given throughout this subsection the technical coefficients A and B. This places us in a short-run perspective.

Keynesian unemployment. The relevant set of equations is reproduced in table 14.1. Suffixes D and S denote demanded and supplied quantities respectively; suffix T denotes transacted quantities. Total final demand FD is defined as private consumption plus an exogenous component that includes public expenditures, investment and exports. Private consumption demand is determined by total disposable income DI. The demand for imports MD is the usual function of total final demand and relative prices. The difference between FD and MD defines the demand for domestic goods YD which, together with other variables such as the previous employment level (not shown), determines the demand for labour. As we are by assumption in a situation of generalised excess supply, transactions on both the goods and the labour markets are determined by the demand side. The wage equation simply says that the expected real wage rate is proportional to the expected productivity of labour. With an elasticity of real wage demands to productivity gains equal to one (as assumed), the proportionality factor is merely the share of total value added claimed by labour. That share is here inversely related to the unemployment rate. The last equation defines the price of value-added by a mark-up on expected average production costs APC. Coefficient π_0 represents the share of total value-added that firms claim over and above interest and depreciation. It is equal to the mark-up rate. It corresponds to pure profits and/or to a margin for incomplete utilisation of factors (labour hoarding, excess capacity).

Table 15.4. *Determination of macroeconomic aggregates in a pure Keynesian regime* ($YD < YP$, $LD < LS$)

Demand for goods:	$\left\{\begin{array}{l} FD = CD(DI) + EXO \\ MD = MD(FD, PF, PM) \\ YD = FD - MD \end{array}\right.$
Demand for labour:	$LD = L(YD)$
Transacted quantities:	$\left\{\begin{array}{l} CT = CD,\ MT = MD,\ YT = YD \\ LT = LD \end{array}\right.$
Wages and prices:	$\left\{\begin{array}{ll} W = \omega_0(LD/LS)^{\omega_1} A^e P^e & \omega_0, \omega_1 \geqslant 0 \\ P = e^{\pi_0} APC^e & \pi_0 \geqslant 0 \\ \text{where } APC = A^{-1}W + B^{-1}V \end{array}\right.$

The basic properties of the real part of the model are well known. For given wages and prices, the levels of output and employment are determined by final demand. To increase employment, one must increase either the exogenous component of final demand or consumption demand. Under reasonable assumptions, higher real wages imply more consumption demand.

The price equation in table 15.4 embodies an assumption of downward price rigidity: the excess supply of goods does not lead to price decreases. Consequently, prices are entirely determined by costs and the only form of inflation is 'cost-push'. Aside from exogenous shocks, a systematic inflationary bias may or may not be present, depending upon the presence or absence of excessive income claims relative to value added. This is most easily seen by looking at a stationary perfect foresight equilibrium.

With correct expectations, the price equation can indeed be rewritten (using the approximation $e^{-\pi_0} \simeq 1 - \pi_0$) as

$$1 = \pi_0 + A^{-1}\frac{W}{P} + B^{-1}\frac{V}{P},$$

that is, total value added is divided into three parts: mark-up π_0, labour income $A^{-1}(W/P)$, and capital income $B^{-1}(V/P)$. Let us assume a fixed capital share κ_0, as if capital usage costs were perfectly indexed on the price of value added. The share of total value-added left for labour is then simply

$$A^{-1}\frac{W}{P} = 1 - \pi_0 - \kappa_0. \tag{5}$$

The desired labour share is in turn obtained from the wage equation as[3]

$$A^{-1}\frac{W}{P} = \omega_0 - \omega_1 UR. \tag{6}$$

Coefficient ω_0 thus represents the share of total value added that would be claimed by workers in a zero unemployment economy.

The income claims represented by equations (5)–(6) include a single *endogenous* influence, namely, that of unemployment on wages. Accordingly, any inflationary bias arising from conflicting income claims can be corrected only through unemployment, a crude specification made popular by the discussion of 'non-inflationary rates of unemployment' (*NIRU*). The *NIRU* is in our case the unemployment rate that reconciles (5) and (6):

$$NIRU = \frac{1}{\omega_1}(\pi_0 + \kappa_0 + \omega_0 - 1) \underset{\text{def}}{=} \frac{1}{\omega_1} DG \tag{7}$$

where DG stands for 'distributive gap', i.e. the relative excess of income claims over value added. The *NIRU* is proportional to the 'distributive gap', with a factor of proportionality equal to the reciprocal of the elasticity of wages with respect to unemployment. In other words, a Keynesian equilibrium with stationarity of both prices and quantities implies an employment level $LS(1 - NIRU)$ uniquely determined by the sum of income claims $(\pi_0 + \kappa_0 + \omega_0)$ and the elasticity ω_1. With $\omega_1 \simeq 0.4$ (see empirical results, Section 4), a discrepancy of four percentage points would imply a *NIRU* of 10 per cent! Notice, though, that the *NIRU* should be lowered by the extent to which firms lower $(\pi_0 + \kappa_0)$ when demand is slack. This is not modelled here. Finally, an oil shock with full indexation of wages on consumer prices is in this setting equivalent to an increase in ω_0, hence in the *NIRU*.

Needless to say, a perfect-foresight stationary Keynesian equilibrium can exist if and only if the *NIRU* defined in (7) is feasible, i.e. if it is non-negative *and* larger than the rate of unemployment that would prevail if all production capacities, were utilised. Otherwise, the economy would end up in either repressed inflation or classical unemployment.

Classical unemployment. The relevant equations are reproduced in table 15.5.

---

[3] We use the approximations $\omega_0(LD/LS)^{\omega_1} \simeq e^{\omega_0 - 1}e^{-\omega_1 UR} \simeq \omega_0 - \omega_1 UR$.

Table 15.5. *Determination of macroeconomic aggregates in a pure classical unemployment regime*
$(LD < LS, YD > YS)$

Demand for goods:	Same as in table 15.4
Demand for labour:	$LD = L(YP) = L'(KA)$
Transacted quantities:	$\begin{cases} LT = LD \\ YT = Y(KA) \\ MT = MD + M(YD/YT) \\ CT = CD \end{cases}$
Wages and prices:	$\begin{cases} W = \omega_0(LD/LS)^{\omega_1}A^eP^e \\ P = e^{\pi_0}(YD/YT)^{\pi_1}APC^e \\ \text{where } APC = A^{-1}W + B^{-1}V \end{cases}$

The goods demand equations remain unchanged. Labour demand and employment are now determined by the availability of capital rather than the demand for goods. The availability of capital determines production, which falls short of the demand for goods.[4] Total imports are therefore the sum of 'structural' imports MD plus a positive component representing the spillover from the domestic goods market $(M(YD/YT) \geq 0)$. Despite the shortage of domestic goods, we still assume that the demand for consumption goods is not rationed $(CT = CD)$. Implicitly, this means that the shortage of production capacities is fully compensated by a combination of increased imports, higher factor utilisation rates (overtime working, for example) and inventory decumulation, although the latter effects are not explicitly modelled here. (Pure rationing could also appear in the form of delivery lags; it seemed wiser not to overemphasise their role in an annual macro-model.)

The wage equation remains unchanged. The price equation includes a positive effect of demand pressure on the mark-up rate. This asymmetric treatment of excess demand versus excess supply amounts to assuming that prices are more flexible upwards than downwards.

Again, the properties of the real part of the model are well known. Output and employment are determined by production capacities – which in turn depend upon available physical capital and real wages. Demand management does not affect output and employment except via investment. Real wages affect employment via capital–labour substitution and investment levels.

[4] Notice however that, because of employment adjustment costs, the observed employment and production levels may also be influenced by past employment and production levels; i.e. LT and YT do not necessarily coincide exactly in the short run with the potential levels of LP and YP defined earlier.

Demand pressures affect prices, which are assumed flexible upwards. Accordingly, there are now two sources of inflation: cost-push and demand-pull. With excess demand for output, demand-pull introduces a systematic inflationary bias. Price stability accordingly requires an offsetting trend in costs. The rate of classical unemployment introduces a downward bias in wages, to be considered jointly with the income claims.

In this framework, the NIRU is a meaningless concept, but one can define a 'non-inflationary rate of excess demand', or *NIRED*, to express conveniently the single endogenous influence on prices and wages.

The properties of the perfect-foresight stationary classical unemployment equilibrium are derived in exactly the same fashion as for the Keynesian regime. In this case, however, the unemployment rate is fully determined by production capacities. At given technical coefficients, this unemployment rate measures the 'capital gap' (*CG*), i.e. the shortage of production capacities relatively to the capacity required to eliminate unemployment:

$$CG = \frac{LS - L(YP)}{LS} = 1 - \frac{L(YP)}{LS}.$$

From the price and wage equations we obtain, respectively,

$$A^{-1} \frac{W}{P} = 1 - \pi_0 - \pi_1 \ln \frac{YD}{YT} - \kappa_0 \tag{8}$$

and

$$A^{-1} \frac{W}{P} = \omega_0 - \omega_1 CG. \tag{9}$$

Combining these two results and solving for the rate of excess demand, $RED = (YD - YT)/YT \simeq \ln YD/YT$, yields the 'non-inflationary rate of excess demand':

$$NIRED = \frac{1}{\pi_1} (\omega_1 CG - DG). \tag{10}$$

It is a positive function of the capital gap (owing to the negative effect of *CG* on wage claims) and a negative function of the distributive gap $DG = (\pi_0 + \kappa_0 + \omega_0 - 1)$. Inflation will develop if and only if $RED > NIRED$. This can be avoided by adequate demand management policies. The *RED* thus becomes the relevant policy indicator in the classical regime, a role played by *UR* in a Keynesian regime.

The stationary classical unemployment equilibrium described by (10) will of course obtain if and only if $NIRED \geqslant 0$ and $CG \geqslant 0$. Given (7), the first condition can also be recast as $CG \geqslant NIRU$. There is otherwise no stationary classical unemployment equilibrium.

Repressed inflation. The relevant equations are similar to those of the classical regime, except for the production and employment levels, which are now constrained by the availability of labour rather than capital ($LT = LS$, $YT = Y(LS)$). Demand pressures are now positive on both the goods and the labour markets.

A stationary 'repressed inflation' equilibrium[5] will not exist unless the distributive gap DG and the capital gap CG are both negative. The first condition would imply weak income claims ($\omega_0 + \pi_0 + \kappa_0 < 1$); the second would imply a potential employment level larger than the supply of labour. If these two conditions are not satisfied, price adjustment will progressively lead to either Keynesian or classical unemployment, depending on the values of DG and CG.

Aggregation. We now abandon the fiction of an homogeneous economy in favour of an explicit aggregation over micro-markets. This procedure calls for specifying a joint frequency distribution over the demand for goods, the supply of labour and the availability of production capacities. Simple assumptions (see Lambert, 1988) lead to an employment equation where the aggregate employment level is a CES function of the aggregate concepts $L(YD)$, $L(YP)$ and LS used so far. This CES function thus replaces the usual 'min' condition. More formally, we have

$$LT = \{L(YD)^{-\rho} + L(YP)^{-\rho} + LS^{-\rho}\}^{-1/\rho}, \qquad \rho \geqslant 0 \qquad (11)$$

where ρ is linked to the correlations between the values across micro-markets of the demand for goods, the availability of production capacities and the supply of labour. The lower the value of ρ, the lower the correlation between these values and thus the more important the mismatch between the distribution of these three quantities across micro-markets. Note that this simple formulation makes impossible the distinction between labour mismatch and capacity mismatch. Such a distinction would require the use of a different exponent for each aggregate variable appearing in (11).

---

[5] The now well-established terminology 'repressed inflation' may seem inappropriate in our case, as all three regimes can actually witness inflation or deflation, depending on the values of the parameters and of starting conditions. We use it only to mean 'generalised excess demand'.

We define as the 'structural unemployment rate at equilibrium' ($SURE$) the unemployment rate that would be observed in a situation of macro-economic equilibrium, i.e. for $L(YD) = L(YP) = LS$. Given (11), one obtains

$$SURE = \frac{LS - LT}{LS} = 1 - 3^{-1/\rho}. \tag{12}$$

It is a negative function of ρ. For $\rho \to \infty$, $SURE \to 0$, structural imbalances disappear, and equation (11) boils down to the usual min condition.

An immediate implication of (11) is that the elasticities of employment with respect to $L(YD)$, $L(YP)$ and LS are all less than unity and correspond to the proportions of firms or micro-markets in each regime (denoted ϕ_K, ϕ_C and ϕ_I, respectively):

$$\eta_{LT \cdot L(YD)} = \left\{ \frac{LT}{L(YD)} \right\}^\rho = \phi_K \tag{13}$$

$$\eta_{LT \cdot L(YP)} = \left\{ \frac{LT}{L(YP)} \right\}^\rho = \phi_C$$

$$\eta_{LT \cdot LS} = \left(\frac{LT}{LS} \right)^\rho = \phi_I.$$

The elasticities of aggregate employment to the wage rate or to the demand for domestic goods will thus be a weighted average of the elasticities in each pure regime, with weights ϕ_K, ϕ_C and ϕ_I, respectively. With respect to the wage rate, we have

$$\eta_{LT \cdot W} = \phi_K \eta_{L(YD) \cdot W} + \phi_C \eta_{L(YP) \cdot W} + \phi_I \eta_{LS \cdot W}. \tag{14}$$
$$+ \qquad\qquad - \qquad\qquad ?$$

As for the demand for domestic goods, we may reasonably assume that it has no short-term effect on production capacities or on labour supply. The elasticity of aggregate employment to YD is then simply

$$\eta_{LT \cdot YD} = \phi_K \eta_{L(YD) \cdot YD}. \tag{15}$$

Because all three regimes are simultaneously present, inflationary pressures are again a mixture of cost-push and demand-pull, as in the classical unemployment regime. The endogenous influences on wages and prices are now twofold, namely, unemployment UR (which moderates wages) and demand pressures RED. They operate against the background of income claims DG and classical unemployment CG. Price stability again requires that demand-pull inflationary pressures be exactly offset by cost-push deflationary pressures. The stationary equilibrium relationship between the rates of unemployment and excess demand is given by the wage and price equations. With perfect foresight we obtain – say from (10), written in terms of observed rates,

$$UR = \frac{1}{\omega_1}(DG + \pi_1 \, RED). \tag{16}$$

To determine the *NIRU* and the *NIRED*, we need a second relationship between these two variables. It is given by the employment equation (11). The latter can be rewritten as

$$1 = \left\{\frac{L(YD)}{LT}\right\}^{-\rho} + \left\{\frac{L(YP)}{LS}\frac{LS}{LT}\right\}^{-\rho} + \left(\frac{LS}{LT}\right)^{-\rho}$$

$$= (1 + RED)^{-\rho} + (1 - CG)^{-\rho}(1 - UR)^{\rho} + (1 - UR)^{\rho}$$

where we use the definitions

$$CG = \frac{LS - L(YP)}{LS} \quad \text{and} \quad RED = \frac{YD - YT}{YT} = \frac{L(YD) - LT}{LT}$$

(with given technical coefficients and no labour hoarding). Simply rearranging the terms leads to

$$(1 - UR)^{\rho} = \frac{1 - (1 + RED)^{-\rho}}{1 + (1 - CG)^{-\rho}}. \tag{17}$$

Equations (16) and (17) are reproduced in figure 15.6. The positively sloped linear function PP' is (16), the negatively sloped nonlinear function LL' is (17). The effects of changes in the parameters DG, CG and ρ are indicated by dashed curves. When ρ decreases and goes to zero (growing mismatch), the negatively sloped curve becomes steeper and steeper; in the limit ($\rho = 0$), it becomes vertical at $UR = 1$. At the other end, when ρ goes to infinity, the curvature of the function increases until it becomes a right angle with vertex at CG on the horizontal axis. The employment equation (11) then boils down to the 'min' condition used in the previous subsections. The intersection of the functions depicted in figure 15.6 determines the stationary equilibrium of the economy. The *NIRU* is seen to be a positive function of the capital gap CG, of the distributive gap DG and of the degree of mismatch ($1/\rho$). The *NIRED* is positively affected by the capital gap and the degree of mismatch, negatively affected by the distributive gap. This is summarised in table 15.6.

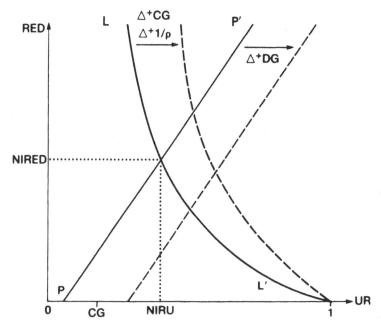

Fig. 15.6. Determination of the stationary equilibrium (equations (16) and (17)).

The table also indicates the effects of DG, CG and $1/\rho$ on the proportion of firms in each regime. The signs of these effects follow from the definitions of ϕ_K, ϕ_C and ϕ_I given in (13):

$$\phi_K = \left\{ \frac{L(YD)}{LT} \right\}^{-1/\rho} = (1 + RED)^{-\rho}$$

$$\phi_C = \left\{ \frac{L(YP)}{LT} \right\}^{-1/\rho} = (1 - UR)(1 - CG)^{-\rho}$$

$$\phi_I = \left\{ \frac{LS}{LT} \right\}^{-1/\rho} = (1 - UR)^{-\rho}$$

with $\phi_K + \phi_C + \phi_I = 1$.

The LL' and PP' curves depicted in figure 15.6 only describe stationary equilibrium conditions. In the very short run, the economy can be off these two curves and in either one of the four regions they delineate. The slow adjustment of labour to its equilibrium value (the so-called labour

Table 15.6. *Effects of increases in DG, CG and* $(1/\rho)$ *on the unemployment and excess demand rates and on regime proportions*

	UR	RED	ϕ_K	ϕ_C	ϕ_I
Distributive gap (*DG*)	+	−	+	−	−
Capital gap (*CG*)	+	+	−	+	−
Mismatch $(1/\rho)$	+	+	0	0	0

hoarding phenomenon) is responsible for deviations from *LL'*; the sluggishness of wage and price expectations or adjustments is responsible for deviations from *PP'*. The rate of change of employment is positive above *LL'*, negative below; the rate of inflation is positive (or more generally larger than its expected value) above *PP'* and negative below. Traditional fix-price models completely disregard the *PP'* curve and proceed as if any point on *LL'* could be reached by adequate demand management policies. This amounts to assuming that, in the very short run, wage-price stickiness enables demand management policies to produce any desired deviation from *PP'*.

4. Empirical results

We have six equations to estimate: the two technical relationships (2), the consumption function, the import and employment equations, the wage and price equations. Ideally, one would like to estimate all these equations jointly by *FIML*, in order to take account in an efficient way of simultaneity and of the many cross-equation restrictions. Because of the strong nonlinearities involved and of the danger of not being able to control effectively an iterative optimization procedure involving all the parameters at once, we used instead a sequential block-by-block limited information procedure. This means (1) joint *ML* estimation of the two technical relationships; (2) OLS estimation of the consumption function; (3) joint *ML* estimation of the import and employment equations (this joint estimation is motivated by the presence in both equations of the unobserved variable *YD*, the demand for domestic goods defined as (observed) total final demand minus (unobserved) structural imports – see p. 377 above); (4) instrumental variable estimation of the wage and price equations.

This sequential estimation procedure implies that the values of the technical coefficients *A* and *B* used in estimating the employment and the price equations are those obtained in step (1) from the estimation of the technical relationships. Similarly, the values of the excess demand indicator

In $YD/YT^* \simeq RED$ used in estimating the price equation are the values previously derived from the estimation of the import and employment equations. The results of this sequential estimation procedure are reproduced in table 15.7. We first discuss each equation separately; these comments are numbered (1)–(16), and those that are specific to our approach are italicised. We then turn to the implied values of the *NIRU* and *NIRED*.

Table 15.7. *Estimated equations*
(Standard errors in parentheses; estimated variables denoted ˜)

(1) $\ln \dfrac{YT}{LT} = 2.58 + 0.022t - 0.013t' + 0.55\,\dfrac{0.27}{1 - 0.73\Lambda}\ln\dfrac{W}{PI} + 0.06\ln DUL$

  (0.27) (0.002) (0.001) (0.05)   (0.04)

  s.e.e. = 0.0075 $DW = 2.00$ sample = 1954–82

(2) $\ln \dfrac{YT}{KA} = 1.55 + 0.022t - 0.013t' - 0.45\,\dfrac{0.27}{1 - 0.73\Lambda}\ln\dfrac{W}{PI} + 0.25\ln DUC$

  (0.27) (0.002) (0.001) (0.05)   (0.06)

  s.e.e. = 0.0149 $DW = 2.00$ sample = 1964–82

Notes to equations (1) *and* (2): Correlation between the residuals of equations (1) and (2): 0.71

  $t' = 0$ before 1974 ($t = 22$), $t' = t - 22$ afterwards

(3) $\Delta\ln CT = 0.28 + 0.22UR - 0.76\Delta UR + 0.013\Delta\ln PC$
    (0.15) (0.17)   (0.30)   (0.10)

     $+ 0.46\Delta\ln DI + 0.42\quad\ln DI_{-1} - 0.47\ln CT_{-1}$
      (0.14)   (0.13)   (0.15)

  s.e.e. = 0.0087 $DW = 2.00$ sample = 1954–82

(4) $\ln MT = -2.08 + 1.14\ln FD - 0.28\ln PM^* + 0.69\ln PF^* + 1.79\ln\dfrac{\widetilde{YD}}{YT^*}$

  (0.0008)(0.00004)   (0.01)   (0.0002)   (0.24)

  s.e.e. = 0.0173 $DW = 2.13$ sample = 1955–82

where $\ln PM^* \equiv (0.70 + 0.20\,\Lambda + 0.10\,\Lambda^2)\ln PM$
  $\ln PF^* \equiv (0.15 + 0.25\,\Lambda + 0.60\,\Lambda^2)\ln PF$

(5) $LT = \{L(YD)^{-\rho} + L(YP)^{-\rho} + LS^{-\rho}\}^{-1/\rho}$

  $\ln L(YD) \equiv 0.014 + 0.73\{-\ln\tilde{A} + (0.96\ln YD + 0.04\ln\widetilde{YP})\} + 0.27 LT_{-1}$
      (0.004) (0.01)   (0.05)   (0.05)   (0.01)

  $\ln L(YP) \equiv 0.023 + 0.73(-\ln\tilde{A} + \ln\widetilde{YP}) + 0.27\ln LT_{-1}$
      (0.000) (0.01)   (0.01)

  $LS \equiv LT + U$
  $\rho \equiv (0.0065 + 0.00012t)^{-1}$
    (0.001) (0.000005)

  s.e.e. = 0.004 $DW = 2.28$ sample = 1955–82

Table 15.7 (*cont.*)

---

(6) $\Delta \ln W = 1.31 \, \Delta \ln P - 0.004 - 0.11 \, UR$
         $(0.22) (0.13) (0.50)$

$$+ 0.55 \, \Delta \ln \frac{YT}{LT} + 0.04 \left\{ \ln \left(\frac{YT}{LT} \right)_{-1} - \ln \left(\frac{W}{P} \right)_{-1} \right\}$$
$$(0.30) \phantom{+ 0.55 \, \Delta \ln \frac{YT}{LT} + 0.04} (0.27)$$

s.e.e. $= 0.0126$ $\qquad$ $DW = 1.70$ $\qquad$ sample $= 1956\text{--}82$

(6') $\Delta \ln WN = 0.91 \, \Delta \ln PC - 0.092 - 0.43 \, UR$
         $(0.17) (0.095) (0.15)$

$$+ 0.48 \, \Delta \ln \frac{YT}{LT} + 0.17 \left\{ \ln \left(\frac{YT}{LT} \right)_{-1} - \ln \left(\frac{WN}{PC} \right)_{-1} \right\}$$
$$(0.25) \phantom{+ 0.48 \, \Delta \ln \frac{YT}{LT} +} (0.15)$$

s.e.e. $= 0.0166$ $\qquad$ $DW = 2.01$ $\qquad$ sample $= 1956\text{--}82$

Instruments: $t, t', DUL, DUC, \ln\left(\dfrac{\widetilde{YD}}{YT^*}\right)_{-1}, \Delta \ln\left(\dfrac{YT}{LT}\right)_{-1}, \left(\dfrac{0.27}{1 - 0.73\Lambda} \ln \dfrac{W}{PI}\right)_{-1}$

---

(7) $\Delta \ln P = 0.038 + 1.04 \ln\left(\dfrac{\widetilde{YD}}{YT^*}\right) - 0.54 \, \Delta \ln\left(\dfrac{\widetilde{YD}}{YT^*}\right)$
         $(0.064) (0.50) \phantom{\ln\left(\dfrac{\widetilde{YD}}{YT^*}\right)} (0.33)$

$$+ 0.63 \, \Delta \ln APC - 0.27 \, \Delta^2 \ln APC + 0.41(\ln APC_{-1} - \ln P_{-1})$$
$$(0.17) (0.16) (0.28)$$

s.e.e. $= 0.010$ $\qquad$ $DW = 1.70$ $\qquad$ sample $= 1956\text{--}82$

$APC \equiv (\bar{A}^{-1} W + \bar{B}^{-1} 0.20 \, PI)$
$\phantom{APC \equiv (\bar{A}^{-1} W + \bar{B}^{-1}} (0.06)$

Instruments: $t, t', DUL, DUC, \ln\left(\dfrac{\widetilde{YD}}{YT^*}\right)_{-1}, \ln\left(\dfrac{YT}{LT}\right)_{-1}, \left(\dfrac{0.27}{1 - 0.73\Lambda} \ln \dfrac{W}{PI}\right)_{-1}, \Delta \ln P_{-1}$

Technical coefficients (equations (1) and (2))

1. The *observed* productivities of labour and capital are not in general equal to the *technical* productivities. This discrepancy is taken into account by using two indicators of factor utilization, DUL and DUC. The former is based on partial unemployment figures, the latter on business surveys in the manufacturing sector. The values of the coefficients of these variables should not be given too much economic significance, except to note that a coefficient of DUC smaller than unity may indicate that the fluctuations in the rate of capital utilisation as reported by firms in the manufacturing sector overestimate the fluctuations at the aggregate level.

2. The coefficients of the trend variables t and t' indicate that the rate

of exogenous technical progress has decreased from 2.2 per cent before 1974 to 0.9 per cent afterwards.

3. The values of the relative factor costs lag polynomial function were generated recursively, according to

$$\left\{\Theta(\Lambda)\ln\frac{W}{V}\right\}_t \equiv \frac{1-\theta}{1-\theta\Lambda}\ln\left(\frac{W}{V}\right)_t$$

$$\equiv (1-\theta)\ln\left(\frac{W}{V}\right)_t + \theta\left\{\Theta(\Lambda)\ln\frac{W}{V}\right\}_{t-1}.$$

The starting value $\{\Theta(\Lambda)\ln W/V\}_{t=0}$ was set at 5.45, close to the 1953 value of $\ln W/V$. This restriction was not rejected by a *LR* test. A value of θ equal to 0.73 means that only 27 per cent of the change in the optimal technical coefficients A and B implied by a change in relative factor costs is realized within a year.

4. In all this, we assumed the capital usage cost V to be proportional to the price of investment goods *PI*, which amounts to assuming, *inter alia*, a constant long-term real interest rate. More elaborate specifications, based on the observed nominal interest rate minus a weighted average of current and past inflation rates, proved unsuccessful.

Consumption function (equation (3))

5. We postulate a constant elasticity of private consumption CT to household disposable income DI. The static specification is written as

$$CT = e^{c_0 + c_1 UR}(DI^e)^{c_2} \tag{18}$$

where DI^e stands for expected disposable income and coefficient c_1 allows for an effect of unemployment on consumption. The dynamic specification is in the form of an error correction mechanism. Simple rearrangements of (18) lead to

$$\Delta\ln CT = c_1 UR + c_2\Delta\ln DI^e + (c_0 + c_2\ln DI_{-1} - \ln CT_{-1}). \tag{19}$$

In words a change in CT may result from an abnormal unemployment rate, from an expected change in disposable income, or from a previous discrepancy between desired and realized values. Let us now assume that only a fraction $\delta_2 \geqslant 1$ of such a discrepancy is corrected in the subsequent period. Let us furthermore define $\Delta\ln DI^e$ as $(\delta_0\Delta\ln DI + \delta_1\Delta\ln DI_{-1})$ and generalise $c_1 UR$ to $(c_{10}UR + c_{11}UR_{-1})$. Equation (19) then becomes

$$\Delta \ln CT = c_0 \delta_2 + (c_{10} + c_{11})UR - c_{11}\Delta UR$$
$$+ c_2(\delta_0 + \delta_1)\Delta \ln DI - c_1\delta_1\Delta^2 \ln DI$$
$$+ \delta_2(c_2 \ln DI_{-1} - \ln CT_{-1}). \tag{20}$$

6. With δ_1 set equal to zero, OLS estimation of (20) yields an elasticity of aggregate consumption to disposable income of $c_2 = 0.90$ in the long run and $\delta_0 c_2 = 0.46$ in the short run. The interpretation of the unemployment rate effect is unclear; the effect appears strongly negative in the short run, but positive in the long run. When added as an explanatory variable, the inflation rate appears insignificant.

Imports (equation (4))

7. The structural demand for imports MD (excluding energy, which is left exogenous) is specified as a log-linear function of total final demand (less public consumption and energy imports) FD, import prices PM and domestic prices PF. That is,

$$\ln \widetilde{MD} \underset{\text{def}}{=} - 2.08 + 1.14 \ln FD - 0.28 \ln PM^* + 0.69 \ln PF^*.$$

8. *As there are always some domestic 'micro-markets' in excess demand, observed imports will always be larger than or equal to the structural demand MD. The discrepancy between the two is a function of the importance of domestic production shortages, measured by* $\ln YD/YT^* \simeq RED \geqslant 0$, *where* YT^* *is the production level that could be reached with currently available inputs and a normal input utilisation rate, after correction for the hoarding of labour.*

9. The dynamics of the price effects turned out to be poorly defined. The weights given to past and current values were fixed at what seemed to be reasonable values in view of the unconstrained estimation results. These restrictions decrease the log-likelihood from 175 to 171 but leave the other parameter estimates basically unchanged. The elasticity of imports to final demand prices is (in absolute value) about twice their elasticity to import price themselves. The bundles of goods involved are perhaps different; or changes in PM may have repercussions on PF, so that their impact is split among the two variables.

10. *The elasticity of imports to total final demand is not very far from unity and substantially below that obtained with traditional methods, i.e. when demand pressure effects are not modelled explicitly but are simply replaced by a term (most often insignificant) involving the degree of capacity utilisation. The demand pressure coefficient is here significant and implies*

that a 1 percentage point increase in the excess demand for domestic goods increases imports by 1.79 per cent. With imports representing about 50 per cent of GDP in the 1970s, about 90 per cent of any excess demand for goods is immediately compensated by additional imports.

Figure 15.7 reproduces the ratio of total imports to structural imports (MT/MD) and of domestic demand to normal domestic supply – given available inputs – (YD/YT*) from 1955 to 1982. These two demand pressure indicators are always larger than one, thereby indicating that there always subsists a certain proportion of firms in the classical and inflation regimes which are constrained by capacity and labour shortages respectively rather than sales. That proportion, however, becomes especially weak in 1958 and after 1980, when the proportion of firms in the Keynesian regime becomes more important (77 per cent in 1982).

Employment equation (equation (5))

11. The employment equation has the form suggested in (11). Variable $\tilde{A}$ is the technical productivity of labour as estimated from equation (1). That is,

$$\ln \tilde{A} \underset{\text{def}}{=} 2.58 + 0.022t - 0.013t' + 0.55\Theta(\Lambda) \ln \frac{W}{V}.$$

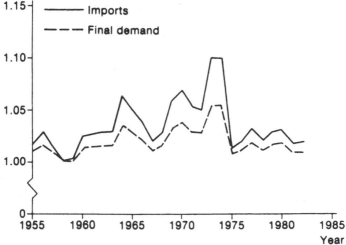

Fig. 15.7. Indicators of tension in the Belgian economy, 1955–82: imports (MT/MD) and final demand (YD/YT^*).

The potential and past employment levels appearing in the Keynesian labour demand function $L(YD)$ represent the effects of adjustment costs and the ensuing hoarding of labour during recessions. The interpretation of LT_{-1} in $L(YP)$ is similar. *The short-run elasticity of the Keynesian demand for labour $L(YD)$ to demand for domestic goods is estimated at*

$$\frac{\partial \ln L(YD)}{\partial \ln YD} = (0.96)(0.73) = 0.70.$$

The short-run elasticity of actual employment can be substantially lower and depends on the proportion of firms in the Keynesian regime ϕ_K:

$$\frac{\partial \ln LT}{\partial \ln YD} = \phi_K \frac{\partial \ln L(YD)}{\partial \ln YD}.$$

A typical value of ϕ_K is 0.55, which would imply a short-run elasticity equal to 0.39.

12. *The mismatch parameter ρ is represented as an inverse linear function of time. The values of ρ_0 and ρ_1 indicate a regular and significant increase in structural imbalances. As a consequence, the structural unemployment rate at equilibrium (SURE) has risen from 1.39 per cent in 1955 to 4.5 per cent in 1982.*

13. *The values of the Keynesian labour demand LK and of the potential employment level LP are reproduced in figure 15.4. They are obtained from $L(YD)$ and $L(YP)$, respectively, after deduction of the labour hoarding effect (no lagged employment effect). Both series remained fairly close to the supply of labour LS throughout the 1960s and early 1970s. In 1975 the Keynesian demand for labour collapsed; it has never recovered since. After 1975, the decline in the investment rate (see figure 15.5) caused the stagnation, and then the decline of potential employment. In 1982 the capital gap (i.e. the discrepancy between the supply of labour and the potential employment level in percentage points) reached about 9 per cent.*

14. The dramatic fall in the Keynesian demand for labour in 1975 resulted mainly from the collapse of the demand for domestic goods, enhanced by the effects of productivity gains (see table 15.8). The change in the demand for domestic goods was itself the result of a similar change in total final demand arising from lower investments and lower exports. By 1976 investments and exports had both recovered, and they produced a strong increase of total final demand. The rise in the demand for domestic goods turned out to be much weaker, however, while the demand for imports rose strongly, with 40 per cent of the increase owing to a

Table 15.8. *Analysis of the changes in the Keynesian demand for labour and its determinants after* 1975
(Percentage points)

	1975	1976	1981	1982
Growth in Keynesian demand for labour	−8.0	+0.7	−3.0	−1.8
of which: wages	−2.8	−3.3	−2.4	−2.2
demand for domestic goods	−5.2	+4.0	−0.6	+0.4
Growth in final demand	−4.4	+7.3	−1.3	+1.2
of which: consumption	+1.2	+4.9	−0.1	+1.3
government spending	+4.8	+3.9	+1.2	−1.5
investment:				
fixed capital	−2.1	+2.8	−16.4	−0.8
total investment	−14.1	+7.1	−17.0	−1.5
exports	−9.4	+11.8	+3.3	+3.4
Growth in imports demand	−2.8	+15.4	−1.1	+3.2
of which: final demand	−7.0	+9.3	−1.9	+1.9
prices	+4.2	+6.1	+0.8	+1.3

significant loss of competitiveness. The years 1981–82 witnessed again an important decrease in investment. This time, however, exports remained steady and there was no additional loss of competitiveness.

Wage equation (equations (6)–(6'))

15. The dynamic structure of the wage equation is similar to that of the consumption function (see above). The wage equation can be written in terms of either labour costs or net labour income per employee. In the former case, the dependent variable is defined as the wage cost per employee, including employers' social security contributions, and the relevant price index is the price of value added. In the latter case, the dependent variable is the net wage rate, after deduction for direct taxes and employees' social security contributions, and the relevant price index is the price of consumption goods. In both cases the observed productivity of labour proved to have a larger explanatory power than the technical concept derived from equation (1). The sign of the unemployment rate coefficient is negative, as expected, albeit not significantly different from zero in the labour cost formulation. In the latter case, also, the coefficient of the inflation rate at 1.31 is larger than (although not significantly different from) unity. This is the sort of result one would expect in the face of an oil shock with wage demands indexed on the price of consumption goods rather than the price of value added. From the

estimates of equation (6) and (6'), one can retrieve the values of ω_0 and ω_1 mentioned in tables 15.4 and 15.5. One obtains from (6) $\hat{\omega}_0 = 0.90$, $\hat{\omega}_1 = 0.1$ and from equation (6') $\hat{\omega}_0 = 0.58$, $\hat{\omega}_1 = 0.43$. One must be aware, however, of the extremely poor precision of these estimates. Further work is obviously needed on this point.

Price equation (equation (7))

16. The dynamic structure is again similar to that of the consumption function. The specification imposes that, in the long run, cost increases are fully passed on to prices. This restriction is not rejected by the data. When freely estimated, the long-run elasticity of prices to average production costs turns out to be 0.97 and not significantly different from unity. The capital usage cost is approximated by a constant α times the price index of investment goods, PI. This amounts to assuming that the sum of the depreciation and real interest rates (corrected for taxation) remains constant at α. The latter is estimated at 0.20. It follows that $\hat{\kappa}_0 \simeq \hat{\alpha}(KA/YP) \simeq 0.4$. One notices the strong and significant demand pressure effect, implying that the mark-up on costs increases by one percentage point for every 1 per cent increase in excess demand. The constant term and the error correction coefficient imply a normal mark-up rate equal to $\hat{\pi}_0 = 0.038/0.4 = 9.5$ per cent, which seems quite reasonable (but again is subject to a high standard error).

Estimates of the NIRU and NIRED

The 1973, 1975 and 1982 estimated values of the *NIRU* and the *NIRED* are reproduced in table 15.9. Each of these three years corresponds to a turning point in the economic developments between 1970 and 1985. 1973 is the last year with rapid growth and one-digit inflation; 1975 coincides with the trough of the recession consecutive to the first oil shock; 1982, the last year covered by our data, is also the starting point of a strict incomes policy.

The values of the capital gap CG and of the mismatch parameter ρ used to compute the *NIRU* and the *NIRED* and reported in table 15.9 are those obtained from the estimation of the econometric model. This is *not* the case however for the values of the distributive gap DG. The extremely poor precision of the parameter estimates underlying DG (especially ω_0 and κ_0), and the crude specification whereby ω_0 and π_0 are constant through time, call for the use of extraneous information. It

Table 15.9. *Estimates of the non-inflationary unemployment rate (NIRU) and non-inflationary rate of excess demand (NIRED)*

	Distributive gap, DG (%)	Capital gap, CG (%)	Mismatch ρ	Equilibrium structural unemployment rate, SURE (%)	Non-inflationary unemployment rate, NIRU (%)	Non-inflationary rate of excess demand, NIRED (%)	Unemployment rate, UR (%)	Rate of excess demand, RED (%)
1973	0.00	−0.41	31.8	3.4	4.5	1.9	3.8	5.6
1975	4.00	0.30	29.6	3.6	10.1	0.3	7.5	0.8
Variant	0.00	0.30	29.6	3.6	5.0	2.1		
1982	0.00	8.77	23.8	4.5	10.8	4.5	16.0	1.0
Variant 1	0.00	0.00	23.8	4.5	6.1	2.5		
Variant 2	4.00	8.77	23.8	4.5	13.4	1.7		

seemed reasonable to us to assume a widening of the distributive gap from 0 per cent in 1973 to 4 per cent in 1975, as a result of the first oil shock. The distributive gap may have been reduced towards zero again in 1982 as a result of the strict incomes policy.

From table 15.9, we draw the following conclusions.

1. The estimated decline in ρ (an inverse function of time, as an approximation) entails a growing mismatch (whether due to the labour market or to the production facilities and product mix), and hence a steadily growing 'structural unemployment rate at equilibrium' (*SURE*).

2. The assumption made about the distributive gap is very important: the difference in the estimated value of the *NIRU* is 5.1 per cent in 1975 and 2.6 per cent in 1982. If $DG = 4$ per cent is indeed more plausible for 1975 and $DG = 0$ is more plausible for 1982, one would estimate that the *NIRU* has not changed much between 1975 and 1982, remaining at the embarrassing level of 10–11 per cent.

3. The factors behind the *NIRU* in 1974–75 and in 1982 are quite different. The main difference comes from the 'capital gap'–the insufficient number of working posts–which accounts for 4.7 percentage points in the 1982 estimate of the *NIRU* ($10.8 - 6.1 = 4.7$). The observed level of unemployment for 1982 could be decomposed as follows:

	(%)
Total unemployment	16.0
due to: the capital gap	4.7
structural mismatch	4.5
need to offset potential demand pressures	1.6
insufficient demand	5.2

An important conclusion is that *stronger demand could reduce unemployment* (in 1982) *by 5 per cent without inflationary pressure*, so long as the 'distributive gap' *DG* remains close to zero. Another important conclusion is that *creation of additional capacity* (*to eliminate the capital gap*) *and better adjustment of supply to demand* (*to eliminate structural mismatch*) *would be needed to reduce unemployment* (*and the NIRU*) *below* 11 *per cent.*

The results of table 15.9 are portrayed in figure 15.8. The figure reproduces the positions in 1973, 1975 and 1982 of the two curves LL' and PP', the intersection of which determines the *NIRU* and the *NIRED*. The 1982 curves are represented by continuous lines. The points E_{73}, E_{75}

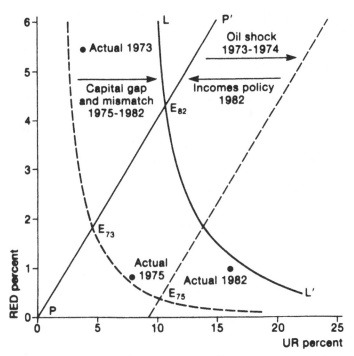

Fig. 15.8.   Actual and non-inflationary values of UR and RED in Belgium,
1973, 1975 and 1982.

and E_{82} describe the values of the $NIRU$ and the $NIRED$ in 1973, 1975 and 1982, respectively.

5.   Concluding remarks

We embarked on this confession with the modest aims of (1) seeking an explanation for the differential rate of growth of Belgian real wages in the 1970s; (2) seeking an explanation for the dramatic decline in employment and increase in gross apparent labour productivity of the Belgian manufacturing sector over the past decade; and (3) summarising what we had learned from the estimation of quantity rationing models.

On the first point, we note that our price and wage equations, crude as their specification may be, track the sample data quite accurately without revealing residual anomalies in the 1970s. At the same time, several coefficients of these equations are estimated with low precision. The equations reflect the interdependence of prices, wages, productivity and employment; caution is needed in drawing conclusions about causal or dynamic structures.

Are the mechanisms of price and wage formation in Belgium apt to create an inflationary spiral? The *estimation* of our equation for the price of value added yields a unitary long-run elasticity to average production costs, and a unitary short-run elasticity to demand pressures. The *estimation* of our wage equation suggest a short-run elasticity of nominal wage costs to prices (of either value added or consumption) close to, and possibly exceeding, unity. Also, the *specification* of our wage equation imposes a unitary long-run elasticity to gross average productivity, which itself is positively related to real wages. In such a model, exogenous inflationary pressures through wages (an oil shock, with full indexation of wages on consumption prices) or prices (a temporarily excessive level of final demand) may easily result in an inflationary spiral. The record of the 1970s confirms that danger, and suggests an alarming sensitivity of the Belgian economy to inflationary tendencies. The manufacturing sector, with its heavy dependence on export sales, bears the brunt of that sensitivity.

On the second and third questions, we reach parallel conclusions: *it is difficult to separate out the respective influences of factor prices (real wages) and effective demand in accounting for the inadequate performance of Belgian employment since 1974. The only safe conclusion is that both aspects matter.*

Looking at history through the filter of quantity rationing models, we feel that the concepts of 'potential employment' and 'Keynesian labour demand' provide a convincing (to us) interpretation, which is still grossly incomplete. These concepts are helpful to portray the supply side and demand side of the economy. It seems definitely useful to evaluate by how much output and employment could be boosted without either additional investment or the high rates of capacity utilisation suspected of 'rekindling inflation'. Expressing these evaluations in terms of 'non-inflationary rates' of unemployment and excess demand is also helpful. As a corollary, one evaluates how many new working posts should be made available (through investment, additional shifts or work-sharing, in order of decreasing contributions to potential output) along the road to full employment to bridge the 'capital gap'. Hopefully, this combination of traditional and disequilibrium concepts may help bridge an 'intellectual gap' as well.

At the same time, one must be careful not to interpret the spread between labour supply (or potential employment) and Keynesian labour demand as being 'due' to insufficient demand. In a country that exports more than one-third of its value added and competes with imports for another third, excess supply may simply reflect excessive, though non-increasing, costs – either marginal (quantity-setting firms) or average (price-setting firms). Thus, *a part of what is commonly labelled 'Keynesian unemployment' may well be the consequence of a real-wage problem.* And that part could be significant in Belgium.

Similarly, one must be careful not to interpret the spread between labour supply and potential employment as being 'due' to factor prices (real wages). When potential employment corresponds to full use of given facilities, and varies over time through scrapping and/or new investments, *one must reckon with the decisive influence of demand expectations on scrapping and investment decisions.* Then, *a part of what is commonly labelled 'classical unemployment' may well be the consequence of an effective demand problem* – and that part could be significant in Belgium.

We must accordingly conclude that an analysis of the employment problem which does not treat exports and investment endogenously is grossly inadequate. If, as suggested by Bauwens and d'Alcantara (1983), the elasticity of exports with respect to domestic production capacity is three times as high as the elasticity with respect to domestic wages, then a better understanding of the investment process deserves first priority on the research agenda. Given the complexity of the problem, it would seem imperative to rely on more disaggregated data, using all available sources of information.

There is an additional reason why such a research strategy commends itself. A number of authors have stressed the growing extent to which labour is now regarded as fixed factor – a remark that is particularly applicable to Europe, and even more so to Belgium. New hirings and new fixed investments are then best viewed as a joint decision, and should be analysed as such – even though the choice of techniques (factor proportions) deserves separate attention.

There is an element of paradox here, since the model of Section 4 suggests instead a quite rapid adjustment of employment to desired levels, as if labour were in fact a variable factor. However, the 'investment' aspect of hiring decisions is much less significant in periods of growth (1963–74) than in periods of stagnation, or high uncertainty about future growth rates (today). Again, that aspect may affect less significantly layoffs (as in the period 1975–83) than new hirings (today?).

Needless to say, the care needed to interpret the result of our disequilibrium econometrics is equally appropriate when interpreting traditional concepts, like the *NIRU* (see in particular our comments about table 15.9).

A related question left unanswered in this confession came up in the first part of Section 3: Is the elasticity of employment with respect to real wages the same in case of wage increases and wage decreases? Or could it be that the relationship of employment to real wages is 'kinky', in a small open economy like Belgium, with a higher elasticity of employment to wage increases than to wage cuts? What prompts us to repeat this interrogation is the feeling that employment in the Belgian manufacturing sector is unlikely to grow, in response to the incomes policy of the 1980s, at a rate comparable to that at which it fell in response (partially at least) to the differential growth of real wages in the 1970s.

There is again an element of paradox here, since contractual and legal measures have attempted to protect labour from easy dismissals. These measures have clearly been of limited effectiveness in the manufacturing sector. One type of situation when they are bound to be ineffective is of course bankruptcy – a phenomenon of quantitative significance, as revealed above, but seldom modelled explicitly in econom(etr)ics. A realistic model of investment decisions should thus treat scrapping and new investment separately, and should consider financial constraints explicitly. A combination of traditional and disequilibrium concepts is also appropriate in that area.

16 Europe's unemployment problem: introduction and synthesis*

1. General presentation

The economic record of Europe over the past thirty years is divided into two contrasting subperiods: a period of fast balanced growth until 1974, a period of slow growth with unemployment since then. The contrast between the two subperiods, and the contrast vis-à-vis the US which has followed throughout a path of relatively slow but sustained growth, are brought out in table 16.1, which gives average growth rates for major macroeconomic variables over the two subperiods. The developments in Europe during the second subperiod are illustrated by figure 16.1, which traces unemployment against excess capacity in manufacturing since 1975. The gradual rise of unemployment and the cyclical behaviour of capacity utilisation are clearly visible.

The originality of the European Unemployment Programme (EUP) consists in presenting the results obtained from estimating the same model (broadly speaking) in ten countries (the US, the eight major EEC countries and Austria)[1] for periods from the late fifties or early sixties to the mid eighties.[2] Thus, the model specification had to be flexible enough to cover

---

* Chap. 1 in *Europe's Unemployment Problem*, J. H. Drèze, C. R. Bean, J. P. Lambert, F. Mehta and H. Sneessens, eds., MIT Press, Cambridge, Mass., 1991. The authors have benefited from the invaluable assistance of Fatemeh Mehta, who has in particular prepared all the tables and figures. Her work was supported by contract II/09602 of DG II at the Commission of the European Communities. We have also benefited from comments and suggestions from Torben Andersen, Michael Burda, Wolfgang Franz, Jean-Paul Lambert, Guy Laroque, Fiorella Padoa-Schioppa and Henri Sneessens. Our main debt naturally goes to the 24 authors of the ten country papers collected in this book.
[1] A related study for Switzerland (Stalder, 1989) also exists.
[2] See Appendix 16.2 for a list of papers and authors.

Table 16.1. Macroeconomic indicators, Europe/US

	Average Real Growth Rates	Europe	US
GDP (table 10)	61–74	4.6	3.6
	75–88	2.1	3.2
Employment (table 2)	61–74	0.3	1.9
	75–88	0.1	1.9
Private Consumption (table 17)	61–74	4.8	3.8
	75–88	2.4	3.2
Public Consumption (table 19)	61–74	3.6	3.1
	75–88	2.3	3.2
Investment (table 21)	61–74	5.0	3.8
	75–88	1.2	3.2
Real Wages (table 29)	61–74	4.6	1.8
	75–88	1.6	0.9
Labour Productivity	61–74	4.3	1.7
	75–88	2.0	1.3
Unemployment Rate (table 3)	1960	2.5	5.5
	1974	2.6	5.6
	1988	11.3	5.5

Source: Statistical Annex, European Economy, No. 38, November 1988, Commission of the European Community.

the diversity of experiences in the different countries, and for each country in the two subperiods. When the research project was initiated in 1986, it was by no means obvious that such an attempt would succeed. The idea came out of the Conference on *The Rise of Unemployment*, held at Chelwood Gate, Sussex, in May 1985, with Proceedings published in *Economica*, Supplement, 1986.[3] At that conference, much was learned from comparing the unemployment experience in a dozen countries.[4] But the reasons for the differences and similarities were difficult to identify, because different authors had adopted different analytical frameworks. It was difficult to separate out real differences from differences of approach. The authors therefore decided to adopt a common framework, combining the best elements from the different papers, and to estimate a set of country models using the same broad specification.

It may be said at the outset that the project has met with at least one measure of success; namely, that the common specification has indeed proven flexible enough to describe the main developments in the different

[3] Also available as a book edited by C. Bean, R. Layard and S. Nickell and published by Basil Blackwell.
[4] The same as here, plus Australia and Japan.

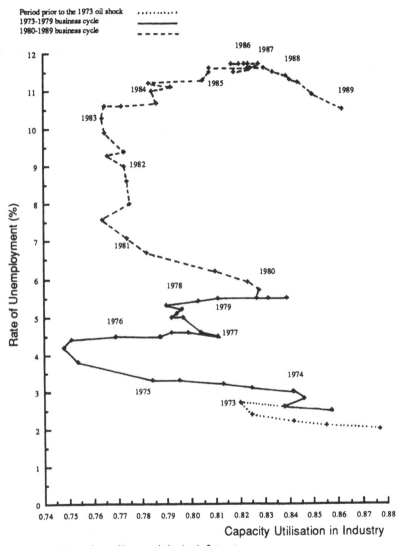

Period prior to the 1973 oil shock ....
1973-1979 business cycle ——————
1980-1989 business cycle − − − − − −

Quarterly observations are shown, with years marked against the first quarter.
Source: European Commission, DG2, 1989.

Figure 16.1   Rate of unemployment and capacity utilisation in industry in the
European Community. Quarterly observations are shown, with the years marked
against the first quarter. *Source: European Economy.*

countries over the different subperiods. Our model has provided a framework within which the advocates of the different analytical approaches could identify more precisely their grounds for disagreement, and evaluate these against empirical findings; and it has provided a framework within which the experience of different countries could be interpreted more (meaning)fully than before.

This paper is an overall report about empirical results, stressing the aspects where a comparison of national findings is instructive and the aspects which are more specific to our model. These empirical results are discussed under two headings: prices, wages and productivity (Section 4); then output, employment and demand (Section 5). In order to permit interpretation of the empirical findings, a brief presentation of the model is given in Section 2, followed by a more detailed presentation in Section 3. A concise, non-technical summary of the main findings is given in Section 6 (to which hurried readers may turn), leading to some policy conclusions.

2.   Overview and microeconomic foundations

2.1.   Broad structure

The model describes the short-run evolution of an open economy in terms of two aggregate domestic commodities: a physical good and labour. The broad structure is outlined in figure 16.2. The model defines for each period (year)[5] the supply and demand of the physical good and of labour. The interaction of supply and demand on the two markets determines simultaneously output and employment and hence also the rates of capacity utilisation and of unemployment.[6] These two variables in turn trigger price and wage adjustments. The evolution of prices and quantities feeds back into the determinants of supply and demand, thereby closing the model.

2.2.   Employment

Our primary concern is (un)employment. At the heart of the model lies the recognition that for a filled job to exist three conditions must be satisfied. First, that there exists a worker in the right place and with the right skills for the job. Second, that there is the capital available to employ the worker. Third, that there is a demand for the worker's output.

[5] Only the French model is estimated from quarterly data.
[6] This joint determination is explained below.

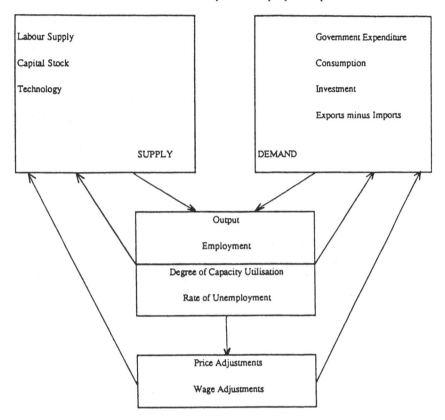

Figure 16.2

The first of these requires little explanation. However, the second and third do require an explanation of the underlying model of production technology and firm behaviour. Within the neoclassical paradigm of perfect competition, with smooth production functions, firms will always vary the capital/labour proportions when relative prices provide incentives to do so, and firms can in principle sell as much as they wish at the prevailing price.

That paradigm seems inconsistent with the results of business surveys. These regularly show a small proportion of firms claiming that capacity is a constraint and a significant proportion claiming to experience demand constraints. Instead, the managers of a neoclassical firm should always claim that capacity is a constraint if they operate with an upward sloping short-run marginal cost curve; and they should never refer to a demand constraint if they face a perfectly elastic demand curve. This suggests replacing the assumption of short-run substitutability between capital and labour by an assumption of limited *ex post* factor substitutability, leading to well-defined concepts of 'capacity output' and 'capacity employment' in the short run. It also suggests replacing the assumption of 'profit maximisation at given prices' by the assumption that firms announce selling prices and then meet demand. Price setting is the natural formulation under imperfect competition, in which case price is set so as to equate (expected) marginal revenue and (expected) marginal cost. It remains valid in the limiting case of perfect competition where marginal revenue is equal to price, so that price is set equal to (expected) marginal cost.[7]

Our setting is thus one where firms set output prices and choose input levels, given their observations or expectations regarding demand conditions and input prices. At any point in time, firms inherit a given capital stock as a result of past investment decisions. If *ex post* factor substitution possibilities are limited (in particular, take time), there is at that point an upper bound to employment dictated by the available number of job slots (capacity employment – *LC*) and an associated upper bound on the level of output (capacity output – *YC*) determined by the level of capital and the embodied technical coefficients.

However, employment may fall short of capacity employment because the firm cannot hire as many workers as it would like. In that case employment will be equal to the available workforce (labour supply – *LS*) and the output level will be determined accordingly (full employment output – *YS*).

Employment may also fall short of capacity employment and labour supply because at the prevailing output price there is insufficient demand forthcoming. In that case output will be determined by effective demand (demand-determined output – *YD*) and the employment level will be determined accordingly (demand-determined employment – *LD*).

These three employment concepts (and their output counterparts) correspond to the three prerequisites for the existence of a filled job, that were outlined at the start of this section. In a given plant or shop *i*, actual

[7] For a rigorous definition of competitive equilibria with price setting firms, see Dehez and Drèze (1988a). That paper extends the concept of competitive equilibrium to the case of fixed costs and increasing returns to scale. A further extension to imperfect competition is in preparation.

employment L_i and output Y_i will correspond to the minimum of these three conceptual levels:

$$L_i = \min(LC_i, LD_i, LS_i) \tag{1}$$

$$Y_i = \min(YC_i, YD_i, YS_i). \tag{2}$$

A word of caution about these relationships is needed. They are introduced here to describe some of the constraints (physical and economic) under which firms operate. The formulation is quite general, and compatible in principle with an equilibrium interpretation as well as a disequilibrium interpretation. For instance, when capacity exceeds demand, it could still be the case that demand is precisely at the level for which the chosen price is optimal, whereas the excess capacity is consistent with minimisation of the total cost of producing that output from indivisible equipment. But it could also be the case that excess capacity is due to a depressed demand level, and will be eliminated (through layoffs or scrapping) if demand expectations do not recover soon enough.

Still relationships (1)–(2) are not the end of the story, because one needs to explain (i) the decisions of the firms about the level of capital, the embodied technical coefficients and the output price; (ii) the clearing of output markets; (iii) the aggregation of firm level variables into macro-economic variables; and (iv) the determination of input prices and 'demand' for output. We take up these four items in sequence.

2.3. The rest of the model

(i) Firms treat factor prices as given when making their pricing and investment decisions. Profit maximisation dictates that prices are set as a mark-up over short-run marginal cost. The markup reflects either the elasticity of demand for output on imperfectly competitive markets, or the margin needed to cover fixed costs at normal rates of capacity utilisation, or both. Short-run marginal cost depends on wages and the level of productivity embodied in the technology, at least when capacity and labour supply constraints do not bite.

However, it is costly to continuously adjust prices, which consequently have to be posted in advance on the basis of demand expectations, If there is a chance that demand will be so high that capacity or labour supply constraints bite, then the firm may wish to increase its mark-up to choke off some or all of the excess demand. Alternatively, it may prefer to maintain a reputation for 'fair' pricing, while running down inventories (generally ignored here)[8] and possibly building up back orders. Which combination of these two policies prevails is an important empirical question; the specification of the price equations needs to be flexible enough to admit either answer.[9]

The embodied technical coefficients and the rate of capital accumulation will depend upon (expected) factor prices. Because the level of demand fluctuates over time, the expected level of utilisation of new machines or facilities matters: having capital lying idle some of the time increases the effective cost of that capital and reduces the profitability of investment. Finally, the investment rate will obviously depend on the gap between the desired stock of capital and existing capital. For these two reasons, investment should be positively related to the degree of capacity utilisation.

(ii) Having set prices, on the basis of their demand expectations, firms which are not constrained by capacity or labour supply will *always* be willing to meet the level of demand forthcoming at the posted price, because that price necessarily exceeds marginal cost. There is no rationing of demand when supply bottlenecks do not operate. On the other hand, supply bottlenecks may lead to excess demand for output, which individual firms may not wish to choke off through price increases. In such cases, the demand for the products of other firms producing close substitutes will increase accordingly. Some of these will be foreign firms, so the level of imports may increase.[10] If some domestic suppliers choose to divert output from the foreign to the domestic market, exports will fall, thereby adding to the deterioration of the trade balance. The upshot is that demand pressures will be associated with a combination of price increases and trade spillovers. These demand pressures will also be accompanied by undesirably high degrees of capacity utilisation, spurring investment. The model assumes that these mechanisms are sufficiently powerful that no quantity rationing of domestic demand is ever observed (in aggregate annual data).

(iii) The aggregation of the employment and output decisions of firms into the corresponding macroeconomic variables recognises the heterogeneity of the situations faced by individual firms. Because there are many products, there will exist simultaneously cases where product

---

[8] The German model does, however, contain an inventories equation.

[9] As explained in Section 4.1, the combined evidence from the 10 countries supports the reputation argument.

[10] This is best understood as reflecting the activity of (wholesale) traders who chase supplies wherever they can be found, either domestically or abroad, when not available from the usual sources.

demand exceeds capacity output, and cases where it falls short of capacity. Similarly, because there are many skills, there will simultaneously exist job vacancies and unemployed workers. Aggregating equations (2), for instance, yields

$$Y = \Sigma_i Y_i = \Sigma_i \min(YC_i, YD_i, YS_i)$$
$$\leqslant \min(\Sigma_i YC_i, \Sigma_i YD_i, \Sigma_i YS_i)$$
$$= \min(YC, YD, YS). \qquad (3)$$

With many firms, skills and products, the min conditions are smoothed by aggregation. A simple functional relationship among the aggregate variables – used in most of the papers – can be derived from plausible (lognormality) assumptions about the distribution across firms of the relative magnitudes of the three proximate determinants of output, viz:

$$Y = [YC^{-\rho} + YD^{-\rho} + YS^{-\rho}]^{-\frac{1}{\rho}}. \qquad (4)$$

This relationship, and in particular the parameter ρ (>0), is discussed in section 3.3 below.

The corresponding employment relationship is

$$L = [LC^{-\rho} + LD^{-\rho} + LS^{-\rho}]^{-\frac{1}{\rho}}. \qquad (5)$$

(iv) Turning to input prices and output demands, the model is fairly standard. For simplicity, the papers generally do not model the financial sector of the economy, instead treating interest rates as exogenous. To the extent that (real) interest rates are determined in global rather than national capital markets, this is a justifiable assumption.

Wages however clearly do not need to be endogenised. In general these will respond to tightness of the labour market, as well as to productivity growth. In addition, there are a number of variables, such as terms of trade movements, changes in taxes and changes in benefit levels that may affect wage settlements. Through the tightness of the labour market, unemployment affects wages; that is the only relationship where unemployment appears explicitly.

Aggregate demand is the sum of: consumption, mostly related to disposable income; investment, whose determinants were mentioned above; government expenditures (exogenous) and export demand minus import demand, both of which are related to the relevant measure of final expenditure (at the world level for exports, the domestic level for imports) and to international competitiveness (world prices relative to domestic prices). Through the trade equations, domestic prices and hence domestic costs (in particular wages) affect aggregate demand, output and employment.

3. The model in detail

A more detailed presentation of the model is conveniently organised around the four blocks of figure 16.2 as spelled out in figure 16.3, namely: supply; demand; output and employment; prices and wages.

3.1. Technology and supply

Labour supply LS is typically exogenous.[11] Capacity output YC is equal to the stock of capital K times the output/capital ratio at full utilisation of capital. The stock of capital is that inherited from the past. The output/capital ratio B, and the associated output/labour ratio A, are assumed to reflect cost minimisation subject to a linearly homogeneous constant elasticity of substitution production function.[12] These ratios are assumed fixed in the short run (over the year), because adjustments in factor proportions take time. This *ex post* Leontief technology is somewhat more extreme than we would like but provides a convenient organising benchmark.

The estimated productivity equations allow for technical progress through time trends and use a distributed lag $\Theta(\Lambda)$ on relative factor prices $\dfrac{W}{Q}$ (where W denotes wages and Q the appropriate user cost of capital). That distributed lag captures both the sluggishness of the adjustment in technical coefficients due to the putty-clay nature of the technology *and* the process by which expectations of future factor prices are formed. The resulting equations for *technical* productivities take the form

$$\left(\frac{Y}{K}\right)_{tech} = B_t = B\left(t, \Theta(\Lambda)\frac{W}{Q}\right)$$

(6)

$$\left(\frac{Y}{L}\right)_{tech} = A_t = A\left(t, \Theta(\Lambda)\frac{W}{Q}\right)$$

(7)

[11] The French, Dutch and British papers contain labour supply equations.

[12] In the Austrian, Belgian, Danish and US papers, the Cobb–Douglas specification is not rejected by the data. The estimated elasticity of substitution is 0.94 in Italy, but much lower in France (0.5) and Germany (0.3).

and are estimated in a log-linear specification. To these technical coefficients correspond the concepts of capacity output $YC = BK$, full employment output $YS = ALS$ and capacity employment $LC = YC/A$.

Capacity output and capacity employment are latent variables, not directly observed. In principle, *measured* average productivities Y/K and Y/L are related to the technical productivities B, A by identities defining the degree of utilisation of the factors of production, DUC and DUL respectively: $DUC = Y/BK$, $DUL = Y/AL$. These two definitions are not quite symmetrical, however. K defines at the same time the aggregate capital stock available to the economy, and the sum of the capital stocks installed in the firms. *Ex post*, that capital may not be fully utilised, because there is insufficient labour to man the machines or (more likely) there is insufficient demand for the output. An empirical measure of DUC is available from business surveys of the manufacturing sector, where firms are asked to report their estimates of $Y/YC = Y/BK$. Such measures are used in most papers. In order to allow for data inadequacies, the estimated equations do not impose that measured capital productivity be equal to B times DUC, but rather to B times DUC^β, where β is a freely estimated elasticity.[13]

The story for labour utilisation is slightly different, because the aggregate labour force available to the economy is not equal to the sum of the labour forces employed in the firms. Hence, DUL is not a measure of unemployment. If labour were a fully variable factor, employment in the firm would be adjusted continuously to production needs, and measured labour productivity would be equal to technical productivity, independently of the ratio of actual employment to capacity employment. But labour is not a fully variable factor in the short run. There are two aspects to this: heads and hours. A straightforward story, quite appropriate for blue collar workers, would say that actual hours correspond closely to production needs, and are reconciled with employment (heads) through departures of actual hours per head from standard hours: overtime, when there are too few heads; part-time unemployment or temporary layoffs, when there are too many heads. Under that story, the number of heads would be explained through, say, a partial adjustment mechanism on the gap between desired and past employment; whereas productivity per head

---

[13] The coefficients β reported in table 16.7 range from 0.3 to 0.7, up to an Italian outlier (0.13).

would be equal to technical productivity times the degree of utilisation of labour, measured by the ratio of actual hours per head to standard hours per head.[14] In many countries, there exist some data on the ratio of actual to standard hours per head (typically, for blue collar workers in manufacturing). These data are used in most papers, again with a freely estimated elasticity parameter α to allow for data inadequacies.[15] That story carries over to white collar workers, with the proviso that their actual hours are typically kept equal to standard hours, with the intensity of work taking up the slack. It is of course rather heroic to assume that the ratio of actual to standard hours per head for blue collar workers in manufacturing alone correctly measures the degree of utilisation of employed labour in the whole economy.

The general form of the estimated equations appears in figure 16.3. The log-linear counterpart appears in the text, with the same numbering, and with lower case letters denoting logarithms. For the productivity equations, we have:

$$y_t - k_t = \beta_0 + \beta_1 t + \beta_2 \Theta(\Lambda)(w - q) + \beta_3 \, duc \qquad (8)$$

$$y_t - l_t = \alpha_0 + \alpha_1 t + \alpha_2 \Theta(\Lambda)(w - q) + \alpha_3 \, dul. \qquad (9)$$

To go from these to estimates of YC and $\underline{LC}$, one simply sets the DUC and DUL variables at their upper limits $\overline{DUC}$ and $\overline{DUL}$ – either unity or the highest level attained over the sample period. This yields

$$yc = y + \beta_3(\overline{duc} - duc); lc = l + \beta_3(\overline{duc} - duc) - \alpha_3(\overline{dul} - dul). \qquad (10)$$

3.2. Demand

The demand side of the model is relatively conventional, except for the introduction of capacity utilisation terms into the trade equations to take account of the supply bottlenecks discussed above.

Government expenditure is treated as exogenous. The consumption function typically uses disposable income of households as the main

---

[14] By the same argument, the DUL variable could meaningfully be introduced in the capital productivity equation. Rien n'est parfait, dit le renard.

[15] The coefficients α reported in table 16.7 range from 0.4 to 1, up to a Belgian (0.05) and an Italian (1.9) ouliers.

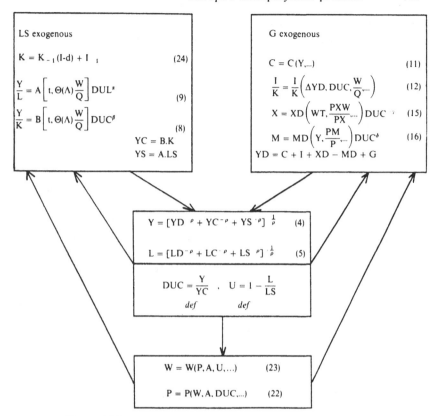

Figure 16.3

explanatory variable.[16] As indicated in Section 5.6 below, it might have been desirable to introduce wage income, transfers and property income as separate arguments – but the merits of that more ambitious specification are not unanimously recognised. As explained in Section 5.3 below, the treatment of investment differs somewhat from country to country. The dependent variable is typically the accumulation rate I/K, but several alternatives come up. Many papers find that the degree of capacity utilisation serves as a useful proxy for expected future capacity utilisation, and possibly also for future profitability.

In line with the general principles outlined above, the models assume that domestic final demand is never rationed. Aggregate demand YD is

[16] A couple of papers treat consumption as exogenous.

the sum of consumption C, investment I, government expenditure G, and export demand XD minus import demand MD. A stylised specification goes as follows:

$$c = \gamma_0 + \gamma_1 y + \cdots \tag{11}$$

$$i - k = \delta_0 + \delta_1 \Delta yd + \delta_2(yd - yc) + \cdots \tag{12}$$

$$xd = \varepsilon_0 + \varepsilon_1 wt + \varepsilon_2(pw - px) \ldots \tag{13}$$

$$md = \eta_0 + \eta_1 yd + \eta_2(p - pm) \ldots \tag{14}$$

where WT denotes world trade with price index PW, whereas PX, PM and P denote export prices, import prices and the value-added deflator respectively.

As explained above, the excess of YD over Y is absorbed by inventories (not modelled) or spills over into the trade balance. Accordingly, realised imports and exports are allowed to deviate from the levels specified in (13)–(14) to an extent that depends upon the degree of capacity utilisation. It is convenient to express that last variable relative to a minimal level $\underline{DUC}$ at which no spillover would occur.[17] This leads to the following specification:

$$x = \varepsilon_0 + \varepsilon_1 wt + \varepsilon_2(pw - px) - \varepsilon_3(duc - \underline{duc}) \tag{15}$$

$$m = \eta_0 + \eta_1 yd + \eta_2(p - pm) + \eta_3(duc - \underline{duc}). \tag{16}$$

As will be seen in Section 5.1, the empirical analysis mostly yields significant parameter values for ε_3 and especially for η_3.

Using (15) and (16), we can express YD as

$$YD = Y + (XD - X) - (MD - M)$$

a relationship that could also be approximated by[18]

$$yd = y + \left(\frac{X}{Y}\varepsilon_3 + \frac{M}{Y}\eta_3\right)(duc - \underline{duc}). \tag{17}$$

---

[17] The introduction of $\underline{DUC}$ is motivated by the desire to obtain a convenient expression for YD (see footnote 18). This amounts simply to redefining the constants ε_0 and η_0. In practice, $\underline{DUC}$ is measured as the lowest value of DUC observed over the sample period.

[18] The approximation comes from

$$YD = Y + X\left[\left(\frac{DUC}{\underline{DUC}}\right)^{\varepsilon_3} - 1\right] - M\left[\left(\frac{DUC}{\underline{DUC}}\right)^{-\eta_3} - 1\right]$$

$$= Y\left\{1 + \frac{X}{Y}\frac{DUC^{\varepsilon_3} - \underline{DUC}^{\varepsilon_3}}{\underline{DUC}^{\varepsilon_3}} + \frac{M}{Y}\frac{DUC^{\eta_3} - \underline{DUC}^{\eta_3}}{DUC^{\eta_3}}\right\}.$$

3.3. Output and employment

The definition of output and employment through aggregation over firms was introduced in (iii) of Section 2.3. Ignoring for the moment the labour supply bottlenecks, one may concentrate attention on the firm level capacity output YC_i and demand-determined output YD_i. Assuming the ratio of these two quantities to be (approximately) lognormally distributed over the set of firms, one obtains by aggregation a simple CES-type relationship between actual output (sales) Y, capacity YC and demand YD, namely

$$Y = (YC^{-\rho} + YD^{-\rho})^{-\frac{1}{\rho}}, \tag{18}$$

where the parameter $\rho > 0$ is related to the variance of the ratio of demand to capacity across firms; see Lambert (1988). That relationship is illustrated in figure 16.4, which shows how the 'CES-bow' replaces the 'min-boomerang' through aggregation. In that figure, b denotes unfilled orders and c denotes unused capacity. At the price which would equate aggregate supply and aggregate demand, b and c would be equal. In terms of equation (18), when $YC = YD$, then $Y = YC \cdot 2^{-\frac{1}{\rho}}$ and $(YC - Y)/YC = 1 - 2^{-\frac{1}{\rho}}$ measures the 'structural underutilisation rate of capacity at equilibrium' (SURE), in the terminology of Sneessens and Drèze (1986a).[19] As ρ tends to infinity, the CES-bow of figure 16.4 tends to the min-boomerang, and SURE goes to zero. As ρ decreases, SURE increases (tending to 1, or 100%, as ρ tends to zero), reflecting a growing 'mismatch' between capacity (supply) and demand at the firm level.

The *demand for labour* by firms is derived from their manpower needs to produce output – say $L(Y) = Y/A$, satisfying

$$L(Y) = \frac{Y}{A} = \left[\left(\frac{YC}{A} \right)^{-\rho} + \left(\frac{YD}{A} \right)^{-\rho} \right]^{-\frac{1}{\rho}}$$
$$= (LC^{-\rho} + LD^{-\rho})^{-\frac{1}{\rho}}. \tag{19}$$

Abstracting from short-term dynamics, actual *employment* will be the minimum of labour demand and labour supply, with the latter operating

---

[19] Referring to the labour market, these authors define SURE as the 'Structural Unemployment Rate at Equilibrium'.

as a binding constraint when the required skills are not available locally. Aggregating again over firms under a lognormality assumption, we obtain another CES-type relationship between aggregate employment L, aggregate labour demand $L(Y)$ and aggregate labour supply LS, say with parameter ρ':

$$L = (L(Y)^{-\rho'} + LS^{-\rho'})^{\frac{-1}{\rho'}}. \tag{20}$$

Inserting (19) into (20), we obtain the general 'nested CES' relationship

$$L = [(LC^{-\rho} + LD^{-\rho})^{\frac{\rho'}{\rho}} + LS^{-\rho'}]^{-\frac{1}{\rho'}} \tag{21}$$

which allows for different degrees of 'mismatch' on the goods markets and on the labour markets. That general formulation is used in the French model and is discussed further in Section 4.3 below. The other country models introduce the assumption that $\rho = \rho'$, so that (21) simplifies to (5). The output and employment determination is then given by (4)–(5).

3.4. Prices and wages

At the level of the firm, demand is uncertain and prices have to be set before the uncertainty is resolved. The technological assumptions imply

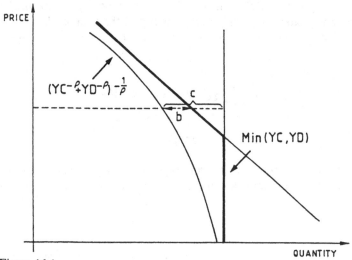

Figure 16.4

that the firm's short-run marginal cost curve is backward *L*-shaped as in figure 16.5. In the absence of capacity or labour supply constraints, therefore, imperfect competition theory suggests that the (value-added) price *P* will be a mark-up over (constant) unit labour costs W/A, where the mark-up depends upon the price elasticity of demand. Alternatively, as for instance in the contestable markets literature (e.g. Baumol *et al.*, 1982), competitive forces may keep the price in line with unit (average) production cost at a 'normal' degree of capacity utilisation DUC^*, i.e. $W/A + Q/B\,DUC^*$. In either case, the level of output and employment will then be determined by the level of demand *YD*.

As explained in Section 2.3 (i), the pricing relationship should also include a term in the expected level of (YD/Y), to pick up any spillover of supply bottlenecks onto pricing behaviour. However, since *YD* is a latent variable which can only be constructed from within the model itself,

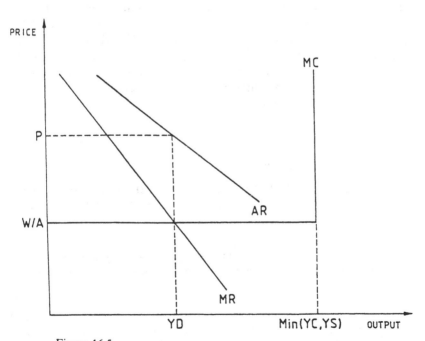

Figure 16.5

most papers pursue a short-cut by using the observed degree of capacity utilisation DUC as a proxy. Thus, the price equation becomes

$$p = \zeta_0 + \zeta_1(w - a) + \zeta_2(q - b) + \zeta_3 duc - \zeta_4(w - w^e), \qquad (22)$$

where the nominal wage surprise $w - w^e$ is included to allow for the possibility that prices may have to be fixed before wage levels are agreed.[20] Several papers impose $\zeta_1 = 1$, $\zeta_2 = 0$ (mark up over unit labour costs), whereas others estimate $\zeta_1 < 1$ (close to the wage share in value added, in agreement with a unit elasticity of prices with respect to average cost at normal capacity).

Finally, we need to consider how wages are determined. Suppressing inessential dynamics, an eclectic specification of the real (product) wage equation might take the form

$$w - p = \xi_0 + \xi_1 a + \xi_2(l - ls) - \xi_3(p - p^e) + \xi_4 z \qquad (23)$$

where $(p - p^e)$, usually proxied by $\Delta^2 p$, is the price surprise reflecting the fact that some wages are set before prices are known, and Z is a vector of shift variables such as the terms of trade, tax rates, benefit levels, the share of long-term unemployed, measures of union power and the like. This equation is open to a variety of interpretations depending on the variables that are included in Z (see Layard and Nickell, 1985). The fact that over long periods unemployment is generally untrended suggests that ξ_1 should be unity, in which case the equation basically relates the wage shares W/PA to the unemployment rate.[21] This equation is discussed at greater length in Section 4.2 below.

3.5. Structural and reduced forms

Equations (4), (5), (8), (9), (11), (12), (15), (16), (22) and (23) form a system of ten equations in the ten endogenous variables, Y, L, DUC, DUL, C, I,

---

[20] In the papers, this is usually proxied by $\Delta^2 w$, the change in wage inflation.

[21] Simultaneously setting $\xi_1 = 1$ in the wage equation, and $\zeta_1 = 1$, $\zeta_2 = 0$ in the price equation, leads to

$$p - w + a = \zeta_0 + \zeta_3 duc - \zeta_4(w - w^e) \qquad (22')$$

$$w - p - a = \xi_0 + \xi_2(l - ls) - \xi_3(p - p^e) + \xi_4 z. \qquad (23')$$

The issue of identification of these two equations should then receive more attention than it has typically been given in this work.

X, M, P and W. (See also figure 16.3.) The system is completed by the identity

$$K_{t+1} = (1 - d)K_t + \dot{I}_t \tag{24}$$

where d is the scrapping rate.

This common structure forms the basis of the ten country papers. The exact specification of each equation was chosen by the country authors to reflect national idiosyncracies. Although the resulting diversity of precise specifications sometimes restricts comparability of results, it turns out to be quite instructive. In particular, the commonality of freely adopted specifications sometimes conveys a significant message, as we shall see.

In principle, the ten equations form a simultaneous system and should be estimated as such. Experimentation with estimation methods performed on the Belgian model has revealed that simultaneous FIML estimation of the ten equations yielded parameter values very close to those obtained by a block recursive method, but at a considerably heavier computational cost. Accordingly, the simpler method was adopted for the other countries.[22] That procedure led to repeated use of an instrumental variables representation for some of the endogenous variables.

In practice, all the equations except (4)–(5) are specified as log-linear. The simultaneous system is non-linear. When formulated in terms of growth rates, however, the system is nearly linear, up to some parameters computed for each observation from the level values of the variables. That property is useful for short term analysis, as illustrated in Section 5.

Whether it be expressed in levels or in growth rates, the ten-equation model is fairly complex, and its qualitative properties may not be immediately obvious; see, however, Sneessens and Drèze (1986a, Section 3) for a discussion of some basic properties.

It is common practice in macroeconomics to seek a condensed representation through a few reduced form relationships, preferably suited for graphical analysis in two dimensions. Given our primary concern with (un)employment, we could try to derive two reduced form relationships describing the labour market, in terms of which the determination and comparative statics of the real wage and (un)employment could then be discussed.

Our reduced form analysis of the labour market is based on two blocks

---

[22] There is one exception: the Italian model was estimated by FIML.

of 4 structural equations each. Treating DUC and DUL as 'state' or 'shift' variables, the productivity equations (8)–(9) and the price-wage equations (22)–(23) can be solved for the four variables A, B, P, W as functions of U and additional shift variables (including Q). We shall deal with these four equations in Section 4. Logically, they could be summarised in a single relationship, say between U and W/P, to be labelled 'wage-price-productivity' equation. (Clearly, the coefficient of unemployment in the wage equation plays the same important role here as in other work.) Such a relationship could be interpreted as giving the unemployment rate which brings about consistency between the wage formation (23), the price formation (22) and the labour productivity (9) – after using (8) to eliminate B from (22). That reduction is illustrated formally in Appendix 16.1 and for a particular specification in Section 4.5. Shifting the 'wage-price-productivity' schedule inwards is a major goal of so-called supply-side policies.

Turn next to the demand block. Treating DUC and K_{-1} as 'state' or 'shift' variables, the four equations (11), (12), (15) and (16) can be solved for the four endogenous variables C, I, XD and MD – hence for YD – as functions of P and of exogenous shift variables like G, WT, PW, PM, ... The role of P comes via the price terms PW/PX and PM/P appearing in the trade equations. For the purposes of the present exercise, it is more convenient to relate trade competitiveness directly to real wages W/P.[23] The reduced equation summarising the demand side would thus relate YD and W/P through competitiveness.

The transition from aggregate demand to (un)employment consists of two steps. One of these relates output to aggregate demand by means of (4), which brings in capacity output YC and full employment output YS – as well as the important parameter ρ capturing microeconomic mismatch between supply and demand. The other relates output and employment through the technical labour productivity $Y/L = A$, itself related to real wages. The net effect of these two steps, detailed in Section 5, is to combine the competitiveness effect with the effects of real wages on factor

---

[23] The standard argument to the effect that rises in real wages impair competitiveness rests on the same relation. Explicit modelling of the links from W/P to PW/PX and PM/P would add to be the complexity of the model ...

substitution, which go in the same direction.[24] This produces a reduced form 'labour demand' equation, whereby employment is negatively related (unemployment is positively related) to real wages; the main shift factors come from exogenous demand (G and WT), from exogenous competitiveness (PW and PM) and from the inherited capital K_{-1}.[25]

Combining this 'labour demand' equation with the previously derived 'wage-price-productivity' equation yields the reduced form description of the labour market. Major departures from previous studies reside in the greater attention paid (i) to technical productivities and factor substitution; (ii) to the possible mismatch of supply and demand; and (iii) to the role of the capital stock in defining the supply potential of the economy.

Some macroeconomic authors (including Blanchard in Drèze *et al.* 1991, Ch. 2) use a particular specification of the price and wage equations, which can then be solved uniquely for the real wage and (un)employment; the reduced form demand equation is then solved for the nominal price level.

At the other end of the spectrum, the first generation of disequilibrium models treated wages and prices as exogenous, then concentrated upon the interplay of effective demand with capacity in the relationships (4)–(5) determining output and employment. Again, this is a particular specification.

These two extremes may be viewed as focussing respectively on the 'wage–price' equation[26] and on the 'labour demand' equation of a labour market reduced form. The present model is more general, because it specifies explicitly and quite generally the structural relationships lying behind each of these two equations. The price paid for increased realism is increased complexity.

4. Prices, wages and productivity

4.1. Prices

A first important empirical regularity of the empirical results is the lack of a significant influence of demand pressure on prices. Table 16.2

[24] As explained in Section 5, the effects of real wages on factor substitution are twofold, in this model. The substitution of capital for labour increases the labour/output ratio, thereby reducing the employment associated with a given level of output. In addition, capital deepening reduces the capacity output associated with a given stock of capital, thereby reducing output (at given levels of effective demand and of the capital stock) and employment.

[25] Note that the productivity equations play a role in the 'labour demand' equation as well as in the 'wage setting' equation.

[26] Productivity is taken as given in the Blanchard chapter and related work.

Table 16.2. *Elasticities of prices (GDP deflator)*

(Upper rows = short run, lower rows = long run)

Variable	Austria	Belgium	Britain	Denmark	France	Germany	Italy	Netherlands	Spain	U.S.
Demand pressure (DUC)	0.225	0.188[1] 0.003	−0.054[3] −0.084	no price equation estimated		0.155 0.277	0.720 0.970		−0.270 −0.443	−0.001 −0.005
Cost push (Wages)	0.510 1	0.749[2] 1	0.880 1		0.490	0.477 0.855	0.740 1	0.163 0.403	1 1	1.361 1

[1] The demand pressure variable is YD/Y, with YD estimated within the model.
[2] The cost variable is average production cost, estimated within the model.
[3] Numerical value not comparable with those for other countries.

reproduces the point estimates of the elasticities of prices (the deflator of GDP) with respect to the degree of capacity utilisation, used as a measure of demand relative to capacity output, and with respect to wages. Nine equations were estimated. In two countries (France, Netherlands), no significant influence of capacity utilisation on prices could be measured. In three countries (Spain, UK, US), a significant but small *negative* elasticity was estimated.[27] In three countries (Austria, Belgium, Germany) a significant but small *positive* elasticity was estimated. In Italy, the estimated elasticity is positive and quite high (0.72) – but it is partly offset by a negative elasticity with respect to the degree of utilisation of labour (measured by the ratio of actual to normal working hours). The prevailing picture is thus one of negligible measured influence of demand pressure on prices. In that light, the reference to high rates of capacity utilisation as a warning that demand stimulation would be inflationary is questionable.

The absence of a significant influence of demand pressure on prices is all the more instructive, because authors sought for such an influence, and tried alternative measures of demand pressure. One must hasten to add that the elasticity of prices with respect to wage costs is substantial everywhere[28] – ranging between 0.5 and 1 in the short run, and typically set equal to 1 (after suitable testing) in the long run. In that light, the more relevant question is whether demand stimulation is likely to generate upward pressure on wages, which would then promptly be transmitted to prices. We return to price-wage dynamics below (Section 4.5).

4.2. Wages

The empirical results concerning wage equations are summarised in table 16.3, which gives the elasticity of real product wages with respect to average labour productivity and the derivatives of the rate of growth of real wages with respect to the unemployment rate (measured in percentage points). In every single European country, measured productivity gains seem to be passed on quite rapidly into wages, with short-run elasticities ranging from 0.4 to 0.8 and with a long-run elasticity close to unity. Similarly, the dampening effect of unemployment on real wage growth is present everywhere, with sensible orders of magnitude, but the coefficients

[27] A negative influence could reflect increasing returns to scale or procyclical movements in perceived demand elasticities.

[28] Except in the Netherlands, where the dependent variable is the price deflator of output and where the equation is estimated for the period 1971–1987; higher elasticities are obtained there when the dependent variable is consumer prices instead of output prices.

Table 16.3. *Wages*

(Upper rows = short run, lower rows = long run)

Variable	Austria	Belgium	Britain	Denmark	France	Germany	Italy	Netherlands	Spain	U.S.
Productivity (elasticity)	0.412	0.882	0.100	0.360	0.420	0.660	0.710	0.562	0.830	0.0017[2]
	1.060	0.821	1			1	1	0.839		0.017
Unemploy. (semi-elasticity)	−0.025	−0.004[3]	−0.011[4]	−0.012[3]	−0.003	−0.004	−0.014			−0.002[3]
	−0.028	−0.007	−0.110	−0.055		−0.004	−0.020		−0.011	−0.013
Vac. rate			0.011[1]					0.025		
			0.110					0.093		

[1] Vacancy rate is estimated from the percentage of firms reporting an excess demand for labour in business surveys.

[2] Productivity is proxied by a time trend; the coefficient, 0.0017, may be compared with the estimated trend coefficient of 0.0023 in the labour productivity equation, suggesting an elasticity of real wages to labour productivity close to 0.8.

[3] Unemployment variable appears with a lag of one period.

[4] The explanatory variable is (U *Effective* − V). The nature of this variable means the numerical value of the semi-elasticity is not comparable with those for other countries.

are not precisely estimated. In the US, measured productivity did not enter significantly, and was replaced by a time trend.

The specification of the wage equations turns out to be quite interesting, and deserves some discussion. We first note that all equations, except the French one based on quarterly data, fit quite well, with estimated standard errors ranging from 0.5% to 1%. This may be compared with the results presented at the first Chelwood Gate Conference, where the standard errors of wage equations ranged between 1.5% and 2%.[29]

These wage equations, which are listed in table 16.4, display two notable features. First, with the exception of France, they all embody an error correction mechanism which relates the *level* of real wages to the *level* of unemployment in the long run. This is in marked contrast to the orthodox 'Phillips curve' relationship (of which the French equation is an example) which links the unemployment rate to the *rate of change* of real wages. This level specification originates in the classic paper of Sargan (1964).

The second notable feature is that, with the exception of the Danish, French and American wage equations, the error correction mechanisms imply that in the long run, it is essentially the share of wages in GNP (rather than the real wage itself) that is related to the unemployment rate. This would seem to correspond to the notion that wage formation in Europe today is dominated by unions who are heavily concerned over distributional fairness, in contrast to the United States.[30] As we shall see below in Section 4.5, this has important implications for the susceptibility of the European economies to inflationary shocks.

Finally there is the issue of the responsiveness of wage demands to unemployment. There are two dimensions to this: the overall size of the effect; and the speed with which it operates. Measuring the overall size by the long-run semi-elasticities of the real wage to the unemployment rate (given in table 16.3), we see that they range from 0.4% in Germany to 2.8% in Austria.[31] In *all* countries this sensitivity of real wages to

[29] See Bean *et al.* (1987) or *Economica*, Supplement 1986. As a further reference, we note that average standard errors of the wage equations estimated by Grubb *et al.* (1983) for 19 OECD countries on annual data 1957–1980 with the parsimonious specification $\Delta w = \alpha \Delta p + (1 - \alpha)\Delta w_{-1} - \gamma u + \delta t + \text{constant}$ was 2.35%.

[30] Hellwig and Neumann (1987) describe as follows the negotiating stand of West German trade unions: 'As political organisations, they are very much concerned with the "fairness" of the distribution of income. In principle, they want to raise or at least maintain the share of wages in GNP.'

[31] The semi-elasticity for Denmark is even larger at 5.5% but as noted in the Danish paper, this equation is less than satisfactory in a number of respects, despite its low standard error, suggesting that it should be treated as an anomalous outlier.

Table 16.4. *Survey of wage equations*

Austria

$$\Delta \ln\left[\frac{WH}{P}\right] = -0.4\left[\ln\left(\frac{WH.L}{P.Y}\right)_{-1} + 0.025U^{-1} - 0.55\ln TAX2_{-1} + \text{const.}\right]$$
$$- 0.65\Delta^2\ln P - 0.025\Delta U + 0.5\Delta\ln TAX2 - 1.2\Delta\ln TAX3 + \text{const.}$$

Belgium

$$\Delta \ln\left[\frac{WN}{PC}\right] = -0.5\left[\ln\left(\frac{WN.L}{PC.Y}\right)_{-1} + 0.01U_{-1} + \text{const.}\right] + 0.88\Delta\ln\left(\frac{Y}{L}\right) + \text{const.}$$

Denmark

$$\Delta \ln\left[\frac{W}{PC}\right] = -0.21\left[\ln\left(\frac{W}{PC}\right)_{-1} + 0.055U_{-1} + 0.3HOURS_{-1} + \text{const.}\right] + 0.36\Delta\ln A - 0.76\Delta\ln\left(\frac{PC}{P}\right) + \text{const.}$$

France

$$\Delta \ln\left[\frac{W}{P}\right] = 0.4\Delta\ln\left(\frac{Y}{L}\right) - 0.6\Delta\ln\left(\frac{PC}{P}\right) - 0.08U + \text{dummies} + \text{const.}$$

Germany

$$\Delta \ln\left[\frac{W}{P}\right] = -0.17\left[\ln\left(\frac{W.L}{P.Y}\right)_{-1} + 0.004U_{-1} + \text{const.}\right]$$
$$- 0.004\Delta U + 0.66\Delta\ln A + 0.18\Delta\ln\left(\frac{W}{WN}\right) + 0.04\Delta\ln\left(\frac{PM}{P}\right) + 0.27\Delta\ln\left(\frac{W}{P}\right)_{-1} + \text{dummies.}$$

Italy

$$\Delta \ln\left[\frac{W}{P}\right] = -0.71\left[\ln\left(\frac{W.L}{P.Y}\right)_{-1} + 0.02U + 0.01\ln DUC - 0.9\ln TAX4 + \text{const.}\right] + 0.2\Delta\ln\left(\frac{PM}{P}\right)$$

Netherlands

$$\Delta\ln\left[\frac{W}{PC}\right] = -0.34\left[\ln\left(\frac{W}{PC}\right)_{-1} - 0.8\ln\left(\frac{Y}{L}\right)_{-1} - 0.1V_{-1} - TAX2_{-1} - 0.64TAX1_{-1} + \text{const.}\right]$$

$$+\ 0.56\Delta\ln A + \Delta TAX2 + 0.4\Delta TAX1 + 0.025\Delta V + \text{const.}$$

Spain

$$\ln\left[\frac{W}{P(1+TAX3)}\right] = 0.16\ln\left(\frac{Y}{L}\right) - 0.01U - 0.27\Delta^2\ln P + 0.8[\text{mismatch} + \text{replacement ratio} + \text{import wedge}] + \text{dummies} + \text{const.}$$

U.K.

$$\Delta\ln\left[\frac{W}{P}\right] = -0.1\left[\ln\left(\frac{W}{P}\right)_{-1} - \ln\left(\frac{YC}{LC}\right)_{-1} + 0.11(U_{Effective} - V) + 0.65\ln(\text{Repl. Ratio})\right] - 0.1\Delta^2\ln P$$

US

$$\Delta\ln\left[\frac{W}{P}\right] = -0.1\left[\ln\left(\frac{W}{P}\right)_{-1} - 0.2t + 0.013U_{-1} + 0.45\text{ Wedge}_{-1} + \text{const.}\right] - 0.001\Delta U - 0.06\Delta DEMOG - 0.32\Delta^2\ln P + \text{const.}$$

TAX1: labour taxes paid by employees
TAX2: labour taxes paid by employers
TAX3: indirect taxes
TAX4: income taxes
WH: hourly wage cost
WN: take-home wage
W: wage cost
PC: consumer prices

unemployment is too low to ensure that unemployment is substantially self-correcting in the face of adverse shocks (see Section 4.5).

As far as the speed of the effect of unemployment on real wages goes, that too varies across countries. For instance in Austria and Germany lags in the response of wages to unemployment are very short[32] – virtually all of the effect comes through in the first year – while for most of the other countries the effect of unemployment on real wages is quite drawn out. Some of these differences whether short or long run, will be attributable to differences in choice of specification and sampling error, but some also no doubt reflect real institutional differences.[33]

4.3.   Shifts of the U–V curve

There is another striking empirical regularity in the results. It is most conveniently described as additional evidence corroborating outward shifts in the so-called Beveridge, or U–V curve. The estimated employment equations, neglecting partial adjustment terms, are of the form

$$L_t = [LD_t^{-\rho_t} + LC_t^{-\rho_t} + LS_t^{-\rho_t}]^{\frac{-1}{\rho_t}}, \tag{25}$$

with $\dfrac{1}{\rho_t} = a + bt, b > 0$, representing a growing 'mismatch' of supplies and demands at the microeconomic level. Table 16.5 reproduces the values of a and b for the different countries, as well as the implied estimates of the 'structural unemployment rate at equilibrium' (SURE) for 1960 and 1986. The rise over time in 'mismatch' is clear everywhere.

The specification of the French employment equation is slightly different, namely

$$L_t = [(LD_t^{-\rho_1} + LC_t^{-\rho_1})^{\frac{\rho_{2t}}{\rho_1}} + LS_t^{-\rho_{2t}}]^{\frac{-1}{\rho_{2t}}}, \tag{26}$$

with $\dfrac{1}{\rho_{2t}} = a + bt, t > 0$ but ρ_1 constant (not a function of t).[34] Let us denote by ELD_t the 'effective labour demand' at t, namely

$$ELD_t = (LD_t^{-\rho_1} + LC_t^{-\rho_1})^{\frac{-1}{\rho_1}}, \tag{27}$$

[32] In these countries, the coefficients of U_{-1} in the error correction term, and of ΔU, are *equal*. Accordingly, a rise in unemployment leads to a lower permanent level of real wages but then calls for no further adjustment (brings no further pressure to bear on real wages).

[33] The earlier Chelwood Gate volume included a discussion of these issues. We do not address them further here.

[34] The French entry in table 16.5 concerns $1/\rho_{2t}$.

Table 16.5. *Mismatch* (1/*RHO*)

Variable	Austria		Belgium	Britain	Denmark	France	Germany	Italy	Netherlands	Spain	U.S.
Constant		0.004	0.0292	found as	−0.008	−0.009	0.016	0.014	0.02	0.008	0.035
	69–72	0.03		a solution							
	73 onwards	0.01									
Trend	1966–1968		0.0005		0.003	0.0028	0.001	0.003	0.000005	0.00098	0.0005
		0.008									
	1969–1972										
		−0.004									
	1981–1986										
		0.004									
SURE 1960		0.004[1]	0.035		0.017	0.0[1]	0.019	0.029	0.022	0.009	0.041
1986		0.036	0.047		0.071[2]	0.033	0.046	0.090[2]	0.022	0.035	0.053

[1] This value is for 1966
[2] This value is for 1984

Table 16.6. *Mismatch*

Variable	Austria	Belgium	Britain	Denmark	France	Germany	Italy	Netherlands	Spain	U.S.
1/RHO2										
Constant		0.199			−0.009		0.024		−0.036	
Trend		0.0018			0.0028		0.003		0.0056	
1/RHO1										
Constant		0.099			0.01		0.01		0.023	

a CES-combination of the notional labour demand LC_t and the labour requirement corresponding to output demand LD_t. We may then rewrite (26) successively as

$$L_t = (ELD_t^{-\rho_{2t}} + LS_t^{-\rho_{2t}})^{\frac{-1}{\rho_{2t}}}, \tag{28}$$

$$1 = \left[\left(\frac{ELD_t}{L_t} \right)^{-\rho_{2t}} + \left(\frac{LS_t}{L_t} \right)^{-\rho_{2t}} \right]^{\frac{-1}{\rho_{2t}}} \tag{29}$$

$$1 = (1 + V_t)^{-\rho_{2t}} + (1 + U_t)^{-\rho_{2t}}. \tag{30}$$

Equation (30) defines a relationship between the unemployment rate U_t and the vacancies rate V_t which, *for a fixed value of* ρ_{2t}, is simply a Beveridge curve. The location of the curve is determined by ρ_{2t}, because, when $U_t = V_t$ (along the diagonal), then $U_t = V_t = 2^{-\rho_{2t}} - 1 > 0$.

To say that ρ_{2t} *is a function of t is to say that the Beveridge curve* (30) *is shifting over time. When* $1/\rho_{2t}$ *increases with t the Beveridge curve is shifting outwards*, as revealed by the intersection of the curve with the diagonal.

The French estimates thus suggest that the degree of matching between supply and demand for goods has remained constant over time, whereas the Beveridge curve has shifted outwards, revealing a growing mismatch between the supply and demand for labour services at the microeconomic level.

It would be interesting to verify whether the French finding applies to other countries as well. A prima facie confirmation of that hypothesis is found in the British, Dutch and Spanish papers, which introduce and estimate a concept of 'effective labour supply'. In the UK, the corresponding 'effective unemployment rate' is hardly trended, suggesting that the rise in measured unemployment since 1975 reflects the growing mismatch, alluded to in the previous paragraph. In the Netherlands, the trend factor in ρ_t is considerably reduced when labour supply is replaced by effective labour supply. In Spain, where an equation explaining ρ_t is estimated, the retained specification changes, and the trend term drops out.

To investigate the matter further, we have used the estimated levels of LD_t, LC_t and LS_t in the Belgian, Italian and Spanish models to test the specification (26) – namely, a constant value of ρ_1 and a trended value for $1/\rho_{2t}$. The results are reported in table 16.6. In the case of Belgium and Spain, the French specification is unambiguously accepted. In the case of Italy, the hypothesis that $1/\rho_{1t}$ is constant is accepted at the 1%, but rejected at the 5% level, against the hypothesis that $1/\rho_{1t}$ is trended. But the trend in $1/\rho_{2t}$ is unambiguously significant under both specifications. The estimated models are thus consistent with outward shifts in the Beveridge curve.

4.4. Productivity

Much effort was directed, in the EUP, at estimating the 'technical' productivity of labour and capital, i.e. productivity at 'normal' or 'full' rates of utilisation of labour and capital. To that end, measures of utilisation rates – DUL and DUC respectively – were introduced in the (productivity) equations used to estimate simultaneously the production function and the first-order condition on desired factor proportions. Both variables proved significant in most cases – particularly the DUC variable (with t-ratios ranging from four to twelve in seven countries). The parameter estimates in the productivity equations are given in table 16.7.

A natural benchmark is the identity relating the rates of growth of output Y, employment L and labour productivity A:

$$\dot{l} = \dot{y} - \dot{a}. \tag{31}$$

Figures 16.6a and 16.6b give plots of the time-series (1960–1986) for the observed values of $\dot{l}$, $\dot{y}$ and the estimated values of $\dot{a}$ at normal rates of factor utilisation. Except for equation residuals and variations in utilisation rates, these three series satisfy equation (31).[35] Also plotted are the growth rates of labour supply, $\dot{ls}$; the vertical difference $\dot{ls} - \dot{l}$ measures the increase in unemployment, and can be cumulated over time to trace the unemployment rate.

The global picture for the seven European countries is one of stationary employment ($\dot{l} \approx 0$ *on average*), with a trend decrease in output growth offset by a trend decrease in productivity growth. By contrast, the US series display no trend in output growth, but portray the so-called 'employment miracle': employment growth is positive throughout – up to short lived recessions – and oscillates around the labour supply series. Labour productivity growth (at normal utilisation rates) was positive in the sixties, but almost came to a halt in 1970.

From the productivity equations, one can obtain a decomposition of labour productivity gains into that part reflecting pure technical progress

---

[35] Two countries (France and the Netherlands) are missing, due to data constraints at the time of writing.

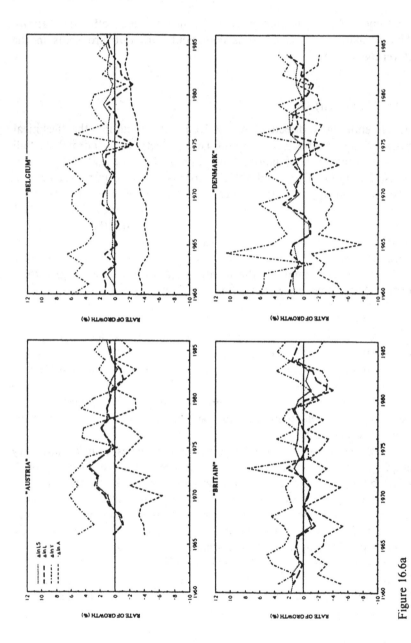

Figure 16.6a

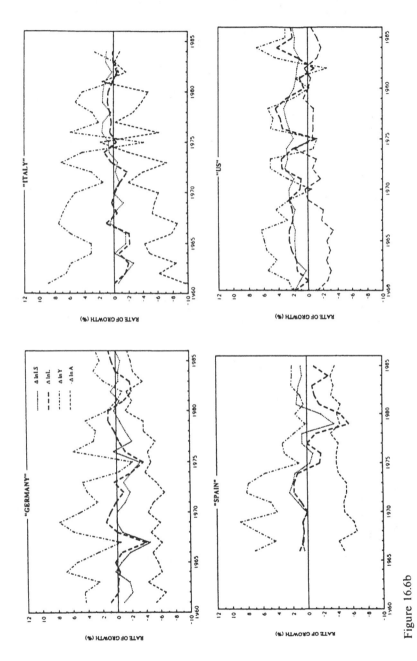

Figure 16.6b

Table 16.7. Technical coefficients

Labour productivity

Variable	Austria	Belgium	Britain	Denmark	France	Germany	Italy	Netherlands	Spain	U.S.
Trend	1966–1972 0.025; 1973–1977 0.007; 1978–1986 0.011	1954–1973 0.02; 1974–1985 0.007			0.004	$0.007t(7-0.1t)$	0.009		1978–1985 0.01	1952–1973 0.02; 1974–1986 0.016
Rel. prices										
SR elasticity	0.1	0.17	0.19	0.46	0.24	0.13	0.18	0.05	0.11	0.02
LR elasticity	0.26	0.59	0.83	0.88	0.48	0.3	0.58	0.18	0.51	0.15
Mean lag in yrs	1.5	2.57	3.37	1.53	1.6	1.35	3.23	2.51	3.55	6.67
DUL										
DUC	0.8	0.05	5.13	0.63	0.46	1.06	1.87	0.81	0.15	0.59

Capital productivity

Variable	Austria	Belgium	Britain	Denmark	France	Germany	Italy	Netherlands	Spain	U.S.
Trend	1966–1972 0.049; 1973–1977 0.041; 1978–1986 0.006	1954–1973 0.02; 1974–1985 0.007			−0.003	$-0.007t(1+0.01t)$	0.014	CONSTANT	1978–1985 0.01	1952–1973 0.004; 1974–1986 0.001
Rel. prices										
SR elasticity	−0.3	−0.11	−0.1	−0.15	0.24	0.13	−0.27		−0.11	0.01
LR elasticity	−0.74	−0.41	−0.44	−0.37	0.48	0.3	−0.36		−0.49	0.07
Mean lag in yrs	1.5	2.57	3.37	2.4	1.6	1.35	4.1		3.55	5.33
DUL							0.35			
DUC	0.65	0.27	6.12	0.75	0.56	0.53	0.13		0.5	0.43
Elasticity of substitution	0.65	0.27	1.27		0.48	0.3	0.94		1	1

and that part reflecting choices of factor proportions induced by changes in relative prices. A common feature of most models is the measurement of the user cost of capital through a price index for investment goods. (Only in the UK and US could an effect from interest rates be detected.) The productivity equations embody distributed lags on relative factor prices – both to model price expectations, and to reflect adjustment lags in technological choices. Mean lags of three years are typical.

The contribution of factor prices to labour productivity is negligible in the US. In Europe, where real wages as well as productivity grew faster than in the US, there is a distinct influence of relative factor prices on technical labour productivity. That influence hovered around 2% to 2.5% per year until the late seventies, then started declining towards levels of 0.5% to 1% around 1986.

Crude as these estimates may be, they have the merit of quantifying a phenomenon about which qualitative evidence seems undisputed, namely that substitution of capital for labour has been an important phenomenon in Europe over the past 30 years, including the period of high unemployment. Whereas productivity growth is the engine of progress under full employment, the substitution of capital for labour is wasteful when there is unemployment.

4.5. *The wage–price–productivity spiral*

The role of relative prices in guiding choices of factor proportions may be linked to the specification of the price and wage equations. To illustrate the phenomenon of induced substitution, we introduce a streamlined example, broadly consistent with the findings reported in this section.[36] With a constant real interest rate, and with prices of investment goods moving closely with output prices, one may approximate relative factor prices by real product wages. Neglecting dynamics and cyclical fluctuations, a streamlined labour productivity equation then reads as follows:

$$a = y - l = \alpha_1 t + \alpha_2(w - p) + \text{constant}, \tag{32}$$

$$\dot{a} = \alpha_1 + \alpha_2(\dot{w} - \dot{p}), \tag{33}$$

where in the constant returns Cobb–Douglas case, α_2 is the capital elasticity of output.

If the error correction term in the wage equation may be written in terms of the labour share, a streamlined version of that equation is:

$$\dot{w} = \dot{p} + \dot{a} + z_1, \tag{34}$$

---

[36] See Appendix 16.1 for a more general specification.

where z_1 denotes additional influences on wages, in particular unemployment. Under the assumption made about the cost of capital, prices are a markup on wage costs, up to additional factors z_2:

$$\dot{p} = \gamma(\dot{w} - \dot{a}) + z_2. \tag{35}$$

The solution to equations (33)–(35) is:

$$\dot{a} = \frac{\alpha_1 + \alpha_2 z_1}{1 - \alpha_2} \tag{36}$$

$$\dot{w} = \frac{\alpha_1}{1 - \alpha_2} + \frac{z_1}{1 - \alpha_2}\frac{1 - \gamma\alpha_2}{1 - \gamma} + \frac{z_2}{1 - \gamma} \tag{37}$$

$$\dot{p} = \frac{z_1 \gamma}{1 - \gamma} + \frac{z_2}{1 - \gamma} \tag{38}$$

$$\dot{w} - \dot{p} = \frac{\alpha_1 + z_1}{1 - \alpha_2}. \tag{39}$$

The rate of growth of labour productivity can thus be decomposed into an exogenous part corresponding to pure technological progress α_1 and an endogenous part induced by relative prices, $\alpha_2(\dot{w} - \dot{p}) = \frac{\alpha_2(\alpha_1 + z_1)}{(1 - \alpha_2)}$ or roughly $\frac{\alpha_1 + z_1}{2}$.

In terms of equation (36) the downward pressure exerted by unemployment on wages (through z_1), will not reverse the capital/labour substitution ($\dot{a} < 0$) unless it reduces real wages at a rate at least equal to $\frac{\alpha_1}{\alpha_2}$, or roughly $3\alpha_1$. Thus, with a typical value of α_1 like 0.02, and a rise in unemployment of one percentage point per year, the coefficient of U (or ΔU) in the wage equation should be as large as -0.06 in order for the downward pressure on wages to bring capital/labour substitution to a halt (after a mean lag of some three years ...). In no single country do we find a coefficient that large. Clearly, the mechanism through which unemployment could be self-correcting is weak. We should not be surprised that unemployment has been persistent, in Europe.

We also note from equation (38), and from the elasticities in table 16.3, that shocks affecting price (z_2) or wage (z_1) inflation are multiplied respectively by a factor of 3 or so $\left(\frac{1}{1 - \gamma}\right)$ and 2 or so $\left(\frac{\gamma}{1 - \gamma}\right)$ – revealing a high sensitivity to inflationary shocks. The sensitivity to wage shocks is less pronounced in the US where measured productivity gains do not seem to be incorporated into wages.[37]

A more refined analysis should consider explicitly the 'wedges' between consumption wages and product wages (including in particular labour taxes, which have increased everywhere), or between the value-added deflator and import prices (as influenced also by exchange rates), as well as between the prices of investment goods and those of consumer goods. In economies as exposed to inflationary spirals as suggested by equations (36)–(38), exogenous shocks affecting these wedges can have serious real consequences.

5. Output, employment and demand

5.1. Trade spillovers

Before reviewing the determination of output and employment in the EUP models, we wish to handle a simple question related to the comment made in Section 4.1 about the price equations. If prices do not react to demand pressure, how does one explain that quantity rationing of demand is hardly ever observed? In the EUP models, it is assumed that demand pressure spills over into foreign trade – either in the form of more imports, or in the form of less exports; see equations (15)–(16). To the extent that domestic producers may be reluctant to give up foreign markets, the penetration of which is a costly investment, the impact of capacity utilisation should be weaker for exports than for imports. (In particular, if export markets receive priority in case of excess demand for domestic output, the size of the import spillover is thereby increased.)

The estimated elasticities from the trade equations are reproduced in table 16.8. Except for a couple of perverse signs in the export equations, suggesting that export *demand* (as distinct from supply) may have failed to be identified, the results are quite straightforward. The spillover terms in the import equations are all significant and quite sizeable. As expected, the quantitative order of magnitude is lower in the export equations.[38]

---

[37] In the US wage equation, $\dot{a}$ is replaced by a trend. Equation (38) then takes the form
$$\dot{p} = \frac{\gamma z_1(1 - \alpha_2)}{1 - \gamma} + \frac{z_2}{1 - \gamma}.$$

[38] In addition to the reason mentioned above, this may also reflect a simultaneity bias, since exports require use of capacity – a bias that might also affect the DUC coefficient in the import equation. An interesting alternative hypothesis was mentioned to us by Michael Burda, namely that import spillovers concern investment goods, acquired in order to restore capacity margins. That hypothesis, verified by Burda on US data, is fully consistent with our discussion of investment behaviour in Section 5.3 below.

Table 16.8. *Trade elasticities*

(Upper rows = short run, lower rows = long run)

Variable	Austria	Belgium	Britain	Denmark	France	Germany	Italy	Netherlands	Spain	U.S.
Elasticities of imports										
Final demand	1.72	1.25		1.22	1.7	1	1	1.22	1.43	0.22
	1		No	1.19		1.98	1	1.52		2.03
Rel. prices	−0.81	−0.63	separate	−0.23	−0.56	−0.74	−0.61	−0.18	−0.29	−0.22
	−1.65		equations	−0.6		−1.47	−3.81	−0.37		−0.11
Spillover	0.62	1.89		0.49		1.46	0.88	0.62	1.15	1.37
	0.62					1.46	2.12	1.31		1.37
Elasticities of exports										
World trade	1.1	1.04	for	2.47	1.33 + 0.006t	0.76	0.28	0.99	1.86	1.64
	1		exports	2.12		1.15	1	1.06		1.01
Rel. prices	−0.47	0.13	and	0.11	−0.74	−0.33	−0.14	−0.65	−1.01	−0.79
	−0.49		imports	0.14		−0.5	−0.5	−1.98		−1.58
Spillover	0.01	−1.77				−0.21	0.62	−0.27	−0.76	−0.35
	0.01					−0.21	−2.07	−0.83		−0.35
Sum of price elasticities										
	1.28					1.07	0.75	0.83		1.01
	2.14				1.3	1.97	4.31	2.35	1.3	1.7
Sum of spillover elasticities										
	−0.62	−3.66		−0.49		−1.67		−0.89		−1.72
	−0.62					−1.67	−4.19	−2.14	−1.91	−1.72

Adding together the import and export elasticities and looking at the median (over the nine countries) of the sums, we obtain for relative prices the values 1 in the short run, 1.5 in the long run; and for capacity utilisation 1 in the short run and 2 in the long run (with no clear relationship to import shares).

These results call for further analysis. We know that rates of capacity utilisation are positively correlated across countries, and that some 70% of the trade of the ten countries in our sample is internal to the group. It would be more satisfactory to take these two facts into account and explain trade flows (and spillovers) through the rates of capacity utilisation at the two ends of the flow.

Returning to the issue of demand pressure, and the lack of justification for the inflationary fears grounded in high rates of capacity utilisation, it must now be recognised that domestic stimulation of demand in a country experiencing demand pressure is likely to generate import spillovers and hence a further deterioration of the trade balance. Since European governments are typically allergic to current account deficits, we find here an alternative explanation for the oft heard reference to capacity utilisation as a ground for cautious fiscal policies.

5.2. *Proximate determinants of growth*

The models estimated under the EUP lead to a natural decomposition of the growth rate of output into three proximate components, corresponding respectively to the growth rates of output demand, of capacity output and of full employment output. The decomposition follows directly from the relationship defining output

$$Y = (YD^{-\rho} + YC^{-\rho} + YS^{-\rho})^{\frac{-1}{\rho}}, \tag{4}$$

$$\dot{y} = \eta_{Y \cdot YD} \dot{y} d + \eta_{Y \cdot YC} \dot{y} c + \eta_{Y \cdot YS} \dot{y} s \tag{40}$$

where $\eta_{Y/YD}$ denotes the elasticity of Y with respect to $YD \left(= \dfrac{Y^{\rho}}{YD^{\rho}} \right)$, and so on. These elasticities satisfy

$$\eta_{Y \cdot YD} + \eta_{Y \cdot YC} + \eta_{Y \cdot YS} \equiv 1. \tag{41}$$

This identity has theoretical foundations in the model of aggregation underlying (4). It leads to an interpretation of the three elasticities as the proportions π_D, π_C and π_S of micromarkets where domestic output is

Table 16.9. *Regime proportions*

Year	Austria		Belgium		Britain		Denmark		Germany
	π_D	π_C	π_D	π_C	π_D	π_C	π_D	π_C	π_D
1965			0.36	0.26	0.40	0.15	0.13	0.65	0.23
1966	0.65	0.23	0.37	0.24	0.50	0.10	0.22	0.35	0.27
1967	0.69	0.09	0.54	0.16	0.72	0.08	0.34	0.18	0.54
1968	0.46	0.21	0.50	0.19	0.53	0.15	0.40	0.30	0.56
1969	0.29	0.36	0.35	0.28	0.46	0.20	0.13	0.60	0.22
1970	0.24	0.52	0.34	0.26	0.50	0.19	0.15	0.69	0.03
1971	0.28	0.42	0.43	0.20	0.71	0.14	0.28	0.46	0.09
1972	0.28	0.53	0.41	0.22	0.73	0.13	0.22	0.54	0.23
1973	0.37	0.16	0.29	0.34	0.33	0.22	0.16	0.76	0.24
1974	0.24	0.11	0.33	0.34	0.37	0.15	0.34	0.45	0.33
1975	0.88	0.01	0.67	0.17	0.75	0.07	0.88	0.03	0.73
1976	0.91	0.01	0.65	0.23	0.75	0.10	0.58	0.32	0.81
1977	0.87	0.01	0.69	0.22	0.66	0.11	0.61	0.32	0.60
1978	0.87	0.01	0.78	0.17	0.67	0.10	0.66	0.29	0.56
1979	0.73	0.04	0.71	0.24	0.65	0.12	0.30	0.63	0.47
1980	0.77	0.04	0.70	0.24	0.86	0.05	0.37	0.53	0.39
1981	0.79	0.08	0.83	0.14	0.91	0.05	0.63	0.28	0.52
1982	0.86	0.03	0.81	0.17	0.92	0.04	0.64	0.26	0.74
1983	0.86	0.03	0.79	0.20	0.86	0.09	0.52	0.34	0.84
1984	0.74	0.06	0.71	0.28	0.78	0.13	0.38	0.44	0.74
1985	0.60	0.19	0.72	0.27	0.71	0.15			0.53
1986	0.58	0.21	0.82	0.17	0.75	0.13			0.40

determined by demand, by capacity and by availability of labour respectively (see Lambert, 1988). In that notation, we may rewrite (40) as

$$\dot{y} = \pi_D \dot{y}d + \pi_C \dot{y}c + \pi_S \dot{y}s, \qquad (42)$$

a linear relationship among growth rates.

Table 16.9 gives the time series of (π_D, π_C, π_S) for various countries. The main message is again the contrast between the European and US patterns. *In Europe the proportion of micromarkets where output is demand-determined grew markedly from 1975 and especially 1981 onwards. In the US, there is little trend in the proportions; π_D moves procyclically, and π_C countercyclically.*

An alternative presentation of that message is offered by figures 16.7a and 16.7b, which display the series $\pi_D \dot{y}d$, $\pi_C \dot{y}c$ and $\pi_S \dot{y}s$ – i.e. the decomposition of output growth into its three proximate determinants.

A remarkable feature of figure 16.7 is the negligible contribution of capacity and labour supply growth to output growth in the eighties, for most European countries and particularly so for Austria, Belgium,

Table 16.9. (continued) *Regime proportions*

Germany	Italy		Netherlands		Spain		U.S.		Year
π_C	π_D	π_C	π_D	π_C	π_D	π_C	π_D	π_C	
0.44	0.28	0.15	0.25	0.29			0.25	0.49	1965
0.37	0.23	0.14	0.32	0.24	0.22	0.20	0.16	0.58	1966
0.18	0.42	0.18	0.55	0.08	0.49	0.06	0.12	0.61	1967
0.17	0.46	0.16	0.54	0.08	0.36	0.15	0.21	0.50	1968
0.42	0.45	0.27	0.36	0.24	0.16	0.23	0.19	0.49	1969
0.79	0.39	0.27	0.25	0.41	0.18	0.14	0.19	0.49	1970
0.69	0.58	0.27	0.36	0.31	0.31	0.25	0.41	0.33	1971
0.33	0.45	0.19	0.61	0.16	0.06	0.66	0.44	0.31	1972
0.36	0.20	0.25	0.48	0.29	0.02	0.76	0.31	0.42	1973
0.34	0.21	0.31	0.66	0.15	0.13	0.63	0.20	0.54	1974
0.13	0.61	0.26	0.79	0.13	0.53	0.27	0.31	0.45	1975
0.10	0.51	0.22	0.78	0.13	0.48	0.31	0.59	0.25	1976
0.22	0.48	0.19	0.76	0.13	0.37	0.46	0.45	0.34	1977
0.25	0.40	0.21	0.66	0.22	0.50	0.43	0.36	0.42	1978
0.31	0.35	0.20	0.41	0.48	0.66	0.30	0.28	0.49	1979
0.38	0.24	0.20	0.43	0.50	0.83	0.15	0.25	0.53	1980
0.29	0.44	0.19	0.64	0.34	0.80	0.19	0.40	0.40	1981
0.16	0.58	0.19	0.85	0.14	0.70	0.29	0.41	0.39	1982
0.12	0.73	0.19	0.83	0.16	0.70	0.30	0.65	0.24	1983
0.20	0.60	0.20	0.65	0.34	0.78	0.22	0.53	0.30	1984
0.36			0.42	0.56	0.81	0.19	0.37	0.40	1985
0.47			0.32	0.65			0.38	0.39	1986

Germany and the UK. The proximate importance of demand for output growth since the second oil shock is thus clearly confirmed – in contrast again to the US, where capacity and labour supply availability retain significance.

Since demand for domestic output is the sum of consumption, investment, government expenditure and the trade balance, it is instructive to decompose in turn the rate of growth of YD into these four components:

$$\dot{y}d = S_C \dot{c} + S_I i + S_G \dot{g} + (S_X \dot{x} - S_M \dot{m}), \qquad (43)$$

where S_C is the ratio of consumption to YD, and similarly for the other shares. That decomposition is presented in figures 16.8a and 16.8b. In comparison to European countries, one may note for the US: (i) the relatively limited amplitude of the foreign trade component in that relatively closed economy; (ii) the positive contribution of government expenditure ever since the mid-seventies and especially in the eighties; (iii) the sustained contribution of consumption, especially again in the eighties. In Europe, the amplitude of the foreign trade component is much

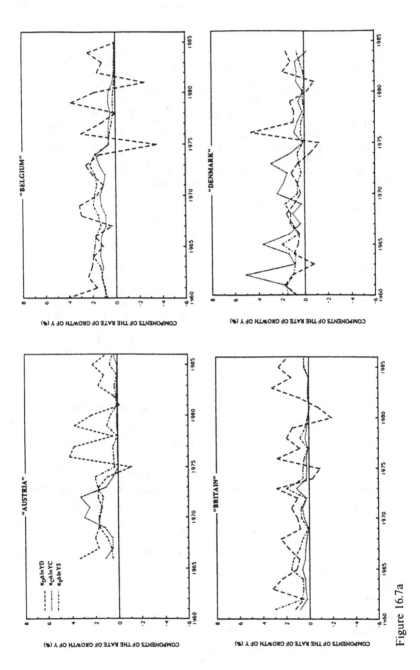

Figure 16.7a

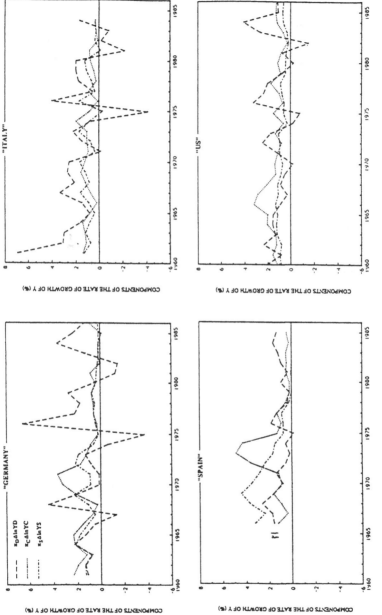

Figure 16.7b

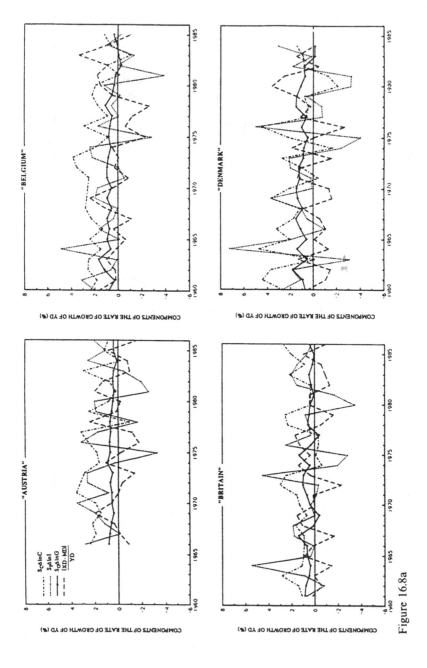

Figure 16.8a

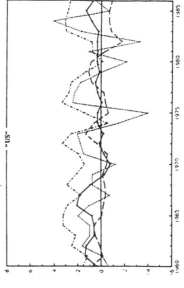

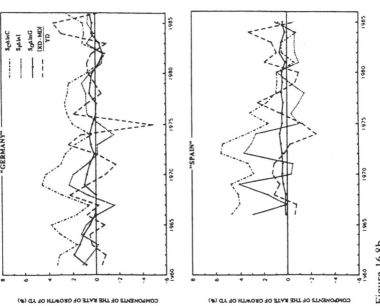

Figure 16.8b

more pronounced, especially in the smaller countries like Austria, Belgium and Denmark.

Another striking feature, shared by Europe and the US, is the amplitude of the *contributions to GDP growth* coming from investment. This is somewhat surprising, because investment amounts to less than 20% of *GDP*; yet, it repeatedly contributes plus or minus four percentage points to *GDP* growth, because it is much more volatile than the other components. In particular, the sharp declines of aggregate demand in 1975 and 1981 (see figure 16.7) are largely due to the collapse of investment in those years. We report accordingly on investment equations, before turning to impact multipliers in Section 5.4.

5.3. Investment

The first impression made by the nine investment equations of the EUP models (investment is exogenous in the French model) is one of disconcerting diversity. The six different dependent variables, the broad array of explanatory variables and specifications, span the corresponding variety of investment theories! Upon closer examination, one notes that four equations are quite similar after all, namely the Austrian, German, Italian and British ones. These express the rate of growth of the stock of capital as a linear function of its own lagged value and of the ratio of output demand to full capacity output – with possibly one or two additional variables, like the rate of growth of output demand (Austria, Italy), a measure of profitability (Austria, UK) or the real long-term rate of interest (Germany). Typical coefficients are near 0.8 for the lagged dependent variable, 0.1 for the log of YD/YC or 0.25 for the sum of the coefficients of log YD/YC and log YD/YD_{-1}. Noting that $\Delta \ln K \simeq I/K$ minus (rate of capital depreciation), the implied long-run elasticity of the net capital accumulation rate with respect to DUC is not too far from unity – a sensible property.

Another four equations explain the level, or the growth rate, of gross investment in terms of a variety of specifications. The main regularity among these is the significance of a DUC variable.

Going back to Section 4.1, note that, in a world where prices are set as a markup on costs with little sensitivity to demand pressures, 'profitabi-lity' is mostly dependent upon the rate of capacity utilisation; hence capital accumulation should depend heavily upon the *expected* degree of utilisation of additional capacity. The currently observed DUC is a natural proxy for that expected DUC – if only because there is little point in *adding* to capacity when unused capacity is currently available.

5.4. Output dynamics

When looking at the evolution of demand components, one must remember first that most of them are endogenous, being simultaneously determined with output; and second that relative prices affect at least the trade component. A partial endogenisation of demand growth is obtained from a stripped version of the demand block consisting of equations (11), (13) and (14). Treating provisionally investment and government expenditure as exogenous, one may rewrite these three equations in growth rates form, then substitute them in (43) and (42), obtaining finally:

$$
\dot{y} = \frac{\pi_D}{1 + S_M \eta_{M \cdot YD} - \pi_D S_C \eta_{CY}} \cdot \{ S_i \dot{i} + S_G \dot{g} + S_X \eta_{X \cdot WT} \dot{w} t
$$
$$
+ S_X \eta_X \cdot \tfrac{PW}{PX} (\dot{p}w - \dot{p}x) - S_M \eta_M \cdot \tfrac{PM}{P} (\dot{p}m - \dot{p}) \}
$$
$$
+ \frac{1 + S_M \eta_{M \cdot YD}}{1 + S_M \eta_{M \cdot YD} - \pi_D S_C \eta_{C \cdot Y}} \{ \pi_C \dot{y}c + \pi_S \dot{y}s \}, \tag{44}
$$

where $\dot{y}c = \dot{k} + \dot{b}$ and $\dot{y}s = \dot{l}s + \dot{a}$.

Although that expression may appear forbidding, its interpretation is in fact quite straightforward. A synthetic formulation would be:

$$
\dot{y} = \pi_D \times \text{open economy multiplier}
$$
$$
\times [\text{contribution from growth rates of investment}
$$
$$
\text{and exogenous demand components}
$$
$$
+ \text{contributions from price effects of trade component}]
$$
$$
+ \text{contributions from } \dot{y}c \text{ and } \dot{y}s. \tag{45}
$$

As is well known, the impact of demand shocks in such models is dampened by the factor π_D, because output adjusts only when it is demand-determined. For the same reason, the multiplier is reduced, because the propensity to consume (in the denominator) generates output only in the proportion π_D. Knowledge of the proportions (π_D, π_C, π_S) of table 16.9 is thus important for policy evaluation.

Remembering that $\dot{b}$ and $\dot{a}$ are functions of $(\dot{w} - \dot{p}i)$, one message of equation (44) is that three relative prices play a role in the short-run dynamics of output and employment, namely $(\dot{p}w - \dot{p}x)$, $(\dot{p}m - \dot{p})$ and $(\dot{w} - \dot{p}i)$. It was already mentioned in Section 3.4 that relative-price 'wedges' could affect the price–wage spiral. We note here that the same wedges also affect directly output and employment dynamics in a manner worthy of further investigation.

Equation (44) also reveals the complexity of the growth process, whereby output growth is related to other physical growth rates (capital, government demand, world trade), to labour supply and productivity growth, and to changes in relative prices. The balanced growth of the sixties and early seventies was characterised in Europe by stable labour supply and relative prices, high productivity growth and parallel growth of output, capital, government demand and trade – see table 16.1.[39] Once the pattern is broken – due to shocks in relative prices and exogenous demand components – it is natural that time be required to regain the balance. It is conceivable, but by no means certain, that we are now approaching again a path of balanced growth – although not necessarily at the same rate.

5.5.   Employment dynamics

In view of the interest attached to a 'reduced form' labour demand equation, as explained in Section 3.5, it is suggestive to examine more closely the counterpart of (42) for employment, namely

$$\dot{l} = \pi_D \dot{l}d + \pi_C \dot{l}c + \pi_S \dot{l}s$$
$$= \pi_D(\dot{y}d - \dot{a}) + \pi_C(\dot{k} + \dot{b} - \dot{a}) + \pi_S \dot{l}s. \tag{46}$$

Using (8)–(9) and (43), we can use this equation to bring out the structure of the short-run elasticity of employment with respect to real wages in the reduced form labour demand equation, namely:

$$\eta_{L \cdot \frac{W}{P}} = \frac{\partial \dot{l}}{\partial(\dot{w} - \dot{p})} = \pi_D \left(\frac{\partial \dot{y}d}{\partial(\dot{w} - \dot{p})} - \frac{\partial \dot{a}}{\partial(\dot{w} - \dot{p})} \right) + \pi_C \frac{\partial(\dot{b} - \dot{a})}{\partial(\dot{w} - \dot{p})}$$
$$= -(\pi_D + \pi_C) \frac{\partial \dot{a}}{\partial(\dot{w} - \dot{p})} + \pi_D \frac{\partial \dot{y}d}{\partial(\dot{w} - \dot{p})} + \pi_C \frac{\partial \dot{b}}{\partial(\dot{w} - \dot{p})}. \tag{47}$$

The first term in (47) captures the impact of real wages on labour productivity; i.e., the impact of the capital/labour substitution induced by relative prices. In the notation of equations (9) and (33), it is equal to $-(\pi_D + \pi_C) \alpha_2 \simeq -\alpha_2$.

The third term in (47) captures the impact of real wages on capital productivity; i.e., the impact of the capital deepening induced by relative prices. In the notation of equation (8), it is equal to $-\pi_C \beta_2 \simeq -\pi_C(1 - \alpha_2)$;

---

[39]The US example is there to remind us that a different growth pattern is possible.

that approximation is exact under a Cobb–Douglas production function. The relevance of that term is open to question, however, to the extent that factor proportions *on existing capital* may prove difficult to adjust *ex post*. The putty–clay models rule out that possibility. We assume that such adjustments take time, thus adopting an intermediate position between the more extreme putty–clay or putty–putty views.

The middle term in (47) captures the impact of real wages on aggregate demand, which is transmitted to employment in a proportion π_D. In the EUP specification of the demand block, that impact comes from the trade equations. Taking multiplier effects into account, but still treating investment, public expenditure and world trade as exogenous, one obtains:

$$\frac{\partial \dot{y}d}{\partial(\dot{w} - \dot{p})} = \frac{S_X \eta_X \cdot \frac{W}{P} - S_M \eta_M \cdot \frac{W}{P}}{1 + S_M \eta_{M \cdot YD} - \pi_D S_C \eta_{CY}}$$
$$\simeq S_M \cdot \eta_{(X - M)} \cdot \frac{W}{P} \cdot \mathcal{M}_D \tag{48}$$

where we have written $\mathcal{M}_D$ for the demand multiplier and assumed (near) equilibrium of the trade balance.

In summary, under these assumptions

$$\eta_L \cdot \frac{W}{P} \simeq -\alpha_2 - \pi_C(1 - \alpha_2) - \pi_D S_M |\eta_{(X - M)} \cdot \frac{W}{P}| \mathcal{M}_D. \tag{49}$$

The three distinct components of this formula have their place in the discussion to follow.

5.6. *Wages and demand*

We may now take up the difficult, but essential, question of the interplay of wages and demand. We should first of all note that the EUP models embody rather crude consumption functions (or no consumption function at all, in Austria, Denmark, Italy and the US). Thus, *the role of wages in sustaining consumer demand is not captured*. According to some, little loss of information is involved, because they regard the hypothesis of a higher propensity to consume out of wage income than out of gross profits as unsubstantiated (presumably, due to the chain from profits to asset prices to wealth to consumption). Even so, there would remain scope for *unemployment* to depress consumption through a 'permanent income' effect. These issues will not be settled by the work under review. (Still, we note that the well-behaved German consumption function implies a fall in consumer demand of 0.25% for a 1% decrease in employment, at unchanged disposable income).

The direct channel through which wages influence final demand in equations (44) and (49) comes from the price elasticities of foreign trade. It is important, in that connection, to draw a distinction between a wage shock in a single country and a wage shock affecting simultaneously several (most) European countries. In the former case, the wage shock being quickly transmitted to prices, and the sum of the price elasticities being of the order of one in the short run and higher in the long run, the impact on final demand is quite sizeable, and roughly proportional to the country's degree of openness, as measured by $S_M \simeq S_X$. In the latter case, the elasticity of prices to wage costs being of comparable magnitude in the different countries, and some 60% of the trade being intra-European, the relative prices would be much less affected, and the influence on final demand would be significantly dampened, both for individual countries and for Europe as a whole (whose degree of openness is roughly comparable to that of the US).

The difficult question concerns the interaction between wage formation and fiscal stance: Have European Governments adjusted their fiscal stance in response to wage shocks? (The adjustment could be contractionary, to fight inflation or to avoid current account disequilibria; but it could also be expansionary to prevent a rise in unemployment, resulting from the loss of competitiveness and from the induced capital–labour substitution.)

The econometric work within the EUP is not instructive in this respect, because government spending is exogenous in all models. But the papers contain a number of interesting anecdotes. These include such classics as the German fiscal contraction following the 'locomotive experiment' of the late seventies. They also include the temporarily successful Austrian and Danish attempts to counter the first oil shock through expansionary fiscal policies – and the reversal to budget consolidation as the public debt built up.

Beyond these individual anecdotes, there is a common experience. Temporary demand stimulation through fiscal policy exerts only temporary effects, in these models. That is, a temporary stimulus does not by itself raise the level of output permanently. It could in principle happen that growing public expenditures become self-financing as the growth rates of other components of final demand match that of government spending. But that would fail to happen if investment and exports lag behind. The fiscal deficit then results in a growing public debt and current account deficit, eventually inducing a reversal of policies. A wise use of the fiscal instrument rests on a comparative assessment of the state of the economy today, and tomorrow at the time of the policy reversal required to reimburse the debt. The chain of events which led European governments to tighten fiscal policy in the wake of the second oil shock was most unfortunate. That episode contains a lesson for the future.

The temporary nature of fiscal stimuli is confirmed by the simulations carried out with some of the EUP models.

5.7. A synthesis

Bringing together the contents of Sections 4 and 5 regarding the influence of wages on employment, we note that the models under review embody two explicit channels and one implicit channel through which that influence exerts itself. The two explicit channels are (i) the demand side, through the foreign trade elasticities – a channel of greater significance in case of single country wage movements than in case of parallel wage movements in several countries; (ii) the supply side, through capital-labour substitution – a channel that is equally significant in the single country case as in the multi-country case.[40] The implicit channel concerns fiscal policy reactions to wage shocks.

It is interesting to speculate briefly about the relative importance of the two explicit channels. From formulae (36)–(38) and (49), and from the figures in tables 16.3 and 16.8, one would guess that the two channels are of comparable importance in the case of single-country shocks – the exact answer being related to that country's degree of openness. In the case of European-wide shocks, the capital-labour substitution channel is probably the dominant one. As noted above, capital-labour substitution induced by the incorporation of productivity gains into wages are wasteful when the economy operates under inefficient unemployment.

One message from the work under review is that wage moderation has to fight the tide, in the supply channel as well as in the demand channel, if it is to pave the way for a reduction in unemployment. As noted in Section 4.5, real wage adjustments will not increase the employment content of growth unless they amount to something like three times the rate of autonomous technological progress; the tide is thus quite strong along the supply channel. In the demand channel, the growth rates of capital, government demand and world trade define another tide. When these rates fall below the growth rate of labour productivity, the effects of wage adjustments on the trade balance again need to overcome that

---

[40] To this should be added all the general equilibrium interactions, like the investment accelerator, whereby the supply side reacts to demand conditions, and so on.

adverse tide before they result in employment growth. Lags in the reaction of wages to unemployment, then in the reactions of prices and factor proportions to wages, slow down the adjustment process. It is always difficult to fight the tide with insufficient boat speed ...

6. Summary and conclusions

6.1. Summary

The broad empirical regularities of the EUP may be summarised as follows.

1. The measured influence of demand pressure on prices is negligible, but the elasticity of prices with respect to wage costs is substantial, ranging from minimal values of 0.5 in the short run to 1 in the long run.

2. Real wages incorporate measured productivity gains quite rapidly in Europe, with short-run elasticities ranging from 0.4 to 0.8 and long-run elasticities close to 1. Measured productivity does not enter significantly in the US wage equation.

3. The level of unemployment typically enters the wage equations through an error correction term, relating the share of wages in value added to the level of unemployment. The estimated coefficients imply a reduction in the wage share, per percentage point of unemployment, ranging from 0.4% in the high unemployment countries to 2.5% in Austria – revealing the weak self- correcting mechanism for unemployment in the former group. That specification is consistent with the view that European labour unions are much concerned with the fairness of the distribution of income.

4. The $U-V$ (Beveridge) curve has shifted outwards, in all countries (including the US).

5. The incorporation of measured productivity gains into real wages induces capital-labour substitution, which is wasteful in economies operating under inefficient unemployment. Employment growth in Europe was curtailed by factor substitution at an average rate of some 2% per year until the late seventies, and 1% per year more recently. If that substitution had stopped when it became wasteful, the rise of unemployment in Europe could have been avoided.

6. Shocks on prices are multiplied by a factor of 2 to 4, and shocks on wages by a factor of 1 to 3, through the wage-price-productivity spiral. The European economies are thus inflation-prone.

7. Demand pressures, which as suggested under point 1 are not choked

off through price increases, spill over into imports, and to a lesser extent exports, thereby deteriorating the trade balance. That robust country-level finding remains to be analysed in a multi-country setting.

8. The main and nearly unique proximate determinant of output growth in the eighties in Europe has been effective demand. The growth of demand is linked to the growth of its exogenous components, namely government expenditures and world trade. It is also linked to the relative growth rates of domestic and foreign prices, through the price elasticities of exports and imports. This last channel is much less significant for Europe as a whole than for individual countries.

9. The degree of capacity utilisation is a significant determinant of investment. (In line with the suggestion under point 1 that prices are geared to costs but not to demand pressures, the profitability of investment should depend largely upon utilisation rates.)

10. Besides affecting employment through their influence on the foreign trade component of demand, wages also affect employment through capital-labour substitution, as noted under point 5. For Europe as a whole, that second channel is probably more significant than the first.

11. Temporary demand stimulation through fiscal policy exerts only temporary effects, in within-sample-period simulations of the EUP models. And the papers contain anecdotes about policy reversals induced by cumulated deficits.

6.2. Conclusions

The empirical findings suggest explaining the contrast between the US 'employment miracle' and the European persistent unemployment in terms of two proximate causes: (i) the wage formation process differs as between the two zones, in particular regarding the incorporation of measured productivity gains into real wages; (ii) whereas the proportion of firms where output and employment are demand determined grew markedly in all European countries in the late seventies and mostly remained high, that proportion is not trended in the US – presumably due to a combination of relative closedness, sustained consumption and lasting deficits.

The European wage-formation process makes non-declining employment dependent upon sustained output growth. In small open economies, this in turn requires parallel growth in exports – as determined by world demand and competitiveness. When some of these elements are missing, fiscal policy alone is not a very effective instrument.

These conclusions must be taken with a … pound of salt! After due pruning, it will probably remain inescapable that the elimination of European unemployment is a very difficult challenge. The work reviewed here suggests strongly that the mechanism through which unemployment could be self-correcting is weak and slow, in Europe. A gradual elimination will tautologically call for a prolonged period during which output grows faster than productivity – a situation not witnessed over the past 30 or 40 years. Because growth of real wages induces gains in measured productivity through capital-labour substitution, the goal will be easier to reach if medium-run expected wage growth is strictly contained. We do not know whether, and how, that condition could be met. Under that condition, the fear that faster output growth would rekindle inflation is probably misplaced – but a temporary deterioration in current accounts would need to be faced. And the expansion would require cooperation among several European countries, if national current account problems are to remain manageable. On the other hand, if demand stimulation through fiscal policy has only temporary effects, the accumulation of public deficits is unlikely to be tolerated.

We do not wish to eschew these dilemmas by resorting to fine tuning. Still the following remarks appear timely:

(a) Public deficits are more tolerable, from an intertemporal perspective, if they correspond to productive investments.

(b) Labour taxes have an obvious role to play in containing, or reversing, the growth of labour costs and medium-run expectations about them; one advantage of tax adjustments is that they are not apt to be perceived as transitory; granted that many among the currently unemployed are at best candidates for low-paid jobs, a reduction in labour taxes should be targeted towards the low end of the wage scale (for example by exempting minimum wages from social security contributions).

(c) In order to alleviate labour market tensions, it is important to increase the supply of those specific skills which are in excess demand; both training opportunities and wage differentials have a role to play here. There is also scope for initiatives to make wage differentials more acceptable, and to limit their unnecessary spreading to other skills. Still, it must be recognised that the required skills will not be supplied by the long-term unemployed; for these, special programs remain needed.

From a longer-run perspective, there is ground to be concerned about the vulnerability of Europe to inflation as well to output and employment fluctuations. The division into relatively open national economies compounds these problems, by creating complex interdependencies between countries. This also leads to a need for international cooperation in demand management, public investment, etc. The proces of wage formation has almost certainly been destabilising in the seventies, and the experience could be repeated. The goal of distributional equity needs to be implemented more efficiently. We need an operational way of separating out technical progress from measured productivity gains associated with capital deepening induced by wage increases. The incorporation into real wages of productivity gains following from capital deepening is entirely desirable when an economy is at full employment, but the resulting substitution of capital for labour becomes wasteful in the presence of unemployment.

Appendix 16.1

Consider the linearly homogeneous constant elasticity of substitution technology

$$Y^{1-\frac{1}{\sigma}} = [\Theta(t)L]^{1-\frac{1}{\sigma}} + [\Phi(t)K]^{1-\frac{1}{\sigma}} \tag{A.1}$$

where $\Theta(t)$, $\Phi(t)$ reflect labour-augmenting and capital-augmenting technical progress respectively. Cost minimisation gives equilibrium factor proportions, $\left(\dfrac{K}{L}\right)^*$, as

$$\left(\frac{K}{L}\right)^* = \left(\frac{\Theta}{\Phi}\right)^{1-\sigma}\left(\frac{W}{Q}\right)^{\sigma} \tag{A.2}$$

where Q is the appropriate user cost of capital. Also,

$$\left(\frac{Y}{L}\right)^* = \Theta\left[1 + \left(\frac{\Theta Q}{\Phi W}\right)^{1-\sigma}\right]^{\frac{\sigma}{\sigma-1}}. \tag{A.3}$$

If prices P are set as a mark-up on average cost, then

$$P = \mu \cdot \frac{WL + QK}{Y} = \mu\frac{WL}{Y}\left(1 + \frac{Q}{W}\frac{K}{L}\right). \tag{A.4}$$

Using (A.2) and (A.3),

$$\frac{WL}{PY} = \mu^{-1}\left[1 + \left(\frac{\Theta Q}{\Phi W}\right)^{1-\sigma}\right]^{-1} \tag{A.5}$$

$$\frac{W}{P} = \mu^{-1}\Theta\left[1 + \left(\frac{\Theta Q}{\Phi W}\right)^{1-\sigma}\right]^{\frac{1}{\sigma-1}} \tag{A.6}$$

$$\frac{WL}{PY} = \mu^{-\sigma}\Theta^{\sigma-1}\left(\frac{W}{P}\right)^{1-\sigma}. \tag{A.7}$$

Equation (A.7) combines the production function and the price equation to yield a (long-run) equilibrium relationship between the wage share and the real (product) wage.[1] It implies that the wage share will be constant if the mark-up rate μ is constant and real wages grow at the same rate as the labour-augmenting technical progress Θ.

Let the wage equation yield a long-run relationship between the wage share and the unemployment rate, say

$$\ln\frac{WL}{PY} = \omega_0 - \omega_1 U. \tag{A.8}$$

Using (A.7), that relationship may indifferently be expressed in terms of the real wage, namely

$$\begin{aligned}
\ln\frac{W}{P} &= \ln\Theta + \frac{\sigma}{1-\sigma}\ln\mu + \frac{\omega_0}{1-\sigma} - \frac{\omega_1}{1-\sigma}U \\
&= \ln\Theta + \omega_0' - \omega_1' U. \tag{A.9}
\end{aligned}$$

(A.9) is the reduced 'wage-setting' equation implied by the production and wage-price block of the model, under the assumptions of this appendix. It can be combined with a reduced 'labour demand' equation to determine equilibrium in the labour market and to investigate its comparative statics properties.

Note that under (A.7) two alternative specifications of the error-correction term in the wage equation, using respectively the wage share and the real wage, are not identified.

---

[1] Two special cases where the relationship is degenerate are:

(i) $\sigma = 1$ (Cobb–Douglas production function), in which case the wage share is uniquely determined by the technology and the mark-up factor;

(ii) $Q \propto P$, say $Q = RP$ (cost of capital proportional to the price of value added), in which case the real wage is given by (A.6) and the wage share is determined by the technology, the mark-up factor and R.

Appendix 16.2

Table of Contents of *Europe's Unemployment Problem*, J. H. Drèze, C. R. Bean, J. P. Lambert, F. Mehta and H. Sneessens, eds., MIT Press, Cambridge, Mass., 1991.

List of symbols

Lower case letters denote logarithms; dots denote time derivatives.

A	Technical (or full capacity) output/labour ratio
B	Technical (or full capacity) output/capital ratio
C	Consumption (real)
DUC	Degree of capacity utilisation
DUL	Degree of labour utilisation by firms (ratio of actual to normal hours)
FD	Final demand $(C + I + G + XD)$ (real)
G	Government expenditures (real)
GDP	Gross domestic product (real)
I	Investment (real)
K	Capital stock
L	Employment (actual) in persons
LC	Full capacity employment
LD	Employment at demand-determined output
LS	Labour supply
M	Imports (actual, real)
MD	Import demand (real)
P	Price deflator of GDP
PI	Price index of investment goods
PM	Price index of imports
PW	Price index of world imports
PX	Price index of exports
Q	User cost of capital
$S_C, S_G, S_I, \ldots$	Shares of $C, G, I, \ldots$ in YD
U	Unemployment rate
V	Vacancies rate
W	Wage rate, nominal
WT	World imports (real)
X	Exports (actual, real)
XD	Export Demand (real)
Y	Gross domestic product, output (real)
YC	Capacity output
YD	Demand-determined output
YS	Full-employment output

VIII Policy

17 Work-sharing: some theory and recent European experience*

1. Introduction

As soon as it became clear that the current recession in Europe was likely to be severe and protracted, commentators and politicians became attracted to the possibility of *redistributing work amongst people so as to reduce involuntary unemployment*, i.e. *work-sharing*. This was not a new development. Similar concern had arisen in the thirties, leading to the dramatic and unsuccessful attempt by the Front Populaire to introduce a 40 hour week in France (see for instance *Economie Européenne*, 1980 or Fontaine, 1984, for a summary account of that earlier development, and Carré *et al.*, 1972, for a survey of French experience). In recent years, a number of policy measures designed to promote work-sharing have been implemented in European countries, and several reports have attempted to assess their impact (Van Den Bergh and Wittelsburger, 1981; Hart, 1984; or Commissariat Général du Plan, 1985). The overall impression conveyed by these reports is one of limited effectiveness in reducing unemployment – at least if one goes by hard evidence – while it is sometimes even asserted that these measures are misdirected and bound to be self-defeating (see Layard *et al.*, 1984). Yet, with youth unemployment rates reaching 25% or more in several European countries, and no major improvement in sight, it is understandable that the motivation to bring about some degree of work-sharing should persist.

* *Economic Policy*, 1, 3 (1986), 562–619; Post-scriptum, Discussion and Appendix (pp. 599–617) not reproduced here. This is a much revised and extended version of a paper (Drèze, 1986a) initially commissioned by the Macroeconomic Policy Group of the Center for European Policy Studies (CEPS) under contract with the Directorate-General for Economic and Financial Affairs (DG II) of the Commission of the European Communities, whose financial support is gratefully acknowledged. The assistance of Yves Leruth in collecting data is also gratefully acknowledged. Hopefully, the revisions will dispel the erroneous impression of early readers that I regard implicit contract theory as an explanation of involuntary unemployment (which it is not) and as the only explanation of relevance to work-sharing. Comments and suggestions by Charles Wyplosz, members of staff of DG II, referees and members of the *Economic Policy* Panel are gratefully acknowledged.

The present paper is not meant to replicate the existing collective reports, but rather to appraise recent European experience and the prospects for work-sharing in the light of the modern microeconomic analysis of labour contracts. This calls for some theoretical considerations (Section 2) before turning to the evidence (Section 4), and I must beg readers to endure the detour. A brief summary of the arguments may serve the dual purpose of providing patient readers with markers, and less patient or less interested readers with an excuse for jumping to the conclusions, or even discarding the paper altogether! It may also help those familiar with my earlier work in this area to assess quickly how my thinking has evolved (see Drèze and Modigliani, 1981; Drèze, 1979c, 1980a).

To begin with (Section 2.1), I shall argue that most people attach a positive value to having a 'regular' job, as opposed to a 'casual' job, or no job at all. There are substantial variations across individuals, and over time for a given individual, in the value of a job and in the supply of hours. From the viewpoint of employers, 'regular' jobs are typically the preferred form of employment, but the provision of such jobs usually entails incurring fixed hiring costs (of screening, training and long-term commitments). In addition there must be a current and continuing need for the additional employee. Accordingly, the supply of regular jobs is inelastic to their short-run cost. Next (Section 2.2), I shall argue that short-run disequilibria on the market for regular jobs can occur, can sometimes become sizeable and are subject to self-aggravating tendencies. In such situations (well illustrated by present circumstances), the elimination of disequilibrium can be very slow. It would be both undesirable and unrealistic to rely on wage flexibility alone to clear the labour market in the short run. The theory of 'implicit labour contracts' predicts that the wages of employees in regular jobs remain downward rigid in periods of slack demand for labour while adjustments take place in the form of partial unemployment or temporary layoffs. These combine labour hoarding by firms with some degree of work-sharing among employees under contract. New entrants to the labour market are not party to these arrangements. There is no market mechanism whereby work could be redistributed efficiently between workers under contract (insiders) and newcomers (outsiders). Instead, as insiders attempt to shelter their wages from competition by outsiders, and the latter seek income insurance or exert market power, a degree of wage rigidity spreads to the new contracts as well. Also the fixed costs of new hirings, coupled with rigidities in the organisation of work, stand in the way of work-sharing among newcomers in the form of part-time employment. An inefficient allocation of regular jobs results, from which many newcomers – in particular the young – are left out. Special measures are needed to correct this inefficiency (Section 2.3), based on three considerations (Section 2.4). First, there are externalities, the most obvious of them being unemployment compensation, which is a cost to society but not to individual agents. Second, there are complex legal provisions, which may or may not facilitate work-sharing. Third, there are many 'public good' aspects to the organisation of working time, providing scope for leadership through public policy.

After a brief interlude (Section 3), which offers a normative alternative to Section 2, I turn to the record in Section 4. Selected fragments of evidence from various sources are organized under three headings:

(i) *Trading jobs*, i.e. replacing a worker under contract by a newcomer (Section 4.1). There is scope for such replacements to the extent that the value of a job varies widely over individuals. The most obvious measure calls for early (voluntary) retirement with mandatory replacement; measures of that kind have been introduced in several countries, pulling large numbers of workers out of the labour force. Although hard figures on new hirings are scanty, those which exist reveal a large measure of success when, but only when, replacement is mandatory.

(ii) *Sharing jobs* can take two forms (Section 4.2). First, a worker under contract is replaced by a newcomer on a part-time basis (typically half-time); while such measures have been introduced in some countries, with negligible effects, surveys suggest substantial potential interest in progressive retirement schemes. Second, newcomers are hired on a part-time basis, so that a single working post is filled by more than one person. This is in principle easier, since no worker under contract is involved. Measures facilitating part-time employment have been taken in some countries, and hiring of public servants on an 80% basis has been introduced in the Benelux countries. There is no indication of growth in part-time work by men; for women growth is concentrated in those countries which have lagged behind in this respect, and reflects a trend towards greater accommodation of worker preferences rather than a cyclical pattern. One specific difficulty seems to arise from rigidities in the organization of working schedules which stand in the way of part-time early retirement and of part-time contracts on a 75% or 80% basis. This is the area where innovative measures, difficult as they may be, seem to offer the greatest challenge.

(iii) *Trading hours for jobs*, i.e. reducing weekly (or annual) working time for workers under contract in order to create new jobs (Section 4.3). This is the most controversial measure and also a difficult one, because large numbers of workers under contract are involved, and because the measure interferes with the organization of work. Firms engaged in labour hoarding will not hire additional employees in response to reductions in hours, whereas expanding firms will resist such reductions; the short-run elasticity of employment with respect to hours worked is probably very small, and we know very little about the long-run elasticity. There is no clear evidence of promising prospects along this line, apart from isolated situations (like continuous operation with multiple shifts).

In conclusion, both short-run and long-run policy prospects are evaluated (Section 5). As the paper covers a broad range of issues, I deal with some of them very briefly. In particular, aspects well covered in accessible documents (like implicit contract theory) will be treated summarily (Chapters 2 and 3 of Okun, 1981, provide an excellent background reference for the whole paper). And I shall refrain from any peripheral developments. This is not a paper on employment policies in general, but specifically on work-sharing. Thus, the issues of the trade-off between work-sharing and other measures, or between employment and other objectives (like price stability), are not taken up. This does not belittle their significance. Promoting overall employment through an adequate combination of supply-side and demand-management measures remains the first priority.

2. Theory

2.1. Regular jobs

2.1.1. Regular and casual jobs. The distinction between the total number of hours worked and the number of persons employed is now part of any serious discussion of labour use and employment (OECD, 1983, 1985). It has also found its way progressively into econometric practice (see Fair, 1969, for an early account). The relevance of the distinction is brought out by the figures on hours worked per person in tables 17.1 and 17.2, which reveal a steady decline, both in the long run and in the recent past.

Another useful distinction concerns 'regular' jobs and 'casual' jobs, as already developed in some detail by Hicks in *The Theory of Wages* (1932). A 'regular' job is an employment relationship that is expected by both parties to have some stability and to last as long as circumstances will permit, with neither party forcing termination whimsically. Stability may be guaranteed through an explicit contract. Due, however, to the difficulty of covering enough relevant contingencies in formal terms, the typical contract will be largely implicit and rely on accepted norms of behaviour to which both parties are expected to conform. 'Regular' jobs should be distinguished from 'casual' jobs, which carry no expectation of stability and require the performance of a specific task over a specific, typically short, time span for a given wage. Neither party commits itself, even implicitly, to continue the relationship.

Table 17.1. *Life hours of work in the United Kingdom*

Year	1891	1911	1931	1951	1971	1981
Men	153	146	126	118	100	88
Women	51	46	41	40	40	40
All Workers	102	96	83	79	69	64

Source: Armstrong, P. J. (1984). 'Technical Change and Reductions in Life Hours of Work', The Technical Change Centre, London.

Table 17.2. *Annual hours worked per person, 1890–1979*

	1890	1913	1929	1950	1970	1979
Austria	2,760	2,580	2,281	1,976	1,848	1,660
Belgium	2,789	2,605	2,272	2,283	1,986	1,747
Canada	2,789	2,605	2,399	1,967	1,805	1,730
France	2,770	2,588	2,297	1,989	1,888	1,727
Germany	2.765	2,584	2,284	2,316	1,907	1,719
Italy	2,714	2,536	2,228	1,997	1,768	—
Japan	2,770	2,588	2,364	2,272	2,252	2,129
Sweden	2,770	2,588	2,283	1,951	1,660	1,451
UK	2,807	2,624	2,286	1,958	1,735	1,617
US	2,789	2,605	2,342	1,867	1,707	1,607
Median	2,770	2,588	2,285	1,982	1,825	1,690

Source: Maddison, A. (1982). *Phases of Capitalist Development*, Oxford University Press, Oxford.

There are many cogent reasons why regular jobs are a superior form of employment, from the viewpoint of firms and workers alike. First, most jobs are performed better with the benefit of experience, including some experience that is specific to the workplace itself; when the job involves teamwork, experience is frequently a team attribute, and needs to be rebuilt whenever a member of the team is replaced. Second, most firms are complex organisations, where individual workers interact with many other members of the firm (supervisors, personnel department, maintenance or inventory services, etc.); such relationships are facilitated by repeated contact. Third, the employer–employee relationship is itself complex, involving a measure of trust and mutual understanding which can only be developed gradually. Fourth, a longer-run employment contract provides opportunities not present in short-lived contracts; thus, rewarding realised performance *ex post*, averaging between good and bad years, or between periods of pressure and slack, is possible with regular jobs, but not with casual jobs.

2.1.2. The viewpoint of workers. The workplace provides one among many examples of areas of life where regular relationships, developed over time on a continuing basis, are essential to the pursuit of human goals. The foremost examples are of course the family and friendship. Medical care, education, community relationships, trade, services, leisure activities, and so on, provide additional examples. An important indirect benefit from a regular job lies in the prospects which it affords for founding a family, buying a house, and establishing consumption patterns. In modern economies, fringe benefits and social security benefits are more extensive for holders of regular jobs, thereby increasing their attractiveness as they form a growing part of overall compensation. It is thus safe to assume that *most individuals attach a positive value to having a regular job.* Within the context of such jobs, they supply hours (and effort) in accordance with the traditional assumption that the marginal disutility of work (relative to leisure) increases with working time, resulting in an upward sloping supply curve for hours. (This eminently sensible view is not incorporated in standard textbook treatments of labour supply, because it is technically unwieldy; it is however incorporated indirectly in the models of 'learning by doing' and 'embodied human capital' or in the models of employment over time under uncertainty.)

For a proper appraisal of work-sharing measures, the significance of regular jobs is twofold. First the distribution of an aggregate number of hours over individual jobs matters, to an extent imperfectly captured by the supply of hours. A distribution over more jobs carries the advantage of shorter hours and more leisure for all concerned; in addition, it carries the advantage of endowing more individuals with regular jobs that are valued positively. Second, the value attached to a regular job varies considerably, both across individuals, and for given individuals over time. That different individuals may attach a different weight to the stability of employment is an immediate corollary of the diversity of tastes. At given wage rates, different individuals would prefer to supply a different quantity of hours. Yet it is a commonplace observation that most regular jobs specify a standard working week, imposed on whole sets of employees, with little room for individual variation. Also, these standard working times vary little from firm to firm. Hopefully, standard working times reflect the preferences of the 'median worker', being too long for half the labour force and too short for the other half. When faced with the choice of either working the standard time, or not at all, each worker takes an all-or-nothing decision. The net value of the job will, other things equal, be higher the closer standard working time comes to an individual's preferences. In particular, those who would prefer appreciably shorter hours will benefit less from holding the job. It would seem plausible that older workers fall into that category and hence place a lower net value on regular jobs. (There are two additional reasons why the value to any individual of having a regular job is bound to decline as the age of retirement draws near. On the one hand, the period over which a stable relationship is anticipated becomes shorter, and hence less significant. On the other hand, the link with other durable patterns of behaviour – family, house, and so on – becomes less important, as these are well established already.) The significance of individual variations on the value of regular jobs is of course that they offer prospects for gains through redistribution – a point that is central to some work-sharing measures, and is taken up in Section 4.1 below.

2.1.3. The viewpoint of firms. First, *the provision of a regular job requires an initial investment on the part of the firm* – which 'toll', discussed at length by Okun (1981, chapters 2, 3) turns labour into a 'semi-fixed factor' (Oi, 1962). Obviously, the benefits of experience acquired on the job, of integration in a work team and in the firm's organization, of mutual trust or of averaging rewards over time and across states, will accrue only progressively after a period of initiation. There will often be a period of training, during which a worker's productivity may be insufficient to cover his or her wage. Furthermore, because workers are heterogeneous, firms will attempt to identify the more promising candidates through screening. Also, to the extent that the firm is offering some degree of income and employment stability, it is undertaking a commitment which may prove costly under adverse circumstances. The present value of whatever costs or risk premium may be associated with that commitment is another component of the fixed cost of a new hiring. An implication of this initial investment is the typical preference of firms for hiring employees on a full-time rather than a part-time basis. By typical, I mean here that special advantages linked to part-time work must be present in order for that form of employment to be offered (the foremost example comes from peak loads within the week, as in retailing, where part-time work is indeed widespread). Otherwise the initial investment is basically the same whether a person works full time or part time. Consequently full-time work is altogether cheaper, and part-time work is typically confined to casual jobs, failing other inducements.

Second, *'regular' jobs are not created at will, they must correspond to some real employment prospect in the firm.* At the start, this requires a place of work, demand for the output, and relative prices at which the additional job is profitable. In addition, the firm must anticipate that the additional employee will remain wanted with sufficient probability for a sufficient time. Adverse anticipations or considerable uncertainty about technological developments, demand or relative prices, would destroy the prospect of potential employment. The disconcerting fact is that so many conditions must be fulfilled *simultaneously* for a regular job to be forthcoming whereas failure of any *one* condition is enough to annihilate the prospect.

An implication is that the supply of regular jobs is bound to be highly inelastic to their short-run cost. Specifically, temporary wage cuts or employment subsidies will not be very effective in increasing the supply of regular jobs: the other elements must be there (places of work and demand for output) and the relevant cost consideration is the long-run cost over the prospective period of employment, of which the short-run cost is only a part. Thus, temporary employment subsidies will at best move forward hirings that were contemplated anyhow, and stimulate casual employment (Phlips, 1978). Desirable as they may be, these effects remain limited in scope.

2.2. Short-run fluctuations

2.2.1. Sources of fluctuations. The short-run equilibrium between supply and demand for regular jobs is subject to numerous hazards – as we know only too well from recent experience. There are several independent factors affecting either the supply or the demand for regular jobs. To begin with the supply of jobs (the demand for labour), four main factors should be listed as exerting macroeconomic influences. (These factors may of course affect specific labour markets differently; the point of interest here is that when these factors affect many specific labour markets in a given country, or set of countries, in the same direction, then macroeconomic implications become noticeable.) First, the demand for output may be slack, due to an excess of savings over investment, a fall in the demand for exports, a contractionary fiscal policy, or a combination of these. Second, labour-saving technological progress may reduce the demand for labour at given levels of output. Third, relative factor prices may induce substitution of capital for labour, or substitution of production elsewhere for production in the home country. Fourth, the capital stock physically available, or open to profitable use, may become insufficient to offer an adequate number of jobs. In a given country at a given time, the first three factors may set in exogenously while the response of fiscal policy is basically an endogenous factor – but that does not guarantee the proper response! Further a self-perpetuating force sets in when public deficits originating in the reduced levels of employment and activity are deemed unbearable and fought through reduced public expenditure. Most significantly, as the demand for domestic output slackens, investment is discouraged, plants are scrapped, and the capital stock is brought down to the level warranted by current output. While the low level of investment further reduces aggregate demand, the fourth factor comes into play: there are no longer enough places of work to generate adequate employment. Reflating the supply of jobs now requires investment in new capacity; the growth of employment is bound to be slow, even in the face of a demand upheaval and demand management is discouraged by the fear that insufficient capacity leads to inflationary pressures.

Turning to the demand for jobs (the supply of labour), the main factors operating in the short run are demographic and migratory movements, and changes in participation rates. In some European countries, female participation rates have gone up steadily over recent decades, resulting in significant increases in labour supply through the recession. There is frequent reference in the literature to the so-called 'discouraged worker effect', but it may also be the case that unemployment discourages some workers, especially married women, from *quitting* jobs which they would otherwise have given up temporarily; at the same time, unemployment may induce others to register as job seekers, even though they might otherwise have postponed entry into the labour force. In this way, unemployment becomes subject to self-perpetuation.

2.2.2. Implications for regular and casual jobs. Because regular jobs entail an initial investment, prospective fluctuations favour casual jobs. In particular, at times of high *uncertainty* about demand, technology and real wages in the future, one may expect a temporary increase in casual employment. Unfortunate as this development may be given the well-founded preference of employees for regular jobs, it is to some extent unavoidable, and still compatible with efficiency. In particular, it may be desirable to postpone investment in a new hiring until it can be directed more effectively. This calls for the development of casual jobs during a recession, while waiting for signs of recovery before incurring the tolls of regular job creation. There is indeed superficial evidence that the private sector relies more intensively on casual employment (including subcontracting and contracting *ad interim*) in times of recession and uncertainty like the present. In the public sector special employment programmes – especially those providing casual jobs for the young – make sense given the relative ease and speed with which they can be set up, their low net costs, and the social value of the associated output.

Because the supply of regular jobs is inelastic with respect to labour costs in the short-run, relying on wage flexibility to clear the markets for regular jobs is not a realistic prospect. Indeed, market clearing wages could drop to very low levels in response to a conjunction of adverse shocks. Market-clearing wages could even drop to a level where a sizeable part of the unemployment becomes voluntary (although the unemployed may still register as seeking work in order to collect benefits)! There are two compelling reasons why that kind of flexibiltiy is undesirable. The first, of a microeconomic nature, is that it would generate excessive income uncertainty for workers holding regular jobs. That argument is taken up in Section 4.1 and extended to a discussion of wage discrimination between workers under contract and new recruits. The second, of a macroeconomic nature, is that a major drop in labour incomes would depress aggregate demand further, leading to an 'equilibrium' with very low levels of output and employment. The fact that the resulting unemployment is labelled 'voluntary' provides little solace. Given our imprecise estimates of the wage elasticity of labour demand and of the income multiplier, not to mention our near ignorance of the implications of wage moderation for government budgets, it is safer to look at incomes policy as a long-run instrument and not to rely on it as a short-run stabiliser of employment.

2.3. Labour contracts and market failures

2.3.1. The theory of implicit contracts. How does one reconcile the idea that most people want to have a regular job and stable income with the prospect of recurrent fluctuations in the demand for labour? This very question is taken up in recent theoretical work on 'implicit' labour contracts. (Azariadis, 1975, Baily, 1974 and Gordon, 1974, are the seminal contributions; Drèze, 1979a, gives a non-technical presentation of the main ideas; more recent accounts appear in the *Quarterly Journal of Economics*, Supplement, 1983, or in the surveys by Azariadis, 1979, Ito, 1982, Rosen, 1985, and Hart and Holmström, 1989). The main implication of this theory is that *efficient labour contracts will embody an element of risk-sharing*, protecting labour incomes from the vagaries of supply and demand shocks to a sizeable extent. If wages were allowed to vary widely in response to these shocks, the resulting income uncertainty would be costly to workers unable to diversify their labour supply, who therefore will be more risk averse than firms whose shareholders can hold diversified portfolios; hence the possibility of welfare improving risk-shifting arrangements, where the *labour contracts include a form of income insurance through reduced wage flexibility*. The insurance premium should be paid partly through lower wages during the early period of employment (explaining to some extent the practice of seniority bonuses), and partly through reduced upward wage flexibility (to an extent compatible with maintaining incentives). An optimal arrangement would combine an efficient degree of risk-sharing (in particular labour incomes become immune from firm-specific risks and bear a less-than-proportional share of economy-wide risks)[1] with privately efficient levels of employment (the marginal value product of labour equals its opportunity cost for workers at all times).

The combination of downward rigid wages and efficient levels of employment implies that wages do not correspond to the marginal value product of labour at all times, but only do so *on average*. In particular, during a recession, wages in many firms will exceed the marginal value product of labour; these firms practise 'labour hoarding' and will not hire new workers, *even at wages lower than those which they currently pay*. New hirings will start only at wages lower than the marginal value product of labour and with all contracted employees working full hours. For these firms (which could well be a majority during a deep recession), the elasticity of employment with respect to wage reductions is zero. This statement applies only to new hirings, however. Retention of workers under contract will be enhanced by wage cuts in firms facing bankruptcy, which can also

---

[1] Violation of this condition is a major drawback of the otherwise attractive profit-sharing scheme advocated by Weitzman (1984). Firm-specific risks should not matter to holders of diversified portfolios. That argument does not apply to privately owned firms, however.

be numerous in a deep recession – see for instance Sneessens and Drèze (1986b).

Another consideration of interest here is that the optimal (Pareto-efficient) level of unemployment is the level which would have occurred with flexible wages: at that level, the marginal value product of labour would equal the reservation wage of workers and all unemployment would be voluntary. With downward wage rigidity, the marginal value product of labour should not fall below the reservation wage of the workers, but should at least fall that far! The difference is that unemployment *appears to be involuntary* – and is definitely perceived as such by the individual worker. Efficient arrangements again call for work-sharing among employees under contract, who should preferably be laid off on a part-time basis at times of slack employment, to the extent compatible with incentives and organisation of work. In practice, that approach seems applicable only to blue collar workers; temporary layoffs, whether on a part-time or full-time basis, are practically unknown among white collar workers (that seniority bonuses are more significant for white collar workers than for blue collar workers is consistent with this observation). And part-time layoffs for blue collar workers are often discouraged by the rules governing unemployment compensation, which is not always available on a flexible, part-time basis.

There is very little hard evidence on the practical relevance of implicit contract theory, beyond the easy observation of widespread downward rigidity of wages, either real (as in most European countries) or nominal (as in the US). An early study by Abowd and Ashenfelter (1981) provided some indication that a higher probability of temporary lay-off is partly compensated by a higher wage when employed – a finding whose interpretation in the contract framework is not entirely straightforward. Further studies by Ashenfelter and Brown (1982) and Card (1985), quoted by Hart and Holmström (1989), apparently suggest little support for the hypothesis that employment levels can be explained by opportunity costs rather than wages, yet numerous macroeconometric studies corroborate the widespread belief that firms practise 'labour hoarding' during recessions. A study by Oswald (1984) of the written terms of actual labour contracts again finds little corroboration of the theoretical predictions. Neither do we know precisely how reductions of labour inputs are distributed over workers under contract – a subject on which some evidence should now be available in Europe. Collecting and analysing that evidence would seem worthwhile, if only for the light it could throw on the related issue of including the unemployed in work-sharing schemes.

2.3.2. Present and future contracts. The theory of implicit contracts asserts that efficient risk-sharing between risk-averse workers and less risk-averse firms justifies some degree of wage rigidity *for holders of regular jobs.* But that argument has not been extended to the market for regular jobs – although the extension is implicitly suggested in an example of Holmström (1981). The question of interest is whether the terms of new contracts should be flexible enough to clear the market for regular jobs at all times under all conditions, or whether efficient risk-sharing between firms and *prospective job-seekers* calls for some degree of rigidity *in the terms of new contracts,* with the associated implication of some unemployment.

It has been known for a long time that keeping wages above the market-clearing level may raise a worker's expected utility (computed with a probability of unemployment equal to the resulting unemployment rate): a sufficient condition is that the wage elasticity of labour demand be small in relation to the risk aversion of workers (see Appendix to chapter 13). That observation is the starting point of the so-called 'union models' of unemployment, surveyed for instance by Oswald (1985), Pencavel (1985) and Lindbeck and Snower (1985). In these models, however, wages are chosen *ex post* so as to maximise a worker's expected utility and are enforced through the market power of unions. The resulting unemployment is inefficient, as could be expected from a monopoly solution. The question raised here is one of *ex ante* efficiency, in an economy with incomplete insurance markets.

In order to address that question, one must introduce explicitly successive generations of workers, and consider *ex ante* the conditions that will be faced by a new generation entering the labour market. The difference with the implicit contract model is that *ex ante* considerations are not exploited in the design of contracts, because workers and firms do not engage in *forward* labour contracts. The contracts come *ex post,* after a new generation joins the labour force. That simple observation has two important implications.

First, future generations are not present when current generations negotiate labour contracts. Therefore, *the allocation of work between successive generations is not covered by the market.* That inescapable market failure introduces a major asymmetry between holders of regular jobs enjoying contractual pre-emptive employment and newcomers, who face a residual labour demand. There is scope for intervention to correct that market failure, for instance through incentives for work-sharing.

Second, because workers do not engage in forward labour contracts, they do not have access to insurance against the possibility of low wages when they enter the market for regular jobs, yet there are other, less risk-averse, agents (the firms and their shareholders) who could supply such insurance on mutually advantageous terms. Downward wage rigidity is a substitute for such insurance – an inferior substitute, to be sure, but sometimes the only available substitute.

Whether or not downward wage rigidity at less than full employment is justified *on efficiency grounds* depends primarily upon the range of feasible alternatives for income maintenance available to workers – both employed and unemployed – when labour market conditions are unfavourable. To see this, consider a generation of workers that will enter the labour market next 'year', under conditions ('states') that may be either 'good' (high market-clearing wages) or 'bad' (low market-clearing wages). Assume for simplicity that workers are risk-averse but firms (shareholders) are risk neutral. If the government could implement a transfer in favour of the workers (whether employed or not) *in the 'bad' state and only in that state*, then it would be optimal to announce such a transfer, and let wages drop to the market-clearing level. Wage rigidity would be inefficient. The *state-contingent* transfer performs for newcomers the insurance function which is embodied in the labour contracts of the earlier generations.

At the other extreme, assume that such state-contingent transfers are not feasible. In that case, wage rigidity in the bad state is the only feasible insurance for newcomers. It is an inferior form of insurance, however, due to the associated loss of output. But when the loss of output is 'small' relative to the insurance gain, then *some degree of downward wage rigidity becomes an efficient second-best policy; the resulting unemployment is individually involuntary, though socially efficient* (the condition that the loss of output be small enough is given in the Appendix to chapter 13). An essential feature is that the wage rigidity is decided before the state is known, whereas the employment decision is taken after observing the state.

An interesting intermediate case arises when the only transfers actively considered take the form of unemployment compensation – financed, say, from a lump-sum tax on profits. In the absence of additional constraints related to incentives, it is then efficient to set the unemployment compensation at a level such that, in 'bad' states, the unemployed are just as well off as the employed newcomers. Thus *unemployment becomes 'voluntary', but the wage is downwards rigid, resulting in less than full employment* (with a marginal product of labour equal to the reservation wage of idle workers collecting unemployment compensation, which thus exceeds the social opportunity cost of labour: see the Appendix to chapter 13).

The special cases provide preliminary insights in a largely uncharted and difficult area, the exploration of which goes beyond the scope of the present paper. They suggest that a form of work-sharing among the newcomers (for instance through part-time jobs) would be desirable when less than full employment is second-best efficient. It would dominate the alternative (full-time work for some, full-time idleness for others), by improving the allocation among newcomers of both regular jobs and hours worked: work-sharing would then be 'first-and-a-half-best'. On that ground alone, it deserves attention.

2.3.3. Wage discrimination and insider-outsider theories. The intriguing stylised fact about downward wage rigidity for new contracts is that we seem to observe little wage discrimination between employees under contracts and new recruits; indeed casual empiricism suggests that wage discrimination *by hiring dates* is not a widespread phenomenon. Of course, some degree of wage discrimination by hiring dates is consistent with the available evidence. Thus teaching assistants hired today by Belgian Universities earn 10% less (at given seniority levels) than those hired a few years ago, whereas bank clerks earn 7% less. In the US, the practice of 'two-tier contracts', introducing explicit wage discrimination between previously employed workers and new recruits, seems to have spread recently, affecting some 25% of union workers outside construction covered by contracts signed in 1983–85 – see Dewatripont (1986) for additional data and analysis. And it is known that the quality of new recruits for given job characteristics improves during recessions and deteriorates during booms – see Okun (1981) and the references given there. Yet in general wages for new workers display little discrimination *vis-à-vis* those of workers already under contract.

It could well be that such discrimination is regarded as impractical by firms and as undesirable by firms and workers alike. Wage settlements, including differentials by occupation and seniority, are complex enough already, and increasing that complexity by adding an extra dimension might be simply impractical. Further, it certainly goes against the grain of accepted ethical norms to accentuate pay differences for equal work. Thus, it could be that wage discrimination by hiring dates has an implicit cost, with the result that the wage rigidities, introduced for the justified sake of risk-sharing in the existing contracts, lead to inefficient involuntary unemployment among newcomers.

An alternative explanation is offered by the so-called 'insider–outsider' theories of unemployment (see Lindbeck and Snower, 1985, for a very useful survey of a growing literature). The point of departure of these theories is 'the observation that, in general, a firm finds it costly to exchange its current, full-fledged employees (the "insiders") for workers outside the firm (the "outsiders")... The turnover cost generates economic rent ... The insiders raise their wage above the entrant wage, *but not by more than the relevant turnover cost*' (Lindbeck and Snower, 1985, p. 47; italics added). This is a sensible explanation which suggests some interesting links between insider–outsider and implicit contract theories.

Thus existing theories of labour contracts typically assume that markets for new contracts at future dates will be competitive. If, as suggested by insider–outsider theories, the wages of employees under contract (insiders) cannot exceed those of new recruits (outsiders) by more than the turnover costs, then it would be in the interest of insiders to keep the wages paid to outsiders as high as possible, i.e. to impose downward wage rigidity for new contracts. In particular, if it could be stipulated that new recruits must be paid the same (or nearly the same) wages as insiders, then the latter would be protected against competition by outsiders. Conversely, implicit labour contracts typically stipulate that insiders will not be laid off and replaced by outsiders. However, such a stipulation could be of limited effectiveness, because it does not prevent expanding firms and new firms from hiring newcomers at lower, market-clearing wages. The position of these firms *in product markets* would thereby be strengthened, whereas the output and employment prospects of the labour hoarding firms would be weakened further. An extreme but suggestive example is offered by the building industry, where new firms are easily organised. If new firms could hire labour at a fraction of the cost applicable to workers under contracts, established firms would have to lower their bids for new building projects commensurately. Thus, insiders in the established firms would face the competition of outsiders *through product prices*; the stipulation that they could not be laid off and replaced by outsiders is ineffective.

It is thus in the joint interest of established firms and their employees to prevent, if they can, the wages specified in new contracts from falling appreciably below the wages of insiders. Of course, this requires market power. That unions in Europe have market power over wage determination is generally accepted. Two additional and new considerations are proposed here. First, union activity on the market for new contracts is not a matter of concern to newcomers only; it is also of direct concern to insiders seeking protection from competition by outsiders via product markets. Second, that very protection is also valuable to established employers.

The resulting coincidence of interests helps to explain the observed practice of industry-level wage settlements, which are binding on new firms and seem to introduce little wage discrimination between insiders and outsiders.

The absence of market mechanisms leading to wage discrimination between workers under contract and new recruits has led to a number of proposals for *marginal employment subsidies* (see e.g. Dornbusch *et al.*, 1983 or Steinherr and Van Haeperen, 1985). As I have noted above, such subsidies should be substantial and durable in order to affect significantly the long-run cost of a regular job, and hence employment. In addition, the argument presented in this section suggests that existing firms, and their employees, may object to such subsidies as generating unfair competition in the product markets.

2.3.4. Summary and implications. Workers seeking employment during a recession (new entrants, and those who have lost their jobs) face two kinds of firms, those engaged in labour hoarding (which are not hiring), and those hiring new workers (including new firms). The former, which may well be a majority during a severe recession, operate at a marginal value product of labour less than the wage costs and equal to the reservation wage of their employees. Routine demographic replacements, which will normally absorb all new entrants in stationary conditions, are not taking place. Newcomers are excluded both from the labour hoarding and from whatever work-sharing is organised among employees under contract. And these firms will not respond to wage cuts by new hirings, until the gap between wage costs and the marginal value product of labour has been bridged: competition between workers under contract and newcomers is shut off. Expanding firms and new firms hire labour to the point where its marginal value product covers wage costs, but not beyond. And they practise little or no wage discrimination between workers under contract and newcomers.

We thus have three groups of workers: first, those under contract in firms which are not hiring, where they are employed at a marginal value product below their wages; second, those employed in new and hiring firms, with a marginal value product equal to their wage; and third, the unemployed. There are two sources of inefficiency in this situation. First, employment should increase in the expanding firms, to the point where the marginal value product of labour is equal to the reservation wage of the unemployed. It is not clear how this can be achieved without some form of wage discrimination between workers under contract and newcomers. Second, the distribution of jobs and hours worked between the employed and the unemployed is inefficient. Indeed, I have presented some quite compelling arguments to the effect that *some* newcomers at least will place a higher value on finding a regular job than *some* workers under contract attach to keeping theirs. (In particular, young workers may be more eager to start a career than workers close to retirement are to bring their own to an end.) Hence, some redistribution of regular jobs between workers under contract and newcomers would be desirable – but will not be naturally forthcoming. In addition, the supply of *hours* being definitely upward sloping, it would be desirable to increase the number of employees and redistribute aggregate hours among them – a standard argument. Thus, whether we look at jobs (valued positively) or at hours of work (valued negatively), we conclude that the allocation of work between newcomers and workers under contract is inefficient. Finally, it is easy to understand why little or no work-sharing takes place among newcomers, in the form of part-time jobs. With firms facing fixed costs of screening and training, and half the newcomers prepared to work more than full-time (as must be the case if standard working time corresponds to median worker preferences), there is ample scope for mutually agreeable contracts on a full-time basis.

The upshot of these arguments is precisely what we observe today in Europe! Namely, a prolonged spell of deeply depressed demand for labour, with employment declining in many firms (especially in the manufacturing sector which is exposed to international competition), downward rigid wages and a modest degree of work-sharing among workers under contract, with very high unemployment rates among the young (and older workers who have lost their previous jobs), and a fair degree of wage rigidity even on new contracts. The resulting allocation of work among all workers is definitely inefficient both because little or no work-sharing takes place between workers under contract and newcomers, and because little or no work-sharing takes place among newcomers finding employment. More efficient work-sharing thus requires special measures.

2.4. The scope for intervention

Market failures provide a motivation for public intervention aimed at correcting inefficiencies. In the case under discussion, that motivation is enhanced by the existence of a social externality. Unemployment is not only a burden on individuals, who are frustrated in their desire to work and to enjoy a stable employment relationship. It also entails additional real burdens for society – for instance when prolonged inactivity leads to delinquency or health deterioration. Of course, the most immediate externality comes from the existence of unemployment compensation schemes. In the light of the arguments reviewed above, it is obvious 'that public unemployment compensation schemes are important and should be maintained, in spite of some obvious drawbacks'.[2] Unemployment compensation accrues to the unemployed at no private cost but it is paid out of public funds which entails a social cost. Any measure resulting in less unemployment also results in less public expenditure on unemployment compensation. More positively, the money spent on unemployment compensation could be spent more profitably on reducing unemployment. *One way is to subsidise work-sharing, thereby providing financial incentives to overcome market failures.*

There are two additional reasons why public measures aimed at promoting work-sharing could *possibly* be effective. First, in most European countries the social security system has become very complex, introducing additional distortions into an already imperfectly functioning labour market. An obvious example arises when ceilings or other regressive formulae for social security contributions (employment taxes) impose a penalty on part-time jobs as compared with full-time jobs. Eliminating those distortions which discourage work-sharing, possibly even creating distortions which favour it, offers scope for public intervention. Second, the organization of working time is a complex social phenomenon, involving coordination of all kinds of activities, with numerous externalities; it falls largely outside the sphere of market allocation. To take again an obvious example, think back to the transition from the 6-day week to the 5-day week. Although 5 days became the norm for blue collar workers shortly after World War II, it took nearly twenty years before that schedule became universal, and it is probably fair to say that consumption patterns are still adjusting to a universal 5-day week. With further reductions in working time below 40 hours per week now emerging here and there, a number of alternative patterns of work are possible. The coordination aspects and externalities provide scope for public initiative in sorting out the costs and benefits *for society* of these alternative patterns, and for public leadership in promoting that which is most desirable.

---

[2] The most fashionable of these drawbacks, namely the negative impact on job search, is of little consequence during a deep recession, when employment is only very weakly linked to labour supply. The possible impact on wages is a more serious matter.

3. Interlude (sorbet)

Before turning to consider specific measures aimed at promoting work-sharing in Europe, it is illuminating to speculate how a substantial temporary decline in the demand for regular labour would be handled in a cooperative environment – like a kibbutz, a network of cooperatives (as in Mondragon in Spain) or an integrated set of family businesses. For concreteness think about a hypothetical kibbutz where the major use of labour (entirely supplied by the members) goes into manufacturing some gadget sold outside. Normally, young members are taken up into the factory work force and trained to replace retiring older members. Assume now that a non-negligible decline in the need for labour input occurs – say due to a major accidental plant destruction, a shortage of raw materials, a sudden fall in the demand for the gadget, the introduction of a new labour-saving technology, or a combination of these. This decline was not perfectly foreseen, although it may perhaps have been contemplated. Also suppose the decline is expected to last for some time, with progressive elimination over a period of months or years at a highly uncertain rate. (That is, long-term corrective action is under way, but will only become fully effective after a while.) How would the kibbutz community react to such an event?

Most likely, a whole set of measures would be combined; diverting some labour to other uses previously endowed with lower priority, such as improving the grounds or repainting the buildings; excusing from work in the factory the older, less able or less motivated workers, or some with high productivity alternatives (like young mothers, or members with valuable personal projects); reducing across the board effective working times, through shorter hours, longer vacations, or occasional days off; calling some of the young workers into the work force on a part-time basis, with the rest of their time devoted to continued education, or to the other work already mentioned.

The list could be extended. The point I wish to make is that various forms of work-sharing would *naturally* be introduced; and it is highly unlikely that a large number of young members would remain totally inactive for prolonged periods.

4. Experience

The digression of Section 3 provides a useful background against which to evaluate the alternative forms of work-sharing which have been considered recently by European policy-makers. I will group them under three headings: *trading jobs*, i.e. replacing a worker under contract by a newcomer; *sharing jobs*, i.e. filling a single working post by more than one person; and *trading hours for jobs*, i.e. reducing working time for workers under contract to create new jobs.

4.1. Trading jobs (early retirement)

Trading jobs between workers under contract and unemployed persons is the simplest, and in a way the most natural, form of work-sharing. In particular, it *does not interfere at all with the organisation of work*. Because the value to individuals of regular jobs varies from one person to the next, there is scope for mutually advantageous trading.[3] By definition, the holders of regular jobs place a non-negative value on their jobs – otherwise, they would quit. But that value could be small – in which case a small 'bribe' would induce the holder to give up the job. If the 'bribe' per year falls short of the level of unemployment compensation, the state can 'buy' the job for an unemployed person, at no net cost (the compensation paid to the quitter is no longer paid to the new employee); this generates a positive externality, namely the value of the job to the new employee. Also, the value of a job is often blown up artificially by social legislation. For instance, some statutory pensions are proportional to average salary over the last five years prior to retirement age; consequently, quitting during these five years entails a cost far in excess of the salary itself (see Hart, 1984). The state could step in to correct the externality – say by neutralising the effect of early quitting on the pension.

These two ideas are combined in early retirement schemes, as introduced in several European countries over the past decade (namely, in the Netherlands and Belgium in 1976, in the UK in 1977, in France in 1981 as a supplement to earlier measures, and in Germany in 1984). Workers close to retirement are natural candidates for giving up jobs, under moderate financial incentives (but subject to suitable adjustments in

[3] Could such trading be organized through markets? In exceptional cases, something resembling a private market for individual jobs exists; but closer scrutiny reveals that the 'jobs' in question are in the nature of independent practice or casual jobs, and lack the dimension of a lasting employment relationship. For regular jobs, the presence of a third party, the employer, complicates the trading: the employer must accept (recruit) the 'buyer' of a job; and if jobs in a firm had positive market values this might provide incentives for the firm to reduce wages and capture the 'rent'. I am not aware of any serious work on this topic. It should also be realised that our complex social legislation does not facilitate market trading of individual jobs. Would a seller be eligible for unemployment compensation? Would a buyer inherit the seniority rights of the seller? Basically, social security rights are not transferable.

pension rules). All the schemes under consideration permit early retirement, at no loss of pension rights after the normal age of retirement, and with an income allowance over the intermediate years. The level of that transitory income, and its source, vary from scheme to scheme; typically, the basic component corresponds to unemployment compensation, with an additional allowance sometimes provided by the firm or by the state. In several schemes, the retired workers must be replaced by a member of the unemployed (a young one, in Belgium), or else, the firm must make a case that it operates with excess labour, so that early retirements are a substitute for dismissals. Although most schemes provide incentives for *voluntary* retirements and none make it compulsory across the board, there are undoubtedly many cases where the worker's hand is forced by the prospect of an unappealing alternative (being laid off, transferred, etc.). And there are undoubtedly cases where the employer's hand is forced towards entering a programme with mandatory replacements.

I have not seen a systematic account and analysis of early retirement programmes at the European level. But the fragmentary country data which I have come across indicate clearly that these programmes can involve substantial numbers of people.

4.1.1. The United Kingdom. Introduced in 1976, the Job Release Scheme offers a weekly allowance to older workers retiring early, provided their employer agrees to replace them by unemployed persons. The allowance is paid until the age of normal retirement, and varies (from £48 to £61 per week) with family and health status. The age of eligibility has varied over time from 64 to 62 years of age for men; it is 59 for women and 60 for disabled men. Participation in the programme is entirely voluntary. According to Davies and Metcalf (1985) there were 272,100 entrants into the programme over the period 1976–1984, with a stock of participants totalling 75,000 persons in 1985. They also quote a replacement ratio (new hirings per entrant) of 92% and claim that 'the Job Release Scheme has the lowest net cost per person off the (unemployment) register' of all the Special Employment Programmes implemented in the UK (namely, £1,650 per person-year in 1985, obtained from a gross cost of £3,250 after netting out the savings in unemployment benefits). They also claim that the scope of the programme could be more than doubled, by extending eligibility to all men aged 60–64.

4.1.2. France. Several early retirement programmes have been implemented. The 'Contrats de Solidarité' were introduced in 1981 and required mandatory replacements. Other programmes without mandatory replacement had been introduced in the past. According to Marchand (1984), by the end of 1983 there were some 700,000 beneficiaries of early retirement programmes, namely 180,000 under 'Contrats de Solidarité', 284,000 in early retirement due to dismissal and 230,000 under voluntary early retirement. According to data presented by Baruh (1986), actual participants in the earlier programmes represented a substantial proportion of potential participants. For 36 sectors, Baruh relates the number of actual participants in 1980–82 to the number of employees at the 1975 census in the relevant age group. He finds the number of actual beneficiaries equal to 51.5% of the 1975 stock, with figures between 40 and 70% in 24 sectors (out of 36), and figures below 40% in only 5 sectors, all of them services. These are crude calculations, but they indicate unambiguously that participation rates for these programmes were high. The replacement ratio is known only for the 'Contrats de Solidarité', where it is reportedly close to 95%. It is of course nil in the case of dismissals, and believed to have been relatively low under the previous schemes which did not require mandatory replacement. The gross cost of these programmes, as estimated from the national accounts, seems to be of the same order of magnitude as in the UK (around £3,200 per beneficiary per year). As of April 1983, the 'Contrats de Solidarité' programme was discontinued; instead, voluntary retirement was offered to all workers aged 60 or more with 37.5 years of labour force seniority. Apparently mandatory replacement is not required.

4.1.3. Belgium. A number of early retirement schemes have been implemented since 1977; the age of eligibility has generally been 60 for men and 55 for women. Except in the case of dismissals, replacement by an unemployed person aged less than 30 is mandatory. Observed replacement ratios reach 63% overall and 83% if dismissals are set aside. As of October 1984, the overall number of beneficiaries totalled 138,000 (see Sonnet and Defeyt, 1984). Thus, in both France and Belgium, some 3 to 4% of the total labour force were involved.

Participation rates for the Belgian programmes are very high, confirming the estimates for France, but also pointing to a possible source of bias. Scarmure (1986) has related the number of actual beneficiaries of early retirement schemes to an estimate of the total number of potential beneficiaries in the 'relevant' age group – namely 60–64 for men and 55–59 for women. He finds participation rates that increase steadily from the date when a programme is launched. These are uniformly much higher for men, increasing from 33% in 1977 to 94% in 1981, than for women, for whom the respective figures are 12 and 38%. For both sexes combined, the rates rise from 24% in 1977 to 60% in 1981 and thence to 85% in 1985 (the breakdown by sex is not given after 1981). There are two sources of bias in these figures. First, on a number of occasions involving firms faced with the prospect of bankruptcy or reorganisation, early retirement schemes have been extended outside the official age bracket (I remember one such instance, where men were forced into retirement at 53 and women at 48). Second, the total number of potential beneficiaries has been obtained by multiplying the figures for the labour force *in the relevant age group* by the percentage of wage and salary earners (as opposed to the self-employed) *in the aggregate labour force*. It would seem likely that labour force participation declines more slowly with age in the case of the self-employed than in the case of wage and salary earners. These two sources of bias reinforce each other. The first is probably the more significant and might explain the high rates of early retirement in France as well as in Belgium.

Scarmure (1986) also provides estimates of the net cost to the Treasury of these schemes. His calculations are more detailed, and probably more comprehensive, than those quoted above for the UK and France. Indeed, he assesses separately the loss of revenue resulting from the termination of employment of an older worker (through lost income tax, social security contributions and indirect taxes), the direct cost of early retirement benefits, the savings connected with removing a young unemployed person from the register, and the gain in revenue from the employment of that young worker. He conducts these calculations separately for white collar workers (where seniority bonuses account for 40% of average end-of-career salaries) and for blue collar workers (where seniority bonuses are insignificant). His figures, translated into sterling, are presented in table 17.3. Although rough, these calculations point to the substantial total cost of early retirement schemes for white collar workers *whose employment would otherwise not have been terminated*. Of course, if a person goes into early retirement *instead of being laid off* (for the good), the net cost is minimal (the French data quoted above suggest that the latter case was more frequent than the former).

    4.1.4. Conclusion. These data are very fragmentary, and leave unanswered many questions worthy of further investigation. In particular, one would like to know: the proportion of the eligible population which has joined voluntary programmes of early retirement, and how that proportion has varied with age, with sex, with qualifications or occupations and with the income maintenance provisions of the programmes; the net impact of early retirement programmes on labour supply, taking into account natural attrition of the labour force in the relevant age groups; the net impact of these programmes on employment, taking into account normal replacement ratios at the times of normal retirement; the effect of mandatory replacement provisions; and the net budgetary costs of alternative programmes.

Table 17.3. *Net cost per capita of early retirement in Belgium (in £)*

		White collar	Blue collar
Loss of revenue from termination of employment of older worker		14,400	8,700
Early retirement benefits		3,700	4,000
	Subtotal	18,100	12,700
Cost of young unemployed		2,700	2,700
Revenue from employment of young worker		7,900	8,700
	Subtotal	10,600	11,400
Net cost		7,500	1,300

Source: Scarmure (1986).

While awaiting results of further research on these points, it seems safe to draw two conclusions from the British, French and Belgian experiences. The first conclusion is that *a mandatory replacement provision seems to make a crucial difference in terms of job creation*. In contrast to the very high replacement rates quoted above for the UK, France and Belgium, figures as low as 10 or 20% are reported for non-mandatory programmes, for instance in the Netherlands (see Commissariat Général du Plan, 1985). Offhand, early retirement without voluntary replacement may be construed as an indication of labour hoarding. It is not implausible that 80 or 90% of the firms adopting early retirement schemes without mandatory replacements were firms with redundant labour. But these figures may be partly illusory, as one might expect replacements to be staggered over time, with the high mandatory rates concealing some hirings unrelated to the scheme and the low voluntary rates failing to take account of subsequent hirings. The second conclusion is that the potential reduction in the effective labour supply *of workers under contract* through early retirement is definitely substantial, as witnessed by the French and Belgian figures. With state pension schemes largely financed by redistributive taxation rather than from an accumulated fund, the official retirement age is (like standard working time) a 'public good', corresponding roughly to the median worker's preferences. In that case, about half the labour force should have a potential interest in early retirement, at a transitory income close to retirement income, the proportion of volunteers increasing smoothly with the income replacement ratio. Surveys conducted in France and the Netherlands confirm these commonsense observations.[4] In the same way that the attractiveness of early retirement varies across individuals, it also varies across firms. One important aspect is the extent of seniority bonuses, which provide an inducement to replace senior workers by less costly beginners. Another aspect is the extent to which firms try to update the skill composition of their work force: early retirement provides advance opportunities for doing so with constant employment.

4.2.   Sharing jobs (part-time work)

This form of work-sharing occurs whenever a single working post is filled by more than one person. Two separate issues will be considered under this heading, namely early retirement on a part-time basis with replacement on the same basis, and part-time work in general.

   4.2.1. Part-time early retirement. In 1982, the UK introduced a 'Job Splitting Scheme', under which (among other provisions) a worker could retire early on a half-time basis, and be replaced on the same basis by one who was unemployed. After 12 months of operation, the Job Splitting Scheme had covered a mere 578 jobs! In 1983, the French 'Contrats de Solidarité', used by 180,000 persons over a two-year span, were brought to an end, and replaced by a scheme offering incentives for half-time early retirement with replacement. That scheme, parallel to the British Job Splitting Scheme, was equally unsuccessful.[5]

   These experiences are definitely sobering, for progressive retirement would seem to convey a number of advantages in comparison with an abrupt end to the working life. Reporting the results of sample polls on the preferences of workers regarding earnings and working time, Van Den Bergh and Wittelsburger (1981) note that diversity of preferences is the

---

[4] According to a survey conducted in France in 1980, 50% of workers would have retired at age 60 instead of 65, if offered the same retirement income. In the Netherlands, when older teachers were given the option of reduced working time in pre-retirement years, 90% of those eligible took advantage of the scheme.

[5] In a sample of 34 firms surveyed in 1984 by a Commission of the French Planning Office, 27 firms had adopted some form of work-sharing or of working-time reduction, but only one case of progressive (part-time) retirement was mentioned; see Commissariat Général du Plan (1985).

rule, with the single exception of German workers who, in a 1979 IFO survey, were 70% in favour of progressive retirement. The apparent failure of progressive retirement schemes in France and the UK should be considered in the light of broader trends concerning part-time work.

4.2.2. Part-time work. The more striking features are the following:

Part-time workers are almost exclusively women and the proportion is rising continuously with age; in the prime age group, it stands uniformly above the average. Although the percentage of men working regularly on a part-time basis has grown somewhat in recent years, the growth is accounted for by older workers or younger workers in special programmes; *there is little or no indication of systematic job sharing among men* (table 17.4).

The percentage of women working regularly on a part-time basis varies substantially across countries, ranging from 40–45% in the UK and Denmark, down to 20% or less in France and Belgium; *variations across countries are much more pronounced than variations over time.*

For women, a high percentage of part-time work tends to be associated with an above average labour force participation rate. When participation rates are adjusted into full-time equivalents as is done in table 17.5, their variability across countries is sharply reduced and adjusted participation rates become independent of the extent of part-time work. This observation suggests that promoting part-time work would increase participation rates, so that the increased employment would not be matched by a commensurate fall in unemployment, nor would it be matched by a commensurate increase in aggregate labour input.

In a country like the UK, where part-time work by women is widespread, the proportion of part-time workers varies substantially with age and family composition (tables 17.6 and 17.7). Also preferences for working time expressed by survey respondents in other countries (like Germany and France), where part-time work is less widespread, imply a desired share of part-time work close to the 40–45% observed in the UK and Denmark (Jallade, 1982). Furthermore, in France with little part-time work, the proportion of part-time workers has increased recently (since 1980), and the increase has been uniform across industries (Drèze, 1986a). On the other hand, in the UK, the percentage of part-time work is stationary. This is consistent with the hypothesis that the extent of part-time work largely reflects the preferences of workers, accommodated by employers, rather than the other way around.

In all countries, part-time work is more widespread in services than in

Table 17.4. *Proportion of employees working part-time by sex and age (% of total employment, regular and casual jobs)*

	Men						Women					
	1975	1983					1975	1983				
	Total	14–24	25–49	50–64	65 up	Total	Total	14–24	25–49	50–64	65 up	Total
Belgium	1.0	3.8	1.4	1.9	18.8	2.0	13.0	14.7	20.4	23.2	37.5	19.7
Denmark	4.7	20.2	2.7	4.8	20.5	6.6	45.2	30.2	44.5	54.4	46.5	44.7
France	3.0	4.5	1.4	3.0	37.6	2.5	16.7	14.4	19.6	25.2	39.2	20.0
Germany	1.9	1.5	0.9	1.6	39.4	1.7	26.7	6.0	36.7	36.5	55.7	30.0
Greece	—	6.7	2.4	3.3	16.7	—	—	10.1	10.9	13.0	51.4	—
Ireland	2.6	5.8	1.6	2.6	—	2.7	16.9	6.9	19.4	27.3	—	15.6
Italy	3.4	3.7	1.1	3.1	25.3	2.4	12.7	7.8	29.8	13.1	29.9	9.4
Netherlands[1]	2.4	11.0	5.3	7.5	46.6	6.9	28.8	22.0	59.9	66.1	55.6	50.3
UK	2.3	6.0	1.0	2.6	57.9	3.3	41.0	15.9	47.1	51.1	74.5	42.1
Europe 10[2]	2.6	4.6	1.4	2.8	35.8	2.8	26.0	12.1	29.8	34.8	—	27.6

Source: Eurostat, *Emploi et Chômage 2*, 1985.
Notes: [1]For the Netherlands, a change in definitions occurred between 1975 and 1983.
[2]Europe 9 for data describing all age groups together.

industry: in the 10 EC countries, the percentage of part-time work is 1.3% in industry and 3.4% in services for men, and 18.0% and 30.3% respectively for women (see Drèze, 1986a). In all sectors, it is concentrated in jobs entailing less responsibility and requiring lower qualifications, as hourly earnings of part-time workers are lower than those of full-time workers (see Jallade, 1982).

Table 17.5. *Adjusted labour-force participation rates, women, 1977*

	Gross participation rate	Proportion of part-time employees	Adjusted participation rate	Unemployment rate
Belgium	25.7	16.7	23.3	10.9
Denmark	38.2	46.3	28.6	8.9
France	33.0	17.8	29.9	6.1
Germany	29.5	28.3	25.2	3.8
Ireland	18.6	18.9	16.7	7.4
Italy	19.9	11.9	18.7	7.0
Luxemburg	22.4	14.4	20.8	1.5
Netherlands	17.6	28.3	15.0	3.3
UK	34.7	40.8	27.3	4.4
Europe 9	28.5	26.4	24.5	5.3
Mean absolute deviation (unweighted)	6.63	10.04	4.55	

Definition: Col (3) = Col (1)$\left[1 - 0.5 \dfrac{\text{Col}(2)}{100} \left(1 + \dfrac{\text{Col}(4)}{100} \right) \right]$.

Source: Eurostat, 'Labour Force Sample Survey', *Emploi et Chômage*, 2, 1985.

Table 17.6. *Proportion of women working part-time by marital status and age, UK, 1977*

Age	14–19	20–24	25–34	35–44	45–54	55–59	60–64	65 up	Total
Married	17.2	19.3	51.5	57.5	48.0	49.4	64.7	80.2	50.2
Unmarried	4.1	4.3	14.9	20.7	21.5	33.3	50.0	70.5	21.1

Source: Jallade (1982). *L'Europe à temps partiel*, Economica, Paris.

Table 17.7. *Proportion of women aged 16–59 working part-time, by marital status and age of youngest child, UK, 1977*

Age of youngest child	0–4	5–9	10–15	16–up	No dependent child
Married	78	78	56	52	31
Unmarried	49	52	35	34	6

Source: Jallade (1982). *L'Europe à temps partiel*, Economica, Paris.

Hours worked by part-time workers are largely concentrated at or near the half-time mark (table 17.8). Yet there is a potential supply of part-time work near the 30 hours, three-quarter-time, mark. According to a survey conducted in the EC countries in the Spring of 1985, 'one in six full-time employed workers in Europe has a very keen interest in a significant reduction in working hours, even if this is associated with a corresponding loss of pay. Ideally they would wish to work approximately 30 hours a week rather than conventional half-time employment.'[6] That supply does not seem to be matched by a corresponding demand.

Table 17.8. *Distribution of hours worked by women employees with regular part-time jobs, Europe 9, 1981*

Hours	0	1–14	15–19	20–24	25–29	30–34	35 up
Industry	6.7	12.5	36.7	11.9	23.2	3.7	5.3
Services	7.1	23.1	35.0	11.6	16.6	2.6	4.0

Source: Eurostat, 'Labour Force Sample Survey', *Emploi et Chômage*, 2, 1985.

An attempt was made in 1984 in the Benelux countries to hire public servants on an 80%, four-day week, basis. No systematic report on that experiment is available yet. Casual evidence suggests that it was not very successful, due to insufficient reorganisation of work. That experiment clearly deserves further study.

4.2.3. Conclusion. Job sharing through part-time work has not developed in Europe as a means of work-sharing to alleviate cyclical unemployment. It has not spread among men. The countries where part-time employment of women is growing are the countries where that form of employment is still infrequent, and where one would expect it to spread irrespective of the recession. Although I have not seen hard data, I suspect that part-time work has not been used as a means of work-sharing for workers under contract in firms with declining employment either. The reasons seem to be a natural preference for full-time contracts, shared by firms and male workers, and a lack of flexibility in providing part-time jobs on a more-than-half-time basis. Indeed, if job sharing were to be

[6] Quoted from European Economy, Supplement B, No. 10, October 1985, where a summary account of the survey is given. The statement quoted in the text is followed by the following comment: 'In practice, these wishes can generally only be realised if the entire work process is organized more flexibly. Only in this way can discrepancies between company and personal working hours be bridged (e.g. in the form of a rolling four-day week).'

used systematically as a way of absorbing fluctuations in the supply of regular jobs, a natural approach would consist in promoting new hirings on a 75% or 80% basis, combined with reorganisation of work aimed at simultaneously extending the rate of utilisation of capital. The latter measures would be particularly appropriate at times when spare capacity is scarce. Some speculative remarks on this theme are offered in Section 5.

4.3. Trading hours for jobs (the working week)

In the long run, reductions in hours worked have been an important component of welfare gains, accounting for something like 25% of overall gains on a crude estimate (see OECD, 1985, quoting Douglas, 1934). At the same time, these reductions have played an important role in reconciling full employment with productivity gains; see tables 17.1 and 17.2 above. (Of course, the extent to which shorter hours have been permitted by, or have triggered, technological progress is not separately identified.) These are long-run trends. The question of interest here relates to short-run fluctuations. During temporary recessions could employment be stimulated (jobs created) by *anticipating* trend reductions in hours? Off-hand, this is a tempting suggestion. In practice, it seems difficult to implement. It was tried in France in the thirties, with little practical impact on effective working time, and a questionable immediate impact on employment. Over the past decade, the theme of a 35-hour week has been the subject of much controversy, as witnessed by the strike of German metal workers in 1979 or official pronouncements in Belgium in 1978, and France in 1981. As of today, there is no indication that stimulating employment through shorter hours is feasible on a significant scale in the short run, and longer-run effects remain subject to much uncertainty. At best, the nature of the difficulties associated with this approach become progressively better understood. I begin by reviewing the theoretical arguments for and against this approach, and then summarise recent experience.

4.3.1. Theory. The theoretical ground for advocating shorter hours during a prolonged recession is of course the prospect of correcting the inefficient distribution of work between employees under contract and job seekers. If a given number of hours is to be shared more efficiently between the two groups, it seems natural to impose shorter hours on both workers under contract and newcomers (at least, this is more natural than laying off workers under contract to hire newcomers). Hopefully new hirings might occur in the same proportion that hours are reduced.

There is an important qualification, however. The logic of implicit contract theory is that firms should use labour up to the point where its marginal value product is equal to the opportunity cost of workers, which is typically well below the full wage cost to firms in a recession. That logic applies to workers under contract – not to newcomers, who are hired only when their marginal value product covers their full wage cost. Consequently, if the hours of workers under contract are reduced, firms operating at a marginal value product of labour below full wage costs will not hire replacements, unless the reduction in hours is sufficient to bring the marginal value product of labour up to the full wage cost. Put more simply, *firms engaged in labour hoarding will not respond to shorter hours by new hirings*, for the same reason that they do not offset natural attrition of their work force by new hirings (such firms will in any case be willing to reduce hours, since they have excess labour). *Shorter hours will induce additional hirings only in those firms which are already hiring* to offset quits or expand employment. Such firms are a minority during a prolonged recession and they are concentrated in specific sectors. Also, these firms will show great reluctance to reduce hours. In order to increase employment, it might be preferable to create incentives for these firms to hire newcomers on a part-time basis – say on a 75% or 80% basis, with the prospects of switching to full-time work as the pressure of unemployment abates.

Of course, had the newcomers been part of a market clearing process *ex ante*, they would be part of the labour hoarding today, and shorter hours would be an attractive alternative to layoffs. The problem is again one of asymmetry between sharing work solely among those under contract, versus sharing work between those under contract and the unemployed. To overcome that asymmetry (to bridge the gap between the marginal value product of labour and full wage costs), the more radical measure of shorter hours with mandatory new hirings should be considered. That is each firm should be required to increase employment by a fixed percentage, while reducing hours for all. Clearly, measures of that kind entail a high degree of arbitrariness and are difficult to implement. To say that new entrants into the labour force would have a job today, if they had been able to contract yesterday, is not to say that employment *in every firm* would thereby be increased *in the same proportion* (that arbitrariness would be alleviated, but not eliminated, if the hiring obligations were tradable among firms). Also, wages today would be different, and so on. Only if the measure under discussion had been fully anticipated could one claim that it was non-discriminatory[7] and it is clear that if such a measure were announced, it would discourage normal hirings to an extent which could be quite harmful.

Two additional pitfalls of a mandatory general reduction in hours should be mentioned (they are discussed at greater length in Drèze, 1980a, where an attempt is also made to quantify their effects). The first concerns effective hours of plant utilisation. In firms operating one or two shifts for a conventional number of hours, reducing weekly hours is likely to simply reduce plant utilisation and output, with no effect on employment. A typical example is offered by automobile plants working two shifts, with little or no possibility of keeping plant hours constant when weekly schedules of workers are reduced by a few hours. It is only when the number of shifts is simultaneously increased that employment will rise naturally, the limiting case being offered by plants operated on a continuous basis, where shorter hours per worker entail the need for additional employees. The second pitfall concerns effective wage costs. If shorter hours result in higher hourly wage cost, whatever positive effects on employment may be associated with the reduction in work hours must be weighed against the negative effects associated with increased labour costs. These may have two sources. On the one hand, effective wage costs may rise due to the fixed costs of hiring and training, now spread over fewer hours, and due to the capital costs, similarly spread over fewer hours if plant utilisation is linked to the working schedules of employees. On the other hand, workers on shorter hours may attempt to protect their disposable income by claiming higher hourly wages, and a less than proportional reduction in take-home pay. The risk that shorter hours result in higher effective wage costs will be tempered if employment-conscious unions substitute hiring claims for wage claims. The difficult question, ultimately, is to assess the long-run incidence of hours worked on effective wage costs. The instantaneous increases arising from shorter hours at unchanged take-home pay may be partly compensated by smaller wage increases thereafter, whereas the instantaneous wage moderation accompanying demands for more employment may be partly compensated by catching up later. In either case, speculation about future wage patterns is needed to draw firm conclusions. Finally, there is a presumption that many firms are able to offset a gradual reduction in weekly hours by productivity increases without new hirings.

---

[7] The existence of an equilibrium under rational expectations and proportional quantity constraints is, however, questionable.

4.3.2. Experience. The salient features of recent European experience with hours worked per week seem to be the following:

(i) Over the past 10 years, average hours worked per week have declined (see table 17.9). The main explanation for this decline lies in the near disappearance of overtime work. On the one hand, there was less need for overtime work, due to the depressed demand for output. On the other hand, unions and governments discouraged overtime work, in order to stimulate new hirings.[8]

Table 17.9. *Average weekly hours worked, blue collar workers, manufacturing*

	Belgium	France	Germany	Italy	Netherlands	UK
1972	41.7	45.0	43.2	41.9	43.9	43.0
1982	34.9	39.4	40.0	37.5	40.6	41.4

Sources: Eurostat, *Gains horaires, durée du travail*, 2, 1983.

(ii) In those cases where a reduction in hours with mandatory new hirings has been put forward, it has met with adamant opposition from employers. Thus, a proposal by the Belgian Government in 1979 to subsidise a reduction of the standard working week from 40 to 38 hours with new hirings corresponding to 3% of employment and with some 'wage moderation', was rejected by the employers and some unions. When offered to individual firms on a voluntary basis, the proposal met with negligible success. In 1982 in France, the 'Contrats de Solidarité' offered inducements to encourage new hirings offsetting either reductions in working time or early retirements; out of some 12,500 contracts signed by September 30, 1982, only 4.5% were concerned with a reduction of working time, and 10 times as many new hirings resulted from early retirement as from shorter hours (see Hart, 1984).

(iii) Where a reduction in standard hours was introduced without mandatory new hirings, it seems to have led to very few new hirings in the short run – with one exception mentioned below. At least, *those who have looked for evidence of new hirings do not seem to have found it.* This was the case, in particular, for surveys conducted in Belgium in 1980 and more recently in France (see Quatrième Congrès des Economistes Belges de langue française, 1980, and Commissariat Général du Plan, 1985). The only clear cases of new hirings came from firms operating on a continuous basis with several (typically five) shifts. Shorter hours per shift necessarily

[8] Rosen (1985) outlines a simple model of 'returns to hours' in a contracts framework, where firms use overtime in good states, layoffs with constant hours in bad states.

implied some (less than proportional) new hirings.

These findings are sobering, and confirm the theoretical warnings that reductions in hours will not create many jobs in the short run. At the same time, advocates of shorter hours seem to proceed from a *presumption* that shorter hours per week somehow imply more jobs in the long run – other things being equal. The reasoning apparently calls on arithmetic and the analogy with wages is instructive. The short-run elasticity of employment with respect to real wages is generally believed to be small, whereas the long-run elasticity at a given output level should be close to unity given the constancy of factor shares. Similarly, the short-run elasticity of employment with respect to hours per week is apparently small, for the reasons just indicated, whereas the long-run elasticity should be close to unity on grounds of arithmetic. Both arguments of course assume that productivity, technology, and output are unrelated to wages or hours, and departures from these assumptions may well prove significant in the long run. Moreover the presumption rests on the unproven *assumption* that hours and workers are perfect substitutes. This is an area where uncertainties are substantial. Several attempts have been made to throw light on the issue by simulating macroeconomic models (see, for instance, Charpin and Mairesse, 1978, Driehuis and Bruyn-Hundt, 1979, or Plasmans and Vanroelen, 1985). Simulations typically compare employment forecasts with and without a reduction in weekly hours, under alternative assumptions about wages. Sometimes explicit hypotheses about the elasticity of output with respect to hours are also introduced. My own attitude towards these simulations is one of polite scepticism. Too little is known about the elasticity of employment with respect to weekly hours *in a context of general recession* for these simulations to be reliable. Estimates of production functions where hours and number of employees appear as separate arguments, based on time series data covering the past thirty years, are not likely to measure that elasticity accurately, and I have not seen estimates based on recent microeconomic data. Accordingly, I regard the fragmentary information from the surveys mentioned under (ii) above as more instructive for short-run purposes and I refrain from drawing long-run conclusions.

5. Appraisal and policy prospects

5.1. *Appraisal*

Hopefully, this essay may have convinced the reader: first, that some form of work-sharing is called for to efficiently absorb sizeable fluctuations in the demand for labour; second, that market institutions fail to bring about work-sharing between workers under contract and job seekers, or among job seekers themselves; and third, that there is scope for public intervention to correct that market failure during deep recessions. It is thus not surprising that interest in work-sharing as a means of alleviating unemployment should be alive in Europe today and that specific measures have been introduced. The brief review of experience with these measures reveals that early retirement schemes with some form of income maintenance have pulled large numbers of senior workers out of the labour force and have led to roughly commensurate numbers of new hirings when and only when the schemes specified mandatory replacements; part-time work has not spread as a means of sharing work among job seekers, or between job seekers and workers under contract (the total failure of part-time early retirement schemes being particularly striking); and those who have looked for evidence of job creation induced by reductions in weekly hours have not found any appreciable short-run effects, leaving open the question of potential longer-run effects which is subject to related uncertainties over capital utilisation, wage costs and productivity adjustments.

These empirical findings are generally consistent with theoretical considerations, to the extent that the (positive) value of holding a regular job varies substantially across individuals and over an individual's working life, suggesting in particular that a substantial proportion of the members of the older generations could be induced to hand over their jobs to new recruits at little cost. Also the fixed costs of hiring and training deter firms from using part-time labour, except in special circumstances (like peak loads within the week), whereas enough workers eager to work full-time are forthcoming. Finally, firms engaged in labour hoarding, which may well be in a majority during deep recessions, will not respond to shorter hours (or lower wages, for that matter), by new hirings, and firms which are hiring new employees will resist reductions in hours.

There are four immediate implications of this essay for policy purposes. (Since every form of work-sharing has both opponents and advocates, none of these implications is original. My only hope is to have convinced the reader that my own stand is consistent with both theory and recent experience.)

(i) *Early retirement with mandatory replacement stands out as the most promising approach to work-sharing in the short-run.* In several countries that approach has hardly been used, and offers a genuine prospect for some alleviation of unemployment – of youth unemployment especially, if replacements are reserved for the young. More detailed work aimed at quantifying that prospect, both numberwise and costwise, should be encouraged.

(ii) *Shorter weekly hours stand out as the least promising and most uncertain approach to work-sharing in the short run.* At a minimum it should not be used indiscriminately. It will produce positive employment effects in those sectors (including metal working?) where plants are operated on a continuous basis, negative output effects without gains in employment in those sectors where hours of plant utilization are given by the working week, and longer-run effects will be negative if shorter hours imply higher effective hourly wage costs.

(iii) If one accepts the view that firms engaged in labour hoarding will not respond to either lower wages or shorter hours by new hirings, *one should concentrate the promotion of work-sharing on expanding and new firms.* In these firms, part-time work by the new employees may well be the more natural pattern of work-sharing.

(iv) *Part-time work stands out as the most disappointing approach to work-sharing, in the sense that its potential to alleviate unemployment, which could be substantial, has not been exploited at all.* This is all the more disappointing since part-time early retirement would seem so much more natural and appealing than abrupt early retirement. Given the substantial measure of success met by early retirement programmes and the overwhelming desire expressed by workers for gradual retirement, it is doubly disappointing to observe the total failure of the timid attempts in that direction. *Although efforts to promote part-time work are bound to be slow in producing their effects, because they call for substantial reorganisation of work, such efforts are worth undertaking from a long-run perspective.*

5.2. Policy prospects

In the longer-run, three interrelated questions must be faced, to which only speculative answers can be given today. First, how long will it take to restore a measure of full employment in Europe (say, with youth unemployment rates of 5% or so)? Second, will the historical trend towards a shorter working week continue itself in the future? Third, how seriously should we take the prospect of other deep recessions, comparable to those of the thirties and the eighties? If full employment will not be restored in Europe for several years to come (and this is my personal reading of the forecasts), and deep recessions may occur again (for the reasons explained in Section 2.2), then one should look seriously at part-time work as a means of sharing jobs during such recessions. In addition since there is no reason why the historical trend towards shorter hours should come to a halt, one should take seriously the issue of maintaining the utilisation of capital and the provision of services. Indeed, as the working week becomes shorter, it is increasingly important to uncouple individual working hours from the period of business activity (over which capital is used and services are provided). Otherwise overhead costs will creep up, and the benefits of additional leisure will be partly offset by the deterioration in availability of services. These two remarks are linked *because uncoupling individual working hours from the period of business activity is bound to open up new prospects for part-time work*, at a gain in overall efficiency as well as in labour market flexibility.

A number of schemes to that effect have been proposed, ranging from the general adoption of half-day shifts six days a week, to rotating vacation periods of up to three months per year (see e.g. Palasthy, 1978, and Van den Broeck *et al.*, 1984). The most appealing scheme to my mind would be a general adoption of the four-day working week with six days of activity. A working post could then correspond to either one full-time and one half-time job, or two three-quarter-time jobs, or three half-time jobs – or one and a half full-time jobs with three full-timers filling two working posts. Aside from the obvious advantages of reducing commuting time for workers by 20% and increasing the use of capital by up to 35% (six days of nine hours versus five days of eight hours), this scheme would generate flexibility in the provision of part-time work especially on a 75% basis. Hopefully, it would also generate flexibility in the provision of part-time early retirement, and facilitate job sharing through part-time work among the new employees of expanding and new firms. A novel perspective would thus be opened for part-time work as a means of work-sharing to absorb fluctuations in the market for regular jobs. Of course, a four-day week with six days of activity is highly speculative as well as controversial. It is speculative, because we lack solid information, beyond the isolated experience of a few firms which have chosen to operate on that basis for reasons of their own.[9] And it is controversial, because six days of activity means Saturday work (typically two weeks out of three) and a reversal of the trend towards longer weekends with less organised activity taking place then. Reversing that trend has an obvious welfare cost, to be weighed against the associated efficiency gains. On the other hand it may be

---

[9] I know of one industrial firm which has adopted the scheme a few years ago to expand capacity by 35% without new investment or multiple shifts; and one savings bank which has adopted the scheme to impose team work on its staff.

indispensable to protect the utilisation of capital, if the working week is to be reduced further as technological progress continues.

I have no particular authority to discuss this speculative proposal. But I may refer back to two points made earlier, which are of relevance here. The first is that, in a world where firms and (male) workers have a common preference for full-time regular jobs, temporary reliance on 75% jobs when there is excess supply of labour will require some inducements. It is a challenging task to think through a coherent approach to this issue. The open questions are numerous, and the answers are not obvious. At a time when only three out of four new entrants into the labour force are employed, if we had a four-day week with six days of activity, should we penalise full-time work, subsidise part-time work, or both? If there is a penalty, should it be levied on the employer or the employee, or is that issue immaterial? Should hours above the average effectively worked, counting the unemployed, carry social security benefits, like rights to pensions and unemployment compensation? A whole set of intriguing questions arise, which require an analysis combining considerations of *ex ante* risk-sharing and incentives. The second point, made earlier in Section 2.4, is that a major reorganisation of work involves numerous externalities and therefore calls for guidelines and coordination from the public sector. In particular, a four-day week with six days of activity requires coordination between production activities, services, leisure activities, schools, etc. Such coordination can only evolve over time, and is facilitated if the new pattern is known ahead of time. It also involves the public sector directly, through the provision of public services. It would certainly make sense for the post office, administrative services open to the public, and the like, to consider six days of activity, with a greater reliance on part-time workers.

18 The two-handed growth strategy for Europe: autonomy through flexible cooperation*

PART I: THE TWO-HANDED STRATEGY

1. The present state of affairs

There is little doubt that over the years 1984–87 economic conditions in Europe have improved. Inflation has fallen to more comfortable levels. Most current account deficits have been reduced, with some countries achieving significant surpluses. Public finances are now sounder in many countries, with the primary budget (i.e. net of interest payments) more often in surplus than in deficit. After a period when the strength of the dollar made European currencies look weak, the much awaited correction has taken place, now raising fears of a hard landing of the US currency. More importantly, the resumption of growth is widespread in contrast to the experience of the early eighties.

Yet there is no room for complacency for at least two reasons. The first one is the unemployment situation. Double-digit unemployment rates are the rule rather than the exception, and no relief seems in sight, in the near future. As of May 1987, there were 16.1 million unemployed (seasonally adjusted) in the 12 countries of the European Community, that is 11.4% of the labour force. Total unemployment has not changed over the last 12 months. Significant decreases in the UK and Portugal have been matched by increases in most other countries. In Germany, while

* *Recherches Economiques de Louvain*, 54, 1 (1988), 5–52. With Charles Wyplosz, Charles Bean, Francesco Giavazzi and Herbert Giersch. This paper appeared as *Economic Papers*, n°60, October 1987, of the Commission of European Communities and as a CEPS paper, n°34, December 1987, of the Center for European Policy Studies. The editors are grateful to both these institutions for their permission to publish this article.

The authors thank Jürgen Kröger for help with the data and Sara del Favero for diligent research assistance.

500

total unemployment has come down by forty thousand, GDP growth has been negative for the last two quarters. Short-run prospects therefore look bleak, with a genuine danger that unemployment may rise once again. Mass unemployment represents a waste of human resources, as well as a major social problem with unpredictable long-run political and economic implications.

The second cause of concern is the disappointingly low rate of private investment, now around 19% of GNP as compared to 22% in the sixties. Although this may be of limited immediate consequence, it bears the seeds of long-term economic stagnation. For some reason Europe is not using and accumulating factors of production as in the past; this is bound to affect future living standards.

This report takes as its premise that Europe still very much needs to enact growth-enhancing policies. We first recall why the present level of utilisation and rate of accumulation of resources are not optimal.[1]

We then consider what corrective actions might be taken. Of course the major reason why these have not yet been carried out is that a certain number of apparent constraints on policy makers stand in the way. It is important to assess the true seriousness of these constraints.

Among these constraints, the question of external balance stands out. Although we regard this concern as largely misdirected, we will consider it in some detail. We stress that the openness of an economy reduces the domestic benefits which a country derives from expanding demand, and conclude that cooperation is a way out of this dilemma. Accordingly, this report's main contribution is to consider how best the EC countries could exploit their differences in size and initial conditions to jointly adopt appropriate policies. In particular, the report highlights the crucial position of Germany, France and the UK in pursuing a set of policies that will enhance growth. It also recognizes that differences in objectives may affect a country's willingness to play the role warranted by the general macroeconomic situation. The result will be a collective loss in overall effectiveness. We believe, however, that the EMS can serve as a focal point for mutually beneficial growth-enhancing policies.

2. Three growth alternatives

One way of understanding why and how Europe fails to adequately exploit its resources is to contrast current forecasts and desirable outcomes.

---

[1] All previous reports of the CEPS Macroeconomic Policy Group have presented similar analysis.

We first review the probable outlook until the end of the decade under existing policies and then consider two alternatives: the EC Commission Cooperative Growth Scenario and the type of performance achieved by Europe in better times during the sixties.

2.1. The baseline

The baseline projection of the EC Commission as presented in its 1986 Annual Report (which is very much in line with forecasts produced by other institutions) is a natural point of departure and is shown in table 18.1. Its main features are slow growth, moderate inflation, sluggish investment and an unacceptably high level of unemployment. Interestingly, given the situation in the rest of the world, such growth rates allow a slight surplus on Europe's overall current account.[2]

Table 18.1. *EC Commission simulations for EC 10*

(Annual average growth rates, 1986–1990, in %)

	Baseline	Cooperative Scenario
1. GDP volume	2.7	3.5
2. GDP deflator	3.3	2.7
3. Employment	0.7	1.2
4. Investment	3.7	6.8
5. Unemployment[a]	10.3	7.1
6. Real unit labour costs	−0.3	−1.3
7. Real wages per head	1.9	1.1
8. Productivity	2.0	2.3
9. Residual[b]	−0.2	−0.1
10. Current account, % of GDP	0.6	0.1
11. Budget deficit, % of GDP[a]	3.4	3.9

[a] 1990 levels.
[b] Residual is (6) − (7) + (8) and is a measure of changes in labour taxes.
Source: European Economy n°30, November 1986, p. 44.

However, in many ways the baseline projection must be considered as rather optimistic. The 1987 figures, which define its starting line, have been revised *downwards* in October 1987, relative to the October 1986 forecasts. In every respect, the aggregate revisions exhibited in table 18.2 are for the worse. Detailed member country figures (not shown) indicate

[2] This is quite important given the assumptions made for the rest of the world: rising oil prices, stable ECU/Dollar and ECU/Yen exchange rates, and a reduction of the US budget deficit to 1 percent of GNP by 1990. These assumptions are not favourable from the point of view of the European current account which may exceed the reported forecasts.

that unemployment is expected to increase in five countries, decrease in five, and stay stable for the other two, as well as remaining stable for the European Community as a whole. Furthermore these revised forecasts do not incorporate the latest disquieting trends reported above.

2.2. The Cooperative Growth scenario

In the Cooperative Growth Strategy proposed by the EC Commission, the overall growth rate is raised to above 3%, which will permit a decline in the unemployment rate to 7% by 1990. This growth scenario shares many of the characteristics of the two-handed approach proposed by the CEPS Macroeconomic Policy Group. It rightly emphasizes the benefits of policy coordination which are at the heart of the present report. Its key elements are a decline in real labour costs achieved through wage moderation and decreased labour taxes, a reduction in income taxes and an increase in public investment. According to the Commission's estimates (see table 18.1) this would produce faster growth and lower inflation, at the expense of a worsening of the current account. But even this rather optimistic scenario fails to bring unemployment down to those rates which prevailed in Europe up to the mid-seventies.

The Cooperative Growth Strategy, as designed by the Commission, calls for a cumulative fiscal expansion through additional public expenditures and tax reductions adding up, over the four years 1987–1990, to 3.2% of EC10 GDP. By concentrating the effort in the three largest countries (Germany, France and the UK), which account for 70% of EC 10 GDP, this scenario actually calls for a cumulative fiscal expansion in these three adding up (over the four years) to 4.6% of their own GDP.

Table 18.2. *Revision of 1987 forecasts for EC 12*

(% change p.a. unless otherwise stated)

	October 1986 Forecast	October 1987 Rev. Forecast
GDP in volume	2.8	2.2
Domestic demand	3.5	3.2
Exports of goods and services	3.7	2.0
Imports of goods and services	6.2	4.6
Nominal unit labor costs[a]	2.8	3.4
Real unit labour costs[a]	−0.7	0.1
Unemployment rate (% of labour force)	11.7	11.8

[a] Relative development of labour costs per head and macroeconomic labour productivity (real: deflated by GDP deflator).
Source: E.C. Commission COM(87)77, Table 1, and the Annual Economic Report.

Such an effort is of an altogether different order of magnitude from the programmes currently under consideration in several countries. The fiscal measures decided in Germany for 1988–90 only amount to about 1% of its GDP; similarly, those enacted in the UK for the fiscal year 1987–88 and projected for 1988–89 constitute a cumulative fiscal stimulus of about 1.5% of its GDP. Jointly, these measures amount to 0.5% of EC10 GDP, to which should be added a further 0.2% increase due to various fiscal changes in other countries. So far then, current fiscal plans envisage a stimulus worth only 0.7% of EC 10 GDP, thus falling substantially short of the Commission's proposed Cooperative Strategy 3.2% target.

2.3.   The golden sixties

The last scenario that we wish to explore is a return to the kind of economic performance achieved by Europe during much of its post-war years. Its characteristics are well known: an average growth rate close to 5% per year and unemployment between 2 and 3%. Such a GDP growth rate does not necessarily translate into employment growth. One benchmark is provided by the Cooperative Growth Scenario. Its policies imply a short-run marginal employment coefficient of one third, so that a 5% annual GDP growth rate would lead to an annual average growth rate of employment of 1.7%, bringing unemployment down to some 5% in 1990 – an attractive prospect. Another benchmark is the experience of the sixties during which employment growth in Europe was a mere 0.3% per annum. These numbers essentially tell us that growth will have to be more labour-intensive than in the sixties if we wish to reduce unemployment.

Are there real obstacles standing in the way of such a growth pattern? Looking at aggregate unemployment figures, it does not seem to make sense worrying about labour shortages. But aggregate figures are often misleading. Current unemployment is concentrated amongst the unskilled and in particular geographical areas. Youth unemployment is particularly high in all countries except Germany. A reduction in the cost of employing unskilled workers may be necessary to erase such inequalities (see Box 1). We return to this issue below.

┌─ BOX 1 ──

One difficult question raised by our hypothetical 'golden sixties' scenario – or by any scenario embodying significant employment growth – concerns the level of skills within the labour force. Unemployment today is largely concentrated amongst the unskilled. There are two ways in which such a situation could have come about. Consider a given decline in aggregate employment – say 8% for illustration's sake – which is accompanied by an increase in unemployment concentrated entirely amongst the unskilled. This could reflect an 8% decline in employment at every skill level, accompanied by a reallocation of some workers to less skilled jobs so that all except the lowest skill groups enjoy full employment, but with a fraction of each group (corresponding to a growing number of people as we move down the skill ladder) accepting employment in less skilled jobs. Thus all the unemployment will eventually be concentrated amongst the least skilled workers. Alternatively, the same *aggregate* picture could emerge if a restructuring of the demand for workers of different skills (possibly induced by inappropriate wage differentials) resulted in a loss of employment at the *lowest* skill level alone, with no reduction in employment at higher levels. The concentration of unemployment amongst the unskilled results from the adaptation of labour supply in the first case, but from the restructuring of labour demand in the second case.

Our illustration is extreme; both labour supply adaptation and labour demand restructuring may take place simultaneously – the relative importance of the two processes is unknown. The supply adaptation (or 'staircase') story is accepted by many as the primary explanation. Recently, our attention has been drawn by Danthine and Lambelet (1987) to the Swiss experience, and in particular to the fact that unskilled migrant workers, numbering some 8% of the Swiss labour force, were repatriated, without this being accompanied by any restructuring of the qualification mix among Swiss workers. That experience lends *prima facie* support to the demand restructuring story. If this is the case throughout Europe a majority of the unemployed in the EC are simply unemployable – unless either their skills are upgraded, or else a reverse restructuring of labour demand is induced, for example by a change in relative prices (i.e., a reduction in the cost of employing unskilled workers).

It matters little whether 'unskilled' is understood in terms of acquired technical skills, or in terms of stable working habits. And it should be clear that putting the long-term unemployed back to work will entail a substantial retraining cost in either case.

Can capital be the binding constraint? It was not in the sixties. But the capital–output ratio has increased in the meantime. With a capital–output ratio as high as 4.5, a growth rate of output at 5% would require a net investment share of 22.5%. With a depreciation rate of 3% this is equivalent to a gross investment share of 36%, which would somehow have to be financed. As an example, the highest gross investment share reached since 1960 for EC10 stood just below 29%. If the capital–output ratio were to drop to 4 (its lowest level was 4.1 in 1973), the required gross investment share would be 32% instead.[3] A traditional savings rate would seem to imply that a 5% growth rate requires either a significant decrease in capital intensity – the kind of decrease which is precisely required for a more labour-intensive growth – or significant borrowing abroad, i.e. current account deficits. It might seem improbable that the trend towards increased capital intensity should be reversed. Such a possibility should not be dismissed outright as fanciful, however. The growth pattern of the sixties was shaped by the short supply of domestic labour (as evidenced by low unemployment rates and the recurrent recourse to immigration). Hopefully, a more balanced growth pattern might emerge naturally in a period of severe unemployment. It would need to be based on capital-widening rather than on capital-deepening investment – hence on relative factor prices more favourable to the adoption of labour-intensive methods employing the categories of workers in the greatest excess supply.

Some reliance on capital imports to finance increased investment would also be justified, despite the implications for the current account. Provided the investment is profitable, it will generate sufficient revenues to finance the increased foreign debt burden. This issue is explored in more detail in Section 3.3.3.

2.4. Assessment

We consider the baseline as a realistic, yet unacceptably pessimistic, forecast. Indeed this report is dedicated to the search for acceptable solutions to avoid its very realisation. The Cooperative Growth Strategy provides a solution which looks satisfactory only when compared to the baseline. Its results are a clear improvement on the current forecast, yet they are quite modest given the size of the unemployment problem. The

---

[3] These calculations are based on data in Mortensen (1984), pp. 62–65. With $K/Y = 4.5$ and $\dot{Y}/Y = \dot{K}/K = 5\%$, the net investment rate is $\dot{K}/Y = (\dot{K}/K)(K/Y)$. With a depreciation rate $d = 3\%$, the gross investment rate is $I/Y = (\dot{K} + d.K)/Y$. The value of d is inferred from the 1984 values as: $d = (I/Y - \dot{K}/Y)/(K/Y) = (22.5 - 9.5)/4.6 = 2.82\%$.

'golden sixties' scenario, on the other hand, looks too good to be true. We fully realize that it may be *politically* unrealistic. What concerns us, however, is whether it is feasible from an *economic* point of view; obviously it requires a different type of growth, but it is not obvious that it is altogether beyond reach. Much depends upon how it is sought. The two-handed approach offers a framework within which policies capable of achieving more ambitious results than the baseline can be developed. It rests on the same logic as the Cooperative Growth Strategy, and may be put to work to pull Europe more forcefully out of its slow-growth, high-unemployment trap.

3. The two-handed approach

3.1. The logical foundation

The two-handed approach, advocated in the previous reports of the CEPS Macroeconomic Policy Group, stresses the need for a simultaneous expansion of supply and demand so as to create additional productive capacity hand-in-hand with the demand for its services.

The logic of the two-handed approach rests on an assessment of the nature of European unemployment and on a parallel assessment of the conditions necessary for job creation. In order for a job to be created, two broad sets of condition must be satisfied. First there must exist a demand for the output generated by that additional worker. Because dismissing a worker is costly, that demand should be sustained long enough to ensure that the additional worker will be required in the foreseeable future. Second, satisfying that demand must be both profitable and physically possible: there must exist spare capacity and the cost of labour (and other inputs) must not be excessive. Keynesian macrotheory stresses the first condition; when that condition fails, unemployment is said to be 'Keynesian'. Classical macrotheory stresses the second condition; when that condition fails, unemployment is said to be 'Classical'. The current European situation requires due attention to both requirements, and the two-handed approach does just that.

The mix of Classical and Keynesian unemployment prevailing at a particular time is of crucial relevance to policy decisions. If unemployment is mostly Classical, then demand policies are useless in the short run, with the stimulus likely to evaporate in price inflation and/or imports. What is called for is an expansion of supply, through increased efficiency and investment. Policy should be 'supply friendly'. If unemployment is mostly Keynesian, then demand stimulation is the required policy, and entails little risk of inflationary pressures. It is thus important to diagnose the relative importance of the two types of unemployment.

Such a classification is always difficult, because it cannot be based on direct indicators, such as the unemployment rate itself, or on national accounts data. Keynesian unemployment is predicated upon the existence of simultaneously unused labour and capital capacity. Classical unemployment would follow either from the absence of physical equipment to be manned by new hirings or from excessive labour costs. Although systematic quantitative analysis along these lines is relatively recent and still fragmentary, the available evidence is entirely consistent in suggesting that European unemployment exhibits *both* Classical and Keynesian features.[4]

We interpret this evidence as indicating that unemployment is Keynesian at the margin, and Classical beyond: a demand expansion would quickly eliminate the Keynesian unemployment component and trigger inflationary pressures as bottlenecks are reached. An indication of the seriousness of the situation is provided by business surveys in industry. Table 18.3 indicates that current use of capacity is slightly below the 1979–80 peak level. The extent to which capacity is reported excessive in relation to demand expectations is much higher (10%) than the 1979 peak level, however, confirming that we currently face a conjunction of low demand and fully used capacity.

This high level of capacity utilisation, despite the low level of demand, is the result of both extensive scrapping and the low rate of new investment which prevailed in Europe over the last decade. Capacity has adjusted to a slow growth environment, transforming a slow growth trap into a capacity trap. Indeed, during a prolonged period of weak demand, it is rational for producers to adjust downwards their capacity to this demand. This constant adaptation of the capital stock to the level of demand is illustrated in figure 18.1: despite continuously growing slack in the use of labour, the degree of capacity utilisation oscillates within relatively narrow margins.

The result is a frustrating situation where no demand stimulus is implemented because of the absence of spare capacity, while there does not exist spare capacity because demand has been, is, and is expected to be weak. *This is the rationale for the two-handed approach: capacity*

---

[4] That evidence arises from a variety of studies based on widely different methodologies: see the special issue of *Economica* (1986, Supplement), *World Economic Outlook* (April 1987), Lambert, Lubrano and Sneessens (1984), Bruno and Sachs (1985), Sachs and Wyplosz (1986). It matters a lot that these studies generally lead to the same conclusion.

Table 18.3. *Capacity utilization and expected capacity constraints in manufacturing industry*

	Degree of capacity utilization							Expected capacity constraints[a]						
	1973 peak	1975 trough	79/80 peak	82/83 trough	1984	1986	1987 April	1973 peak	1975 trough	79/80 peak	82/83 trough	1985	1986	1987 April
Belgium	85.4	70.4	79.1	74.4	76.0	79.4	78.8	−12	+58	+35	+53	+29	+26	+27
Denmark										+10	+38	+3	+8	+20
Germany	88.1	74.8	86.0	75.3	80.2	84.7	83.8	−3	+56	+12	+49	+17	+13	+20
Greece				74.4	75.5	77.0	76.8							
France	87.8	76.6	85.3	81.1	81.9	83.3	83.2	−24	+45	+11	+48	+37	+31	+26
Ireland		68.1	56.8	61.5	67.3	73.0	80.8		+34	+2	+40	+25	+18	+19
Italy	78.8	68.0	77.3	69.1	72.0	75.2	77.2	+1	+63	+17	+58	+37	+37	+24
Netherlands	86.0	76.0	83.0	75.8	82.3	83.4	83.0	−3	+60	+14	+51	+4	+4	+8
U.K.	90.6	75.5	87.6	73.0	82.5	85.1	87.0				+63	+23	+28	+17
EC[b]	86.4	75.0	83.9	76.4	79.1	82.2	82.7	−7	+54	+14	+50	+26	+24	+21

[a] Balance of respondents expecting to be more than sufficient (+) or less than sufficient (−) in relation to production expectations. Thus (+) indicates excess capacity, (−) capacity too small.
[b] Weighted average of available country data.
Source: European Economy, Sup. B, n°5, May 1987.

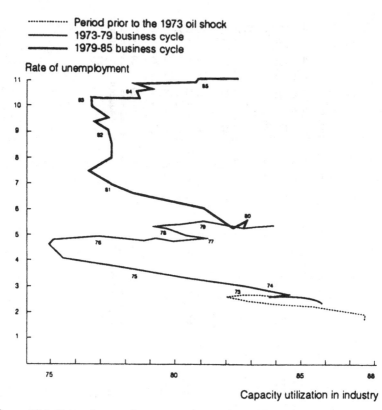

Figure 18.1. Rate of unemployment and capacity utilisation in industry in the Community (Quarterly observations are shown, with the years marked against the first quarter).
Source: European Economy, 26, November 1985.

constraints must be eliminated via appropriate supply-side policies while demand must expand to trigger an upward adjustment of productive capacity.

3.2. The agenda

If Europe is to break out of the capacity trap and grow faster, more efficient use must be made of available production possibilities, extended through capacity-widening investment. The profitability of investment and hirings requires a conjunction of adequate profit margins and adequate demand expectations. The policy challenge is to bring about these two conditions *simultaneously*: either of them in isolation would be ineffective.

Ideally, one would like to see capacity expand first, in an anticipation of a growing demand, that could then be satisfied without resistance. It is unlikely that business investors would harbour such confident expectations, however, leaving governments with the option of implementing policies that remove inefficiencies and raise profit margins whilst at the same time raising effective demand in anticipation of the prospective growth of supply.[5] The policy mix is thus bound to be comprehensive. Success is predicated upon determination in using the two hands, and can be further enhanced by selecting measures which have beneficial effects on both supply and demand.

Starting with policies aimed at raising productive efficiency and the profitability of investment, they should consist of the following:

1. medium-run labour cost reductions achieved through a combination of continued wage moderation and cuts in labour taxes;

2. wage differentiation, i.e., a more pronounced reduction in overall wage costs for unskilled workers and for workers in depressed areas;

3. public infrastructure investments likely to raise productive efficiency, especially in regions with high unemployment and a correspondingly high growth potential;

4. elimination of wasteful subsidies and the introduction of measures to speed up the creation of an internal Common Market (deregulation, liberalisation, etc.);[6]

5. measures to enhance the efficient use of capital and labour through more flexible working schedules, hopefully including some uncoupling of worker time and company time.[7]

The first point is essential to generate the medium-run profitability expectations underpining new investment and hirings. Visible progress has been accomplished recently on the front of wage moderation: in every country, except the UK, real unit labour costs have declined – the average decrease in the Community being 2.5% over the past two years (see table 18.4). Continuing wage moderation is essential and, in particular, adverse terms of trade movements should not lead to compensating changes in wages. In some countries this would require altering formal or informal indexation clauses: we do not underestimate the far reaching implications of this measure, yet we wish to stress its importance for the medium-run evolution of labour costs.

---

[5] The rationale for a demand stimulation that leads the expansion of supply (but not the measures designed to bring it about) has been expounded by Giersch (1987b) under the label of the 'Schumpeter Case'.

[6] See Giersch (1987a).

[7] See Drèze (1986b).

Table 18.4. *Growth in real unit labour costs* in % p.a.

	1974–1981	1982–1986	1987
Belgium	1.4	−1.5	0.4
Denmark	0.2	−1.6	3.4
Germany	0.0	−1.3	0.6
Greece	2.6	−0.6	−3.8
Spain	−0.2	−2.5	−0.9
France	1.1	−1.0	−1.6
Ireland	0.7	−2.1	0.3
Italy	0.6	−0.9	0.3
Netherlands	−0.2	−1.6	2.1
Portugal	1.5	−4.8	−0.7
UK	−0.1	−0.1	0.8
EC 12	0.4	−1.2	0.1
USA	0.0	0.0	0.2
Japan	0.8	−0.5	0.0

[a] Wage bill divided by value added.
Source: EC Commission.

However, only so much can be achieved through wage moderation. Fortunately, labour cost reductions can also be achieved through lower labour taxes. The scope for labour tax reductions is best shown by considering the costs incurred when an unemployed worker is hired. The employer will face the full cost, which includes wages and all labour taxes (social security, income). For society as a whole, though, not only do taxes no longer appear as a cost, but in addition there is the extra saving of the unemployment benefits which need not be paid. The size of this divergence between privately incurred costs and their public, i.e. budgetary, equivalent is documented in table 18.5, which gives some numbers based on average labour taxes and social security contributions (we look at the *marginal* cost of moving an *average* worker from the situation of being unemployed to the situation of being employed). Ideally we would like to have comparable figures for unemployment benefits. In the absence of such data for most countries, we have for all countries assumed a replacement ratio (the ratio of average unemployment benefits to average earned income) of 50% based on estimates provided by Layard and Nickell (1985) for the UK.[8] Of course a better measure would use the figures applicable to a marginal worker. Because of such imperfections, table 18.5 should be interpreted with due caution. From table 18.5, we learn that the various taxes which contribute to raise the cost of labour, although

[8] Limited evidence for other countries presented in OECD, *Employment Outlook* 1984, confirms that this ratio is a reasonable number.

Table 18.5. *Costs of reducing unemployment in 1985-% of GDP*

	Net wages and salaries (1)	Social contributions (2)	Income tax paid by labour (3)	Total labour taxes[d] (4)	Total cost faced by employer[e] (5)	Ratio = $\dfrac{\text{Budgetary cost[f]}}{\text{Private cost}} \times 100$ (6)
Belgium	41.9	13.5	11.0	24.5	66.4	68.5
Denmark	51.9	1.9	24.2	26.1	78.0	66.7
Germany	29.1	16.9	7.9	24.8	53.9	73.0
Greece	32.8	10.3	2.8	11.1	43.9	64.3
Spain	34.1	12.1			46.2[c]	63.1[c]
France	32.9	21.3	3.4	24.7	57.6	71.4
Ireland	48.9	5.8	10.2	16.0	64.9	62.3
Italy	43.0	12.6	5.1	17.7	60.7	64.6
Netherlands	25.9	25.4	7.2	32.6	58.5	77.9
Portugal	37.8	10.8	2.4	13.2	51.0	62.9
UK	44.9	10.7	8.9	19.6	64.5	65.2
USA	46.0	9.0	10.5[b]	19.5	65.5	64.9
Japan[a]	48.4	15.2	6.5[b]	21.7	70.1	65.5

[a] 1984;
[b] Income tax;
[c] Excluding income taxes;
[d] Total labour taxes include social contributions and labour income taxes (4) = (2) + (3);
[e] The private cost faced by an employer is the sum of net wages and salaries and of total labour costs (5) = (1) + (4);
[f] The budgetary cost is the private cost less labour taxes and less the reduction in unemployment benefits (assumed to be 50% of net wages); hence, (6) = [(4) + 1/2(1)]/(5).
Source: EC Commission.

somewhat different from country to country, are sufficiently large to offer a sizeable room for manoeuvre.

The significance of the wedge between the private and public cost of labour can be expressed alternatively in terms of the wedge between the private and public marginal efficiency of capital, for a capacity-widening investment. In the private calculations, the additional labour employed to operate the new facilities enters at its private cost. From a public viewpoint, part of that cost disappears – namely all labour taxes, plus the unemployment benefits no longer accruing to the newly hired workers. Thus, from a public viewpoint, the marginal efficiency of capital is higher and the private level of investment is too low. Put more simply, *the additional investment draws into use previously unemployed labour resources*, thereby generating a positive externality for the government budget.[9] The full externality is the difference between the private and *social* cost of the labour drawn into use by the additional investment.

Turning to policies aimed at raising effective demand, they should consist of fiscal measures (as detailed below) resulting for Europe as a whole in temporarily larger public deficits. (However this does not mean higher deficits in every country; we discuss at length in Section 7 the country-specific aspects of this general policy.) These temporary deficits are to be financed primarily by borrowing and to be offset by future surpluses with a clear commitment not to resort to inflationary finance. Money growth should only accommodate any anticipated growth in potential output. In what follows, the fiscal expansion is assumed to take this form. We explain in Section 3.3.2 why such a policy of substituting taxes tomorrow for taxes today will indeed be effective in raising demand.

As for the fiscal measures themselves, cuts in labour taxes are probably the most efficient means to reduce the wedge between the private and budgetary cost of labour and to discourage capital deepening, hence our recommendation to focus on them. Although this is not the place to discuss in detail alternative schemes of labour tax cuts, we would favour maximising their employment impact by concentrating their effects on segments of the labour force where the underutilisation of labour is greatest, e.g. the long term unemployed, the young, the unskilled, and the depressed areas.[10] The immediate effect of a cut in labour taxes is to raise

[9] Our reasoning assumes that the added capacity will be used. Otherwise, the investment would not take place. We are thus led back to our previous point that investment and employment require both sufficient profitability and adequate demand expectations.

[10] For instance, the objective of giving priority to the unskilled may be satisfied through an exemption level below which social security contributions are waived or reduced; see Blanchard *et al.* (1985, p. 32) or Drèze (1987b, p. 30).

profits. This affects both consumption and investment. The effect on consumption is indirect via higher dividend income and stock-market wealth. The effect on investment is more direct. Both channels however involve substantial lags. This suggests complementing labour tax cuts with reductions in income taxes. Lower income taxes would, of course, significantly help to promote wage moderation. It is thus comforting to note that both the UK and Germany have recently announced income tax reductions. In addition to these tax cuts, there is scope for increased investment in public services and in the infrastructure, both at the national and European levels. This is an area which has been excessively squeezed in recent years. Any project which yields an adequate social rate of return fits naturally into the proposed fiscal measures. We advocate measures which simultaneously have desirable effects on both supply and demand. We will henceforth refer to this set of measures as a supply-friendly fiscal expansion.

3.3. The risks

In one form or another, the two-handed approach has now been advocated for some time, e.g. the Cooperative Growth Strategy. We cannot therefore avoid asking why progress is so slow. Of course it may be simply that the logic of the two-handed approach is not (yet) readily apparent, but it is likely that other concerns prevent its adoption. The current emphasis on patience is most likely explained by governments' fears of three possible consequences of any fiscal expansion, no matter how supply friendly: (i) a resurgence of inflation; (ii) escalating budget deficits; (iii) a deteriorating current account. We believe that these fears are largely unfounded. Let us briefly sketch our arguments.

3.3.1. Inflation. It is perfectly understandable that governments which have invested so much effort and reputation into the battle against inflation now wish to solidify their success. Emphatically, we share this view. It is important to note that the policies that we advocate rely on supply-expanding and cost-reducing measures, so that by their very design they are unlikely to present major inflationary risks. Quite to the contrary, they have a built-in *anti*-inflationary bias. This is why we believe that the inflationary risks of a supply-friendly fiscal expansion are limited, especially in comparison to the costs of remaining caught in the present slow-growth trap.

3.3.2. Budget deficits. The budgetary picture shares many features with inflation. The process of financial consolidation is still under way in most European countries, so that the time might seem ill-chosen to contemplate measures which will result in heightened deficits. Budget deficits are a natural source of concern, in particular because they result in higher public debts. In the long run, the main issue is the public debt and the ability to meet the required interest payments. To the extent that the proposed strategy generates faster growth and more employment, it will not only generate welfare gains by releasing unused resources, but also additional receipts for servicing the burden of the additional debt.

This is not the place to review the literature on the burden of the public debt. We shall only consider a point which has received limited attention so far.[11] It concerns the question whether raising the debt today serves a useful purpose, given that fiscal policy will have to be eventually tightened in order to honour the debt. This will be the case if aggregate output is currently insufficient so that the deficit serves the useful purpose of inducing an intertemporal substitution in the demand for labour, away from a (future) period of full employment towards a (current) period of unemployment. The net gain is measured by the difference between the private and public costs of labour at a time of underemployment. This argument assumes that when the deficit is later eliminated, the reduction in labour-market distortions will have achieved 'full' employment.[12]

Of course the argument just presented rests upon two important premises. First the fiscal expansion must not be undercut by the crowding-out effect of an interest rate increase or an exchange rate appreciation. Second, it must be credible that the debt will be repaid through a future budget surplus, rather than through the inflation tax. The second condition is not likely to be met in countries where the debt-GNP ratio has already reached very substantial levels. This is why the Cooperative Growth Strategy is right in advocating a fiscal expansion only in those countries where the debt–GNP ratio is lowest – Germany, the UK and France. The relevant data are given in Section 7.

3.3.3. External constraints. The last fear concerns the external balance. As in the case of a budget deficit, the current account feeds into the external debt which is the main external constraint. Upon considering an increase in the external debt the same criterion should apply, namely

---

[11] Barro (1979), Lucas and Stokey (1983), Persson, Persson and Svensson (1986) discuss the optimal intertemporal pattern of taxes and public debt.

[12] The case under consideration is also one where Barro's (1974) argument, that a fiscal expansion is fully offset by a reduction in private demand, does not apply.

whether the resources borrowed abroad will generate the proper returns. A fiscal expansion accompanied by monetary accommodation is bound to lead to a 'deterioration' of the current account (reduction of an export surplus) so that net foreign indebtedness will increase (capital outflows reduced). To the extent that the current account deficit corresponds to additional investment, the additional foreign debt simply means that the country is relying on the international capital markets to finance its expansion.

A useful benchmark case is one where the government budget remains balanced, but the supply of private domestic savings falls short of domestic private borrowing needs. Then the current account deficit arises because of an increase in private investment as the government budget remains balanced. Rational firms will borrow only if the return on their investment is at least equal to the cost of capital. Much the same applies when investment is carried out by the government, provided that it abides by the same rentability criterion. As long as this condition is satisfied, borrowing abroad actually increases national wealth, and the additional net foreign debt is more than offset by the present discounted value of the stream of future earnings. Because the latter is not measurable, a country's net foreign asset position, which only values its financial assets and liabilities, may be almost as unreliable an indicator as its current account.

Does this imply that if the current account deterioration reflects increased current consumption, the country is 'living beyond its means'? The correct answer is that the country is facing a solvency constraint. There is an important case when there is actually no such constraint: this occurs when the country's growth rate exceeds the real interest cost of the debt so that any fraction of income earmarked for debt repayment, no matter how small, will be sufficient.[13] Otherwise solvency requires that current deficits be matched by future surpluses. If the country's ability to generate sufficient surpluses is in doubt, the main outcome will be a pressure towards exchange rate depreciation, which in some instances may take the form of a speculative crisis. But, whatever the mechanism to establish solvency, what is ultimately required is a reduction in aggregate spending relative to income, and this represents the true external cost of the fiscal expansion.

A simple calculation illustrates the point. Up to the mid-seventies most European countries were running current account surpluses more often

[13] The point is made in Cohen (1985).

than deficits so that it is natural to assume that they then started with little or no net external indebtness. Assuming a real interest rate of 5% and a growth rate of 2%, a current account deficit representing 2% of GNP over ten years amounts to a foreign debt of the size of 23% of GNP. This is the worst situation that we envision for most countries. To consider an extreme case, with deficits as high as 5% for ten years, the debt would represent 58% of GNP. (Only Denmark and Ireland may be in a worse situation.) What is the current account surplus needed to *stabilise* the debt at such levels? For the lower level of 23%, a surplus of 0.7% is sufficient and this figure rises to 1.8% when the debt level represents 58% of GNP. While these numbers are purely illustrative, they suggest that the eventual sacrifice imposed by *continuous* deficits of the size mostly observed in Europe is quite moderate. Several of the arguments of this section are illustrated with a stylised numerical allegory presented in Appendix 18.1.

3.3.4. Deficits or debts? While for both the public budget and the external account, the appropriate constraint is the corresponding debt level (a stock), policy makers typically express concerns about deficits (a flow).[14] What is the proper criterion? In terms of *constraints*, solvency is the correct criterion and the debt level is one way to measure it.[15] But in terms of policy-making the deficit may also be a relevant criterion. The debt is a 'first-order' burden as resources will eventually have to be committed to its service and possible repayment. The deficit is a 'second-order' burden because of the associated macroeconomic adjustment costs of shifting from deficit to balance or surplus. For any target debt level, the wider the present deficit, the larger the needed adjustment will be, and the worse its welfare implications. The deficit is also a more immediate concern and thus attracts the policy makers' attention more forcefully than the debt which cannot be dealt with in anything but the long run.

4. The bottom line

The policy challenge for Europe today boils down to Europe being caught in a low-growth, high-unemployment trap, characterised by: (i) substantial unused labour resources and a correspondingly high growth potential; (ii) production facilities which have adjusted downwards to low

[14] See Viñals (1986).
[15] Buiter (1985) discusses these issues in great detail.

levels of effective demand. A return to faster growth requires both an acceleration of growth in supply and a revival of demand expectations. The prevailing uncertainty surrounding the supply responsiveness generates fears in some official quarters that demand stimulation would evaporate in inflation and imports, without any lasting effects on output and employment. These fears breed inaction – and hence low investment.

To break the vicious circle, a two-handed strategy of the kind outlined above, is needed. Unwillingness to follow such a two-handed strategy may reflect a lack of confidence in the prospective effectiveness of the action of either hand. It is inescapable, that confidence in the effectiveness of both the supply-side and the demand-side components is needed today.

The ultimate fear is perhaps that the supply-side measures will be too timid, or the response of supply too slow, to avoid inflationary and exchange rate pressures as the fiscal expansion proceeds. We can only repeat that the more vigorous and productive the supply-side measures, the less likely, and the less severe, such pressures will be.

We do not claim that risks of inflationary or exchange rate pressures are totally absent. We can only repeat that they will depend upon the mix to be chosen and that some of them are worth taking, given the current underutilisation of resources and the danger of a further extension of unemployment in the near future. Each government has to balance its fear of inflation and deficits against its commitment to fight unemployment. As we explain in Section 7, the differences in initial conditions and policy objectives of the European countries will influence both their choice of policy mix and their willingness to expand.

But there is an important additional dimension to the policy challenge, to which we now turn. Due to the high degree of openness of European economies, cooperation in pursuing the two-handed strategy is important to overcome specific constraints on national policies and in internalising some important non-priced externalities.

PART II: AUTONOMY THROUGH FLEXIBLE COOPERATION

5.   Openness and the case for cooperation

5.1.   Effects of openness on fiscal policy effectiveness

The analysis of Part 1 presented the basis for, and content of, the proposed two-handed growth strategy. This analysis has largely overlooked the fact that some European economies are quite open.

Openness plays a crucial role as it may profoundly affect the cost-effectiveness of the proposed policies. This part considers the role of openness and demonstrates the crucial importance of cooperation for policies designed to enhance demand.[16]

In an economy with unemployment and with a sizeable wedge between the private and public costs of labour, the effectiveness of a fiscal expansion is measured by the additional output and employment resulting from it. Its cost is indicated by the associated increase in the public and current account deficits. The very fact that an economy is open reduces the (domestic) effectiveness and raises the (domestic) costs of the fiscal expansion. Furthermore, the more open the economy, the more pronounced the effect.

5.1.1. Reduced policy effectiveness. The reduced effectiveness results directly from the dampening effect of additional imports, as measured by the marginal propensity to import. A given initial stimulus to demand will produce fewer jobs at home because some of the demand leaks abroad. Although foreigners in turn may spend some of their increased income on domestically produced goods, the feedback will be staggered over time, and will be less than complete if a fraction of the income generated abroad is hoarded. Of course, the import leaks are not lost at the world level – they benefit the suppliers of imports as an externality, if they experience a similar discrepancy between the private and budgetary costs of labour; we shall return to that point.

The fact that the feedback is *staggered* matters when the whole purpose of the fiscal stimulus is to induce an intertemporal substitution in demand,

---

[16] One member of the group (H.G.), while fully supporting the two-handed strategy described in Part 1, wants to take exception to Part 2 to the extent that it deviates from the following position: coordination is not a necessary condition of the strategy. Instead of waiting for others, individual countries can start on their own, e.g. Germany. This country should take the lead, with or without prior coordination, by adopting measures to improve the competitiveness of its domestic locations in the worldwide market for capital and direct investment in order to transform its current account surplus into an additional stock of capital for more permanently productive jobs within its area: in given circumstances, the social returns of investment in Germany would far exceed the rate of interest earned from exporting capital. Even smaller countries could move ahead without time consuming prior coordination. Going alone, however, requires that the measures taken promise as much positive effects on the supply side as they increase demand. The supply-side effects are to improve the competitiveness of domestic producers so that the expanding country captures more of total world demand at the time when part of the domestic demand stimulus leaks out to raise imports. What matters is the balance of demand and supply effects. Coordination takes only care of the demand side. Stressing the coordination issue involves neglect of the supply effects and their importance. It thus runs into the danger of creating a moral hazard problem: a demand expansion may too easily be considered sufficient.

from the future to the present. How staggered the feedback will be, depends on the origin of the imports: Belgian imports from France, which in turn addresses 10% of its own import demand to Belgium, will induce a quicker feedback than Belgian imports from Spain, which addresses less than 2% of its own imports to Belgium. Detailed linked econometric models would be needed to estimate the length of the lags, but the argument that the feedback is less than complete, if part of the income generated abroad is hoarded, is standard. One aspect of that argument is not commonly spelled out, however, yet that aspect is important for our purposes. In Europe, average rates of gross taxation (ratios of public receipts to GDP) are close to 50% in many countries. For a country engaged in fiscal stabilisation, this implies an automatic hoarding of about half of export-led increases in income. For the partner country which contemplates a fiscal expansion, it means that some 50% of the hoped-for feedbacks would be sterilised – at least temporarily. Again, detailed econometric models would be needed to assess the precise magnitude of this effect, but the numbers are bound to be large. Given the current stress in Europe on fiscal consolidation, fears of foreign sterilisation are quite natural and probably go a fair way towards sustaining the expectation that the feedback will be *slow* and *incomplete*, substantially reducing the *effectiveness* of fiscal policy in any single open economy.

5.1.2. Increased costs. The increased cost of the fiscal stimulus derives from the externality corresponding to a private cost of labour in excess of its budgetary cost: the cost of domestic labour to the country is its budgetary cost, while the cost of foreign labour is the full private cost. The difference between the two accrues to the foreign country (with only limited feedback to be expected). To illustrate, if the Belgian government hires formerly unemployed Belgian workers to tend the public parks of Antwerp, the net cost to the Belgian taxpayers is the difference between the net earnings of the workers and the unemployment benefits that they used to receive (labelled budgetary costs in table 18.5). If instead Dutch gardeners are hired the net cost to the Belgian taxpayers is the full gross cost (labelled private costs in table 18.5). Obviously, this increase in cost will be greater the more the increase in demand, the associated increase in employment, leaks abroad, i.e. the higher the marginal propensity to import.

5.1.3. Openness. Thus, as the marginal propensity to import rises, the domestic cost effectiveness of the expansion is affected, reducing the country's incentive to carry it out on its own. The importance of this point has been illustrated vividly by the 'early-Mitterrand' French expansion of 1981–82, the associated current account deterioration quickly leading to a reversal of policy (see Sachs and Wyplosz (1986)). However, if several countries together form a relatively closed area, they can reap the full benefits of an expansion just like a closed economy. We shall argue that this is the case today in Europe, and particularly that it is more reasonable to advocate a simultaneous expansion by France, the U.K. and Germany than to ask Germany to play the locomotive role again while France and the U.K. postpone action until the German expansion takes momentum.

In Appendix 18.2, we explain why import shares, corrected for the import content of exports, provide an operational measure of the degree of openness of an economy, which is well suited for a discussion of the cost effectiveness of fiscal policy. Some figures on import shares, net import shares (imports less import content of exports), and marginal propensities to import are collected in table 18.6. It is clear that openness is inversely related to country size, and directly related to the extent of economic integration with neighbouring countries. EC10 as a whole is about half as open as the least open of its members. In spite of its larger

Table 18.6. *Measures of openness (1985)*

	Import Share	Net Import Share	Marginal propensity to import [a]
Belgium	76.1	44.2	53.0
Denmark	36.7	19.8	23.8
W.Germany	28.7	19.8	23.8
Spain	20.2	15.7	18.8
France	24.9	15.6	18.6
Ireland	58.5	40.0	48.0
Italy	28.6	18.9	22.7
Luxemburg	94.4	-	-
Netherlands	59.4	25.0	30.0
Portugal	41.9	25.5	30.6
UK	28.2	18.7	22.4
Greece	32.5	26.0	31.2
EC 10	13.4	-	-
USA	10.1	-	-
Japan	11.4	-	-

Note:[a] (1.2) × (net import share).
Adjustment for import content of exports based on input-output tables when possible.
Source: EC Commission. From country desks, based on national sources.

size, measured by GDP or population, EC10 is still more open than either the US or Japan. In part, this reflects a more limited endowment of natural resources (relative to the US), and in part closer links to former colonies or other non-community European economies. But the degree of openness of Europe as an entity is much closer to that of the US or Japan than to that of a typical member country.

The figures in table 18.6 prompt us to the conclusion that Europe as a whole is sufficiently closed to pursue autonomous fiscal and monetary policies, provided it can define and implement these policies on a cooperative basis. The need for cooperation among European countries derives from their high degree of individual openness, which imposes severe constraints on autonomous policy actions by individual countries.

We thus see openness as a major explanation for the reluctance of European governments to implement the two-handed strategy.

5.2. The case for cooperation

The case for policy cooperation is quite simple and well known.[17] A sufficient condition is that the private and budgetary costs of any factor or commodity (labour for example) diverge at home and abroad. Then, if governments make their policy decisions based only on the effects on domestic welfare, they will ignore any effect on the allocation of resources abroad. In the absence of any wedge between the private and social costs, this does not matter, since the allocation of resources is efficient. However, when, for example, unemployed labour abroad is brought into use by a domestic fiscal expansion, the home country ignores this beneficial effect in deciding how large an expansion to make. The essential point is that there exists an externality which is not properly 'priced'. Hence, we find a strong temptation for each country to act as a caboose in the hope that the other ones will play the role of the locomotive. Thus in assessing the success of the German-led expansion following the Bonn Summit of 1978 – the 'locomotive' experiment – one should take into account the effects of Germany's action on its trading partners. While Germany experienced a deterioration in its current account and some acceleration in inflation, it also raised the level of activity abroad.[18] It should be noted that coordination of policies is emphatically *not* the same as their synchronisation. Thus the

[17] Hamada (1976), Cooper (1984), Sachs (1983).
[18] Unfortunately the second oil shock and the contractionary fiscal and monetary policies it engendered prevent any firm conclusion about the overall success of the experiment; see Bean (1985).

worldwide inflation of 1973 was engendered by the simultaneous but *un*coordinated fiscal and monetary expansion pursued by the industrialised economies. The result was chronic overheating.[19]

One natural domain of cooperation concerns the fears of sterilisation through attempts at budget consolidation by trading partners, as explained in Section 5.1. If two countries are both inhibited in their implementation of a desirable fiscal expansion by such fears, it would be natural for them to reach mutual assurance that each country's expansion will not be partly offset by the other country's fiscal stance. Cooperation is then conducive to more successful policies in both countries.

The logic of the case is elementary and widely recognised at different levels. It is the same logic of 'coordination failure' which plays an important role in microeconomic reasoning, to explain why individual firms operating below capacity do not find it advantageous to expand output and employment individually, in anticipation of the demand that would materialise if all firms expanded simultaneously.

The case for cooperation is intimately linked to the two-handed approach. One hand, that directing the supply side, by and large does not require cooperation.[20] The need for cooperation follows from the determination to use the second hand, that of the demand side. Indeed, most of the supply-side measures under consideration can be implemented at national levels by individual countries acting on their own. Not only the measures, but also their effects, are of a primarily domestic nature. The incentives to adopt them are there, whether or not other countries do likewise. Further, these supply-side measures work towards improving competitiveness, so that external considerations reinforce the domestic motivation. (The same cannot be said of measures encouraging market integration or trade liberalisation. These are appropriately approached at the supranational level.)

The fact that macroeconomic policy cooperation is bound to stress the demand element in the policy mix, has a disadvantage. It leads to a rhetoric that neglects the supply side, where a lot of hard work is to be done. This disadvantage is particularly obvious in Section 7 of the present report, which of necessity is devoted almost entirely to demand-side

---

[19] Indeed, it is not generally the case that the lack of coordination leads to over-contractionary policies. It can also result in over-expansionary policies, particularly under a fixed exchange rate regime.

[20] There exist some supply-side measures which would still benefit from cooperation (e.g. when they affect the internal terms of trade, or market liberalisation which spills over abroad), but the magnitude of the gains from cooperation in these cases is likely to be small.

policies. Hopefully, our insistence on the complementarity of the two sides should be clear to the reader from Part 1. For some of us, the anticipatory demand expansion is even viewed primarily as a means of facilitating the removal of supply rigidities, the completion of the internal market and the liberalisation of world trade. However, even though the emphasis placed on the two sides may differ, there is no doubt in our minds that only a two-handed strategy can restore acceptable rates of growth in Europe. There lies the most important message.

6. Europe and the rest of the world

6.1. Little promise for policy cooperation

The income flow measures in Section 5.1 capture adequately the size of the externalities which make the case for cooperation. They reveal clearly that large countries, or country groups, are relatively closed. Table 18.7 summarises the relevant data. As might be expected, the cross-country income multipliers between such areas are quite small. Table 18.8 reports the multipliers from the COMPACT Model – a model yielding results for the European Community as a whole (EC10).[21] The only sizeable entry (0.4) concerns the impact of the US on Japan. Those for Europe are uniformly small (0.1 or 0.2).

Table 18.7. *Trade flows between major countries or groups* (1986)

	USA	EC 12	Japan
Imports as % of own GDP	10.2	9.5[a]	6.6
Exports as % of own GDP	6.8	9.7[a]	11.5
Imports of EC 12 as % of EC 12 GDP	1.9	13.1[b]	1.1
Exports of EC 12 as % of EC 12 GDP	2.6	13.1[b]	0.4

[a] is extra-EC trade
[b] is intra-EC trade
Source: European Economy, July 1987, n°33. Tables 35 and 36.

As a consequence, the need for policy cooperation between such large but closed entities is not great. That conclusion is confirmed by the welfare computations performed by Oudiz and Sachs (1984) reported in Box 2.

[21] Where comparable, results from other models (for instance those of the Interlink model used at OECD, or the MCM model used at the Federal Reserve Board, or of the EPA in Tokyo) are not markedly different. See, e.g. Oudiz and Sachs (1984), pp. 20–21.

Table 18.8. *Cross-country income multipliers*

1% of GDP increase in public expenditures (non-wages) with non-accommodating monetary policy

% discrepancy w.r.t. baseline simulation

Country taking action	EC 10			USA			Japan		
	1 year	2 years	3 years	1 year	2 years	3 years	1 year	2 years	3 years
EC 10	1.1	1.3	0.9	0.1	0.2	0.2	0.1	0.1	0.1
USA	0.15	0.2	0.2	1.3	1.2	1.0	0.3	0.4	0.4
Japan	0.05	0.1	0.1	0.1	0.1	0.1	1.1	1.2	1.4

Source: COMPACT Model

BOX 2: Welfare gains from cooperation

The welfare calculations by Oudiz and Sachs (1984) were based on two large models which measure the links between the US, Japan and Germany (the MCM model of the Federal Reserve Board and the Japanese EPA model). Given contemporary forecasts for the three years 1984–86, they looked for the policy actions which would improve the welfare of all three countries, without hurting any of them; welfare is measured in units (percent) of GNP and corresponds to the perceived costs of falling below potential GNP, inflation, and current account imbalances. The striking feature of their results, reported in table 18.9, is how little is achieved through *optimal* coordination: the 0.33 obtained for Germany means that, compared to uncoordinated policy making, full coordination would only improve that country's welfare by an equivalent of 1/3 of one percent higher GNP over the three years period. Clearly, if the best that can be achieved is of this magnitude, there is little incentive in undertaking the kind of elaborate negotiations that full coordination requires.

Table 18.9. *Welfare gains from cooperation*

	USA	Germany	Japan
MCM	0.17	0.33	0.99
EPA Model	0.03	0.03	0.32
MCM Modified	0.54	0.56	2.96

Unit of welfare gain equivalent to a percentage of GNP averaged over three years. Target values are: inflation, zero; current account-GDP ratio, zero for the US, 2% for Germany and Japan.

The last line is based on a modification of the MCM with Germany enlarged three-fold and called 'Europe'.

Source: Oudiz and Sachs (1984).

The scope for coordination is best approached as an exercise in cost-benefit analysis. Small gains may indeed be worth reaping if the cost in obtaining them is minimal, whereas larger gains may sometimes fail to cover their cost. Pending such a quantitative analysis, we feel safe in concluding that the (political) difficulties of coordinating policies at a world level are such that the effort may scarcely be worthwhile.[22]

6.2. A careful exchange rate policy

Another important channel of transmission of policy impacts across countries is the terms of trade. Unfortunately, the effects of fluctuations in the terms of trade are more difficult to capture through econometric models than income effects. Still, in table 18.10, we report cross-country exchange rate multipliers as estimated by the COMPACT Model. The picture emerging from that table confirms our general intuition: the impact of a depreciation of the US dollar against all other currencies exerts less influence at home, and more influence overseas, than a comparable depreciation of the ECU, or even more so of the yen. Presumably, the same conclusion would hold for an appreciation.

Looking at tables 18.8 and 18.10, we note that a 10% change in the value of the dollar has roughly the same medium-term impact on the GDP of EC 10 as a 2.5% change in US national income. But exchange rates are much more volatile than national incomes, so that Europeans are justifiably concerned by the real consequences of the dollar instability. The current situation is dominated by a considerable amount of uncertainty. The sharp appreciation of the dollar from 1980 to 1985 has been mostly undone by its equally sharp depreciation since then. While the full impact of this depreciation remains to be felt, a further sizeable depreciation is seen by some (see Dornbusch and Frankel (1987)) as a distinct possibility. The effects on the exchange rate of an acceleration of growth in Europe must be considered in such a context. If existing macroeconomic models provide any guide to the future (and doubts are legitimate ...), then faster growth in Europe would put downward pressure on its currencies. If current parities are close to their sustainable equilibrium levels (and here too there is ample room for doubt), then it would be desirable to accompany the fiscal expansion with a monetary policy which would avoid significant short-and-medium-term swings.

[22] This does not mean that Europe does not stand to benefit from some policy actions in the US. Given the strong linkages between financial markets, a reduction of the US budget deficit would be welcome in Europe. The exchange rate aspect of these linkages is taken up in the following section.

Table 18.10. *Cross-country exchange rate multipliers*

(10% depreciation against all currencies)

Country taking action	EC 10 1 year	2 years	3 years	USA 1 year	2 years	3 years	Japan 1 year	2 years	3 years
EC 10	0.15	0.5	0.8	−0.1	−0.15	−0.2	−0.1	−0.1	−0.2
USA	−0.1	−0.3	−0.5	0.2	0.3	0.35	−0.3	−0.6	−0.8
Japan	−0.05	−0.1	−0.1	−0.05	−0.1	−0.1	0.4	0.7	1.1

Source: COMPACT model.

On the other hand, the experience of the present decade is one where currency movements have been dominated by the dollar and policy initiatives in the US. Under such conditions it is dangerous for Europe to try to stabilise its exchange rates *vis-à-vis* the dollar as it would mean a severe loss of monetary policy independence, an undesirable outcome given the limited gains from transatlantic coordination as shown earlier. Europe should therefore use monetary policy to offset exchange rate pressures caused by its own fiscal actions (this prescription concerns Europe as a whole *vis-à-vis* the rest of the world; internal European exchange rate policies are discussed in some detail in Section 7.2). Our proposed fiscal-monetary mix has precisely that property.

Offsetting exchange rate pressures may not be appropriate, however, in the presence of other shocks. Unfortunately, given the amount of existing uncertainty, we cannot provide succinctly a comprehensive analysis of the appropriate monetary policy responses to the many disturbances which may occur.

6.3. *Policy implications: Europe's autonomy*

The implications of the discussion so far are clear. It would be futile to aim at finely-tuned coordination of economic policies between Europe, the US and Japan. Our simple, clear conclusion cuts through an issue where the interplay of economics and politics has turned into a complex, confused debate. *We believe that Europe should assume responsibility for its own economic policies and regard itself as an autonomous economic entity.*[23] This conclusion is somewhat at variance with the spirit of efforts initiated at summit meetings of the Group of Seven, and endorsed in

---

[23] To avoid ambiguities: we are not arguing that Europe is more efficient in achieving coordination, rather the gains from coordination within Europe are that much greater due to the more open and interrelated nature of its constituent economies.

particular in Section 4.7 of the EC Annual Report 1986–87 – a point to which we return in Section 7.1.

Being autonomous does not mean disregarding the actions of others, of course. What other countries do is relevant to European policy choices, and must be taken into account. We refer in Box 3 to common responsibilities which Europe shares with others at the world level. Rather autonomy requires accepting one's responsibilities without blaming others for one's difficulties. That is exactly how Europe should approach its severe unemployment problem. The recent experience of a large US trade deficit and an overvalued dollar with its negligible impact on European employment,[24] confirms that we should not expect miracles from increased exports to the US which presently account for only 4% of Europe's GDP.

While world macroeconomic policy coordination does not seem to pass the cost-benefit test, there are nevertheless other areas of cooperation that we wish to mention briefly. One is the international monetary system, a second is trade liberalisation, and the third concerns the LDCs. They are discussed in Box 3.

BOX 3: Three items for world cooperation

The prominent issue is the macroeconomic adjustment required by the LDC debt problem and the US current account deficit. The more developed countries should cooperate actively in improving the growth potential and living standards of the LDCs. Beyond the technical steps needed to organise more realistic terms for the debt and more efficient risk-sharing between rich and poor countries, the main long-run concern should be to promote stable growth of LDC exports. This calls for sustained demand for these exports from the main industrialised areas. As the US attempts to reduce its own external deficit, it is important that the European surplus be reduced and reversed to make room for a surplus by the LDCs, without which their debt situation can only worsen. In this respect the policy mix advocated in this paper – which implies a reduction in the Europe-wide current account surplus, possibly turning it into a deficit – is consistent with Europe's responsibilities in the world economy.

---

[24] Of course, that impact could have been increased, had the supply responsiveness in Europe been greater. That lack of responsiveness in turn was probably influenced by the conviction that the US deficit and overvalued dollar were temporary.

A second area for cooperation is a significant reduction of the role played by the dollar on the international scene. As noted by Oudiz and Sachs (1984, p. 7, table 2 reproduced here in table 18.11): 'The US dollar remains the linchpin of the world monetary system. As shown in table 18.11, the currency of denomination of international reserves, Euro-dollar loans, new issues of Eurobonds, and OPEC portfolio wealth remains to a far higher extent in US dollars than the US share of world GNP would suggest. The special role of the dollar leads to important asymmetries between the effects of US policies on Europe and Japan, and the effects of European and Japanese policies on the United States. Shifts in the value of the dollar can have significant income redistribution effects throughout the world that may also have important demand consequences; changes in the value of the European currencies or the Japanese yen do not have such effects.' With all the prudence called for in this difficult area, we feel that the primary need remains that of developing better alternatives to the US dollar as international instrument of reserves, transactions and liquidity.

The third issue, trade liberalisation, was discussed extensively in the latest report prepared by the CEPS Macroeconomic Policy Group (H. Giersch (1987a)). It would of course be partly self-defeating to work towards smoother trade flows through stabilisation of the dollar, while at the same time accepting other impediments and distortions through tariffs, import restrictions and other barriers. Trade liberalisation can contribute to supply expansion and output growth in all parts of the world. It should be promoted now, and Europe should exercise leadership in that respect. This issue cannot be overemphasised at a time when protectionist pressures are rising on both sides of the Atlantic.

Table 18.11. *The role of the US dollar in international finance*

	Share of US dollars		
	1975	1978	1981
Official reserves	79.4	76.9	70.6
Eurodollar loans	73.7	67.6	70.6
Eurobond issues	47.2	48.2	80.2
US share of world GNP	24.3	25.0	n.a.

Source: Reproduced from Oudiz and Sachs (1984), Table 2.

7. Policy cooperation within Europe

7.1. Cooperation and the EMS

So far, the EMS has brought about some cooperation in monetary, and to a lesser extent, in fiscal policies, but this is not by itself a guarantee that the required policies will emerge naturally. In this section, we briefly review the benefits that member countries have reaped from participation in the EMS, its role in encouraging cooperative behaviour, and the requisite conditions for cooperation in the two-handed strategy.

The primary objective of the EMS is to deliver bilateral exchange rate stability. Trade flows between European countries will be more stable if they are not subject to volatile exchange rate movements. Given the large share of exports in value added, greater stability in trade carries over to greater stability in output and employment. Thus, exchange rate stability helps to insulate the real economy from monetary shocks.[25] In addition, the EMS has been instrumental in enhancing the effectiveness of anti-inflationary policies in the early eighties, when all European countries were sharing the common objective of reducing their excessive rates of inflation. The EMS constraint of maintaining stable exchange rates proved helpful to that end in two ways:

(i) It eliminated the temptation for individual countries, especially the more open ones, to export their inflation through currency appreciation – a policy that obviously could not succeed if pursued by all.[26]

(ii) It also enabled member countries to borrow the anti-inflationary reputation of the Bundesbank to help reduce domestic inflationary expectations.[27]

It was thus important for all concerned to adhere as strictly as possible to the agreed exchange rates. The automatic success of the EMS as an implicit tool of policy coordination resulted from the fact that the tool was ideally suited to the main priority of the day – the elimination of inflation – an objective which was shared by all countries.

---

[25] There is some debate whether these objectives have been met. Rogoff (1985) finds that the EMS has made bilateral exchange rates more predictable, not necessarily more stable. De Grauwe and Verfaille (1987) compare exchange rate variability before and after 1979 and conclude that there is no obvious evidence that the variability of bilateral exchange rates has decreased more inside than outside the EMS.

[26] Giavazzi and Giovannini (1986) show, however, that the EMS has introduced long-run trends in intra-European competitiveness, and suggest that the system has not prevented some European countries – at least Italy – from using currency appreciation to export inflation.

[27] See Giavazzi and Pagano (1988).

To the extent that the system functions as it should (and has done so far), it reduces substantially the leeway for independent interest rate policies in the member states. *Participation in the EMS amounts to a surrender, by all but one country, of domestic interest rates as an unrestricted policy instrument.* It also implies the surrender of the exchange rate as an instrument for equilibrating the current account. Rather, it entails an implicit commitment to achieve long-run external solvency by price adjustment alone. At the same time, the EMS countries retain the option of floating together *vis-à-vis* the rest of the world, thereby achieving external balance in a manner which individual member countries have forfeited by joining the EMS.

The EMS, however, does not enforce automatic cooperation of fiscal policies. It may provide a useful framework for cooperation, but does not substitute for the sort of negotiation required to enact mutually beneficial policies.[28] An important feature of the environment in which cooperation must take place is the fact that the various European countries start from different initial conditions. With different initial conditions, there is still room for cooperation, but it may lead to varied policy actions in the different countries. We call this 'flexible' cooperation. We address this issue in the next section. We shall then consider another aspect which also complicates the matter: the possibility that policy objectives may differ among the various countries.

7.2. Cooperative growth with differentiated initial conditions

7.2.1. The setting. Differences in initial conditions matter because they alter the constraints on policy choices. In the present context, we have identified three such constraints (Section 3.3): inflation, the public debt, and the external debt. We have already stressed that inflation need not be a threat because the two-handed approach incorporates significant contributions to cost and price stability. Looking at the current situation we note that, for the first time in twenty years, Europe's average inflation rate (as measured by the CPI) has receded to its level of the mid-sixties. Yet differences between countries remain substantial, with the four Mediterranean countries well above the European average, the UK close to it, and the remaining countries below it. The inflationary position of the southern countries should thus be kept in mind, while the respite in

---

[28] The EMS merely reduces the possible policy choices of its member countries but does not restrict them completely, leaving room for coordination, or the absence of it. See Begg and Wyplosz (1987).

trend inflation is put to good use. The relevant data are displayed in figure 18.2.

Differences in the state of the public finances amongst the European nations are clearly recognized in the Annual Report of the EC Commission. In particular the Report stresses that budget deficits in several member countries are already so high that they must be reduced rather than increased further – for otherwise the burden of public debt would soon grow beyond control. (Figure 18.3 clearly brings out the association between public debts and deficits.) Hence the Commission's recommendation that fiscal expansion should start in Germany, with France and the UK following.

This internal constraint now has to be connected to the other important one, namely, the external constraint. The two-handed growth strategy should be viewed against the background of figure 18.4, where the twelve EC countries (Belgium and Luxemburg combined) are located in terms of their net government debt/GNP ratio (horizontally) and of their current account deficit/GNP ratio (vertically).[29] Each country is represented by a circle, its size proportional to the country's GNP. Two solid lines are drawn at the (weighted) averages of the ratios for EC 12.

7.2.2. The principles. A supply-friendly fiscal expansion, with monetary accommodation, should lead to a temporary increase of the net debt/GNP ratio and to a temporary deterioration of the current account/GNP ratio. This implies that the EC *averages* in figure 18.4 should move north-east.

The movement of the averages does not, however, require that each individual country moves north-east. Actually, the position of some countries in figure 18.4 is such that they would prefer to move in a different direction. In particular, Italy, Ireland and Belgium are trying to move westward, so as to reduce the weight of their public debt (indeed, the Annual Report of the EC Commission recommends that these countries continue their efforts at budget consolidation). Similarly, Denmark and

---

[29] In principle, we would prefer to measure the external constraint through the net external debt rather than through the current account. However, official figures for net external debt are often lacking, and therefore seldom used, so we use the more familiar figures. On the basis of cumulative current account data since 1960, we have constructed net external debt estimates and used them in figure 18.5. The picture does not differ much from that of figure 18.4 and may be used interchangeably. We have already discussed this issue in section 3.3.4 and will return to it below.

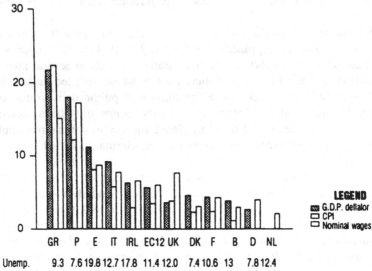

Three Measures of Inflation – 1986

LEGEND
- G.D.P. deflator
- CPI
- Nominal wages

	GR	P	E	IT	IRL	EC12	UK	DK	F	B	D	NL
Unemp.	9.3	7.6	19.8	12.7	17.8	11.4	12.0	7.4	10.6	13	7.8	12.4
Growth 86	-0.4	3.9	2.7	2.7	3.2	2.5	2.6	2.5	2.3	2.0	3.5	1.7

Figure 18.2

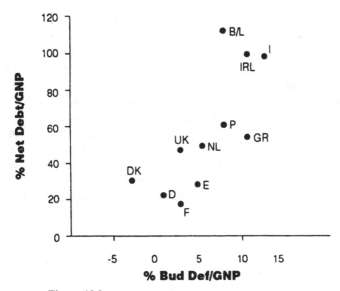

Figure 18.3

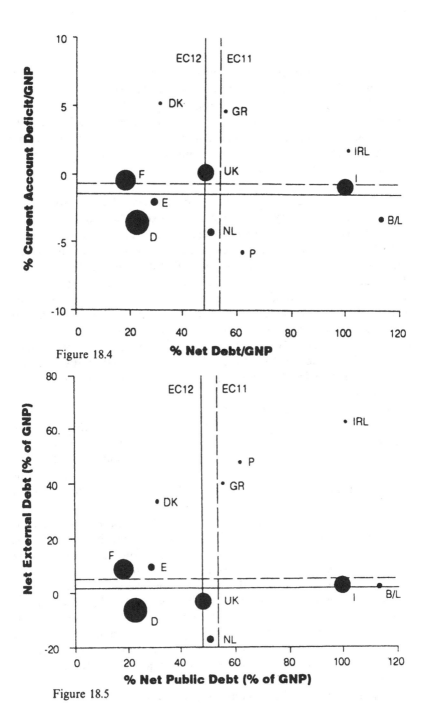

Figure 18.4

Figure 18.5

Greece would like to move southward, to reduce their external deficit. (We return to these specific country tendencies below).

Flexible cooperation, as distinct from policy synchronisation, does not require all countries to move in the same direction. Instead, it tries to define country-specific policies that tend to the common goal, while duly taking into account the differences in initial conditions. What does this mean, in present circumstances?

7.2.3. Flexible cooperation. Countries located in the south-west quadrant need not worry about their debt or external position – Germany is the obvious and well-known instance. It can adopt the two-handed strategy wholeheartedly. As a consequence, Germany moves north-east and pushes the EC average (aggregate) in that direction. As that happens, the remaining countries benefit from an externality (the additional imports of Germany) which would tend to push them in a south-westerly direction if they remained passive, i.e., if they kept their public spending and tax rates unchanged. Indeed, they export more, which improves their current accounts, raises their GNP (by a smaller percentage) and reduces their public deficits. The net effect for EC 12 aggregates is still a displacement north-east, but by less than the initial impulse which is dampened by the externalities.

In order to avoid the dampening, it is desirable that the countries located near the boundary of the south-west quadrant should also follow the two-handed strategy and move north-east of their own initiative. Looking at figure 18.4, we see that France, the UK and the Netherlands fall in that category. Spain is in the same quadrant as Germany and on the surface shares the same degree of freedom; due account should, however, be given to the fact that Spain (as well as Portugal and Greece) is in a difficult transition phase as it gradually integrates its economy into the Community. Together, France, the UK, the Netherlands and Spain account for some 51% of EC 12 GNP. Adding Germany, we now have 77% of the community engaged in the supply-friendly fiscal expansion and unambiguously pushing the aggregate north-east, in spite of some residual dampening from the remaining smaller countries. The two-handed growth strategy for Europe is then definitely under way. It seems clear to us that such cooperative action is far more effective than a repeat of the 'German locomotive experiment'. The bulk of the impact comes from the joint initiatives of Germany, France and the UK which together account for 65% of EC 12 GNP.

What about the remaining countries? If they remain passive, they move south-west. Although their dampening effect on the aggregates is now reduced, it is still there. Could it be avoided? It could indeed, because their antisymmetrical positions relative to the new averages allows for offsetting movements which eliminate the dampening. More specifically, if Denmark and Greece moved south-east, whereas Belgium and Italy moved north-west, the aggregate of these four countries could remain roughly unchanged, allowing the expansion initiated in the other countries to work out its full effects without dampening. Let us look at the implied policies.

The clearest case is that of Belgium. This country is currently engaged in an effort to reduce its budget deficit. Although this effort will be facilitated by the faster growth of neighbouring countries, it should still be pursued. The current account will then display an even larger surplus, whereas the country should move *north*-west. The surplus will naturally be reduced in due time by a currency appreciation. The same policy conclusion holds for Italy, although the implied appreciation would be less marked (both because the initial position involves a smaller surplus and because the smaller degree of openness leads to less pronounced externalities). Conversely, Denmark would see its current account improve under the export pull. This country should adopt a more expansionary fiscal stance, in order to move eastward (contrary to the westward tendency associated with a passive fiscal stance). If the fiscal expansion did more than offset the current account improvement, then a slight currency depreciation would follow. The same applies to Greece, although to a lesser extent. We thus see how Belgium, Italy, Denmark and Greece could play their role by ensuring that no dampening of the initial impulses occurs. The required policies imply some ancillary currency realignments, involving mainly the Belgian franc and the Danish crown. Finally, Ireland could remain 'passive' and move against the tide – but that country accounts for less than 1% of EC 12 GNP or trade.

What remains to be spelled out are the accompanying monetary policies. Given that in each country fiscal policy is set as suggested above, choosing a particular monetary policy is equivalent to the choice of an exchange rate policy, which leads to a consideration of the role of the EMS (assuming that the UK, although not part of the EMS, stabilises the ECU value of the pound). As discussed above, one of the main merits of the EMS is the fact that it provides a credible nominal anchor for price levels across Europe. The system has proven flexible enough to accommodate divergent trends periodically, but it has also penalised (through loss of competitiveness) the more inflation-prone countries in Europe. It has thus provided a credible incentive not to resort to inflationary policies.

All this is crucial for the policies we advocate. A strong commitment to the EMS lends credibility to the announcement that a temporary budget deficit will not be paid for through inflationary finance: it thus reduces the pressures towards exchange rate depreciation that arise whenever the government's ability to generate future budget surpluses is in doubt. Of course the enhanced credibility provided by the EMS cannot eliminate the possibility of speculative attacks: these should be *jointly* resisted by the central banks of the member countries.

In the long run, we cannot rule out the possibility that the fiscal actions necessary to implement the two-handed strategy may require an adjustment of relative prices among European countries. However, the size and even the sign, of these adjustments are difficult to anticipate, as they depend on a number of (often counteracting) factors: the degree of substitutability among debt issued by different governments and denominated in different currencies is, for example, an important one, and one of which we know very little. The flexibility built in the EMS will prove valuable in making these relative price adjustments possible – if and when the time comes.[30]

The foregoing analysis suggests unambiguously that the cooperative growth strategy is feasible, in spite of substantial differences in initial conditions. It also illustrates vividly that cooperation should not be confused with synchronisation.

7.3. Differences in policy objectives

The strategy outlined in the previous section assumes common policy objectives among all countries, namely a high priority given to the fight against unemployment. Yet Denmark has recently gone through a period of drastic budget consolidation, and might be reluctant to go into deficit again. More significantly, Germany has a deep-rooted aversion to inflation, and might be reluctant to participate in a strategy where the fiscal expansion anticipates the acceleration of growth in supply. Even though we believe that hesitation is ill-advised, it is nevertheless instructive to discuss its implications. If Germany did not participate in the cooperative growth strategy, the remaining countries would have to choose between

---

[30] For an analysis of these effects see Sachs and Wyplosz (1984). Needless to say we fully recognize the merits of the relative stability of exchange rates within the EMS. The formulation in the text assumes that our policy recommendations become implemented from a starting situation characterised by sustainable exchange rates. If that was not the case, one should distinguish carefully the consequences of the starting situation from those of the policy actions.

giving up that strategy altogether, or carrying it out on their own. What would the latter alternative look like?

The bulk of the expansion would now come from France, the UK, Spain and the Netherlands. As noted above, these four countries account for 51% of EC 12 GNP, as opposed to 77% with Germany. A rough calculation suggests the extent of the collective loss incurred by carrying out the strategy without active German participation. Using the ratio to GDP of extra-community imports of goods as a rough measure of openness, we get a figure of 13.4% for EC 10. Leaving out Germany, the corresponding figure for the remaining 9 countries jumps to 18.6%, up by a full 5%. In relative terms, the degree of openness of EC 10 goes up by nearly 40% if Germany is left out. The cost to the remaining 9 countries of Germany's failure to participate in the concerted expansion is thus serious, in terms of import leakages and terms of trade deterioration.

Now France and the UK are in the frontline (the dotted lines on figures 18.4 and 18.5 show the EC averages when Germany is left out) and are quite vulnerable with respect to their external position. Furthermore, a fiscal expansion without Germany may well entail some loss of credibility for the monetary authorities and put additional pressure on the exchange rates of the expanding countries. In practice, this amounts to an effective appreciation of the DM. In fact, what is required, is an agreement with Germany to disagree, namely a revaluation of the DM within the EMS; in a sense this would be the German contribution to cooperation. If of a proper magnitude, and if accompanied in the devaluing countries by wage and price moderation – the overriding condition of success in any case – such a realignment would ensure that the collective current account of the expanding countries does not become a source of major concern. Besides this general change, the rest of the recommendations of the previous section apply, except that the fiscal expansion is stronger (even though less effective) wherever it is enacted, and the overall expansion is dampened by Germany's passive fiscal stance.

In addition to being less effective overall, that alternative entails the additional cost of more pronounced currency realignments. And it entails Germany losing competitiveness through appreciation and ending up with increased unemployment. Through that channel, an inflation/unemployment trade-off seems inescapable, even in a country to which the Phillips curve analysis is sometimes considered inapplicable.[31] Thus, not only the expanding countries suffer from the lack of German cooperation, but

[31] Phillips curve equations for Germany appear to have been successfully estimated, among others, by Franz (1985), Franz and König (1986), and Bean, Layard and Nickell (1986).

Germany ends up with more unemployment (and less inflation) that in the alternative scenario of the previous section. This confirms the advantages of cooperation, but also suggests that cooperation may arise indirectly: faced with a one-sided expansion elsewhere in Europe, it would still be to Germany's advantage to adopt the two-handed strategy.

8. Conclusion

We have restated the reasons why Europe needs policy actions to extricate itself from its slow-growth, high-unemployment trap. Because of the complex reasons lying behind the underutilisation of the productive resources, and the continuing failure to speed up the accumulation of resources, the required policies must work on both the supply and the demand sides. The two-handed strategy aims at making the economy more efficient in mobilizing its existing resources and readier to increase them. It works on the supply side through a mix of competition enhancing measures as well as cost-cutting fiscal action. It simultaneously works on the demand side through labour tax cuts. Demand feeds into supply by providing the producers with the necessary long-term demand incentives to hire labour and increase productive equipment. Simultaneously, all available opportunities for productive public investment should be seized, both by the EC itself and by member countries. Productive public investments may without reservation be financed by capital inflows. We regard the inflationary risk of this strategy as moderate and well worth taking.

In reviewing the reasons behind the past reluctance to adopt the two-handed strategy, we have emphasised the role of openness, and found it useful to separate the situation of individual countries from the position of the European Community as a whole.

The EC itself is quite closed. The current account constraint, while not to be overlooked, is therefore relatively unimportant. The implication is that the EC should not make the adoption of the two-handed strategy contingent on reaching a cooperative agreement with the US and Japan. Europe should assert its autonomy and adopt the policies that suit it best. This, of course, does not mean that Europe should completely ignore the external effects of these policies, nor that it should renege on its obligations towards the rest of the world. Two important issues emerge in this connection. First, the financial links are important, fast and powerful. This implies that exchange rate management requires considerable caution. However, this is not a one-sided issue and avoiding disruption will require some cooperation with the US and Japan. In particular, a better functioning international monetary system remains a desirable objective. The second important issue concerns the LDC debt problem. At a time when the US must close its external deficit, current account surpluses in the indebted LDCs will require deficits elsewhere, particularly in Europe. The two-handed strategy would bring this about.

Cooperation within the EC is an altogether different matter. An important implication of openness – and all EC countries are very open – is that a fiscal expansion is both less effective and more costly, the more open is the economy. Supply-side policies, on the other hand, tend to become more desirable as the degree of openness rises. The inescapable conclusion is that the external constraint is likely to play havoc with the two-handed strategy: it favours only one hand, supply-side policies. A full commitment to the strategy therefore requires that the external constraint be loosened and that requires fiscal cooperation.

Cooperation is not synonymous with synchronisation. Because economic conditions (chiefly inflation, the public and external debts) differ across countries, policies too will have to differ. Flexible cooperation recognizes this fact and calls for a clear understanding of the role of different initial conditions. Rather than repeating the Bonn Summit approach of staging a fiscal expansion with Germany taking the lead and France and the UK following suit, we think that it would be more effective for the three countries to move simultaneously. The other countries may move less, or not move at all, or use their exchange rates in accordance with their particular initial conditions.

A particularly difficult situation arises when there is disagreement on the policy objectives, especially if a large country is concerned. This would be the case should Germany put a higher weight, relative to other countries, on stabilising its public finances and pursuing disinflation, and a lower weight on resuming growth and reducing unemployment. This would leave much of the burden on the two remaining large countries which can afford to adopt fiscal measures. We think that Europe can resume faster growth even without fiscal expansion in Germany, but this would inevitably cause a significant appreciation of the mark within the EMS, would entail a less favourable outcome on inflation and unemployment in France and the UK, and pose a serious threat of rising unemployment in Germany.

As is often the case, black and white conclusions are deceptive. The choice is not necessarily between a fully coordinated two-handed strategy or the continuation of the status-quo. Each country stands to benefit from the strategy. The more each country expands, the more favourable is the outlook in the remaining countries. The larger is the number of expanding countries, the larger are the gains to each of them individually. Thus, all that is needed is that all, or some of, those countries which can afford it, and fortunately the larger countries can, adopt the two-handed strategy. The others will then either follow, when they can, or simply share in the benefits. How far each country travels the proposed route in the end will depend on its starting position.

Appendix 18.1.   Fiscal expansion in an open economy

In the Island of Flexco, there is an output potential of one mumm per period, controlled by a multinational company and produced with labour alone. The island has two inhabitants, Richard and Mason, and a combined treasury-central bank, the Bank of Flexco (BOF). The local currency, called uce, exchanges for yens one to one. In period 1, Richard holds 100 uces and the central bank's reserves amount to 100 yens. Richard has decided to buy one mumm, which costs 100 uces, in period 2. Accordingly, he deposits his 100 uces at the central bank for one period and will receive an interest of 50%. In what follows his situation will remain unchanged: in period 2 he will own one mumm and 50 uces. The BOF also earns a 50% interest per period on its yen holdings.

Mason would like to buy one mumm as soon as possible but has no money. He has offered his labour services to the company but is not hired in period 1 due to lack of demand. He will be hired in period 2 to produce the mumm ordered by Richard, for which he will get a salary of 100 uces and will then be able to purchase a mumm for himself, but is upset to have to wait. He could borrow from Richard, but they do not know each other. The result is that Mason will order his mumm in period 2 and receive it in period 3. Are there possibilities of improving the island's welfare relatively to the baseline situation just described?

One possibility is for the BOF to give to Mason the 100 uces deposited by Richard as a pure transfer, and announce a tax of 60% on labour income. Mason will then order one mumm at once and will be hired by the company to produce it. Practically, he will pay the mumm upon ordering, will receive his salary at time of hiring, immediately pay a tax of 60 uces and deposit the remaining 40 uces at the BOF. All this happens simultaneously at the beginning of period 1, with interest of 50% accruing at the beginning of period 2. The situation of Mason has now improved. In period 2 he owns a mumm since period 2 plus 100 in cash (his period

1 net earnings of 40 augmented of 20 in interest and his period 2 net earnings of 40). As for the BOF, it has used the 50 yens it earned on its reserve holdings in period 2 to back the creation of 50 uces required to pay back Richard 150 uces in capital and interest, as it only received from Mason 60 in taxes and 40 in deposit. (In period 3 it will use the 60 uces levied as taxes from Mason to pay back his deposit of 40 plus interest of 20.) Relative to the baseline situation, the net addition to the island's assets is the locally produced mumm of Mason. The tax-subsidy mix has raised demand during the slack period, with a balanced inter-temporal budget, and has boosted real income to the same extent.

Suppose however that Mason uses his subsidy to buy yens from the BOF and import a Japanese mumm. The BOF loses its reserves and the associated interest income, which forces it to raise income taxes to 100%. This, of course, allows Mason to order immediately a Japanese mumm which, we assume, he will receive in period 2 (given the remoteness of Japan from the Island of Flexco). On the other hand, Mason is not hired in period 1 to produce his mumm which is imported from Japan, so he foregoes period 1 income and all his period 2 income is taxed away. The BOF ends up with no assets and a liability of 50 uces to serve Richard's interest. One could argue that these uces (the monetisation of the deficit) are worthless – or equivalently that a tax of 100% of interest income would be needed to avoid the liability. The change relative to the baseline is the one-period-ahead mumm of Mason at the loss of the BOF's foreign reserves – i.e. no net gain.

While endless variations of this allegory are possible, it illustrates two important points about a fiscal expansion in an open economy. Firstly, that demand failures offer a prospect for welfare gains. Secondly, that openness, more precisely the marginal propensity to import, works towards cancelling that prospect.

Appendix 18.2. How to measure openness

An economy is open if international trade and financial movements are important for its functioning, and thereby for the welfare of its people. Financial movements affect the interest and exchange rates and may have real effects as well as impose a constraint on policy making. This is an issue that we will consider later on. The importance of trade can take several forms. One of them is the dependence on imports for essential procurements like food or energy. Another is the dependence on exports for marketing domestic resources, like natural resources or labour. An absolute measure of that importance would call for a comparison of welfare levels with and without trade. Such a measure is difficult to construct and its practical significance is limited by the very nature of the question raised – a rhetorical question in most cases since autarky is hardly a realistic option.

Rather, we are concerned with the macroeconomic policy implications of openness. That is a very different, and quite specific question. As shown in the previous section, it arises only in the presence of some disequilibrium which requires, and justifies, the use of macroeconomic policies. In that case, the degree of openness affects the cost and effectiveness of macroeconomic policies through two channels: income flows and the terms of trade. For these specific purposes a rough measure of the degree of openness of an economy is the ratio of imports or exports to national income. That measure is too rough, though, when exports themselves have a significant import content. A corrected measure, the ratio to national income of imports net of import content of exports, coincides with the share of value added which is exported when the trade account is in balance.

To understand how these ratios represent income flows, it helps to consider first the extreme case where exports have a negligible import content, and consist basically of value added. When domestic demand expands, the increment is distributed between imports and domestic output in proportions corresponding to the *marginal* propensity to import. The *average* propensity to import is only relevant in this context because of the *empirical* observation that elasticities of imports with respect to national income are much more similar across countries than marginal propensities to import.[32] Although measures of import elasticities tend to be biased upwards away from unity because of the growing structural independence over the sample period, with the size of the bias likely to vary from country to country, measured elasticities seem to be clustered remarkably around 1.3, implying corrected elasticities around a value of 1.1 or 1.2. Marginal propensities to import dM/dY are then well approximated by a stable (across countries) multiple of import shares M/Y, say $1.2 M/Y$. The degree of import leakage is thus proportional to the import share.

---

[32] The estimated elasticities of imports with respect to final domestic demand range from 1.2 to 1.8 in the COMET model, and from 1.1 to 1.6 in the DESMOS model, both of which include all major European countries. The COMPACT elasticity for EC 10 as a whole is 1.3. Scattered import equations for individual European countries, that we came across more recently, give similar figures.

Turning now to terms of trade effects, and still neglecting the import content of exports, consider a depreciation which leaves unchanged the value-added deflator. The welfare cost is measured to the first order by the volume of imports times the rate of depreciation. As a percentage of national income, that cost is equal to the import share M/Y times the rate of depreciation. It is thus proportional to the import share for a given rate of depreciation.

This argument would be deceptive if the rate of depreciation needed to correct a given imbalance were itself inversely proportional to M/Y, leaving the product independent of the degree of openness. It is difficult to rule out this possibility generally, in particular without reference to the imbalance to be corrected. An interesting case, of direct relevance to our discussion in the report, arises when the imbalance is a trade deficit generated by an expansion of domestic demand. In such a case, the required rate of depreciation is proportional to the rate of demand expansion, with the factor of proportionality depending upon trade elasticities and being thus, to a first approximation, independent of the degree of openness. Write both exports X and imports M, evaluated in foreign currencies, as functions of (among other things) a 'relative price' variable p, which might be world prices PW divided by the product of home prices (or costs) PH times the exchange rate e. The trade account A is $X - M$, so that, writing η for elasticities,

$$\frac{dA}{de} = -\frac{X}{e}\eta_{Xp} + \frac{M}{e}\eta_{Mp}, \qquad \frac{de}{e} = \frac{dA}{M\eta_{Mp} - X\eta_{Xp}}.$$

Expansion of domestic final demand D by a given percentage α will affect the current account in an amount $\alpha D.(dM/dD)$. The adjustment in the exchange rate needed to restore the current account balance is thus given by:

$$\frac{de}{e} = \frac{\alpha D \dfrac{dM}{dD}}{M\eta_{Mp} - X\eta_{Xp}} = \alpha \frac{\eta_{MD}}{\eta_{Mp} - \dfrac{X}{M}\eta_{Xp}} \simeq \alpha \frac{\eta_{MD}}{\eta_{Mp} - \eta_{Xp}}.$$

Of course, we need to correct for the import content of exports. The simplest way is to net them out so as to consider net imports. Indeed an increase in domestic demand will not by itself influence the volume of exports, at least if we neglect the feedback effects. (To take into account the feedback effects would require more complex calculations involving matrices of bilateral flows.) Neglecting the feedback effects leads us to understate openness but the bias is not important in the short run, and only marginally related to the degree of openness itself. Neglecting the import content of exports would introduce a severe bias more or less proportional to the degree of openness itself because exports are nearly equal to imports. Actually, the import content of exports is likely to rise with openness, making the bias an increasing function of openness.

References

Abowd, J. and O. Ashenfelter (1981), 'Anticipated Unemployment and Compensating Wage Differentials', in S. Rosen, Ed., *Studies in Labour Markets*, University of Chicago Press, Chicago.

Adams, F. G., Clavijo, F. and R. Orsi (1973), 'A Macroeconomic Model of Belgium: ANELISE', *Recherches Economiques de Louvain*, 39, 303–326.

Allais, M. (1953), 'L'extension des théories de l'équilibre économique général et du rendement social au cas du risque', *Econometrica*, 21, 269–290.

Armstrong, P. J. (1984), *Technical Change and Reduction in Life Hours of Work*, Technical Change Centre, London.

Arrow, K. J. (1953), 'Le rôle des valeurs boursières pour la répartition la meilleure des risques', *Econométrie*, 41–47, CNRS, Paris; translated as 'The Role of Securities in the Optimal Allocation of Risk-Bearing', *Review of Economic Studies* 31, 91–96.

(1965), *Aspects of the Theory of Risk-Bearing*, Yrjö Jahnsson Foundation, Helsinki.

Arrow, K. J. and F. H. Hahn (1971), *General Competitive Analysis*, Holden-Day, San Francisco.

Artus, P., Laroque, G. and G. Michel (1984), 'Estimation of a Quarterly Macroeconomic Model with Quantity Rationing', *Econometrica*, 52, 1387–1414.

Ashenfelter, O. and J. Brown (1982), 'Testing the Efficiency of Employment Contracts', mimeo, Princeton University, Princeton, NJ.

Aumann, R. J. (1975), 'Values of Markets with a Continuum of Traders', *Econometrica*, 43, 611–646.

Aumann, R. J. and J. H. Drèze (1986), 'Values of Markets with Satiation or Fixed Prices', *Econometrica*, 6, 1271–1318; reprinted as ch. 6 here.

Aumann, R. J. and L. Shapley (1974), *Values of Non-Atomic Games*, Princeton University Press, Princeton, NJ.

Azariadis, C. (1975), 'Implicit Contracts and Underemployment Equilibria', *Journal of Political Economy*, 83, 6, 1183–1202.

547

(1979), 'Implicit Contracts and Related Topics: A Survey', in Z. Hornstein *et al.*, eds., *The Economics of the Labour Market*, HMSO, London.

Baily, M. (1974), 'Wages and Employment under Uncertain Demand', *Review of Economic Studies*, 41, 1, 37–50.

Balasko, Y. (1978), 'Budget Constrained Pareto-Efficient Allocations', mimeo, Paris.

Banque Nationale de Belgique (1978), 'Politique de change: choix et implications', *Bulletin de la Banque Nationale de Belgique*, avril.

Barro, R. J. (1974), 'Are Government Bonds Net Wealth?', *Journal of Political Economy*, 82, 1095–1117.

(1979), 'On the Determination of the Public Debt', *Journal of Political Economy*, 87, 940–971.

Barro, R. J. and H. I. Grossman (1971), 'A General Disequilibrium Model of Income and Employment', *American Economic Review*, 61, 82–93.

(1976), *Money, Employment and Inflation*, Cambridge University Press, Cambridge.

Barten, A. P., d'Alcantara, G. and G. J. Carrin (1976), 'COMET: A Medium-Term Macroeconomic Model for the European Economic Community', *European Economic Review*, 7, 63–115.

Baruh, M. (1986), 'La réduction du temps de travail en Europe: historique, effets et stratégies d'avenir', Mémoire, Département des Sciences Economiques, Université Catholique de Louvain, Louvain-la-Neuve.

Basevi, G. (1973), 'Commodity Trade Equations in Project Link', in J. Ball, ed., *The International Linkage of National Economic Models*, North-Holland, Amsterdam.

Baumol, W. J., Panzar, J. C. and R. D. Willig (1982), *Contestable Markets and the Theory of Industry Structure*, Harcourt Brace Jovanovitch, New York.

Bauwens, L. (1979). 'Analyse bayésienne d'un modèle d'exportation', Mémoire de Statistique, Faculté des Sciences, Université Catholique de Louvain, Louvain-la-Neuve.

Bauwens, L. and G. d'Alcantara (1983), 'An Export Model for the Belgian Industry', *European Economic Review*, 22, 265–276.

Bean, C. R. (1985), 'Macroeconomic Policy Coordination: Theory and Evidence', *Recherches Economiques de Louvain*, 51, 267–283.

Bean, C. R., Layard, P. R. G. and S. J. Nickell (1986), 'The Rise in Unemployment: a Multi-Country Study', *Economica*, 53, Supplement, S1–S22.

Bean, C. R., Layard, P. R. G. and S. J. Nickell (eds.) (1987), *The Rise in Unemployment*, Basil Blackwell, Oxford.

Beato, P. and A. Mas-Colell (1985), 'On Marginal Cost Pricing with Given Tax-Subsidy Rules', *Journal of Economic Theory*, 37, 356–365.

Begg, D. and C. Wyplosz (1987), 'Why the EMS? Dynamic Games and the Equilibrium Exchange Rate Regime', in R. Bryant and R. Portes, eds., *Global Macroeconomics, Policy Conflicts and Cooperation*, Macmillan, London.

Bénassy, J. P. (1975), 'Neokeynesian Disequilibrium Theory in a Monetary

Economy', *Review of Economic Studies*, 42, 502–523.

(1982), *The Economics of Market Disequilibrium*, Academic Press, New York.

Berckmans, A. and F. Thys-Clément (1977), 'BREUGHEL II, Modèle belge à moyen terme de politique économique', *Cahiers Economiques de Bruxelles*, 76, 475–535.

Bergström, T. C. (1976), 'How to Discard "Free Disposability" at No Cost', *Journal of Mathematical Economics*, 3, 131–134.

Blanchard, O., Dornbusch, R., Drèze, J. H., Giersch, H., Layard, P. R. G. and M. Monti (1985). 'Employment and Growth in Europe: A two Handed Approach', CEPS Paper 21, Brussels.

Blanchard, O. and S. Fischer (1989), *Lectures on Macroeconomics*, MIT Press, Cambridge, Mass.

Blaug, M. (1986), *Who's Who in Economics*, Wheatsheaf, Brighton.

Bleeckx, F., Devuyst, P., Mandy, P. and F. Prades (1978), 'A la recherche des causes du chômage', mimeo, Institut des Sciences du Travail, Université Catholique de Louvain, Louvain-la-Neuve.

Blomme, R. (1978), *Etude des propriétés dynamiques d'un modèle stochastique: application au cas du modèle ANELISE*, Faculté des Sciences Economiques, Sociales et Politiques, Université Catholique de Louvain, Louvain-la-Neuve.

Böhm, V. and H. Müller (1977), 'Two Examples of Equilibria under Price Rigidities and Quantity Rationing', *Zeitschrift für Nationalökonomie*, 37, 1/2, 165–173.

Boiteux, M. (1956), 'Sur la gestion des monopoles publics astreints à l'équilibre budgétaire', *Econometrica*, 24, 22–40.

Bonnisseau, J. M. and B. Cornet (1988), 'Existence of Equilibria when Firms Follow Bounded Losses Pricing Rules', *Journal of Mathematical Economics*, 17, 119–147.

Borch, K. (1960), 'The Safety Loading of Reinsurance Premiums', *Skandinavisk Aktuarietidskrift*, 43, 163–184.

(1962), 'Equilibrium in a Reinsurance Market', *Econometrica*, 30, 3, 424–444.

(1968a), 'Indifference Curves and Uncertainty', *Swedish Journal of Economics*, 70, 19–24.

(1968b), 'General Equilibrium in the Economics of Uncertainty', in K. Borch and J. Mossin, eds., *Risk and Uncertainty*, Macmillan, London, pp. 247–258.

(1976), 'The Monster in Loch Ness', *Journal of Risk and Insurance*, 43, 3, 521–525.

(1985), 'Theory of Insurance Premiums', *The Geneva Papers on Risk and Insurance*, 10, 132–208.

Breeden, D. (1979), 'An Intertemporal Asset Pricing Model with Stochastic Consumption and Investment Opportunities', *Journal of Financial Economics*, 7, 265–296.

Bronsard, C. and E. Wagneur (1982), 'Second rang et déséquilibre', *Cahiers du Séminaire d'Econométrie*, 24, 71–92.

Brown, D. J., Heal, G. M., Khan, M. A. and R. Vohra (1986), 'On A General Existence Theorem for Marginal Cost Pricing Equilibria', *Journal of Economic*

550   *References*

Theory, 38, 371–379.

Brown, D. J. and A. Robinson (1972), 'A Limit Theorem on the Cores of Large Standard Exchange Economies', *Proceedings of the National Academy of Sciences of the USA*, 69, 1258–1260.

Bruno, M. and J. Sachs (1985), *Economics of Worldwide Stagflation*, Basil Blackwell, Oxford.

Buiter, W. (1985), 'A Guide to Public Sector Debts and Deficits', *Economic Policy*, 1, 13–79.

Card, D. (1985), 'Efficient Contracts and Costs of Adjustment: Short-Run Employment Determination for Airline Mechanics', mimeo, Princeton University, Princeton, NJ.

Carré, J. J., Dubois, P. and E. Malinvaud (1972), *Croissance Française: un Essai d'Analyse Causale de l'Après-Guerre*, Seuil, Paris.

Cartter, A. M. (1959), *Theory of Wages and Employment*, Irwin, Homewood.

Champsaur, P. (1975), 'Cooperation Versus Competition', *Journal of Economic Theory*, 11, 394–417.

Champsaur, P., Drèze, J. H. and C. Henry (1977), 'Stability Theorems with Economic Applications', *Econometrica*, 45, 2, 273–294.

Charpin, J. and J. Mairesse (1978), 'Réduction de la durée du travail et chômage', *Revue Economique*, 1, 189–205.

Chetty, V. K. and P. R. Nayak (1978), 'Drèze Equilibria for Polyhedral and Strictly Convex Price Sets', Discussion Paper, Indian Statistical Institute, New Delhi.

Clarke, F. H. (1975), 'Generalised Gradients and Applications', *Transactions of the American Mathematical Society*, 205, 247–262.

(1976), 'A New Approach to Lagrange Multipliers', *Mathematics of Operations Research*, 1, 165–174.

(1983), *Optimisation and Non-Smooth Analysis*, Wiley, New York.

Clower, R. W. (1965), 'The Keynesian Counterrevolution: A Theoretical Appraisal' in F. H. Hahn and F. Brechling, eds., *The Theory of Interest Rates*, Macmillan, London.

(1967), 'A Reconsideration of the Microfoundations of Monetary Theory', *Western Economic Journal*, 6, 1–9.

Cohen, D. (1985), 'How to Evaluate the Solvency of an Indebted Nation', *Economic Policy*, 1, 139–167.

Commissariat Général du Plan (1985), *Aménagement et Réduction du Temps de Travail*, La Documentation Française, Paris.

Cooper, R. (1984), 'Economic Interdependence and Coordination of Economic Policies', in R. Jones and P. Kenen, eds., *Handbook of International Economics*, North-Holland, Amsterdam.

Cornell, B. (1981), 'The Consumption Based Asset Pricing Model: A Note on Potential Tests and Applications', *Journal of Financial Economics*, 9, 103–108.

Cornet, B. and G. Laroque (1980), 'Lipschitz Properties of Constrained Demand

Functions and Constrained Maximisers', Working Paper 8005, INSEE, Paris.

d'Alcantara, G. (1983), *SERENA: A Macroeconomic Sectoral Regional and National Accounting Econometric Model for the Belgian Economy*, Katholieke Universiteit Leuven, Leuven.

d'Alcantara, G. and Associates (1979), 'The International Trade Sector, SERENA Model Report', mimeo, Belgian Planning Bureau, Brussels.

Danthine, J. P. and J. C. Lambelet (1987), 'The Swiss Case', *Economic Policy*, 5, 149–179.

Davies, G. and D. Metcalf (1985), *Generating Jobs*, Simon and Coates, London.

Debreu, G. (1959), *Theory of Value*, Wiley, New York.

——— (1962), 'New Concepts and Techniques for Equilibrium Analysis', *International Economic Review*, 3, 257–273.

——— (1972), 'Smooth Preferences', *Econometrica*, 40, 603–615.

Debreu, G. and H. Scarf (1963), 'A Limit Theorem on the Core of an Economy', *International Economic Review*, 4, 225–246.

De Carvalho, F. (1979), *Planning Public Consumption under Restricted Information: A Process-Oriented Contribution*, Facultés des Sciences Economiques, Sociales et Politiques, Université Catholique de Louvain, Louvain-la-Neuve.

De Grauwe, P. and C. Holvoet (1978), 'On the Effectiveness of a Devaluation in the EEC-Countries', *Tijdschrift voor Ekonomie en Management*, 23, 1, 67–82.

De Grauwe, P. and G. Verfaille (1987), 'Exchange Rate Variability, Misalignment, and the European Monetary System', unpublished, University of Leuven, Leuven.

Dehez, P. and J. H. Drèze (1984), 'On Supply-Constrained Equilibria', *Journal of Economic Theory*, 33, 1, 172–182; reprinted as ch. 3 here.

——— (1988a), 'Competitive Equilibria with Quantity-Taking Producers and Increasing Returns to Scale', *Journal of Mathematical Economics*, 17, 209–230; reprinted as ch. 4 here.

——— (1988b), 'Distributive Production Sets and Equilibria with Increasing Returns', *Journal of Mathematical Economics*, 17, 231–248.

den Hartog, H. and H. S. Tjan (1976), 'Investments, Wages, Prices and Demand for Labour', *De Economist*, 124, 32–55.

Dermine, J. and J. H. Drèze (1981), 'La Belgique dans la crise et la contrainte de balance des paiements', *Recherches Economiques de Louvain*, 47, 55–76.

Deschamps, P. (1976), *Second-Best Pricing with Variable Product Quality*, Faculté des Sciences Economiques, Sociales et Politiques, Université Catholique de Louvain, Louvain-la-Neuve.

Dewatripont, M. (1986), 'Two-Tier Contracts as Labour Market Adjustment', Working Paper 8603, Université Libre de Bruxelles, Bruxelles.

Diamond, P. and J. Mirrlees (1971), 'Optimal Taxation and Public Production', *American Economic Review*, 61, 8–27, 261–278.

Dierker, E., Guesnerie, R. and W. Neuefeind (1985), 'General Equilibrium when Some Firms Follow Special Pricing Rules', *Econometrica*, 53, 1369–1393.

Dixit, A. (1978), 'The Balance of Trade in a Model of Temporary Equilibrium with Rationing', *Review of Economic Studies*, 141, 393–404.

Dornbusch, R., Basevi, G., Blanchard, O., Buiter, W. and P. R. G. Layard (1983), 'Macroeconomic Prospects and Policies for the European Community', CEPS Paper 1, Brussels; in O. Blanchard *et al.*, eds., *Restoring Europe's Prosperity*, MIT Press, Cambridge, Mass., 1986.

Dornbusch, R. and J. Frankel (1987), 'Macroeconomics and Protection', in R. M. Sterm, ed., *US Trade Policies in a Changing World Economy*, MIT Press, Cambridge, Mass.

Douglas, P. (1934), *The Theory of Wages*, Macmillan, New York.

Dramais, A. (1986), 'Compact – A Prototype Macroeconomic Model of the European Community in the World Economy', *European Economy*, 27, 111–160.

Drazen, A. (1980), 'Recent Developments in Macroeconomic Disequilibrium Theory', *Econometrica*, 48, 283–306.

Drèze, J. H. (1960), 'Quelques réflexions sereines sur l'adaptation de l'industrie belge au Marché Commun', *Comptes Rendus de la Société d'Economie Politique de Belgique*, 275, 3–37; translated as 'The Standard Goods Hypothesis' with a post-scriptum by the author, in A. Jacquemin and A. Sapir, eds., *The European Internal Market: Trade and Competition*, Oxford University Press, Oxford, 1989.

(1964), 'Some Postwar Contributions of French Economists to Theory and Public Policy', *American Economic Review*, 54, 1–64.

(1974a), 'Axiomatic Theories of Choices, Cardinal Utility and Subjective Probability: A Review', in J. H. Drèze, ed., *Allocation under Uncertainty: Equilibrium and Optimality*, Macmillan, London, ch. 1; reprinted as ch. 1 in Drèze (1987a).

(1974b), 'Investment under Private Ownership: Optimality, Equilibrium and Stability', in J. H. Drèze, ed., *Allocation under Uncertainty: Equilibrium and Optimality*, Macmillan, London, ch. 9; reprinted as ch. 14 in Drèze (1987a).

(1975), 'Existence of an Exchange Equilibrium under Price Rigidities', *International Economic Review*, 16, 301–320; reprinted as ch. 2 here.

(1979a), 'Human Capital and Risk-Bearing', *The Geneva Papers on Risk and Insurance*, 12, 5–22; reprinted as ch. 17 in Drèze (1987a).

(1979b), 'Demand Estimation, Risk-Aversion and Sticky Prices', *Economics Letters*, 4, 1–6; reprinted as ch. 9 here.

(1979c) 'Salaires, emploi et durée du travail', and 'Salaires, emploi et durée du travail: Réponse à Paul De Grauwe', *Recherches Economiques de Louvain*, 45, 17–34 and 123–132.

(1980a), 'Réduction progressive des heures et partage du travail' in *Les Conditions de l'Initiative Economique*, 4ème Congrès des Economistes de Langue Française, Commission 3, 2–4 and 57–83.

(1980b), 'Public Goods with Exclusion', *Journal of Public Economics*, 13, 5–24; reprinted as ch. 7 here.

(1981), 'Inferring Risk Tolerance from Deductibles in Insurance Contracts', *The*

Geneva Papers on Risk and Insurance, 20, 48–52; reprinted as ch. 5 in Drèze (1987a).

(1982), 'Decision Criteria for Business Firms', in M. Hazewinkel and A. H. G. Rinnooy Kan, eds., *Current Developments in the Interface: Economics, Econometrics, Mathematics*, D. Reidel, Dordrecht, pp. 27–51; reprinted as ch. 15 in Drèze (1987a).

(1983), 'Stability of a Keynesian Adjustment Process', mimeo, Université Catholique de Louvain, Louvain-la-Neuve.

(1984a), 'Autogestion et équilibre général', *Revue Européenne des Sciences Sociales*, 22, 66, 209–229.

(1984b), 'Second-Best Analysis with Markets in Disequilibrium: Public Sector Pricing in a Keynesian Regime', in M. Marchand, P. Pestieau and H. Tulkens, eds. *The Performance of Public Enterprise: Concepts and Measurement*, North-Holland, Amsterdam, pp. 45–79; and in *European Economic Review*, 29, 3, 263–301, 1985; reprinted as ch. 8 here.

(1985a), '(Uncertainty and) The firm in General Equilibrium Theory', *Economic Journal*, 95, Supplement: Conference Papers, 1–20; reprinted as ch. 16 in Drèze (1987a).

(1985b), 'Aux prises avec l'économique, être chrétien, qu'importe?' *L'Entreprise et l'Homme*, 4, 177–184.

(1986a), 'Work-Sharing: Why? How? How Not ...', CEPS Paper 27, Brussels.

(1986b), 'Work-Sharing: Some Theory and Recent European Experience', *Economic Policy*, 1, 3, 561–619; reprinted as ch. 17 here.

(1987a), *Essays on Economic Decisions under Uncertainty*, Cambridge University Press, Cambridge.

(1987b), 'Underemployment Equilibria: From Theory to Econometrics and Policy', *Europen Economic Review*, 31, 9–34; reprinted as ch. 1 here.

(1989a), *Labour Management, Contracts and Capital Markets, A General Equilibrium Approach*, Basil Blackwell, Oxford.

(1989b), 'L'arbitrage entre équité et efficacité en matière d'emploi et de salaires', *Recherches Economiques de Louvain*, 55, 1, 1–31, 1989; English version: 'Wages, Employment and the Equity-Efficiency Trade-Off'; reprinted as ch. 12 here.

(1989c), 'The Role of Securities and Labor Contracts in the Optimal Allocation of Risk-Bearing', in H. Loubergé, ed., *Risk, Information and Insurance. Essays in the Memory of Karl H. Borch*, Kluwer Academic Publishers, Boston; reprinted as ch. 11 here.

(1990), 'Stability of a Keynesian Adjustment Process', to appear in W. Barnett, B. Cornet, C. d'Aspremont, J. Jaskold Gabszevicz and A. Mas-Colell, eds., *Equilibrium Theory and Applications*, Cambridge University Press, Cambridge, forthcoming; reprinted as ch. 10 here.

(1990), 'European Unemployment: Lessons from a Multicountry Econometric Study', *Scandinavian Journal of Economics*, 92, 2, 135–165.

Drèze, J. H. and C. Bean (1991), 'Europe's Unemployment Problem: Introduction

554   References

and Synthesis', in J. H. Drèze, C. Bean, J. P. Lambert, F. Mehta and H. Sneessens, eds., *Europe's Unemployment Problem*, MIT Press, Cambridge, Mass., ch. 1; reprinted as ch. 16 here.

Drèze, J. H., Bean, C., Lambert, J. P., Mehta, F. and H. Sneessens (eds.) (1991), *Europe's Unemployment Problem*, MIT Press, Cambridge, Mass.

Drèze, J. H. and D. de la Vallée Poussin (1971), 'A Tâtonnement Process for Public Goods', *Review of Economic Studies*, 37, 133–150.

Drèze, J. H. and C. Gollier (1989), 'Risk-Sharing on the Labour Market', mimeo, Université Catholique de Louvain, Louvain-la-Neuve.

Drèze, J. H. and K. Hagen (1978), 'Choice of Product Quality: Equilibrium and Efficiency', *Econometrica*, 46, 3, 493–513.

Drèze, J. H. and M. Marchand (1976), 'Pricing, Spending, and Gambling Rules for Non-Profit Organisations', in R. E. Grieson, ed., *Public and Urban Economics, Essays in Honor of William S. Vickrey*, Lexington Books, Lexington, pp. 59–89, reprinted as ch. 19 in Drèze (1987a).

Drèze, J. H. and F. Modigliani (1972), 'Consumption Decisions under Uncertainty,' *Journal of Economic Theory*, 5, 308–335: reprinted as ch. 9 in Drèze (1987a).

(1981), 'The Trade-Off between Real Wages and Employment in an Open Economy (Belgium)', *European Economic Review*, 15, 1, 1–40; reprinted as ch. 14 here.

Drèze, J. H. and H. Müller (1980), 'Optimality Properties of Rationing Schemes', *Journal of Economic Theory*, 23, 150–159; reprinted as ch. 5 here.

Drèze, J. H., Wyplosz, C., Bean, C., Giavazzi, F. and H. Giersch (1988), 'The Two-Handed Growth Strategy for Europe: Autonomy through Flexible Cooperation', *Recherches Economiques de Louvain*, 54, 1, 5–52; reprinted as ch. 18 here.

Drèze, J. P. (1982), 'On the Choice of Shadow Prices for Project Evaluation', Discussion Paper, Indian Statistical Institute, New Delhi.

Driehuis, W. and M. Bruyn-Hundt (1979), 'Enige Effecten van Arbeidstijdverkorting', *Economisch Statistische Berichten*, 1964, 289–300.

Duffie, G., Shafer, W., Cass, D., Magill, M., Quinzii, M. and J. Geanakoplos (1988), 'Lectures Notes on Incomplete Markets', BoWo Discussion Paper A-192, Universität Bonn, Bonn.

Economie Européenne (1980), *Aménagement du Temps de Travail*, EEC, Strasbourg.

Emerson, M. (1988), *What Model for Europe?*, MIT Press, Cambridge, Mass.

European Economy (1984), *Annual Economic Report 1984–85*, EEC, Strasbourg.

Eyskens, M. (1978), 'Budget: Situation et perspectives', Secrétariat d'Etat au Budget et à l'économie régionale flamande, Bruxelles.

Fair, R. C. (1969), *The Short-Run Demand for Workers and Hours*, North-Holland, Amsterdam.

Fama, E. F. and G. W. Schwert (1977), 'Human Capital and Capital Market Equilibrium', *Journal of Financial Economics*, 4, 95–125.

Fisher, F. M. (1983), *Disequilibrium Foundations of Equilibrium Economics*, Cambridge University Press, Cambridge.

Fontaine, C. (1984), 'L'évolution de la durée annuelle du travail en France depuis 1930', *Chronique d'Actualité*, SEDEIS.

Franz, W. (1985), 'The Past Decade's Natural Rate and the Dynamics of German Unemployment: A Case Against Demand Policy?', *European Economic Review*, 21, 51–76.

Franz, W. and H. König (1986), 'The Nature and Causes of Unemployment in the Federal Republic of Germany since the 1970's: An Empirical Investigation', *Economica*, 53, Supplement, S219–S224.

Gérard, M. and C. Vanden Berghe (1984). 'Econometric Analysis of Sectoral Investments in Belgium (1956–1982)', *Recherches Economiques de Louvain*, 50, 89–118.

Giavazzi, F. and A. Giovannini (1986), 'The EMS and the Dollar', *Economic Policy*, 2, 456–485.

Giavazzi, F. and M. Pagano (1988), 'The Advantage of Tying One's Hands: EMS Discipline and Central Bank Credibility', *European Economic Review*, 32, 1055–1082.

Giersch, H. (1987a), 'Internal and External Liberalisation for Faster Growth', CEC, DG for Economic and Financial Affairs, Economic Paper 54, Brussels.

(1987b) 'Economic Policies in the Age of Schumpeter', *European Economic Review*, 31, 35–52.

Ginsburgh, V. and I. Zang (1978), 'Price-Taking or Price-Making Behavior in Export Pricing', Discussion Paper 7805, CORE, Université Catholique de Louvain, Louvain-la-Neuve.

Gollier, C. (1988), *Intergenerational Risk-Sharing and Unemployment*, Faculté des Sciences Economiques, Université Catholique de Louvain, Louvain-la-Neuve.

Gordon, D. F. (1974), 'A Neo-Classical Theory of Keynesian Unemployment', *Economic Inquiry*, 12, 431–459.

Gourieroux, C., Laffont, J. J. and A. Montfort (1984), 'Econométrie des modèles d'équilibre avec rationnement: une mise à jour', *Annales de l'INSEE*, 55/56, 5–38.

Grandmont, J. M. (1974), 'On the Short-Run Equilibrium in a Monetary Economy', in J. H. Drèze, ed., *Allocation under Uncertainty: Equilibrium and Optimality*, Macmillan, London, ch. 12.

(1977), 'Temporary General Equilibrium Theory', *Econometrica*, 45, 535–572.

(1978), 'The Logic of the Fix-Price Method', *Scandinavian Journal of Economics*, 80, 169–186.

Grandmont, J. M. (ed.) (1988), *Temporary Equilibrium: Selected Readings*, Academic Press, San Diego.

Grandmont, J. M., Laroque, G. and Y. Younès (1978), 'Equilibrium with Quantity Rationing and Recontracting', *Journal of Economic Theory*, 10, 84–102.

Greenberg, J. and H. Müller (1979), 'Equilibria under Price Rigidities and Externalities', in O. Moeschlin, ed., *Game Theory and Related Topics*, North-Holland, Amsterdam, pp. 291–300.

Grossman, S. J. and R. J. Shiller (1982), 'Consumption Correlatedness and Risk

Measurement in Economies with Non-traded Assets and Heterogeneous Information', *Journal of Financial Economics*, 10, 195–210.

Grubb, D., Jackman, R. and P. R. G. Layard (1983), 'Wage Rigidity and Unemployment in OECD Countries', *European Economic Review*, 21, 11–39.

Guesnerie, R. (1975a), 'Un formalisme général pour le "second rang" et son application à la définition des règles du calcul économique public sous une hypothèse simple de fiscalité', *Cahiers du Séminaire d'Econométrie*, 16, 87–116.

(1975b), 'Pareto Optimality in Non-Convex Economies', *Econometrica*, 43, 1–29.

(1977), 'On the Direction of Tax Reform', *Journal of Public Economics*, 7, 179–202.

(1980), 'Second-Best Pricing Rules in the Boiteux Tradition: Derivation, Review and Discussion', *Journal of Public Economics*, 13, 51–80.

(1981), 'Analyse microéconomique normative du modèle keynésien élémentaire', mimeo, CEPREMAP, Paris.

Guesnerie, R. and K. Roberts (1984), 'Effective Policy Tools and Quantity Controls', *Econometrica*, 52, 59–86.

Guesnerie, R. and J. Tirole (1981), 'Tax Reform from the Gradient Projection Viewpoint', *Journal of Public Economics*, 15, 275–293.

Hahn, F. H. (1978), 'On Non-Walrasian Equilibria', *Review of Economic Studies*, 45, 1–17.

Hamada, K. (1976), 'A Strategic Analysis of Monetary Interdependence', *Journal of Political Economy*, 84, 677–700.

Harsanyi, J. (1955), 'Cardinal Welfare, Individualistic Ethics and Interpersonal Comparisons of Utility', *Journal of Political Economy*, 63, 309–321.

Hart, O. D. and B. Holmström (1989), 'The Theory of Contracts', in T. Bewley, ed., *Advances in Economic Theory*, Cambridge University Press, Cambridge, pp. 71–155.

Hart, R. A. (1984), *Shorter Working Time*, OECD, Paris.

Hart, S. (1977a), 'Asymptotic Value of Games with a Continuum of Players', *Journal of Mathematical Economics*, 4, 57–80.

(1977b), 'Values of Non-Differentiable Markets with a Continuum of Traders', *Journal of Mathematical Economics*, 4, 103–116.

(1980), 'Measure-Based Values of Market Games', *Mathematics of Operations Research*, 5, 197–228.

Hellwig, M. and M. Neumann (1987), 'Germany under Kohl', *Economic Policy*, 5, 103–145.

Hendry, D. F. (1982), 'Whither Disequilibrium Econometrics?', *Econometric Reviews*, 1, 65–70.

Henin, P. Y. (1980), 'A Suggestion for Unifying the Theory of Unemployment: A Model of Process Equilibrium under Quantity Rationing', Discussion Paper, Université de Paris I, Paris.

Hicks, J. R. (1932), *The Theory of Wages*, Macmillan, London.

Hildenbrand, W. (1974), *Core and Equilibria of a Large Economy*, Princeton University Press, Princeton.

—— (1981), 'Short-Run Production Functions Based on Microdata', *Econometrica*, 51, 1095–1125.

—— (1982), 'Core of an Economy', in K. J. Arrow and M. D. Intriligator, eds., *Handbook of Mathematical Economics*, Volume II, North-Holland, Amsterdam, ch. 18.

—— (1983), 'On the Law of Demand', *Econometrica*, 51, 997–1019.

Holmström, B. (1979), 'Moral Hazard and Observability', *The Bell Journal of Economics*, 10, 1, 74–91.

—— (1981), 'Contractual Models of the Labour Market', *American Economic Review*, 71, 2, 308–313.

Houthakker, H. (1955), 'The Pareto Distribution and the Cobb–Douglas Production Function in Activity Analysis', *Review of Economic Studies*, 23, 27–31.

Ito, T. (1982), 'Implicit Contract Theory: A Critical Survey', Discussion Paper 82-165, Center of Economic Research, University of Minnesota, Minneapolis.

Jallade, J. P. (1982), *L'Europe à temps partiel*, Economica, Paris.

Kannai, Y. (1966), 'Values of Games with a Continuum of Players', *Israel Journal of Mathematics*, 4, 54–58.

Keynes, J. M. (1936), *The General Theory of Employment, Interest and Money*, Harcourt Brace, New York.

Kooiman, P. (1984), 'Smoothing the Aggregate Fix-Price Model and the Use of Business Survey Data', *Economic Journal*, 94, 899–913.

Kooiman, P. and T. Kloek (1985), 'An Empirical Two-Market Disequilibrium Model for Dutch Manufacturing', *European Economic Review*, 29, 3, 323–354.

Koopmans, T. (1957), *Three Essays on the State of Economic Science*, McGraw-Hill, New York.

Kuipers, S. K. and H. F. Bosch (1976), 'An Alternative Estimation Procedure of a Clay–Clay Type of Vintage Model: The Case of the Netherlands, 1959–1973', *De Economist*, 124, 56–82.

Kurz, M. (1982), 'Unemployment Equilibrium in an Economy with Linked Prices', *Journal of Economic Theory*, 26, 100–123.

Lambert, J. P. (1988), *Disequilibrium Macroeconomic Models, Theory and Estimation of Rationing Models Using Business Survey Data*, Cambridge University Press, Cambridge.

Lambert, J. P., Lubrano, M. and H. Sneessens (1984), 'Emploi et chômage en France de 1955 à 1982: un modèle macroéconomique annuel avec rationnement', *Annales de l'INSEE*, 55–56

Layard, P. R. G., Basevi, G., Blanchard, O., Buiter, W. and R. Dornbusch (1984), 'Europe: The Case for Unsustainable Growth', CEPS Paper 8/9, Brussels; in O. Blanchard *et al.*, eds., *Restoring Europe's Prosperity*, MIT Press, Cambridge, Mass, 1986.

Layard, P. R. G. and S. J. Nickell (1985), 'The Causes of British Unemployment', *National Institute of Economics Review*, 111, 62–85.

Leijonhufvud, A. (1968), *On Keynesian Economics and the Economics of Keynes*, Oxford University Press, Oxford.

Leroy, R. (1962), *Signification du chômage belge*, Office Belge pour l'Accroissement de la Productivité, Brussels.

Lévy-Lambert, H. (1968), 'Tarification des services à qualité variable', *Econotrica*, 36, 564–574.

(1969), *La Vérité des Prix*, Seuil, Paris.

Lindbeck, A. and D. Snower (1985), 'Explanations of Unemployment', *Oxford Review of Economic Policy*, 1, 2, 34–59.

Lucas, R. and N. Stokey (1983), 'Optimal Fiscal and Monetary Policy in an Economy without Capital', *Journal of Monetary Economics*, 12, 55–93.

Machina, M. (1987), 'Choice under Uncertainty: Problems Solved and Unsolved', *Economic Perspectives*, 1, 1, 121–154.

Madden, P. (1978), 'Some Results on Drèze Equilibrium', mimeo, Manchester University, Manchester.

Maddison, A. (1982), *Phases of Capitalist Development*, Oxford University Press, Oxford.

Malinvaud, E. (1971), 'Procédures pour la détermination d'un programme de consommation collective', *European Economic Review*, 2, 187–217.

(1972), *Lectures on Microeconomic Theory*, North-Holland, Amsterdam.

(1977), *The Theory of Unemployment Reconsidered*, Basil Blackwell, Oxford.

(1980), 'Macroeconomic Rationing of Employment', in E. Malinvaud and J. P. Fitoussi, eds., *Unemployment in Western Countries*, Macmillan, London.

(1982a), 'An Econometric Model for Macro-Disequilibrium Analysis', in M. Hazewinkel and A. H. G. Rinnooy Kan, eds., *Current Developments in the Interface: Economics, Econometrics, Mathematics*, D. Reidel, Dordrecht.

(1982b), 'Wages and Unemployment', *Economic Journal*, 92, 1–12.

Malinvaud, E. and Y. Younès (1977a), 'Une nouvelle formulation générale pour l'étude de certains fondements microéconomiques de la macroéconomie', *Cahiers du Séminaire d'Econométrie*, 18, 63–112.

(1977b), 'Some New Concepts for the Microeconomic Foundations of Macroeconomics', in G. C. Harcourt, ed., *The Microeconomic Foundations of Macroeconomics*, Westview Press, Boulder; Macmillan, London (1978).

Mangasarian, O. L. (1969), *Nonlinear Programming*, McGraw-Hill, New York.

Marchand, M. (1973), 'The Economic Principles of Telephone Rates under a Budgetary Constraint', *Review of Economic Studies*, 50, 507–515.

Marchand, O. (1984), 'L'emploi en 1982–83: simple répit dans la divergence entre demande et offre', *Economie et Statistique*, 166, 25–38.

Marshall, A. (1920), *Principles of Economics*, 8th edition, Macmillan, London.

Martin, C. (1986), 'Disequilibrium Modelling of the Demand for Corporate Borrowing in the UK: An Application of Linear Disequilibrium Estimation', mimeo, Birkbeck College, London.

Mas-Colell, A. (1977), 'Competitive and Value Allocations of Large Exchange Economies', *Journal of Economic Theory*, 14, 419–438.

Mayers, D. (1973), 'Non-Marketable Assets and the Determination of Capital Asset Prices in the Absence of a Riskless Asset', *Journal of Business*, 46, 258–267.

McDonald, I. and R. M. Solow (1981), 'Wage Bargaining and Employment', *American Economic Review*, 71, 5, 896–908.

McKinnon, R. (1969), 'Portfofio Balance and International Payments Adjustment', in R. A. Mundell and A. Swoboda, eds., *Monetary Problems of the International Economy*, Chicago University Press, Chicago, pp. 189–234.

Meade, J. E. (1982), *Wage Fixing*, Allen, London.

Mertens, J. F. (1980), 'Values and Derivatives', *Mathematics of Operations Research*, 5, 523–552.

(1988), 'The Shapely Value in the Non-Differentiable Case', *International Journal of Game Theory*, 17, 1, 1–65.

Mifflin, R. (1976), 'Semi-Smooth and Semi-Convex Functions in Constrained Optimization', RR–7621, International Institute for Applied Systems Analysis, Laxenburg.

Modigliani, F. and T. Padoa-Schioppa (1977), 'La Politica Economica in Una Economia con Salari Indicizzati al 100 o piu', *Moneta e Credito* 117.

(1978), 'The Management of an Open Economy with 100% plus Wage Indexation', *Essays in International Finance*, 130, Princeton University Press, Princeton.

Morishima, M. (1976), *The Economic Theory of Modern Society*, Cambridge University Press, Cambridge.

Mortensen, J. (1984), 'Profitability, Relative Factor Prices and Capital/Labour Substitution in the Community, the United States and Japan, 1960–1983', *European Economy*, 20, 33–67.

Mossin, J. (1966), 'Equilibrium in a Capital Asset Market', *Econometrica*, 34, 768–783.

(1977), *The Economic Efficiency of Financial Markets*, Heath and Co, Lexington.

Muellbauer, J. (1978), 'Macrotheory vs Macroeconometrics: The Treatment of Disequilibrium in Macromodels', Discussion Paper 29, Birkbeck College, London.

Negishi, T. (1961), 'Monopolistic Competition and General Equilibrium', *Review of Economic Studies*, 28, 196–201.

Neyman, A. and Y. Tauman (1979), 'The Partition Value', *Mathematics of Operations Research*, 4, 236–264.

Nyssens, A. and E. Wittman (1976), 'Comparaison internationale des salaires et de la productivité', *Les Dossiers Wallons*, 3–4–5, 165–255.

Oates, W. E. (1966), 'Budget Balance and Equilibrium Income: A Comment on the Efficacity of Fiscal and Monetary Policy in an Open Economy', *Journal of Finance*, 21, 489–498.

OECD (1983), *Employment Outlook*, Paris.

(1984), *Employment Outlook*, Paris.

(1985), *Employment Growth and Structural Change*, Paris.

Oi, W. Y. (1962), 'Labour as a Quasi-Fixed Factor', *Journal of Political Economy*, 70, 538–555.

Okun, A. (1981), *Prices and Quantities: A Macroeconomic Analysis*, The Brookings Institution, Washington; Basil Blackwell, Oxford.

Oswald, A. (1984), 'Efficient Contracts are on the Labour-Demand Curve: Theory and Facts', mimeo, Oxford University, Oxford.

(1985), 'The Economic Theory of Trade Unions: An Introductory Survey', *Scandinavian Journal of Economics*, 82, 2, 160–193.

Oudiz, H. G. and J. Sachs (1984), 'Macroeconomic Policy Coordination among the Industrial Economies', *Brookings Papers on Economic Activity*, 1, 1–75.

Palasthy, T. (1978), 'Six heures de travail par jour', *Les Dossiers Wallons*, 6, 3–40.

Pencavel, J. (1985), 'Wages and Employment and Trade Unionism: Microeconomic Models and Macroeconomic Applications', *Scandinavian Journal of Economics*, 87, 2, 197–225.

Persson, M., Persson, T. and L. Svensson (1986), 'Time Consistency of Fiscal and Monetary Policy', IIEP Seminar Paper 331, Stockholm.

Phelps, E. S. (1963), 'Substitution, Fixed Proportions, Growth and Distribution', *International Economic Review*, 4, 265–288.

Phlips, L. (1974), *Applied Consumption Analysis*, North-Holland, Amsterdam.

(1978), 'Selective Manpower Policies in Germany, with Special Reference to Wage-Cost Subsidies', in *European Labour Market Policies*, National Commission for Manpower Policy, Washington.

Picard, P. (1982), 'Prix fictifs et déséquilibre en économie ouverte', mimeo, Centre de Mathématiques Economiques, Université de Paris-I, Paris.

Pigou, A. C. (1928), 'An Analysis of Supply', *Economic Journal*, 38, 238–257.

Plasmans, J. and A. Vanroelen (1985), 'Arbeidsuurverkorting: Een Mogelijke Oplossing voor (Jeugd) Werkloosheid?', mimeo, UFSIA (SESO), Antwerp.

Pratt, J. (1964), 'Risk Aversion in the Small and in the Large', *Econometrica*, 32, 127–136.

Quandt, R. E. (1986), *Bibliography of Quantity Rationing and Disequilibrium Models*, Mimeo, Princeton University, Princeton, NJ.

Quatrième Congrès des Economistes Belges de Langue Française, (1980), *Réduction Progressive des Heures et Partage du Travail*, Commission 3, CiFOP, Charleroi.

Ramsey, F. P. (1927), 'A Contribution to the Theory of Taxation', *Economic Journal*, 37, 47–61.

Roberts, K. (1982), 'Desirable Fiscal Policies under Keynesian Unemployment', *Oxford Economic Papers*, 34, 1–22.

Rockafellar, R. T. (1970), *Convex Analysis*, Princeton University Press, Princeton.

(1979), 'Clarke's Tangent Cones and the Boundary of Closed Sets in R^n', *Non-Linear Analysis, Methods and Applications*, 3, 145–154.

Rogoff, K. (1985), 'Can Exchange Rate Predictability be Achieved without

Monetary Convergence? – Evidence from the EMS', International Finance Discussion Paper 245, Federal Review Board, Washington.

Rosen, S. (1985), 'Implicit Contracts: A Survey', *Journal of Economic Literature*, 23, 3, 1144–1175.

Roth, A. E. (1977), 'The Shapley Value as a von Neumann-Morgenstern Utility', *Econometrica*, 45, 657–664.

Rowthorn, B. and A. Glyn (1987), 'The Diversity of Unemployment Experience since 1973', Applied Economics Discussion Paper 40, University of Oxford, Oxford.

Roy, R. (1942), *De L'Utilité – Contribution à la Théorie des Choix*, Hermann, Paris.

Sachs, J. (1983), 'International Policy Coordination in a Dynamic Macroeconomic Model', NBER Working Paper 1166.

Sachs, J. and C. Wyplosz (1984), 'Real Exchange Rate Effects of Fiscal Policy', NBER Working Paper 1255.

(1986), 'The Economic Consequences of President Mitterrand', *Economic Policy*, 2, 261–321.

Sandmo, A. (1974), 'Two-Period Models of Consumption Decisions under Uncertainty', in J. H. Drèze, ed., *Allocation under Uncertainty: Equilibrium and Optimality*, Macmillan, London, ch. 2.

Sargan, J. D. (1964), 'Wages and Prices in the UK: A Study in Econometric Methodology', in P. Hart, G. Mills and J. Whitaker, eds., *Econometric Analysis for Economic Planning*, Butterworths, London.

Scarf, H. (1986), 'Notes on the Core of a Productive Economy', in W. Hildenbrand and A. Mas-Colell, eds., *Contributions to Mathematical Economics, Essays in Honor of Gérard Debreu*, North-Holland, Amsterdam.

Scarmure, P. (1986), 'Réduction, aménagement et redistribution du temps de travail: état de la question et évaluation des politiques en Belgique', Mémoire, Département des Sciences Economiques, Université Catholique de Louvain, Louvain-la-Neuve.

Schmeidler, D. and K. Vind (1972), 'Fair Net Trades', *Econometrica*, 40, 637–642.

Shafer, W. and H. Sonneschein (1975), 'Some Theorems on the Existence of Competitive Equilibrium', *Journal of Economic Theory*, 11, 83–93.

Shapley, L. (1953), 'A Value for n-Person Games', in H. W. Kuhn and A. W. Tucker, eds., *Contributions to the Theory of Games*, Volume II, Princeton University Press, Princeton, pp. 307–317.

(1969), 'Utility Comparisons and the Theory of Games', in G. Th. Guilbaud, ed., *La Décision*, CNRS, Paris, pp. 251–263.

Sneessens, H. (1981), *Theory and Estimation of Macroeconomic Rationing Models*, Springer-Verlag, Berlin.

(1983), 'A Macroeconomic Rationing Model of the Belgian Economy', *European Economic Review*, 20, 193–215.

(1987), 'Investment and the Inflation-Unemployment Trade-Off in a Macroeconomic Rationing Model with Monopolistic Competition', *European Economic Review*, 31, 3, 781–808.

Sneessens, H. and J. H. Drèze (1986a), 'A Discussion of Belgian Unemployment, Combining Traditional Concepts and Disequilibrium Econometrics', *Economica*, 53, S89–S119; reprinted as ch. 15 here.

(1986b), 'What, if Anything, Have We Learned from the Rise of Unemployment in Belgium, 1974–1983?', *Cahiers Economiques de Bruxelles*, 110/111, 21–26.

Solow, R. (1962), 'Substitution and Fixed Proportions in the Theory of Capital', *Review of Economic Studies*, 29, 207–218.

Sonnet, A. (1985), 'Valeur ajoutée, contenu en emplois et en travail', *Service de Conjoncture*, IRES, Université Catholique de Louvain, Louvain-la-Neuve.

Sonnet, A. and P. Defeyt (1984), 'Le marché du travail en Belgique', *Bulletin de l'IRES*, 94, 1–99, Université Catholique de Louvain, Louvain-la-Neuve.

Stalder, P. (1989), 'A Macroeconomic Disequilibrium Model for Switzerland with Continuous Regime Transitions and Endogenous Investment', *European Economic Review*, 33, 863–893.

Steinherr, A. (1975), 'Economic Policy in an Open Economy under Alternative Exchange Rate Systems: Effectiveness and Stability in the Short and Long Run', *Weltwirtschaftliches Archiv*, 111, 24–51.

Steinherr, A. and B. Van Haeperen (1985), 'Approche pragmatique pour une politique de plein-emploi: les subventions à la création d'emplois', *Recherches Economiques de Louvain*, 51, 2, 111–151.

Stigler, G. J. (1942), *The Theory of Price*, Macmillan, New York.

Sweezy, P. (1939), 'Demand under Conditions of Oligopoly', *Journal of Political Economy*, 47, 568–573.

Tauman, Y. (1981), 'Value on a Class of Non-Differentiable Market Games', *International Journal of Game Theory*, 10, 155–162.

Thys-Clément, F., van Rompuy, P. and L. De Corel (1973), *RENA, Un modèle économétrique pour l'élaboration du plan 1976–1980*, Belgian Planning Bureau, Brussels.

Tobin, J. (1952), 'A Survey of the Theory of Rationing', *Econometrica*, 20, 4, 512–553.

Van Den Bergh, R. C. and H. Wittelsburger (1981), *Working Time Reductions and Unemployment*, Conference Board in Europe, Brussels.

Van den Broeck, J., Hendericks, E. and L. Coenaerts (1984), *Roterende Vakantie*, RUCA, Antwerp.

Van der Laan, G. (1980), 'Equilibrium under Rigid Prices with Compensation for the Consumers', *International Economic Review*, 21, 63–74.

(1982), 'Simplicial Approximation of Unemployment Equilibria', *Journal of Mathematical Economics*, 9, 83–97.

(1984), 'Supply-Constrained Fixed Price Equilibria in Monetary Economies', *Journal of Mathematical Economics*, 13, 2, 171–187.

Vandoorne, M. and W. Meeusen (1978), 'The Clay–Clay Vintage Model as an Approach to the Problem of Structural Unemployment in Belgian Manufacturing: A First Exploration of the Theoretical and Statistical Problems', Working Paper 7808, Faculty of Applied Economics, State

University Centre, Antwerp.

van Moeseke, P. (1965), 'Stochastic Linear Programming: A Study in Resource Allocation under Risk', *Yale Economic Essays*, 5, 196–254.

Viñals, J. (1986), 'Fiscal Policy and the Current Account', *Economic Policy*, 3, 711–744.

Vohra, R. (1988), 'On the Existence of Equilibria in Economies with Increasing Returns: A Synthesis', *Journal of Mathematical Economics*, 17, 179–192.

Waelbroeck, J. and A. Dramais (1974), 'DESMOS: A Model for the Coordination of Economic Policies in the EEC-Countries', in A. Ando, R. Herring and R. Martson, eds., *International Aspects of Stabilisation Policies*, Federal Reserve Bank, Boston.

Weddepohl, C. (1979), 'An Equilibrium Model with Fixed Labour Time', *Econometrica*, 47, 921–938.

Weitzman, M. L. (1984), *The Share Economy: Conquering Stagflation*, Harvard University Press, Cambridge, Mass.

Wilson, R. (1968), 'On the Theory of Syndicates', *Econometrica*, 36, 119–132.

Younès, Y. (1975), 'On the Role of Money in the Process of Exchange and the Existence of a Non-Walrasian Equilibrium', *Review of Economic Studies*, 42, 489–501.

Index

566   *Index*

Printed in the United States
By Bookmasters